# Finding & Buying Your Place in the Country

*4th Edition*

Les Scher and Carol Scher

Real Estate
Education Company
a division of Dearborn Financial Publishing, Inc.

This publication is designed to provide accurate and authoritative information in regard to the subject matter covered. It is sold with the understanding that the publisher is not engaged in rendering legal, accounting or other professional service. If legal advice or other expert assistance is required, the services of a competent professional person should be sought.

Acquisitions Editor: Christine E. Litavsky
Managing Editor: Jack Kiburz
Cover Design: Paul Perlow Design
Artwork: Roger Bayless and Pearl Hurd
Editorial Production Service: Saxon House Productions

Published by Real Estate Education Company, a division of
Dearborn Financial Publishing, Inc.®

Printed in the United States of America

96 97 98  10 9 8 7 6 5 4 3 2 1

**Library of Congress Cataloging in Publication Data**

Scher, Les.
    Finding & buying your place in the country / Les & Carol Scher.—
4th ed.
        p.        cm.
    Includes bibliographical references and index.
    ISBN 0-7931-1785-2 (pbk.)
    1. Country homes—United States—Purchasing. 2. Country homes—Canada—
Purchasing. 3. Vacation homes—United States—Purchasing. 4. Vacation homes—
Canada—Purchasing. I. Scher, Carol.
II. Title.
HD256.S27 1996
643′.2—dc20                                                    96-11562
                                                                 CIP

# Dedication

To Howard Wilcox
November 9, 1920–August 28, 1994

# Contents

## APPENDIXES 387

# Acknowledgments

Since the first edition of our book was published in 1974, we have received many letters from readers offering their own stories and new ideas. This fourth revised edition brings together over 20 years of new information and research. It has been completely updated as to every aspect of buying property and includes the latest advances in technology and communication to help you gather vital information.

An exhaustive job was done by our two technical research assistants, Holly Vetter and Ron Vetter.

We are grateful to our editor, Chris Litavsky, for her efforts in helping us publish this new book for the landbuyers of the nineties.

As always, we thank our friends, neighbors and clients who continue to make our life in the country a beautiful experience.

Les Scher
Carol Scher

# Introduction

*My father told me when I was very young the first thing a man must do is to own a piece of land. When you go into a store and you buy something it's chattel, but when you own a piece of land, that's real. And that's where the words* real estate *originated.*

—Chuck Berry

We have now been living in the country for more than 25 years, having purchased our place during the rural land movement of the late sixties. Our land was undeveloped, except for an open-framed horse barn. When we handed our down payment to the real estate agent, I can remember wondering if we were making the biggest mistake of our lives. Fortunately, it was one of the best decisions we have ever made.

We soon learned about carpentry, cement, plumbing and electric wiring; about springs, pumps and holding tanks; about tree-planting, gardening and dirt-road maintenance; and about alternative energy systems. We now supply our own power, using solar cells, a water turbine and storage batteries, with a propane generator as a backup. Our house is built, as are a shop, laundry room and game room. We have fresh fruit and vegetables and a business in town that supports us.

My commute to my office in the small rural town of Garberville, in the redwood-tree country of northern California, is only a 30-minute drive through the hills, along the river and under the redwoods. We can still drink pure water from a spring and breathe clean air. And I know that thousands of other people across the United States and Canada have had similar good fortune in their moves to the country, and many more seek to leave the congestion of the major cities and suburbs.

A recent Gallup poll commissioned by the National League of Cities found that one-third of those residing in municipalities of 50,000 or more would migrate to the country if they had the chance. Beginning in the mid-seventies, for the first time in 150 years, the flow of population in the United States switched direction away from the cities and their immediate surroundings.

This pattern remains the same today. The population seems to be responding naturally to overcrowding, congestion, pollution, depersonalization and a decline in the quality of life in urban areas, as well as to the increasing high cost of living in a metropolitan area.

The past 20 years have seen new kinds of cars and trucks especially suited to the rural lifestyle, rugged and economical to operate. Rural roads and accessibility of rural areas to the city are being improved at an accelerated rate. It is easier now than at any other time in history to live in a rural area and reasonably commute to the heart of a major city, if that is what you choose to do.

However, the creation of the information highway can help many people commute to any city without ever leaving home. Computers, modems, fax machines, the Internet, cable television and scanners, with the help of Federal Express, the United Parcel Service and the U.S. Postal Service, are rapidly enabling many people to move their businesses to rural areas or to start up new businesses in remote locations where it was previously impossible to do so. We have included in this book the means for you to use this new technology in researching your purchase of a place in the country.

Folks in retirement continue to seek a peaceful rural community to live in, and they bring their hard-earned life savings with them, making more opportunities for people who work and have businesses in the area. Retirees see the value in selling their urban or suburban property at a high price and buying a comparable property in the country for one-third the price, putting the rest of the money in savings, kicking back and enjoying life.

Younger pioneers are willing to accept the lower income in rural areas for the joys of country living. However, the net disposable income is often increased because the cost of living is lower.

A 1995 report issued by the American Resort Development Association found that interest in recreational property purchases increased substantially since 1990. 60.3 percent of households now feel they have a chance of purchasing recreational property by 2005. This is believed to result from the end of the recession, aging of the baby-boom generation and the decline in mortgage interest rates. A single-family vacation home or cabin is the dream of more Americans than any other type of recreational property, and recreational land is in more demand than resort condominiums. Surprisingly, the under-40 age group has the strongest belief that they will purchase recreational property in their lifetime.

The second-home or vacation-home market is also healthy. Any owner of a vacation retreat, as long as it is not rented out for more than 14 days per year, is allowed to deduct mortgage interest payments, property taxes and casualty losses. If the property is rented for more than 15 days during the year, the tax laws become complex and you should consult a tax attorney or accountant. (Tax deduction rules regarding vacation homes are found in Internal Revenue Code Section 280A.)

Therefore, I do not expect to see a decline in the desire to own a second home as a retreat. In fact, many owners of vacant rural lots will likely start developing them to take advantage of the tax breaks.

The Federal Department of Housing and Urban Development recently pointed out that in 1976, 1 in 12 American families owned either a second home or a vacant recreational lot, and that by 1985 that figure had doubled.

Although prices were high and interest rates ridiculous in the late seventies and early eighties, things have now returned to normal. It now appears that the late nineties and well into the next century will be excellent years to purchase rural real estate, not necessarily as a get-rich investment but as an investment in a better lifestyle.

## How To Use This Book

This book is meant to be a tool that you should carry with you as you go through the processes of finding and buying your place in the country. You will have to read parts of it more than once to absorb all of the information. Many of the things I discuss will become much clearer when you actually get out and start dealing with real estate agents, looking at land and delving into the public records at the local city hall. If you have the time and inclination to follow the course of investigation I outline, you will be protected, with minimal need for a lawyer. Even when you retain counsel for some aspect of the purchase, such as inspecting the final draft of your contract of sale or title documents, it will be very helpful for you to have this background information available.

The chapters in this book are divided into ten parts, and there are Appendixes at the end of the book. Part I, "Looking for Land," should be used in conjunction with the Appendixes. This first section gives basic information on how to find out about land for sale, and it teaches you how to protect yourself when dealing with real estate agents by explaining the role they play and the sales tactics they use. Part II, "Checking Out the Land," outlines in detail the factors you should consider when choosing the general location of the land and evaluating the various aspects of a specific parcel, especially the soil, the water and the condition of the structures. Part III, "The Land and the Law," explains in an easy-to-follow manner the legal protections you need and how to investigate them. Part IV, "Deciding on a Fair Price," will help you evaluate the fair market value of the land and bargain skillfully with the seller to get his asking price down to a figure you consider reasonable. Part V, "Financing Your Purchase," explores the types of financing, the sources of loans and available government programs. Part VI, "The Contract of Sale," presents a model form that you can copy from the book, modify for your own transaction and thus help to ensure that you will be adequately protected in your purchase. This is the heart of the book and the most important section. You must get everything in writing when you are dealing with real estate. Nothing you are told verbally is legally binding, unless you can prove what was said, and that is often impossible. Part VII, "Going Through Escrow," demystifies the escrow process and explains title searches, abstracts of title and title insurance. The various forms of co-ownership are outlined, and a Model Owners Agreement is included. Different types of deeds are then described. Part VIII, "Canada," contains information and resources for evaluating property purchases in this unique area. Part IX, "Using a Lawyer," discusses how to select and use a lawyer. Part X, "Property Evaluation Checklist," sums up the entire book in a simple checklist that you should take with you every time you go property hunting. It contains a complete and basic summary of all points raised throughout the book, and

it will remind you of every question you need to ask and every piece of information you will need to obtain to be a safe and wise buyer.

The "Useful Resources" at the ends of the chapters and the Appendixes at the end of the book contain hundreds of addresses and sources of information for everything from real estate catalogs to solar energy systems and prefab log houses. When writing for any of the pamphlets, also ask for a recent catalog or list of publications to get the most recent information and prices. You may find publications that you are particularly interested in that we have not included.

The "Useful Resources" also include material available from government and private agencies, and books, magazines and other data not readily available in local libraries or bookstores. Even if you send for only the free resources, you will have a valuable personal library of information that will aid you both before and after you purchase your place in the country.

## Electronic Information

This book has been updated to include electronic information. It is exciting to now have information available at our fingertips, or rather phone lines. Nothing can replace a library or the feel of a good book, but with time and distance sometimes a factor (especially here in the country), it is nice to have new information sources.

We found information on the Internet, from bulletin board systems (BBS), through faxes and a new system called FaxBacks. We have supplemented the old "snail mail" addresses (the electronic-age term for the U.S. Postal Service) and libraries with these new sources. Some electronic addresses are preceded by the initials URL, which stand for Uniform Resource Locator. This is the standard descriptor for World Wide Web addresses.

With this new information highway we found a whole new set of terms.

### E-Mail

When you see the term *E-mail*, it refers to an electronic way to leave a message for someone or some group. In order to use E-mail you need to have a way to deliver it. You must have a modem, appropriate software and be a subscriber to a service like America On-Line, Genie, or CompuServe, or have an Internet account. We have an Internet account with Northcoast Communications (northcoast.com).

### Internet

An *Internet site* in this book refers to a site from which you retrieve information. It may be an actual site where the resource is found or it may be a starting point to look for more information. The Internet has Gopher sites that have text based information and Web sites that have graphical information. We found that the government supports its Internet sites. Most government sites at one time were Gopher sites. Now many have switched to Web sites. It is therefore necessary to have a good web browser. We used Netscape and found it worked well at all sites. You can use your search engine, a program designed to search the many Internet servers, to look up a topic to then get specific sites. You use it like an index or card catalog. The links between sites are becoming more sophisticated and run smoother every day. We found categories like "Real Estate" and "Alternative Energy" with the search. These catagories gave us relevant information, as well as referred us to other sites.

### BBS

*Bulletin board systems (BBS)* require a communication package. We encourage you to feel comfortable using yours before going on line. (We used Qmodem Pro). Bulletin boards either have information posted or files that can retrieved. When calling up most government BBSs, you'll be instructed step by step what to do. You will be asked for a password on most of them. Our suggestion is to decide on a password that you will use for all government BBSs that is different from the one you use to access your provider accounts. An example would be "BOOK," which was our password for this book.

### FaxBack

If you don't have telecommunicating capabilities, but have access to a fax machine or fax capabilities on your computer, then this type of service is becoming more available. With the use of *FaxBack systems*, you phone up a number and are faxed a list of available information. After deciding which publications you'd like sent, you simply phone back and request, usually up to three, documents. Then in a matter of moments your request is faxed back to you.

We include telephone numbers, TDD for the deaf, and fax numbers for offices listed in the "Useful Resources" sections when available. With the elimination of offices and departments due to government restructuring, some of your mail may be returned and you will need to telephone to reach the correct person. A phone call can also put you on the trail of information at a faster pace. Remember though, once securing your place in the country, you might prefer going back to the slower "snail mail" pace of country life.

The introduction of electronic information as a rural resource is very exciting. Some Internet sites may not have exactly what you want but just keep looking. Remember to keep good bookmarks because when you hit on information there can be so much that it is hard to retain it all. It is nice to be able to return to the site again for more information or as a starting point for further adventures. Any questions or comments regarding using electronic information in your investigations can be directed to our consultants, Ron and Holly Vetter, at vetter@northcoast.com.

# PART
# I

# Looking for Land

# CHAPTER

# 1 How To Start Your Search

*This is a dream as old as America itself; give me a piece of land to call my own, a little town where everyone knows my name. It's a dream we are dreaming with a new heart-and-gut-felt urgency. More than the romance of the country, it's a promise of safety, of comfort, and of old-fashioned values.*

—Faith Popcorn, *The Popcorn Report*

Purchasing land should be done as carefully as selecting the person with whom you will share it. Even if you are not currently ready to buy land, you should begin looking because it takes time to find the right place; you want to learn as much as you can about country property before you buy. The more land you see, the more you will learn about differences in value and about your expectations. When land hunting, try to keep an open mind. People often find that after seeing many kinds of

places, they choose a different type of environment than they had originally sought. Take your time, and approach your search with a relaxed but probing attitude.

Take your outdoor camping equipment or your trailer, if you have one, when you go land hunting. Some real estate agents and sellers will allow you to stay on the land for a day or two so that you can get a sense of what it is like. (The aspects of the land that you can explore while camping on it or visiting it are discussed in Part II, "Checking Out the Land.") Unless you spend some time on it, you can't begin to get an idea of whether the property will be right for you. Try to stay at least a day on the land, although you will probably only be able to do this if it is vacant.

Make an effort to see the property at its best and at its worst. Most land is sold in the spring and early summer, from April through July, usually the

2

most beautiful time of year. The weather is getting warm, the wildflowers are in bloom, the grass is green and water is plentiful. People are beginning to think of getting a place to spend the approaching summer and those to follow. Sales usually drop a little during the driest summer months but increase again in the early fall, from September through October. Land prices are highest during these seasons because the demand is greater. (The effect of the number of interested buyers on the price of a piece of property is discussed in Chapter 20, "Bargaining To Get the Seller's Asking Price Down.")

The best time to buy is in the late fall and winter, when the number of buyers diminishes and prices are at an annual low level. Few people will venture forth to look at land in the dead of winter, when many country roads are impassable. If you see some land you like in the spring, try to wait to see it again when the weather gets drier and hotter. Not only will you be able to see it under both good and bad conditions, but you will probably get it for a much better price. If you still like the land when the roads are muddy and rutted and the skies are overcast—and you also like it when it is hot, humid and dry—you know you will be happy with your purchase. Similarly, if you see some land for the first time in the middle of winter when it is covered with snow, do not buy it until you see it after the snow melts. A beautiful covering of snow can disguise a poor piece of land.

If possible, try to live in the area in which you want to buy before you make your purchase. You may find that you do not like the area as well as you imagined you would. It is usually easy to find a house or cabin to rent for a few weeks or a month. If you ask around, you may be able to find a job as caretaker of someone's property. This is an economical way to live in the country while looking for your own piece of land. (See "Useful Resources" at the end of Chapter 7 for instructions on how to obtain information on caretaking positions in the country.)

If you are a resident, you will probably hear about places for sale that an outsider would not find out about. To avoid paying an agent's commission, many people do not sell their land through real estate agents. Some do not even advertise in the local paper or post signs but simply rely on friends passing the word. There are several common ways to find out about property for sale without living in the area, however.

Most real estate agencies print up listings of available properties, which they will send to you on request. Go to the main branch of your local library or telephone company and ask to see the yellow pages of the directory for the area in which you are interested. You can then send letters to all the real estate agents in that area asking for their listings and telling them what you want. They will send you the current listings and let you know if something comes into their offices that might interest you.

Large real estate agencies publish land catalogs listing various pieces of property they have for sale. In Appendix A at the end of the book, I list the catalogs now available free from major real estate companies that have local franchises throughout the rural areas of the United States. (One of the most famous companies is United National Real Estate.) The different catalogs are fun to look at and they will give you an idea of prices in various areas of the country; but their major purpose is to lure you into the local offices so that the agents can show you whatever properties they have available—not necessarily the ones they advertise. Because of the lag time in printing catalogs, properties listed often are already sold before the catalog comes out. Other deals that sound fantastic in the catalog may prove disapointing because of the subjective nature of describing and advertising a piece of property.

When reading any real estate advertisement, notice what is excluded as well as what is included. Any piece of land can be written up to sound good or can look beautiful in a tiny photograph. An ad always refers to a parcel's good qualities. For example, if no mention is made of water availability, there is a good chance that water supply will be a problem.

Another common advertising technique used by many real estate agencies is illustrated by the following quote from a real estate promotion:

> From this brochure select the property or section that suits you best and see it now! Delay might mean that someone else might beat you to the bargain you have chosen. The brochure will be in the hands of thousands of other people in every corner of the U.S., and the first person on the ground with the necessary deposit is the one who gets the place of his choice!

Don't let such ads scare you into thinking that you must buy land immediately because nothing will be left if you don't. Lots of land is still available, and more becomes available every day as large landholdings, ranches and farms split up. Although land prices continue to fluctuate, good deals are constantly coming up. If you know what you are doing, you will be able to get a good piece of land at a reasonable price for many years in the future.

Another common way to locate land for sale is to look in the local papers in the area and in the classified ads of major newspapers of a nearby city. The Sunday editions of large newspapers carry the most real estate advertisements, and many rural brokers advertise in the urban areas because that is where the market is. Often there is a separate classification for "Country Property."

When you go to an area, prepare index cards containing a description of the type of land you want. Hang these cards on local bulletin boards with an address at which you can be reached. You can also place an ad in the local paper for a small fee.

It is possible to purchase land from other than a private party. Although homesteading is no longer possible, even in Alaska, the federal and state governments still sell and lease land to the general public. A program exists, for example, whereby summer homes can be leased in the national forests. Information on how to obtain all the available literature on the above subjects is given in the Appendixes.

Land also can be purchased at tax sales, held when property taxes have not been paid by the owner. This land seems to be a bargain, but many technical aspects are involved. I do not recommend that you buy such land without consulting an attorney. In most cases, you must pay cash for the land, and after you buy it, the owner still has a legally specified period of time in which to pay the back taxes and redeem the land. If this happens, you will get your money back with interest, but you will lose the land. Tax sales are discussed in Chapter 17, "Property Taxes and Assessments." You can get all the facts on the local laws in your area from the county tax collector.

A variation on buying land at a tax sale is to look in the tax collector's public file in the county tax collector's office to find parcels that have back taxes due on them. You can then contact the owners and ask them if they would like to sell. You might find an owner who is desperate and willing to sell his place at a bargain price.

Buying land at a foreclosure or trustee sale also involves technical legal problems and should not be attempted without hiring an attorney to explain the intricacies of these sales and how to protect yourself.

You will not have any problems finding land for sale. Your main concerns will be the quality of the land and improvements, the price you will pay for it, the inclusion in your contract of sale of all the necessary legal protections and the method of financing your purchase. The remainder of this book is devoted to these topics.

# 2 Real Estate Brokers and Salespersons

*Remember—the seller's real estate agent is working for the seller and does not get paid without making a sale.*

## Brokers Serve a Useful Function

Over the years I have grown to appreciate the value of real estate brokers in the world of country property. Unlike their urban counterparts, country brokers spend time ferrying buyers over hill and dale to show them property. They can't just give out an address and send the buyer out to look at a house; personal touring must be done, and this is time-consuming. A broker may have to drive an hour or

more to each home, on numerous occasions, before a property is sold. And a broker can show a property many times and never sell it. Although it may seem that brokers make an unfair amount of money (5 to 10 percent of the sales price) on a deal, often the effort never leads to a sale. Brokers incur high advertising costs running newspaper ads and mailing out brochures. Such costs are part of the broker's overhead, not a separate cost to the seller. Because many sellers of rural property are not available to show their property, they would have a difficult time selling their property without the help of a good real estate broker.

Brokers also lead the effort to keep country property available for sale. They often help fight over-restrictive laws against subdividing and developing land, thereby protecting their own livelihood while keeping a country home an option open to you.

Brokers counteract the tendency of some rural residents to close the door to newcomers, which helps us all to realize our dream of finding and buying a place in the country.

## Caveat Emptor—
## Let the Buyer Beware!

In the past 20 years land buyers have become considerably more sophisticated. Because of that sophistication, less scrupulous real estate agents have fared badly. Federal and state agencies also have been more vigorous in regulating new subdivisions and elevating the standards of agents. Nevertheless, some agents have adopted more subtle tactics; others just are not well-informed. So, whether you are dealing with the honest or the subtle, the well-informed or misinformed, remember the cardinal rule: Caveat Emptor—"Let the buyer beware!" You will be pleased to know, however, that the old Latin saying has taken on a new dimension since the mid-seventies. The agent and the seller are no longer free, under state statutes and codes of professional ethics, to treat an uninformed buyer as fair game. The buyer is entitled by law to fairness and disclosure by all parties to the transaction.

You'll soon have the knowledge and ability to double-check anything a real estate person tells you. Demand all important statements in writing. Never let a real estate salesperson intimidate you to a point where you refrain from asking questions or from cross-checking anything he or she tells you. To play the game of real estate you must know who the players are.

## Differences Between Brokers
## and Salespersons

Persons are licensed to sell real property by the states, either as real estate brokers or real estate salespersons. The term *agent* applies to both.

### The Real Estate Broker
State agencies generally require that a person aspiring to become a licensed broker serve as an apprentice to another licensed broker's firm for a specified period of time, complete some college-level courses and pass a comprehensive examination on real estate law and conveyancing. Most states also subject broker candidates to a financial condition and credit audit. After obtaining a license, the broker is required to take periodic continuing education in real estate courses.

The real estate salesperson or broker acts as liaison throughout the negotiations between you and the owner who is selling his or her land. For example, if you want to make an offer to buy land, you give your offer to the agent to deliver to the seller. The seller then gives his or her response to the agent, who delivers it to you. The agent cannot legally refuse to inform the sellers of any facts involving a possible sale, even if the amount of money or the terms you offer seem outrageous. An agent can usually accept a deposit from you on behalf of the seller, though the agent rarely has the power to actually accept your offer and sign a purchase agreement on the seller's behalf. Some states permit real estate agents to write certain documents, such as purchase agreements and deposit receipts. Other states consider the drafting of a purchase agreement to be the practice of law, an illegal activity for a real estate agent who is not a licensed attorney.

### The Real Estate Salesperson
To become a real estate salesperson, one is required to pass an examination on principles, law and conveyancing. Salespersons work under the supervision of a licensed real estate broker and can sell land only under that broker's authority. A salesperson usually cannot sign any documents or receive any commission directly, but can do so only through the broker.

### The REALTOR®
To ensure professionalism for the land-selling industry, the 700,000-member National Association of REALTORS® adopted a code of ethics. Only licensed agents who have taken an oath to ascribe to that code of ethics are entitled to call themselves "REALTORS®"—in some parts of the country, salespeople are designated "REALTOR-Associates." local area REALTOR® boards have a grievance panel of members to hear cases involving member REALTORS® who have violated that code. This panel is available to home buyers and sellers at no cost to them, and offers speedier resolution than the court

process. A salesperson working under a member broker is kept under close supervision by that broker. You can always identify a brokerage firm that belongs to the NAR by the sign in the window that displays the big blue and gold "R."

The following true story is a good example of how a purchaser can get in trouble. I know the principals involved in this case personally.

A salesperson convinced a buyer to purchase some land by assuring him that a beautiful creek ran across the property. The buyer, without double-checking anything the salesperson told him, signed a contract, paid the purchase price and closed the deal. Then he decided to get a survey done before beginning to build his house, to be sure that it would be within the property lines. He should have demanded that a survey be conducted before he bought the land, for the survey showed, to the buyer's surprise, that the creek was not on his property. Since the land was worthless without water from the creek, he went to the former owner to try to get his money back, but was unsuccessful. The former owner had never promised the buyer that the creek was on the property; in fact, the two had never even met.

The buyer then tried to locate the salesperson, but he had left the broker's employ. The broker claimed he had never told his salesperson that the creek was on the property. But the broker did admit that when the salesperson asked if the creek were on the property, the broker answered that he thought it might be but could not be sure without a survey.

Getting nowhere, the buyer filed a complaint with the district attorney against the salesperson and broker for fraud. The district attorney found the salesperson and brought him in for questioning. At that time the salesperson stated that he knew nothing about the property other than what the broker had told him and that the broker *did* say the creek was on the land. The district attorney refused to get involved and referred the victim to a private attorney. However, the buyer had nothing in writing to prove that he had been told the creek was on the land. After consulting several lawyers about suing the parties involved, the buyer decided that the costs and fees were too high. He decided to spend the money on a well instead. The buyer did not get what he paid for and will have to pay still more for the well. This all could have been avoided by demanding a survey before the close of the sale.

Even if you are positive that you have the law on your side and that you will have no problem proving your case, you still have to hire an attorney, pay court costs and follow through with lengthy and costly litigation. And if the defendant agrees to settle the matter out of court, you will still have legal fees to pay. In many areas, the courts are jammed with cases, and a year or two or more may pass before you can even get into court. If you do not have evidence in writing, you will have a difficult time proving your case.

Never depend on your ability to bring a successful case against someone, should he or she defraud you. Your goal is to investigate the property so thoroughly before you buy that you will not have any reason to bring a court action later. As a safety factor, make sure your contract of sale specifies all terms and conditions of the deal, so that you will have a good case if those terms are not met.

## The Real Estate Agent Works for the Seller

A basic fact to remember when dealing with real estate agents is that agents generally are hired by sellers and owe what is called *fiduciary obedience* to those sellers.* Agents are not independent persons who simply try to find buyers for pieces of property. Usually a seller has signed a form of listing contract, making an agent the employee of the seller. When the agent finds an acceptable buyer, the seller will pay the broker's firm a commission. Agents are directly responsible and owe complete loyalty to the sellers who engage them. (But the law does not require an agent to comply with illegal or unscrupulous instructions by the seller. Rather, it forbids such compliance.) Because agents' commissions are based on a percentage of the selling price, it is in their interest to get the highest price possible for land. (The agent's role in setting the asking price for the property is explained in Chapter 20.)

Because an agent showing property usually represents the seller, he or she is obligated to seek the highest possible price for the seller. The agent, however, may be unwilling to advise you as to whether the seller will accept a lower price.

If you reveal to the agent the top price you are

---

*Throughout the remainder of this book, I will refer to the owner of the land as the *seller* and the person who sells his land for him as the *broker* or real estate *agent*.

willing to pay for the property, the information may be passed on to the seller without your knowledge or approval—in truth, it is part of the agent's job. That revelation could result in the seller's asking for that higher price and your paying more than you otherwise might have paid had you not confided in the agent. As a buyer do not disclose that sort of information to an agent who does not represent you.

### Buyer Agency

You may hear of *buyer agency*—it is a coming type of brokerage in many areas, and it may work to your advantage. Skipping the technicalities, it is simply your hiring an agent to work for *you* as the buyer. That agent works for you alone; you may speak freely and know that your agent is looking for the best price for you, not for the seller.

It costs no more; instead of a seller's paying, say $5,000 to the selling broker, the seller pays $2,500 to the selling broker and you take $2,500 you might have paid to the seller for the property, and pay that to your "buyer's broker." It is not quite that simple, but it is not much more complicated, either.

## The Types of Listings

A seller usually gives his property to an agent under one of the following common types of listing contracts. The most desirable contract for an agent is an *Exclusive Right To Sell*, which means that the broker is the only person or firm allowed to sell the land during the period the contract is in force. If the property is sold by anyone else, *including the owner,* the listing broker is entitled to the commission. No other agent can show the land without the listing broker's permission, and if the seller finds a buyer on his own, the broker under contract is still entitled to a commission.

Often, a broker will invite other agents to show the property under a *multiple listing* arrangement, and if another broker finds a buyer for the property, both brokers will share the commission. (Note: Both brokers are working for, and owe allegiance to, the seller.)

A second form of listing is one called an *Exclusive Agency* contract, similar to an Exclusive Right to Sell, except that the sellers reserve the right to sell the land by themselves without being obligated to pay any commission to the agent. If another agent sells the land, the listing agent is entitled to the full commission.

The third type of agreement (which is seldom a formal contract) is an *open listing,* under which the sellers list their land (frequently verbally) with several different brokers. The first agent to find a satisfactory buyer gets the commission. The sellers also can sell the land themselves and not pay anyone a commission. Most brokers avoid this type of agreement because they are competing with everyone else in town; they will show open-listed land only after showing protected exclusive listings—their own or other offices'.

Because most sellers add the amount of the commission to their asking price to pass the expense on to the buyer, the lack of a commission due a broker in a direct sale may be used as bargaining chip in negotiation for a lower sales price.

Land seekers are occasionally successful in locating property owners and purchasing directly from them when the property is not even being advertised for sale. Many owners of rural land, particularly if it is underdeveloped or used only for a second home, do not live in the area of the property. But if you can identify the parcel on an assessor's map, then get the owner's name and address from the public record in the county tax receiver's office, you may be able to get negotiations underway.

## How To Protect Yourself

### Get It In Writing!

An agent makes money only if he sells some property, and competition for listings in rural areas is extremely tough. Some real estate agents will take any listing they can get, regardless of the condition of the property. It might be lacking adequate water, legal access, well-drained soil, or other features of good land, but that won't stop some agents from taking the listing. Eventually someone may buy it.

Some agents are not going to volunteer the bad points of a piece of property. Only by asking the right questions and demanding specific answers do you stand any chance of learning the facts. Don't be satisfied with equivocal statements, such as, "I think so," "I don't think there's been a problem in the past," or, "Nobody can make a guarantee about that in this area." This type of statement is meaningless. While *full disclosure* is demanded by state laws and the REALTOR® code of ethics, it is sometimes up to you to pursue all the facts of the situation. In giving an ambiguous response to your question, the agent is not committing to anything.

**Figure 2-1.  How To Read a Real Estate Ad**

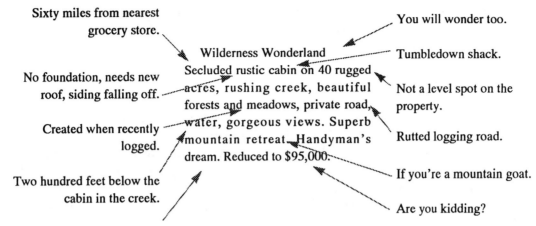

Even a definite statement, unless you get it in writing, is worthless. You must receive more than ambivalent, worthless statements when preparing to part with thousands of dollars.

**Work Out Everything**
**Before the Deal Is Closed**
Never buy land on the agent's assurance that a problem can be worked out after the deal is closed. For example: You will share a well with adjoining landowners, but no agreement has been reached for pump maintenance or allocation of water. The agent may tell you that your neighbors are great people and that you will have no problem working out an arrangement after you buy the land. This is a common-and dangerous-sales technique. Once you take title, the agent is out of the picture. If your neighbors should not turn out to be so nice, you are in real trouble!  Don't assume the agent is going to help you with problems once he gets his commission-if he can't arrange the details in writing *before* you buy the land, he certainly will not do so after closing.

**These Lines Are Always Good for a Laugh**

- "I'll let you in on a secret about the seller."
- "I'm going to show you something nobody else has seen."
- "The land is really worth more than the seller is asking."
- "So far, nobody else has seen this property."
- "If I had the money, I'd buy this piece myself."
- "Look, a lot of people are interested in this property, so you better make up your mind quickly."
- "If your creek or spring dries up, you can always drill a well."
- "I am sure the seller will not negotiate."
- "You have a prescriptive right-of-way; you don't need a deeded easement."

You should also read ads with a skeptical eye. (See Figure 2–1.)

**Understand the Broker's**
**Psychological Approach**
After dealing with countless real estate agents I have found two standard psychological approaches used in selling country property. The first I call the "Welcome to the country, smile and don't worry about a thing" approach. The second is the "Why are you trying to complicate the deal by asking all those questions?" approach.

**"Welcome to the Country, Smile and**
**Don't Worry about a Thing"**
The rural land dealer often exudes this attitude. The first thing you notice is the informal, unbusinesslike appearance. But don't let the absence of a necktie or a silk blouse lull you into thinking that the agent is less sophisticated than some slick, high-pressure city agents. Coming from the city, you may be easily mesmerized by the country ambiance. The agent will try to make you feel completely at ease and will offer to help you find a nice piece of land. He or she can convince you that your interests are

paramount, in the hope that you won't question anything you are told.

Extreme caution should be used when dealing with developers who fly prospective customers to subdivisions for the weekend, provide free meals and drinks, let them ride horses and swim, and then make a big sales pitch. These sales gimmicks place extreme pressure on the captive buyers. A purchase agreement should never be signed until you have returned home and taken a few days to cool off and think about what you are getting yourself into. Most states now regulate the previsit motivational meetings, require the advance distribution of a property prospectus approved by the state and further require a cooling-off period that grants the buyers several days to rescind the contract without losing their deposit.

Several brokers have given their personal tips for showing property in the country. The most interesting one is to make sure the owner-seller has bread baking or coffee brewing when the prospective purchaser is shown the home. These are two favorite smells for most people and lend a pleasant but subconscious edge to a sales pitch. One broker makes sure the house is warm and a big fire is going in the fireplace, with drinks available and fresh flowers on the table.

### "Why Are You Trying To Complicate the Deal?"

This approach is extremely effective, particularly when used with buyers who know little about what they are doing. Nobody wants to admit ineptitude. Thus, when a buyer asks too many questions, the real estate agent gives him a look that implies, "What's the matter, can't you follow this?" Most agents dislike anyone who asks a lot of questions, especially lawyers who "complicate things with all kinds of trivial conditions." The broker would have you believe that buying land is simply a process of finding a parcel that looks good to you and signing the purchase agreement. All the rest is just "paperwork." This fact is exemplified by the statement made by a few brokers that the Purchase Agreement and Deposit Receipt is just a receipt for some money and only one of many forms the buyer will get. Many buyers do not know that once the deposit receipt is signed by both parties, it becomes the binding contract for the land purchase.

Experienced agents know very quickly whether a buyer is going to be an "easy sale." They base their judgment on how much knowledge you appear to have about real estate, how much money you intend to spend and whether you seem to have "buyer's fever." Thus, when a buyer starts asking questions about extremely important legal matters such as title insurance, easements, water rights, building permits and financing, some brokers pass the topics off as if they are merely secondary to the deal. They are secondary to the broker, whose goal is to sell the land. There will be no commission generated unless the property sells. The broker will try to avoid anything that delays the sale.

But these matters are *not* secondary to you. Once you have read this book, you will have many questions to ask the agent selling the property, about every aspect of your purchase—you may even sound like a lawyer. Never let an agent's accusation that you are paranoid, uptight or concerned with minor points embarrass you while investigating your purchase. Brokers have nothing to lose when they take your deposit. You are the only one who can lose anything.

## Many Brokers Will Negotiate Loans

An agent might volunteer to assist you with your financing. Brokers often have very close ties with local banks, savings and loan associations and other residential lenders. But you have to be careful of two things: First, a broker may charge you for this service without disclosing the charge in advance. Second, the loan might have a higher interest rate, origination fee or other costs than another loan you can get elsewhere. Some say "Brokers sell homes, bankers sell money." In most states, individuals must have state licenses to act as a loan broker. In any event, you should always compare the terms of a loan the broker might arrange for you with those of other available lending institutions. (See Chapter 25.)

## A Real Estate Agent and His or Her Reputation

A real estate agent develops a reputation very quickly in a small town. Spend some time in the local restaurants, at the gas station, in the hardware store, in the retail shops. Talk to folks about your interest in moving to the area. Ask for recommendations about a broker and pay attention to what you hear. When I first came into my area looking for land, every time I asked the locals who not to deal with in town, I was given the same two names. Those two brokers are no longer in business, and for good reason.

The fact that a broker shows you a piece of property does not commit you to patronize him. If you hear that a particular broker has lost his license or is being investigated by the district attorney or local real estate board, find out if this is true. Write to your state department of real estate and ask what the current status of the broker is and whether he or she has been charged with fraudulent sales practices in the past. It is illegal for persons to claim they are brokers if they are not, and most states require a person to be licensed to sell property that belongs to others.

## Preparing To Deal with an Agent

Many real estate agents prefer that you write or call to make an appointment to view land rather than just drop in. Go to the phone company or to the public library and get a copy of the phone book for the area you want to investigate. Look under "Real Estate" in the Yellow Pages, write down the addresses of all the brokerage firms in town, then send duplicate letters to those agencies telling them when you will be in the area and requesting an appointment to view their properties. Most brokers will send you pamphlets describing what they have for sale. If some of the described properties are already sold, businesslike brokers will mark them with a "Sold" stamp.

The brokers want to know what kind of property you are looking for and how much money you have to spend. If you are restricting your search to land with electricity to the site, that is not more than 15 minutes from the nearest town and has a year-round creek running through it, the firm will determine whether they have any listings that will interest you. You should always try to get them to show you everything they have that meets your requirements. Never tell brokers the actual amount of money you have to spend; you will be in a better position to

bargain, to get the purchase price down later. Simply tell them the price range of property you can afford. Always act like a serious customer, however, or the brokers may not show you the best of what their firms have listed, particularly if properties are distant from their offices.

If you do not like any of the properties a broker shows you, you can leave your name with that broker and tell him or her to write you if something comes up that matches the description of what you want. The conscientious broker who realizes that you are serious will notify you when a new property comes on the market. You should keep the contact open by communicating regularly with agents.

## Warning—Never Try To Cheat an Agent

Unfortunately, some buyers try to cheat brokers out of commissions. I have successfully sued both buyers and sellers for doing so. A buyer is shown a parcel of land by a broker, and the buyer makes contact directly with the seller and negotiates a selling price. The buyer and seller close the deal without informing the broker, hoping that the broker never finds out. This is a breach of the seller's listing contract with the broker. The buyer is liable for damages for interfering with the contractual relationship between the seller and broker and for conspiring with the seller to deprive the broker of his lawful commission. Should the broker sue for his commission, both will lose in court.

## Useful Resources

The following pamphlet is free from:

Federal Trade Commission
Office of Consumer and Business Education
Bureau of Consumer Protection
Washington, DC 20580

"Real Estate Brokers"

# Checking Out the Land

# 3 Climate

## Do You Know What To Expect?

The first thing a person who moves from the city to the country notices is the weather. As a resident or worker in the city you probably spend most of the day indoors under artificial lighting, insulated from the climate by sealed and tinted windows and air-conditioning. You imagine that when you move to the wide open spaces you will delight in the smell of the earth after a light rain and the warmth of the early morning sun shining on fields and trees. But getting in and out of an isolated area on a slippery, rutted dirt road in the snow and rain; trying to start your car in subfreezing weather; using a cold, damp outhouse; having your water pipes freeze; and keeping yourself and your animals warm are also part of country life.

Urban expatriates often make the mistake of

moving to an area of the country where the weather is completely different from what they are used to, and they often find they are unable to adjust to the new climate. I strongly recommend that you spend part of each of the four seasons—preferably a whole year if you intend to buy land in an unfamiliar area—to assure yourself that you are willing and able to keep yourself happily alive in that area's climate.

## Climate Regions Map

The basic elements of climate that you should consider and research when land hunting are temperature, humidity, rain and snow, drought, floods, winds, frost, sunshine, fog, cloudiness, hurricanes, cyclones, tornadoes, and dust storms. The United States Department of Agriculture Climate Regions

Map divides the 48 contiguous United States into 32 separate climate regions. It is reprinted here as Figure 3–1, followed by a description of each region.

*Region 1* comprises the Pacific Coast west of the Coast Range from Santa Cruz Bay to the Canadian line. Its characteristics are cool, dry summers with frequent fogs and heavy winter rainfall with lowest temperatures 8 to 10 degrees below freezing in the north to about freezing in the south.

*Region 2* includes the Willamette Valley in Oregon and the region of similar climate north of it in Washington, including the shores of Puget Sound. The summers are warmer and drier than in Region 1, and the average lowest temperatures are from 10 degrees to 20 degrees F.

*Region 3* includes the Sacramento and San Joaquin valleys in California. This region has hot, dry summers and mild winters with 10 to 20 inches of rainfall. The temperature drops to 8 to 10 degrees below freezing on the valley floor, with slightly higher temperatures on the hillsides.

*Region 4* includes the Sierra Nevada and Cascade mountain ranges. This region has hot, dry summers, except for occasional scattered showers in the mountains. Most of the winter precipitation, from 20 to more than 50 inches, falls on the western slopes, where winters are moderate to cold. East of the mountains, wide variations in temperatures occur frequently. The Sierra Nevadas have snow annually at elevations as low as 2,000 feet. Throughout this entire area, conditions vary considerably according to elevation.

*Region 5* comprises the area west of the Coast Range from Santa Cruz to Santa Barbara, thence to San Diego, Redlands and Riverside, including what is popularly known as Southern California. The summers are dry, cool on the coast and warm inland; the winters are moderately rainy, from 30 inches in the mountains to 10 inches in the valleys, and are nearly free from frost on the coast and in the foothills.

*Region 6* is the Columbia River Valley in eastern Washington. The summers are warm; the winters have ordinary temperatures of 10 degrees to 15 degrees F, with extreme occasional lows of zero. The annual rainfall varies from 7 to 20 inches, mostly in winter and spring.

*Region 7* includes the plateau of the eastern part of the state of Washington and the valleys of northern Idaho and western Montana. The summers are warm, and the lowest winter temperatures range from zero to 15 degrees F, with an annual rainfall of 10 to 20 inches.

*Region 8* is the Snake River Plains and the Utah Valley. It is semiarid country with water available for irrigation. The summers are hot, and the winters

**Figure 3–1. Climate Regions Map**

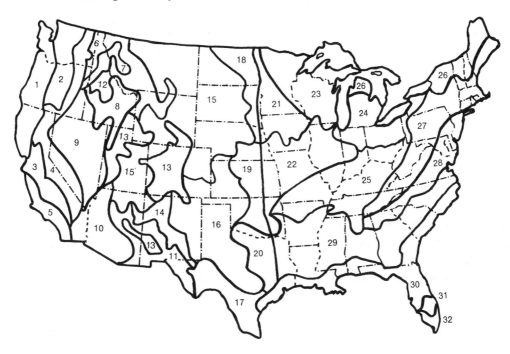

often have minimum temperatures of zero to -10 degrees F, with a rainfall of 9 to 15 inches, mostly in winter.

*Region 9* is the northern part of the great arid interior plateau located mainly in the states of Oregon, Nevada and Utah. Its characteristics are hot days and occasional frosty nights in summer, with cold winters and about 10 inches of rainfall annually.

*Region 10* includes all the southwestern desert, including portions of California, Arizona and a corner of Nevada. The climate is hot to scorching, with a rainfall of 3 to 10 inches.

*Region 11* comprises the southern part of the great arid interior plateau that is located in New Mexico and Arizona. Its characteristics are the same as the plateau farther north (Region 9), except that the temperatures are higher.

*Region 12* is that part of the Rocky Mountains included in Idaho, Montana and Wyoming. The temperature and rainfall vary greatly, depending on elevation and exposure.

*Region 13* includes the Rocky Mountains of Utah and Colorado. It is similar to the region farther north, except that the temperatures for the same elevation are about 7 degrees warmer.

*Region 14* includes the Rocky Mountains of Arizona and New Mexico. It is similar to the region farther north, except that temperatures for the same elevation average about 6 degrees warmer than Region 13, and 13 degrees warmer than Region 12.

*Region 15* is the northern Great Plains area south to Kansas and Colorado, extending from the 5,500-foot contour on the west to the black soils on the east. It is extremely cold in winter in the northeastern portions, usually dropping to -30 degrees or -40 degrees F, while close to the mountains it is 20 degrees warmer. The summers are moderately warm. It is generally recognized as the northern part of the dry-farming area, with annual rainfall of about 15 inches.

*Region 16* is the central portion of the Great Plains, including the plains portion of Kansas, Oklahoma and New Mexico, as well as portions of the plains in Colorado and Texas. It extends eastward from about the 6,500-foot contour on the west to the black soils on the east. Rainfall varies from 12 to 22 inches annually. The climate is warmer and has greater evaporation than Region 15. It is the southern portion of the dry-farming area.

*Region 17* is the dry, hot portion of southwestern Texas, with 12 to 22 inches of rainfall annually, but with excessive evaporation.

*Region 18* is the subhumid black-soil country lying east of the dry-farming area of the northern Great Plains and is intermediate as to moisture between Region 15 and the more humid area to the east of it. The winters are very cold and dry.

*Region 19* is the subhumid black-soil area of Kansas, southern Nebraska and much of Oklahoma. There is more moisture than in the dry-farming country to the west of it and less than in the area farther east. It is a locality of sudden variation in winter temperatures and of hot winds in summer.

*Region 20* is the subhumid or transition region of central Texas with black and chocolate-colored soils. In moisture conditions it is intermediate between the dry-farming regions farther west and the humid climate of eastern Texas.

*Region 21* is the northern part of the prairie country, with frequent droughts of more than 30 days in the western portion and cold winters with drying winds. Annual rainfall is 20 to 30 inches, occurring mostly in the summer season.

*Region 22* is that portion of the prairie country that has higher temperatures than Region 21 but is subject to similar cold, drying winds in winter. Annual rainfall is 30 to 40 inches.

*Region 23* is the western part of the Great lakes forest area. The eastern portion is slightly warmer and more humid than the western portion, the latter much resembling Region 21.

*Region 24* is largely that part of the country influenced by the Great Lakes, lying east of Lake Michigan and extending south into Ohio and eastward to Lake Ontario. There is considerable moisture in the atmosphere, in addition to an annual rainfall of 30 to 40 inches, rather well distributed through the year. The winter temperatures are more moderate than in Region 23.

*Region 25* includes the Ohio and lower Tennessee River valleys and the Ozark Mountain region. The winter temperatures are rather moderate with much alternate freezing and thawing, while the summer is warm with a 30-day drought often occurring near its close. Rainfall is 40 to 50 inches annually.

*Region 26* includes the colder sections of the eastern United States, comprising much of Maine, New Hampshire, and Vermont, the mountainous portions of New York and a portion of northern Michigan. It is characterized by cold winters with heavy snowfall and short summers of long days and cool nights.

*Region 27* is the Appalachian Mountain country, including much of New England and New York, most of Pennsylvania, and the mountainous portion of the states southward. The rainfall is abundant, usually from 35 to 50 inches a year, and is well distributed through the season. In the colder parts the snowfall is abundant.

*Region 28* lies just east of Region 27 and includes the Piedmont and some adjoining sections with similar growing conditions. It extends from northern Alabama northeastward across the Carolinas and Virginia to New Jersey and the coast of Massachusetts. It is warmer than Region 27, with abundant rainfall except in late summer, when 30-day droughts often occur. The winters are open, with much freezing and thawing, and there is little snow protection to be relied on.

*Region 29* includes most of the cotton country, extending from what is known as east Texas eastward and northward to the Atlantic Ocean in North Carolina and Virginia. It lies between the Piedmont region and the swampy lower coastal plain that borders the Gulf of Mexico and the Atlantic Ocean. Rainfall is abundant, from 45 to 60 inches annually, and is well distributed, except toward the last of the rather warm summer, when a long drought frequently occurs, particularly in the western portion.

*Region 30* is the swampy coastal plain from Wilmington, North Carolina, southward along the Atlantic Ocean and westward along the Gulf of Mexico. It has moderate summer temperatures with hot sunshine, short winters, an abundance of rainfall (50 to 60 inches), except in the Texas portion, and is almost subtropical.

*Region 31* is southern Florida, with the exception of the subtropical fringe. It is subject to annual frosts, often becoming sufficiently cold to kill the tops of tender plants without killing their roots, and has rather warm summers and a rainfall of about 50 inches.

*Region 32* is the tropical coast of southern Florida. It has slight range of temperature with no killing frosts and annual rainfall of 50 to 60 inches.

## Geographical Differences Between East and West

The East is less mountainous than the West, and geographic changes are relatively gradual from one section to another. Likewise, temperatures generally increase slowly as you go from north to south. The West, on the other hand, contains large rugged mountain ranges with great differences in elevation over short distances. For example, Mount Whitney, the highest peak in the continental United States outside Alaska (14,495 feet), and Death Valley, a desert wasteland containing the lowest point in the United States (276 feet below sea level), are less than 85 miles apart. These extremes of topography cause the climate to be much more diverse throughout the West than in the East. Temperature differences tend to be based on elevation and can vary greatly within a small area. When looking for land, especially in the West, don't assume that the climate of your prospective homestead is the same as the climate of the nearest town 20 miles away. For instance, the areas around our home often get fog in the mornings and afternoons, whereas our valley, protected from the ocean on one side and the river valley on the other by two mountain ranges, gets almost no fog throughout the year.

## Rain and Snow—The Humid East and Arid West

An average of 30 inches of water falls as rain or snow in the United States each year, but this precipitation is not divided evenly over the country. There is a dividing line between the humid East and the arid West.

The heaviest mean annual rainfall is more than 100 inches near the North Pacific Coast, and several other locations in the West have a mean annual precipitation in excess of 40 inches. But most of the West, from Texas through the Great Plains area north to Montana and the Dakotas, averages less than 20 inches of rainfall annually, and much of the Southwest averages less than 10 inches a year.

Overall, the East gets considerably more rain because of the mixing of Arctic air with the semitropical air masses from the South. The warm southern air flow curves across the Gulf of Mexico, up the Mississippi, and then turns east over the Appalachians to the Atlantic. The Arctic air mass from the north pushes the warm air upward, which lowers the temperature, resulting in heavy rains in both summer and winter. Figure 3–2 shows the great difference in average annual precipitation between the humid East and the arid West. The eastern half of

**Figure 3–2. Average Annual Precipitation**

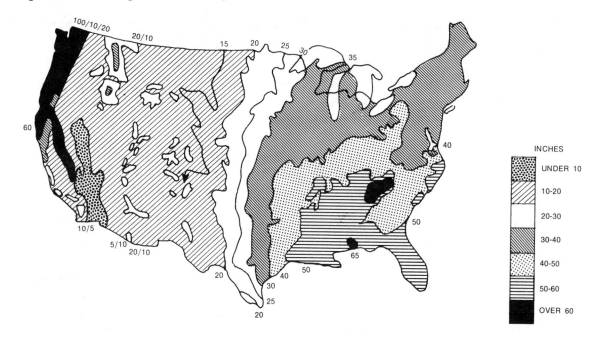

the United States, which contains about 40 percent of the country's total land area, gets 75 percent of the rain and snow. Most of the floods occur in the eastern part of the country because of this excessive precipitation.

### Floods

In whichever part of the country you are looking, if the land is next to a river or stream, you should seriously consider the possibility of a flood. In our area, a devastating flood wiped out several towns along our main river in 1964. I have met a few people who have bought land along that river since that time. They all know about the 1964 flood, but none has actually studied the history of flood damage or the likelihood of future floods occurring. They know only that their homesteads may be wiped out some winter and have accepted perennial anxiety. Most county libraries maintain a local history section that contains a large collection of information on past floods, including photos, newspaper and magazine articles and maps that indicate where the worst damage occurred. These libraries also have information on flood-control measures subsequently taken by the county.

Unfortunately, some of the finest land is located in vulnerable floodplain areas along large rivers, but most rural areas are developing flood-control projects, which lessen potential hazards. Examine the progress of local flood-control plans if you are looking for land along a watercourse. Be especially

cautious when buying land along a river that has had a forest fire or extensive logging operations conducted along its banks. Removing trees increases the amount of surface water runoff and greatly increases the potential for floods where none have occurred in the past. Heavy grazing and farming also help to cause floods by destroying the natural ground cover.

The size of a stream does not indicate its propensity to flood. Even the smallest streams have sent several feet of water into living rooms during heavy storms. Carefully balance your desire to live in a flood area with the potential dangers to your homestead.

### Flash Floods

In many parts of the United States flash floods are a threat. These are local floods of great volume and short duration that generally result from heavy rainfall. They are often the most damaging floods, because they occur on short notice and are highly unpredictable. Some of the states seriously affected by flash floods are Maine, New Jersey, North and South Carolina, Ohio, Virginia, and West Virginia, although flash floods are not limited to the East. The National Weather Service is setting up automatic alarm systems in flash-flood areas throughout the East. If an alarm system has been installed in your area, the price of the land may increase slightly, but the added cost will be worthwhile.

Storms of flash-flood proportion occur in the Great Plains states when warm, moist tropical air moves up over the plains and collides with cold, dry polar air, causing heavy rains, thunder and lightning. In these storms, one-third of the average annual precipitation can fall in 24 hours; occasionally, one-fifth of the annual supply falls in one hour, and then four months may pass without any rain at all.

**Drought**

Too little rain and snow can be as bad as too much. Drought is a serious threat to many areas of the country. The usual problems in the arid West have already been mentioned, and they will be described in greater detail in Chapter 4, "Is There Enough Water on the Land?" Recurring droughts are a normal feature of the climate in southern parts of the Great Plains area, which has had four major droughts since 1880. The most severe occurred during the 1930s throughout the Dust Bowl and caused many farmers to lose their land. The latest drought in that area lasted for four years in the 1950s.

Major water supply crises also occur in other parts of the country. Between 1961 and 1966 most of the 14 northeastern states suffered a serious lack of water. The areas most affected extended from eastern Massachusetts to eastern Pennsylvania. Many rural inhabitants found their wells completely dry during most of the year, and trees, grass, flowers, and crops showed the serious effects of the long water shortage. In addition, wells along the Atlantic Coast were contaminated by seawater, which seeped into the ground as large amounts of fresh water were withdrawn during dry periods. Other parts of the humid East suffered major droughts in the 1930s and in 1949, as well as through the sixties.

In 1986 the South suffered the worst drought in more than 100 years, and the devastating effects of the summer of 1986 will be felt for many years to come. As of 1992, California has been in a five-year drought, and many historically good springs are drying up. A depleted water table can take years to revive.

A thorough study of the drought history of an area and the community's ability to meet future crises will give you the best indication of what might be in store for you if you buy property there.

## Frost and Sunshine— The Length of the Growing Season

If you are interested in growing your own food, you will want to know the number of frost-free days the area has, because many fruits and vegetables cannot tolerate freezing weather. Check local conditions, visit farms and nurseries in the area, and talk to long-time residents about the weather, the length of the growing season, and the crops that are grown there.

## Personal Health

The effect a particular climate may have on your health should not be overlooked. Hot, humid climates often aggravate asthma, allergies, hyperhidrosis, eczema and other conditions. Those of you who are allergic to ragweed pollen should avoid southern New England, the mid-Atlantic states, the southern Great Lakes area, and the northern and central states of the Midwest east of the Rockies.

Rheumatic and arthritic problems are increased in cold, moist areas. High altitudes cause shortness of breath and are undesirable for people with lung difficulties and cardiac conditions.

The rainfall in the coastal regions is considered healthier than that in the inland areas because of the salt air, and dry air in general is healthier than humid air. These are among the reasons many older people move to Florida or Arizona. If you have health problems, consider the effect of climate carefully when selecting land, and consult your doctor regarding your choice.

## A Final Word

I have discussed only a few of the major problems caused by weather, but there are many others. If you stay in an area a while and study its climate history, you will know if you want to live there permanently. The most desirable areas of the country are those with the most temperate climate conditions, and land prices there are much higher than elsewhere. Rural costs generally decrease in proportion to the harshness of the winters. Do not be attracted to cheap land unless you are prepared to meet the exigencies of the area's climate. I have found that weather and its attendant problems have been one of the major factors in causing people to leave their newly purchased country land and return to the city.

## Useful Resources

### Climate Maps, Tables, Data, Satellite and Weather Information

Complete climate information is available for every state and most major cities from the following agency. Weather and Satellite data can also be requested at the following address. To get a complete catalog of all available resources with current prices and ordering information, write to the National Climatic Data Center and request copies of their available publications, including the *Selective Guide to Climatic Data Services* and *Selective Climatological Publications*.

U.S. Department of Commerce

National Oceanic and Atmospheric Administration

National Environmental Satellite Data and Information Service

National Climatic Data Center

Federal Building
Asheville, NC 28801-5001
Phone: (704) 271-4800
Fax: (704) 271-4876
E-mail: satorder@ncdc.noaa.gov
URL: http://www.ncdc.noaa.gov/

Examples of some of the titles available from the National Climatic Data Center, either by mail or over the electronic information highway, are:

- "Climatic Information for Those Planning a Move to Another Area."
- "Climate of Each State." Includes a narrative climatic summary of the states; monthly and annual norms of maximum, minimum, and mean temperatures, precipitation, heating-degree days and cooling-degree days; and freeze data. Specify state desired.
- "Solar Radiation Atlas." A resource atlas is available for each state; includes direct and diffuse solar radiation data.
- "Wind Energy Resources Atlas." Prepared for each state, identifying annual average wind power, wind power maps, major wind resource areas and wind data sources.
- "Daily Means and Extremes of Temperature, Precipitation, and Snowfall for Each State and Local Climatological Data."
- "National Thunderstorm Frequencies for the U.S."
- "U.S. Soil Temperature." Depth of soil temperature measurement, soil type and daily measurement.

### Local Sources of Information

Local and county libraries have local weather statistics, including information on disasters such as floods and droughts. County agriculture agents have weather charts and data on the variations of the growing seasons in their areas.

Chambers of commerce have brochures that contain local climate information. Local airports and fire departments will have weather stations with thorough records of their areas' climates. Such weather stations often have the most accurate local statistics. Local boards of health or county health departments have pollen count statistics and other climate data that relate to health problems.

# 4 Is There Enough Water on the Land?

*Of all our natural resources, water has become the most precious.*

—Rachel Carson, *Silent Spring*

Your land can have the most beautiful view in the world, but without water it is useless. Never buy land without a proven source of adequate water.

## Dry Land Isn't Always in the Desert

Most people buy land in the spring and early summer when creeks are full, spring water is bursting from the hills and meadows are green. In late August and September, early buyers are often shocked to find that all of their water has dried up. If you have lived primarily in urban areas where water has always been just a turn of the tap away, you don't realize the work and expense involved in bringing water where you want it. Just to get running water

into your house might involve installing a generator, pump, pipeline, holding tank and well. You might see land with a beautiful creek and not realize that it is too far away from the nicest building site to be of any use.

If there is no water visible on the land, you may be told that everyone in the area uses wells and that if you dig deep enough you will find water. The facts are that not all land has underground water, finding any is often difficult and drilling a well is expensive. A big creek or a good well on a neighboring property does not mean there is water on your land. Do not be fooled by such misstatements.

To get a complete picture of the general pattern of water distribution throughout the United States, read Chapter 3, "Climate." Even if you have a year-round creek running through your land, you will be restricted in taking water from it by your state's water laws. A complete discussion of water rights is contained in Chapter 10, "Water Rights."

## Types of Water Sources

Water sources are either on the surface or underground. Surface waters include rivers, streams, creeks, lakes, ponds, bogs, marshes, mud flats, springs and cisterns. Water is trapped underground in two types of areas: in aquifers, loose water bearing materials like gravel, sand and clay, or in consolidated water bearing rocks, notably limestone, basalt and sandstone. In many cases, surface water sources are excellent for irrigation, livestock, fire fighting, ponds and other uses, but cannot be used for drinking. Therefore, a well is often a necessity, regardless of the presence of surface water.

The following sections cover the various aspects of each type of water source.

## Surface Waters

### Rivers, Streams and Creeks

Rivers, streams and creeks differ primarily in size and length. Rivers are large watercourses that are often navigable and public. Although you should have enough water available for your use, you may find that you have to share your river with motorboats, water skiers and swimmers, although swimming may be unpleasant because of the film of gas and oil left on the water's surface by motorboats. Look upstream to see if there are factories, lumber mills or other polluters that might make the river unpleasant to swim in and dangerous to drink. If you are interested in fishing, ask the local bait shop about the fishing potential of the river.

How much logging has occurred upstream? According to the Environmental Protection Agency, streams in logged areas contain up to 7,000 times more sediment after logging. The resulting siltation kills mature fish, smothers spawning beds, destroys stream vegetation and clogs smaller creeks.

Check to be sure that there are no plans to build dams on the river that will flood your land. Get a copy of the master water plan for your area from your state water resources department. This is particularly important if you are buying along a major river. When dams are built, many homesteads along the river are condemned by the government and will become the bottom of a new lake. (See Chapter 15, "Eminent Domain and Condemnation.")

Streams and creeks are much smaller than rivers and often do not flow continuously throughout the dry season, especially in the arid West. The only way you can tell if your stream or creek will flow year-round is to see it flowing during the driest part of the summer, usually August or September. Don't accept the word of a real estate agent that a creek never goes dry. Even if the agent is not deliberately misleading you, he or she probably has never lived on the land and has no idea how much the flow decreases. If a creek is your only year-round source of water, your activities will be limited by the amount of water in it during its lowest period.

Check with the local farm adviser, health department or U.S. Geological Survey (USGS) office to see if the stream has ever been *gauged*, or measured. Talk to other people who live along the creek or stream to see what their experience has been. Look at their crops and those on the land you want to buy, if there are any, to get some idea of what the stream can support. If you are buying land that has never been lived on and nobody knows the performance of the stream, you should definitely see the stream at its lowest water level to determine if it will support your homestead.

You will probably want to know if you can fish in your stream. Many streams are classified as spawning grounds where fishing is prohibited. Check the state fish and game code, usually obtainable in the local bait shop, to find out how your stream is classified. Often, extremely heavy penalties are levied for fishing in spawning areas.

A unique problem along the coasts is the flow of salt water into inland streams and creeks. if you buy land near the ocean, be sure your stream does not have this problem. Salt water is unsuitable for both agricultural and household use.

### Lakes and Ponds

If you purchase land on a lake you will have many of the same problems you would on river land in terms of recreational disturbances and polluted water. Lakeside land is a very desirable place to live, but before you buy you should consider how crowded yours will become during the summer. Figure 4–1 indicates the location of each type of lake property.

You might be lucky and find a parcel of land with a pond on it. If you do, find out the source of the water that feeds it. If a creek or spring feeds the pond, make sure the flow is sufficient to keep the pond full year-round. The presence of fish in the water is a good sign of a healthy pond. If they can live there, it probably doesn't get stagnant in the summer, but you should still test the water before assuming you can swim in it safely. Ask about the mosquito problem in the summer. This is often an undesirable side effect of a pond. If the pond is a good one, it is worth the extra money you will pay for the land.

It is much more likely a real estate agent will show you a possible "pond site" rather than a pond. He or she might show you some springs or creeks that could be used to feed a man-made pond and tell you that the site has already been researched. Never assume a pond can be built unless a reliable source, such as a geologist, your local farm adviser or a Soil Conservation Service agent investigates the site and determines its feasibility as a pond site. Successful ponds depend on the soil's ability to retain water, an adequate and continuous water flow and proper geological conditions. I have seen ugly mud holes where hopeful new landowners had put a lot of energy into creating beautiful ponds, only to find that their soil wouldn't hold water.

Building a pond requires heavy-duty equipment, expensive building materials and possibly a system to divert water to the pond from a water source. The mere presence of an "excellent pond site" should never be your primary reason for buying a piece of land. A "pond site" is a common sales gimmick used to make land seem more attractive and justify a high selling price. Don't be swayed by such tactics. I could go on any piece of land and point out a possible "pond site." So could you.

**Bogs, Marshes and Mud Flats**

The presence of bogs, marshes and large mud flats can present advantages or disadvantages. Occasionally, geographic layout will be such that you can build a dam and create a pond. Usually, however, these areas will be nonproductive breeding grounds for mosquitos and other pests. When such areas exist on the property, you are paying for land that cannot be used. Remember, too much water can be just as great a problem as too little water. (See the section entitled "Drainage" in Chapter 5.) Use this as one of your arguments when bargaining to lower the selling price.

**Springs**

In many areas, springs are the primary source of water. A spring occurs where water seeps to the surface from a crack in the rock formation or where a

**Figure 4–1. Location of Types of Lake Properties**

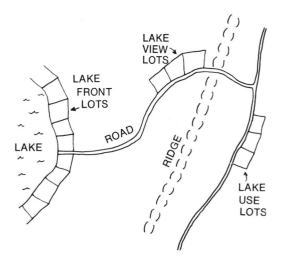

road cuts through a water vein. Artesian wells are like springs, except that the water is forced up by underground pressure.

Often a spring will be only a tiny trickle of water coming out of a hillside. Don't underestimate its value until you measure its rate of flow. If a spring produces 1 gallon of water a minute, which looks like a trickle, it produces 1,440 gallons every 24 hours. If you have a large holding tank to collect the water as it flows to the surface, this amount could support a small homestead.

When you are looking at land with springs, take along a gallon jar and measure the flow per minute using a watch with a second hand. Multiply this amount by 60 to get the flow per hour, then multiply that result by 24 to get the flow per day. Of course, you will have to see the spring during the driest part of the year to be certain that the flow is still sufficient for your needs. (See "How Much Water Will You Need?" later in this chapter.) The rate of flow can often be increased if a spring is properly dug out and opened up. But never attempt to do this without the advice of an expert, because you might cut open too much and cause the spring to go underground.

If you want to locate a spring on some land, maps are available that indicate springs and groundwater sources. These can be good quadrangle maps or special water maps. You may obtain maps of your area from the local Natural Resources Conservation Service (NRCS) or farm adviser. The USGS and the Army Corps of Engineers might also have results of water studies done in your area. (See "Useful Resources" at the end of this chapter.) Even if you can't locate a water source on a map, you should go over the land on foot searching for new or undiscovered

**Figure 4–2. Cones of Depression**

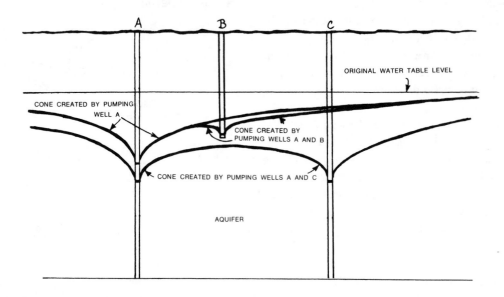

springs. Look for plants that indicate water is beneath the surface. (See the section, "Plants as Indicators of Groundwater," later in this chapter.) Do some research to find out what trees and shrubs in your area indicate water. Remember that the presence of springs on neighboring land does not mean that any exist on your land. Water may flow out of one side of a mountain and not the other.

### Cisterns

Cisterns are large circular or rectangular storage tanks, either completely open at the top to collect rainwater or open only enough to allow a pipe to enter and bring in water from roofs or fields. Cisterns are made of cement, wood or metal. The collected water is rarely used for drinking because of the possibility of contamination. However, it can be used for swimming and irrigation.

Examine any cisterns on the land for leaks, holding capacity, connections to the water sources and general condition of the structures and their enclosures. If a rain-gathering cistern is the only water source for the property, your activities will be limited by the amount of water gathered during the rainy time of year.

## Underground Water

### Wells

In the United States, 80 percent of rural water comes from underground sources and is pumped to the surface through wells. Underground water, or groundwater, is preferred for drinking because it is purer than surface water. Groundwater can be brought up at any point and thus can be obtained close to where you need to use it. Because surface water flows away swiftly and is subject to tremendous evaporation, the water supply in a stream or creek varies more than the steady supply of groundwater. The primary difficulty with a well is the high cost of digging, casing and sealing it and the necessity for a pump to bring the water to the surface.

If electricity is not available, you will have to use a generator to run your well pump. You might have a motor running several hours every day. This is a noisy, polluting, expensive operation, and mechanical breakdowns can be frequent. If you can use a windmill or produce your own electricity with wind, solar or water power, your life on the land might be more pleasant. (See Appendix F for information on windmills, pumps and alternate sources of energy.)

### Problems

If you are going to use a well, find out the history of water problems in the area before you buy. When large quantities of water are pumped, a *cone of depression* forms, which lowers the water table underlying the land. (See Figure 4–2.) Sometimes too much water is pumped out to allow an adequate rate of water replenishment, and the shallower wells in an area may dry up as the water table gets lower. Once the water table is lowered, it may take several years for it to be replenished; and all the wells in the area will have to be dug deeper, at great expense to the landowners. Surprisingly, this has been more of a problem in the eastern half of the United States, although it has occurred in some areas of the West. Often farming areas will experience a very bad underground water exhaustion problem for several years until a flood year replenishes the underground water basin.

A common problem in areas near salt water, especially on the East Coast, is saltwater seepage into wells, often caused by too many wells or faulty wells. Be very careful of this when looking at land near a body of salt water.

### Wells Already on the Land

If you look at land that has a well on it, ask the seller to show you any available records that indicate the amount of water pumped at various times of the year. Does the well need to be dug deeper to get a larger flow to meet your intended needs? Remember, the depth and size of a well do not necessarily coincide with its capacity to yield water.

A well must be located a safe minimum distance from any sewage disposal system before it will be approved by the county health department. If the well does not meet these requirements, you may be prohibited from using it after you buy the land. Has the seller had the well approved and does he or she have the certificate of approval? (See Chapter 13, "Building and Health Codes.")

The well *casing* is a metal or plastic pipe inserted into the well hole to prevent the sides from collapsing. It is perforated with holes or slits to allow water to seep in and be stored during the "recharge period." Can you tell what condition it is in?

A well must have a watertight pump-mounting surface seal around the top if it is to prevent contamination from the entry of foreign matter into the well casing. This sanitary seal consists of a 12-inch concrete base above the surface of the ground and a 30-inch concrete casing that goes at least 30 inches below the ground level. Is this casing cracked or leaking?

Examine the pumping setup to see if it is in good condition. Is a new pump or motor needed? Ask the seller to start the pump, and watch it operate for a few hours. Ask the seller what brand of pump he or she is using and what its capacity is. How old is the equipment and when was it installed?

Who drilled the well? Go to the well-driller and ask to see the drilling log or driller's report to read

what information was recorded regarding the quality of the well and its capacity. Sometimes a driller will not show you this document without the owner's permission. If the seller will not grant you permission to inspect the report, you should be suspicious of the quality of the well. Figure 4–3 is an example of such a report.

### Analyzing Land with No Visible Water

If there is no surface water on the land, before you buy it you must know whether you will hit a decent supply if you dig a well. Ninety percent of all water beneath the surface of the ground occurs in the top 200 feet, and the average depth of all domestic water wells in the United States is slightly less than 50 feet.

Groundwater exists only in the area called the *zone of saturation*. This is the area beneath the ground in which all the openings and pores in the soil, sand, gravel or rock are filled with water. Developing a well involves drilling a hole into the zone of saturation. Water then drains by gravity from the saturated earth into the well, from which it is pumped to the surface and is replaced by other water flowing toward the well. (See Figure 4–4.) The rate at which this new water moves into the well, its *recharge rate*, determines the amount that can be withdrawn at any one time. Thus you will want to know not only if there is underground water present but also its quantity and rate of flow. The total groundwater in an area is replenished every year by new precipitation, which controls the amount of water present in the zone of saturation. It is estimated that 95 percent of the total fresh water available is groundwater.

## Locating Underground Water

### Plants as Indicators of Groundwater (Phreatophytes)

One method used to locate underground water is to find certain plants, called *phreatophytes*, that exist only when their root systems can reach the water table. (The name phreatophyte is derived from two Greek words meaning *well plant*.) Some phreatophytes indicate not only the presence of groundwater but also the quality and approximate depth of the water below the surface. For instance, in arid regions willows or cottonwood trees usually mean that good-quality water is available within 20 feet of the surface. Some species of birch, maple,

**Figure 4–3. Sample Well-Driller's Report**

**WATER WELL DRILLER'S REPORT**
(Sections 7076, 7077, 7078, Water Code)

**THE RESOURCES AGENCY OF**

*Do Not Fill In*
**N⁰ 117312**

State Well No._____
Other Well No._____

**(1) OWNER:**

Name    Gabriel Stern

Address    Anywhere

U.S.A.

**(2) LOCATION OF WELL:**

County  Somewhere          Owner's number, if any—

R. F. D. or Street No. Section 21, Township 4 South,
Range 2, East
10 miles west of Eugene on
south side of Hwy. 135
Riverside Ranch

**(3) TYPE OF WORK** *(check):*

New well ☒    Deepening ☐    Reconditioning ☐    Abandon ☐

*If abandonment, describe material and procedure in Item 11.*

**(4) PROPOSED USE** *(check):*

Domestic ☒  Industrial ☐  Municipal ☐

Irrigation ☐  Test Well ☐  Other ☐

**(5) EQUIPMENT:**

Rotary ☒
Cable ☐
Dug Well ☐

**(6) CASING INSTALLED:**

SINGLE ☒ DOUBLE ☐

If gravel packed

| From | ft. to | ft. | Diam. | Gage or Wall | Diameter of Bore | from ft. | to ft. |
|---|---|---|---|---|---|---|---|
| " 0 | " 184 | .65/8 | 10 | " | 9 | 0 | 184 |
| " | " | " | " | " | | | |
| " | " | " | " | " | | | |
| " | " | " | " | " | | | |

Type and size of shoe or well ring

Describe joint  Welded

Size of gravel: 1/2"

**(7) PERFORATIONS:**

Type of perforator used  Torch

Size of perforations  6  in., length, by  3/16  in.

| From | ft. to | ft. | Perf. per row | Rows per ft. |
|---|---|---|---|---|
| " 164 | " 184 | " | 2 | 1 | " " " |
| " 124 | " 164 | " | 4 | 1 | " " " |
| " | " | " | | " " " | " " " |
| " | " | " | | " " " | " " " |

**(8) CONSTRUCTION:**

Was a surface sanitary seal provided? ☒ Yes ☐ No  To what depth  20  ft.

Were any strata sealed against pollution? ☐ Yes ☒ No  If yes, note depth of strata

From        ft. to        ft.

" " "

Method of Sealing  Cement on pack

**(9) WATER LEVELS:**

Depth at which water was first found                        ft.

Standing level before perforating                        ft.

Standing level after perforating            114  ft.

**(10) WELL TESTS:**

Was a pump test made? ☐ Yes ☒ No  If yes, by whom?  Bail

Yield:  25  gal./min. with  30  ft. draw down after  1  hrs.

Temperature of water  Cool  Was a chemical analysis made? ☐ Yes ☒ No

Was electric log made of well? ☐ Yes ☒ No

**(11) WELL LOG:**

Total depth  184  ft. Depth of completed well  184  ft.

Formation: *Describe by color, character, size of material, and structure.*

| | | | |
|---|---|---|---|
| 0 ft. to | 13 ft. | Brown clays |
| 13 " | 34 " | Clayee brn. & yellow sand (very soft) |
| 34 " | 44 " | Brown clays |
| 44 " | 45 " | Brown sandstone |
| 45 " | 49 " | Sandy grey clay |
| 49 " | 65 " | Fractured blue rock |
| 65 " | 67 " | Hard blue rock |
| 67 " | 69 " | Grey clay |
| 69 " | 90 " | Blue fractured rock w/streaks of clay |
| 90 " | 103 " | Brown rock w/streaks of brown clay |
| 103 " | 107 " | Brown clay w/rock |
| 107 " | 109 " | Fract. brn. rock w/stks. of clay |
| 109 " | 129 " | Fract. hard rusty grey rock |
| 129 " | 138 " | Very hard fractured greywackie |
| 138 " | 145 " | Blue and grey rock |
| 145 " | 151 " | Hard grey clay with rock streaks |
| 151 " | 157 " | Grey rock (rough) |
| 157 " | 162 " | Hard grey clay with rock streaks |
| 162 " | 167 " | Hard black and grey rock with fractures |
| 167 " | 174 " | Hard grey clay with rock streaks |
| 174 " | 176 " | Hard black rock |
| 176 " | 181 " | Hard grey clay with rock streaks |
| 181 " | 183 " | Hard black rock |
| 183 " | 184 " | Hard grey clay with rock streaks |

Work started  9/20  19 73  Completed  9/28  19 73

**WELL DRILLER'S STATEMENT:**

*This well was drilled under my jurisdiction and this report is true to the best of my knowledge and belief.*

NAME  Wilcox Drilling & Pump Company
        *(Person, firm, or corporation)*        *(Typed or printed)*

Address  Anywhere

U.S.A.

[SIGNED]_____

Well Driller

License No.  32890    Dated_____, 19____

sycamore, alder, bay and live oak also indicate groundwater at shallow depths. Unfortunately, the value of these plants as indicators is reduced in humid regions where there is an abundance of water in the soil. Some of the principal plants that indicate groundwater in arid regions are shown and briefly described in Figure 4–5. Each area of the country has its own phreatophytes. Your local well-driller, farm adviser, agriculture experiment station, or other advisory agency (see "Useful Resources") will know the ones to look for in your area.

### Witching, Dowsing and Divining To Find Groundwater

An ancient method used to find water that is still used today is witching or dowsing for water with a divining stick or rod. As far back as the sixteenth century, farmers walked across their land carrying a forked branch in front of them, waiting for it to point down to the ground over a water source. A forked or straight twig from a peach, willow, hickory, dogwood or cherry tree is the most common tool used by diviners. The twig is held between both hands facing out and up and is supposed to roll down or spin around when held over water. Almost every rural area has its well-known diviners. Some work for nothing and others charge a fee for their divining services. Some claim to be able to tell which way the water flows and how deep it is by the movement of the divining rod. However, the USGS has concluded that not one scientifically conducted

experiment using water witches to locate optimal sites for water well location has ever yielded conclusive, reproducible support for water witches' claims. I would not buy land solely on the basis of their findings, but they might confirm some other appraisals made by a well digger or farm adviser.

### Well-Driller's Appraisal of Groundwater

The local well-driller will probably give you the most complete and accurate appraisal of the availability of water on your land and the cost of pumping it. Get the appraisal from the driller you intend to hire to drill the well, because all or part of the appraisal fee will be refunded when you finally hire the company to do the drilling. In our area, the appraisal fee is $20 an hour, and there is a 50 percent refund if the well is put in within a year. The appraiser will compare your land to other property in the area where that company has drilled wells. Each company keeps accurate logs of drilling depths and of the quantity and quality of water that is finally pumped. They also examine the soil, vegetation and geography to estimate the location of water.

Unfortunately, a company generally won't guarantee its appraisal, but a test drilling can be done for a smaller charge than a complete well. If your decision to buy land is contingent solely on whether water is present, a test drilling is advisable.

When selecting the company to do the drilling, compare appraisal fees, refund provisions, costs for

### Figure 4–4. Sources of Groundwater

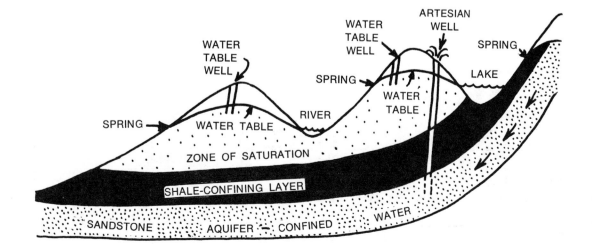

**Figure 4–5. Phreatophyte Examples**

Rushes, sedges, and cattails indicate good-quality water at or just below the surface.

Reeds and cane indicate good-quality water within 10 feet of the surface.

Saltbush is a reliable indicator of variable-quality water near the surface. It usually grows along the margins of salt flats.

Pickleweed indicates mineralized water near the surface. It usually grows on salt flats in soil that has between 1 and 2 percent salt content.

**Figure 4–5.  Phreatophyte Examples (*continued*)**

Arrowweed indicates good-quality water 10 to 20 feet below the surface.

Elderberry shrubs and small trees indicate water within 10 feet of the surface.

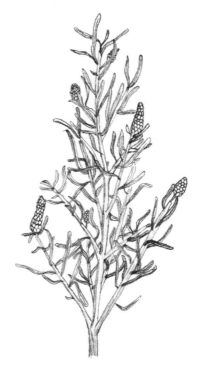

Rabbit brush indicates water within 15 feet of the surface.

Black greasewood indicates mineralized water 10 to 40 feet below the surface.

**Figure 4–5. Phreatophyte Examples (*continued*)**

Mesquite indicates good quality water 10 to 50 feet below the surface.

drilling methods and the grade of casing to be used. Ask for recommendations from the local health department and people living in the area. A good well-drilling contractor will sign a written contract with you, will operate well-maintained equipment and will provide insurance protection for you. Such a contractor will estimate the cost of the job step by step, including a breakdown of unit prices, and give you a specific drilling price in advance. When the job is completed, the contractor will provide a record of the strata penetrated by the well and a statement of work performed and materials used.

Check to see if prospective contractors are members of the state and national associations of well-drilling contractors, evidence that they keep abreast of new developments in their field. Hire the driller with the best reputation, regardless of price. When it comes to well construction, like anything else, it's worth paying more for good quality.

## Types of Wells

The following basic introduction to the types of wells should help you estimate the costs of sinking a well on land you intend to buy and evaluate wells already on the land.

### Dug Well

The oldest type of well is the dug well. Usually 3 to 4 feet in diameter, it is dug with a pick and shovel to a maximum depth of 50 feet. These wells are dangerous and painstaking to dig, and they often go dry because they are so shallow. Their main advantage is the large storage area, but this permits contamination more easily than other wells because of seepage through the well walls and from the large opening on top. Dug wells are probably more common in Canada these days than in the United States. (See Figure 4–6.)

### Bored Well

Bored wells are similar to dug wells, except that they are often deeper and smaller in diameter. An auger bucket, either power or hand-operated, is used to dig these wells, which often run to 100 feet in depth and are cased all along the inside wall. The bored well is practically obsolete today because of the more efficient driven and drilled wells.

### Jetted or Hydraulic Well

This type of drilling can be done only in soft, sandy soils such as are found in some coastal areas. The well is drilled by applying a high-pressure stream of water that cuts through the earth and washes it out of the hole. As this is done, a 1½ inch pointed

**Figure 4–6. Dug Well**

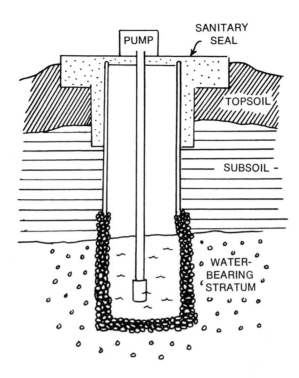

jetting tool is shoved down into the loose sand as far as it will go, and when it stops the well is complete. If you take a garden hose and jet the water into the ground, you do the same thing. This method is useless if rock or clay is reached.

### Churn, Spud or Percussion-Tool Drilled Well

To drill this type of well, a large, chisel-shaped bit is pounded into the ground over and over again by lifting it high into the air and dropping it. With each fall, the bit digs deeper into the ground. During this process, water is poured into the developing hole to transform the loosened dirt into mud, which is then drawn out of the hole. It takes a long time to drill a well in this manner, but it is still effectively done by commercial drillers.

### Drilled Well

Drilled wells are the most common type of wells being used today. The method was first used when oil drillers built special power equipment to drill oil wells. The type of drill used is the rotary tool, which rotates into the earth like a drill rather than pounding the surface as the percussion tool does. The drill has a sharp cutting bit on the end, and the shaft is hollow. As the drill turns into the earth, water is forced down into the drill stem, and the pressure of the water sends the cut dirt and rock to the top of the hole. As the drill goes deeper into the

ground, additional sections of stem are screwed on to increase the length of the drill. (See Figure 4–7.)

### Driven Well

A driven well is usually cheaper to construct than a drilled well. Pipe sections several feet long are

**Figure 4–7. Drilled Well**

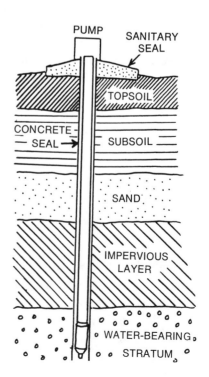

**Figure 4–8. Driven Well (Horizontal)**

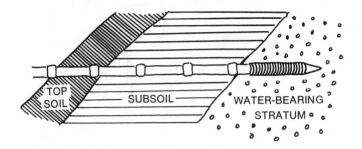

TOP SOIL — SUBSOIL — WATER-BEARING STRATUM

screwed together with a sharp well-point and screen on one end. The pointed end is pounded into the ground until it reaches below the water-table level and a sufficient amount of water can enter the well through the screen. The ground must be soft enough to take a driven well, since hard rock and clay cannot be penetrated. The depth is limited to a maximum of 50 feet, and only a small flow of water will be attained. Occasionally, several driven wells are joined together with a single pump to get a greatly increased flow. As with all wells, a driven well may be cut into the earth horizontally or vertically. (See Figure 4–8).

## Cost of Well Drilling

The cost of well drilling is based on the depth of the well in feet, the toughness of the earth and the accessibility of the area. The usual cost for drilling with a standard air rotary or mud rig quoted by one of the most reputable companies in our area under normal conditions is $10 per foot to drill and $10 per foot to case, with an additional charge to get the equipment in if you are in a remote location. Using a bucket rig in our area can cost up to $35-$40 per foot plus the cost of the casing. The casing includes lining the inside of the well with a steel or plastic casing to protect it from contamination and collapse and pouring a concrete or grout seal around the top. Different companies have different qualities of casing so compare the quality of the casing when you compare prices of the various well drillers in your area. A drilled well can go to a depth of 1,000 feet. You can find out the normal well depth in your area from the local well drillers and thus estimate the approximate cost to you. In our area, wells are usually between 150 and 300 feet deep. At $10 per foot

to drill and $10 per foot to case, a well can cost from $3,000 to $6,000. Most companies have a minimum depth charge, even if they hit water before that depth.

Keep in mind that there is always a chance you will not hit water. No driller is going to guarantee water when he starts drilling. He just tells you his price per foot and then drills until he hits water or you can't afford to pay for another foot. You can pay several thousand dollars for a dry hole, and that is one of the biggest risks of buying country land. Even in areas where water is plentiful, drilling is successful only about 85 percent of the time. The people representing the other 15 percent are simply out of luck and money. You must be certain there is water before you buy.

## Is the Water Drinkable?

If water is declared potable by the county health department it is safe to drink. The safety is determined by examining the water at your source and the conditions around it. You will probably not be surprised to learn that animal manure and soil bacteria are usually harmful to a water supply. Human sewage and poisonous sprays are the primary causes of contaminated water.

Drinking, tasting or smelling water will tell you little about its potability, because even clear, good-tasting water may be contaminated. However, your local county health or sanitation department will gladly conduct a free or inexpensive water analysis for you. A health inspector will come out to collect the sample and to examine the source and surrounding area. The inspector will determine if an existing or intended septic tank, outhouse or cesspool is too close to the water source. If the water flows through farmland or irrigated land, it can be tested for the presence of insecticides. Hazardous-waste disposal sites are an increasing source of groundwater contamination. If your land is very isolated, the health inspector will give you a sanitized bottle and tell you how to properly collect a water sample for testing. The basic water test includes a coliform bacterial count, which reflects the amount of human and other warm-blooded-animal excreta in it. If you want a more complete mineral and bacterial analysis, which is not usually necessary, you will have to pay to have it done by a commercial laboratory.

Underground well or spring water is usually safer than surface water. Underground water has been sifted through the porous earth, which purifies it, whereas contaminated surface water must travel a long distance to get the cleansing effect of underground sifting.

I recommend that you always get the basic water test done, no matter what the history of the drinking water on the land is. The family living there now may have been drinking the water for 50 years, but pollution can occur virtually overnight. Polluted water can cause cholera, typhoid fever, amoebic dysentery, infectious hepatitis and possibly polio. Don't take any chances.

### Groundwater Pollution

If you are relying on groundwater from a spring or well, you might also want to check the surrounding area for groundwater pollution, especially if there are any industries located in your area. More and more we are finding that industrial products and wastes have been improperly stored and are leaking into the groundwater. For instance, about 30 square miles of a shallow aquifer were contaminated by aldrin and dieldrin, both toxic substances, at the Rocky Mountain arsenal and surrounding area. The wastes, by-products from the manufacture of pesticides and chemical warfare agents, had been stored in unlined holding ponds, and huge quantities of the wastes had been seeping from the ponds for years. Sixty-four domestic, stock and irrigation wells had to be abandoned.

In heavily fertilized areas, such as farming communities, nitrates from decomposed ammonia fertilizer infiltrate the groundwater and pollute it. Nitrate-rich water leads to a serious disease in infants known as *methemoglobinemia*.

Animal feedlots provide a huge volume of waste compared to their size. For example, a 10-acre feedlot, with 1,000 head of cattle produces wastes equivalent to those of a town of 6,000 people. One public water-supply well in northwestern North Dakota continued to be contaminated by livestock wastes more than 40 years after a nearby livery stable was abandoned. If you are buying in a farming or livestock area, always have the available drinking water tested before you purchase property there.

If you are looking at land that is in a floodplain, and if there are several other homes in that floodplain that use septic tanks and wells, it is very possible that the effluent from the septic tanks will pollute the groundwater. Check with the local health officials to see if there are periodic outbreaks of hepatitis due to an increase in coliform bacteria during times of high water.

If you suspect some kind of pollution of the groundwater in an area you are looking at, check with the local health department to see if they can give you any information.

### Watch Out If the Land Is Too Cheap

A recent news article told of a city in Florida that sold seven acres it knew to be saturated with toxic wastes to a virtually penniless veteran. From 1958 to 1967 it had been a hazardous waste site where Allied Petroleum Products, Inc., dumped toxic sludge containing PCB's, heavy metals and organic compounds. At one time a dike had broken and 200,000 gallons of poisonous sludge had oozed into a nearby creek, threatening the community's drinking water as PCB's leached into the groundwater. The city finally graded the site and covered it with sod in 1980. Then they offered it for sale for $992.74 in back taxes, and the veteran bought it.

When environmental officials arrived to study the site for a Superfund cleanup, the owner first threw them off his land. The state then went to court to order him to clean up his land to the tune of $225 million. Now he is fighting back with a lawsuit, but meanwhile he has suffered a great deal and still has to cope with it.

### Minerals in the Water

The quality of water may also be affected by an excessive amount of calcium and magnesium, which causes it to become hard. Try to work up a lather with a bar of soap and a dish of water. The harder the water, the less sudsing you'll get. Hard water is less desirable for washing, cooking and heating, but is generally not a serious detriment. Water-soften-ing equipment can be purchased and installed at any time.

Other minerals may affect the quality and taste of the water. Iron in water affects the flavor of cooked vegetables, coffee and tea. It stains clothes, water pipes and bathroom fixtures and causes a reddish-brown sediment or oily scum to appear on the surface. Hydrogen sulfide gas and sulfates give water a rotten-egg odor and taste, which you will find highly objectionable. The water may also have silt suspended in it, which gives it a muddy or cloudy effect. These and other mineral problems can be corrected through the use of chlorination and filtration equipment, which will be an added expense to you and good cause for demanding a reduction in the purchase price.

## How Much Water Will You Need?

Without water you cannot cook meals or grow vegetables, flowers or orchards. You cannot raise animals, bathe, wash, swim, fight fires or quench your thirst. Although water needs differ, depending on various factors, the U.S. Department of Agriculture lists the following daily water requirements:

| Needed by | Gallons per Day |
|---|---|
| Each person (includes such activities as drinking, cooking, bathing, washing clothes and dishes, flushing toilets) | 55–80 |
| Each milk cow | 35 |
| Each horse | 6–15 |
| 25 chickens | 1–3 |
| Each hog | 2–4 |
| Each sheep | 2 |
| Garden (1,000 sq. ft., say 50 × 20 ft.) | 70 (or 700 every 10 days) minimum |

The following are estimates of how much water is used for various domestic purposes:

| Item | Gallons |
|---|---|
| Taking a bath | 0–40 |
| Taking a shower | 20–30 |
| Running a washing machine (1 load) | 20–30 |
| Washing dishes | 8–10 |
| Flushing a toilet | 4–6 |

If you intend to have a large garden or plant an orchard, berries or flowers, you will need a much greater supply of water than you need for animals alone. If you must pump your water, you will not want to run your pump 24 hours a day, even if it is electric. Be sure that both the well and the pump have the capacity to deliver the amount of water you will need as quickly as you want it.

Always overestimate your water needs, because after buying your land, your ability to develop it will be limited by the amount of water available.

## The Water Supply System

If you are looking at undeveloped land, you must determine its suitability for a water supply system. The water supply system is the means by which you get the water from its source to your house, garden, trees, fields and animals. The standard equipment includes pipe or hose, one or more holding tanks, a pump house and various pieces of hardware such as valves and faucets. If you are looking at land that already has a developed water system, you will want to know if it was well designed and built and if it is still working properly.

The purpose of the following sections is not to tell you how to develop a water system but to give you an idea of what to look for and think about in terms of developing or repairing a water system on land you might buy. Each type of water system has its own maintenance problems. Setting up an adequate water system can cost thousands of dollars. Before you buy a piece of land, estimate the costs required to develop a new water system or repair an existing one. If the expense is beyond your means, do not purchase that land.

### Gravity–Flow System

The cheapest and easiest way to bring water where you need it is by using the force of gravity. To do this, the water source must be higher in elevation than the place to which you want to bring the water, so that when you lay your hose or pipe the water will flow freely of its own accord to the lower point. However, because air is lighter than water, the hose between the two points must drop steadily downhill, or air bubbles will collect in the high spots of the hose and slow down or stop the flow of water. If you cannot avoid laying the hose over a high spot, you can prevent air from entering it by putting in the proper valves for bleeding the lines or by keeping both ends of the hose constantly submerged in water.

If a hill is situated above a building site but you cannot find a spring or other water source on it, you might consider drilling a horizontal well into the side of the hill to get water to flow out without using a pump. Ask a well-driller to appraise the possibility of finding water this way on land you might buy. It is difficult to determine different elevations over a long distance on a piece of land with the naked eye, and special meters are needed. The well-driller has this equipment, or you can rent it from a local surveying rental service and run your own test.

The only materials needed to set up a gravity–flow water system are a holding tank, which might be a spring box, lake, pond or dammed-up portion of a creek; the necessary pipe or hose; storage tanks; and various valves, faucets and other hardware. This system is the cheapest and easiest to maintain because no pump is necessary.

**Siphon System**

The siphon system is similar to the gravity-flow system in that the source must be higher in elevation than the point to which you eventually want to bring the water. However, any rise in the ground that is higher than the source requires siphoning to get the water to flow over it. This is done by sucking the water up over the rise and down the other side far enough so that it begins to flow of its own accord. As long as you don't lose the siphon, the water will continue to flow. Every time the siphon is broken by air getting into the hose, you must suck the water to get it going again. You can use the same methods to prevent air from entering the hose that you would use in the gravity–flow system. The difference between these two systems is that in a pure gravity–flow system, none of the high spots in the hose are higher than the source, so no sucking is required to start the system.

If the rise is too high or the distance too great to begin the siphon by sucking with your mouth, you will need a pump to get it going. Otherwise, the siphon water system requires the same equipment as a gravity-flow system and costs the same to install and maintain.

**Pumping Your Water Using Gas,
Electricity or Wind**

Unless you are fortunate enough to have a water source positioned so that the water will flow by a gravity or siphon system, you will need a pump.

The most common pump used for shallow wells and surface water sources is the gasoline-powered centrifugal pump, which sucks water up and pushes it out with great force. A two-horsepower pump of this type can suck the water to a height of about 20 feet. However, if you can place the pump at the source, say alongside a stream or pond, it can push the water several hundred feet up a bank or hill.

If your source of water is a deep well, you will need an electric pump. The one horsepower electric jet pump can suck water from a maximum depth of 110 feet. However, the electric submersible well pump is more commonly used today and can pump much higher. It is a long, cylindrical pump that is placed at the bottom of the well. A one horsepower submersible pump can push 10.2 gallons of water per minute to a height of 220 feet.

Because these pumps require electricity, you will have to either bring it in or supply it with a generator. Generators are powered by gasoline, propane or diesel fuel. There are also wind generators that look like windmills, and they produce electricity that charges a set of storage batteries. If wind conditions are suitable, you can run an electric pump using this system without the noise and pollution of a gas or diesel generator. (See Appendix F, "Alternative Energy Resources.")

You can also use a windmill to pump water directly from a well. A windmill is cheap, non-polluting and quiet, compared with a gasoline powered pump or generator. Today in the southernmost parts of the country, notably Texas, and in parts of Pennsylvania, windmills are still widely used in place of the combustion engine or electric pumps. If one already exists on the land, find out if it still functions and what its capacity is. You will be fortunate if there is one on your land, but don't let its quaint but magnificent beauty persuade you to purchase land that is otherwise not what you want, or pay a higher price for the land than it is really worth.

If you will need a pump and possibly a generator, find out the cost of buying and installing equipment sufficient to meet your needs before you buy the land. You can't do anything on the land until you have water, so you should figure the cost of a motor and pump into the purchase price as part of your initial investment.

If a pump is set up on the land, ask the owner or real estate agent to start it up so you can see how well it works and how much water is pumped. Watch it pump for at least a half hour to be sure it operates well. Get the brand names and numbers of the motor or generator and pump so you can check with the local dealer to see how much they are worth and what their specifications are. Find out how long the owner has used the equipment and if there have been any problems with it. Does the owner have any repair bills, and is there still a valid warranty for the equipment? (See "Useful Resources" at the end of this chapter for available pump information.)

**Holding Tanks**

Unless you have a lake, pond or other large natural body of water situated higher than your homestead area, you will need at least one holding tank in your water system to keep a large quantity of water available. The greater your water needs, the larger the tank will have to be. If you want to irrigate an orchard and garden or grazing fields for your animals, you will need a large tank. For instance, if you plan to have a half-acre garden, it will require the equivalent of one inch of rain, or about 11,350 gallons, every ten days. If you want to water once every five days, you will need a tank that holds at least 5,675 gallons just to water your garden once. Fruit trees need to be watered less frequently than smaller plants, but they need a large amount of water when irrigated because their roots go extremely deep.

If there is a holding tank on the land, determine its capacity to be sure it is large enough for your intended needs. To figure out the volume in cubic feet of a cylindrical tank, multiply the area of the base in feet by its height in feet. (To refresh your memory, the formula is $\pi r^2 h$, where $\pi = 3.1416$, $r$ = radius and $h$ = height of the tank.) The volume in cubic feet of a square or rectangular tank is figured by multiplying the length times the width times the height in feet. Once you get the volume in cubic feet, you have to transform the result into gallons. To do this, multiply the number of cubic feet by 7.4805, which is the number of gallons in 1 cubic foot.

For example, assume you have a cylindrical tank with the following dimensions: the height is 10 feet and the diameter of the base is 12 feet. Thus, the radius is 6 feet. Plugging these numbers into the formula, we get $3.1416 \times 6^2 \times 10 = 3.1416 \times 36 \times 10 = 3.1416 \times 360 = 1,130.98$ cu. ft. To translate this figure into gallons of water, multiply $1,130.98 \times 7.4805 = 8,460.30$ gallons.

Check the tank to be sure it doesn't leak. Examine the structure that supports it to see if it is sturdy. The tank might be inside a well house. If so, is that in good shape? Holding tanks are expensive, and repairing or replacing a damaged one could be costly. Mention any necessary repair work to the owner, and either ask the owner to have it fixed before you buy the land or use this as another reason why he or she should lower the asking price. Price the existing tank at the local supply house. Wooden tanks are always more expensive than metal ones. Ferroconcrete tanks are being used more frequently these days, and are usually very suitable for most places. If you have to develop your own water system, include the cost of purchasing and installing a holding tank and its supporting structure.

In cases where electricity is available on a continuous basis, a pressure pump will be used to move the water to a pressure tank in the house, so that when a faucet is turned on, the pressurized flow will always be available. These pressure tanks look like big hot-water heaters and are most commonly used where the water source is from a well.

**Pipes and Fixtures**

Check the pipe works on the land to see if there are sufficient domestic and irrigation works to suit your needs. Look for leaks or evidence of recent repair. Has steel, concrete or plastic pipe been used? Is the system constructed so that water will not freeze in the pipes in winter? Each type of pipe has its own merits.

The water system, if one exists, will be included in the selling price of the land, so you should evaluate its quality and value before buying. Often the system has been used for many years and the owner underestimates the depreciation in its value. look for things that need improvement or parts that need replacement, and point out these things when bargaining to get the price down.

**An Example To Help You Visualize Your Water System**

Figure 4–9 shows an example of possible ways to develop a water system. It is included to help you learn how to look at a piece of land and visualize its possibilities for water development. The three systems shown all use a large holding tank (5,000 gallons) situated on a high point of land above the house, garden, orchard and animals, so that gravity flow can be used.

System 1 carries water from a holding box built around a spring that was exposed when a road was cut into the side of the hill. The spring is higher in elevation than the holding tank, so gravity brings a

**Figure 4–9. Possible Ways To Develop Water**

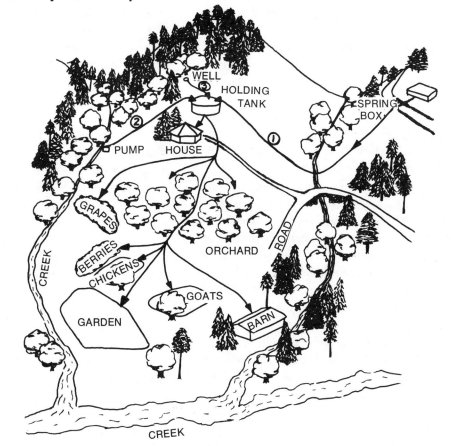

continuous flow to the tank. However, the spring produces only about 700 gallons a day in the driest part of the summer, which is not enough to support the needs of a family with a garden, orchard and animals. The garden alone requires about 600 gallons a day. Because the young fruit trees, berries, flowers, animals and people all need water, another method that will provide more water must be developed.

System 2 illustrates the most inexpensive and logical next choice, which is to pump water from the nearest creek up to the holding tank. Have the creek water tested for potability. (See "Is the Water Drinkable?" earlier in this chapter.)

System 3, which might be cheaper in the long run, requires drilling a well above the holding tank. A row of bay trees is growing up the side of the hill behind the holding tank, which indicates underground water. Because this is on the side of a hill, a horizontal well could be drilled, which would allow a gravity–flow of water into the holding tank. Although this system would not require a pump, the amount of water this source would produce is un-

known. Alter spending the money to drill a well, the rate of flow might not be sufficient to meet the needs of the family.

The three year-round creeks alone assure the family that it has a more than adequate water supply. If you plan your purchase carefully, you should always have enough water for your needs.

## Outside Water Supplies—Public Utility Companies, Private Water Companies, Public Water Districts

Some rural areas, especially those containing large farms in arid regions, have established irrigation companies, mutual water companies and public or private utility companies that handle the task of supplying water within their service districts. The legal and operational setup is different for different agencies. If you have to purchase water from a private profit-oriented water company or a public utility company, you will pay rates regulated by the Public Utilities Commission. If you are supplied by a mutual water or irrigation company, you will have to join a private, nonprofit association of landowners who have organized to supply water to themselves.

Real estate ads will usually indicate if water is supplied by a private water company. The following are statements made in recent ads for land in Colorado: "good water shares available," "water line goes by property, irrigation dependent on classification by water users," "ditch irrigation, 500 water shares" and "35 tillable acres now ditch irrigated, 35 water shares with land."

The right to receive water often is based on ownership of shares of stock in the company. Instead of receiving monetary dividends, the shareholder receives water according to the amount of stock he or she owns. The price of stock can be quite high in areas where water is scarce. For instance, if you are buying land on which you intend to irrigate one acre and five shares of stock are needed to get enough water to irrigate that acre, you will have to buy those shares, either from the seller at the time of purchase or from the company after you own the land. If each share is worth $100 on the current market, it is going to cost you an extra $500 to get water to your land. If the owner includes shares of stock with the land, make sure you are not being overcharged for the water, because the seller will undoubtedly add the cost of the shares to the asking price.

Investigate the company to find out how dependable it is, how many of your neighbors belong to it and what the value of the shares is.

It is always better to buy the owner's water shares with the land, because sometimes shares are not easy to obtain. There may not be any surplus water available to a new owner or, because these companies are private, the members may not like your lifestyle and may refuse to sell shares to you under some pretext. The ad that says "irrigation dependent on classification by water users" means that the members of the water company have control over how much water, if any, will be sold to a landowner. Also, if an ad says "water shares available," that does not mean that you will be able to get them. If shares do not come with the land, you had better be sure that you can purchase some or lease some before you buy, or have the seller buy what you need and then add the cost to the price of the land. Do not buy on an assurance that you can get shares after the deal is closed. You might be left high and dry.

Public water or irrigation ditches are formed by state and local legislatures to provide water to their inhabitants. Each district has definite boundaries, local control and, most importantly, the power to tax and assess property within the district. You are familiar with the idea of paying property taxes for school districts. Water districts operate the same way.

If your land is within the boundaries of a water district, you will want to know how you can get water and what the present and future tax assessments will be. Generally the value of land within such a district increases, even if the land has its own independent source of water. Whether or not you use district water, you will have to pay assessments, just as you pay school taxes even if you do not have children. If you want to buy land but need to obtain your water from a district, be sure the land is within the district. Many districts will extend their services to land not previously within their boundaries if circumstances warrant. To obtain this service you will have to go before the county planning commission, board of supervisors or water district board and petition them to allow your land into the service area. It will be easier to have the seller of the land do this before you buy. Accompany the seller to the hearings. If you cannot be serviced from the district and water is unavailable from any other source, the land is worthless. You had better start looking somewhere else.

## Sharing Water with Others

You will frequently encounter a situation in which several parcels share one or more water sources. For example, the piece you are buying might have deeded water rights to take a percentage of water produced by a spring or creek on a neighbor's property, or the water right might be limited to taking a certain maximum number of gallons per day. This is a tricky situation. You must go to the water source on the neighbor's land and determine the output. Often, a land developer subdivides a single parcel into several smaller parcels and allots more water than is actually available. The fact that the county or local governing agency approves the subdivision does not mean there is an adequate water supply. Often, the first people to develop their land have enough water, but as more development takes place, the water supply becomes inadequate. If your water source is being shared, talk to the persons you will share the water with and determine what the history of usage is. It is a fact of life that people do not like to share water when water is scarce. Find out what the situation is before you buy. If you are to share water, you will need deeded rights to install and maintain your water system on the neighbor's property, and you will need deeded rights to lay and maintain a pipeline to your property and possibly deeded access to drive to the water source to construct a tank and maintain a pump.

On the other hand, surrounding landowners may have the right to come onto your property and take water. Do you want land that one or more persons have the right to enter for purposes of constructing and maintaining pumping facilities?

I recommend that you never buy land in an area of scarce water unless you have your own water source on your own property free from interference by others. People are now moving into rural areas where homesteads may never have been developed, and as development proceeds, water may become a precious commodity. The legal battles in the future will be over water. Think about the future of your water supply before you buy.

## The Water Protection Clause in the Contract of Sale

Never buy land without a written guarantee that a year-round source of water exists that is sufficient to meet your needs. Two guarantees are provided in the Model Contract of Sale in Chapter 27. Clause 16(c) is a warranty by the seller that a visible water source delivers a specified minimum amount of water throughout the year. If the water dries up after you buy the property, the seller will be liable for a breach of this warranty. The fact that the seller makes the warranty, however, does not relieve you of the responsibility of examining the water situation during the critical dry months before you buy the land.

Clause 17(f) is a condition to the sale that should be used if no water source presently exists on the land. You want to have at least a test drilling and preferably a completed, productive well drilled before, not after, you finalize your purchase. The ideal situation is to have the seller pay to drill the well. If the seller locates a good water supply, the price of the well can be added to the purchase price. If water cannot be located, you will not have to proceed with the purchase, the contract will be re-

scinded and your money will be returned to you. If the seller resists such a condition, you can offer a compromise by agreeing to pay for half the drilling costs, even if no water is found on the land. Do not agree to pay the entire cost if no water is found; if you do, you could spend a few thousand dollars drilling a dry well on land you do not own.

You do not want to make your land purchase on promises alone. Sellers who are not willing to guarantee that there is water on the land do not care if they cheat you. Never buy land without such a condition in the contract, unless you like high-stakes gambling.

Always read the documents that pertain to your own water rights or others' rights to take water from your land. If you have any questions about these documents or don't understand any portion of them, contact an attorney who is experienced in real estate matters so that he or she can explain them to you.

## Useful Resources

**Publications on Water, Wells, Pumps and Ponds**
Following are some sources and a list of some of their publications on water and related subjects.

From:   ANR Publications
        (Division of Agriculture and Natural
        Resources)
        University of California
        6701 San Pablo Avenue
        Oakland, CA 94608-1239
Voice:  (510) 642-2431
        (800) 994-8849
Fax:    (510) 643-5470
E-mail: anrpubs@ucdavis.edu

| | |
|---|---|
| "California's Groundwater Resources," #21393 | $1.50 |
| "California Water Resources," #21379 | $1.00 |
| "Water Conservation: The Potential," #21382 | $1.00 |
| "Water Wells and Pumps: Their Design, Construction, Operation & Maintenance," #1889 | $4.50 |
| "Cost Comparison between Electric Motors and Engines for Irrigation Pumping," 1994 #1933 | $3.00 |
| "Drip Irrigation," #2740 | $1.50 |
| "Drip Irrigation Management" #21259 | $3.50 |

"Grading land for Surface Irrigation,"
#2692                                                  $2.50
"Irrigation Costs," #2875                    $1.75
"Irrigation on Steep land," #2825         $2.00
"Measuring Irrigation Water," #2956     $2.00

From:  State Water Resources Control Board
       Division of Water Rights
       P.O. Box 2000
       Sacramento, CA 95812-2000
Voice: (916) 657-2170
URL:   http://www.swrcb.ca.gov
BBS:   (916) 657-9722

"Water Wells and Pumps: Their Design, Construction, Operation and Maintenance"

From:  Superintendent of Documents
       U.S. Government Printing Office
       Washington, DC 20402
Voice: (202) 512-1800
Fax:   (202) 512-2250
Fax on demand: (202) 512-1716
E-mail:  help@eids05.eids.gpo.gov
URL:   http://www.access.gpo.gov (Subject
       Bibliographies are available online)
FTP:   eids04.eids.gpo.gov
Bulletin Board: (202) 512-1387 or telnet:
       federal.bbs.gpo.gov

*Manual of Individual and Non-Public
   Water Supply Systems,*
   S/N 055-000-00375-1                      $ 7.50
*Ground Water Manual*  S/N 024-003-
   00172                                         $23.00
*Drainage Manual*  S/N 024-003-00177-5  $15.00
*Earth Manual*: A Water Resources
   Technical Publication
   S/N 024-003-00173-2                      $15.00
*Rain: A Water Resource*  S/N 024-001-
   03589-8                                        $1.00
*What is Water?* S/N 024-001-03588-0    $1.00

From:  United States Department of Agriculture
       (USDA)
       Natural Resources Conservation Service
       (NRCS)
       Washington, DC 20250-1300
Voice: (800) THE-SOIL

The NRCS has available many publications. They

request a self-addressed stamped envelope for their
free brochures. Some are:

"Flood Plain Management"
"The Water Cycle—Nature's Recycling System"
"What is a Watershed?"
"Small Watershed Projects"
"Publication List"

From:  Deep Rock Mfg. Co.
       5192 Anderson Road
       Opelika, AL 38601

"How To Drill Your Own Water Well"

Bulletins on water conditions in California from
1977 until now may be obtained from the following
agency. Ask for the publications list, then select the
years you want.

       State of California Resource Agency
       Department of Water Resources
       P.O. Box 942836
       Sacramento, CA 95812-2000
Voice: (916) 657-2203
Fax:   (916) 657-1485
BBS:   (916) 657-9722 (Log in BBS)
URL:   http://www.swrcb.ca.gov

"Water Wells and What You Should Know About
   Them."                                        Free
"Small Earth Dams Circular," #467          Free
"Soil and Water Management for Home
   Gardeners," AXT-111                         $1.00
"What Does Water Analysis Tell You?"
   ATX-118                                        $1.00

From:  Water Education Foundation
       717 K Street, Suite 517
       Sacramento, CA 95814
       (916) 444-6240

Layperson's Guide Series to:

Water Rights                                      $4.00
Ground Water Law                                  $4.00
Drinking Water                                    $4.00
California Water Map                              $7.50
Landscape Designs Easy and Efficient       $1.00
Landscape Design II                              $1.00

The following are free from any U.S. Geological
Survey Earth Science Information Center. See

"Useful Resources" at the end of Chapter 5 for the addresses of the Earth Science Information Centers (ESICs):

"Ground Water"

"Ground Water and the Rural Homeowner"

"Ground Water: The Hidden Resource"

"Ground Water: An Under Valued Resource"

"Ground-Water Contamination—No 'Quick Fix' in Sight"

"Ground Water Studies" Fact sheet

"How Much Water in a 12-ounce Can?"

"NASQAN: Measuring the Quality of America's Streams"

"Natural Steam for Power"

An Overview of the Stream-Gaging Program

"Save Water . . . Save Money"

"Rain: A Water Resource"

"State Hydrologic Unit Maps"

"The Hydrologic Cycle"

"Toxic Waste—Ground-Water Contamination

"Water in the Urban Environment: Erosion and Sediment"

"Water—Managing a National Resource

"Water-Use Information?"

"Water Dowsing"

"What Is Water?"

"Water Resources Division Information Guide"

"Are Fertilizers and Pesticides in the Ground Water?"

## U.S. Geological Survey
## Water Resources Division

The USGS Water Resources Division, under the U.S. Department of the Interior Water Resources Division, includes within it the National Water Information Clearinghouse (NWIC), which answers general questions on hydrology, water as a resource, and hydrologic mapping, as well as on the products, projects and services of the Water Resources Division. NWIC offers free subscriptions to "National Water Conditions," a monthly summary of water resource conditions in the U.S. and Southern Canada.

You can call the NWIC toll-free at 1-800-426-9000, or write to:

National Water Information Clearing House
U.S. Geological Survey
423 National Center
Reston, VA 22092

The USGS also operates EarthFax, a fax-on-demand system, at (703) 648-4888. General Water Resource Information and USGS fact sheets are available. Below are selected topics.

| Document Number | Title |
|---|---|
| 5000 | Index to Water Resources Information currently available from EarthFax |
| 5001 | "Water on the Web: USGS Water Home Page" |
| 5052 | "Federal State Cooperative Water Resources" |
| 5058 | "Ground-Water Studies" |
| 5501 | "What is Ground Water?" |
| 5525 | "Ground Water Atlas of the United States" |

Questions related to water resources in a particular area should be directed to the appropriate Water Resources Division District Office of the USGS. Specific information for each state is available through the World-Wide Web at http://www.H20.usgs.gov. When writing to a state office, add the specific address, as given in the list below, to the following three lines:

Water Resources Division
District Office
U.S. Geological Survey

Alabama
520 19th Ave.
Tuscaloosa, AL 35401
Voice: (205) 752-8104
Fax: (205) 752-9086
E-mail: jeffcoat@usgs.gov

Alaska
4230 University Dr., Suite 201
Anchorage, AK 99508-4664
Voice: (907) 786-7111
Fax: (907) 786-7150
E-mail: pbrooks@usgs.gov

Arizona
375 S. Euclid Ave.
Tucson, AZ 85719
Voice: (602) 670-6671
Fax: (602) 670-5592
E-mail: nmelcher@usgs.gov

Arkansas
401 Hardin Rd.
Little Rock, AR 72211
Voice: (501) 228-3602
Fax: (501) 228-3601
E-mail: ralidwin@usgs.gov

California
Federal Building, Room W-2233
2800 Cottage Way
Sacramento, CA 95825
Voice: (916) 979-2605
Fax: (916) 979-2669
E-mail: shulters@usgs.gov

Colorado
Bldg. 53, Denver Federal Center
Mail Stop 415, Box 25046
Lakewood, CO 80225
Voice: (303) 236-4882 Ext. 258
Fax: (303) 236-4912
E-mail: dlystrom@usgs.gov

Connecticut
Ribicoff Federal Building, Room 525
450 Main St.
Hartford, CT 06103
Voice: (203) 240-3063
Fax: (203) 240-3783
E-mail: cthomas@usgs.gov

Delaware
208 Carroll Building
8600 LaSalle Rd.
Towson, MD 21286
Voice: (410) 512-4801
Fax: (410) 512-4810
E-mail: jgerhart@usgs.gov

District of Columbia
See listing for Maryland

Florida
227 N. Boronough St., Suite 3015
Tallahassee, FL 32301
Voice: (904) 942-9500 x3011
Fax: (904) 942-9521
E-mail:jvecchio@usgs.gov

Georgia
Peachtree Business Center, Suite 130
3039 Amwiler Rd.
Atlanta, GA 30360-2824
Voice: (770) 903-9100
Fax: (770) 903-9199
E-mail: twhale@usgs.gov

Hawaii
677 Ala Moana Blvd., Suite 415
Honolulu, HI 96813
Voice: (808) 522-8290
Fax: (808) 522-8298
E-mail: wmeyer@usgs.gov

Idaho
230 Collins Rd.
Boise, ID 83702-4520
Voice: (208) 387-1316
Fax: (208) 387-1372
E-mail: jlhughes@usgs.gov

Illinois
102 E. Main St., 4th Floor
Urbana, IL 61801
Voice: (217) 344-0037
Fax: (217) 344-0082
E-mail: sfblanch@usgs.gov

Indiana
5957 Lakeside Blvd.
Indianapolis, IN 46278-1996
Voice: (317) 290-3333, Ext. 175
Fax: (317) 290-3313
E-mail: lswain@usgs.gov

Iowa
P.O. Box 1230
Iowa City, IA 52244
Voice: (319) 358-3600
Fax: (319) 358-3606
E-mail: rgbrown@usgs.gov

Kansas
4821 Quail Crest Pl.
Lawrence, KS 66049
Voice: (913) 832-3505
Fax: (913) 832-3500
E-mail: waucott@usgs.gov

Kentucky
: 2301 Bradley Ave.
Louisville, KY 40217
Voice: (502) 635-8080
Fax: (502) 635-8009
E-mail: rbsee@usgs.gov

Louisiana
: 3535 S. Sherwood Forest Blvd. Suite 120
Baton Rouge, LA 70816
Voice: (504) 389-0281, Ext. 3107
Fax: (504) 389-0706
E-mail: ehmartin@usgs.gov

Maine
: 26 Gansnestom Dr.
Augusta, ME 04330
Voice: (207) 622-8201
Fax: (207) 622-8204
E-mail: dcowing@usgs.gov

Maryland
: 208 Carroll Building
8600 LaSalle Rd.
Towson, MD 21286
Voice: (410) 512-4801
Fax: (410) 512-4810
E-mail: jgerhart@usgs.gov

Massachusetts
: 28 Lord Rd., Suite 280
Marlborough, MA 01752
Voice: (508) 490-5002
Fax: (508) 490-5068
E-mail: wsonntag@usgs

Michigan
: 6520 Mercantile Way, Suite 5
Lansing, MI 48910
Voice: (517) 887-8903
Fax: (517) 377-1627
E-mail: cbarton@usgs.gov

Minnesota
: 2280 Woodale Dr.
Mounds View, MN 55112
Voice: (612) 783-3106
Fax: (612) 783-3103
E-mail: garklavs@usgs.gov

Mississippi
: Federal Building, Suite 710
100 W. Capitol St.
Jackson, MS 39269
Voice: (601) 965-4600 Ext. 5595
Fax: (601) 965-5782
E-mail: glryan@usgs.gov

Missouri
: 1400 Independence Rd., Mail Stop 200
Rolla, MO 65401
Voice: (314) 341-0825
Fax: (314) 341-0805
E-mail: sherrill@usgs.gov

Montana
: Federal Building, Room 428
3015. Park Ave.
Helena, MT 59626-0076
Voice: (406) 449-5302
Fax: (406) 449-5497
E-mail: moreland@usgs.gov

Nebraska
: Rm 406 Federal Building
Lincoln, NE 68508
Voice: (402) 437-5082
Fax: (402) 437-5139
E-mail: lsweiss@usgs.gov

Nevada
: 333 West Nye Lane, Rm 203
Carson City, NV 89706
Voice: (702) 887-7600
Fax: (702) 887-7629, 7621
E-mail: jonowlin@usgs.gov

New Hampshire
: 525 Clinton St.
Bow, NH 03304
Voice: (603) 225-4681
Fax: (603) 224-8714
E-mail: bmrazik@usgs.gov

New Jersey
: 810 Bear Tavern Rd., Suite 206
West Trenton, NJ 08628
Voice: (609) 771-3901
Fax: (609) 771-3915
E-mail: dc_nj@usgs.gov

New Mexico
Pinetree Office Park, Suite 200
4501 Indian School Rd., N.E.
Albuquerque, NM 87110-3929
Voice: (505)262-5301
Fax: (505) 262-5399
E-mail: livingst@usgs.gov

New York
425 Jordan Rd.
Troy, NY 12180
Voice: (518) 285-5602
Fax: (518) 285-5601
E-mail: lgmoore@usgs.gov

North Carolina
P.O. Box 30728
Raleigh, NC 27622
Voice: (919) 571-4044
Fax: (919) 571-4041
E-mail: jfturner@usgs.gov

North Dakota
821 E. Interstate Ave.
Bismark, ND 58501-1199
Voice: (701) 250-4606
Fax: (701) 250-4252
E-mail: wfhorak@usgs.gov

Ohio
975 West Third Ave.
Columbus, OH 43212
Voice: (614) 469-5553 Ext. 112
Fax: (614) 469-5626
E-mail: shindall@usgs.gov

Oklahoma
202 N.W. 66 St., Building 7
Oklahoma City, OK 73116
Voice: (405) 843-7570
Fax: (405) 843-7712
E-mail: kdpeter@usgs.gov

Oregon
10615 S.E. Cherry Blossom Dr.
Portland, OR 97216
Voice: (503) 251-3202
Fax: (503) 251-3470
E-mail: ddlynch@usgs.gov

Pennsylvania
840 Market St.
Lemoyne, PA 17043-1586
Voice: (717) 730-6910
Fax: (717) 730-6997
E-mail: gnpaulac@usgs.gov

Rhode Island
28 Lord Rd., Suite 280
Marlborough, MA 01752
Voice: (508) 490-5002
Fax: (508) 490-5068
E-mail: wsonntag@usgs.gov

South Carolina
720 Gracern Rd.
Stephenson Center, Suite 129
Columbia, SC 29210
Voice: (803) 750-6107
Fax: (803) 750-6181
E-mail: gpatter@usgs.gov

South Dakota
1608 Mt. View Rd.
Rapid City, SD 57702
Voice: (605) 394-1780
Fax: (605) 394-5373
E-mail: kllindsk@usgs.gov

Tennessee
810 Broadway, Suite 500
Nashville, TN 37203
Voice: (615) 736-5424 Ext. 3123
Fax: (615) 736-2066
E-mail: hmattraw@usgs.gov

Texas
8011 Cameron Rd., Building 1
Austin, TX 78754-3898
Voice: (512) 873-3002
Fax: (512) 873-3090
E-mail: rohawkin@usgs.gov

Utah
1745 West 1700 South
Rm 1016 Administrative Building
Salt Lake City, UT 84104
Voice: (801) 975-3350
Fax: (801) 975-3424
E-mail: hlcase@usgs.gov

Vermont
See listing for New Hampshire

Virginia
     3600 West Broad St., Rm 606
     Richmond, VA 23230
     Voice: (804) 771-2427
     Fax: (804) 358-0476
     E-mail: pahamilt@usgs.gov

Washington
     1201 Pacific Ave., Suite 600
     Tacoma, WA 98402
     Voice: (206) 593-6510
     Fax: (206) 593-6514
     E-mail: cgoodwin@usgs.gov

West Virginia
     603 Morris St.
     Charleston, WV 25301
     Voice: (304) 347-5131
     Fax: (304) 347-5133
     E-mail: dbrown@usgs.gov

Wisconsin
     6417 Normandy Lane
     Madison, WI 53719-1133
     Voice: (608) 276-3801
     Fax: (608) 276-3817
     E-mail: wagebert@usgs.gov

Wyoming
     2617 E. Lincolnway, Suite B
     Cheyenne, WY 82001
     Voice: (307) 778-2931, Ext. 2728
     Fax: (307) 778-2764
     E-mail: bdlewis@usgs.gov

In addition to the above offices, you may find useful information at any of the USGS offices listed under "Useful Resources" at the end of Chapter 5. Additional publications on water data are available from the National Water Information Clearinghouse at:
     U.S. Geological Survey
     423 National Center
     Reston, VA 22092
     Voice:  (800)H20-9000
     URL: http://H20.gov

### United States Topographic Maps

The USGS topographic maps indicate the following water features: perennial and intermittent seasonal streams, wells and springs; intermittent lakes; marshes; inundated areas; dry lake beds; water tanks; dams; bridges; rivers; and perennial lakes.

Most real estate brokers keep such maps in their office. Local sporting goods stores and bookstores usually sell them. You can also purchase the maps for your and other areas by following the instructions given in the "Useful Resources" for Chapter 5, under the heading "Topographic Maps and Other USGS Map Products."

### Local Well-Drilling Companies

If you look in the local Yellow Pages, you will find one or more well-drilling companies. They are extremely helpful in determining the availability of water on your land. For a fee they will do a test drilling or surface appraisal. They can show you any available drilling logs and reports for wells already on the land or on neighboring land. The logs indicate the depth of the wells, the type of water-bearing material that has been drilled through and the capacity and output of the wells. Get the opinion of more than one company as to the possibility of water on your land. Ask a lot of questions. Sometimes they may not release the information without the seller's consent. Sellers who refuse to consent are often hiding something.

The following nonprofit trade association has a lot of valuable information.

     National Ground Water Association
     6375 Riverside St.
     Dublin, OH 43017
     Voice: (800) 551-7379
     Fax: (614) 761-3446

You can request their "Ground Water and Well Technology Catalog" by writing or faxing. The following pamphlets are also available and cost $.50 each, unless noted otherwise.

"Before You Hire a 'Water Witch'"
"Ground Water Heat Pumps"
"Domestic Water Treatments for Homeowners"
"Everything You Wanted to Know About Septic
     Tanks, But Didn't Know Whom to Ask"
"Ground Water Pollution Control: It Depends on
     You"
"America's Priceless Ground Water Source"
"Water Conservation in Your Home"
"Rural Drinking Water—Private Wells or Public
     Water Supply"
"When You Need a Water Well"

"Buyers Guide and Directory of Manufacturers— Water Well Products and Services," #J011, $4.00

## Environmental Protection Agency

The Environmental Protection Agency has some pamphlets available by writing to:

> U.S. Environmental Protection Agency
> Information Access Branch
> Public Information Center (PIC)
> 401 M Street, SW 3403
> Washington, DC 20460
> Voice: (202) 260-2080
> Fax: (202) 260-6257
> URL: Public-Access@epamail.epa.gov
> Safe Drinking Water Hotline: (800) 426-4791
>    in Washington, DC (202) 382-5533

"Ground Water Protection: A Citizen's Action
   Checklist"
"Is Your Drinking Water Safe?"
"Pesticides in Drinking-Water Wells"
"Lead in Your Drinking Water"
"Citizen Monitoring: Recommendations to
   Household Well Users"

## NRCS and Other Sources

When looking for information on water, streams, and the water cycle you can also contact the United States Department of Agriculture's Natural Resources Conservation Service (NRCS). Their Public Affairs Department can let you know what publications are currently available. They can also direct you to the correct office to answer your questions.

> Natural Resources Conservation Service
> (NRCS)
> U.S. Department of Agriculture
> Washington, DC 20250-1300
> URL: http://www.usda.gov

Information can also be obtained from:

> National Rural Water Association
> P.O. Box 1428
> Duncan, OK 73534
> (405) 252-0629

There are State Agencies dedicated to issuing water permits and determining allocation of water re- sources within each state. Check your phone book for their phone number and address.

## Local Boards of Health

You can locate the nearest health department through the telephone directory. It will have brochures on water testing and potability. You can arrange to have it test your water for you and give you a chemical analysis as well as a bacterial and coliform count. Boards of health have minimum standards for contamination of water and will tell you if your water is safe to drink. They do all of this as a public service or, in some cases, for a slight fee.

## Local Water Districts, Irrigation or Reclamation Districts, and Water Agencies

It is possible that your land is within an area that is provided with water by a public or private water company, agency or district. You should be able to find out if this is the case by asking the real estate broker or seller. Go to the offices of the water facility and find out what its services are, how much water you can receive and how much it will cost you. Even if your land is not covered by its operation, it might be able to give you information regarding the availability of water on your land.

## Other Sources of Water Information

County Agriculture Agent or Farm Adviser
Local Agricultural Experiment Station
Forest and Range Experiment Station
Army Corps of Engineers
Natural Resources Conservation Service
Local Universities and Colleges
Various departments, such as the Department of Geology, conduct water surveys and investigations, and they may have some useful information.

The following are available from local, state or county farm bureaus:

"Groundwater and Environmental Pollution Self
   Help Checklists for Farmstead and Farm Fields"
"Protecting Our Groundwater: A Grower's Guide"

## The County Engineer

Most counties have a civil engineer responsible for investigating and documenting water and flood conditions, drainage and other geological problems. He or she might have valuable information.

# CHAPTER 5

# The Earth—Soil, Vegetation and Topography

*What then of the man who hears these words of mine and acts upon them? He is like a man who had the sense to build his house upon rock. The rain came down, the floods rose, the wind blew and beat upon that house; but it did not fall, because its foundations were on rock.*

—Matt. 7:24–26

When real estate agents show property, they emphasize its best features. They are not going to walk buyers across an acre-long gully or tell them that the land turns into a giant undrained mud puddle for six months during the rainy season. They won t explain that a property is on a north slope and gets no sun all winter. They will show some beautiful "homesites," but it will be up to buyers to determine if these sites can actually support buildings and gardens. You cannot tell by just looking at the soil, for instance, if a piece of land will be able to support an on-site sewage disposal system. Never buy land without first either securing the necessary permits for installing your own sewage disposal system or ensuring that you can hook up to a public sewage system.

Finding answers to questions about the condition of the soil, its drainage patterns and its ability to grow things is essential in analyzing the land you intend to buy. If the soil is good, you will have abundant vegetation and few problems with erosion, drainage, slipping foundations and flooding. You should inspect the geography, seek advice from experts and study maps and photographs.

## Topsoil

Topsoil is the loose upper layer of the soil. It is usually richer and darker than the subsoil because it contains humus, or decayed vegetable matter, which is almost black in color and rich in plant nutrients. A dark, thick topsoil rich in humus indicates high fertility. (See Figure 5–1.)

Almost 60 percent of the topsoil in the United States has been lost or destroyed by poor management. Heavy farming has depleted nutrients from the soil, and heavy grazing, logging and fires have destroyed much of the cover vegetation that held the topsoil together. With the vegetation gone, erosion began. The action of water and winds removed the surface soil, washing it into the rivers and oceans. To get an idea of how much earth is carried off in a storm, fill a jar with water from the nearest creek the next time it rains and let the dirt settle to the bottom.

Good land should have at least 10 to 14 inches of loose topsoil. Ground that is rocky and hard lacks topsoil. If the earth is soft enough to poke a stick into easily, it has some topsoil. Generally, land near the ocean tends to be rocky and barren.

The health and abundance of either natural or planted vegetation gives a good and simple indication of the soil quality. Land with too much vegetation on it is often better than land with not enough. Undesirable brush and weeds can be cleared away quite easily with the right equipment, but bringing in lost topsoil that has been washed away because of poor ground cover is an enormous task. Uncleared brushy land will probably be cheaper to buy than land that has been cleared and is ready to build on. Ten of our 80 acres are flat land completely overgrown with thorny brush that could be cleared to make another homesite area. Because this area can't be used as it is, however, instead of increasing the value of the land, as flat land usually does, it did not affect the purchase price.

Although erosion is one of the easiest problems to spot, it is difficult to repair. In an eroded gully

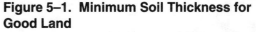

## Figure 5–1. Minimum Soil Thickness for Good Land

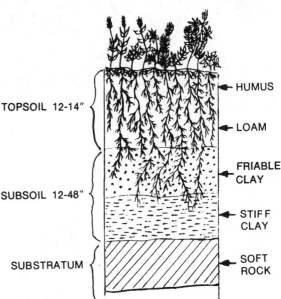

TOPSOIL 12-14″
SUBSOIL 12-48″
SUBSTRATUM

HUMUS
LOAM
FRIABLE CLAY
STIFF CLAY
SOFT ROCK

that has lost topsoil, plant roots will have a difficult time getting started in the hard subsoil. The gully makes a natural channel for excess rainwater to run off the land. Consequently, baby plants that do get a foothold quickly drown or are swept away by the force of the water.

Sandy soils, steep slopes with little vegetation and land that has been logged by the clear-cut method are particularly susceptible to erosion. Not all land that has been logged is bad, however. If enough trees were left to hold most of the soil in place, it may be beautiful land that can be purchased at a much lower price than virgin timberland. You must carefully inspect the land for signs of erosion, though, and be wary if the land has been stripped of its trees.

If you are planning to farm for a living, you should carefully choose land with highly fertile soil. However, if you plan to have a family vegetable and flower garden and perhaps a small orchard, you might consider buying less fertile land with the idea of building up a rich topsoil. The process is a slow one and requires that you cart in loads of organic matter such as spoiled hay, grass clippings, leaves, wet garbage and dirt, but it is a rewarding process.

## Soil Texture

The texture of soil is important for healthy plants, good drainage and building construction. There are four basic soil textures: gravel, sand, loam and clay. Gravel and sand are made up of large particles, whereas clay consists of very tiny particles. Loam, the most common soil in the United States, consists of about equal parts of clay and sand. Because gravel and sandy soils are very loose, they quickly lose valuable nutrients, which are leached out in water, and gain and lose heat rapidly, causing quick thawing and freezing. On the other hand, compact clay soil becomes mushy and sticky when wet, cutting off oxygen to plant roots and making cultivation difficult. A loamy soil is preferred by most plants because it contains the best aspects of both sand and clay. To correct either a highly sandy soil or a heavy clay soil, you will have to build up the amount of humus in the soil.

The best way to determine the texture of the soil is to rub some in your hand and between your fingers. How does it feel? Sand is loose and gritty; clay is heavy and compact when dry and sticky and doughy when wet. Clay is usually gray or yellow. Loam will crumble in your hand and is black.

Dig some holes at different places on the land. Is it hard to dig? How soon do you hit rock? If you dig for several feet and still find a good loam and loose earth that is not too sandy, you have fine soil. If the whole area is rocky and hard, you will have problems. If a road has been put in, look at and feel the various layers of soil that are exposed where the road cuts into the earth.

## Drainage

Drainage refers to the amount of water that can be absorbed by the soil before it becomes saturated. At the saturation point, the water collects on the surface or runs off into the nearest creek or drainage ditch. Most plants will not grow where drainage is poor because their roots cannot tolerate being in more water than they can absorb. These plants actually drown.

A layer of rock or other impervious material, such as hardpan or claypan, near the surface or a high water table can make drainage poor. A few types of soil, like adobe, have very poor drainage. When adobe gets wet, it swells up and prevents water from draining through it. Generally land in the humid eastern United States and in the northern central states is most likely to have drainage problems.

Water-loving plants such as sedges, cattails or rushes or such trees as willows, some maples or bays dotting a meadow indicate poor drainage, although those same plants located in a row or in a small clump would probably indicate the presence of an underground stream or spring.

### Hardpan and Claypan

Hardpan (a compacted layer that is impenetrable by roots) and claypan (a hardpan consisting mainly of clay) occur naturally in the soil or result from years of intensive plowing. Poor plowing practices ruin the soil structure. The fine soil particles are tightly compacted, which destroys the pore spaces in the subsoil and forms a dense, stone like layer that cuts off the topsoil from the subsoil. These hard layers are usually impenetrable by plant roots or water. Plants trying to grow in the soil above the hardpan or claypan will have shallow roots that are easily injured by drowning and drought. The plant roots drown because water collects around them without being able to sink into the ground, and they dry up because they cannot escape the hot sun by penetrating deeper into cooler, moist ground.

### Drainage Tests

If little is growing on land that was once heavily farmed, be careful. Look at the land during and after a rainstorm. If the area becomes a huge mud puddle or the water runs off the surface without penetrating into the ground more than a few inches, the drainage is obviously bad, and the subsoil might be an impervious material.

A dry test involves digging six or more holes 4 to 12 inches in diameter and at least three feet deep at various places on the land, especially where your house and garden will be. Does the ground feel as if you are chopping into rocks? If so, you have an indication that the soil is bad. When you have finished digging, take a knife and scratch the sides of each hole. If the dirt crumbles easily, the soil is not impervious, but if the dirt is tightly compacted and hard to crumble, some kind of hardpan exists.

After you have examined the sides of the dry holes, you are ready to do a *percolation test*. (See Figure 5–2.) A percolation test determines how quickly and effectively water drains through a porous substance. First, roughen the sides of each hole so that water can enter the soil easily, remove any loose dirt from the bottom and add two inches of gravel to prevent sealing. Fill each hole with at least 12 inches of water. Keep the water level 12 inches above the gravel for four hours or more by adding water when needed. If you are doing this test during the dry season, keep the hole filled for at least 12 hours. The ground must simulate its condition during the wettest season of the year. When the dirt is thoroughly wetted, let the water level reach six inches above the gravel. Measure the drop in the water level every 30 minutes for four hours if the water drains out slowly. If the water drains out quickly, measure the drop in the water level every ten minutes for one hour. Add water after each measurement to bring the level back up to six inches above the gravel. Multiply the last measurement of the drop in the water level by 2 if you are measuring every 30 minutes or by 6 if you are measuring every ten minutes to get the percolation rate in inches per hour. If the percolation rate is less than 2½ inches per hour, the permeability of the soil is insufficient for good plant growth and sanitation.

Water will collect after a heavy rain, drowning your plants and flooding your septic tank.

A faster test involves pouring several gallons of water on dry ground. Wait a few minutes and dig into the soil to see how far the water has penetrated. If the soil is still dry a few inches beneath the ground, drainage could be a problem.

Ask your local health inspector if you can get a professional percolation test done. You may have to pay to have this test done by a licensed soil engineer or geologist in some locations. For more information on drainage problems in your area and on how to test the soil, go to the state Agricultural Experiment Station or local office of the Natural Resources Conservation Service. A soil map will also state the drainage qualities of each soil in the area. (See "Useful Resources" at the end of this chapter.)

**Figure 5–2. Percolation Test**

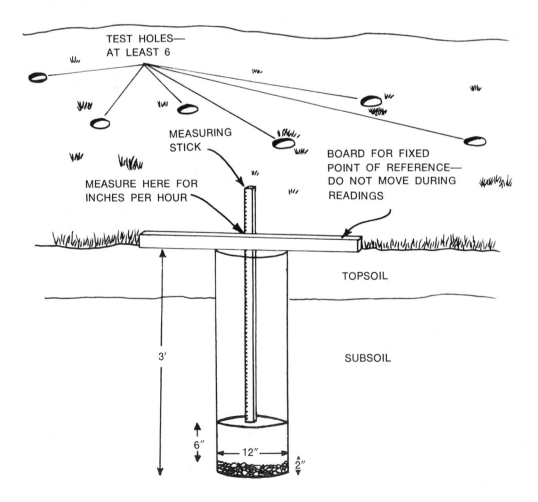

**Poor Drainage Affects Septic Tanks, Cesspools, Basements and Building Foundations**

Poor drainage often causes flooding in basements and septic tank systems. If there is a house with a basement on the property, go down and look at it carefully. Are there signs that it floods? Do the owners have a sump pump in the basement for pumping out water?

If you are planning to build a house on land with drainage problems, you can dispense with a basement but not with a sewage disposal system. If your soil will not allow proper drainage, and if the building codes require the installation of a septic tank with a house, building and health inspectors will not allow you to construct a dwelling. (See Chapter 13, "Building and Health Codes.") If water will not drain properly, the water and sewage flushed into the septic tank and drained out by leach lines will float to the surface of the ground during a rainstorm. I have seen this happen in areas where drainage was poor, and it makes living conditions very unpleasant. The soil must be deep and permeable to effectively absorb the effluent, or discharge, from a septic tank. A rock layer or seasonal high water table in the upper four feet of the ground could make the area unsuitable for sewage disposal.

Where drainage is poor, you also will be required to construct special building foundations with extra stability. If water stands for a long period of time under a house, it will cause wood rot and mildew, which greatly decrease the value and life of the house. It is important that you have the building and health inspectors view the land before you buy so that you know you will have no problem obtaining permits afterward.

**Correcting Drainage Problems**

Correcting poor drainage is an expensive operation, requiring the construction of artificial drainage ditches or the laying of drainage tiles. Drainage tiles are pieces of tube with holes in them. The tiles are spaced closely together directly above the impervious layer of soil, and they collect and carry excess water out to a drainage area. (See Figure 5–3.) If the land has already been laid with tiles, be sure they are in perfect condition, because finding and correcting broken or separated tiles is an expensive and time-consuming job. You should see the drainage system in full operation under the most arduous water conditions before buying. The owner should show you a complete diagram of the

**Figure 5–3. Drainage Tile**

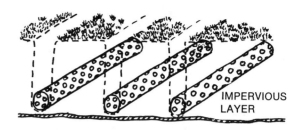

tile pattern so that you can conduct a thorough investigation.

Drainage ditches are usually made of concrete and are spaced farther apart than tiles. The ditches are above the ground, and water is carried in them to a creek or channel. They are also expensive to construct.

If proper drainage of land you want to buy requires a runoff system to deliver the water into a nearby creek or drainage ditch, you need a legal easement to cross neighboring lands. (See Chapter 9, "Easement Rights.") If you divert water from your land onto adjoining lands, you may be held liable for damages unless you have the legal right by the laws of your state or by a written document to divert the water. (See Chapter 10, "Water Rights.")

In areas where drainage is a problem, your land may be within a drainage district established to take water from all land in the district through a common system of canals. Membership in a drainage district is similar to membership in an irrigation district, except that the purpose of the organization is different. (See Chapter 4, "Is There Enough Water on the Land?" to see how an irrigation district operates.) Find out whether your land is within such a district and, if so, whether the seller is already a member. How much are the assessments on the land? Before you buy, speak to the drainage district adviser about any drainage problems and about what will be involved in bringing the land within the district if it is currently excluded.

If you plan to buy land that will require the laying of drainage tiles or construction of ditches, add this cost to the purchase price because it is something that must be done before you can live on the land. If you buy land that has a drainage system already installed, the price will be higher because of this improvement. You should consider whether the added expense is really worthwhile, because it might be possible to find land in the area with good drainage for much less money. Occasionally, the physical conditions of a particular parcel of land prevent good drainage, regardless of what is attempted to alleviate the problem.

## Planning To Install a Septic Tank

If you are planning to have a septic tank, pick up a copy of the sanitary regulations from the local health or pollution-control department.

The soil will have to be tested for permeability or percolation as described above. The groundwater level and bedrock should be at least four feet below the bottom of the trench field or seepage pit. Low areas should be avoided because after a rain, the water may collect there. Also avoid land that slopes more than 15 degrees because the water will flow too rapidly through the drainage pipes.

There should be enough room on the land to install a second drainage or leach area if the first one clogs up. The size of the drainage field depends on the soil's percolation rate and the number of bedrooms in the house. The more trench you have above the minimum required, the better, because the leach field will last longer. However, trenches should not be any longer than 100 feet at most. The usual drainage field occupies 1,000 to 2,000 square feet, so you will want to have 2,000 to 4,000 square feet of space available for a leach field.

If you are going to obtain your water from a well, it should be 100 feet or more from the leach field and preferably uphill from it. The minimum-size parcel for both a well and a septic tank is about a half acre. If you are buying property on the edge of a town that has a sewage treatment system, and if it is possible that in a few years that system may be extended to include your property, try to see if you can put the leach field between the house and the street. That way it will be easier to connect to the public sewer if it becomes available. It will also be easier to reach with a septic tank cleaner's pumper truck. However, if the property is downhill from the street and will also have a well, you may have to locate the septic tank and leach field in the back and the well in the front near the street. In this case you may want to install an extra sewer connection in front if you are certain that a sewer will be available in the future.

The best septic tanks are made of concrete. Although wooden and steel tanks are available, they are usually about the same price but last only ten

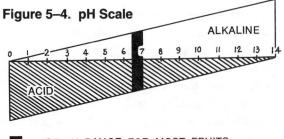

**Figure 5–4. pH Scale**

■ BEST pH RANGE FOR MOST FRUITS, VEGETABLES, AND FLOWERS

years or so, whereas a concrete tank may last as long as the house does. Generally, for a one-bedroom or two bedroom house, the recommended tank size is 750 gallons; for three bedrooms, 1,000; four bedrooms, 1,250; five or six bedrooms, 1,500 gallons. These capacities take into account garbage disposal, automatic dishwashers and washing machines. Most septic tank systems include a distribution box between the tank and the leach field to equalize the flow of effluent into the various pipes. When you lay out your leach field you may want to have the pipes interconnect if the ground is fairly level. That way, if one end of a pipe gets clogged up, effluent can still enter through the other end. See Chapter 6 for more information on septic tanks.

## Acidity and Alkalinity

The acidity or alkalinity of the soil has a tremendous effect on the vegetation. Acidity and alkalinity are measured on a pH scale that goes from 0 to 14, 0 being extremely acid and 14 being extremely alkaline. A soil with a pH factor of 7.0 is neutral. Nearly neutral soils, testing in the range of 6.5 to 7.0, are best for most fruits, vegetables, field crops and flowers. (See Figure 5–4.) Soil that is too acid or alkaline locks valuable nutrients into it, making them unavailable for plant use.

An extremely acid or alkaline soil may be difficult to remedy. To correct an acid soil requires the annual application of quantities of lime. An alkaline soil requires sulfur or gypsum. If you cannot correct the soil deficiency, you will be limited to growing only certain items. For example, the only crops that will grow on a highly acid soil are berries, potatoes, peanuts, radishes and watermelon.

For centuries farmers used to taste the soil to test for acidity or alkalinity. If the soil tasted sour, it was too acid; if it tasted bitter, it was too alkaline; but if it tasted sweet it was good for raising crops. Today there are two other simple ways you can test your soil to determine "sweetness." One uses reagents; the other uses litmus paper. For both tests you should collect moist soil samples from a depth of about six inches (where plant roots are) from various parts of the land, because different areas may have different pH factors.

The reagent test requires that you purchase an inexpensive soil-test kit. You can get one at any gardening supply house. Put a bit of the sample earth into a test tube or small clean container and mix in some of the liquid reagent that comes in the kit. The reagent is a chemical that changes color according to the pH factor. look at the color that results from the mix and compare it with a color chart that comes with the kit to determine the acidity or alkalinity.

The cheaper test is done with litmus paper. You can purchase neutral litmus paper with a pH factor of 7.0 at a drugstore or garden supply center. Press a piece of litmus paper into the moist soil sample. If the paper remains the same color and just gets wet, the soil is neutral. If it turns blue, the soil is alkaline; if pink, acid.

After testing the soil, test the water source on the land to see if it is acid or alkaline. The water you use to irrigate your plants will affect them as much as the soil will.

You can get a more thorough test done by the local farm adviser, Soil Conservation Service, or college agricultural or soil department. After analyzing your soil, they will tell you what kinds of things you can grow on the land.

## Pesticides in the Soil

You may want to know if pesticides, herbicides or other poisons have been used on the land or on neighboring land, because many of these poisons are long-lived and can be carried to surrounding water supplies by rainwater and irrigation water seeping through the soil. If you are interested in organic gardening, you will want "pure" soil. Ask the owner what has been used on his or her plants. Look for poisons and spray containers in the barn, garage, basement or greenhouse. The best insurance that you are getting unpoisoned soil is to buy land that has never been cultivated or lived on.

## The Building Site

Every real estate ad makes a point of mentioning that there is a building site on the land being sold. "Numerous building sites," "pretty building sites," "site to build a cabin or home," "excellent view homesite" and "many level building sites" are examples of how this may be advertised. When you evaluate so-called building sites, remember my warning about pond sites in Chapter 4. Just as anybody can point out a supposed pond site, it is easy to call an area a building site. But it takes careful analysis to determine whether a place is truly suitable for the construction of a home. A favorite tactic used in selling rural land is to take prospective buyers to a spot on the property where there is a nice view or a fairly level clearing and call it a homesite. The site looks beautiful, and its view overlooking the valley or lake captures the buyer. The person who buys this parcel may discover too late that the land is too steep to build on, that it is impossible to construct a road into the site or that the drainage is insufficient for a septic tank.

Many considerations that do not apply to a city lot are necessary to determine the suitability of a country homesite. Most important of these are the feasibility of building a road, of getting utilities and of getting water to the site. For instance, if a homesite is on a ridge high above a creek that is the only source of water, you might find it impossible or very costly to bring water to the site, especially if no electricity is available. (Refer to Chapter 4, "Is There Enough Water on the Land?", for the problems involved in getting water to the homesite and garden areas.) If no road presently exists, you must get an estimate of the costs of constructing one before you buy. The terrain or the soil might make building a solid road to the site an impossible task. If an access road does exist but it is dirt, find out what the average annual maintenance costs are to keep the road in good condition. You may find that the road becomes impassable in the winter, especially in snow country, which may mean a long walk from the county road with groceries. For heating, cooking and lighting you might want to have a large propane fuel storage tank, which must be filled periodically by a large tanker truck. Your road must be kept in good enough condition for the truck to get in and out, and your homesite must have an area for the tank that will be accessible to the truck.

**Figure 5–5.  Site's Exposure to Sun**

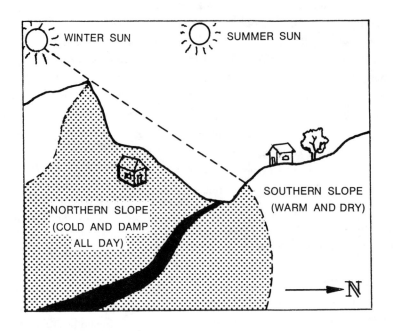

Consider the site's exposure to the elements. A house on a southern or southeastern slope will always be warmer because it gets the winter sun. A building site at the bottom of a hill facing north, on the other hand, will probably be cold and damp all winter long. (See Figure 5–5.) Another major decision is whether to buy on a mountaintop with a view or in a valley. On a ridge you will probably be more exposed to high winds, a hot sun all day and all the noises from the valley below. Valleys tend to be cooler, quieter and closer to water sources. Even if you have your heart set on a spectacular view, consider all the other aspects of the location, too.

The type of ground on which you build your house is important. You will have problems if it is either extremely hard or extremely soft. A rocky surface will not provide a good anchor for your foundation, and water runoff may be a problem. Soft dirt will be unstable and incapable of supporting a heavy structure, and it will be susceptible to land slides and subsidence.

A major problem in areas of silty clay soil, commonly called *adobe*, is *soil creep*, which occurs when the earth slowly oozes downhill in wet weather months. During the dry summer months the soil shrinks as the water content decreases, and huge cracks may open up in the ground. When the winter rain comes, the unstable soil slips under the force of gravity until the particles settle into more stable positions. The greatest amount of soil movement occurs at the onset of the winter rains.

Soil creep varies with the soil depth and pitch of the slope. Tests have shown that on a slope of only eight degrees, soil five feet deep can move an average of half an inch each year at the surface. Soil creep can cause serious damage to foundations and walls. When examining an area, look for indications of poor soil stability, such as large cracks in the surface and leaning fence posts, power poles and structures.

The possibility of land collapsing into *sinkholes* must be considered in many areas of the country. Sinkholes occur when the roofs of underground caverns suddenly collapse, leaving a huge pit in the ground. This is believed to be caused by either natural or man-induced lowering of the water table. Where the necessary conditions exist, sinkholes are an extremely serious and frequent problem. For example, in Shelby County, Alabama, more than 1,000 sinkholes have occurred in the past 25 years. In fact, all of central and northern Alabama has soil susceptible to cave-ins of this type. When investigating your soil, always ask about the occurrence of sinkholes and other regional soil problems.

With increasing frequency, large areas of swamp and marshlands, river beds and flooded areas are being filled in with dirt in an attempt to gain more land on which to develop housing and make a larger profit. Do not buy real estate where the building sites consist of landfill. You will have no end of troubles. Before buying, find out if the ground will support a house and other structures without creating excessive settling or cracking of the foundation.

The most common building problems are slipping and cracking foundations and walls, sliding hillsides and flooded basements. The best ground to build on has soil at least five feet deep, allows good drainage of water, does not flood or lie over a high water table and is level or moderately sloping. Steep slopes are generally poor building sites because they can slide and erode. The steeper the building site, the more difficult it will be to construct a solid foundation.

A level homesite is an asset to a piece of property and always raises the land's value. (See Chapter 19, "Evaluating the Price of the Property.") If you plan to have only a house, garden and small family orchard, you need only a few level acres. large stock animals, such as cows or horses, usually need at least one acre per animal for grazing. One way to get level land for a low price is to buy an area thickly covered with brush, because it is worth less than land that already has been cleared. Although considerable work may be required to clear the area, the soil is likely to be very rich, having been protected and fed by the brush for years. Be careful to protect the newly uncovered earth from erosion, and you will have some valuable land for very little money.

## Native Building Materials
## and Fuel on the Land

In this country you will be lucky if you find land at a reasonable price with enough trees on it to construct a house. Such abundance is found mostly in Canada, where many people still construct their homes from standing timber on the land. In the United States you will probably have to rely on such materials as rock and adobe rather than trees if you want to build from available resources.

In many areas where land has been logged, enough wood may be lying on the ground to use as fuel for cooking and heating your house for several years. Brush that must be cleared or dying trees that should be cut also can be used for fuel. If you are buying in isolated country, wood fuel on the land is practically a necessity.

## Poison Oak, Poison Ivy and Other Allergies

If you are sensitive to poison oak, ivy or sumac, do not buy land that is covered with it. These prolific plants are difficult to get rid of. They have to be dug up by the roots or continually sprayed with poisons. If you are allergic to them, you cannot do this yourself. Goats and donkeys will eat the stuff, but you will need quite a herd to make a dent.

Other allergies to plants, such as hay fever, can also make life in the country unpleasant. Try to avoid those plants that are particularly irritating to you. Visit the land in the worst season for your allergies, and if you start to wheeze and sniffle, look somewhere else. Ask a local health department official for information on local plant and pollen conditions.

## Earthquakes and Fault Lines

Although California and Alaska are the areas most noted for their earthquakes, faults do exist in other regions of the country. A few major quakes have been recorded in New England; in South Carolina; in the Mississippi Valley; and in the western mountains of Montana, Wyoming, Utah, northern Arizona and New Mexico. In most areas of the country, earthquakes are a minor problem. Even if a major quake occurs, you will be safer in the country away from toppling buildings and the chaos of panicking people. Make sure that you don't build your house or access road on top of a fault line, because minor shifting of the earth will cause you endless problems. Check with your state division of mines and geology or your local farm adviser to determine whether fault lines exist in your area. Both sources have maps showing where all the earthquake areas are located. Further information can be obtained from the U.S. Geological Survey (USGS), National Earthquake Information Center, Stop 967, Box 25046, Denver Federal Center, Denver, CO 80225.

## Landslides

If you look at a house built on a steep hillside or if you are planning to build your house on a hillside, carefully check out the structure of the soil on the hill. You don't want to have your beautiful country house go sliding down the hill during an unusually heavy rainstorm.

During heavy rains landslides may occur on steep hills with surfaces of loose, fragile or slippery rocks and soil. The term *landslide* includes slumps, earth flows, mud flows, rock slides, soil creep and rock avalanches.

Often shallow surface flows of mud and debris will take a house in a landslide. But in deep-soil areas, moisture will work its way down until it reaches layers of impervious clay or siltstone underneath the more porous rock and soil. The water accumulates to form a slick plane a few feet to many yards beneath the surface. If more heavy rains occur, the entire block of hillside may slip away with the house or other structures on it.

If you are buying land in a subdivision, find out if there is a soils and geology report or an environmental impact report available. Check with the USGS to see if any maps have been made of the land you are looking at (see "Useful Resources" at the end of this chapter for addresses). The USGS has prepared elaborate maps of many slide-prone areas in the United States. However, the less populated an area is, the fewer studies will have been done. Check with your local planning or zoning commission to see if it has any information.

If a house is built on a steep hill or the building site for your dream house is on a hill, you want to put a contingency in your contract that the close of escrow is subject to your approval of an inspection and a report prepared by a civil engineer, a registered geologist or a soils engineer.

You also want to find out how much it will cost to protect an existing house that is situated on a hill that might slide. The geologist or soils engineer may recommend that you build diversion walls, add deep piers to your foundation to anchor the house to solid bedrock or stabilize the hill. Some of these measures could be very expensive, and you must consider these costs in calculating the cost of your purchase.

## Minerals

I explain the importance of mineral rights and how to investigate them in Chapter 11, "Mineral, Oil, Gas, Timber, Soil and Other Rights." You may be shown land that does not possess mineral rights. These rights may be held by the seller, another party or the U.S. government. Try to find out why the party in possession is holding onto the rights, and investigate the geology of the area to determine the possibility of their ever wanting to exercise these rights.

You can do this by finding out what minerals are known to be on the land and in the general area. The same agencies that have earthquake information will have studies of the area's geology and facts about past and present mineral explorations in every part of the state. If it appears that the land does not have any minerals currently being used or sought after, you will probably be safe in buying it without mineral rights. Often the government or individuals will hold on to mineral rights without ever intending to use them. Sometimes the government will keep the mineral rights to a piece of land it sells as a matter of policy.

## Maps and Aerial Photographs

When requesting information on the maps and photographs described in the following sections, include a description of the property you want covered. If it is within an area described by the United States Rectangular Survey, give the base and meridian, section, township, range, county and state in which the parcel is located. (See Chapter 8, "Land Descriptions and Surveys.") If the land is in an area not described by the Rectangular Survey, describe its location as precisely as possible according to the particular survey system used.

Whenever ordering a map or photograph, ask for the most recent one available, because older maps and photos will not include new roads, highways and buildings. To receive your map or photo in good condition, you must specifically request that it be sent in a mailing tube so that it will not be folded by the sender or the post office.

### Soil Maps and Other Soil Information

Every state is represented by a regional field office of the United States Forest Service, which has soil maps available to the public at little or no charge. (See "Useful Resources" at the end of this chapter.) A soil map, which breaks down the soil types throughout a given area, gives much information regarding the soil itself and what is growing on it (see Figure 5–6). Each map has an accompanying chart and leaflet that explains how to read the symbols. Before buying land, get all the maps you can find to help you really know the geography of the area. Soil information can be obtained from most of the resources listed at the end of this chapter.

Figure 5–6 is a portion of a U.S. Department of Agriculture (USDA) Forest Service soil map that covers our land. It is based on aerial photos and onsite inspection and classification. Each symbol details important aspects of the soil and vegetation of the area. For example, the symbols D, T, M, 812/5, and III represent the following information:

**Figure 5–6. Sample Soil Map**

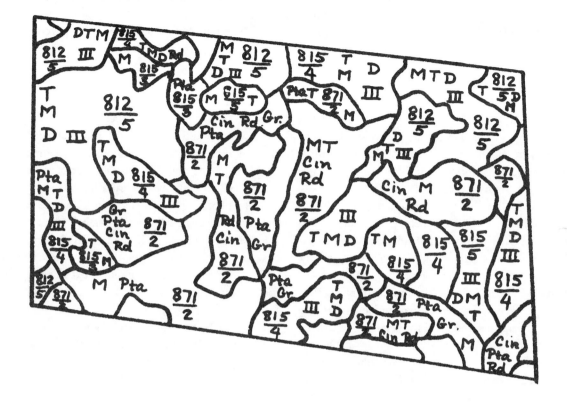

- D—Douglas fir; will not usually sprout if top is killed by fire; negligible browsing value for horses, cattle, sheep, goats and deer.
- T—tan oak tree; will sprout following a fire; negligible browsing value for horses, cattle, sheep, goats and deer.
- M—madrone tree; will sprout following a fire; negligible browsing value for horses and cattle and poor to negligible value for sheep, goats and deer.
- 812/5—Hugo soil series; over four feet deep, loam texture, slightly acid, light grayish brown in color; rolling to steep uplands topography; good permeability for movement of water, air and roots through the soil; drainage good, no toxins present; annual rainfall is 65 to 75 inches; good to very good for commercial timber, and fair for grasses.
- III—the height that the average Douglas fir tree reaches at the age of a hundred years on this soil is 140 feet.

Another source of soil maps and descriptions is the Natural Resources Conservation Service (NRCS), which publishes soil surveys for each state. (See "Useful Resources" at the end of this chapter.)

Included in the map and survey are soil land capability groupings; productivity ratings for trees and farm and horticultural crops; soil ratings and limitations; soil morphology, the relation of soils to their environment; principles of soil classification; and a general description of the climate and other features significant to soil problems of the area.

**Vegetation and Timber Stand Maps**
These maps are similar in style to soil maps. If an agency such as the Forest Service has soil maps for your area, it will probably also have timber stand and vegetation maps. (See "Useful Resources" at the end of this chapter.)

**Topographical Maps**
The topographical map is an essential aid to understanding the lay of the land. The unique aspect of the "topo" map is the use of contour lines to indicate elevation. The distance between contour lines is usually 40 feet measured along the ground. Thus, the closer the lines, the steeper the terrain. These maps also show roads, railroads, cities, towns and water features. By comparing aerial photographs of each area with actual ground inspections, the USGS

has prepared topographical maps for the entire United States.

Topographical maps also are called quadrangle maps because each unit of area surveyed is a quadrangle. You can get either 7½-minute or 15-minute quadrangle maps. Chapter 8, "Land Descriptions and Surveys," explains how an area is broken into quadrangles. The 7½-minute quadrangle map is drawn to a scale of 1:24,000, which means that 1 inch on the map equals 24,000 inches or 2,000 feet on the ground. Thus, 2 inches on the map equals approximately 1 mile. The 15-minute quadrangle map is drawn to the scale of 1:62,500, which makes 1 inch equal to about 1 mile on the ground. Thus, the 7½-minute maps give much greater detail.

The USGS publishes an index to topographic maps for each state, which you can obtain free by writing the main office or visiting your nearest USGS office. Each index lists the map for each specific geographic region, or quadrangle, within the state by name and the year in which it was charted.

The index also lists special maps available and the addresses of local map reference libraries, local map dealers and federal map distribution centers. Order blanks and a list of prices are included. When you write for your state's index, also ask for the free booklet describing topographical maps and symbols.

Because of the popularity and importance of topographical maps, local sport shops, stationery stores and dealers in civil engineering equipment usually sell them.

### Aerial Photographs and Status Maps

Aerial photographs are taken with special automatic cameras that are held vertically while an airplane flies at a constant altitude above sea level along carefully laid-out sky trails. Each snap of the camera's shutter captures an area of ground that overlaps the ground covered in the last photograph by about 60 percent. Each strip of film covers a certain strip of ground. When the plane flies over the adjoining parallel strip of ground, the overlap between strips is from 30 percent to 50 percent. These photo strips are then laid out side by side to form a photo index showing the entire area.

Although aerial photography did not begin on a national basis until 1930, most areas of the United States have been covered. Some areas have been photographed by more than one agency, and the quality of reproduction tends to vary according to who took the pictures and the date they were taken.

A good photo can help you study the geography of the land, including the extent of erosion, vegetation and timber growth.

An aerial photo also can be used to get an idea of the location of a parcel's boundaries if they have not been marked on the ground or if only the corners have been marked by a surveyor. Draw in the boundaries, according to the description of the land, on a topographical map, and compare it to an aerial photo done to the same scale. Topographical maps are drawn using aerial photos, so you should be able to locate and draw in the boundaries on the aerial photo quite easily. From the features shown in the photograph, you can then locate the boundaries on the ground fairly accurately.

The best way to look at an aerial photograph is with a set of paired stereoscopic prints. Placing two consecutive overlapping photos next to each other and using a stereo viewer or lens stereoscope, you can see the photo in 3-D. The effect is beautiful, and each feature sticks out at you as if you were hovering over the land in a helicopter. If you have ever looked at a 3-D movie or comic book using a red and green viewer, you know the effect. You can use a stereo viewer or a similar device at any of the agencies listed at the end of this chapter. You can buy a stereoscopic viewer at stores that sell surveying or engineering equipment or from Forestry Supplies, Inc., 205 W. Rankin St., P.O. Box 8397, Jackson, MS 39204. Also, army surplus stores and scientific supply houses occasionally have them for sale. The folding pocket type is the least expensive.

Each agency that sells aerial photos issues free status maps showing the photos that are available for your area. Each status map indicates the area photographed, the date the photos were taken, the various sizes of photos available and the prices, and includes order blanks.

## Useful Resources

### United States Geological Survey (USGS) and Earth Science Information Centers (ESICs)

The USGS has offices around the country that can assist walk-in customers and also answer inquiries by mail or telephone.

In addition to assisting the public in selecting and ordering all USGS products, the ESICs provide counter service for USGS topographic, geologic, and water-resources maps and reports. The offices furnish information about the USGS and its programs and are linked to information held by state and other federal offices. Most ESICs maintain libraries of recent USGS book reports and are regional depositories for Open-File Reports.

Listed below are ESIC locations and the regions that each covers. These offices include local ESICs that provide information about geologic, hydrologic, topographic and land-use maps, books and reports, as well as aerial photographs. For information, call 1-800-USA-MAPS.

Alaska

Anchorage-ESIC
4230 University Dr., Room 101
Anchorage, AK 99508-4664
Voice: (907) 786-7011
Fax: (907) 786-7050

California

Menlo Park-ESIC
Building 3, Rom. 3128, MS 532
345 Middlefield Rd.
Menlo Park, CA 94025 -3591
Voice: (415) 329-4309
Fax: (415) 329-5130
TDD: (415) 329-5092

Colorado

Lakewood-ESIC
Box 25046, Federal Center, MS 504
Building 25, Room 1813
Denver, CO 80225-0046
Voice: (303) 202-4200
Fax: (303) 202-4188

Colorado

Lakewood Open Files-ESIC
Box  25286, Building 810
Denver Federal Center, MS 517
Denver, CO 80225
Voice: (303) 202-4210
Fax: (303) 202-4695

District of Columbia

Washington, DC-ESIC
U.S. Department of the Interior
1849 C St., NW, Room 2650
Washington, DC 20240
Voice: (202) 208-4047
Fax: (202) 208-6297
TDD: (202) 219-1510

Missouri

Rolla-ESIC
1400 Independence Rd., MS 231
Rolla, MO 65401-2602
Voice: (314) 341-0851
Fax: (314) 341-9375
TDD: (314) 341-2716

South Dakota

Sioux Falls- ESIC
EROS Data Center
Sioux Falls, SD 57198-0001
Voice: (605) 594-6151
Fax: (605) 594-6589
TDD: (605) 594-6933

Mississippi

Stennis Space Center-ESIC
Building 3101
Stennis Space Center, MS 38529
Voice: (601) 688-3541
Fax: (601) 688-2230
TDD: (601) 688-3315

Utah

Salt Lake City-ESIC
2222 West 2300 South, 2nd Floor
Salt Lake City, UT 84119
Voice: (801) 975-3742
Fax: (801) 975-3740
TDD: (801) 975-3744

Virginia

Reston-ESIC
507 National Center
Reston, VA 22092
Voice: (703) 648-6045
Fax: (703) 648-5548
TDD: (703) 648-4119

Washington

Spokane-ESIC
U.S. Post Office Building, Rm. 135
904 West Riverside Avenue
Spokane, WA 99201-1088
Voice: (509) 353-2524
Fax: (509) 353-2872
TDD: (509) 353-3235

**Main and Branch Libraries of the USGS**

The library system of the USGS is open to the public. Most of the materials in the library system may be borrowed by the public through interlibrary loans. Holdings include 1.1 million monographs and serials, 385,000 maps, 355,000 pamphlets and 340,000 reports and dissertations in microform, all relating to geological matters within the United States.

For more information write:

California

   Library, U.S. Geological Survey
   Mail Stop 955
   345 Middlefield Rd.
   Menlo Park, CA 94025
   (415) 319-5029

Colorado

   Library, U.S. Geological Survey
   Mail Stop 914
   Box 25046, Federal Center
   Denver, CO 80225
   (303) 326-1000

Virginia

   U.S. Geological Survey Library
   National Center, Mail Stop 950
   12201 Sunrise Valley Dr.
   Reston, VA 22092
   (703) 648-4302

**USGS Photographic Library**

The USGS photographic library contains a collection of more than 250,000 photographs (mostly black and white) taken during USGS studies. The photographic library may be used by the public. Persons who wish to obtain prints or enlargements, copy negatives or duplicate transparencies are encouraged to visit the library to make their selections. The library staff will prepare lists of selected photographs in response to specific requests. Photographs are indexed by subject and by geographic location and include aerial photographs of most areas within the United States.

**Book and Text Products Section of the USGS**

The Book and Text Products Section distributes popular publications of general interest, such as leaflets, pamphlets and booklets. Write for the catalog to:

U.S. Geological Survey
Book and Sales Reports
Federal Center
Box 25425
Denver, CO 80225
Voice:  (303) 236-7477
Fax: (303) 236-1972

**Topographic Maps and Other
USGS Map Products**

The USGS Map Products Section sells geologic, hydrologic, topographic, land use and land cover maps over the counter and by mail. To order, write to:

Branch of Distribution
U.S. GEOLOGICAL Survey
Box 25286 Federal Center
Denver, CO 80225
(800) 435-7627

Order by map name, state and series. To obtain this information, first write for a free index for your area of interest and a booklet describing topographic maps available. The indexes show available published maps. Index maps show quadrangle location, name and survey data. Also listed are special maps and sheets, with prices, map dealers, federal distribution centers, map reference libraries and instructions for ordering maps. Although the distribution offices described above provide counter service for their products, they are primarily mail-order outlets. For maps, ESICs are the main over-the-counter sales outlets of the USGS (see addresses above).

**Publications on Soil,
Maps and Aerial Photographs**

The following pamphlets are free from the USGS Main Office or its Public Inquiry Offices (see addresses above).

"Cartography at the USGS"
"Catalog of Maps"
"Maps of the U.S."
"New Publications of the Geological Survey" (ask
    to be put on the list for future monthly mailings)
"Popular Publications of the USGS"
"Index to Small-Scale Maps of the United States"
"Information Sources and Services"
"The U.S. Geological Survey"
"Tools for Planning Topographical Maps"
"Topographic Maps"
"Topographic Mapping"
"Topographic Map Symbols"

"United States Geological Survey Library"
"Public Inquiry Offices of the U.S. Geological Survey"
"Photographic Library of the Geological Survey"
"Geologic Maps, Portraits of the Earth"
"Active Faults of California"
"Earthquakes"
"Elevations and Distances in the United States"
"Maps of the United States"

**Aerial Photography**
Below is a list of sources for aerial photos and the names of the status maps available.

*United States Geological Survey (USGS)*
Ask for "Status of Aerial Photography in the United States and Status of Aerial Mosaics." These publications list the government agencies that have photographed each area of the country and the commercial aerial photographers who sell prints of their photos, and they tell how you can order the photos. Order these publications from the USGS offices listed above or from the Photographic Library and Distribution Service or Map Information Office noted below. Also write for the following publications:

"How to Obtain Aerial Photographs"
"How to Order Maps on Microfilm"
"Looking for Old Aerial Photographs"
"NHAP and NAPP Photographic Enlargements"

Give your state name and ask for the "Catalog to Topographic and other Map Coverage" for the date you are interested in and the "Index to Topographic and other Map Coverage" for your state.

Photographic Library
U.S. GEOLOGICAL Survey
Mail Stop 914 Box 25046, Federal Center
Denver, CO 80225

or

U.S. GEOLOGICAL Survey
Map Distribution Federal Center
Building 41, Box 25286
Denver, CO 80225
Voice: 1-800-USA-MAPS
URL: http://www.usgs.gov/esic/map.html

**Local Commercial Aerial Photographers**
Most areas have private businesses that engage in aerial photography. The cost of hiring a plane and photographer would be prohibitive, but in many cases they have already photographed your land,

and for a small fee, you can purchase a copy of a picture of your land. Inquire at local photography stores and airports, and look in the telephone directory under "Photographers-Aerial." In some cases, it might not cost you much to charter a flight on a small plane for an hour to take your own aerial photographs.

One company that does aerial photography is WAC Corporation. They have both photos and CD-ROMS. Their new series of CDs are called *Cities on CD*. Photos start at $30.00 and CDs at $349.00. They can be reached at:

WAC
520 Conger Street
Eugene, OR 97402-2795
Voice: (800) 845-8088
Fax: (503) 342-5169

*City Halls or County Courthouses*
Many cities and counties have photographed large areas within their borders. Ask the Planning Commission if they have commissioned any aerial photographs of your area.

*U.S. Department of Agriculture (USDA-FSA)*
The USDA packet gives information on available aerial photographs, their sizes, types, scales and so on. The Aerial Photography Field Office (APFO) library includes photographs used by the Farm Service Agency (FSA) and the U.S. Forest Service (USFS). You can order information free from:

USDA-FSA
Aerial Photography Field Office
2222 West, 2300 South
P.O. Box 30010
Salt Lake City, UT 84130-0010
Voice: (801) 975-3503
Fax: (801) 975-3532

Each FSA county office has a photo index of the county or counties it serves. You may visit your state or county ASCS office, select the photo you need from this index and obtain assistance in preparing an order.

If you are interested in an aerial photograph of a distant county, you may wish to purchase a line or spot index or a digital index, each $4.00, of the area you are interested in to make your selection. Or you may send a legal description, including state, county and township with section and range numbers or coordinate location, or a copy of a county or city map or USGS topographic map with the area you are interested in outlined in red to the APFO office above.

*Ordering Older Photos*
Aerial photo negatives from 1941 and earlier were transferred to the National Archives. To order any of these older photos, write to:

> National Archives and Records Service
> Cartographic Archives Division
> General Services Administration
> 8601 Adelthi Road
> College Park, MD 20740-6001
> Voice: (301) 713-7040
> Fax: (301) 713-7488

*National Oceanic and Atmospheric Administration National Ocean Service*
This agency specializes in research of coastal areas and regions around navigable rivers. Send all inquiries regarding aerial photos to:

> Support Section, N/CG-236
> Nautical Charting Division
> National Ocean Service, NOAA
> Rockville, MD 20852
> Voice: (303) 497-6826
> Fax: 303) 497-6513
> URL: http://www.info@ngac.noaa.gov

**U.S. Forest Service (USFS) Regional Field Offices**
The USFS has information on soil studies in areas near U.S. forests and also has aerial photographs. Write to the U.S. Forest Service at the following regional offices.

> United States Forest Service
> Department of Agriculture
> 201 14th St., S.W.
> Washington, DC 20250-6090
> URL: http://www.fs.fed.us/intro/directory/fs_ofc.html

Northern Region (Idaho, Montana, North Dakota, NW South Dakota)
> Federal Building
> P.O. Box 7669
> Missoula, MT 59807
> (406) 329-3316

Rocky Mountain Region (Colorado, Nebraska, South Dakota, Eastern Wyoming, Kansas)
> P.O. Box 25127
> Lakewood, CO 80225
>
> or
>
> 740 Simms St,
> Golden, CO 80401
> (303) 275-5350

Southwestern Region (Arizona, New Mexico)
> Federal Building
> 517 Gold Ave., SW
> Albuquerque, NM 87102
> (505) 842-3292

Intermountain Region (Southern Idaho, Nevada, Utah, Western Wyoming)
> Federal Building
> 324 25th St.
> Ogden, UT 84401
> Voice: (801) 625-5605
> Fax: (801) 625-5127

Pacific Southwest Region (California, Hawaii)
> 630 Sansome St.
> San Francisco, CA 94111
> (415) 705-2870

Pacific Northwest Region (Oregon, Washington)
> 3335 W. 1st St.
> P.O. Box 3623
> Portland, OR 97208
> (503) 326-3625

Eastern Region (Illinois, Indiana, Iowa, Ohio, Maine, Maryland, Massachusetts, Michigan, Minnesota, Missouri, New Hampshire, New Jersey, New York, North Carolina, Pennsylvania, Rhode Island, Vermont, West Virginia, Wisconsin)
> 310 W. Wisconsin Ave.
> Milwaukee, WI 53203

Southern Region (Alabama, Arkansas, Florida, Georgia, Kentucky, Louisiana, Mississippi, North Carolina, Puerto Rico, South Carolina, Tennessee, Texas, Virginia)
> 1720 Peachtree Rd., NW
> Atlanta, GA 30367

Alaska Region
> Federal Office Building
> P.O. Box 1628
> Juneau, AK 99802

**State and Private Forestry Offices**

The state and private forestry offices are located in the same buildings as the USFS Regional Field Offices (see above) with the exception of the following area:

Northeastern Area (Connecticut, Delaware, Illinois, Indiana, Iowa, Maine, Maryland, Massachusetts, Michigan, Minnesota, Missouri, New Hampshire, New Jersey, New York, Ohio, Pennsylvania, Rhode Island, Vermont, West Virginia, Wisconsin)

> 6816 Market Street
> Upper Darby, PA 19082

**State Forestry Offices**

These are state agencies that manage and protect a state's forest resources. They have information you will need if you intend to purchase land adjacent to or near state forest lands. You can locate your local office by looking in the telephone book under the state listings and subheading for "Forestry Department."

Mail all inquiries regarding land-related subjects such as soil conditions, water availability, erosion problems and farming to the local Cooperative State Extension Services. Always request a list of available publications.

> Cooperative State Research, Education, and
>   Extension Services
> USDA
> Washington, DC 20250-9000
> Voice: (202) 720-3029
> Fax: (202) 720-0289
> URL: http://www.csreesc@reeusda.gov

Your local Cooperative State Extension Service can be located through your local farm adviser. The main offices are located at the following universities (listed alphabetically by state):

Auburn University, Auburn, Alabama
University of Alaska, Anchorage and Fairbanks
University of Arizona, Tucson
University of Arkansas, Fayetteville
University of California at Davis
Colorado State University, Fort Collins
University of Connecticut, Storrs
University of Delaware, Newark
University of the District of Columbia,
   Washington, DC
University of Florida, Gainesville
University of Georgia, Athens

University of Hawaii at Manoa, Honolulu
University of Idaho, Moscow
University of Illinois, Urbana
Purdue University, West Lafayette, Indiana
Iowa State University, Iowa City
Kansas State University, Manhattan
University of Kentucky, Lexington
Louisiana State University, Baton Rouge
University of Maine, Orono
University of Maryland, College Park
University of Massachusetts, Amherst and Boston
Michigan State University, East Lansing
University of Minnesota, Minneapolis, St. Paul
Mississippi State University, Mississippi
State University of Missouri, Columbia
Montana State University, Bozeman
University of Nebraska, Lincoln
University of Nevada, Las Vegas
University of New Hampshire, Durham
Rutgers University, New Brunswick, New Jersey
New Mexico State University, Las Cruces
Cornell University, Ithaca, New York
North Carolina State University, Raleigh
North Dakota State University, Fargo
Ohio State University, Columbus
Oklahoma State University, Stillwater
Oregon State University, Corvallis
Pennsylvania State University, University Park
University of Rhode Island, Kingston
Clemson University, Clemson, South Carolina
South Dakota State University, Brookings
University of Tennessee, Knoxville
Texas A&M University System, College Station
Utah State University, Logan
University of Vermont, Burlington
Virginia Polytechnic Institute and State University,
   Blacksburg
Washington State University, Pullman
University of Wisconsin, Madison
University of Wyoming, Laramie

**Natural Resource Conservation Service (NRCS)**

This federal agency, formerly the Soil Conservation Service (SCS), works with local soil and water conservation districts. Most rural areas contain one or more conservation districts and a local Soil Conservation Service. They have maps and conduct onsite inspections and evaluations of soil quality and water resources. To locate your local office look in the telephone book under U.S. Government, subheading "U.S. Dept. of Agriculture, Natural Resources Conservation Service," or ask the local farm adviser. You should request a list of published soil maps and surveys and other information for your state from the main office:

> Natural Resources Conservation Service
>   (NRCS)
> U.S. Department of Agriculture
> Washington, DC 20250-1300
> Voice: (800) THE-SOIL
> URL: http://www.nalusda.gov

The NRCS state offices can be contacted by the adresses listed below or through the following World-Wide Web address: http:// www/crcs.usda. gov/soils/nssc.html.

Alabama
>   665 Opelika Rd.
>   Auburn, AL 36830
>   Voice: (205) 887-4506
>   Fax: (205) 821-0250

Alaska
>   949 E. 36th Suite 400
>   Anchorage, AK 99508-4362
>   Voice: (907) 271-2424
>   Fax: (907) 271-3951

Arizona
>   3003 N Central, Suite 800
>   Phoenix, AZ 85012-2945
>   Voice: (602) 280-8810
>   Fax: (602) 640-5137

Arkansas
>   Fed Bldg., Rm. 5804
>   700 W Capitol
>   Little Rock, AR 72201-3228
>   Voice: (501) 324-5445
>   Fax: (501)324-6138

California
>   2121 C 2nd St.
>   Davis, CA 95616
>   Voice: (916) 757-8262
>   Fax: (916) 757-8382

Colorado
>   655 Parfet St.,  Rm. E200C
>   Lakewood, CO 80215-5517
>   Voice: (303) 236-2886
>   Fax: (303) 236-2896

Connecticut
>   16 Prof Park Rd.
>   Storrs, CT 06268-1299
>   Voice: (860) 487-4013
>   Fax: (806) 487-4054

Delaware
>   1203 College Park Dr., Suite 101
>   Dover, DE 19904-8713
>   Voice: (302) 678-4160
>   Fax: (302) 678-0843

Florida
>   P.O. Box 141510
>   2614 NW 43rd St.
>   Gainesville, FL 32614-1510
>   Voice: (904) 338-9500
>   Fax: (904) 338-9574

Georgia
>   Fed Bldg., Box 13
>   355 E. Hancock
>   Athens, GA 30601-2769
>   Voice: (706) 456-2272
>   Fax: (706) 546-2145

Hawaii
>   Federal Bldg., Rm. 4316
>   300 Ala Moana Blvd.
>   Honolulu, HI 96850-0002
>   Voice: (808) 541-2605
>   Fax: (808) 541-1335

Idaho
>   3244 Elder, Rm. 124
>   Boise, ID 83705-4711
>   Voice: (208) 334-1601
>   Fax: (208) 334-9230

Illinois
>   1902 Fox Dr.
>   Champaign, IL 61820-7335
>   Voice: (217) 398-5267
>   Fax: (217) 398-5310

Indiana
>   6013 Lakeside Dr.
>   Indianapolis, IN 46278-2933
>   Voice: (317) 290-3200
>   Fax: (317) 290-3225

Iowa

    Fed Bldg.
    210 Walnut St., Suite 693
    Des Moines, IA 50309-2180
    Voice: (515)284-4261
    Fax: (515) 284-4393

Kansas

    760 S. Broadway
    Salina, KS 67401
    Voice: (913) 823-4565
    Fax: (913) 823-4540

Kentucky

    771 Corporate, #110
    Lexington, KY 40503-5479
    Voice: (606) 224-7390
    Fax: (606) 224-7399

Louisiana

    3737 Government St.
    Alexandria, LA 71302-3727
    Voice: (318) 473-7751
    Fax: (318) 473-7682

Maine

    5 Godfrey Drive
    Orono, ME 04473
    Voice: (207) 866-7245
    Fax: (207) 866-7262

Maryland

    339 Busch's Frtg Rd., Suite 301
    Annapolis, MD 21401-5534
    Voice: (410)757-0861
    Fax: (410) 757-0687

Massachusetts

    451 West Street
    Amherst, MA 01002-2995
    Voice: (413) 253-4351
    Fax: (413) 253-4375

Michigan

    1405 S. Harrison Rd.
    East Lansing, MI 48823-5202
    Voice: (517) 337-6701
    Fax: (517) 337-6905

Minnesota

    600 Farm Credit Bldg.
    375 Jackson St.
    St Paul, MN 55101-1854
    Voice: (612) 290-3675
    Fax: (612) 290-3375

Mississippi

    McCoy Fed Bldg.
    100 W. Capitol St.
    Jackson, MI 39269-1399
    Voice: (601) 965-5205
    Fax: (601) 965-5178

Missouri

    601 Business Loop 70W
    Parkade Ctr., Ste. 250
    Columbia, MO 65203-2546
    Voice: (314) 876-0900
    Fax: (314) 87600913

Montana

    10 E. Babcock, Fed. Bldg.
    Bozeman, MT 59715-4704
    Voice: (406) 587-6813
    Fax: (406) 587-6761

Nebraska

    Fed Bldg., Rm. 152
    100 Centennial Mall North
    Lincoln, NE 68508-3866
    Voice: (402) 437-5300
    Fax: (402) 437-5327

Nevada

    Bldg. F, Ste. 220
    5301 Longley Lane
    Reno, NV 89511
    Voice:  (702) 784-5863
    Fax: (702) 784-5939

New Hampshire

    Federal Building
    Durham, NH 03824-1499
    Voice: (603) 868-7581
    Fax: (603) 868-5301

New Jersey

    1370 Hamilton St.
    Somerset, NJ 08873
    Voice: (908) 246-1662
    Fax: (908) 246-2358

New Mexico
    6200 Jefferson, NE
    Albuquerque, NM 87109-3734
    Voice: (505)761-4400
    Fax: (505) 761-4462

New York
    441 South Salina St.
    5th Floor, Suite 354
    Syracuse, NY 13202-2450
    Voice: (315) 477-6505
    Fax: (315) 477-6550

North Carolina
    4405 Bland, Suite 205
    Raleigh, NC 27609-6293
    Voice: (919) 790-2888
    Fax: (919) 790-2881

North Dakota
    220 E. Rosser Ave., Room 278
    Bismarck, ND 58502-1458
    Voice: (701) 250-4421
    Fax: (701) 250-4478

Ohio
    200 N. High St., Room 522
    Columbus, OH 43215-2478
    Voice: (614) 469-6962
    Fax: (614) 469 2083

Oklahoma
    100 USDA Agr. Bldg., Suite 203
    Stillwater, OK 74074-2655
    Voice: (405) 742-1200
    Fax: (405) 742-1201

Oregon
    101 SW. Main St. 1300
    Portland, OR 97204-3221
    Voice: (503) 414-3262
    Fax: (503) 414-3277

Pennsylvania
    One Credit Union Pl., Suite 340
    Harrisburg, PA 17110-2993
    Voice: (717) 782-2202
    Fax: (717) 782-4469

Rhode Island
    60 Quaker Ln., Ste. 46
    Warwick, RI 02886-0111
    Voice: (401) 828-1300
    Fax: (401) 828-0433

South Carolina
    1835 Assembly, Fed. Bldg., Room 950
    Columbia, SC 29201-2489
    Voice: (803) 253-5681
    Fax: (803) 253-3670

South Dakota
    Federal Bldg.
    200 Fourth, SW
    Huron, SD 57350-2475
    Voice: (605) 352-1200
    Fax: (605) 352-1270

Tennessee
    801 Broadway
    Nashville, TN 37203-3878
    Voice: (615) 736-5471
    Fax: (615) 736-7764

Texas
    101 S. Main Poage Fed. Bldg.
    Temple, TX 76501-7682
    Voice: (817) 774-1214
    Fax: (817) 7741388

Utah
    Fed. Bldg.
    125 S. State St., Room 4402
    Salt Lake City, UT 84138
    Voice: (801) 524-5050
    Fax: (801) 524-4403

Vermont
    69 Union Street
    Winooski, VT 05404-1999
    Voice: (802) 951-6795
    Fax: (802) 951-6327

Virginia
    1606 Santa Rosa Rd.
    Richmond, VA 23229-5014
    Voice: (804) 287-1691
    Fax: (804) 2887-1737

Washington
    W. 316 Boone Ave., Suite 450
    Spokane, WA 99201-2348
    Voice: (509)353-2337
    Fax: (509) 353-2354

West Virginia
   75 High St., Rm. 301
   Morgantown, WV 26505
   Voice: (304) 291-4484
   Fax: (304) 291-4628

Wisconsin
   6515 Watts Road, Suite 200
   Madison, WI 53719-2726
   Voice: (608) 264-5577
   Fax: (608) 264-5483

Wyoming
   Fed Bldg.
   100 East B. Street, Room 3124
   Casper, WY 82601-1911
   Voice: (307) 261-5201
   Fax: (307) 261-5512

**State Soil Conservation Offices, State Department of Agriculture and Agricultural Extension Service, and Farm and Home Adviser**

The State Soil Conservation Offices State Department of Agriculture and Agricultural Extension Service, and Farm and Home Adviser coordinate programs to conserve and protect the state's soil and are sources of information regarding the evaluation of soil conditions. These state agencies provide general information useful for rural homeowners and can be located by looking in the telephone directory first under the state heading, and then the subheading for "Agriculture" or "Agricultural Extension Service."

**Other Sources of Soil Information**

*Local Board of Health*
*or County Health Department*
Will test the soil for its suitability for septic tanks or other types of sewage systems. Some land is unsuited for sewage systems because of the poor drainage, and the health department will not issue the necessary permits. Get the soil checked before you buy.

*Local Building Inspector*
Has information on soil types, drainage and erosion as they pertain to the suitability for construction of a dwelling. Get the inspector to look at your land before you buy and tell you if you will be able to get a permit for your intended construction.

*Local Universities and Colleges*
Various departments study local soil and vegetation conditions. Check for information at such departments as forestry, soils, plant nutrition, geology and mining.

*State Mineral Agencies*
Every state has an agency in charge of mineral and geology studies within the state. For example, South Dakota has a state geological survey, Oregon has a Department of Geology and Mineral Industries, California has a Division of Mines and Geology and Texas has a Bureau of Economic Geology. You can get the address of your state mineral agency from your local farm adviser, your nearest USGS office, or the *Research Centers Directory*.

*Research Centers Directory*
The reference section of most libraries has a publication entitled *Research Centers Directory,* edited by Archie M. Palmer and published by the Gale Research Company. This book lists every agency involved in agricultural research and services in each state. By looking under your state, you can find all the available sources of information and assistance in the evaluation of the land you are investigating.

*Books and Pamphlets*
The following is available from:

   Superintendent of Documents
   U.S. Government Printing Office
   Washington, DC 20402

*Drainage Around Your Home,*
   SIN 001-000-03455-3                 $1.00

The following are a few titles that have been available for free. There are more titles becoming available so contact your local office (See addresses at end of this chapter) from:

   NRSC-Public Affairs
   U.S. Department of Agriculture
   Washington, DC 20250

"Soil Erosion By Water"
"Soil Erosion By Wind"
"Conservation Planning—You and Your Land"
"Plant Material for Conservation"
"Farmers and Ranchers: Soil Surveys Can Help You"
"Soil Surveys Can Help You"
"List of Published Soil Surveys"

The following are available from:

ANR Publications
University of California
6701 San Pablo Ave.
Oakland, CA 94608-1239

"Forest Grazing Management in California,"
    #21388                $1.50
"Management of Small Pastures," #2906    $1.50
"Managing and Modifying Problem Soils,"
    #291                 $2.00
"Managing Compacted and Layered Soil,"
    #2635                $1.50
"Planning for Your Mountain Property,"
    #21360                $1.50
"Protecting Trees When Building on Forested
    Land," #21348            $1.75
"How to Grow Your Own Firewood, 1990,"
    #21484                $2.50
"Landscape for Fire Protection," #2401    $1.50
"Soil and Water Management for Home
    Gardeners," #2258         $1.75
"Forest Management Information Services: A
    Guide" for California Landowners,"
    #21443                $2.00
"Planting California Forest Land," #2925    $2.00
"Preliminary Guildlines for Managing California's
Hardwoods Rangelands," #21413    $5.00

For more information regarding minerals, see Chapter 11, including the "Useful Resources."

**Recent Earthquake Data—National Earthquake Information Service (NETS)**
The National Earthquake Information Service computes and publishes epicenter locations for earthquakes worldwide and provides general information pertaining to the geographic location, magnitude and intensity of recent earthquakes. Write for a list of current publications or CD software:

National Earthquake Information Center
U.S. Geological Survey
Federal Center
Box 25046, Mail Stop 967
Denver, CO 80225-0046
Voice: (303) 273-8406
Fax: (303) 273-8450
E-mail: hdf@neis.cr.usgs.gov
BBS: (303) 273- 8508 Password: GUEST

**Road Building**
The following publications are available from:

Mendocino County Resource Conservation
District 405 S Orchard Ave.
Ukiah, CA 95482
(707) 468-9223

*Road Building*               $ 5.00
*Stream Channel & Gully Grade*
*Stabilization Structures*        $ 2.00
*The Handbook For Forest And Ranch Roads*
                         $20.00

**CHAPTER**

# 6  Evaluating Houses, Manufactured Homes and Other Structures

*But what of the man who hears these words of mine and does not act upon them? He is like a man who was foolish enough to build his house on sand. The rain came down, the floods rose, the wind blew and beat upon that house; down it fell with a great crash.*

—Matt. 7:26–27

Whether you want to buy land with a house already on it or to build your own house is a basic decision.

An existing house adds a considerable amount to the price of land. If you are willing to put in the necessary labor, building your own house can be fairly cheap, and you can realize your dream house. Even if you hire a professional builder, you might save money in the long run by buying undeveloped land and building the kind of house you want.

However, if you find a good piece of land with a house on it that is within your price range, you must be able to inspect the house to be sure it is soundly built and will be safe and comfortable to live in. If you want to refurbish an older house, you must determine how much work will have to be done and how much it will cost; the house might be too dilapidated to bring up to current building code standards. Faults in the structure that you find during your inspection can be used later in bargaining to get the purchase price down. (See Chapter 19, "Evaluating the Price of the Property," and Chapter 20, "Bargaining To Get the Seller's Asking Price Down.")

This chapter takes you through every part of the house and tells you what to look for. Each item is listed to make it easier to refer to. Take this book with you on your inspection, along with a pencil, pad of paper, flashlight, pocketknife and some old clothes. Look at the house several times under both good and bad weather conditions, in the daytime and at night, and you will have a good idea of how livable it will be for your family.

## The Neighborhood

If the property is in a populated area, the first thing you will notice is how the house looks in comparison with other houses in the neighborhood. If it looks shabbier than surrounding homes, the price might reflect the value of the community, whereas the actual worth of the house may be much less.

## Placement of the House

Before examining the structure itself, study the placement of the house in relation to both the surrounding area and the environment as a whole.

Is the house placed so you have the privacy you desire? Can you see other houses? Can you be seen by neighbors and passersby? If so, is the situation disagreeable to you, and can it be easily remedied by constructing a fence or planting shrubs and trees?

What kind of view is there from the most frequently used rooms in the house? Is the view appealing to you? A good view increases the price of a house, but it makes life much more enjoyable.

Is the house placed so it receives the maximum amount of winter sun? The south side of the house should have the most windows and be where the most frequently used rooms are located. It should also have an overhanging roof or some other means of shading the inside of the house from direct sunlight in summer. (See Figure 6–1.)

**Figure 6–1. Exposure of the House to Summer and Winter Sun**

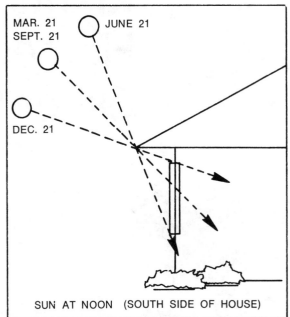

SUN AT NOON   (SOUTH SIDE OF HOUSE)

Does the vegetation around the house allow enough sunlight in, or is the house usually dark and damp? Many homes in the woods have a serious dampness problem because they are too well-shaded by large trees. Some types of forests, such as redwood forests, are much damper than others. If you see the structure in the dry season, imagine what the conditions are like in winter.

Is the house conveniently situated in relation to the rest of the property? For example, are the gardening and recreational areas near the dwelling? Are the outbuildings and other structures, such as the pump house, storage tank and generator, nearby? Climbing up a steep, distant hill to fix the water pump in pouring rain or a snowstorm can be miserable.

Despite their importance, many of the above factors are given little consideration by builders.

## Blueprints and Original Building Contract

Before you inspect the house itself, find out if the original blueprints of the house and other specifications are available for inspection. If the house was built by a contractor or someone hired to do the job, ask the seller if he has the original contract, which might have warranties in it that guarantee against any defects in construction, including labor and materials.

## Foundation

The foundation is the supporting structure of the house. The house might be built on poles; on posts and concrete; on a concrete, stone or brick perimeter foundation or concrete slab; or on a basement of stone, brick or concrete.

Pole construction is used primarily where the building site is not level. Huge poles are sunk deep into the ground, and the house is built around them, up in the air. The following list spells out some of the things to look for:

- If the poles are wooden, at least the buried part should be chemically treated to prevent them from rotting.
- Have poles or posts near the ground been treated against wood rot and termites? If so, when and by whom? Talk to the termite service that did the job and ask them what they know about the house.
- Has there been a chemical coating applied to the concrete or brick foundation to prevent dampness and water from getting beneath the house? If so, how long ago was this applied? Are there any cracks in the dampproof coating? Does water ever stand under the house?
- If the house has a stone or brick foundation or is supported on masonry piers, check for cracks and crumbling mortar. Minor cracks can usually be repaired. More extensive deterioration may indicate that major repair or replacement will be necessary.
- If the house is built on posts sunk in concrete, the concrete might be under each post or it might be under the entire perimeter of the house.
- Examine the concrete with your flashlight, either from the basement or from the crawl space, to see if there are any cracks. Minor cracks can usually be repaired. Large open cracks may get progressively worse and usually indicate a major problem.
- Concrete beneath posts should show above the ground. No dirt should touch the posts, because the concrete protects the wood from rotting.
- Is the foundation sinking into the ground? Do all doors swing easily? Badly fitting doors are one of the first indications of sinking, because the doorways are no longer square.

- Do the floor joists, or supports, sag?
- Have the posts separated from the floor at any point?
- Are there any irregularities in the foundation that you can see?
- Check for wood rot, termites, tunnels and other indications of pests, such as holes with fine sawdust under them. Has the foundation ever been chemically treated against termites? When and by whom? Talk to the termite service that did the job and ask them what they know about the house.

If the entire house is set on a concrete slab, examine it at all visible points. This kind of construction is often difficult to inspect.

- Does the slab appear to be tilting or sinking into the ground at any point?
- Has the floor become separated from the slab at any point?
- Can you see any large cracks in the cement? Hairline cracks are usually not important.
- Check for termites and wood rot. Take a screwdriver or some sharp tool and probe the wood. Does the tool enter easily? Does the wood break across the grain with little splintering?
- Slab construction offers greater protection to termites once they have invaded the wood. Is there any termite shielding around the house? Has the concrete been chemically treated? When and by whom? Talk to the termite service that did the job for information about the condition of the house.
- If the house is in earthquake country, the house should be bolted to the foundation.

### Crawl Space

The crawl space is the area under a house between the ground and the bottom of the house. Crawl space houses usually have a foundation wall or piers supporting the floor joists. Check for cracks and settlement of these supports.

If the house has foundation walls of poured concrete, minor hairline cracks have little effect on the structure. Open cracks indicate a failure that may get worse. It is difficult to tell without observing it over several months.

If the house is supported on wood posts and piers, check to be sure the wood posts are properly preserved and up off the ground on metal pedestals on adequate concrete supports. Wood should not be directly on or in the concrete, because it absorbs moisture and rots at the contact point. Inspect posts for decay and insect damage. The bottom of the house must be a minimum of 18 inches from the ground. Walk around the house looking for vent openings into the crawl space. If none or an insufficient number exist, there will be excessive moisture from condensation under the house. This deteriorates the floors, foundation and other parts of the structure and promotes wood rot. Vents are also necessary for safety if heating units are located within the crawl space and if gas and sewer lines run under the house. You have to crawl into this space to see the foundation and the underside of the floor. (This is why you should wear old clothes.) Find the opening, take your flashlight, and crawl in.

- Has ground-cover paper or roofing paper been laid over the surface of the ground under the crawl space? This helps ventilation and insulation. What kind of condition is the paper in? Where this paper is used, vents are usually smaller. If the paper has deteriorated, the vents might be too small to prevent excessive moisture from forming.
- Is the heating unit located under the house? If so, inspect it as outlined later in this chapter, under "Heating System."
- Look at all visible pipes. Any leaks or corrosion?
- Look at the wiring. Do you see any loose, frayed or broken wires?
- Inspect the foundation as specified above.

**The Basement**
Many rural homes have a basement or cellar. It serves as an insulator for the house, and it may be used as a workroom, storage area, food and wine cellar or recreation room. The most severe problem in basements is flooding and dampness. All basements are vulnerable to water at one time or another.

- A sump pump is turned on automatically or manually to pump water from a flooded basement. If you see a sump pump in the house, you know there are problems. Ask the owner why it is there, how often it is used, and why the basement floods. The problem might be corrected by placing drainage pipes or ditches around the house. It is more severe if the slope of the land itself is at fault. Talk to the building inspector about the problem and get an estimate of what has to be done to correct the problem.
- Other evidence of dampness is water stains on the walls and floors. Are there drainage holes in the floor? Are there signs of mud anywhere? Use your flashlight to inspect the basement carefully. Look for signs of water penetration, such as rust at the base of the heater or steel posts, stains, discoloration or decay on wood partitions, wood posts, damaged floor tiles or mildewed carpeting, a white salt buildup (efflorescence) on foundation walls, stains or mildew on objects stored on the floor. Is there a musty smell? Do you see mold? Does it feel damp? Can you find any standing water or excess moisture?
- If there is a floor drain, the floor should slope toward it.
- Even if the basement doesn't flood, it might have poor ventilation. Condensation causes moisture to form on basement walls unless there are open windows or vents. Are there sufficient vents or windows? Damp spots on walls or the floor could be due to condensation, rather than to water leaking in from outside.
- Are the basement walls and floor cement, wood or dirt? A cement basement floor is the best kind. Do you see cracks in the walls or floor? Cracks cause water leaks and indicate structural defects. Has any kind of waterproofing been used on the walls and floors?
- If the basement is damp, it might require the installation of a dehumidifier. Is one already installed? How old is it and what is its service history?
- While you are in the basement, inspect the foundation and look for evidence of termite infestation and wood rot.

Damp or leaky basement walls may require major repair. Possible causes of the dampness are clogged or broken downspouts, clogged drain tile, cracks in the walls, lack of slope of the finished grade away from the house foundation or a high water table. Check for dampness by examining the basement a few hours after a heavy rain. Most of these problems can be remedied. However, a high water table is more serious and very difficult to remedy.

There are no miracle cures for a wet basement, so be very cautious if you see evidence of flooding.

## Destructive Insects

### Termites

Regardless of the age of the house or the type of construction used, it can be infested by termites and other damaging insects. The most common and serious troublemaker is the subterranean termite. A heavily infested house can have 250,000 termites constantly eating away at it. Even if the seller has had the house fumigated recently, termites can return within a short time. The problem may be so serious that further fumigation is worthless. Although termites are found throughout the United States, they are particularly numerous in the South Atlantic and Gulf Coast states and in California. Termites inhabit more than 200 million homes and cause $500 million damage a year.

Termites need two things to survive: wood and water. A termite will die in 24 hours if it is deprived of moisture. Good ventilation and dry ground under the house are essential in preventing termites. In heavily infested areas, a chemical barrier in the ground around the home is necessary.

There are several ways to detect termites: The first is the presence of *termite highways*. Termites live in underground nests and burrow into the foundation and the rest of the structure. You can see paths along the foundation where they burrow up into the wood. look for veins or streaks along the wood.

The second is the *termite tube* or *tunnel*. These flattened tubes are made of mud suspended directly from the underside of the floor to the earth. The termites travel through these tunnels to get from their nests in the moist ground to the wood. You will see these tubes in crawl spaces and basements. They also can be built up the sides of the foundation, the walls, the water and drain pipes, and the chimney.

The third way to find termites is with a knife or screwdriver. Termite activity usually occurs inside wood that looks fine from the outside. Take your tool and make jabs at different parts of the house. If the wood is soft, you have termites or wood rot.

During your inspection, look for termites and discarded termite wings around anything that touches, or is near, the ground, including the foundation, basement walls, floor joists, the underside of the floor, house beams and posts, window frames, porches, drain and water pipes, along chimneys, on the attic walls, on roof beams and on the underside of the roof.

### Other Destructive Pests

There are other insects that can seriously damage a building. Some of these include the powder-post beetles, which occur throughout the United States; the house borers found in the eastern United States, from Florida through Massachusetts; the carpenter ants and bees; and two other types of termites. Your county building inspector can give you information on local pest problems and how to examine a structure for pest damage.

## Wood Rot (Dry Rot)

Wood rot is more damaging than termites. It is a major problem in the North. When wood becomes wet, either from direct contact with water or by condensation, a fungus grows, causing the wood to decay. These organisms cannot colonize or decay wood that has a moisture content of less than about 30 percent. A properly constructed and maintained home has a moisture content of less than 15 percent. When this fungus is present, the wood takes on the appearance of being dried out. This is why wood rot is often called "dry rot." Once wood rot sets in, the entire structure can become dangerously weakened, and the value of the house is greatly diminished. To prevent dry rot, the house must be dry and well insulated. Wood rot commonly occurs in attics, basements, crawl spaces and under porches. As you inspect the house, maintain constant vigilance for wood rot. Use your flashlight to inspect every dark corner.

When you see an area that looks rotten, take your pocketknife or screwdriver and scratch the wood. How easily does it break down? Stick the tool into the wood. If it sinks in easily, the condition is severe and probably too costly to repair.

## Floor Supports

Check the floor supports in the basement ceiling or, if there is no basement, from the crawl space under the house. Wood posts should not be embedded in a concrete floor. Examine the base of wood posts for decay even if they are set above the concrete.

Check wood girders for sag and also for decay at

the exterior wall bearings. A small sag is not usually a problem unless parts of the house have obviously become distorted.

Check the sill plates or joists and headers that rest on top of the concrete foundation. They are exposed to moisture and are subject to decay or insect attack.

Check at the framing of floor joists around stair openings. Some builders estimate that 50 percent of the houses built have inadequate framing around stairs. If floors are sagging, you may have to relevel and reinforce them.

## The Living Area

### Floors

Do the floors slope? A tilting floor indicates serious foundation problems.

Loose and noisy floorboards indicate foundation problems. Walk over the floor slowly to feel if there is any sagging or give.

Are the wooden floors nicely sanded and finished?

Look at the point where the floors meet the walls. Are the joints tight with no evidence of warping?

If the floor is concrete covered with asphalt tile or wood flooring, are there any cracks in the covering?

If the kitchen and bathroom floors are covered with linoleum or tile, look for cracks and chipped areas where water has entered and rotted the floor underneath. Is the tile or linoleum well laid and properly fitted around fixtures and along the walls? Has any of the covering come loose from the floor?

### Interior Walls

Dry walls are wood, fiberboard, sheetrock or gypsum wallboard nailed or taped onto the frame. Plastered walls are lath and plaster. Both types of walls may be either painted or papered.

Do the walls bulge or buckle?

Is the plaster or paint cracking, or the paper peeling? Moisture, vapor and condensation could cause these things to happen.

Is a new paint job or wallpapering needed?

Have the walls recently been painted or papered? If so, a defect may be hidden. Feel the walls and examine them closely. Wallpaper placed over the old covering might later peel.

If you don't like the wall colors, you will have to figure in the cost of repainting or repapering.

If there are water stains on the walls, the plumbing is deteriorating or the roof leaks.

### Ceilings

Water stains on the ceiling indicate a leaky roof or bad plumbing.

Look for recent plastering, taping or painting as a warning that the roof leaks or the ceiling is in a weak condition. It may have already begun to collapse in these places.

Check the ceiling of the room directly underneath the bathroom for leaks.

### Doors

Open and close all the doors. Are they snug without sticking? Is any warping evident? Examine the walls around doors, particularly over the tops of doors. Cracks indicate a lack of proper bracing over and around a door opening.

Is there weather-stripping on the doors leading outside? Is it in good condition, or are there large cracks between the door and the door frame? Do you feel a draft when the doors are closed?

Do all the doors latch properly?

Are there screen doors? In what condition is the screening?

Are storm doors necessary?

Do the doors need refinishing or painting?

Are the doorways large enough for you to move your furniture through them?

### Windows

Open and close all the windows to see if they are snugly installed. Is there a draft when they are closed?

Is weather-stripping around the frames in good condition?

Is there any broken or cracked glass?

Are there warped sashes? (The sash is the frame holding the pane of glass.) Are windows loose, or is putty chipped badly?

If any of the windows have been painted or nailed shut, find out why.

Is there any chipped paint? In an older house built before 1960 lead based paints were used. Lead is a potentially dangerous element. This paint will have to be carefully removed.

Are storm windows or shutters needed?

Is there screening on all the windows? Are there any holes in the screens?

Are there shades or blinds?

If any windows are covered by shades or curtains, look behind the coverings. Is there enough light in the house from properly sized and placed windows? Pay special attention to lighting in the kitchen.

Are there any skylights? Look for evidence of leaking around the edge.

### Bathroom

Is the bathroom conveniently located?

Inspect floor and wall tiling for leaks, cracks, looseness and sloppy workmanship.

Is there any indication that water leaks from the shower, bathtub, sink or toilet? Is caulking chipped or cracked?

Is there a shower, and is it a good solid tiled or ceramic one, or is it a cheap metal semiportable type? If it is tiled, are any tiles buckling or cracked, indicating rot beneath the tiles? (Also see "Plumbing," below.)

### Kitchen

Is the kitchen large enough for your needs and well laid out?

If you are bringing in your own appliances, will they fit easily? If not, you will have to change the layout or buy new appliances.

An older kitchen might be less adaptable to modern conveniences, and this decreases the value of the house.

The kitchen and bathrooms are the most expensive to remodel. Keep this in mind.

## Appliances and Equipment

Are appliances and equipment going to be included in the sale (for example, stove, refrigerator, freezer, dishwasher, washing machine, clothes dryer, microwave, tractor and lawn mower)? Examine and operate all appliances and equipment (including motors) to be sure they are in good working order. Ask to run the dishwasher and washing machine through a complete cycle while you are checking through the house, checking them periodically to be sure they work properly. Check the age, brand name and original cost of each item. Have any been repaired or overhauled recently? If so, get a receipt of payment for the overhaul that indicates what work was done and whether there is a guarantee on it. Don't be afraid to ask questions.

All appliances included with the home must be itemized in writing and included in the contract of sale.

## Water Heater

There are two kinds of water heaters: the instantaneous tankless type and the storage-tank type. The instantaneous type heats the water as it passes through small tubes in a combustion chamber, such as a firebox, and goes directly to the faucet. The storage-tank type heats the water in an insulated tank, and the water remains in the tank until it is used. When the tank is emptied it takes time to heat up a new tank of water. Most houses use the storage-tank water heater.

Examine the water heater. If it bears the label of the National Board of Fire Underwriters, it meets normal safety requirements.

The manufacturer's label on the tank gives the size of the tank in gallons. If the heater operates on gas or oil, a family of four needs a tank with a capacity of 30 gallons. Electrical water heaters take longer to heat up, so a minimum size of 50 gallons is recommended. A full load of clothes in an automatic washer takes 25 to 40 gallons of hot water; dish washing and rinsing average 2 to 4 gallons; a tub bath takes 10 to 15 gallons; and a shower uses 9 to 12 gallons.

Any evidence of leaks in the heating system? How old is it? Does the hot water appear rusty? This indicates a rusting heating system that needs to be replaced.

## Plumbing

Faulty plumbing is the most expensive thing to repair in a home.

Good water pressure is important. Turn on all the faucets individually. Is there good pressure at each faucet? Turn on two or three faucets at the same time. With the water running at full force in the kitchen, is there adequate pressure in the bathroom? How is the pressure on the second floor? With the faucets on, flush the toilet and see if the water flow is affected. Poor plumbing will cause bursts of hot or cold water from a faucet or shower head when the toilet is flushed. This can be unpleasant or even dangerous when taking a shower or washing. Is the pressure sufficient to permit you to install additional outlets or water facilities, such as another bathroom or a dishwasher?

Do the faucets drip or leak? Look for water stains in the bathtub and sinks.

Fill the sink and bathtub with water. Is the water rusty or clear? Old pipes or water heaters produce rusty water.

Watch the water drain. Is there good drainage, or are some drains plugged?

Drop a fistful of toilet paper or a cigarette into the toilet and flush it. Does it flush well, refill quietly and shut off completely?

Do you like the fixtures: the sinks, tub, shower, toilet, faucets, and so on? Generally, the older the fixtures, the less value they add to the house. In older houses, the hot and cold faucets are separate units, which makes it difficult to wash. Are any of the fixtures chipped or scratched? Find out the cost of installing modern fixtures, and figure it into the other expenses of bringing the house up to contemporary standards.

Is there a problem with pipes freezing in the winter? The building inspector in the area will know the depth at which pipes should be buried to prevent freezing under local winter conditions. Determine from blueprints, questioning the seller and physical inspection whether the pipes are situated to prevent freezing.

Does a plumbing diagram exist showing where all the pipes are in the house? How easy is it to make repairs on the system? There should be a main valve that shuts off the water supply to the house. Is it conveniently located? In addition, does each faucet have its own shutoff valve so that you can repair one outlet without shutting off all the water to the house?

Is there a water softener or filtration system for improving the quality of the water? If so, does it serve its purpose well? Get the brand name and price it. How old a unit is it, and what is its service history? When was the last time a plumber was called to make repairs? Get the plumber's name and talk to him or her about the condition of the plumbing.

If the house is more than 80 years old, there is a possibility that the plumbing may still contain lead or lead alloy pipes. Check to see if the pipes are dull gray instead of copper. If they are gray, they are probably lead.

Even if the house is newer and the pipes are copper, there may be a problem of contamination from lead solder, which until recently was used to join copper pipes. Contamination is most serious if the area has soft water, which is slightly acidic and therefore corrodes the lead solder, or if the copper pipes were installed using lead solder within the last five years, because lead dissolves most easily in the first five years. There are alternatives to lead solder, however. For instance, tin-antimony solder is a good alternative, though more expensive than lead solder, and may have been used in recently installed plumbing.

If you suspect lead contamination, call the local health department to see if it will test the tap water for lead and other contaminants. If the department does not do the testing itself, it can refer you to a private lab that will test the water.

It has become evident that lead is a highly toxic metal and that even the "maximum safe levels" of lead may not be safe enough. Lead can damage the nervous system, blood-forming process, kidneys and reproductive system; it can cause learning and behavioral disorders and stunted growth in young children and raise blood pressure in adults.

The seller may say that you can just install a water filter. However, charcoal water filters won't remove lead. The only type recommended by the Environmental Protection Agency (EPA) is one with a reverse osmosis filtering process; but these are expensive, energy intensive and difficult to maintain. Although cheaper initially, they may be more expensive than replacing the plumbing in the long run.

If there is serious lead contamination, you should consider replacing the plumbing if you decide to buy the house. Find out how much it will cost and add that amount to the price of the house. See Chapter 4, "Is There Enough Water on the Land?" for a discussion of wells, pumps and other aspects of the plumbing system.

## Sewage Disposal System

If the house is connected to public sewerage lines, is there any indication of broken pipes or bad connections? If there is no public sewerage connection, does the house use a septic tank system installed on the property? A septic tank is a large wooden, steel or concrete box with a filtration system in it. The entire system is buried underground. Leach lines carry the strained effluent from the tank through an underground absorption field, from which the fluid drains into the earth.

First find the tank. Often, property owners don't even know where it is. Some people have a map, or there is one on record with the local health department. However, the tank shouldn't be too hard to find. Just look for where the sewer line exits the house. The tank is usually five to ten feet from the house and should be no more than a foot below ground. Poke into the ground with a strong stick or preferably an iron pole, and you should be able to locate it. Just hope that the owner hasn't built a beautiful patio or perhaps a lovely flower garden over it.

The tank has a cover on it that is lifted off to pump it out. Find the cover and see if it is easy to remove. If it is covered with vegetation, that is a good indication that the tank has not been properly maintained.

Is the septic tank an old wooden one, a steel one or a new single-unit concrete one? The concrete ones are far superior to the others.

Try to find out the results of any percolation tests done on the property. Find out when the septic tank and leach field were installed and who did it. Find out the type and location of the leach field. If the owner has a diagram of the system (see Figure 6-2), take a look at it, then go out and see if you can tell where the leach field is located.

There should not be any vehicles moving over this area or any deep-rooted vegetation growing over it, either of which might damage the tank or leach lines. If you see one area of the lawn that is much greener than the rest, it may be irrigated by leaking effluent. Inspect the ground for effluent or raw sewage. You should not smell any sewage in the area. If you do, you may not want to buy the house. Installing a new drainage field can cost as much as building a whole septic tank system for a new house and is usually much harder to do if there are landscaped gardens and yards to be careful of.

A septic tank should be cleaned periodically to remove unfiltered material. This is done by a cleaning service that uses a tank truck, pump and hose to pump the material from the septic tank. When was the tank last cleaned? Get the name and number of the cleaning company. Ask the company to show you the service history of the tank and give you an opinion of its condition. Normal maintenance requires the tank to be inspected and cleaned every three to five years.

What is the liquid capacity of the septic tank? The proper size is based on the number of people living in the house and the number of facilities con-

**Figure 6–2. Septic Tank System Arrangements**

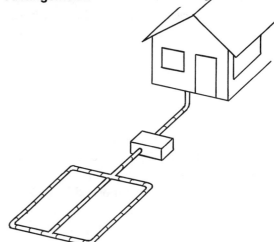

Closed or continuous tile septic tank system arrangement for level ground.

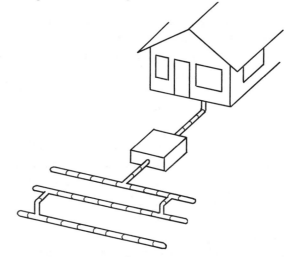

Serial distribution septic tank system arrangement for sloping ground.

nected to the tank. If you have more people in your family than the previous owners had, or if you intend to add more water-using equipment to the house, you must be sure the septic system can absorb the extra load. Get advice on this from the dealer who installed the tank or presently services it. The local health department also has this information.

If the system looks okay so far, challenge the system by flushing all the toilets three times in succession and filling up the bathtub with five or six inches of water and letting it drain. Then check the lowest drain in the house, for example, the drain in the basement laundry sink, to see if the water has backed up in it. If the system withstands this test, it may not matter when the owner had the system pumped.

Even if the water does back up due to your test, if you are still interested in the house, ask the owner to have a septic tank company come to see if the line from the tank to the leach field is blocked. That may cost as little as $30 to $50. You will want to be there when the work is done so you can ask the septic tank workers questions.

Ask the owner how the system is maintained. Are the owners careful not to overload the system by doing three or four loads of laundry in one day but instead, spacing them out over the week? Are they careful not to throw anything that is not biodegradable into the septic tank (even filters from cigarettes)? Also, bulky paper items like paper towels shouldn't be allowed to go into the septic tank.

Caustic chemicals are very hard on septic systems, including those intended for septic systems that are supposed to soften solids. Flushing yeast or store-bought enzymes for septic tanks are totally unnecessary, though they usually aren't harmful. However, care should be taken not to destroy the anaerobic bacteria inside the tank that digest the sewage. Therefore, substances like the salt solution used to recharge water softeners should be piped to a special seepage pit, because salty water can shorten the life of a septic tank. *Moderate* use of disinfectants, bleaches and drain cleaners is not usually a problem.

A cesspool is a hole or tank in the ground that simply collects sewage. It does not contain a filter system or leach lines and is grossly inferior to a properly installed and maintained septic tank. Although a cesspool is regularly pumped, it is often smelly and prone to overflow in heavy rains because of its lack of an absorption field. You should not place much value on a cesspool. Figure in the cost of replacing it with a septic tank.

Regardless of the kind of sewage system the property has, has it been approved by the local health department? (See Chapter 13, "Building and Health Codes.")

## Electrical System

Is there electricity in the house? If not, and you want to receive it, you will incur a major expense wiring the house. (For the expense involved in bringing in electricity to the land, see Chapter 7, "Amenities of the Area.")

If there is electricity, is the house adequately wired to meet your needs? This will depend on the amount of electricity that the house is wired to accept and the availability of outlets. Older houses have thin wire incapable of safely conducting a large amount of amperes and usually have few outlets. Often there is no overhead lighting.

Does each room have outlets? The kitchen is the most important room to check. Are there enough outlets for your appliances? If not, the wiring is probably not sufficient, because you should not overload the outlets.

How many electrical appliances are presently being used around the house?

Are any wires loose or frayed?

The electrical system uses either a circuit breaker or a fuse box. If a fuse blows or the circuit breaker is tripped, the electrical outlets on that line go dead. This often occurs when the system is overloaded or short-circuited. Does the house use fuses or a circuit breaker? Circuit breakers are used in modem systems.

The local electric company can tell you how much load the present system can carry. Does the present system meet building codes and has it been approved?

If the house has to be rewired to bring it up to current building code standards or to meet your needs, you should get an estimate of the costs involved from a local contractor. It is an expensive undertaking.

## Heating System

Many different kinds of heating units are in use today. Central heating warms the entire house from one source, either by blowing hot air through outlets, vents and ducts in each room, or by circulating hot water through pipes in the walls, floors or ceilings of each room. The former is called conductive heating; the latter is called radiant heating. Instead of central heating, each room might have its own space heater, such as a radiator, wall heater, fireplace or other type of unit. The heating system might use electricity, oil, gas, coal or wood fuel. The best way to eliminate drafts is to locate heating units along outside walls, under the windows. Baseboard heating is the most efficient draft eliminator. Ask the following questions:

- What heating system does the house have?
- Where are the individual outlets located?
- How much does it cost to run in the winter?
- Is heat supplied to each room in the house?
- How rapidly and effectively is the house heated? Turn on the heating units to find out.
- Does the heater make a lot of noise during operation?
- How old is the heating unit? What is the service history? Ask the local dealer what the life expectancy of such a unit is. Most heaters run trouble-free for only seven or eight winters.
- Look on the heater for the specifications. The BTU output is the amount of heat a furnace will emit. Write down the figure and see if its capacity is normal for the area.
- If the furnace is gas-fired, do you smell gas around it? The local gas company will inspect it free and tell you about its efficiency and cost of operation.

**Fireplace and Chimney**

Your winter heating bills can be lowered considerably if you have an efficient fireplace, fireplace insert or wood stove. A standard fireplace is extremely inefficient. As much as 90 percent of the heat value in the wood can be lost up the chimney. Fireplaces with heat exchangers are usually better, but they still do not solve the problem of air combustion. In "airtight" stoves or furnaces you can control the flow of air through the stove or furnace. These provide the most efficient way to extract heat from wood. Modern wood-burning stoves approach the efficiency of modern gas or oil furnaces, with more than half of the heat energy in the fuel being converted into usable heat in the room or dwelling. Don't be sold automatically on a big, old-fashioned fireplace. A good "airtight" stove or fireplace insert is far more valuable. A good one is worth paying a little more for. However, some fireplaces and wood stoves are poorly designed or improperly maintained and can cause many problems.

Whatever is used for heating, inspect it carefully. When was it last cleaned and by whom? It should be cleaned annually.

Are the walls and floor around the fireplace or wood stove adequately protected? Do you see any smoke marks on the walls? There might be some draft problems.

If there is a fireplace, have the owner show you how to operate the damper. Does it work easily? Does it open all the way? Are the bricks in good condition? Does it have vents on the side for extra heating efficiency? Is it large enough for good-size logs? Is it in a good location?

Look where the chimney goes through the ceiling. Is it well protected? Any evidence of burning? If metal stovepipe is visible, tap the pipe. Do you hear flakes of creosote falling from the inside walls of the stovepipe? If so, it needs to be cleaned.

When you go outside, examine the chimney. Any cracks, crumbling mortar or missing bricks? Does the top extend far enough above the roof to be safe and to create a good draft? When you go up on the roof, examine the top of the chimney. Is the opening protected so that sparks don't escape? Does it need cleaning?

The building inspector can tell you if the fireplace or wood stove is in good condition or what has to be done to bring it up to code. But the best way to evaluate a fireplace or wood stove is to see it in action. Ask the owner to light a fire for you.

**Insulation**

The house must have good insulation as well as good heating. A house is insulated to prevent heat loss in the winter and to keep out heat in the summer by placing a layer of material between the inside and outside walls of the house to keep the air still. If a large air space between the walls is the only insulation, the air will move and heat will escape by convection. Common types of insulating materials include foil, fill, slab or board.

Ask if there is any place in the house where you can see the insulating material. What kind is used? Older houses may have sawdust or newspaper, which are fire hazards.

When the temperature outside falls, the inside surfaces of windows and exterior walls get colder. As the air within the house comes into contact with the cold windows and walls, it chills and settles to the floor, creating a draft as it moves across the floor. (As you walk through the house, does it feel as though it were well-insulated? Is it uniformly warm? Do you feel cold drafts, especially on the floor?)

If there is snow on the roof, how much of it is melted? Compare it with other houses in the area. Rapidly melting snow indicates heat is escaping through the roof because of poor insulation. (See Figure 6–3.)

Extremely cold climates require up to six inches of fiberglass insulation in the walls, and more in the roof, whereas temperate areas need only a thin

**Figure 6–3. Insulation**

WELL INSULATED

POORLY INSULATED

layer. Ask the local building inspector or building supply store about the standards of the area.

## Ventilation

As you walk through the house does the temperature seem too warm or too cold? Is the air clammy or stuffy? The first problem is caused by poor insulation, the second by improper ventilation.

Proper ventilation allows good air circulation and is usually accomplished by opening windows on opposite sides of the house to create a slight breeze. If the openings on the cooler side of the house, usually the north side, are low and small and the openings on the hot side of the house, usually the south side, are high and large, the ventilation will be improved.

Is the house comfortable in the summer?

Ventilation in the winter when all the windows are closed is very important. In a properly constructed house the air will flow by its own convection currents.

## Air-Conditioning

In most areas of the country, air-conditioning is a must for comfort. If the house you are looking at does not have air-conditioning, beware if you are told that it will be simple to install by using the existing forced-warm-air or other heating system. An efficient heating system will have ducts or vents near the floor because heated air rises. But because cooler air falls, if you use the heating ducts for air-conditioning, all the cool air will remain on the floor. Also, cool air needs larger vents, and if small

heating vents are used, the cold air won't come into the room fast enough for comfort.

For maximum efficiency, there should be separate, overhead air-conditioning properly sized for the house in which it is installed.

If there is air-conditioning, what kind of system is it? Where are the individual outlets located? How much does it cost to run in the hot months? Is cool air supplied to each room in the house?

Turn on the system to see how rapidly and efficiently the house is cooled. Does the system make a lot of noise during operation? How old is the unit? What is its service history? Ask the local dealer what the life expectancy of such a unit is.

If no air-conditioning system presently exists, will you want one? If so, what will be the cost of installing an adequate system?

## The Attic

Eighty percent of the heat lost from a house escapes through the roof. Therefore, an attic helps insulate a house because it creates an air space between the ceiling and the roof. The floor of the attic should contain insulation.

First of all, of course, is there an attic? If not, is the roof itself insulated? If there is an attic, are the floor and the roof insulated?

An attic must have good ventilation and air circulation. There should be louvered openings on the sides of the attic to aid ventilation. A louver is a slatted opening with wire screening on the inside. These vents should always remain open. If they are closed or if none exist, condensation occurs, and the moisture deteriorates the ceiling, walls and roof. Does any light shine through the roof? If so, that could be a leaky spot. Take out your flashlight and look for water stains on the attic floor, walls and underside of the roof. If you see any, the roof leaks or ventilation is poor.

Look for dry rot and termite damage. Does the roof sag? Does the attic look solid?

Does it seem possible to convert the attic into another room? If not, is it a good storage area? Keep in mind that the attic is always the hottest place in the house because heat rises. If it has already been converted into a room, what is the quality of the workmanship?

## Stairways, Balconies and Terraces

Check the condition of all stairways in the house. Are they brick, wood, concrete or steel? Do they have sufficiently safe railings? This is important if you have young children or older people in the family who could fall easily. Are there any loose boards or cracks in the concrete?

Examine the condition of the balconies and terraces. Are there good railings? Is the flooring solid? Are there any leaks in the protective coverings against rain and sun?

## Closets, Cabinets, Built-ins and Storage Areas

As you go from room to room, look in the closets and other compartments. Does each bedroom have a closet? Are the closets numerous enough and sufficiently roomy to meet the needs of your family?

Well-designed built-ins always impress a buyer and increase the value of a house, particularly in kitchens, where storage space is built in and appliances are set into the woodwork. Notice the quality of the design and construction of shelves, cupboards and cabinets. Do they have glass, metal or wooden doors that open and close easily? Are the joints solid?

## A Porch and Extra Rooms

An enclosed porch in some areas is an essential feature and will add value to the house. If the house has a porch, check the condition and construction of both the inside and the outside. Is the porch sup-

ported as well as the house itself? Is the crawl space underneath the porch well ventilated and dry? Are the screens in good condition? Check for termites and wood rot.

Any additional rooms, such as recreation and rumpus rooms, a laundry, workshop, darkroom or storeroom are going to increase the cost of the house, and you should evaluate their worth to you. If you plan to add on a room or two, is it feasible to do so? It might be cheaper to get a bigger house.

## Siding, Exterior Walls and Trim

Siding is the external covering of the house, whether boards, shingles or some other material. How does it look? Are there any holes, cracks or signs of patch jobs?

Is any paint peeling? Peeling paint can be caused by water getting into the walls or by condensation forming on the back of the siding because of moisture in the house and poor ventilation. Paint will also peel if it is an inferior or improper type or if too much repainting has been done. Talk to the local paint dealer about possible causes and the expense of correcting the condition. Find out when the house was last painted, what kind of paint was used, who did the job and how much it cost.

Examine the exterior trim for signs of wood rot or termites. Has it been painted recently? Is it fitted evenly?

Do all the walls and doors square with each other, or is there sagging or sloping? These are signs of major structural defects.

## Roof, Gutters and Drain Pipes (Leaders)

Get up on the roof. What kind of roofing is used—shingles, tar paper, gravel, plywood, and so on? Are any shingles missing, curling or broken? If any are distinctly lighter in color, they are newer. Ask when they were put on and why. Is the roof material fireproof? Is the tar paper ripping or cracking? When was the roof last worked on, what was done to it and who did the work?

Look at the places where the roof joins the chimney, at pipes, and at the connection where two roof slopes meet. Is metal flashing installed in these places? Flashing is used to weatherproof joints and edges. Is it rusted and corroded? Are there cracks at any of these points?

Is there any evidence of roof leaks?

Does the roof extend out from the house sufficiently to prevent rain or melted snow from running down the walls of the house? If it extends out far enough and you see water stains on the external walls, the roof might be leaking.

Is there a complete gutter system around the roof? Any rust or corrosion? Are there drain pipes coming down from the roof? Are they in good condition and unclogged? Clogged pipes can cause water to back up and leak through the roof.

## Drainage

Where does the water drain off the roof? If water stands around the house, it can seep through the foundation and cause wood rot and basement flooding.

Look at the slope of the ground around the house. The ground should be graded so that water runs away from the house.

Are there, any drainage ditches or other drainage devices in the ground? Are they in good condition? (See Chapter 5, "The Earth—Soil, Vegetation and Topography.")

## Walks and Driveway

Are the walkways in good condition? If they are cement, are there cracks anywhere? If there is a driveway, is it in good condition?

## Fencing

If the house or garden area has a fence around it, is it beginning to lean to one side and fall apart in places, or does it look strong? Does it need a paint job?

When was the fence built?

If there is no fence and one is needed, what would it cost to erect one? Figure this into the house cost.

## Outbuildings

The most common outbuildings in the country are garages, barns and workshops. Often these build-

ings will be included in the deal at much less than their actual worth because they are used as extra selling points by the owner. Generally, these structures are not in as good condition as the house. The greater the emphasis the seller places on these buildings to justify his asking price, the more you should inspect them for defects.

### Garage
Is there any evidence that the roof leaks?

Is it big enough to hold your car?

Does it have a workshop or tool space in it?

If it is connected to the house, give it as thorough an inspection as you give the house.

### Barns
Many barns have not been maintained well and will be in poor condition.

Is there any evidence that the roof leaks?

Is the foundation sound? Is the wood rotting?

Is there any evidence of termites?

If you want to keep horses, cows or goats, is it big enough for them?

Is it insulated? Heated? Are any utilities supplied to it?

Does it have potential as a human dwelling?

What has it been used for in the past?

### Other Outbuildings
There might be a number of other assorted buildings on the land, including poultry houses, pig pens, rabbit hutches, feed storage sheds, silos, granaries, game rooms, a water tank housing, a tool and tack house, well houses, greenhouses and generator houses.

What utilities are supplied to the buildings?

Are these buildings worth whatever additional value the seller places on them? Find out how the seller breaks down the total asking price, what he thinks the house is worth and what the other buildings are worth. You should not hesitate to ask this question. Find out how the tax assessor has assessed the value of these buildings for tax purposes. (See Chapter 17, "Property Taxes and Assessments.")

### Storage Tanks
Underground gasoline storage tanks can lead to a very expensive environmental hazard. Note if the

tank is still used. Check to see if the tank has been tested for leaking.

## Radon Inspection

The Environmental Protection Agency (EPA) now recommends that before you purchase a new or existing home that it be tested for radon. Radon is a cancer-causing radioactive gas. You cannot see, taste or smell it, but breathing it can increase your risks in getting lung cancer. Radon is found in all areas of the United States.

Radon comes from the natural breakdown of uranium in soil, rock and water. Radon typically moves up through the ground to the air above and into your home through cracks and other holes in the foundation. Any new or old home can have a radon problem. Nearly 1 out of every 15 homes have elevated radon levels.

Part of every house inspection should now include a test for dangerously high radon levels.

## Environmental Hazards

Much new research is being conducted on environmental hazards in the home. Because these problems are often found in the construction materials themselves, if you are chemically sensitive or are concerned about your living environment, you will want to consider the potential problems.

For example, there is a growing body of medical research that suggests some diseases may be caused by factors that affect indoor air quality, such as molds and toxins from building materials. Of particular concern are diseases caused by molds and the off-gassing of toxins by synthetic materials such as paneling, chipboard, caulking, linoleum, and carpets. Indoor air syndromes caused by residential houses are becoming increasingly common. This can cause nasal congestion, chronic fatigue and other ailments.

With respect to mold, a damp basement should be considered a red flag; a musty-smelling basement even more so. You should check out the extent of any mold. If it has spread throughout the basement, it may be too far gone to control. Check out the source of water in a damp basement.

Synthetic paneling may need to be replaced with gyprock for some chemically sensitive people. Car-

pets and linoleum may also need to be replaced. Carpets have been linked to many health problems. There are chemicals used in the manufacturing process and there is a tendency for molds and chemicals and debris to accumulate in certain carpets. One test is to put a small piece of carpet in a jar for a few hours and then open it and smell. If there is no odor, it is probably all right. Look under the carpet in a home and see if particleboard or chipboard is underneath. This might create a problem for you.

The most controversial cause of medical problems is formaldehyde. This can be found in certain kinds of home insulation and has been classified by the U.S. Environmental Protection Agency as a "potential human carcinogen." It also comes from outgassing from particleboard, hardboard, paneling, plywood, and other manufactured wood products. Particleboard is often used in factory-built kitchen cabinets, shelves, and furniture.

Vinyl wall coverings may have outgassing from plasticizers, and some wallpaper glues contain fungicides and mildewcides.

The hazard of lead paint in older houses is well known. But oil-based or alkyd paints can contain toxic hydrocarbon solvents, stains, and varnishes. Water-based latex paints can contain fungicides and other biocides.

The above health concerns are only some of the problems we face from modern building materials. See the "Useful Resources" at the end of this chapter for more information on this increasingly important topic.

## Landscaping

Landscaping is always emphasized in real estate ads. Such things as "spacious lawn," "plenty of shade trees around house" and "numerous ornamental plantings in a beautifully landscaped setting" can raise the price of land considerably. You must decide whether these things are important enough to you to warrant the extra cost.

If the land is a small parcel and you have neighbors close by, trees and shrubs might afford needed privacy. Orchards and other land improvements that take many years to develop before they produce are valuable assets if they are free from disease and have been well cared for. An orchard that has been neglected for many years, however, will take time and work to bring it back to productivity, and you should not have to pay extra for it. Flowers and vegetables are nice, but their value is minimal. It is easy to be swayed by a lovely garden and pay an inflated price for the property. If you are buying land that is carefully landscaped, be sure you estimate its true value by placing most of the emphasis on the house and the land itself rather than the frills.

## Added Attractions— Don't Let Them Blind You

The seller might try to entice buyers with many extras, such as animals, animal feed and maintenance equipment, a satellite dish, carpets, drapes, furniture, air-conditioning, appliances of all kinds, tractors, compost shredders, lawn and patio furniture- and almost anything else you can think of. Be careful about letting these extras attract you to a deal that otherwise might not be what you want. I have heard people talk more about the extras that come with a house than about the home and land itself. Real estate agents often exploit this tendency by placing great emphasis on these added features to keep the buyer's mind off the important things.

If extras are included, note the condition of the items, their age and service history and their brand names, if applicable. Price the items yourself, and then ask the seller how he or she computes the value in the total asking price. Have the seller operate each item for you. Is he or she overpricing the frills?

## Final Consideration

Now that you have seen the house, the other buildings on the land and the extras that come with the deal, think about the house again.

- How is the general quality of workmanship and materials?
- Would you feel comfortable living in it?
- Is it your idea of a relaxed home in the country?
- Does it blend in well with the land?
- Do you like the size of the rooms and the way they are laid out?
- Will your furniture fit in well?

- Is the house large enough for your present and future family needs?
- Will it lend itself well to any additions you might want to make? Can you get a building permit to construct additional rooms?
- Can the house be securely locked and sealed while you are away?
- If you are buying an old house and want to refurbish it, can you get the proper permits? Is it economically feasible to rebuild the structure?

No house is perfect. There may be things wrong with the house that can be fixed for only a few hundred dollars. Get estimates on the costs of repairing deficiencies. Armed with these figures you have three choices:

1. Have the seller make the repairs before you buy the house.
2. Bargain to have the price reduced at least by the amount needed to make the essential repairs.
3. Do not buy the house because it is too dilapidated and the seller is not willing to cooperate with you.

## Using a Professional Inspector's Service

If you have decided that the land and the house are definitely what you want, you might like to get a professional evaluation of the house to double check your evaluation. Within the past 20 years or so, real estate inspector services have sprung up around the country to inspect and evaluate the present physical condition of structures and estimate the current cost of making necessary repairs. (An inspector does not estimate the value of the house; that is done by an appraiser.) You can accompany the inspector when he or she inspects the house. The inspector will point out the defects to you and will write up a detailed report that you can use when bargaining with the seller.

A good inspector can tell you whether those water marks in the basement indicate a chronic seepage problem or are the result of a single incident and if serious structural problems are hiding under a fresh coat of paint. All aspects of the house from top to bottom and from the heating and air-conditioning, electrical and plumbing systems to the foundation and insulation are covered by a professional inspection.

Especially if you are not willing to snoop around, digging in every cranny of the house, a complete inspection is well worth the price so that you can get a good idea of the condition of the house before you buy. However, even if you are willing to do your own inspection, it may be worth getting a professional inspection. Professional prospectors have inspected hundreds, perhaps even thousands of homes in their careers and can remain unbiased in their inspections, something you may not be able to do.

Shop around and compare inspection fees. Fees vary from one geographic area to another. Within one area fees can vary, depending on where the house is located, how large it is, the age of the house, special structures or other features and how long it takes to complete the inspection. The charge is usually somewhere between $250 and $500.

House inspector services are an unregulated business, so you must carefully check reputations and qualifications before you hire one. Try to hire an inspector who is also a licensed contractor or a licensed inspector. You could get recommendations from the county building inspector. (Be cautious in hiring anyone recommended by the seller or real estate agent.)

Inspection services will be listed in the Yellow Pages of the phone book under "Home Service" or "Building Inspection Service." A registered civil engineer is also qualified to inspect structures. One nationwide group, named the American Society of Home Inspectors, Inc. (ASHI), was formed in 1976 as a nonprofit voluntary professional society. It has developed formal inspection guidelines and a professional code of ethics, and gives homeowners an assurance of quality and professionalism. If you use an ASHI member you can be assured of a complete detailed inspection.

Rather than get a complete structural inspection, you may just want to get a termite and wood rot evaluation. This type of damage is the most destructive to a home and the most expensive to repair. A pest and fungus inspection costs less than a complete evaluation of the house and is considered essential by lenders and builders.

When selecting a pest control service, again be cautious. Membership in the National Pest Control Association or a state or local pest control association is a good sign that a company is established. Such associations usually have codes of ethics

members agree to, and members have access to the latest technical information on chemicals. Check with your local Better Business Bureau, Chamber of Commerce, county extension agents or consumer office.

When getting a pest inspection, ask what sanitary conditions might invite infestations, the extent and location of a pest problem found at the time of the inspection, what existing or potential avenues of entry there are for a pest infestation, and if there are structural deficiencies serving as actual or potential breeding sites for insects, rodents and other pests. A sample structural pest-control inspection report is shown in Figure 6–4.

The Model Contract of Sale (see Chapter 27) contains a warranty that the house is free of termite infestation and wood rot. (See clause 16[e] and the accompanying explanation.) You can also condition the purchase on your approval of a complete or partial structural report. Clause 17(b) can be used for a complete inspection, and clause 17(d) specifically provides for a pest and fungus report. You can thus sign a contract to buy the property, but the deal cannot be closed unless you approve the results of a structural and termite report. If you receive an unfavorable report, you can terminate the agreement to purchase or have the price reduced by the amount needed to make the repairs. (See clause 17[a] of the model contract.)

Sellers who are unwilling to warrant the condition of a house or allow the inclusion of these conditions may have something to hide. Actually, the seller should pay the inspection costs. You can compromise and pay half if you want. Sometimes, if you demand a report, the real estate agent will pay for it if it will help make the sale.

You can include other warranties of the condition of the property you are buying; for example, that the house is structurally sound, that all the appliances and machinery are in perfect working order and that the livestock are in excellent health.

## Will You Need To Renovate?

If you like the house but will need to renovate it or modify it in some way to make it suit your needs, it still needs to be basically sound.

You will want to reject a house for renovation:

- if the foundation is poor and irreparable. It is occasionally possible to move a house onto a

**Figure 6–4. Standard Structural Pest-Control Inspection Report**

| (WOOD-DESTROYING PESTS OR ORGANISMS) | | | | |
|---|---|---|---|---|
| *This is an inspection report only—not a Notice of Completion.* | | | | |

| ADDRESS OF PROPERTY INSPECTED | BLDG. NO. | STREET | CITY / CO. CODE | DATE OF INSPECTION |
|---|---|---|---|---|

FIRM NAME AND ADDRESS

Telephone:

*Affix stamp here on Board copy only*
↓ A LICENSED PEST CONTROL OPERATOR IS AN EXPERT IN HIS FIELD. ANY QUESTIONS RELATIVE TO THIS REPORT SHOULD BE REFERRED TO HIM.

| FIRM LICENSE NO. | CO. | STAMP NO. |
|---|---|---|

Inspection Ordered by (Name and Address) _____

Report Sent to (Name and Address) _____

Owner's Name and Address _____

Name and Address of a Party in Interest _____

Original Report [X]   Supplemental Report [ ]   Limited Report [ ]   Reinspection Report [ ]   No. of Pages ____

| YES | CODE | SEE DIAGRAM BELOW | YES | CODE | SEE DIAGRAM BELOW | YES | CODE | SEE DIAGRAM BELOW | YES | CODE | SEE DIAGRAM BELOW |
|---|---|---|---|---|---|---|---|---|---|---|---|
| | S | Subterranean Termites | X | B | Beetles—Other Wood Pests | | Z | Dampwood Termites | | EM | Excessive Moisture Condition |
| | K | Dry Wood Termites | | FG | Faulty Grade Levels | | SL | Shower Leaks | X | IA | Inaccessible Areas |
| X | F | Fungus or Dry Rot | X | EC | Earth-wood Contacts | X | CD | Cellulose Debris | X | FI | Further Inspection Recom. |

1. SUBSTRUCTURE AREA *(soil conditions, accessibility, etc.)*    Sub basement—See #1 #2 #3 #4 & #5
2. Was Stall Shower water tested?   None   Did floor coverings indicate leaks?  -----
3. FOUNDATIONS *(Type, Relation to Grade, etc.)*    Concrete—See #6
4. PORCHES ... STEPS ... PATIOS    See #7 #8 #9 & #10
5. VENTILATION *(Amount, Relation to Grade, etc.)*    None
6. ABUTMENTS ...   Stucco walls, columns, arches, etc.    None
7. ATTIC SPACES *(accessibility, insulation, etc.)*    None
8. GARAGES *(Type, accessibility, etc.)*    None
9. OTHER    See #11

DIAGRAM AND EXPLANATION OF FINDINGS   (This report is limited to structure or structures shown on diagram.)

new foundation, but the rest of the house must be in extremely good condition to make this economically feasible.

- if the entire frame of the house is considerably out of square, or if the framing is infested with termites, wood rot or something else.
- if there are so many repairs and replacements necessary that they make the job extremely uneconomical.

Be sure to check with the local building department. Sometimes what seems like a minor addition or repair may require a major revamping of the entire structure to comply with the building codes.

Remember, if the cost of buying and renovating the house does not exceed the fair market value of other houses in the area, it is probably a sound investment.

When you sign your contract, put in a condition that the deal is contingent on your getting a contractor to renovate the house for an amount that is within your budget.

## Purchasing a Manufactured Home with the Land

Many of you will be considering the purchase of a manufactured home. Purchasing a manufactured home is less expensive than building a conventional home of the same size. There are four basic types of structures that fall into this category: the older mobile homes, and modular, panelized and precut homes. Examples of modular, panelized and precut homes are prefabricated log or wood homes, domes and yurts as well as conventional-looking homes. Some of these come as kits. All require a foundation installed separately from the cost of the home, often after the home has been delivered to the house site.

The newer manufactured homes are of good quality because quality control is maintained at the factory level and because manufactured homes must comply with a building code developed by the Department of Housing and Urban Development (HUD). Housing made in factories now accounts for 40 percent of all new single-family home pur-

**Figure 6–4.  Standard Structural Pest-Control Inspection Report** *continued*

General Description _____ wood frame—occupied _____

_____ Inspection Tag Posted (Location) _____ In basement _____

Other Inspection Tags _____ None noted _____

The closed finished stucco and plastic walls, ceilings, areas beneath floor coverings, areas concealed by built-in cabinets, storage, and furnishings were inaccessible for inspection.

Since no visible evidence of infestation or damage was noted in the accessible portions except as set forth in this report, any further inspection of these areas would be impractical. We assume no liability for these areas.

Areas subject to moisture, except as outlined in this report, such as roofs, gutters, windows, shower enclosures, and plumbing leaks are to be maintained by homeowners. This Company assumes no liability for these areas. If work as outlined in this report is performed by others, and a building permit is posted, we wil reinspect the property at an additional cost.

Reseating of toilets and caulking and sealing guaranteed for 60 days. Repairs and treating guaranteed for one year.

We assume no liability for damage, infection, or infestation in inaccessible areas, including sealed stucco walls and soffits. Further inspection of these areas will require openings and be performed on request with permission of authorized parties. No personal belongings, chattels, storage, or carpets were moved at time of inspection. Attics will be inspected when a release from possible damage is received and at additional cost.

State law requires that you be given the following information: CAUTION: PESTICIDES ARE TOXIC CHEMICALS. Structural Pest Control Operators are licensed and regulated by the Structural Pest Control Board, and apply pesticides which are registered and approved for use by the California Department of Food and Agriculture and the United States Environmental Protection Agency. Registration is granted when the state finds that based on existing scientific evidence, there are no appreciable risks if proper use conditions are followed or that the risks are outweighed by the benefits. The degree of risk depends upon degree of exposure, so exposure should be minimized.

If within 24 hours following application, you experience symptoms similar to common seasonal illness comparable to the flu: Contact your physician or poison control center and Comstock Termite and Pest Control immediately. For further information, contact any of the following: Comstock Termite Control 566–0600, County Health Department—588–2466, Poison Control Center—666–2845, County Agriculture Commission—558–3284, Structural Pest Control Board—1430 Howe Ave., Sacramento, CA. 95825 (916) 924-2291. The pesticide or pesticides proposed to be used are ☐ Chlordane ☐ Copper Napthanate ☐ Dursban (Chlorpyrifos)

1. Prior work has been performed.  YES___X___ NO____

2. Some windows and/or doors and surrounds in need of paint and maintenance or replacement.  YES___X___ NO_____ No cost for sash work as this work should be referred to proper trade.

3. Stall shower tested in presence of _____ and did not leak. We assume no liability for any leakage that may or may not appear in the future.

4. Bases of curtain walls and/or steps resting on/or slightly imbedded in concrete.  YES_____ NO___X___

5. This is a reinspection of our original Report #_____ Stamp #_____ Dated_____

6. At the direction of _____ this inspection is limited to the areas as outlined and described below. No other inspection or representation is made or intended.

7. This is a supplemental to our original report #_____ Stamp #_____ Dated_____

8. All work as outlined in our original report has been completed by others. We assume no liability for work performed or permits procured or not procured by others.  YES_____ NO_____

9. Sealing of stairs or decks to be performed by owner as part of general building maintenance.

10. No roofing work, inspection, or representation made by this company as we are not licensed in this field.

SUBSTRUCTURE:

1 & 2. Wood soil contact and infestation noted in window framing and under deck. B-F-EC on diagram.
RECOMMENDATION: Cut out all damage and repair as necessary. Treat all areas of infestation with Dursban.

3. Cellulose debris in sub area soil. CD on diagram.
RECOMMENDATION: Remove and dispose of all cellulose debris.

4. Wood soil contact at base of curtain wall. EC on diagram.
RECOMMENDATION: Cut off base of curtain wall and re-support as necessary.

5. Wood soil contact at base of studding and braces in front sub area. EC on diagram.
RECOMMENDATION: Remove and dispose of non-functional studding. Install new bracing supported on concrete.

**Inspected by** _____ **License No.** _____ **Signature** _____

**Figure 6–4. Standard Structural Pest-Control Inspection Report** *continued*

FOUNDATION:
6. Wood soil contact and damage at base of wall in area indicated. F-EC on diagram.
RECOMMENDATION: Cut out lower framing to remove all damage and to bring all framing above grade. Install new raised concrete footing.

STAIRS:
7. Wood soil contact at base of stairs. Area under lower landing and stairs is inaccessible, however, this appears to be newly built. EC-IA-FI on diagram.
RECOMMENDATION: Lower grade to clear stringers. Install access opening under lower landing for further inspection and recommendations.

STEPS:
8. Damage at base of stairway. F on diagram.
RECOMMENDATION: Cut off base of stairs and resupport as necessary.

STAIRS:
9. Wood soil contact and fungus under new stairway. EC-F on diagram.
RECOMMENDATION: Lift two stairs to gain access to this area. Remove and dispose of cellulose debris. Cut off support framing and resupport as necessary. Replace stairs used for access. (No paint.)

PORCHES & STAIRS:
10. Damage in stairs and ramp left from prior repairs. EC-F on diagram.
RECOMMENDATION: Cut out all damage and repair as necessary. Flash off joists at sidewalk.

OTHER:
11. The following conditions were found in units:
UNIT #1—Lift brick around kitchen sink and repair framing. Reinstall brick. Remove tile around bathtub. Install new waterproof Sheetrock. Retile around tub.

NOTE: A large section of front and rear sub areas has insufficient clearance to crawl. However, from the inspection that can be made of these areas, we find them to be clear and dry.

chases. This increased demand for manufactured homes has caused the manufacturers to improve styles and features. Some manufacturers give you options regarding various features that allow you to customize your home. You may choose to have 2" × 6" exterior walls, 4" in 12" roof pitch, composite shingle roofs, walls extended or deleted, fireplaces and hardwood exteriors to name a few options. It is sometimes hard to tell the difference between a stick built home and a high-end manufactured home. Some of the better manufacturers also follow up after the home is installed and correct problems that develop within the first year.

Do beware of older metal *mobile homes*, although this name is deceiving since fewer than 5 percent are ever moved off the owner's original site. Many are poorly constructed and do not have the durability of frame construction or brick or stone dwellings. They are often small and lack adequate wiring and plumbing. Leaking is a problem, as is proper insulation. They are also far more prone to fire than regular houses. Unlike the newer manufactured homes, the older mobile homes are often taxed on a special personal-property tax basis, rather than as part of the real estate, although many

states will tax them as part of the real estate if they are on permanent foundations. An extremely important point to be aware of is that you usually need the consent of a lender to assume existing liabilities on a mobile home. Because it is sold like a car or personal property, the lender holds the "pink slip" until the home is paid for. However, once on the property, it is included as part of the real property. Always contact the lender regarding your assumption of an existing loan, because lenders usually require that you qualify on your own to assume the loan. If you purchase the home without the lender's approval, it could accelerate the loan and call for it to be paid off immediately. In addition, the state might not recognize the transfer of ownership to you, nor will the insurance company put you on the policy as the insured owner.

You must check out the condition of a manufactured home as carefully as you check that of a conventional home. Test all the appliances, check all sockets with a light and make sure the home is level. You can check to see if the home is level by taking a ball and placing it on a floor with a hard surface to see if it rolls and by opening and closing all interior and exterior doors. If any doors scrape against their jambs, the home may not be level. Turn on all faucets, and flush the toilets. Look for the seal near the doorway or on the outside rear or side of the home. This is placed there to inform you that HUD building standards have been complied with. Have the seller show you all the warranties on the manufactured home, along with the purchase papers.

See what kind of foundation the home sits on and how it is secured. It must be properly anchored to the ground to prevent severe winds and earthquakes from damaging it. If the home is in sections, like a double-wide home, carefully check the seams where they join together for evidence of leaking or loose-fitting areas. Proper leveling of the home is one of the most important aspects of setting up a manufactured home. If done improperly it could cause floors or walls to buckle. Even if it was installed properly when first placed on the site, in time foundation supports may settle unevenly and can cause serious damage.

You can obtain FHA/HUD and VA loans for the purchase of manufactured homes as well as for the real estate. See the "Useful Resources" in Chapter 21, "Types of Financing: Land Contract, Mortgage, Deed of Trust" for all addresses of local offices that can supply current information on loan availability. Other conventional sources of financing are available.

If you are planning to purchase vacant land and then place a manufactured home on it, you should be aware of several points. The zoning must allow placing a manufactured home in your location. Certain areas prohibit such homes or require a certain size and exterior appearance. Check the local planning and land-use department for zoning restrictions.

In some subdivisions, manufactured homes are totally prohibited, according to covenants, conditions and restrictions on all parcels. You will know this if you request and read the restrictions before the close of escrow. If you intend to purchase a manufactured home, write into your purchase agreement a condition that your purchase and the close of escrow is contingent on your obtaining a building permit to place a manufactured home on the property. The parcel of land must have a site accessible to the large truck that will have to haul the home to the site, the site must be as level as possible, the soil must be graded and sloped properly and compacted. This will have to be done by professionals, so you should figure that cost into your

projections. In a rural area it is very important that you have an adequate access road for getting your home to the site.

## Straw-Bale Construction

There is a new movement to bring back an old building technology, *straw-bale construction.* Straw-bale construction was developed in Nebraska by homesteaders who lacked timber and so built their homes out of stacked straw bales plastered with mud. Many of their homes are still in good shape after almost 100 years, a testament to the durability of this material. In the recent revival of this method, the primary building material used is "rice straw," the agricultural by-product from rice production. Bales of straw are fastened together with rebar, wire and a minimum of wood or steel.

Depending on how complex the structure is, a straw-bale house can be relatively inexpensive and easy to build for a do-it-yourselfer. Some very simple structures have been built by a group of friends in a weekend or two for a little as $7.00 per square foot. On the other hand, a complex structure built by a contractor who has never seen this type of construction before will probably be more expensive than standard construction. However, enthusiasts point out that tests have shown that straw-bale homes are more fire retardant than wood homes and can last as long, that straw is one of the most energy-efficient materials you can use to build a home, with insulation values up to four times higher than well-insulated modern homes, and that straw-bale homes reduce the amount of timber needed in construction and provide an alternative to the annual burning of hay and straw fields, a source of air pollution in some areas.

Straw-bale construction seems especially suited for homes in the southwestern United States. In New Mexico where the revival is very strong, straw-bale promoters have successfully pushed the state to add straw-bale construction to its building codes. Arizona, Texas, California, and Oregon are also considering this change. In our area, a home was recently approved and completed in Mendocino County, California.

However, in most areas of the country, building code inspectors and bankers have never heard of straw-bale construction, and permits, financing, and insurance are often very hard to get. If you plan to purchase land with the idea that you will build with straw-bale, be sure to include a condition in the contract that your purchase is subject to your being able to get the necessary permits, financing and insurance before escrow closes.

## Useful Resources

The following are publications to help you inspect a home's physical condition, construct a home and learn about energy efficient home construction.

From:  R. Woods
       Consumer Information Center, Y-6
       Pueblo, CO 81002

"Home Inspection and You," 337B          $.50
"Home Buyer's and Seller's Guide to
    Radon," 129B                         $1.50
"Indoor Air Quality and New and New
    Carpet—What You Should Know"         *free*

From:  National Pest Control Association
       8100 Oak St.
       Dunn Loring, VA 22027

"How To Select and Use Pest Control Services"
"The Uninvited Guest"
"Buying or Selling a Home"
"The Truth about Termites"
"Wood Decay in Structures"

(You can also request a list of member firms of the NPCA.)

From:  University of Illinois
       Building Research Council
       One Fast Saint Mary's Rd..
       Champaign, IL 61820
       (800) 336-0616

| | | |
|---|---|---|
| "Moisture Condensation" | F.6. | $2.00 |
| "Heating the Home" | G3.1 | $2.50 |
| "Maintaining the Home" | Al .5 | $1.50 |
| "Plumbing" | G5.0 | $1.00 |
| "Inspecting the Home" | Al.l | $2.00 |
| "Financing the Home" | A1.3 | $2.50 |
| "Solar Orientation" | C3.2 | $1.00 |
| "Solar Water Heaters" | G5.7 | $1.50 |
| "Gutters and Downspouts" | F13.1 | $2.00 |

"From Roof to Foundation," (30 minute VHS video) on home inspection" is available for $29.95.

Write for a copy of the Council's list of publications for a more complete list.

From:  ANR Publications
       University of California
       6701 San Pablo Ave.
       Oakland, CA 94608-1239

"Do You Want A Home In the Country?" 2210
                                         $1.75
"Landscape for Fire Protection," 2410    $1.50

The following publications also can be obtained from HUD regional area and services offices throughout the country. (See Chapter 21 for regional addresses.)

HUD User,
P.O. Box 6091
Rockville, MD 20850
Voice: (800) 245-2691 or (301) 251-5154
TDD: (800) 483-2209
Fax: (301)251-5747
E-mail: HUDUSER@ASPENSYS.COM
FaxBack: (800) 245-2691

"Blueprint Catalogue, A List of Affordable Housing
    Plans."
"HUD User, A Guide to Publications and Services"
"Minimum Property Standard for Housing," HUD
    4910.1

For information on indoor air pollution, call Indoor Air Quality Information (IAQ INFO) at (800) 438-4318.

If you are interested in finding information regarding toxic substances and pesticides, call the National Pesticide Telecommunications Network at (800) 858-7378.

The following pamphlets are available for free from:

Environmental Protection Agency
Mail Stop SSOP
Washington, DC
20402-9328

"The Inside Story: A Guide to Indoor Air Quality"
"A Citizen's Guide to Pesticides"
"Pesticides in Drinking-Water Wells"
"Home buyers and Seller's Guide to Radon"

"A Citizens Guide to Protecting Yourself and
   Your Family From Radon"
"Model Standards and Techniques of Control
   of Radon in New Residential Buildings"
"Reducing Lead Hazards When Remolding
   Your Home"
"Access EPA"
"Indoor Air Pollution—An Introduction for Health
   Professionals"
"Targeting Indoor Air Pollution—EPA's Approach
   and Progess"
"Indoor Biological Pollutants"
"Residential Air-Claning Devices—A Summary of
   Available Information"
"Flood Cleanup: Avoiding Indoor Air Quality
   Problems"
"Carpet and Indoor Air Quality"

The Environmental Protection Agency's hotline is
(800) 424-9065.

Other federal information service phone numbers
are:

Indoor Air Information Clearinghouse
   (800) 438-4318; (202) 484-1307
National Radon Hotline (800) SOS-RADON
Lead Information Center (800) LEAD-FYI
National Lead Information Clearinghouse
   (800) 424-LEAD

The following pamphlets are available free from:

   Indoor Air Quality Information
      Clearinghouse
   P.O. Box 37133
   Washington, DC 20013-7133
   Voice: (202) 484-1307 or 1 (800) 438-4318
   Fax: (202) 484-1510

"Fact Sheet: Sick Building Syndrome,"  IAQ-0004
"Fact Sheet: Asbestors in Your Home,"  IAQ-0023

For information on asbestos and a list of free pamphlets, contact:

   Asbestos Information Center
   Curtis Hall-Tufts University
   471 Boston Avenue
   Medford, MA 02155
   (617) 628-5000

For information on formaldehyde and other pollutants in the home, and a list of available free
brochures, send a self-addressed stamped envelope
to:

   Consumer Fedreation of America
   1424 16th Street NW
   Suite 604
   Washington, DC 20036
   (202) 387-6121

The Housing Resource Center hosts the annual
Blueprint for a Healthy House Conference, and
prints an index of testing and mitigation products.
Contact them at:

   The Housing Resource Center
   1820 W. 48th Street
   Cleveland, OH 44102
   (216) 281-4663

The following publications are available at the
stated prices from:

   Human Ecology Action League
   P.O. Box 49126
   Atlanta, GA 30359
   (409) 248-1898

| | |
|---|---|
| "Chemicals Can Affect Your Health" | Free |
| "Water Testing" | $2.00 |
| "Water Treatment" | $2.00 |
| "Non-Toxic Home Consultants, Supplies, for Safe Interiors" | $4.00 |
| "Home Building Pollution" | $2.00 |

Another source for medical information is:

   American Academy of Environmental
      Medicine
   Denver, Colorado
   (303) 622-9755

If you have concerns about indoor air there are a
few more sources for information:

   David Miller
   Argricultural Plant Research
   (613) 759-2309

   American Academy of Environmental
      Medicine
   Denver, CO
   (303) 622-9755

**Radon**

The USGS has available (address in "Useful Resources," Chapter 4):

"The Geology of Radon"

From:   Council of Better Business Bureau
        Publication Department
        4200 Wilson Blvd., Suite 800
        Arlington, VA 22203

The Better Business Bureau has available booklets for $2.00 each:

"Home Inspection"          07-24-261
"Manufactured Homes"       07-311-03227
"Radon Testing"            07-24-246

**Underground Storage Tanks**

There is a superfund available for underground storage tank removal. For more information call (800) 813-FUND.

   In California the State Water Resource Board can answer your questions. Address is found in Chapter 4, or call (916) 227-4400.

**Manufactured Homes**

From:   R. WOODS
        Consumer Information Center A
        P.O. Box 100
        Pueblo, CO 81002

"How to Buy a Manufactured Home," 339B $.50

Write to the following agency for current literature on manufactured home standards.

        National Manufactured Housing and
           Construction Safety Standards Division
        Department of Housing and
           Urban Development
        Room 9156
        Washington, DC 20410

The following publication can be obtained from HUD regional area and services offices throughout the country (see Chapter 21 for addresses) or from:

HUD User,
   P.O. Box 6091
   Rockville, MD 20850
   Voice: (800) 245-2691 or (301) 251-5154
   TDD:  (800) 483-2209
   Fax: (301)251-5747
   E-mail: HUDUSER@ASPENSYS.COM
   FaxBack: (800) 245-2691

"Manufactured Housing: A HUD User
   Resource Guide," ACCN-6245          $4.00

A good book about modern manufactured homes is:

*Manufactured Houses—Finding and Buying
   Your Dream Homes for Less*          $14.95
   Written by: A.M. Watkins
   Published by Dearborn Financial Publishing
              155 Wacker Drive
              Chicago, IL 60606-1719

Another source of information is:

   Manufactured Housing Institute
   1745 Jefferson Davis Hwy., Suite 501
   Arlington, VA 22202
   (703) 413-6620

**Log Homes and Domes**

The National Association of Home Builders includes the Log Homes Council and the National Dome Council. Write to the association at the address below for a list of the major log and dome home manufacturers in the United States, Canada and other locations.

   National Association of Home Builders
   Building Systems Councils
   15th & M Sts., NW
   Washington, DC 20005
   (202) 822-0576

   The Log House Builders Association of
   North America
   22203 S.R. 203
   Monroe, WA 98272
   (206) 794-4469

**Yurts**

   The Yurt Foundation
   Bucks Harbor, ME 04618

Vital Designs
David and Annie Raitt
P.O. Box 18
Talmage, CA 95481
Voice: (800) 664-9878
E-mail: cayurts@pacific.net

**Straw-Bale Construction**

If you are looking for information on straw-bale construction, would like to attend a workshop or find out about other straw-bale consultants contact:

David Booth
Synergistic Solutions
P.O. Box 391
Miranda, CA 95553
(707) 943-3061

A newsletter, videos, and several publications on straw-bale are available from:

Out on Bale-by-Mail
1037 E. Linden St.
Tucson, AZ 85719
(602) 624-1673

A report by the Technical University of Nova Scotia regarding moisture, thermal and mechanical properties of straw-bale houses is available from:

Straw House Herbals
R.R. #1
Ship Harbour, Nova Scotia
Canada, BOJIYO
(902) 845-2750

For written materials, including "Straw Bale Construction and the Building Codes" by David Eisenberg, videos, test results, workshops, work tours, contact:

The Canelo Project
Athena and Bill Steen
HC1 Box 324
Elgin, AZ 85611
(520) 455-5548

For more information, call Mother Earth News' Bookshelf at (800) 888-9098 and ask for "The Straw Bale Package."

Two books on straw-bale are:

*Build It with Bales—A Step-by-Step Guide to Straw Bale Construction* by S. O. MacDonald and Matts Myhrman.

*The Straw Bale House* by Steen et al. Available through the Real Goods Company, (800) 762-7325. Real Goods also has two videos on straw-bale construction.

# CHAPTER

# 7 Amenities of the Area

*I don't mind on a given day—let's say a beautiful fall day or something—I can see getting into the car and driving up to the country and getting out and walking around and looking at the lake and leaves and that kind of thing and then getting back into the car and coming home. That I can see. To go and spend two hours, five hours in the country, something like that. I can't see bedding down in the country overnight. I see nothing in that.*

*I like to know, although I've never done it, I like to know that if at two o'clock in the morning, I get a sudden urge for duck wonton soup, that I can go downstairs, find a taxi-cab, go to Chinatown, get it and come back home. This is important to me.*

*I like the idea that it's a live, active city. I don't like to know that if I go outside, it's all trees and bushes and paths.*

—Woody Allen

The life amenities desired by actor/director Woody Allen preclude his living in the country. He is a city person through and through.

*Amenities* is a term often used by real estate

agents to describe those aspects of an area that make it an attractive, enjoyable place to live. The amenities sought by people can differ greatly. Whether you are buying a permanent country residence or a second home for seasonal use, you want a place that meets your needs. The factors that might influence your choice of location are discussed in this chapter.

A good way to find out about an area is to talk to everyone you meet while visiting there. However, if you can rent a house or get a job in the area as a caretaker, you will get a much deeper insight into whether you want to live there permanently.

## The Human Factor

### How Many People in the Area?
If you really want to live in the country, be careful about choosing land in an area that is presently, or soon likely to be, experiencing a land boom. A few states and most small towns near cities are gaining population rapidly. Watch for ads for recreational

94

subdivisions or residential developments as indications that an area is being developed. Unless you are interested mainly in investment in a rapid growth area, you may not be prepared for some of the drastic changes your sleepy little town will undergo in adjusting to its new growth. You may not recognize the place a few years after you buy. The area will be bustling with activity, taxes will go up and zoning and building codes will be more stringently enforced.

On the other hand, if the population of an area is on the decline, land prices and taxes will be lower than in a developing area. It may be harder to find a job or open a business, however, and there may be a deficiency of available services.

According to government statistics, towns and cities with 2,500 to 10,000 people are the fastest growing population centers in America. If you want to live in a place that will retain its rural qualities for a while, choose an area with fewer than 2,500 inhabitants; avoid areas in which packaged recreational or permanent-home subdivisions are being promoted. These developments are like small cities in the country. Between 1970 and 1990, the population of rural areas of all sizes grew, but the most rapid growth occurred in the country outside villages and hamlets recognized as separate entities.

Some exceptional rural areas have witnessed extensive new settlement and growth, notably in Florida and portions of the far West. In the Northeast, rural areas continue to grow faster than metropolitan areas. Since 1960, the pattern has been one of net migration from the Northeast and Midwest and net migration to the South and West. States with the largest net population gains into the 90s were located in the South and West, with California, Texas and Florida leading. Although some losses have occurred in rural areas, there has been population growth in non-metropolitan areas that are attractive to retirees, such as the Ozarks, the Texas Hill Country, Northern Michigan and Wisconsin.

The best source for statistical information about an area's population is the local field office of the Bureau of the Census. These offices are listed in the "Useful Resources" section at the end of this chapter.

### Who Are Your Neighbors?

If you find a nice piece of land, meet your prospective neighbors and talk to them about your plans. They will probably be happy to meet you and proud to show you what they have done with their places. Spend an afternoon with them, and you will learn a lot about the community. You will want to be able to call on them occasionally to look after your place while you are away, to feed your animals or water your garden, and they will want the same from you. If you are moving to an isolated area, your neighbors might be more important to you than if you are living close to town.

If you have children, you will probably want neighbors with children in the same age group, particularly if you plan to live there permanently. On the other hand, if you don't have children, you may not want any nearby children who will climb your apple trees, or adolescents, who will race their cars. If most of your neighbors are young couples, you should expect an increase in the number of children in the area.

A unique problem with neighbors occurs in some areas where ranching is practiced. Many states still observe the "open range" law, which permits animal owners to let their livestock roam free. The burden of fencing in land is on any landowner who does not want the wandering herds to enter his or her property. Thus, if you buy a place next to a cattle ranch and you don't want cows wandering through your land, you will have to build a fence to keep them out. This is a costly project and should be figured into your purchase price.

### Employment

Unless you are independently wealthy or interested in a vacation home only, you will have to decide how you want to support yourself. You may want to live near enough to the city so that you can continue to work at your present job, or you may intend to work in the country, either near or on your land. Your decision will depend to a great extent on what you do to make money and what area you pick to live in. Many artists and artisans have no trouble working in their homes in the country and traveling to the city occasionally to sell their wares. Some artisans set up their studios in nearby towns that have a tourist trade.

Since we bought our land several years ago, many individuals have opened successful businesses in town: several women's, men's and children's clothing stores, including a used-goods store; a shoe store; a bookstore; a movie theater; automobile repair shops; a health clinic; a veterinary office; a law office; several new restaurants, a restaurant and bar and an ice cream parlor; real estate agencies; a grocery store; a vitamins and herbs store; an alternative energy store; a toy store; gift shops; a horseback-riding business; a canoeing and rafting business; and a motel. As rural areas become more populated with residents and tourists, business opportunities will increase, especially for service industries.

If you are thinking of opening a business in your area, consider the demand for your kind of service, the competition and anticipated trends in the area before you decide. Does the area attract an ample tourist trade to support your business? If there are other businesses similar to yours already in existence, is there enough demand to support another one? If the community is growing rapidly, what new facilities are wanted and needed by the newer residents?

Talk to other businessmen in the community, ask questions at the local Chamber of Commerce, read the newspapers thoroughly, look in the Yellow Pages to see what businesses are already established and keep your eyes and ears open to the needs of the business and residential community. Check the local taxes and the zoning and building codes. Talk with the supervisors from the Small Business Administration (SBA), a federal agency specializing in loans to businessmen, and the Farmer's Home Administration. (See "Useful Resources" at the end of this chapter.) These agencies will have information on how to start a business, what the chances of success are, based on past results, and how to get financial assistance. The SBA puts out a pamphlet entitled "Checklist for Going into Business" that is quite helpful. If you intend to buy an existing country business, thoroughly investigate it before purchasing, and find out why it is being sold. You may need the advice of a lawyer and an accountant to be safe.

Many people make part or all of their income in the country from home businesses such as raising animals; selling homemade clothing, pottery, weaving, furniture or jewelry; running repair shops and other services; painting signs; selling antiques; and selling homegrown produce. The greater your imagination and abilities, the more likely you will think of a lucrative home business. You might have to buy property on a well-traveled road if you want to operate a business from your home. Several of my clients operate very successful mail-order businesses, selling records, children's cassettes and video tapes, rare books, alternative energy supplies and musical instruments. With the advent of fax machines, express mail service and overnight delivery services, it is becoming much easier to operate a business in a rural area. The *Mother Earth News* is still the best source of inspirational stories of people making it in the country. (See Appendix A for the address.)

Some of you are probably thinking about farming as a means of survival. The problems of setting up such an operation are far beyond the scope of this book, but the following government statistics reveal much about the current farm situation.

Since the early 1900s, the number of farms in the United States has steadily declined. In 1986, approximately the same number of farms existed as there were in 1860. Between 1950 and 1990, loss of farmland averaged about 5.4 million acres per year.

Reductions in the number of farms and total farmland area are attributable to a combination of factors, including a chronically depressed farm economy, farm production technologies that have reduced labor requirements, consolidation of small farms into larger operating units, government-sponsored land retirement programs and conversion of farmland to non-farm use.

The amount of land in farms of 1,000 acres or more has increased significantly over the past several decades, whereas farms of 500 acres or less has declined. Land in operations having at least 1,000 acres now comprise about 60 percent of the total farmland. Much of the increase in farm size is the result of smaller-sized farms being absorbed into larger operations.

The per acre value of U.S. farm real estate increased 1 percent to 3 percent in 1991. In 1990 farm values rose 2 percent to an average of $682 per acre. The current average remains 17 percent below the record $823 per acre in 1982. Farm values posted their strongest 1990 gains in the Lake states (8 percent) and Mountain (7 percent) regions. In the Northern Plains, the 9 percent average annual increase in values during the preceding three years tapered off to 3 percent in 1990. Corn Belt values rose 25 percent from 1987 to 1990. California had a 5 percent increase from 1987 to 1990.

Values declined 1 percent in the Northeast, 5 percent in Appalachia and 3 percent in the Southern Plains. They were unchanged in the Southwest. In 1990 and 1991 about 9 percent of farm transfers resulted from foreclosure, bankruptcy and condemnation sales and transfers.

In 1990 and 1991 owner-operators participated in 59 percent of purchases, involving 57 percent of the acres sold and 62 percent of the total value of sales. In 1990, foreign interests acquired an additional 1.6 million acres of farm land, raising total holdings to 14.45 million acres as of December 31, 1990. Foreign-owned land constituted over 1 percent of all privately owned farm land and 0.6 percent of all U.S. land.

Net farm income has declined since 1990. The general economic slowdown in 1990 and 1991 dampened investor activity, particularly near urban areas. This, in turn, reduced the demand for farmland for nonagricultural uses, putting downward pressure on farmland prices.

Despite this generally gloomy situation, I believe it is possible to generate at least part of your income by operating a small farm business. With the leveling off of land values and the probable splitting up of large ranches, the next decade could be a good time to begin farming on a smaller scale. There are several informative and inspirational magazines on setting up such an operation that are published regularly. The addresses of some of these publications are given in the list of "Useful Resources" at the end of this chapter and in Appendix A.

If you want to find employment in the country, try the small businesses, the farms and ranches, and the local industrial employers to see if anyone is hiring. Any rural area has a high rate of unemployment, so you must be realistic. However, those with special skills or credentials—teachers, nurses, doctors, lawyers, surveyors and engineers—are usually in demand. Consult the publication put out by the federal government entitled County Business Patterns for the state and county you are interested in. It gives information for civilian jobs based on Social Security statistics, and lists businesses located in the county, where they are located, what wages are paid and how many people are employed. A new report for each state is issued every May. (See "Useful Resources" at the end of this chapter.)

Each state and county also operates its own employment research agency, which keeps vital statistics on employment within the state. You can get more detailed information about local conditions from the nearest Department of Human Resources Development (HRD) or employment agency. Try calling on some employers when you visit the area, and ask about work opportunities. You might be surprised at what is available.

If you want to live in a rural area and continue to commute to a city job, you can do so in most parts of the country. Most cities are relatively compact, and the country is not far away. Figure out how long it would take to get home from your place of employment in the city. It may take a half-hour to go the first five miles, but once you are out of the city, you may be able to go another 30 miles in the next half-hour. Many people are now moving to rural areas and getting to work by driving to a commuter train or bus station, parking there for the day and taking the commuter run into the city, thus avoiding the daily traffic jam. Decide how much time you are willing to spend commuting each day, get a map of your area and pinpoint your place of work. Then draw a circle with that point as the center that encloses the areas within your desired time limit for commuting. You then have a large area to choose from. Don't make your circle too small. If you become too concerned about your commuting time, you might end up looking at suburban property instead of real country land. Another ten minutes and you might find yourself in the heart of the backwoods. It's much closer than you think. Figure 7–1 is an example of how to plot the distances from your land to the places that are important to you.

Basically, this idea simply reverses the usual trend, which has been to live in the city and commute to a vacation home in the country. With ever-increasing mass transportation, this will become an option for a greater number of people who will realize that they can have their city income and their country relaxation simultaneously.

## Services

### Utilities—Water, Sewerage, Gas, Garbage, Electricity, Phone, Mail Delivery and Cable Television

In most areas of the country, you will have to take care of your own utility provisions. The local town will not furnish water and other services beyond its limits.

Setting up a water system and a sewage disposal system are standard country procedures, and you must determine the costs involved before buying your land. (See Chapter 4, "Is There Enough Water on the Land?" and Chapter 13, "Building and Health Codes.") If you want gas or liquid fuel, most rural areas have companies that will install a large tank behind your house that is refilled periodically by a tanker truck. You can usually get propane or diesel fuel in this manner. Talk to the local propane

**Figure 7–1. Distances from Land to Places Important to You**

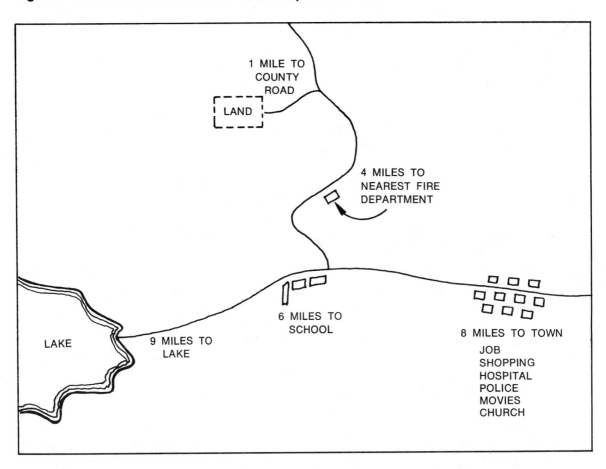

dealer about charges for setting up and servicing the system. You will then have to get appliances that use these fuels.

Do not expect a garbage truck to come by your home unless you are living in town. Most people use county and town dumps, for which there may be a small fee. In the country, you will probably recycle most of your garbage anyway.

Electricity seems to be the one thing most people can't do without. If you think you don't need it, try living without any for a while before buying land. Can you do without electric lights, a record player, television and modern appliances, including power tools? If not, you will need land near existing electric lines. Electricity is extremely expensive to bring in from far away, and for most people a gas or diesel generator is too expensive, noisy and polluting to be practical for full-time use. Before you buy, be sure you have an easement to bring in utility lines, and check into the costs involved. Only the electric company office nearest to the land can give you a complete estimate.

The cost of bringing in electricity is determined by the number of electrical appliances you have and the number of feet of line that will be needed to bring power from the nearest available source. You will get credit for each type of appliance. For example, in our area, Pacific Gas & Electric (PG&E) gives 300 feet free for lighting, 275 feet for an electric hot water heater, 75 feet for an electric refrigerator, 150 feet for an electric range, and so on. These credits are cut for second homes. PG&E charges $10.55 for each foot minus the amount of credit received for each appliance for above-ground, pole-strung wires. If you want the line buried, you will have to pay two to three times more, even if you dig your own trench. If other people living nearby want to join you in bringing in electrical lines, the cost can be shared among you.

There is always a maximum distance the electric company will string lines, even if the customer is willing to pay the entire cost. For example, in some areas of Maine, service will not be extended farther than a quarter of a mile, and in our area after one-half mile the cost jumps drastically.

You might consider installing photovoltaic cells

or water or wind generators to generate your own electricity if you are beyond the reach of the local electric company. Breakthroughs are occurring rapidly now in photovoltaic's. The price of photovoltaic cells dropped from approximately $40 per watt in the 1975 to $10 per watt in 1985 to $7 per watt in 1992, and there have been new discoveries that may drop the price even further. One new chip, known as the point contact photovoltaic cell, "shows potential to provide electricity at costs comparable to conventional power plants, such as those burning fossil fuels, in sun-rich areas like the southwestern United States," according to a report prepared by the Electric Power Research Institute. (See Appendix F for information on alternative energy.) In our home 90 percent of our electricity is produced by solar panels and a water turbine hydro powered unit in our creek.

Phone lines are often extended into areas where electricity is not provided. But check with your local phone company to see where service is given and how much it will cost to bring in phone lines to your intended home.

Mail is usually delivered to mailboxes along the public county roads, so that should not be a problem. Ask about the mail service at the nearest post office.

Cable television is often available in small towns but not usually beyond the town boundaries. Check with the local cable television company listed in the Yellow Pages.

### Fire and Police Protection

Many small towns do not have their own fire and police departments. Often fire protection is maintained on a community volunteer basis. The greatest danger of fire exists in western mountainous areas where forest fires are an annual disaster. If you intend to buy forest land, you should learn something of the history of forest fires in the area and how quickly and successfully they were contained. The local forest ranger station or farm adviser, as well as old-time residents, will have this information. In most areas, fire stations are manned only during the critical dry months. If possible, you should have a large reserve water supply and pump on your land if your area is susceptible to fires. Also trim the lower branches off trees near your house, and keep fire hazards in mind when building a house or planting near the house.

You shouldn't have much cause to call the police if you live outside the cities and suburbs. However, if you are going to be absent from your home or land for a large part of the year, the local law enforcement officers may be able to keep an eye on your place for you. If you want to keep hunters or trespassers off your land or if your land is too inaccessible for normal police protection, sometimes you can hire permanent residents to patrol it for a small fee. Your neighbors may also be willing to help you.

### Road Maintenance

Frequent maintenance of public roads is a necessity in the country. You will have endless difficulties in areas where heavy snowfalls occur if the roads are not swiftly cleared each day. You might be late for work often, and you could be prevented from leaving your house for a long time. In areas where rainfall is heavy, roads need frequent attention and may need frequent repair, depending on the type of soil under the road.

Notice how the roads look as you drive around. Ask old-time residents in the area about the quality and frequency of roadwork. You might not want to purchase a home so far away that it is the last area to be cleared each day. Consider the problems involved if you have only a dirt access road. Check with your local department of roads to see what kind of service is provided for private roads. Usually a fee is charged for private road maintenance.

## Other Considerations

### Educational Facilities
### and Cultural Attractions

If you have children, you will want to know about the schools in the area. Most children in the country are bused to a centrally located public school, and you will want to live near a bus pickup point. Usually the schools are small and have fewer facilities and teachers than city schools, but that does not mean they are not as good. Many country schools are excellent. A few private schools and "alternative schools" are appearing in the country, but they vary widely in quality. Never depend on such a school unless you determine its stability, cost and quality of education. The Chamber of Commerce and local board of education can tell you the locations of the schools in your area and the busing routes. Visit the schools, talk to the teachers and see what facilities they have. Take your children with you.

If you are interested in going to school yourself, many colleges sponsor basic extension courses in rural secondary schools. If you want an extensive variety of courses or want to attend concerts, movies or amateur theatrical and sports events, you might buy in an area near a college or university. Excellent new colleges have been built near rural towns in the past 20 years. Visit the college to see what it offers before you buy in the area. land is usually more expensive in areas where large schools and colleges are located.

### Medical Facilities

Local doctors, hospitals and veterinarians are always an asset in the country. If you are in need of ongoing medical treatment, you must be sure that good service is available in your area from doctors you can trust. Ask your present doctor if he knows a good area in which to settle where the medical facilities are reputable and not overly expensive. Do not be surprised at the informal, relaxed atmosphere in a country clinic. This does not necessarily mean the treatment is inadequate.

Two of the three principal kilers of Americans are heart attacks and strokes. In the case of both, a key factor in survival and recovery is speed of response time for emergency treatment. The consequence is that proximity to hospitals should be, for some, an important consideration in locating their country home.

### Shopping Area

If you have a large family, a nearby shopping center or general store may be a requirement. Check out the shopping facilities in your area, particularly grocery stores, drugstores and Laundromats. How are the prices? Remember that prices for nearly everything will be higher in the country.

If you are 15 miles away from the nearest store, it is a 30-mile drive to pick up groceries. In the winter this can seem like a very long distance.

### Churches and Social Organizations

Many of you will want to have the church of your choice in your new community. Look in the phone book for local churches. Attend a religious service, and talk to the religious and lay leaders and members of the congregation.

If you are interested in social groups, ask the Chamber of Commerce about clubs in the area, such as bridge, gardening and service groups. Your children may want to know about local scouting groups, agricultural clubs and athletic teams. You can visit meetings and functions of such organizations to get a feeling for the kinds of things they are doing and their receptivity to newcomers.

### Recreational Facilities

If you intend to buy a vacation home, the recreational facilities of the area will be a major consideration. The local Chamber of Commerce will have maps and brochures detailing the area's vacation resources. If you are interested in water sports, like fishing, boating and swimming, be sure you buy where public water facilities are available. Whether you are interested in hunting, golfing, skiing, mountain climbing, horseback riding, bowling, spas, movies or good restaurants, recreational facilities are rapidly expanding in rural areas, particularly where the number of seasonal residents is increasing. You do not have to buy land in a massive, expensive, planned "recreational development" to satisfy your needs. Buy yourself a piece of land centrally located in relation to the facilities you want. You will save a lot of money and have a true feeling of living in the country. For more on the disadvantages of "package deal" subdivisions, see Chapter 14, "Subdivisions and Condominiums."

## The Government As a Neighbor

Many real estate agents use the fact that land is located next to federal or state land as a selling point. You will frequently see ads stating that "property borders national forest," "property sits next to U.S. government land" or "adjoining BLM land will provide thousands of acres of recreation." Be very careful when buying such land. Any federal land under Bureau of Land Management (BLM) control can be used for grazing, logging, mining, removal of oil and gas and industrial and recreational development under the Multiple Use Classification system. You can contact BLM regarding livestock grazing at (202) 452-7742 0r fax them at (202) 452-7701.

The Bureau of land Management, an agency of the United States Department of the Interior, controls the use of more than 450 million acres of public lands. You can phone BLM real estate at (202) 452-7779 or their fax number is (202) 452-7708. Before buying property adjoining any of these holdings, write or go to the local BLM office (see Appendix B for addresses) or office of the Department of the Interior and ask for a full report on the present and intended future use of that government land. It will have a map indicating all uses planned for the land for the next five years. Examine it thoroughly. What kind of activities are planned in the area near your land? Logging, mining or a large influx of tourists can destroy your peace and quiet. If the land is to be preserved and presents no problems as a neighbor, however, you may actually find yourself with a backyard of thousands of acres in which to play.

The same problems exist if your land adjoins a national park or other public lands. You must be extremely careful when investigating privately owned land for sale *within the boundaries* of federally owned or state-owned land. The government may have offered to buy or trade the property for government land located elsewhere to unify its holdings. Eventually the owners of that land could be forced to sell through condemnation. (See Chapter 15, "Eminent Domain and Condemnation.")

## Local Politics

You can get a good sense of the political climate in a community by reading the local newspaper, listening to the nearest radio station and attending a board of supervisors' meeting. These meetings are open to the public and announced in advance in the local paper and at the local courthouse or city hall. They are informative and a change of pace from big-city politics. The board legislates and approves the county budget, local improvements and appeals for zoning changes and variances. The governing bodies and local media are better indicators of the flavor of life in the community than anything else.

## A Sample Report on the Area

See the example of a Final Subdivision Public Report (Figure 14–3) in Chapter 14, "Subdivisions and Condominiums," to get an idea of what kind of information on the land you should look for. The report includes facts on geological conditions, water, fire protection, electricity, gas, telephone service, sewage disposal, streets and roads, public transportation, schools and shopping facilities.

## Noise

Many people buy land without realizing that they are near enough to a road to hear the sound of every car and truck that passes by. Heavy trucks, particularly industrial or logging trucks, often run only on weekdays or late at night, so if you look for land on holidays and weekends and do not spend at least one night on the property before you buy, you may not realize the full impact of the traffic.

Every sound in the country is greatly magnified. It comes out of the silence like a roar. If you live near a steep grade, the big trucks will be downshifting as they crawl up the hill. If your house is on the outside of a curve in a road, it might be directly in the path of oncoming headlights. When you look at property, stop to listen for sounds and see how the place is situated in relation to nearby roads.

If you live on a mountaintop, you will hear everything that goes on for miles around—traffic, chain saws, construction noises. Valleys, by comparison, are relatively quiet because the mountains or hills on either side muffle the sounds. The noise factor is a major disadvantage to living on top of a ridge in a populous rural area.

Even if no road is close enough to bother your sleep now, one may be planned for the near future. Most areas have official county and city maps that indicate future street and road development. Talk to the people at the planning department and the department of public roads in your county or the state highway commission to determine where new construction will take place. With the increasing rural population, new road construction is proceeding at a rapid pace and represents a threat to the land buyer in terms of greater noise and possible condemnation. (See Chapter 15, "Eminent Domain and Condemnation.")

Living in snow country exposes you to the new menace of the snowmobile's roar. Unless you intend to have one, you probably will not want to be anywhere near a snowmobile road. Many such roads are being developed throughout the country, officially and unofficially, and you might want to determine if any will be in the neighborhood of your new home.

Not until I spent some time as a caretaker on a large ranch did I realize the importance of avoiding a home under an airplane flight path. Every evening as I was quietly enjoying the beautiful sunset, a jet would roar directly overhead and spread its dirty exhaust across the sky. I made certain when we bought our land that no flight paths existed overhead. Most maps will tell you where military bases and public and private airports are located. You will have to determine how their presence affects your land.

Be aware also of private landing strips on nearby farms and ranches. Many wealthy landowners now have their own planes and runways. Don't think this isn't much of a problem. An airplane is a toy in the hands of many private pilots. Even when used only for business, a low-flying plane that is flown directly over your place several times a day could make your life miserable. Ask your future neighbors if planes or jets are a problem.

Never buy land within sight or sound of a gravel extracting operation or a rock-crushing business.

## Smells and Smoke

Lumber mills, paper mills, factories of all kinds, asphalt plants, garbage dumps and rendering plants are some of the air polluters that you do not want as country neighbors. Legislation controlling air pollution is slow in coming, so don't buy land under the false hope that the local mill will be forced to close down. I have seen rural areas with worse smog than any city I have been in. When we bought our land, we made certain that the two local lumber mills that had recently been closed down had no intention of reopening. During the period when they were going full blast, a clear blue sky was rarely seen.

Look at local maps to determine where such pollution sources exist in your community. Find out from the Chamber of Commerce or planning commission where new industries intend to locate, and check the zoning to see if industrial development is permitted in the area. (See Chapter 12, "Zoning Laws.")

## Pollen

Allergies can cause people to move from one location to another. When relocating to the country, remember that with the increase of vegetation comes an increase in certain types of pollens and molds. The amounts and kinds of pollen in the air are highly variable. Publications and data are available to help you learn about the kinds and amounts of pollens you may encounter in your new area. Check the local library, or write to the American Academy of Allergy and Immunology, 611 East Wells Street, Milwaukee, WI 53202. For a fee, a computerized pollen guide is available by zip code from Hollister Steir Laboratories. Their toll free number is (800) 541-5707.

## Crop Dusting

Crop dusting is a method of spraying insecticides from small planes flying low over field crops. The poisons are easily carried in the wind to neighboring lands and can be a threat to the health of members of your family, particularly the very young, the very old, the ill and pregnant women.

## Useful Resources

### Making a Living
If you are thinking of making your living from the land or conducting your own business in the area, the following publications will be helpful.

From:   Superintendent of Documents
        U.S. Government Printing Office
        Washington, DC 20402

*Forest Owner's Guide to Timber Investments*,
    S/N 001-000-04540-7                $7.00
*Financial Management: How to Make a Go
    of Your Business*, S/N 045-000-00233-1 $2.50
*Starting and Managing a Business from Your
    Home*, S/N 045-000-00232-2         $1.75
*Rural Development Perspectives*,
    S/N 701-031-00000-8                $6.50
*Residents of Farms and Rural Areas; 1991*,
    S/N 803-005-00073-7                $4.00
*Income Opportunities in Special Forest
    Products—Self-help Guide for Rural
    Entrepreneurs*, S/N 001-001-00653-0 $13.00
*Financial Management: How to Make A Go Of
    Your Business*, S/N 045-000-00233-1  $2.50

From:   U.S. Department of Commerce
        National Technical information Service
        Springfield, VA 22161

BLA 74 *Entrepreneurship Theories and Their Use in Rural Development* $8.00
AIB 574 *Rural Land Transfer Survey* $5.50

From: ERS NASS
P.O. Box 1608
Rockville, MD 20850

RDRR 72 *The Farm Entrepreneurial Population*, SB 782 $5.50

From: R.Woods
Consumer Information Center-A
P.O. Box 100
Pueblo, CO 81002
URL: http://www.access.gpo.gov

"Starting and Managing a Business from Your Home," 144X $1.75
"The Small Business Handbook," 573X free
"Guide to Business Credit for Women, Minorities and Small Businesses," 458X $0.50
"Financial Management: How to Make a Go of Your Business," 143X $2.50
"Money Matters," 422X free
"Consumer's Resource Handbook" free

From: Federal Trade Commission
Washington, D.C. 20580

"Work at Home Schemes"

For a list of publications written especially for small-scale farm producers, write to:

Appropriate Technology Transfer for Rural Areas (ATTRA)
P.O. Box 3657
Fayetteville, AR 72702
(800) 346-9140

In 1987, the Appropriate Technology Transfer for Rural Areas program (ATTRA) began to offer free technical assistance to farmers about sustainable agriculture and low-input farming. ATTRA is managed by the National Center for Appropriate Technology. Their information is available free to anyone. Sustainable agriculture techniques can lower farm production costs, improve soil and water quality, increase farm productivity and enhance wildlife habitats.

If you are thinking of retiring to the country, there are free booklets that can be ordered from:

American Association of Retired Persons
Consumer Affairs Program Department
1909 K St., N.W.
Washington, DC 20049

An encouraging book for those looking to start a new life in the country is:

*Country Bound* $19.95

Published by
Communication Creativity
P.O. Box 909
Buena Vista, CO 81211
(719) 395-8659

**Employment Services**
Each state and county has offices to provide job counseling, testing and placement. Consult your local telephone directory for your local Employment Development Department.

An extremely useful publication for anyone interested in caretaking a place in the country in order to learn rural skills and investigate the area is *The Caretaker Gazette*. It is full of caretaking opportunities across the United States and is published bimonthly. A one-year subscription is $24.00 and is available from:

The Caretaker Gazette
2380 NE Ellis Way, Suite C16
Pullman, WA 99163–5303
Voice: (509) 332-0806
E-mail: garydunn@pullman.com

**Other Sources of Information an Area and Its Facilities**

*Chambers of Commerce or Visitors' Bureaus*
Look for listings in the local telephone directory.

*City or County Agencies*
The county or city agency in charge of promoting the area's assets is one of the first places you should visit for information on employment, recreational facilities, schools, cultural and social activities, shopping and medical facilities, and churches. Take a bunch of their free brochures.

*Local Newspapers and the Yellow Pages*
These will give you an idea of the type of businesses in the area and a feel for what the local attitudes and social life are like.

*Utility Company*
Only the local power company can give you accurate information on the availability and cost of supplying electricity and gas. It also has its own studies of population growth in the area and can give you some predictions on where the future growth is to occur and how soon.

*Telephone Company*
Information on available installation and costs.

*Board of Education*
Information on educational facilities and busing service of public and private schools.

*Forest Ranger Station and Farm Adviser*
Information on available fire protection service.

*Department of Roads*
The county, city and state road departments have information on when roads are cleared and whether private roads can be cleared by the public road crews.

*Small Business Administration (SBA)*
This is a federal agency in charge of providing information on how to commence and operate a small business. It also makes loans for this purpose. Write for the address of your local office or look in your local telephone directory for SBA field offices under United States Government. Almost any type of business you can think of is covered in SBA pamphlets. Write and request a list of available pamphlets in the following series:

"How to raise Money for a Small Business"
"How to Start a Small Business"
"How to Start a Home Based Business"

Address all requests and inquiries to:

U.S. Small Business Administration
Washington, DC 20416
Voice: (800) 8-ASK-SBA
Fax: (202) 205-7064
TDD: (202) 205-7333
BBS: (800) 859- INFO (2400 baud)
(202) 205-7265(in D.C.)
(800) 697-INFO (2400 baud)
(202) 205-9600 (in D.C.)
URL: http://www.sba.gov

You can get any information about the results of census activities in each state from any of the field offices of the Department of Commerce located in each state. Look in your local telephone directory under United States Government. The department also has resources that you can use in the office or purchase that will give you just about any kind of information you desire, from the history of the population growth to the age of the residents.

You can contact the Federal Information Center for information about how to contact *any* federal agency. They can be reached at (800) 688-9889.

# The Land
# and the Law

# CHAPTER 8

# Land Descriptions and Surveys

*Cursed be he that removeth his neighbor's land-mark. And the people shall say, amen.*

—Deut. 22:17

*Remove not the ancient landmark which thy fathers have set.*

—Ps. 22:28

Never purchase a piece of land without being sure where its surveyed boundaries are located.

Throughout history most problems of land ownership have arisen from boundary disputes. Precise surveying was begun by the Egyptians nearly 7,000 years ago, and several references to boundary marking can be found in the Bible, but even today most land has not been accurately surveyed and boundary disputes continue to be a major problem for the landowner. The three most common areas of

litigation for rural property owners involve easements, boundary lines and water rights.

Laws require only that a deed contain a legal "description" of the land which defines the parcel in such a way that it cannot be confused with any other piece of land. However, this description does not tell you where the boundaries are precisely located on the ground. That is done by a survey, based on the land description. Because surveys are expensive, many rural parcels are sold without them, despite their importance to the buyer. I will explain why you should demand to have a survey taken on land before you buy after I explain some of the principles involved in land descriptions and surveys.

In the United States parcels are legally described in one of the following three ways:

1. By reference to section, township and range, which are part of the United States Government Survey or *rectangular survey system.*
2. By metes and bounds, also known as the monument and marker system.
3. By reference to a recorded map, plat or tract system.

## Descriptions by Reference to a Section, Township and Range

The U.S. Government, under the direction of the U.S. Surveyor General, began to survey its original public lands in 1784, using the rectangular survey system (the cadastral system), which divided the land into sections, townships and ranges. Large portions of land were broken up into rectangles on a map, then located and marked on the ground by a survey team. By using these marked points, any parcel within a rectangle can be precisely described and located today.

The U.S. rectangular survey system is the most common form of land description used in the country today. Twenty-nine states use it, including Alabama, Alaska, Florida, Mississippi and all of the states north of the Ohio River and west of the Mississippi except Texas. It was the form used when we purchased our land, and I will use it throughout this book.

The description in our deed states that we own

The South Half of the Northwest Quarter of
Section 21, Township 4 North,
Range 2 East,
Mt. Diablo Meridian.

The government started its survey by dividing the land into portions, each of which was given a vertical line running north and south, called the *principal meridian,* and a horizontal line running east and west, perpendicular to the principal meridian, called the *base line.* There are 36 principal meridians in different parts of the country. (See Figure 8–1.) Each meridian is individually named; for example, the Mount Diablo Meridian, Indian

**Figure 8–1.  Principal Meridians of the U.S. Rectangular Survey System**

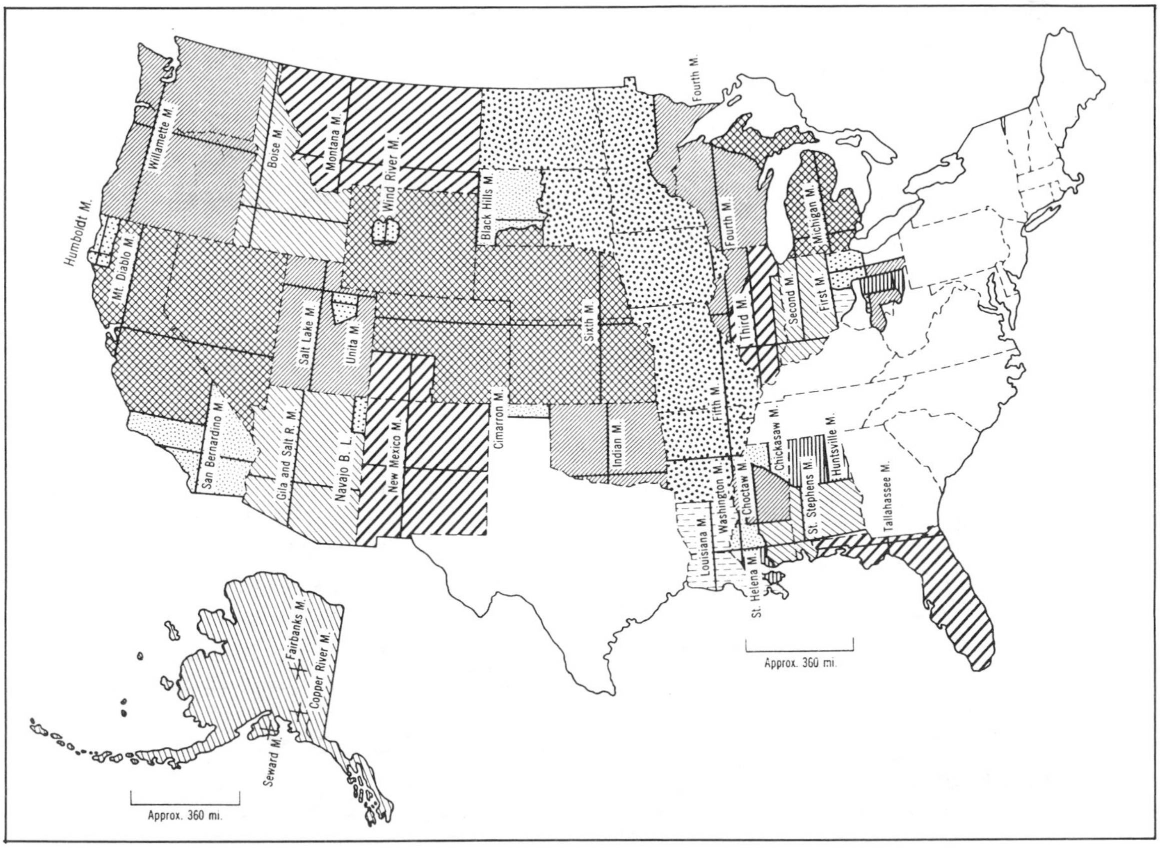

**Figure 8–2. Dividing into Ranges**

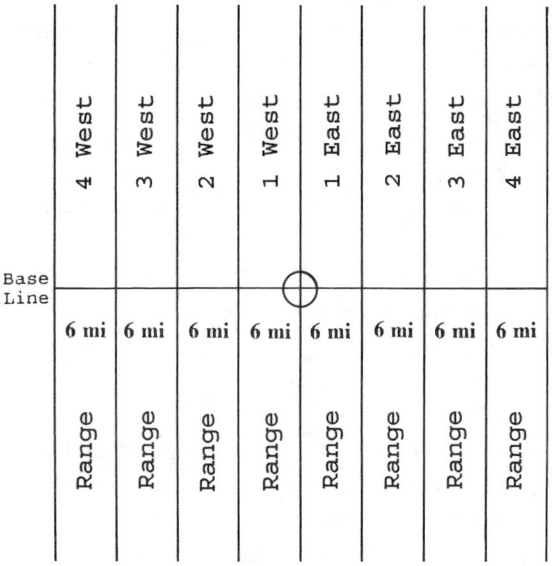

Meridian and Second Principal Meridian. A description that includes the name of the principal meridian locates the area in which the land is situated. You then work backward in the description.

On both sides of the principal meridian, the land is cut into equal strips six miles wide called *ranges.* (See Figure 8–2.) On both sides of the base line, the land is cut into equal strips six miles wide called *townships.* (See Figure 8–3.) Together these strips form a "land checkerboard." Each square of the "checkerboard" is called a *township* and has boundary lines six miles long on all four sides. (See

Figure 8–4.) The range and township strips are numbered outward from the meridian and base lines and can be used in the same way as you use a highway map or atlas to find any township.

In Figure 8–4, I indicate the township that contains our land. It is a square located two ranges to the east of the principal meridian and four townships to the south of the base line. Thus, it is described as "Township 4 South, Range 2 East."

Because a township is a square six miles on a side, it contains 36 square miles (area = length × width). Thus, each township is divided into 36 one-square-mile *sections,* each containing approximately 640 acres and having sides about one mile long. (See Figure 8–5.) (An acre is a square approximately 208.71 feet long on each side with an area of 43,560 square feet or 4,840 square yards.) Because of the primitive methods used for the original surveys, many sections may actually be severely distorted and contain much less, or much more, than 640 acres, the theoretical number of acres in a section. The sections in each township are numbered, starting in the northeast corner and moving alternately right to left, then left to right, concluding in the southeast corner. Figure 8–5 indicates how Township 4 South, Range 2 East is divided into 36 sections. Section 21, in which our land is located, is shaded.

Each 640-acre section is then quartered into 160-acre parcels, called *quarter sections,* designated as the northeast, southeast, northwest, and

**Figure 8–3. Dividing into Townships**

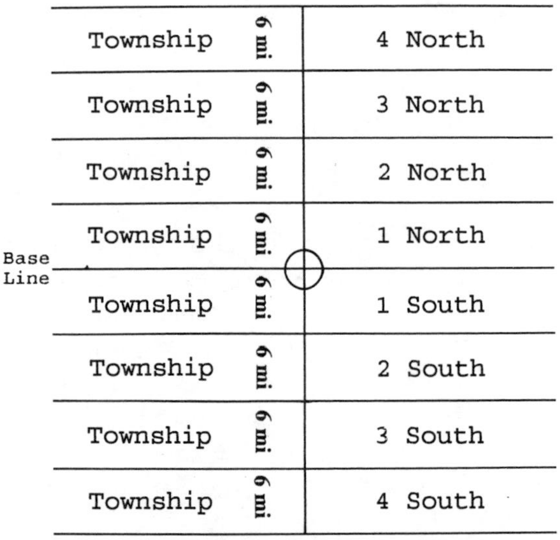

**Figure 8–4. Resulting Townships**

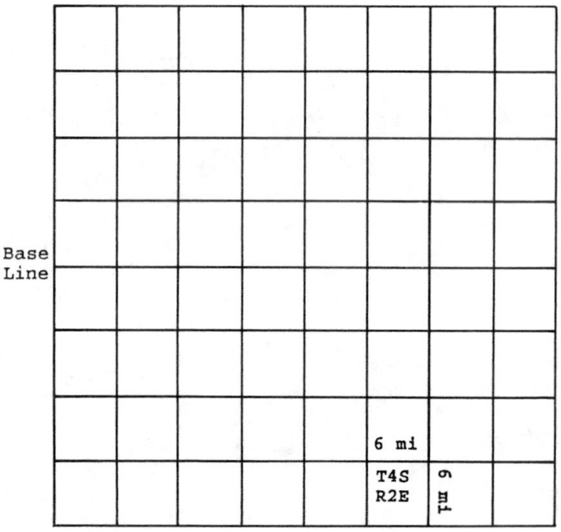

**Figure 8–5. Dividing Townships into Sections**

| 6 | 5 | 4 | 3 | 2 | 1 |
|---|---|---|---|---|---|
| 7 | 8 | 9 | 10 | 11 | 12 |
| 18 | 17 | 16 | 15 | 14 | 13 |
| 19 | 20 | 21 | 22 | 23 | 24 |
| 30 | 29 | 28 | 27 | 26 | 25 |
| 31 | 32 | 33 | 34 | 35 | 36 |

← 6 MILES →

6 MILES (vertical)

southwest quarters. Quarter sections are then quartered into parcels, called "40s" or *square forties,* since each one contains approximately 40 acres. A square forty can then be quartered into four 10-acre parcels, which might be subdivided further into four 2½-acre parcels, and so forth. Figure 8-6 indicates the possible subdivisions of Section 21. The location of our 80 acres is the shaded portion of the section.

When we found the land we wanted to buy, the real estate agent gave us a copy of its description as it would appear in our deed. Using a large quadran-

**Figure 8–6. Dividing a Section into Quarters and Smaller Parcels**

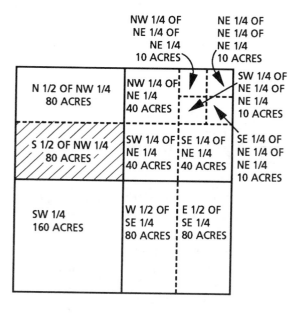

gle map, based on the U.S. rectangular survey that covered the proper meridian and township, we located Section 21. Taking a pencil, we quartered the section and then halved the northwest quarter horizontally. Thus, we located the south half of the northwest quarter of Section 21. The map depicted geographical land features, and we could see what roads and creeks went through the land parcel. (Figure 9–1 in Chapter 9, "Easement Rights," is a copy of what we saw on the map.) Thus, without actually finding the corners and walking the boundaries, we got an approximate idea of what we would be buying. By superimposing the map over an aerial photograph of the same scale, we saw a more accurate picture of the land.

You will notice that Section 21 in Figure 9–1 is not a perfect rectangle. Because of the curvature of the earth or inaccurate measurements at the time of the original survey, the sections may not be equal in acreage. For instance, our land seems to include 80 acres. In fact, on the ground the area covered only 78½ acres. With large parcels, often slightly more acreage is advertised than is actually sold. You can find out the true amount by referring to a legal survey of the land. A survey might already exist and be filed in a volume entitled *Record of Surveys, Book of Maps* or *Official Records* in the county or local recorder's office, or the seller might have a copy of a survey. In cases where no survey presently exists, you will need to be protected in the contract of sale if a subsequent survey shows that less land is present than is advertised. (See clause 2, clause 3, and clause 17[b] of the Model Contract of Sale in Chapter 27.) If you are buying land advertised as 40 acres at $1,000 an acre and, in fact, you are only receiving 38½ acres, such a safety clause could save you $1,500. Most sellers cover themselves by indicating that the acreage is approximate, for example, 40+ acres.

In the 1800s, the Government land Office (now known as the Bureau of Land Management) surveyed each area of the United States where the rectangular survey system exists. The purpose of these surveys was to compile township maps. The maps were first divided into townships and sections on the drawing board. Then the government land office contracted out to surveyors who went throughout the country and established and marked corners, generally every one-half mile around the perimeter of sections. They did this until they completed a survey of each township. They then completed a township plat that was returned to the U.S. government. Once approved, it was then the basis for issuing land patents to the original homesteaders.

These numbered and lettered markers are the starting points for private surveyors hired to locate subdivided parcels within the sections. The surveyors from the Government Land Office took thorough survey notes, called *field notes*, that are used by subsequent surveyors to find section corner markers.

You can get a copy of the original survey maps and notes indicating the location of section markers in your area from the BLM office in the state. (See Appendix B for addresses of BLM offices.) You might also be able to get a copy of these notes and maps from the county surveyor or county engineer. However, you will probably only need the latest survey on which is indicated the location of monuments and how they are marked or *scribed*; for example, a blaze on a tree or a metal pipe in the ground.

## Descriptions by Metes and Bounds

Although most of the United States is within the U.S. rectangular survey system, many deeds describe land using the method of *metes and bounds*. *Metes* are measures of length, such as inches, feet and yards. *Bounds* are natural and artificial boundaries, such as rivers and roads or previously established boundaries. This system, which has been described as a treasure hunt, follows a course from one fixed point, called a monument or marker, to other fixed points until the area of land is entirely enclosed.

In a description by metes and bounds, a fixed starting point that can be easily identified is found on the ground—an unusual tree, a pile of rocks, a creek, the mouth of a stream, a known and fixed point or some other object. If a unique object cannot be found, the position is identified by a measurement from the nearest government land corner or some other accepted property control. Other similarly identified objects must be found at various points around the land so that a boundary line can be formed that encloses the area. Often the markers are highly variable, such as rivers or dirt roads, or impermanent, such as rock piles or trees. You may have heard stories of a landowner moving boundary markers to increase the size of his land. It is easy to get away with such tactics under this kind of system. For this reason, a metes-and-bounds descrip-

tion should be used only as a last resort. The system is usually used when irregular land shapes are sold and in areas that have not been laid out according to the U.S. rectangular survey system.

Below is an example of a metes-and-bounds description.

> Beginning at a point that is 500 feet South and 200 feet East of the Northwest corner of Section 5, Township 2 South, Range 3 West;
> Thence North 100 feet, thence East 200 feet to the West boundary of Jim Jones's property described in Book 60 of Deeds, page 102 of the Official Records of Bloomingdale County; Thence South along said line 100 feet; Thence West 200 feet to the point of beginning.

This tract as described contains approximately 200 acres.

Regardless of how the parcel is described, you must be able to find the boundaries of your land on the ground by using the description. The description must describe a boundary that totally encloses the parcel. That is, it must start and end at the same point. If this is not the case, do not buy the land until the description is legally perfected.

## Map, Tract or Plat System

The third common method used to describe a parcel of land is by reference to another recorded instrument that identifies the land and usually contains a survey. You will probably not encounter this type of description unless you purchase land as part of a large rural or second-home subdivision or a minor subdivision or parcel-split. In that case, all the lots should already be surveyed and recorded with the county recorder in a final parcel map, subdivision map, tract map or plat. (Figure 14–2 in Chapter 14, "Subdivisions and Condominiums," is an example of a parcel map.) Each parcel within the subdivision is described by referring to its location on the recorded map. For example:

> The real property in the County of Goshen, State of Arkansas, described as Lot 80, Happy Home Subdivision (per map recorded July 2, 1988, at page 46 of Book 8 of Maps), Office of the County Recorder of Goshen County.

If you look up page 46 in Book 8 of Maps you will find a map of the subdivision divided into parcels or lots. Be sure the lot number on the map corresponds to the lot you think you are purchasing. The subdivision map will show the location of markers on the ground that delineate the boundaries of each parcel. Using the map, locate the markers for your lot, and you will see what you are buying. You should purchase a copy of the recorded map from the local office where it is recorded.

If your land is described by reference to another document, the document should be properly recorded with the county recorder and must definitely identify your parcel of land.

## Legal Surveys

A legal survey is made by a team of licensed surveyors or civil engineers who carefully lay out in bearings (angles) and distances the exact location of the property on the ground. The survey is based on the description of the parcel given in the deed. So that you will have no delusions as to where your boundaries lie, be sure that they are precisely surveyed and marked on the ground by a legal survey.

An example of metes and bounds description is shown in Figure 8–7. Trace out the boundary line in the illustration by following the description. The parcel of land taking in the northeast quarter of the northeast quarter of Section 21 goes to the road, giving it an irregular shape. A description by metes and bounds of this land could read like this:

> Beginning at the Southwest corner of the Northeast Quarter of the Northeast Quarter of Section 21, Township 4 South, Range 2 East, Mt. Diablo Meridian; proceed a distance of 1,320 feet North along the western line of said Northeast Quarter of the Northeast Quarter of Section 21 to the Northwest corner of the Northeast Quarter of the Northeast Quarter of Section 21 a distance of 1,535 feet to the paved county road, the County Road; thence southerly along the road a distance of 2,012 feet to the southern line of the Northwest Quarter of Section 22; thence west along the southerly line of the Northwest Quarter of the Northwest Quarter of Section 22 a distance of 2,310 feet to the Point of Beginning.

**Figure 8–7. Example of Metes-and-Bounds Description**

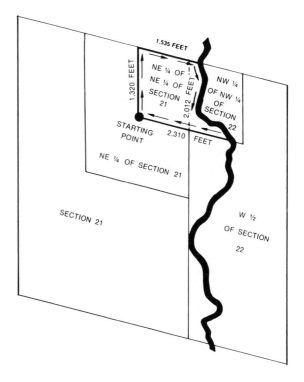

An example of a different type of metes and bounds survey description is

> Beginning at corner No. 1, a hemlock post, 4 in. square, 24 in. above ground, located on the Takotna Highway about ¼ mile southeasterly from its intersection with the left bank of Kuskokwim River and in approximate latitude 62°52' N., longitude 155°40'W. Corner No. 2 of U.S. Survey 999 bears N. 26°59' W., 327.6 ft.

## The Survey and Your Land Purchase

If the seller or real estate agent has a copy of a survey in his or her possession that he or she claims identifies the boundaries of the land for sale, check these points:

- Was the survey conducted by a licensed surveyor or registered civil engineer?

- Is it recorded in the recorder's office as an official survey of the land?
- By using it, can you locate on the ground exactly where the boundaries are? Have permanent markers been placed in the ground by the surveyor and/or have the boundary lines been flagged?

In most cases, only the corners of the property are marked with permanent stakes. Sometimes, a line will be flagged, that is, plastic ribbons tied on trees or bushes or spiked into the ground all along the line. Often trees will be blazed at certain points of the surveyed line. *Blazing* means cutting a notch out of a tree, usually with an axe, that will last as a permanent marker. If you can locate all the corners, you might be able to estimate the boundary lines fairly accurately yourself with a compass, a tape, a flag on a tall post and a friend or two. However, if an important part of the property you are buying, such as a spring, creek, road or house, appears to be close to a boundary line, you should definitely get a licensed surveyor to run the line between the corner points before you buy.

If no survey of the land exists, you can only estimate from a map where the boundaries lie. When 1 inch on a map equals 1,000 feet on the ground, it only takes the thickness of a pencil lead to put a valuable stream either on or off the property.

Surveys are expensive. The average fee in our area is $600 a day for a two-person crew. The rates vary across the country from $75 to $150 an hour for a two-man crew, which is the most common-sized crew used for private surveys. The total cost depends on the amount of time it takes to find the corners, run the boundaries and complete the office research, calculations and mapping, as well as other technical details. If no surveys have been done in the area around the land and the locations of marked section corners or other starting points are far away, the job could take a week or more and cost more than $5,000. Often large sections of land in rural areas have been sparsely or inaccurately surveyed. The job also will take longer if the terrain is rugged, if the parcel is large or if you want the surveyors to run and mark the entire length of the boundary lines rather than just stake out the corners. Always go to the local surveyor and ask what he or she knows about the land. You can find surveyors by looking in the Yellow Pages under "Surveyors—Land." A local surveying firm will give you an estimate of what a total survey would cost

or the cost of just flagging a line. It can also calculate the acreage you are buying once the survey is complete. It will also tell you if any surveys have been done on the total property or along any of its boundary lines. You might also need a road easement surveyed, and the firm can tell you the cost of that service as well.

If you want a guarantee that you are getting what you are paying for, you must demand a legal survey before you buy a parcel of land. If you have a choice between a civil engineer and a licensed surveyor, I recommend using a licensed surveyor, because they are specialists in their field. Sellers should pay to have a survey done if one does not already exist. Naturally, sellers will be reluctant to provide you with a survey if it will cost them any money. But sometimes they have already added the estimated cost of a survey into their asking price, anticipating that the buyer will demand a survey. Thus, in reality, you are already paying for it.

In many cases, a seller will state that the price will have to be increased if the buyer wants a legal survey. If you are certain that you want the land and the purchase price is otherwise satisfactory, you should insist on a survey and pay the seller the cost involved. You will get your money back when you sell the land, because property is more valuable when it is surveyed. It is also easier to sell. But don't give in to the seller without a fight. At least, try to get him or her to pay half of the survey cost.

I have encountered instances where the real estate agent paid for a survey to make a sale to a demanding buyer. An agent would rather make half a commission than none at all. If the seller is hesitant, never hesitate to ask the agent to get the survey done.

A few states have laws that prohibit a seller from conveying land without a legally recorded survey. Most subdivision laws governing the creation of new parcels require surveys of each parcel to be sold. The Model Contract of Sale in Chapter 27 has protective clauses in it that make the closing of the deal subject to buyer's approval of a legal survey, so the buyer will know how much land he or she is acquiring and where the boundary lines are. (See clause 2, clause 3, clause 16[b] and clause 17[b] of the Model Contract and the accompanying explanation in Chapter 27.)

You will undoubtedly encounter real estate agents who will tell you that it is not customary to get land surveyed in the area and that your neighbors agree on where the property lines are. For such an agreement to be legally binding, there must be a recorded boundary line agreement in the county recorder's office. The agent will point out to you where the approximate boundaries of the property are. Unfortunately, many people who buy land on this basis find out later that the boundaries are not where the agent thought they were. Several years ago in our area a highly publicized lawsuit was initiated against a well-established real estate agent in town who sold the same waterfall to three different land buyers. Had the buyers demanded surveys before they bought, this would have been avoided.

As a general rule, never buy land without a condition in the contract giving you the right to approve a survey prior to the close of escrow. Then see that you have a survey done if there is any question in your mind about the location of essential features of your intended purchase, such as a house site, creek, spring or grove of trees.

**Measurements**

Following is a list of measurements commonly used by surveyors with their definitions:

*Measurements Used in the Rectangular Survey*

   Township = 36 square miles = 6 miles on each side.

   Section = 1 square mile = 640 acres = 5,280 feet on a side.

   Quarter-section = 160 acres = 2,640 feet on a side.

*Measurements That Might Be Used in Any Type of Survey*

   1 link = 7.92 inches.

   1 rod = 16.5 feet = 25 links = 5.5 yards.

   1 chain = 66 feet = 4 rods.

   1 pole = 1 rod.

   1 mile = 5,280 feet = 80 chains = 52.8 engineer's chains = 320 rods.

   1 furlong= 40 rods.

   1 acre = 10 square chains = 1/640 of a square mile = 43,560 square feet = 4,840 square yards = 160 square rods. If it is a *square acre* it will be    208.71 feet on a side.

These measurements are used in old surveys. More recent surveys are conducted with a steel tape and electronic measuring instruments, rather than a chain.

Even more recently, modern technology has re-

**Figure 8–8. Measurements Taken as Though Ground Were Flat**

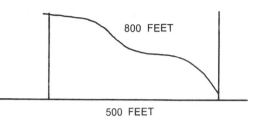

placed the more traditional measuring tapes, compasses and solar transits with electronic instruments. Microwave, light wave, laser beam, photogrammetry and gyroscopic orientations are among the new, high-tech equipment bringing changes to an occupation dating back to biblical times. A surveyor today often goes out into the field with thousands of dollars' worth of equipment to make the most accurate survey possible. The latest technology being used involves utilizing satellite pictures to determine the location of boundary lines. This method does not, however, mean that it is not necessary to locate the boundary lines on the ground.

Measurements are taken on the ground without regard for height variations in the earth's surface. Thus, if the measurement is a line 500 feet long it is taken as if measuring along a level water surface.

In Figure 8–8, the 800-foot walking distance is measured as 500 feet because the measurement is taken as though it were along a level water surface. If it were not done this way, surveys and land descriptions would be even more ambiguous and fluctuating than they are at the present time.

**Common Surveying Terms**

Following is a list of terms commonly used by surveyors with their definitions:

- *bearing tree*—A marked tree used as a corner accessory; its distance and direction from the corner being recorded. Bearing trees are identified by prescribed marks cut into their trunks; the species and sizes of the trees are also recorded. The marks are made by blazing the trees.

- *corner*—A point on the earth, determined by the surveying process, that defines an extremity on a boundary.

- *field notes*—The official written record of a survey conducted by any surveyor and used by the surveyor to draft his or her final map, which becomes the official record of the survey. In many areas this map will he recorded with field notes on it at the county recorder's office.

- *meander line*—A traverse of the margin of a permanent natural body of water or any line that meanders, for example, along a road, creek or lake.
- *monument*—The physical object that marks the location of a corner point.
- *Original Survey*—A cadastral survey that creates land boundaries and marks them for the first time.
- *plat*—A graphic representation drawn to scale depicting the actual survey as described in the official field notes.
- *resurvey*—Cadastral survey to identify and re-mark the boundaries of lands that were established by an earlier survey.
- *traverse*—A sequence of lengths and directions of lines connecting a series of stations that are field points on the ground.
- *witness corner*—A monumented point usually set back on the true line survey near a corner point that cannot be physically occupied or that falls at a place subject to destruction by the elements. The witness corner is then a reference to the true corner point.

# 9 Easement Rights

Most of the country land we looked at was located some distance away from a public road. One or more people usually owned land between the property and the road. This was true of the land we bought, which is a mile in from the public county road with access to it by a single private dirt road. The dirt access road passes through three individually owned parcels. Before we signed any papers, we wanted to be guaranteed that we would have a legal right to cross the private land between the county road and our place. In legal language, we wanted a *deeded easement* for ingress and egress.

Easement conflicts frequently cause legal disputes both in and out of court, but there is no reason why you should have any problems if you do a thorough job of investigating and negotiating before you buy. When you are shown a piece of land with no direct access to a public road, the first thing you should do is ask the agent if there are deeded easements to it. Ask him to show you a map that identifies all intervening parcels and their owners. If he tells you there are no existing deeded easements to the land, then it is presently worthless. What value is land if you don't have a legal right to get to it? As foolish as it may seem, people have unknowingly bought such land in the past and will continue to do so.

An agent may tell you that it is okay; there is a prescriptive easement to the land or some other type of unrecorded easement, such as an easement by necessity. These kinds of easements are not binding until after they have been granted by a court of law; then the judgment granting such an easement will appear in the public records. If your agent cannot show you a written recorded easement, then no legal easement presently exists. Getting a written recorded easement granted in a court of law is not automatic. Never rely on an agent's promise that you can get one. Even if you can eventually get an easement, you may have to spend many months, perhaps even years, involved in costly litigation. (See the section entitled "Unrecorded Easements," later in this chapter.)

Never buy land without deeded access rights to get to it.

## Acquiring an Easement

In most cases, the seller already has a proper easement. If he or she does not, then you should demand that the seller or the real estate agent obtain a legal right of way from each owner of the intervening properties. Once you have a recorded easement in your deed, it will last forever in your favor unless stated otherwise in the description. Landowners will probably charge for the right to cross their land with a vehicle. Sellers who have to pay for an easement will undoubtedly add that cost onto the total purchase price. Sometimes the real estate agent will urge you to buy the land, assuring you that he or she can get the right-of-way permission you need at a later date. However, you should buy only *after* you get the easement, not before.

## How To Check the Deeded Access on a Map

You will understand the concept and importance of an easement if you study the maps in Figures 9–1 and 9–2. I will use our own situation to show you how to check an easement description against a quadrangle map. Figure 9–1 is a portion of the

quadrangle map of our area and is the type of map found in any real estate agent's office. (Chapter 8, "Land Descriptions and Surveys," explains how this quadrangle map was created.) Figure 9–2 shows the same area as Figure 9–1, but land features, roads and houses are indicated. The numbered areas in Figure 9–2 are parcels of land owned by private parties. These parcels do not necessarily follow the regular section and quarter divisions in Figure 9–1 because land parcels are split up in many different ways.

Before signing anything we asked the real estate agent to type up a description of the easement we were to get exactly as it would appear in our purchase contract and deed. According to what he typed, we were purchasing:

**Figure 9–1. Easement Example**

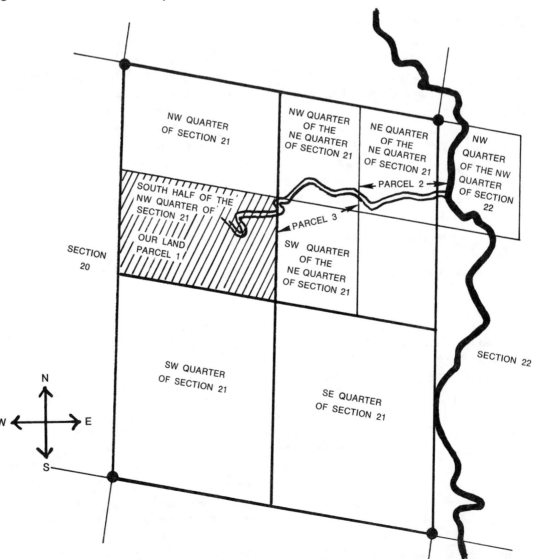

**Figure 9–2. Easement Problems**

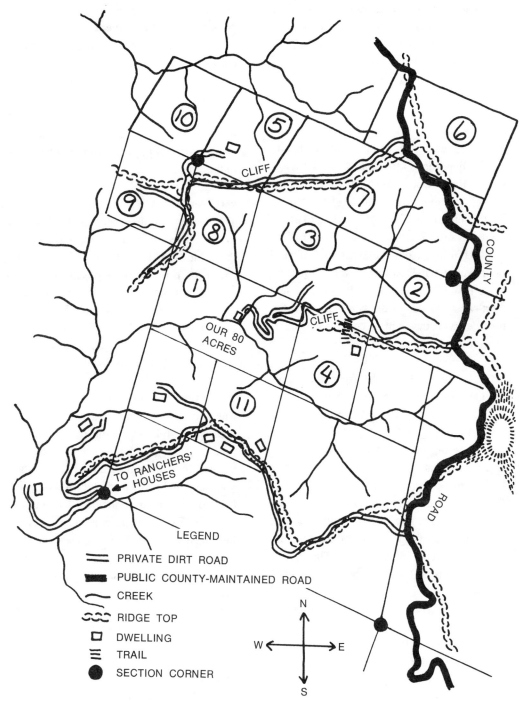

That real property situated in the County of Humboldt, State of California, described as follows:

PARCEL ONE

The South Half of the Northwest Quarter of Section 21, Township 4 South, Range 2 East, Humboldt Meridian.

PARCEL TWO

A non-exclusive easement 60 feet in width over the existing road located in the Southerly portion of the Northeast Quarter of the Northeast Quarter of Section 21 and in the Southerly portion of the Northwest Quarter of the Northwest Quarter of Section 22, in

Township 4 South, Range 2 East, Humboldt Meridian, and extending from the West line of said Northeast Quarter of the Northeast Quarter, Easterly to the West line of the County Road, together with the right to convey said easement to others.

PARCEL THREE

A non-exclusive easement 60 feet in width over the existing road located in the Southerly portion of the Northwest Quarter of the Northeast Quarter and the Northerly portion of the Southwest Quarter of the Northeast Quarter of Section 21, Township 4 South, Range 2 East, Humboldt Meridian, and extending from the West line of said Southwest Quarter to the Northeast Quarter, Easterly and Northerly to the East line of said Northwest Quarter of the Northeast Quarter, together with the right to convey said easement to others.

Follow the above descriptions on the maps. PARCEL ONE is our 80 acres. It is shaded on Figure 9–1 and marked with a 1 on Figure 9–2. Numbers 2, 3 and 4 on Figure 9–2 indicate land parcels owned by three different individuals. You can see that the dirt road that runs from the county road to our 80 acres crosses through these parcels.

PARCEL TWO in the deed includes the dirt road starting at the western side of the county road and running to the western edge of the northeast quarter of the northeast quarter of Section 21. This area is marked 2 on Figure 9–2, and is labeled PARCEL 2 on Figure 9–1.

PARCEL THREE in the deed then brings the easement through the area marked 3 and 4 on Figure 9–2 and labeled PARCEL 3 on Figure 9-1, to the point where the dirt road touches our land and remains on it.

It may take you a while to completely understand the above description, but once you do, you will have no problems when you make your own purchase. It is essential that you understand how to determine what your easement description includes. The above-described parcels assure us that we own a right-of-way from the county road all the way to our building site. Check your easement against a quadrangle map in a similar fashion to ensure that you are getting unquestionable access rights.

## Terms Defining the Easement

### "Nonexclusive" Easement

You will notice that the preceding description of our easements specifies that they are to be "non-exclusive." This means that we are not the only people permitted to use this road; neighboring property owners share this easement with us. It is important to know what this means in actual practice. I discuss the mutual problems of road maintenance later in this chapter.

### "60 Feet in Width"

The description also specifies that the easement is to be "60 feet in width." Actually, the road is not this wide. The right of access is set at 60 feet because there is always a possibility that the road might wash out and have to be reconstructed next to the previously existing road. Because the road is only 20 feet wide now, we have a 40-foot leeway. A minimum allowance of 60 feet is necessary as a safety clause in any easement.

### "Over the Existing Road"

The phrase "over the existing road" means that our access route follows the dirt road in existence at the time of purchase, rather than some other route not yet developed. If a road already is constructed into your land and it is satisfactory for your needs, then be sure that your deed includes the phrase "over the existing road," so there is no misunderstanding at a later date which route your easement is to take. If the road itself has been specifically surveyed, then the survey description should be used because of its precision. It is often preferable to have the road surveyed so there is no question of its location in the future, and because it is then insurable by a title company.

### "The Right To Convey
Said Easement to Others"

The clause in our deed that allows us "the right to convey said easement to others" is important because we might wish to sell our 80 acres in the future. Although most courts have ruled that an easement that benefits the easement holder in the use of his or her land automatically goes with the land, the inclusion in writing of the right to convey makes it specific. It is always best to express the full intent of an agreement in the purchase contract and deed. If we choose to subdivide our land, there is always a question of whether we can pass the easement on to two or more parcels. A property owner is not allowed to overburden an easement, and litigation often arises over such issues. It is best to have language in the easement allowing you to grant it to subdivisions of your parcel.

## Make Sure Your Access Description Includes the Entire Route

One land buyer I interviewed has a serious problem caused by his failure to examine his easement carefully before his purchase. He discovered too late that he did not have the access he thought he had. Although his land is actually several hundred miles from my property, I have, for example purposes, indicated his parcel as 5 on Figure 9–2. When he bought his land, there was already a road running from the county road to his building site. In his deed, the easement was described as the road going through Parcels 6 and 7, leading to his boundary line. You can see that the dirt road hits his land just above the lower left comer of Parcel 7. But notice that the access road then crosses through his land at the lower right corner, goes off his land, courses through three other people's property, 8, 9, and 10, and then circles back onto his land, terminating at his house.

Because this road was already in existence when he purchased his land, he assumed that his easement covered the entire route. The real estate agent told him only that he had "deeded access to his land." The title company did a title search before closing and insured him for the access outlined in his deed, which only went from the county road to his boundary line. But at the point where the road enters his land there is a cliff, which makes it impossible for him to build a road from there to his house. The cliff is indicated on the map.

Thus he is now negotiating with the owners of 8, 9 and 10 for easement rights across their property. He will probably have to pay a large sum of money for those rights, should they decide to give them to him. They are not bound to do so. This landowner does not have a case against the agent or title company because they only guaranteed him access to his land, which he had. The easement just didn't go all the way to his house, as he assumed it did. It was the landowner's fault because he failed to

check. his easement description against a map and survey of his property prior to purchase.

## Easements Where No Road Exists at the Time of Purchase

If you are buying land that does not have an access road already built, you must carefully examine the easement you are to be given in terms of its suitability for a road. Ideally you should get the seller to put in the road before you buy. He or she will probably add this cost to the selling price, but constructing a road involves many problems, so it is better to have the seller assume the risks.

If you wish to put the road in yourself, have the following condition or safety clause inserted for your protection into the Model Contract of Sale (see Chapter 27):

> The Buyer shall make a diligent effort to construct a permanent access road along the route designated by the Easement in the Contract of Sale and the Deed. The road shall be no less than 20 (twenty) feet in width, and shall extend from the most accessible public road to the Buyer's building site. The road shall be adequate for ingress and egress of heavy-duty vehicles. The Buyer shall construct the road by any means of his choosing and the maximum cost the Buyer is willing to assume is $_____. If the Buyer cannot locate and develop an adequate access road for his needs, as specified herein, and he has performed all of the conditions herein, then this Contract is rescinded immediately and the Buyer shall receive all money he has paid to the Seller, and the Buyer shall suffer no further liability under this Contract. Furthermore, Seller shall reimburse the Buyer for the total amount the Buyer has expended in his attempt to construct an access road.

Have a local contractor, construction company or road builder examine the area and determine the best route to your land before you purchase. They will probably do this for free, as well as give you an estimate of costs, because they anticipate being hired for the job. Give the contractor's written report to the seller, and tell him that you want an easement that covers every part of that route because it is the most feasible access route to your land. If he cannot deliver easement coverage over that area, then you should not buy the land. If you do not take the above precautions, you might discover too late that you have been given an easement unfit for the construction of a low-cost permanent road.

## Know Where Your Access Enters Your Property

When you get an easement, be sure it goes to the most desirable place for entry to serve your proposed building site. A difficult situation developed for some people we know in a neighboring county. Although their property is 100 miles from my property, for example purposes only I have shown their property as number 4 on Figure 9–2. They use a dirt road to get to their property. But notice where it hits their property line in the upper left-hand corner of 4. Their only good building sites were in the upper right-hand corner of their land, so they built their house there, as indicated on the map. Directly below the house is a trail that the owners find much more convenient to use than coming up from the point where the access road meets their property. However, you can see that the trail leaves the access road and crosses part of the property belonging to 3. Thus, they are trespassing at that point. Legally, they need another easement to cross that small portion of their neighbor's land. Instead of asking the owner of Parcel 3 for an easement, the owners went ahead and built some steps up the cliff along the short trail to their house and left their truck on the easement. The man who owns Parcel 3 was very upset about the trespassing and the trail across his property. He could sue the owners of Parcel 4 for trespass and damage to property. He may win in court, and the trespassers will be forced to enter their land far from their house at the point where their right of way first touches their own land. They may also have to pay some money for damages.

## Determining the Validity of Your Easement

An easement is a property right; therefore, it should be documented in writing in a grant or deed and shown in an abstract of title or title report. This is very important. Easements should also be filed with the county recorder. When you get a title search before closing, easement rights will be shown, if they are to be included in your deed or title. If no easements show on your title report, stop the deal and question the title company or abstractor about your easement rights.

## Preliminary Easement Check

You can do your own preliminary easement check. Find out from the real estate agent who owns each parcel between your land and the public road. If he doesn't have this information, you can get it from the local tax assessor. If possible, find out the year each landowner, including the person you are buying land from, purchased his or her property. Copies of all recorded deeds are kept in the county recorder's office, which is usually in the county courthouse or local city hall. Look in the deed index or grantee index, which is often filed by year, under the name of the present owner to see where to find a copy of his or her deed. In that deed you should usually find a description of the easement to the property. (For a thorough discussion on searching the records, see Chapter 30, "The Title Search, Abstract of Title and Title Insurance Policy.") Easements are often conveyed by documents separate from a deed; in such a case you will be able to determine them only by ordering a title report.

## Sharing and Maintaining an Easement

In the usual nonexclusive easement, when several people have the same easement rights over a single road to their respective properties, there is often no indication of who will be responsible for the upkeep of the access road. Usually this responsibility is shared by the people who hold the easement. Here is our situation.

You can see that three other landowners, numbered 2, 3 and 4 in Figure 9–2, share the easement with us. These owners help us repair the road each summer. We share the cost on a pro rata basis, and we pay the largest share because we are at the end of the road. Thus, we share the $400 annual expense with three neighbors.

When other people use the same easement access that you will use, speak to some of them before you buy. Ask about the average cost of road repairs and who pays for them. If you find out this information beforehand you may foresee future difficulties with noncooperative neighbors. Many states have laws that state that a person who shares an easement is responsible for a proportionate share of road maintenance according to his use.

If you are the only person who has an easement over a road, you alone will be responsible for maintenance. The landowner of the parcel through which your easement runs cannot interfere with your use of the road and does not have to maintain your access. If both of you use the same access, legally each of you is responsible for upkeep. This maintenance cost will be greater the farther you are from the public road. Before you buy your land, be sure you can afford your isolation.

When you examine your access road, notice how much permanent improvement has been made that will decrease yearly maintenance expense. Look for. culverts, which are steel or concrete pipes placed under the road surface to drain water away from the road. Culverts are essential to prevent a dirt road from becoming impassable because of large ruts and puddles that result from winter rain or snow. They are expensive, and if other landowners use your road you will want all of them to cooperate when it comes to upkeep and improvement. One large culvert in our road cost $300, and a dump truck of rock cost $90.

## Getting the County To Maintain Your Easement

Real estate agents will sometimes tell prospective buyers that the road they will be using will be taken over and maintained by the county after the buyers purchase the land. Be very skeptical of such claims. There are always stiff requirements that must be met before public tax money is spent on any road. For example, in California, if a group of property owners want their road to be taken into the county system, they first must bring the road up to county standards at their own expense. This requires ditching, putting in culverts and laying a minimum amount of surface gravel or asphalt, which is very costly. In addition, once this work is done and the county takes over maintenance of the road, by law it becomes permanently open to the public.

## Easements over Public Lands

Each year thousands of individuals apply to the Bureau of Land Management and state governments to obtain a right-of-way. The federal government charges an application, monitoring and annual rental fee. It grants easements only by permit and generally will not grant permanent easement rights. If you sell your property and if it is served by an easement over public lands, you must obtain permission to assign your easement rights. If you are purchasing land served by a road over government land that is not a general public road, check with the government agency about your access rights before the close of escrow. A good pamphlet discussing easements over federal property is "Obtaining a Right-Of-Way on Public Lands," available free from the U.S. Department of the Interior, Bureau of Land Management, Washington, DC 20240. You can also call BLM at (202) 452-7782 or fax them at (202) 452-7708.

## Does a Neighbor Have an Easement over Your Land?

Easement problems also occur if an access across your land is owned by other landowners. Then it is your land that is being crossed, and it is said to be *encumbered* by or subject to an easement. You often can determine if your land is subject to an easement by personally examining it. Obviously, if a road runs through your place and continues onto another person's land and you can see that someone is using it, you should suspect that an easement exists. Others' rights to cross your land will usually show up in a title report or abstract of title, unless such rights are unrecorded.

## Unrecorded Easements

How does an unrecorded easement become legally binding and "of record"?

There are three situations in which an unrecorded easement might be proved to exist in a court of law. If you see evidence of a road that does not show up in your title search, you should suspect that there may be one of the following three types of unrecorded easements: an easement by prescription, an easement by implication, or an easement by necessity. Although unrecorded easements usually physically exist, a title search will not reveal them, nor will they be protected by a policy of title insurance until such time as the easements are declared to exist by a judge in a court case and that judgment is recorded in the public records. Obtaining a judgment can be very expensive and often difficult to prove because essential witnesses may be dead or hard to locate.

### Easement by Prescription

If a person openly crosses someone else's land continuously for a prescribed number of years as if he or she has a right to do so but, in fact, the owner has not given permission, the user might be able to get an *easement by prescription,* commonly called a *prescriptive easement.* Use of the easement must be open, hostile, notorious, continuous for the specified period of time and under a claim of right. The time period required varies in each state. In California it takes 5 years to establish, whereas it takes 10 years in New York, Louisiana and Oregon; 15 years in Minnesota; 20 years in Illinois, Maine and Wisconsin; and 21 years in Ohio. British Columbia, on the other hand, has abolished the right to prescriptive easements. Regardless of where you are, a prescriptive easement cannot be gained over government property.

### Easement by Implication

If one piece of land is divided into two or more parcels, and if the owner sells one of the parcels, A, without reserving an easement across his or her own parcel, B, but a road exists to A across B that the new owner of A uses openly and obviously with the knowledge of B's owner, the court might grant an easement by implication to the owner of A, even though A may have another way out to a public road. (See Figure 9–3.) This type of easement is often very difficult to obtain, because such an easement would burden B and the courts do not like to create a burden on property unless necessary.

### Easement by Necessity

An easement by necessity is similar to an easement by implication, except that an easement by necessity is granted when A is completely landlocked by B. The expressed intentions of the parties are very

### Figure 9–3. Easement by Implication

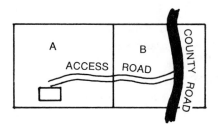

important in this type of case.

All of these types of easements are complicated and their existence is difficult to prove. If you suspect that an unrecorded easement exists on land you are looking at but you are still sufficiently interested in the property, be sure to consult an attorney who specializes in easement law to see what you will be getting involved in. If it turns out that you have another *recorded* easement so that you do not need to pursue one of these types of easements in court, you will be able to purchase the land with peace of mind. If, on the other hand, the lawyer tells you that you will face costly litigation and possibly years of hassling, you will be glad that you can back out of the deal now and look for something else.

## It Is Your Duty To Inspect the Parcel

The implied easement and prescriptive easement will not appear in the County Records and will not be covered by your policy of title insurance. For this reason it is important that you personally walk over and examine your land in its entirety. Make a thorough investigation of any roads or paths that cross the land, whether or not they appear to be well traveled; perhaps the road is only used at certain times of the year. The burden is placed on you to inspect the premises before you purchase to determine the existence of unrecorded easements. Once you have taken title, you will have little chance in court of preventing someone from crossing your land who possesses a legally sound unrecorded easement and who can prove the elements necessary to win such a case.

## Is the Easement over Your Land Going To Bother You?

When one or more landowners have the right to cross your land at any time, such activity could seriously interfere with your peace and quiet. The burden will be greater if the road runs next to your best building site than if it merely crosses the corner of the land far from the living area. Your own access problems also could be greater because the number of people who use the access road. If an encumbering easement breaks up the unity of some land you are interested in, you should use this to get the price down. However, evaluate the situation carefully before you buy. The following story illustrates the importance of predicting the future impact of an easement on the enjoyment of your land. It is fictional, but it could easily have happened.

Some neighbors who live on the ridge above our valley bought 40 acres that were originally part of a large ranch that now extends to the south and southwest of them. Their land is numbered 11 on Figure 9–2. When the ranchers sold the 40 acres, they reserved easements for themselves and others along the dirt road that crosses the neighbor's land. You can see the road running along the ridge from the county road to the ranchers' houses. The only available building site on the 40 acres was next to the dirt road, which is where the owners built their dwelling. Their quiet days were frequently interrupted by jeep, truck and car traffic, as ranch hands entered and left the ranch.

In addition, the ranchers used heavy-duty vehicles on the road, which inevitably produced much dust in the summer and huge ruts during the winter rains. This made winter access difficult for the family, which had only lightweight two-wheel-drive vehicles. When the ruts got too deep, the owners had to walk into their land until the road could be repaired the following summer. They had a difficult time getting the ranch to share road improvement and maintenance costs. They could have filed an action in the courts to compel the ranchers to share in the road maintenance costs, but such action is costly and time consuming. So they lived with this encumbering easement for a couple of years and then put the land on the market and sold out. The new buyers will now have to live with these road problems. But would you want to?

You cannot know the use patterns of an easement unless you spend some time on the land before buying it. Be certain that if there is an easement within eyesight and hearing of the homestead area that the future traffic patterns will not interfere with your desired peace in the country.

## Easements in Gross

An *easement in gross* is one that does not serve a specific parcel of land but is a generalized easement for crossing a parcel; for example, for log hauling or hunting. If an easement in gross has been reserved over your land, together with the right to grant it to others, you could have an unlimited number of persons crossing your property in the future. If the easement is in gross, the deed will normally state that.

## Utility Line Easement

Easements are not restricted solely to personal access. The right to bring utility lines along the easement route can be included. Your easement should provide for "ingress and egress and public utilities." Even if you don't want electricity brought in yourself, it is helpful to have this in your deed if you ever decide to sell your land. A future buyer might want the easement to specifically include utilities.

You will also want to be aware of a utility easement across your land. Although you might be willing to see a car go by a few times a day, you might not enjoy the sight of telephone and electrical poles and wires strung across your property, particularly if they are large distribution lines constructed on huge towers.

## Pipeline Easements

A person who has the right to take water off your land will also have a pipeline easement over your land to transport the water. If you are receiving water rights from another parcel, make sure you have an easement for "laying and maintaining a pipeline" from the water source to your property.

**Figure 9–4. Road Frontage Description**

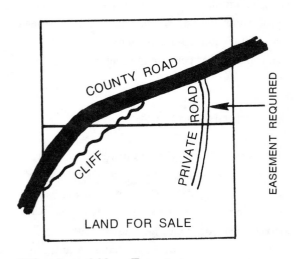

## "The Land Has Frontage on the County Road"

You will frequently see the above phrase in real estate advertisements. Don't make the assumption that road *frontage* necessarily means direct road *access*. The side of the property that borders the county road might be a cliff or a ravine. In such cases, entrance must be gained by crossing a neighbor's land. Figure 9–4 shows road frontage with easement access required.

## An Easement Warranty— Your Best Insurance

An excellent means of obtaining extra easement protection if there is any question in your mind about access is to include a warranty clause in the contract of sale. You may want to include a clause in your Contract of Sale that states that the seller warrants the buyer that he or she will receive legal access, or easements, over the most accessible route between the public road and his or her building site. This warranty covers the problems discussed in this chapter and assures you of legal recourse against the seller if any undisclosed easement problems arise after the deal is closed. You may also want to include a clause stating that all warranties and representations by seller shall survive delivery of the deed. This keeps the warranty binding even after you receive the deed to the property. If your purchase is subject to your prior approval of a title report or abstract, you will have the opportunity to re-

view the easements shown in the report prior to closing. If they are not adequate, stop the deal until the seller can make them sufficient. (See Chapter 27, "The Model Contract of Sale.")

## A Final Warning

The importance of understanding easements and knowing when and where they are located cannot be over stressed. Beware of the real estate agent who tells you, "Don't worry about getting an easement. The former owner of this land has been using it for years. Everybody is real friendly. Nobody around here ever gets easements." Tell the agent that if nobody cares if you use the road, then he or she should have no problem getting the landowners to sign deeds granting such an easement formally.

Think about the future. The people who now own the land you cross might not care whether you do so, but the next owners might not be so gracious. Or the present owners might not like your looks and decide that they are not going to treat you as they did the last owners. All they have to do is put up gates and tell you not to cross their land if you don't have deeded access. These situations are very common in the history of real estate disputes.

You must also protect yourself against easements that could interfere with your use of the land. A thorough personal inspection of your prospective purchase is mandatory for uncovering evidence of easements. It is helpful to discuss the situation with the sellers and their neighbors. Question the real estate agent thoroughly on the matter.

A deeded easement should be described as precisely as possible, in terms of location and purpose. Remember that an easement may not always be revealed by a title search. Thus a comprehensive general warranty is necessary. Easements crossing the seller's land should be used to your advantage when negotiating the selling price if it depreciates the land value by diminishing the peace and quiet of the country isolation you would like.

Prior to the close of escrow, order copies of all documents referred to in the title report or abstract and read through them to see what the easement situation is. Finally, never buy land that does not have deeded recorded adequate easement rights from a public road all the way to the parcel. If you do, you are almost assured of eventually getting into litigation.

# 10 Water Rights

*The water right is a property right. It is a valuable right. And it is real estate. The holder of a water right in an area in which the competition for water is keen needs to be constantly on guard to protect his right against infringement or loss. It is said that eternal vigilance is the price of a good water right.*

—Wells A. Hutchins,
leading water rights expert

The importance of having water on your land has been pointed out in great detail in an earlier chapter. The mere presence of water on your property, however, does not necessarily ensure that you have unfettered rights to use it. Every state has specific and detailed laws regarding water rights and how they may be obtained and lost that apply to all users of the water. It is impossible for me to detail all of the water laws in each individual state, but I will explain the basic theories and their applications to different types of water sources. Contact your state department of resources or your local farm adviser

to find out how you can get a pamphlet detailing the water laws of the state where your land is located. For example, in California you can write to the California State Water Resources Control Board in Sacramento for a pamphlet entitled "Information Pertaining to Water Rights in California: Statements of Water Diversion and Use." (See "Useful Resources" at the end of this chapter.) Similar guides are put out in other states.

## The Purpose of Water Laws

All water is classified as either surface water or underground water. These waters are regulated by different laws, as enacted by state legislatures and interpreted by the state and federal courts. The primary aim of the water laws is to prevent the waste of water and to use what is available in the most beneficial manner possible.

**Figure 10–1. Acquisition of Surface Water Rights**

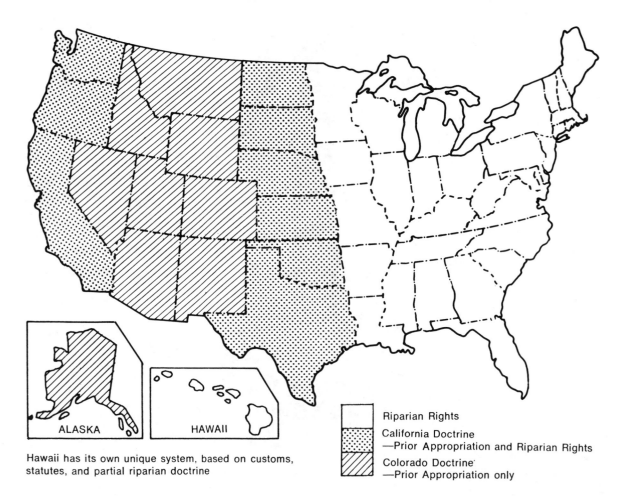

Hawaii has its own unique system, based on customs, statutes, and partial riparian doctrine

☐ Riparian Rights

▨ California Doctrine
—Prior Appropriation and Riparian Rights

▨ Colorado Doctrine
—Prior Appropriation only

## Surface Waters

Surface waters include lakes, rivers, streams, springs, ponds, marshes and any other visible water. Most rivers and lakes are considered to be navigable public waters, and the federal government has control over them. If your land abuts or includes navigable waters, you have water rights as long as they do not interfere with public use.

However, it is more likely that if your land has surface water on it, it will be a *non-navigable* stream, spring or pond. Whether navigable or not, all surface water in the United States is subject either to riparian laws or prior appropriation laws, or to combinations of the two.

These two separate areas of water law, *riparian rights* and *prior appropriation rights,* developed because the water needs in the arid West differ greatly from those in the humid East. Generally, east of the one-hundredth meridian west longitude line, rainfall is abundant throughout the year, whereas west of that line, rainfall is sparse and

nearly all of it falls during the winter months. (See Chapter 3, "Climate.") Figure 10–1 shows the distribution of the types of rights to surface water used by each state throughout the country.

### Riparian Rights

Water laws, like the rest of our laws, evolved from the English common law brought here by the early settlers. Because these settlers first established themselves in the humid eastern portion of the country where water is plentiful, the riparian laws of England, itself a humid country, were nicely suited to the region. Thus, it was logical that we accepted them as our first water laws.

A riparian landowner is one whose land is directly adjacent to the water source. The amount of land actually touching the water is usually irrelevant. The majority of land for sale with surface water contains springs rather than a definable stream. If a spring does not pass beyond the boundary of the land on which it is located, the owner of the land has sole rights to use the water as he wishes. But if that spring is the source of a natural stream that flows across other lands, it falls within the laws of riparian rights. Where many riparian landowners have property adjacent to a single stream or lake, riparian laws are used to determine how much water each is allowed to use.

Originally this country followed the doctrine, inherited from English law, that required that each riparian landowner must let the stream flow in its "natural state" to lower lands. Thus, the flow could not be diminished in quantity or impaired in quality by a riparian user, and any water diverted had to be returned to the stream before leaving the user's property. The purpose of this rule originally was to ensure the free passage of water downstream from one mill wheel to the next. As of this writing, eight states still follow this natural flow method of allocating water. They are Georgia, Maine, Mississippi, Missouri, New Jersey, Pennsylvania, South Dakota and West Virginia. Because this method results in the wasteful loss of much water into the sea, today the majority of state courts and legislatures more often follow the *reasonable use* rule in determining riparian rights.

Reasonable use is a priority system that follows the rule that a riparian landowner can use all the water he needs for "ordinary" or "domestic" purposes without regard to the effect of such use on the water flow to lower riparian landowners. Domestic uses include taking water for washing, cooking, drinking and watering domestic stock animals and gardens. Often a state will fix a maximum quantity considered reasonable for domestic use. For example, some states permit 18.5 gallons per day per 100 square feet for irrigation of home gardens. For a house with a sink and flush toilet, each person is permitted a maximum of 40 gallons per day. *Extraordinary* uses, often referred to as *artificial* uses, include taking water for irrigation of commercial crops, manufacturing, mining and other commercial uses. All domestic uses by all riparian landowners on the stream must be fulfilled before any one of them can use surplus water for artificial uses. Sometimes an upper riparian landowner in using water only for domestic purposes takes all the available water and none flows to lower riparian landowners. This is allowed as long as the use is "reasonable." You should be aware of use patterns upstream when buying land with the expectation of receiving a good steady flow of water.

In determining which artificial uses take priority after all domestic uses have been fulfilled, many

**Figure 10–2. Sale of a Riparian Right**

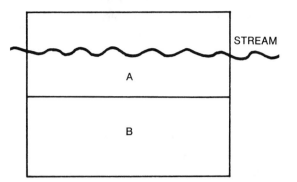

facts are considered, including the length of the stream, the volume of water, the extent of riparian land ownership and the purpose and extent of the use. Using water for aesthetic and recreational purposes, such as swimming and fishing, is far down on the list of preferred uses. Taking water out of a stream to store for later use is usually not allowed under the riparian system. Only if every other riparian owner has enough for domestic and artificial uses can water be taken and stored. Fortunately, the riparian system predominates mainly in the eastern half of the United States where water is plentiful and storage is not usually necessary. The states that follow the *reasonable* use riparian laws exclusively are Alabama, Arkansas, Connecticut, Delaware, Florida, Illinois, Indiana, Iowa, Kentucky, Louisiana, Maryland, Massachusetts, Michigan, Minnesota, New Hampshire, New York, North Carolina, Ohio, Rhode Island, South Carolina, Tennessee, Vermont, Virginia and Wisconsin. Those states discussed later that follow a combined riparian appropriation system generally recognize the reasonable use concepts with regard to riparian rights.

Riparian rights can go with the land itself and cannot be lost because of disuse. They always remain with the land adjoining the water unless specified otherwise. Figure 10–2 shows one effect of a sale of riparian land.

Parcels A and B were originally one unit of land owned totally by Owner C. When Parcel B was sold, Buyer D did not automatically get riparian rights to the stream because Parcel B does not adjoin the stream. However, if C included riparian rights and access rights in the deed to D, then D can use the stream and the rights run with the land. This is legal because Parcel B is in the watershed and was originally a part of the riparian land. The sale simply divided the riparian land into two parcels, when it had all previously been owned by one person. But some states might reclassify Buyer *D* as an *appropriator* with rights secondary to those of a riparian owner.

Once a riparian right is lost, the loss is permanent and can never be regained. If *D*, in the above example, did not get riparian rights reserved in his or her deed, Parcel B can never regain those rights unless it is resold to *C* and reunited as one parcel of land adjoining the stream. If you are buying land that is being severed from a riparian piece of land, riparian rights will attach to your land only if expressly reserved in writing in your deed.

If you buy land with a stream or other surface water on it, you will pay for that water because it increases the value of the land. Sellers who reserve riparian rights and easement rights to cross your land and use the stream for themselves or for the buyer of another parcel should greatly reduce their asking price because such a reservation means you must share the stream on your land with others. A seller may try to reserve these rights for other parcels he or she is selling because it makes any property not adjoining the water a better sales prospect. Carefully evaluate the effect on your home if other property owners have the right to come onto your land, run water lines to their property and take water from your land. Generally, you should not buy land under such circumstances.

When you buy riparian land or land with riparian rights granted in the deed, you can be sold only those rights the seller possesses already. Therefore, you must find out what the seller's rights include. Be certain that the seller has not previously granted his or her riparian rights to another user, leaving no rights for you. Because this information may not show up in the deed, be sure that it is covered in your title search. Courts are destroying riparian rights in legal disputes where they cannot absolutely be shown to exist, so if there is any doubt about your rights, resolve them before taking title to the land.

As a riparian landowner your right to have an adequate water flow includes a right to pure water. Lawsuits between riparian owners over the issue of pollution are fairly common. However, a private action is not as effective as an action by a state agency to prevent pollution. If you want adequate relief, you should file a complaint with the appropriate state agency as well as with the court. Upstream polluters are also liable for damages and possible criminal charges. In some areas, however, pollution that occurs as a result of bathing or watering stock animals is permissible.

In many states you are not free to stock and take fish from some streams or lakes that are adjacent to your land. We cannot fish in our creek under any circumstances because it is classified as a "spawning creek" by the state Department of Fish and Game. The fines for fishing illegally are often several hundred dollars. Look up your stream's classification in the state fish and game regulations before you buy your land if fishing is a major reason for your move to the country. You might also want to check the local rules regarding fish stocking. You generally need a permit to stock your stream or lake, and the type of fish you can use is selected by state officials to protect nearby public waters.

As a riparian landowner you own the rocks in the stream bed and may remove them for use on your land as long as you do not disturb the flow of the water to lower riparian users, although you may need a permit from your state fish and game or wildlife office.

Although the property line of land bordered by a non-navigable stream generally extends to the middle of the stream, it is wise to have this written into your deed if a creek or stream is used as a boundary line of the land. The property line of land on a navigable stream or lake extends to the low-water mark. On a non-navigable stream, as the course of the stream gradually shifts through the years, the property lines shift with the stream. The soil that is slowly deposited on your land during the shifting process is your gain and your neighbor's loss. This process is called *accretion.* However, if the stream changes course as a result of a sudden storm or flood rather than by a gradual process of change, the rule of accretion does not apply, and the boundary lines do not change.

All riparian owners are eligible to take and use the water only on land within the *watershed,* that area that drains into the stream, river or lake. (See Figure 10–3.) If you buy a large piece of land on a stream and want to pump water from the stream over a hill to use on a section of your property that is in another watershed, you will be appropriating the water and thus be subject to *appropriation laws,* rather than riparian laws. Legal action could be taken against you by other riparian owners downstream and by *prior appropriators,* because you are illegally depriving them of stream water.

**Figure 10–3.  Watershed**

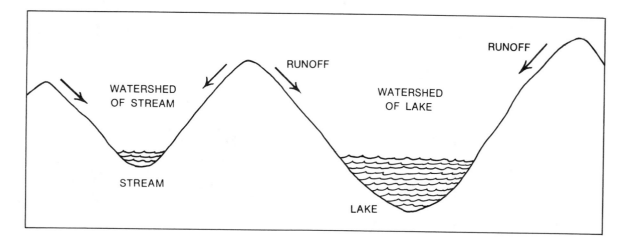

## Prior Appropriation Rights
## (Alone or with Riparian Rights)

In 1849 gold was discovered in California, and people swarmed into the West. Mining towns, army camps and trading posts grew up around major water routes. At first gold was mined directly from the streams in the Sierra Nevada Mountains by using the naturally flowing stream water to wash the sand out of the sifting pans, leaving the gold on the bottom. As gold processing became more advanced, however, long ditches were dug to create more water pressure to separate the gold, and tremendous amounts of water were required. It also became necessary to store huge quantities of water in large reservoirs so that mining could continue during the long dry summer months. New laws were needed to define who could use the limited supplies of water, and prior appropriation laws were adopted.

The basic principle involved in the law of prior appropriation is "first in time is first in right." The first user, often called the *prior* or *senior appropriator,* is permitted to take all the water in the stream he can put to a reasonable and beneficial use to the exclusion of all others higher or lower on the stream who want to take water after him. This rule came into being to avoid wasting water in dry periods. The feeling was that it was preferable to let one individual water user take all the available water needed in a drought rather than to distribute the water in amounts inadequate for each of several users.

As the amount of gold gradually dwindled, many miners and new settlers turned to farming. They began to construct ditches to divert water from streams for a new purpose, to carry it to their lands for irrigation. By 1880, the feasibility of raising large crops by irrigation had been proved, and intensive land development in the West began. Many of the prior appropriation laws developed by miners carried over to this new use of the water resources.

Prior appropriation rights specified that the first settler in an area could choose the land he wanted and build irrigation ditches from the nearest stream to his fields. It was irrelevant whether his land was contiguous, or riparian, to the stream, because nobody else was using the water. The next settler to come to the area had second choice of the land and secondary rights to appropriate the available water to irrigate his land. This pattern was repeated with subsequent settlers.

Thus, because of the scarcity of water and the needs of mining and agriculture, the original riparian laws that the East had adopted from England gave way to the new doctrine of prior appropriation. Nine of the most arid western states now follow the *Colorado doctrine,* which only recognizes prior appropriation laws and does not differentiate between riparian and nonriparian lands. These states are Alaska, Arizona, Colorado, Idaho, Montana, Nevada, New Mexico, Utah and Wyoming.

The other nine western states follow the *California doctrine,* which does distinguish riparian lands but also has coordinated the principle of prior appropriation into the laws. These states are California, Kansas, Nebraska, North Dakota, Oklahoma, Oregon, South Dakota, Texas and Washington. In these states, appropriators are nonriparian users only. Riparian users always have priority over ap-

**Figure 10–4. Relation Between Riparian and Appropriation Rights**

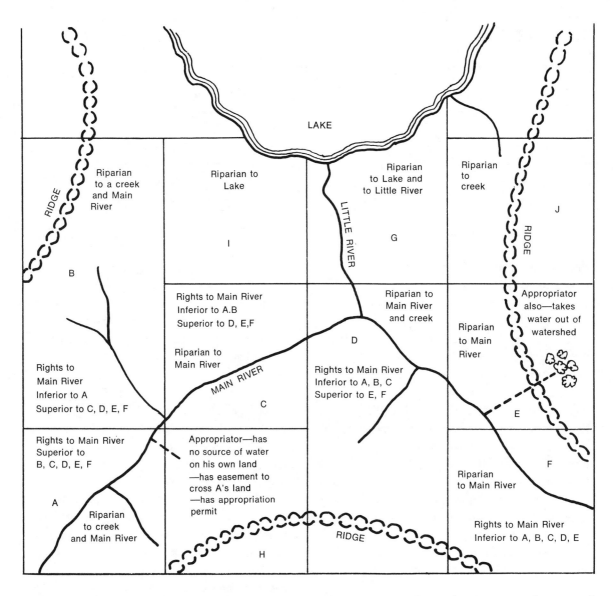

propriators. (See Figure 10–4 to see the relationship between riparian rights and appropriation rights.) Hawaii has a unique system derived from custom and ancient rights that is beyond the scope of this discussion.

The appropriator in every prior appropriation state except Montana must apply to the state for a permit and license to take water. The time of appropriation and priority to use the water dates from the time formal application is made to the state under an appropriation permit. When buying land in one of these states, you should investigate the history of water applications on your stream. You should not only determine what legal steps have been taken to secure water rights on the seller's land but also similarly investigate other lands adjoining the stream.

If you intend to divert a large amount of water and expect to invest a substantial sum of money in diversion equipment, you would be wise to have a survey taken by a local engineer who knows the river. Establish where diversions have already been made, how much water is taken out of the river by prior appropriators, and whether there will be enough left for your use. You can write to the state resources agency or state engineer and ask if any permits have been sought or licenses issued to appropriate water on your stream or river.

This research for prior appropriators is difficult and often inconclusive, but at least make some preliminary investigations because the standard policy of title insurance does not guarantee water rights. You do not want to find your stream dry in August because your upstream neighbor is pumping out all the water before it reaches your property line and you can do nothing about it because he has a ten-year permit from the state to do so. If you are in an appropriation state that does not recognize riparian rights, you have no recourse. If you are in one of the nine appropriation states that do recognize riparian rights, you might be able to force the appropriator to allow enough water through to meet your water requirements, but only after engaging in expensive litigation.

**Obtaining a Permit**

The procedure for obtaining an appropriation permit is similar in each state. I have reprinted a typical application form as Figure 10–5. You can obtain the application forms and rules for filing in your state from your state resources agency or state engineer in charge of water allocation. The procedure I describe below is only an example and may not be applicable in your state.

As you can see, the application is quite detailed and specific. It calls for a description of the diversion works, including location and amount of water to be diverted, a schedule of when the work is to be completed, once you have your permit, and a description of the proposed use. Another form requires environmental information on the effect of the appropriation on fish and wildlife and how you are prepared to deal with such effects. You are also required to pay filing fees and include copies of a project map.

You should file for a permit as soon as possible because the filing date determines who is prior in time. After you have filed your application, notice of the filing is issued and posted in public places and at the stream, so that anybody else who may be prior in time to you or who may have objections can protest. Persons wishing to object to your application have to submit a written protest to the agency and to you, the applicant, within a specified time period. You then have 15 days to answer the protest, and you must reply to the specific complaints. You must file this answer with the agency and send a copy to the complainant.

A hearing is then held before a division of the state water resources agency, which has the authority to grant permits. At this time witnesses and any other evidence regarding the case are heard. If the agency feels the information is insufficient, it may order a field investigation at which you and the protester may be present. Data obtained from this investigation are used to help the agency make a final determination. If it approves your intended diversion, a permit is issued, and you can begin to take the water. Approval by the agency does not ensure water rights. It only indicates that you have been granted permission by the state to use water, and this permission establishes a priority date for you. If others have prior permission and use up all the water, there is nothing you can do.

Once the permit is granted, you must act with reasonable diligence to begin diverting and putting the water to good use. After you begin doing this, the agency grants you a license. You can keep this license forever, as long as there are not three successive years in which no use is made of the diversionary works, in which case you would lose your appropriation rights. Whenever requested, you must report to the agency on what you are doing so that it can be sure the water resources are being put to the best and most efficient use possible.

**Dams and Reservoirs**

If you wish to dam your stream, you should be acquainted with any regulations in your state regarding dams. Generally, even though you are riparian to a stream, if you build a dam for the purpose of storing water for swimming, fishing, or irrigation, you are appropriating that water and must meet the regulations regarding water appropriation in your state. However, mere regulation of the flow of a stream is not an appropriation if it only detains but does not reduce the flow of the water. For instance, dams that are built to create enough head on a stream to drive a power plant do not diminish the actual flow.

Many states have set standards for dam and reservoir construction. A dam usually must exceed certain specified limits before it qualifies for state control. For example, although California regulates dams, it does not supervise any dams that are less than six feet high or that hold less than 15 acre-feet of water. For any larger construction the builder must file for a permit and pay set fees. You can find out your state's requirements, if any, from the same agency that supervises the water uses described above. If an upstream user builds a dam that endangers your water supply, you should file a written complaint to the appropriate department in your county or state.

At least ten states have enacted Mill Acts, which permit a dam to be built by an upper riparian landowner for the purpose of supplying water

**Figure 10–5. Application Form To Acquire Water Rights**

☐ **APPLICATION TO APPROPRIATE WATER BY PERMIT**

(Check one box only)

**or**

☐ **REGISTRATION OF SMALL DOMESTIC USE APPROPRIATION***

(If this form is used to register a small domestic use appropriation, the terms "application" and "applicant" herein, and in related forms, shall mean "registration" and "registrant".)

**Application No.** _____

(Leave blank)

**1. APPLICANT**

_____     ( ___ ) ___ - _____

(Name of applicant)     (Telephone number where you may be reached between 8 a. m. and 5 p. m. - include area code)

_____

(Mailing address)     (City or town)     (State)     (Zip code)

**2. SOURCE**

a. The name of the source at the point of diversion is _____

(If unnamed, state that it is an unnamed stream, spring, etc.)

tributary to _____

b. In a normal year does the stream dry up at any point downstream from your project? YES☐ NO☐ If yes, during what months is it usually dry? From _____ to _____

What alternate sources are available to your project should a portion of your requested direct diversion season be excluded because of a dry stream or nonavailability of water? _____

**3. POINTS of DIVERSION and REDIVERSION**

a. The point(s) of diversion will be in the County of _____

| b. List all points giving coordinate distances from section corner or other tie as allowed by Board regulations i. e. California Coordinate System | Point is within (40-acre subdivision) | Section | Township | Range | Base and Meridian |
|---|---|---|---|---|---|
| | 1/4 of     1/4 | | | | |
| | 1/4 of     1/4 | | | | |
| | 1/4 of     1/4 | | | | |

c. Does applicant own the land at the point of diversion? YES☐ NO☐

d. If applicant does not own the land at point of diversion, state name and address of owner and what steps have been taken to obtain right of access: _____

**4. PURPOSE of USE, AMOUNT and SEASON**

a. In the table below, state the purpose(s) for which water is to be appropriated, the quantities of water for each purpose, and the dates between which diversions will be made. Use gallons per day if rate is less than 0.025 cubic foot per second (approximately 16,000 gallons per day). Purpose must only be "Domestic" for registration of small domestic use."

| PURPOSE OF USE (Irrigation, Domestic, etc.) | DIRECT DIVERSION | | | | STORAGE | | |
|---|---|---|---|---|---|---|---|
| | QUANTITY | | SEASON OF DIVERSION | | AMOUNT | COLLECTION SEASON | |
| | RATE (Cubic feet per second or gallons per day) | AMOUNT (Acre-feet per year) | Beginning Date (Mo. & Day) | Ending date (Mo. & Day) | Acre-feet per annum | Beginning Date (Mo. & Day) | Ending date (Mo. & Day) |
| | | | | | | | |
| | | | | | | | |
| | | | | | | | |
| | | | | | | | |
| | | | | | | | |
| | | TOTAL AMOUNT | | | | TOTAL AMOUNT | |

b. Total combined amount taken by direct diversion and storage during any one year will be _____ acre-feet.

*Not to exceed 4,500 gallons per day by direct diversion or 10 acre-feet per annum by storage.*

WR 1 (12/88)

**Figure 10–5. Application Form To Acquire Water Rights,** *continued*

**5. JUSTIFICATION OF AMOUNT** (For small domestic use registration, complete item b. only)

a. IRRIGATION:   Maximum area to be irrigated in any one year is _____ acres.

| CROP | ACRES | METHOD OF IRRIGATION (Sprinklers, flooding, etc.) | ACRE-FEET PER YEAR | NORMAL SEASON | |
|------|-------|-------|-------|-------|-------|
| | | | | Beginning date | Ending date |
| | | | | | |
| | | | | | |
| | | | | | |

b. DOMESTIC:  Number of residences to be served is _____ . Separately owned ? YES ☐ NO ☐
   Total number of people to be served is _____ . Estimated daily use per person is _____
   Total area of domestic lawns and gardens is _____ square feet.    (Gallons per day)
   Incidential domestic uses are     _____
                                     (Dust control area, number and kind of domestic animals, etc.)

c. STOCKWATERING:  Kind of stock _____  Maximum number _____  Describe type of operation:
   _____
                                     (Feed lot, dairy, range, etc.)

d. RECREATIONAL:  Type of recreation:   Fishing ☐    Swimming ☐    Boating ☐    Other ☐

e. MUNICIPAL:  (Estimated projected use)

| POPULATION 5-year periods until use is completed | | MAXIMUM MONTH | | ANNUAL USE | | |
|------|------|------|------|------|------|------|
| PERIOD | POP. | Average daily use per capita (gal.) | Rate of diversion (cfs) | Average daily use (gal. per capita) | Acre-foot (per capita) | Total acre-feet |
| Present | | | | | | |
| | | | | | | |
| | | | | | | |
| | | | | | | |
| | | | | | | |

   Month of maximum use during year is _____ . Month of minimum use during year is _____ .

f. HEAT CONTROL:  The total area to be heat protected is _____ net acres.
   Type of crop protected is _____
   Rate at which water is applied to use is _____ gpm per acre.
   The heat protection season will begin about _____ and end about _____
                                               (Date)                              (Date)

g. FROST PROTECTION:  The total area to be frost protected is _____ net acres.
   Type of crop protected is _____
   Rate at which water is applied to use is _____ gpm per acre.
   The frost protection season will begin about _____ and end about _____
                                                (Date)                              (Date)

h. INDUSTRIAL:  Type of industry is _____
   Basis for determination of amount of water needed is _____

i. MINING:  The name of the claim is _____ . Patented ☐   Unpatented ☐
   The nature of the mine is _____ . Mineral to be mined is _____
   Type of milling or processing is _____
   After use, the water will be discharged into _____
                                                                (Name of stream)
   in _____ 1/4 of _____ 1/4 of Section _____ , T_____ , R_____ , _____ B. & M.
      (40-acre subdivision)

j. POWER: The total fall to be utilized is _____ feet. The maximum amount of water to be used through the penstock
   is _____ cubic feet per second. The maximum theoretical horsepower capable of being generated by the
   works is _____ . Electrical capacity is _____ kilowatts at _____ % efficiency.
            (Cubic feet per second x fall ÷ 8.8)        (Hp x 0.746 x efficiency)
   After use, the water will be discharged into _____
                                                                (Name of stream)
   in _____ 1/4 of _____ 1/4 of Section _____ , T____ , R____ , _____ B. & M.  FERC No. _____
      (40-acre subdivision)

k. FISH AND WILDLIFE PRESERVATION AND/OR ENHANCEMENT:  YES ☐  NO ☐   If yes, list specific species
   and habitat type that will be preserved or enhanced in item 17 of Environmental Information form WR 1-2.

l. OTHER:  Describe use: _____ . Basis for determination of amount of water needed is

   _____

**Figure 10–5. Application Form To Acquire Water Rights,** *continued*

## 6. PLACE OF USE

a. Does applicant own the land where the water will be used? YES ☐ NO ☐ Is land in joint ownership? YES ☐ NO ☐
(All joint owners should include their names as applicants and sign the application.)
If applicant does not own land where the water will be used, give name and address of owner and state what arrangements have been made with the owner.

_____

_____

b.

| USE IS WITHIN (40-acre subdivision) | | SECTION | TOWNSHIP | RANGE | BASE & MERIDIAN | IF IRRIGATED | |
|---|---|---|---|---|---|---|---|
| | | | | | | Number of acres | Presently cultivated (Y/N) |
| 1/4 of | 1/4 | | | | | | |
| 1/4 of | 1/4 | | | | | | |
| 1/4 of | 1/4 | | | | | | |
| 1/4 of | 1/4 | | | | | | |
| 1/4 of | 1/4 | | | | | | |
| 1/4 of | 1/4 | | | | | | |

(If area is unsurveyed, state the location as if lines of the public land survey were projected, or contact the Division of Water Rights. If space does not permit listing all 40-acre tracts, include on another sheet or state sections, townships and ranges, and show detail on map.)

## 7. DIVERSION WORKS

a. Diversion will be by gravity by means of _____
(Dam, pipe in unobstructed channel, pipe through dam, siphon, weir, gate, etc.)

b. Diversion will be by pumping from _____ Pump discharge rate _____ Horsepower _____
(Sump, offset well, channel, reservoir, etc.) (cfs or gpd)

c. Conduit from diversion point to first lateral or to offstream storage reservoir:

| CONDUIT (Pipe or channel) | MATERIAL (Type of pipe or channel lining) (Indicate if pipe is buried or not) | CROSS SECTIONAL DIMENSION (Pipe diameter or ditch depth and top and bottom width) | LENGTH (Feet) | TOTAL LIFT OR FALL | | CAPACITY (Estimate) |
|---|---|---|---|---|---|---|
| | | | | Feet | + or - | |
| | | | | | | |
| | | | | | | |
| | | | | | | |

d. Storage reservoirs: (For underground storage, complete Supplement 1 to WR1, available upon request.)

| Name or number of reservoir, if any | DAM | | | | RESERVOIR | | |
|---|---|---|---|---|---|---|---|
| | Vertical height from downstream toe of slope to spillway level (ft.) | Construction material | Dam length (ft.) | Freeboard Dam height above spillway crest (ft.) | Approximate surface area when full (acres) | Approximate capacity (acre-feet) | Maximum water depth (ft.) |
| | | | | | | | |
| | | | | | | | |
| | | | | | | | |

e. Outlet pipe: (For storage reservoirs having a capacity of 10 acre-feet or more.)

| Diameter of outlet pipe (inches) | Length of outlet pipe (feet) | FALL (Vertical distance between entrance and exit of outlet pipe in feet) | HEAD (Vertical distance from spillway to outlet pipe in reservoir in feet) | Estimated storage below outlet pipe entrance (dead storage) |
|---|---|---|---|---|
| | | | | |
| | | | | |

f. If water will be stored and the reservoir is not at the point of diversion, the maximum rate of diversion to offstream storage will be _____ cfs. Diversion to offstream storage will be made by: ☐ Pumping ☐ Gravity

## 8. COMPLETION SCHEDULE

a. Year work will start _____ b. Year work will be completed _____
c. Year water will be used to the full extent intended _____ d. If completed, year of first use _____

**Figure 10–5. Application Form To Acquire Water Rights,** *continued*

**9. GENERAL**

a. Name of the post office most used by those living near the proposed point of diversion is _____

b. Does any part of the place of use comprise a subdivision on file with the State Department of Real Estate? YES ☐ NO ☐
If yes, state name of the subdivision _____
If no, is subdivision of these lands contemplated? YES ☐ NO ☐
Is it planned to individually meter each service connection? YES ☐ NO ☐ If yes, When? _____

c. List the names and addresses of diverters of water from the source of supply downstream from the proposed point of diversion: _____

d. Is the source used for navigation, including use by pleasure boats, for a significant part of each year at the point of diversion, or does the source substantially contribute to a waterway which is used for navigation, including use by pleasure boats? YES ☐ NO ☐ If yes, explain: _____

**10. EXISTING WATER RIGHT**

Do you claim an existing right for the use of all or part of the water sought by this application? YES ☐ NO ☐
If yes, complete table below:

| Nature of Right (riparian, appropriative, groundwater.) | Year of First Use | Purpose of use made in recent years including amount, if known | Season of Use | Source | Location of Point of Diversion |
|---|---|---|---|---|---|
| | | | | | |
| | | | | | |
| | | | | | |

**11. AUTHORIZED AGENT (Optional)**

With respect to ☐ all matters concerning this water right application ☐ those matters designated as follows:
_____

_____ ( ) -
(Name of agent)    (Telephone number of agent between 8 a. m. and 5 p. m.)

_____   _____   _____   _____
(Mailing address)    (City or town)    (State)    (Zip code)

is authorized to act on my behalf as my agent.

**12. SIGNATURE OF APPLICANT**

I (we) declare under penalty of perjury that the above is true and correct to the best of my (our) knowledge and belief.
Dated _____ 19___, at _____ , California

(If there is more than one owner of the project, please indicate their relationship.)

Ms. Mr.
Miss. Mrs._____
(Signature of applicant)

Ms. Mr.
Miss. Mrs._____
(Signature of applicant)

*NOTE:*
*If this application is approved for a permit, a minimum permit fee of $100 will be required before the permit is issued. There is no additional fee for registration of small domestic use.*

**Figure 10–5. Application Form To Acquire Water Rights,** *continued*

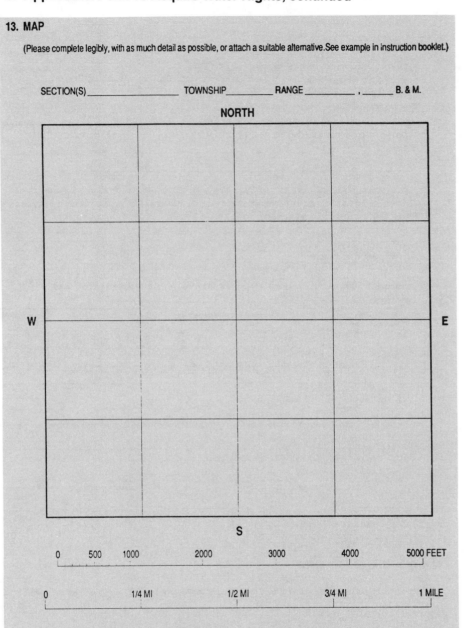

13. MAP

(Please complete legibly, with as much detail as possible, or attach a suitable alternative.See example in instruction booklet.)

SECTION(S)_____ TOWNSHIP_____ RANGE _____ , _____ B. & M.

(1)  Show location of the stream or spring, and give name.

(2)  Locate and describe the point of diversion (i. e. the point at which water is to be taken from the stream or spring) in the following way: Begin at the most convenient known corner of the public land survey, such as a section or quarter section corner (if on unsurveyed land more than two miles from a section corner, begin at a mark or some natural object or permanent monument that can be readily found and recognized) and measure directly north or south until opposite the point which it is desired to locate; then measure directly east or west to the desired point. Show these distances in figures on the map as shown in the instructions.

(3)  Show location of the main ditch or pipeline from the point of diversion.

(4)  Indicate clearly the proposed place of use of the water.

14. SUPPLEMENTAL INFORMATION

a. If you are applying for a permit, Environmental Information form WR1-2 should be completed and attached to this form.

b. If you are registering a small domestic use, Fish and Game Information form WR1-3 should be completed and attached to this form.

c. If you are applying for underground storage, Supplement 1 to WR 1 (available upon request) should be completed and attached to this form.

power, regardless of any detrimental effects on lower riparian users as long as they are compensated for damages. The states that have this stipulation for water are Connecticut, Georgia, Kentucky, Nebraska, New Hampshire, North Carolina, North Dakota, Rhode Island, South Dakota and Virginia.

## Lakes

If you buy property on or near a lake, find out the rights and regulations regarding lakes in your state. A lake, like a river, can be navigable or non-navigable, but the same rules apply in most cases. In most states, the government owns the beds of navigable lakes, but the owner cannot prevent the public from freely using the lake and taking water from it as long as the public has access to the lake. In all states, the ownership of the shore goes with the adjoining property, and the public may be prevented from using that part of the shoreline.

You may have more rights if you are on a non-navigable lake. As a riparian landowner you own the bed of the lake along with all other riparian owners. You have the right to use the entire surface of the lake for recreation, although your property may adjoin the lake for only a small distance along the shoreline. A minority of states, including Illinois, require that ownership of the lake bed must be specified in your deed before you may use the water, and some states restrict your use to the area within the boundaries of your part of the lake bed.

If you are buying property that is not directly on a lake but the seller assures you that you have a right to use it, investigate his assurances. You will probably need an easement across someone's land to get to the lake, and you may need separate rights reserved in writing in your deed to use the lake. If you desire docking facilities for a boat, you will need written permission from the person who owns the docks. The permission should be permanent, otherwise you might be charged an excessive fee to renew the right at a later date. All of these rights are valuable assets to the property; they must be recorded in the public records and in your deed to be legally binding. Your title search should investigate your rights to use a lake if you expect to do so after you purchase your land.

## Underground Water

Wells capturing underground waters provide most rural landowners with their own water supply. Underground waters, usually called groundwater or percolating waters, form from the rain or snow runoff that drains beneath the surface rather than over it and is held in aquifers, porous earth formations such as gravel and sandstone. Some states divide underground waters into several categories, such as underground streams, underflow of streams and percolating water, and apply different laws to each type of water.

Whereas numerous surface water laws were enacted centuries ago, only a handful of laws relating to underground water had been passed prior to World War II because large-scale development of groundwater resources did not occur before that time. Underground water laws are extremely confusing, partly because legislation has not kept up with scientific research on the patterns of underground water movement. In this chapter I can give you only a general idea of the types of laws in force today. The variables are so great throughout the country that you must investigate your state's particular laws to gain a complete knowledge of your rights and liabilities.

Different types of water rights laws have developed for underground waters, as they have for surface waters. These are the English common law *doctrine of absolute ownership,* the American *rule of reasonable use,* the California *rule of correlative rights,* and the *prior appropriation doctrine.*

### The Doctrine of Absolute Ownership

The original rule established in England drew no distinction between underground water and the soil around it. Thus, no rights to groundwater as a separate entity were recognized. The owner of a parcel of land owned the water within it as part of the land. He could extract as much water as he desired, even if he drained all the water from the soil of adjoining landowners. This rule of unlimited withdrawals is now the prevailing doctrine in all the states of the humid Midwest and East, although statutes have been passed modifying the rule to various degrees in many of these states. The main reason for this lack of advancement in underground water laws is that water shortages in the East are not as great a problem as they are in the states of the arid West. Texas is the only arid state that still follows the law of absolute ownership and unlimited withdrawal.

### The Rule of Reasonable Use

A few arid states employ the American rule of reasonable use, which is simply a variation of the English rule of absolute ownership. It holds that a landowner can pump water from beneath his land, even if he draws water from a neighbor's land, so long as the amount he takes is reasonable in relation to the rights of surrounding landowners. Of course, reasonableness is difficult to determine, and therefore the reasonable use rule has not been applied in many states. Only Arizona, Nebraska and Oklahoma continue to use it today.

### The Rule of Correlative Rights

California is the only state that recognizes the rule of correlative rights. Under this rule, if a source of water is shared by two or more neighboring landowners and these landowners use their water reasonably and beneficially, all must share a shortage according to their respective ownerships. No priorities exist among them. One landowner cannot use more than his or her share if the rights of another neighboring landowner will be injured thereby. The purpose of this doctrine is to ensure that all landowners get some water as long as any is available, regardless of how little.

### The Prior Appropriation Doctrine

Priority between appropriators of underground water is based on the same "first in time is first in right" rule that is used for surface waters. All of the western states except Nebraska and Texas have some form of prior appropriation law for underground water. Often this law is applied in combination with another doctrine for particular types of underground sources. The 16 states that use prior appropriation are Alaska, Arizona, California, Colorado, Idaho, Kansas, Montana, Nevada, New Mexico, North Dakota, Oklahoma, Oregon, South Dakota, Utah, Washington and Wyoming.

Thirteen of these states require a permit for all groundwater extractions, regardless of whether the appropriator is an overlying owner, unless the water is to be used only for domestic purposes or for watering stock, lawns or gardens. The other three states, Arizona, California and Montana, require landowners to apply for permits to pump water in only a few designated areas, although all states require a permit to drill a well. Arizona has a new groundwater statute under which groundwater may not be used and wells may not be drilled in statutorily designated active management areas, except pursuant to previously established water right or permit. This is to prevent further development in areas of water shortages.

As with surface-water prior appropriation, the date of issue of a permit determines one's priority in time of shortage. Once a permit is issued, it can be revoked if no water is used for a period of two to five years, depending on the state's requirements.

### Investigating Potential Well Disputes

Even in areas of plentiful water, pumping can sometimes lower the water table sufficiently to cause problems. Many cases of water depletion due to an overabundance of wells in one water basin area have been recorded. When the basin dries up, all well owners suffer. Legal battles often arise between overlying owners because one of them causes the water level to drop below the well depth of the adjacent user. For example, the first landowner pumps from a 100-foot well. A second landowner constructs a 200-foot well and pumps twice as much water as the first well owner. There is still water available for the latter's use, but the well will have to be extended deeper to get it. (See Figure 4–2 in Chapter 4, "Is There Enough Water on the Land?")

The courts have arrived at various solutions to such problems. The second well owner may be ordered to diminish pumping in hopes that the water level will rise or be required to pay the costs of lowering the first landowner's well to the new depth of the lowered water table. A court might consider any use that lowers the natural water table to be unreasonable and enjoin such use. If the first user had a permit, the second user might be prohibited from drilling a well in the first place.

When you are looking for land, be sure enough water is available for your intended needs, because if you deplete the water source or lower its level, you could be liable for damages or enjoined from pumping. Ask adjacent landowners how much water they use and if they know the extent of the underground waters and the level of the water table. In prior appropriation states, check the county recorder's office, state engineer's office or state water agency for permits that have been filed and approved that affect the extent of current pumping and the priorities of other well owners.

Many states regulate well drilling, and certain

requirements must be met by both the landowner and the well driller. You may be required to file a statement of intent and file for a permit if you plan to dig a new well, dig one deeper or repair an old one. The work may have to be inspected by a county or state official, and a permit fee may be demanded. The well driller might be required to file reports, or logs, with the state engineer, geologist or surveyor. The water's potability may have to meet certain legal standards. if you buy land that already has a well on it and if the state or county has any ordinances governing wells, you want to be sure the seller has complied with all the regulations. (See Chapter 13, "Building and Health Codes.")

## Losing Water Rights by Prescription

The necessary elements for prescriptive water rights are the same as those for adverse possession. The prescriptive user must take and use the water in a hostile, actual, notorious, exclusive and continuous manner under a claim of title. (These elements are explained in Chapter 16, "Adverse Possession.")

One of the most common ways to lose water rights by prescription is when an adjoining landowner runs a pipe to a spring on a neighbor's property, either intentionally or by mistake. For example, an owner might think a spring is on her land (the boundary lines have not been surveyed), so she begins to take the water, improve her property and act as if the water is rightfully hers. After ten years, the adjoining property is sold and the purchaser conducts a survey for the first time. The survey shows that the spring, in fact, is on the purchaser's property, and he states his intention to disconnect the neighbor's line, claiming that she is trespassing.

The neighbor then can go to court and file a legal procedure, usually called a *quiet title action,* to establish that she has the permanent right to take the water by prescription, because she has taken it in excess of the required time period, continually, openly and without permission under a claim of right as if she had the right to take the water. Further, she has improved her property, relying on the water. She will likely win her case and will obtain a permanent right to take the water, even though she has nothing in writing giving her the right and originally began the taking with a mistaken belief that the spring was on her land.

This shows the importance of surveying and inspecting your land before the purchase, looking for any uses being made of the property. If there are pipelines on the property that run to a neighbor's land: make immediate and probing inquiry of the seller and the neighbor to find out why water is being taken off the land, and have a survey done. In that way you will find out if there is a potential problem. You will save yourself thousands of dollars in legal expense and much grief if you discover these things before you become the owner of the property.

## Diffused Surface Water

In some areas, "diffused" surface water produced by rain, snow or spring runoff creates serious problems. Often landowners who try to protect their land from flooding by diverting a large amount of runoff away from their houses or fields will, in the process, damage neighboring property. If such a situation is likely to occur on land you might buy, find out about the laws regarding diffused surface waters for your area.

A majority of states permit landowners to pave or regrade their land to alter the flow of surface runoff only if they can do so reasonably, with little danger of harm to adjoining lands.

Twelve states, Arizona, Arkansas, Hawaii, Indiana, Missouri, Nebraska, New York, North Dakota, Oklahoma, Virginia, West Virginia and Wisconsin, follow the common enemy doctrine, which takes the view that flood and runoff waters are enemies landowners may combat by any means necessary, even if their self-defense creates increased dangers for their neighbors. In other words, your neighbor can divert flood waters onto your land, you can divert them onto the next adjacent land, and so on. Although this may seem ridiculous and unreasonable, it was the original approach taken by the courts.

If you are buying land in one of these 12 states, you must inspect the land for signs that it has been flooded or is in danger of being inundated by runoff from a neighbor's land. Since you will probably be a newcomer to the neighborhood, older residents might attempt to take advantage of you. Talk to them before you buy about the problems, if any, that result from excess water runoff. This is most important where your parcel is small and is surrounded by many other parcels.

A few states have formulated an approach to runoff surface water exactly opposite to the common enemy doctrine. This rule, called the *natural flow doctrine,* prohibits a landowner from interrupting or affecting the flow of water even if he or she is harmed by the inaction. The theory is that fewer people will be harmed this way. The states that follow this doctrine are Alabama, California, Georgia, Illinois, Kansas, Kentucky, Pennsylvania and Tennessee.

Sometimes farmers approach drainage problems on a large scale with the combined help of many landowners. Since large areas of flat fertile land would be useless without adequate drainage or flood control, many areas have formed drainage districts. A *drainage district* is created when landowners in an area petition the state for permission to build an extensive system of drains and ditches across large areas for the purpose of protecting valuable land. A vote is held in the affected area, and if the issue passes, a district is organized. Private lands can be purchased for easements to lay drainage tile and ditches; if the owners refuse to sell, their lands may be condemned and taken by the government's right of eminent domain. (See Chapter 15, "Eminent Domain and Condemnation.") Tax assessments increase in the area because of the additional benefits afforded by the efficient large-scale drainage organization, and the price of land within the district generally increases. If your land is within a drainage district, find out what your assessments will be and how your land will be serviced by the district.

## Water Supply Districts and Companies

Water companies and districts are organized to supply water to landowners where large areas need irrigation and the available water resources are inadequate.

Irrigation districts are organized in the same manner as drainage districts, except that the irrigation district brings water to the land, rather than removing water from the land. Water costs in a district are regulated by the state public utilities commission. Sometimes a special assessment will be levied by the district on each property owner to pay for the water development.

Occasionally, instead of forming an irrigation district, farmers band together and organize their own mutual irrigation or water company. Each farmer owns shares in the company. The company purchases, stores and distributes water to its shareholders. These private, nonprofit associations of landowners pool their separate water rights in the company and work together for the purpose of helping each other.

More common today are private commercial water companies that sell water as their "product." The amount of water to be received by a landowner is determined by a contract between the landowner and the company or by the amount of corporate stock bought by the purchaser. If the landowner has stock, his "dividends" are in water rather than money. In most cases, water can be used only on the land for which the stock was issued. If you purchase land being serviced by a mutual or private water company, be sure you are to receive stock or a contract to get water as part of your purchase.

A public utility water company may be set up to sell water to anyone requesting it within its service area. This kind of water company operates like any other public utility company that serves a large city. You will be charged a rate established by state regulations according to the amount of water you use.

## A Final Caution

You now have a basic knowledge of the potential problems that can arise among water users. You can take steps before purchasing land to protect yourself. The seller may not be aware of many potential problems regarding the water on his or her land. He or she may never have used the water for the purposes you intend to use it for. The seller may have been appropriating water without getting a permit, and you will fail to have seniority. You should understand what your rights will be before you buy the land, lest you be unable to get what you need when it is too late. You should also know the water problems explained in Chapter 4, "Is There Enough Water on the Land?"

If you are to take water from somebody else's property, you will need your rights specifically defined and recorded, so that you cannot be cut off in the future at the whim of the landowner. If you ever do have a water problem that you cannot settle by dealing with your fellow water users on a personal level, you may have to hire an attorney. Your attorney will probably initiate legal actions of quieting title and declaratory relief to settle boundary and water usage disputes. If immediate relief is sought, the attorney will file a temporary restraining order and a permanent injunction to prevent you from having your supply completely cut off. He or she might also file an action for damages. These expensive actions can be avoided by careful planning before you complete your purchase.

The various laws discussed throughout this chapter are subject to change at any time. Legislatures are constantly enacting new laws and eradicating old ones. Courts are always coming up with new decisions. It is your responsibility, unless you want to pay a lawyer to do the work, to investigate current water rights laws in your state and to determine the potential for future problems.

Without a doubt, the legal battles of the twenty-first century will be over water, the one commodity we can't live without. You should expect to see water rights mentioned in the press and on television with greater frequency in the years to come. Many rural places where folks are now settling have never had developed homesites at any time in the past, with people using water on a daily basis for all their needs. There is no question that the population is expanding in many rural areas where the water supply is insufficient to meet the needs of all the landowners. Where I live, I get clients in my office practically every week complaining about water hassles they are having with their neighbors. You cannot be too cautious in evaluating the water situation for any property you are thinking of buying.

## Useful Resources

**Local Farm Adviser, Agricultural Experiment Station, State Department of Water Resources and State Engineer**
Any of these sources should have information regarding your state's water laws and how the land

you want to buy is affected by them. The addresses of the experiment stations can be found in your local telephone directory under "Agriculture," either at the state or county levels.

Every state has a department of water resources. There is usually an agency within the department that has specific control over water resources and that issues water regulations and oversees all water use. (See the list of state water resource departments in the "Useful Resources" for Chapter 4.) The director of this agency is usually called the state engineer or water commissioner. If you write to your state's water agency, they will send you complete information on the laws for your state with an application form for an appropriation permit where applicable.

Although the pamphlets and application forms listed below apply only to California, they are good examples of the types of information you can obtain from any state you are in. They can be obtained free from:

> State Water Resources Control Board
> Division of Water Rights
> P.O. Box 2000
> Sacramento, CA 95810

"Information Pertaining to Water Rights in California: Statements of Water Diversion and Use"
"Regulations Pertaining to Appropriation of Water in California"
"How To File an Application Registration To Appropriate Water in California"
"Statutory Water Rights law"
"A Guide to California Water Rights Appropriations"
"The Water Right Process"

# CHAPTER

# 11 Mineral, Oil, Gas, Timber, Soil and Other Rights

When we decided on the property we wanted to buy, we were surprised during our preliminary investigation and after receiving our preliminary title report to discover that our deed would include a reservation of mineral rights in favor of the federal government. The reservation read:

> The Seller grants said land to the Buyer excepting therefrom all coal, oil, gas, and other hydrocarbon rights and mineral rights in said land together with the right to prospect for, mine, and remove the same as reserved by the United States of America in Patent recorded June 8, 1928, in Book 24, page 214 of Patents in the Office of the County Recorder of said County.

Mineral rights, oil and gas rights, timber rights, rights to take water, crops and anything else in or near the earth can be reserved in a deed when the seller of a piece of land wants to keep a right to take these things. Once these rights have been legally reserved, they become encumbrances on the land title, regardless of who buys the land. The right to take something from another's land is called a *profit* or *reservation*. In our case, the federal government retained, or reserved, a profit to take oil and natural gas when it originally sold the land to a private buyer on June 8, 1928. The original deed was recorded in the patents books, which are on public file in the county recorder's office; thus, it is binding on us and anyone else who buys the land after us. When the government first deeded land out of the public domain, it used a patent, which is like a deed. Every patent usually reserved mineral rights as standard procedure, without regard to whether or not useful minerals actually existed. There is now a procedure that allows

**142**

landowners to reacquire the mineral rights to their own land, provided the government determines that there are no minerals likely to be found on the land.

## Investigating a Reservation

You are probably wondering why we bought the land, knowing the government could come in and extract minerals at any time. Before we bought, we conducted a full-scale investigation of the history of mineral exploration in our area. We went first to our state Division of Mines and Geology, cornered an official and spent the day with him going over technical mineral maps of our area and discussing the possibility of the government's ever exercising its reservation rights. Tracing the history of oil exploration in our area, we found that in 1861 the first producing oil wells in California were drilled in a town just 20 miles north of us. The first shipment of oil came out of the area in 1865, when 100 gallons of oil were carried out of the hills in goatskin bags on the backs of mules. Drilling continued for only four months at that location, and a total of 100 barrels of oil were pumped. In the late 1800s and early 1900s, oil rigs were put up in three other towns, all within 15 miles of our place. None of those derricks produced a substantial amount of oil, and pumping was terminated. That activity was the extent of oil drilling in our area. There was no evidence that large-scale mining of coal or other minerals had occurred, although during World War II nitrates had been mined about ten miles from us for a short period of time. We also checked with the federal Office of Minerals and found no new information.

Thus we knew that our land was not another Alaskan oil field, and it was the unofficial opinion of the government official that the reservation would probably never be exercised. The federal government always reserves oil and mineral rights when it sells its land, and although it could always sell its profit to some enterprising company that might drill on pure speculation, we decided that the chances of that happening during our ownership of the land were not very high. We also took into consideration the fact that the government had held the profit since 1928 without using it. This reservation of oil and natural gas was the only defect or encumbrance on the title, so we decided to take the risk and buy the land because everything else about the deal was excellent.

In general I don't recommend buying land that has a reservation of a profit in the deed. After a thorough investigation, however, if you think that the reserved right will not be exercised during your ownership and if everything else in the deal is perfect, you might consider buying the land, although the price should reflect the fact that there is a reservation of rights against the title.

I told you about our investigation to give you an idea of the kind of search you should conduct to ascertain the potential danger of a reservation of the right to remove something from the land. You should consider the length of time between the reservation and your purchase and whether the profit has ever been exercised. Another important consideration is the potential damage that would be done to the land if the profit were ever used. For example, if oil were extracted, rigs would be used until all the oil was removed. They would then be removed. If the right to take gravel were reserved, a whole river bottom could be dug up. If timber rights were reserved, all the trees on your land could be cut. One of the most frequently reserved, and potentially dangerous, rights is the right to cut and remove timber.

## Timber Rights

If your deed includes a reservation of timber rights, the owner of the profit can come onto the property to remove the trees at any time. When this reservation exists, the real estate agent or seller might say that the land has already been logged once and there cannot possibly be another cutting for a hundred years. Depending on how extensive the last cutting was and on how fast the trees grow, this may or may not be true. Even if it is true, you will have a harder time selling the land to someone else as the time approaches for the trees to be cut; and you can never cut any of the trees yourself without incurring potential liability to the timber owner.

As with mineral rights, if timber rights were previously sold separately from the land, this sale is recorded in the county recorder's office. You should be aware of the special meanings of the words used to reserve the right to cut timber. If the original sale specified only that "timber is reserved," the holder can cut only the timber growing at the time he or she received the profit. Thus, if trees have been cut once by the person who reserved the timber on your land and the cutting was done after the date of the reservation, that person no longer holds any right to cut trees. You own the timber rights. If the timber was already cut, the land might look so bad that you wouldn't want it anyway. If you were told that the timber is no longer subject to the right to be cut, then you should request that a deed be obtained that clears this encumbrance from the land title. Timber that has been cut and is lying on the ground does not automatically pass with the land. Once a tree is cut, it becomes personal property and loses its status as real property. If trees have recently been cut on your land, be sure that the deed specifically states that you will acquire the fallen timber with the land and that the seller has not already sold the fallen timber to anyone else.

## How To Find Out If There Is a Reservation in the Deed

Even if the seller or real estate agent does not inform you that you are not getting clear title to the entire land, you will know the truth when you receive an abstract of title, or preliminary title report. Any profit given in a transaction before the sale to you will be recorded in the public records and will be uncovered by a title search. If it is not recorded and you do not know about it, then it will not be legally binding on you. If you become aware of the presence of a prior reservation, go to the county recorder's office and examine the original document that contains the reservation, so you will know all the details of the encumbrance. This knowledge will help you conduct your investigation to determine the probabilities of the profits being exercised in the future. It is easy to look up the document when you know the book and page number.

### Right of Entry

If someone has been granted the right to extract something from your land, the right of entry is implied in that right, unless specified otherwise. When the holder of a profit has the right of entry, he can use the surface of the land in any reasonable manner to perform drilling or other operations for the purpose of extracting the materials that are the subject of the profit.

You will be in a much safer position regarding a reservation if the deed specifies that the holder does not have a right of entry. For example, the reservation in the deed might read like this:

> The Seller grants the land to the Buyer reserving all oil, mineral, gas and other hydrocarbon substances below a depth of 500 feet under the real estate described in the deed, without the right of surface entry.

If the holder of the profit does not have the right of entry to your land, you can refuse him entrance to your property or you can charge him a fee for this privilege. In the above example, if you refuse entry, the holder of the profit can only dig on an adjoining parcel and take whatever is below a 500-foot depth under your land. This type of reservation is used mainly for gas and oil, for which the right of entry is not essential, because a well dug on someone else's land can pump the gas and oil that flows beneath your land to the well.

### Right To Remove Crops

If you are buying farm land that has crops growing on it, ascertain whether the crops have been sold by the owner to another party before you buy the land. If the crops are already sold, then the price of the land should be reduced accordingly. The crops on the land the season you buy might be all that have been sold or the owner might have a long-term contract with a buyer that will be binding on you if you purchase the land. Read any such contracts carefully to ascertain their terms.

### Grazing Rights

If land is subject to someone else's rights to graze livestock on it, you probably don't want the property. Livestock can cause considerable damage to land and seriously disrupt your quiet enjoyment of your property. If cattle are grazing on your land when you inspect it prior to purchase, inquire as to why they are there, how they will be removed and what rights, if any, the livestock owner has to have them there. Grazing and wandering horses, cattle and sheep are a serious problem in many areas of the country, particularly where open grazing is allowed.

### Royalty Rights

If the title is subject to a profit that was sold by the present or an earlier owner, the person who sold the profit probably retained royalty rights to part of the income arising from a future taking of any materials. Try to determine from the recorded documents, the real estate agent or the seller if any royalty arrangements have been made. If so, and you are considering buying the land, attempt to have such royalty rights transferred to you with the property. Then, if the property is disturbed by oil drillers or anyone else, you will reap some benefit from the situation.

## If the Seller Wants To Reserve a Profit

If your seller wishes to reserve the right to take something from the land after he sells it to you, then your situation is different from the one we confronted when we bought our land. It is one thing when the government reserved mineral rights as a matter of policy 50 years ago and has never exercised the right. But it is much different when your seller wants to hold on to some rights when he or she sells you the land. Be extremely cautious in such a situation. Why does the seller want to reserve a profit? If the seller refuses to sell the land without reserving the right to remove something, I recommend that you start looking somewhere else.

## Getting a Loan When Profits Are Reserved

If you intend to borrow money with your land as collateral, some lending agencies might be reluctant to help you if it seems likely that excavations will occur on the land. They may feel that you and your land are not a good risk because your ownership might be interfered with at a later date. You can determine the effect of any reservation in your deed on possible loans by talking to a few lending agencies before you buy. Obviously, if a reservation prevents you from getting the loan you need to buy the land, you had better look for another piece of land.

## Profits by Prescription (Prescriptive Profits)

I have already discussed prescriptive easements in Chapter 9, "Easement Rights." Profits can also be gained by prescription. The requirements are the same as for adverse possession except that the situation is different. (See Chapter 16, "Adverse Possession."). To gain a prescriptive profit, the person claiming the right must have been removing the materials for the legally prescribed length of time, which is set by the statute of limitations. For example, if an adjoining landowner has been taking fruit from trees on the seller's land under the conditions required for adverse possession, and he has done so for the required amount of time, he can claim a prescriptive profit to take the fruit for as long as he wants to continue to do so.

You can discover a prescriptive user only by inspecting the land. If you see evidence that rocks, soil, water, timber, crops or other materials are being removed, find out what the situation is. A title search or abstract of title will not detect a prescriptive use.

## Reservation of Profits in the Contract of Sale

All recorded reservations in the deed and against the title will show up in a title report or abstract of title, which should be shown to you for your approval prior to the close of escrow. You should have a copy of any reservation before you close escrow or approve the reservation, so that you know what is not included in the title to the property.

If you find that a reservation exists and you do not want to buy the property unless the reservation is cleared from the title, then you should disapprove of the title report or abstract of title and demand that the reservation be removed before the close of escrow. You can write your objection in the following manner:

> Buyer disapproves of the condition of title and demands the removal of the existing reservation which states that _____
>
> _____
>
> _____
>
> This reservation must be removed as an encumbrance on the title to said property, by an appropriate document recorded with the County Recorder, before the time scheduled for closing of escrow. If the condition is not satisfied, Buyer has the right at his election to terminate the agreement or waive the condition.

## Useful Resources

**United States Geological Survey**
**Earth Science Information Centers**

Questions about all aspects of geology can be directed to the Geologic Inquiries Group of the USGS. This office answers questions on topics such as earthquakes, energy and mineral resources, the geology of specific areas and geologic maps and mapping.

Information on geologic map indexes for the States is also available. Contact:

> Geologic Inquiries Group
> U.S. Geological Survey
> 907 National Center
> Reston, VA 22092

or any local USGS–ESIC office listed in "Useful Resources" for Chapter 5.

If you are interested in finding out about minerals in your state, contact one of the State Geo-Science Agencies (SGA) offices listed below or one of the state USGS–ESIC offices listed in Chapter 5.

Alabama
> Geological Survey of Alabama
> P.O. O
> University, AL 35486
> (205) 349-2852

Alaska
> Geodata Center
> Geophysical Institute
> P.O. Box 757320
> Anchorage, AK 99775-7320
> (907) 474-6960

Arizona
> E.S.I.C.
> U.S.G.S.
> 340 North Sixth Ave.
> Tucson, AZ 85705-8325
> (602) 670-5584

Arkansas
> Arkansas Geological Commission
> 3815 W. Roosevelt Rd.
> Little Rock, AR 72204
> (501) 296-1877

California
> California Department of Conservation
> Division of Mines and Geology
> 801 K St., MS 14-34
> Sacramento, CA 95814-3532
> (916) 327-1850

Connecticut
> Department of Maps and Publications
> 79 Elm St.
> Hartford, CT 06106-5127
> (203) 424-3555

Delaware
> Delaware Geological Survey
> University of Delaware
> 101 Penny Hall
> Newark, DE 19716-7501
> (302) 831-8262

District of Columbia
> Library of Congress, Federal ESIC
> Washington, D.C. 20540
> (202) 707-8533

Florida
> Florida Resources and Environmental
>    Analysis Center
> 361 Bellamy Bldg.
> Tallahassee, FL 32306-4015
> (904) 644-2883

Georgia
> Mapping Center Office
> 1200 Equitable Bldg.
> 100 Peachtree St.
> Atlanta, GA 30303
> (404) 656-5527

Hawaii
> University of Hawaii at Manoa
> Thomas Hale Hamilton Library Map
>    Collection
> 2550 The Mall
> Honolulu, HI 96822
> (808) 956-6199

Idaho
> University of Idaho Library
> Map Collection
> Moscow, ID 83843-4144
> (208) 885-7552

Illinois

    Illinois State Geological Survey

    615 E. Peabody Dr., Room 121

    Champaign, IL 61820-6964

    (217) 244-0933

Indiana

    Purdue University

    Laboratory for Applications of Remote

        Sensing

    1158 ENTM 220

    West Layfayette, IN 47907-1158

    (317) 494-6305

Iowa

    Iowa Dept. of Natural Resources

    Geological Survey

    109 Trowbridge Hall

    Iowa City, IA 52242-1319

    (319) 335-1575

Kansas

    Kansas Geological Survey

    1930 Constant Ave., Campus West

    The University of Kansas

    Lawrence, KS 66046-2598

    (913) 864-3965

Kentucky

    Kentucky Geological Survey

    University of Kentucky

    228 Mining & Mineral Resources

    Lexington, KY 40506-0107

    (606) 257-3896

Louisiana

    Louisiana Geological Survey

    Louisiana State

    Box G, University Station

    Baton Rouge, LA 70893-4107

    (504) 388-5320

Maine

    Maine Geological Survey

    Department of Conservation

    State House, Station 22

    Augusta, ME 04333

    (207) 287-2801

Maryland

    Maryland Geological Survey

    2300 St. Paul St.

    Baltimore, MD 21218

    (410) 554-5524

Massachusetts

    University of Massachusetts

    Cartographic Information

    Blaisdell House

    Amherst, MA 01003

    (413) 545-0359

Michigan

    Land and Water Management

    Stevens T. Mason Building

    P.O. Box 30028

    Lansing, MI 48909

    (517) 373-9123

Minnesota

    University of Minnesota

    S76 Wilson Library

    Minneapolis, MN 55455-0414

    (612) 624-4549

Mississippi

    Mississippi Institutions of Higher Learning

    MARIS

    3825 Ridgewood Dr.

    Jackson, MS 39211

    (601) 982-6354

Missouri

    Department of Natural Resources

    Division of Geology and Land Survey

    P.O. Box 250

    Rolla, MO 65401

    (314) 368-2125

Montana

    Montana Bureau of Mines and Geology

    Montana Tech, Publications

    1300 West Park St.

    Butte, MT 59701-8997

    (406) 496-4167

Nebraska

    Conservation and Survey Division

    The University of Nebraska

    113 Nebraska Hall

    Lincoln, NE 68588-0517

    (401) 472-7523

Nevada

> Nevada Bureau of Mines and Geology
> University of Nevada
> Reno, NV 89557-0088
> (702) 784-6691

New Hampshire

> Diamond Library
> University of New Hampshire
> Durham, NH 03824-3592
> (603) 862-1777

New Jersey

> New Jersey Geological Survey CN-029
> Trenton, NJ 08625-0427
> (609) 292-2576

New Mexico

> Earth Data Analysis Center
> University of New Mexico
> 2500 Yale SE., Suite 100
> Albuquerque, NM 87131-6031
> (505) 277-3622

New York

> Map Information Unit, State Office Campus
> N.Y. Dept. of Transportation
> Building 4, Room 105
> Albany, NY 12232
> (518) 457-3555

North Carolina

> North Carolina Geological Survey
> P.O. Box 27687
> Raleigh, NC 27611-7687
> (919) 733-2423

North Dakota

> North Dakota Geological Survey
> 1022 East Divide Ave.
> Bismark, ND 58505-0840
> (701) 328-4109

Ohio

> Ohio Department of Natural Resources
> Fountain Square, Building B
> Columbus, OH 43224
> (614) 265-6770

Oklahoma

> Geological Library
> The University of Oklahoma
> 100 East Boyd, R-220
> Norman, OK 73019-0628
> (405) 325-6451

Oregon

> Department of Geology and
>    Mineral Industries
> 800 Northeast Oregon St.
> P.O. Box 5
> Portland, OR 97232
> (503) 872-8750

Pennsylvania

> Bureau of Topographic and
>    Geological Survey
> Department of Environmental Resources
> P.O. Box 8453
> Harrisburg, PA 17105-8453
> (717) 783-8077

South Carolina

> South Carolina Land and Resource
>    Information Center
> 2221 Devine St., Suite 222
> Columbia, SC 29205-2474
> (803) 734-9100

South Dakota

> South Dakota Geological Survey
> Science Center
> University of South Dakota
> Vermillion, SD 57069-2390
> (605) 677-5227

Tennessee

> TVA
> Maps and Surveys Branch-ESIC
> 1101 Market St.
> Chattanooga, TN 37402-2801
> (615) 751-MAPS

Texas

> Texas Natural Resources Information System
> P.O. Box 13231
> Austin, TX 78711-3231
> (512) 463-8337

Utah

    Utah Geological Society
    2363 South Foothill Dr.
    Salt Lake City, UT 84109-1491
    (801) 467-7970

Vermont

    University of Vermont
    Map Room
    Bailey/Howe Library
    Burlington VT 84109-1491
    (802) 656-2503

Virginia

    Virginia Division of Mineral Resources
    P.O. Box 3667
    Charlottesville, VA 22903
    (804) 293-5121

Washington

    Washington State Library
    Document Section—State ESIC Office
    P.O. Box 42478
    Olympia, WA 98504-2460
    (206) 753-4027

West Virginia

    West Virginia Geological and
        Economic Survey
    P.O. Box 879
    Morgantown, WV 26507-0879
    (304) 594-2331

Wisconsin

    State Cartographer's Office
    Science Hall, Room 160
    550 North Park St.
    Madison, WI 53706-1404
    (608) 262-3065

Wyoming

    Geological Survey of Wyoming
    P.O. Box 3008
    University Station
    Laramie, WY 82071-3008
    (307) 766-2286

# 12 Zoning Laws

Zoning is one of the public rights to regulate an individual's land use, without compensation to the owner, for the health, safety and general welfare of everyone. Building and health codes and subdivision laws are also included in this public regulatory power. Depending on your reasons for buying land, zoning laws can be either excellent protection or a damper on your freedom. An investigation of the zoning in your area is an essential aspect of your purchase.

More than 80 percent of the 3,000-plus counties in the United States have zoning power. Each county is first divided into districts, or zones, according to a master plan created by the local planning or zoning commission. The basic zones are industrial, business, residential and agricultural, but there can be many other types. The following list of some of the common types of zones is a good example of how land use can be broken down.

| Zone Symbol | Description |
| --- | --- |
| A | Agriculture |
| Al | Agriculture; residential-agriculture; single-family |
| A2 | Agriculture; poultry and rabbit raising |
| A3 | Heavy Agriculture; floriculture |
| AC | Arts and crafts |
| AE | Agriculture; agriculture-exclusive |
| AL | Limited agriculture |
| AR | Agriculture-residential; administrative research |
| AV | Airport |
| B | Buffer |
| C | Business; commercial |
| C1 | Limited commercial; retail |
| C1S | Shopping center |
| C2 | General commercial; limited commercial; neighborhood shopping |

C3   General commercial; regional shopping; community shopping

C4   Unlimited commercial; service stations

CA   Commercial-agriculture

CH   Highway commercial

CM   Commercial manufacturing

Co   Commercial-office; professional office

CR   Restricted commercial; recreational commercial; community reserve

D2   Desert-mountain

E2   One-family residence; estate; executive; small farms

E3   One-family residence; estate; mountain estate

FP   Flood plain

FR   Forestry-recreation

GA   General agriculture

GR   Guest ranch

HI   Highway

IA   Industrial-recreational; industrial-administrative research

Ll   Light industrial

M    Industrial; manufacturing

MI   Light manufacturing; residential

M3   Heavy industrial

O    Open space; official

P    Parking; parks

PC   Planned community

PF   Public facilities

PR   Park and recreation

Q    Quarries

RI   Single-family residential

R1H  Residential hillside

R2   Duplex; multiple-family

R3A  Multiple-family; mountain resort

R4   High-density multiple-family; suburban residential

R5   Tourist accommodations

R15  Single-family, low density

PA   Residential-agriculture

RE   Residential estate

RF   Recreation-forestry

RR   Rural residential; resort-recreation; residential-resort

RRB  Restricted roadside business

RT   Recreational-tourist; residential transitional

RWY  Railway

SR   Recreation; scientific research

T    Trailer park

TPZ  Timber Preservation Zone

U    Unclassified; hog ranch

WA   Watercourse area

WR   Watershed-recreational

After the county has formed the zones, the specific regulations for each division limit the dimension of the buildings, the size of the building lots and subdivision limits, the density of the population and the number of houses permitted, and the purposes for which the buildings and land can be used.

## Find Out the Zoning Laws Before You Buy

Because zoning is not covered in an abstract of title or title insurance policy, you will have to do some research on your own to ensure that the land you want to buy is in an area that permits the specific activities you want and prohibits those you want to avoid.

All zoning regulations for a particular area are kept by the county board of supervisors, the zoning commission, the planning commission or the building inspector. Ask to see the master plan of the entire area so you can determine the direction of future development. To determine the zoning for a specific parcel of land, you should have its legal description, which you can get from the seller or real estate agent. You might then have to see the tax assessor and get the tax or parcel number for the land if that is how it is listed in the planning books for your community. If the area you are looking at has been incorporated into a town or city, it will be regulated by town or city ordinances; otherwise, separate county ordinances will apply. In some areas, no zoning ordinance will exist at all.

If your area has not been zoned yet, you will have to exercise extreme care in the selection of your country home. After you purchase the land, somebody might come along and construct a bar, junkyard, rendering plant, chicken farm, shopping center, recreation center, second-home subdivision, trailer park or factory. You cannot predict the future in an unzoned area. Do not assume that just because the land is far away from a town or city, no ordinances exist. A piece of land can be very isolated and still be in an industrial zone, where any big business can put up a factory and you might not be allowed to build a residence, or you might not want to. I had a recent case where a homesite was along a beautiful river that turned out to be a gravel extraction area, and there was nothing the landowner could do to stop daily rock crushing.

## Common Zoning Restrictions To Watch For

Zoning law enforcement is usually carried out by the building and health inspectors. They will refuse to issue a permit to build if a proposed building or use of the land violates the zoning restrictions of the area. The penalties for violating these laws are harsh, and enforcement in the more populated areas is relatively efficient. (See Chapter 13, "Building and Health Codes.")

Among zoning restrictions that commonly hinder rural land buyers who want to live on their land are the following:

*Seasonal Dwelling Restrictions*
Some secluded areas are zoned for second-home summer use only. You will not be permitted to live on the land the entire year.

*Number of Homes Permitted*
Most rural areas restrict the number of homes that can be built in an area. For example, only one dwelling will be permitted for every 20 acres of land, or one dwelling per parcel, regardless of size.

*Minimum Size of a Parcel for a Dwelling*
No home can be built on a parcel of less than a specified minimum area.

*Prohibition of Further Subdividing*
Your parcel might already be of a size that prohibits further dividing. If you plan to split off and sell a parcel to raise money to pay for your remaining parcel, be sure the zoning will allow this. Also be aware of this if you buy with partners and intend to split up the land between you at a later date. You might not be able to do so.

*Floodplain Zoning*
An area with a history of flooding might be zoned as a floodplain on which all home construction is prohibited.

*Trailers and Mobile Homes*
Zoning laws often prohibit the use of mobile homes, trailers, buses and vans for dwellings. Mobile homes and trailers, if permitted, are usually restricted to a specified area to prevent them from "cheapening" the value of surrounding houses.

### Variances and Use Permits

If you want to use your land in a way prohibited by the zoning regulations, you must seek a variance or nonconforming-use permit. The purpose of issuing such permits is to retain flexibility in the zoning laws so that land may be used for activities that are compatible with the surrounding area or only temporary. For example, if a trailer is prohibited as a dwelling, you could apply for a use permit to live in a trailer on your land while you are building a permanent residence.

An application must be made to the board of appeals, board of supervisors or planning commission for a variance. The petition application must show that the intended use will not detrimentally affect the surrounding area or create problems for the regular uses permitted in the zone.

Variances are not issued automatically. If they were, the whole purpose of zoning would be defeated. If a real estate agent tells you to go ahead and buy the property because getting a variance will not be a problem, do not listen to him. Always get a necessary variance before you buy. Clause 17(c) of the Model Contract of Sale in Chapter 27 can be used to condition the closing of the deal on your ability to get a use permit. If the permit has not been granted by the close of escrow, you can either terminate the contract or extend the closing date.

### Zoning Warranty

Clause 16(d) in the Model Contract of Sale is a warranty stating what the zoning is at the time the contract is signed and that it will continue to be so zoned at the close of escrow. This is to prevent a situation in which a rezoning that could prohibit your intended use of the land occurs before escrow closes. If the zoning is changed, the contract can be terminated or you can sue the seller for breach of warranty.

Clause 16(f) is a warranty by the seller that there are no violations of any zoning ordinances that have resulted from any activity on his property at the time of sale, whether or not he has actually been cited by the county for a zoning violation.

## Useful Resources

Information on local zoning in your area can be obtained from the county Planning Commission, the county Zoning Commission, the Board of Supervisors or the county Building Inspector.

**Coastal Zone Management**
There are state agencies that plan and implement programs for the orderly development of coastal zones and may have their own separate zoning and building rules controlling development of ocean and inland water coastal properties. You will find their addresses in the local phone book or call the local planning department for more information. Use the addresses below, look for local offices in your phone book or call the local planning department for more information.

Alabama
Environmental Management Department
1751 Cong. W. L.
Dickinson Dr.
Montgomery, AL 36130

Alaska
Division of Governmental Coordination
Office of the Governor
P.O. Box AW
Juneau, AK 99811

California
Coastal Commission
631 Howard St., 4th Floor
San Francisco, CA 94105

Connecticut
Planning and Coastal Area Management
Environmental Protection Department
165 Capitol Ave.
Hartford, CT 06106

Delaware
Department of Natural Resources
    and Environmental Control
89 Kings Hwy.
Dover, DE 19901

Florida
Coastal Zone Management
Environmental Regulation Department
2600 Blairstone Rd.
Tallahassee, FL 32399-2400

Georgia
Coastal Resources Division
Department of Natural Resources
1200 Glynn Ave.
Brunswick, GA 31523-9990

Hawaii
Coastal Zone Management Program
Office of State Planning
State Capitol
Honolulu, HI 96813

Illinois
Division of Water Resources
Department of Transportation
310 S. Michigan Ave., Room 1606
Chicago, IL 60604

Indiana
Division of Water
Department of Natural Resources
2475 Director's Row
Indianapolis, IN 46241

Louisiana
Office of Coastal Management
Department of Natural Resources
P.O. Box 4487
Baton Rouge, LA 70804-4487

Maine
State Planning Office
Executive Department
State House Station, #38
Augusta, ME 04333

Maryland
Tidewater Administration
Department of Natural Resources
Tawes State Office Building
Annapolis, MD 21401

Massachusetts
Coastal Zone Management
Executive Office of Environmental Affairs
100 Cambridge St.
Boston, MA 02202

Michigan
> Great Lakes SHoreland Section
> Department of Natural Resources
> 500 Lafayette Rd.
> St. Paul, MN 55155-4001

Mississippi
> Bureau of Marine Resources
> 2620 W. Beach Blvd.
> Biloxi, MS 39531

New Hampshire
> Office of State Planning
> 2½ Beacon St.
> Concord, NH 03301

New Jersey
> Division of Coastal Resources
> Environmental Protection Department
> 501 E. State St., CN 401
> Trenton, NJ 08625

New York
> Department of State
> 162 Washington Ave.
> Albany, NY 12231

North Carolina
> Coastal Management Division
> Natural Resources and Community
>   Development Department
> 512 N. Salisbury St.
> Raleigh, NC 27604-1148

Ohio
> Division of Water
> Department of Natural Resources
> Fountain Square, Building E
> Columbus, OH 43224

Oregon
> Policy Division, Land Conservation and
>   Development Department
> 1175 Court St., N.E.
> Salem, OR 97310

Rhode Island
> Coastal Resources Management Council
> Department of Environmental Management
> 9 Hayes St.
> Providence, RI 02903

South Carolina
> Coastal Council
> 1201 Main St., SUite 1520
> Columbia, SC 29201

Texas
> Governor's Offices of Budget Planning
> Box 12428, Capitol Station
> Austin, TX 78711

Virginia
> Council on the Environment
> Ninth Street Office Building
> Richmond, VA 23219

Washington
> Division of Aquatic Lands
> Department of Natural Resources
> 202 Cherberg Building
> M/S: QW-21
> Olympia, WA 98504

West Virginia
> Division of Natural Resources
> 1800 Washington St., E.
> Building 3, Room 669
> Charleston, WV 25305

Wisconsin
> Coastal Management Section
> Department of Administration
> P.O. Box 7864
> Madison, WI 53707

# 13 Building and Health Codes

*I sometimes think men do not act like reasonable creatures, when they build for themselves combustible dwellings in which they are every day obligated to use fire.*

—Benjamin Franklin,
letter, 1787, entitled "Building Acts Anticipated"

Building and health codes, like zoning ordinances, are included in the right of the government to regulate individual land use for the health, safety and general welfare of the people. The county may also regulate the construction of private roads that lead onto public county roads to protect those public roads. In this chapter I discuss building codes, permits and enforcement; health codes and permits; road encroachment permits; and how to protect yourself in the contract of sale so you can be sure no code violations exist on the property you are buying.

## Building Codes

The first recorded building code in America was passed in New York (then called New Amsterdam)

in 1625. The code specified types of roof coverings and locations of dwellings to prevent roof fires. In 1648 New York prohibited wooden or plastered chimneys, and inspections by firemasters were initiated. By 1656 straw and reed roofs were prohibited and ordered removed from all houses. Philadelphia went a step farther in 1701 by passing a law providing that any person whose chimney caught on fire would be prosecuted and fined. From the very beginning, building laws were enacted only after disasters had occurred. Although fire prevention was the primary issue in the first building codes, today all aspects of construction are regulated.

Building laws are designed to protect people's financial investments as well as to ensure their personal safety. Often the appearance of a structure is regulated, and unusually designed houses may be discouraged. (I talk more about this later in this chapter.)

Today most building regulations throughout the United States are based on the Uniform Building Code, which was established by the International Conference of Building Officials (ICBO) in 1927.

The Uniform Building Code's stated purpose is to prevent people from being hurt physically or financially by providing minimum uniform standards of building construction.

The Uniform Building Code sets standards for foundations, building materials, design, size and location of rooms, means of exit, windows and ventilation, fireproofing in construction, load and stress of materials for particular purposes, chimneys, stairways and guards, sanitary equipment, plumbing and electricity. Reprinted here are some requirements from the Uniform Building Code that are good examples of the kinds of details covered.

1.  With each application for a building permit, two sets of plans for construction shall be submitted.

2.  Plans shall be drawn to scale upon substantial paper and shall be of sufficient clarity to indicate the nature and extent of the work proposed and show in detail that it will conform to the provision of the Uniform Building Code.

3.  Plans shall include a plot showing the location of the proposed building and of every existing building on the property.

4.  Minimum room sizes:
    a.  At least one room of 120 sq. ft.
    b.  Rooms used for both cooking and living or living and sleeping at least 150 sq. ft.
    c.  Rooms used for sleeping two persons 90 sq. ft. Each additional person—50 sq. ft.
    d.  Kitchen at least 50 sq. ft.

5.  Minimum horizontal dimension of any habitable room shall be 7'-0". Minimum ceiling height in habitable rooms, service rooms, and toilet rooms shall be 7'-0". Where sloping ceilings occur, the required ceiling height shall be provided in at least 50% of the room and no portion of any room having a ceiling height of less than 5' shall be considered as contributing to the minimum required areas. Minimum ceiling height in hallways, corridors, and closets shall be 7'-0".

6.  No water closet (toilet) space shall be less than 2'-6" wide and shall have a minimum of 2'-0" clear space in front of the water closet.

7.  Required window area and opening:
    a.  Bathrooms and water closet compartments not less than 3 sq. ft. nor ⅛ of the floor area, ½ openable.
    b.  Kitchens, rooms used for living, dining or sleeping purposes not less than 12 sq. ft. nor ⅛ of the floor area, ½ openable.

8.  Every dwelling shall be provided with a kitchen. No kitchen shall be used for sleeping purposes.

9.  Every dwelling shall have the following minimum sanitary facilities: water closet, lavatory, tub or shower and kitchen sink. All kitchen sinks shall be provided with hot and cold water. All of the above items shall be properly trapped, vented, and connected to an approved sewage disposal system.

10.  There shall be no opening from a room in which a water closet is located into a room in which food is prepared or stored.

11.  The specifications on this sheet are for conventionally framed dwellings and persons wanting unusual type construction should consult a professional designer.

Of the 3,000-plus counties in the United States, 2,000 follow the ICBO standards, although some areas make changes when necessitated by climatic or topographical conditions and local administrative procedures. The local building inspector's office will have copies of the area's building requirements, including standards for building construction, electrical wiring and plumbing.

## Permits and Fees

Before you build or renovate a structure, you must submit your plans to the local building inspector for approval and pay the applicable permit fees. If the building is a standard-construction "conventionally framed dwelling" of stud wall or masonry construction, you can submit your own plans. The inspector will examine the plans for compliance with the codes. If they are suitable, they will be approved. Then you pay a permit fee based on the number of square feet in the building. There is a standard fee list for each area that you can see before you pay the fee. At the time plans are approved, one-half of the stated building fee must be paid.

Other permits must be obtained for plumbing and electrical facilities and additional fees paid. These fees are based on the number of outlets to be built into the dwelling.

## Inspections and Certification of Occupation

Once your plans are approved and a permit is issued, you can build the house yourself. The law does not require you to hire professional builders. During construction many building departments make four inspections. The first is to look at the foundation after it is laid. The second is a frame inspection after the roof framing and basing are in place and pipes, chimneys and vents are complete. The third is the wall inspection before plastering and siding is commenced. The fourth and final inspection comes after the building is completed and ready for occupancy. Many rural areas only require a single inspection after the house is completed.

Before a house can be lived in and after the final inspection, the building department often is required to issue a certificate of occupancy. If you are buying a newly constructed house, be sure it has been certified properly.

## Getting an Unconventional Structure Approved

If you intend to build an unusually designed dwelling, you will be required to write to the ICBO to see if they have any approved plans for such a structure. (See "Useful Resources" at the end of this chapter.) They have approved standard plans for common unconventional designs, such as domes, yurts and round houses. In most areas, you must have specific plans drawn up by a licensed engineer or contractor.

## Test for Structural Strength

The Uniform Building Code provides that if a structure does not meet normal code requirements, the local building inspector may conduct a test for structural strength on the building before it is approved. In many cases, you will have to hire a structural engineer to conduct these tests to the satisfaction of the building department.

Because of the growing popularity of domes, some companies have conducted strength tests on plywood domes. If you plan a dome, write for the results of tests undertaken by any of the members of the National Association of Home Builders' National

Dome Council. The National Association of Home Builders is a national organization whose membership includes manufacturers of dome buildings. (See "Useful Resources" in Chapter 6 for the address.)

You can contact these manufacturers for questions and information on designs, specifications, prices and builder/dealers in your particular area. These companies sell sets of dome and even yurt plans that may get automatic approval from any building inspector working under the Uniform Building Code. The reason for this is that the ICBO has already tested these designs and approved them. Most building inspectors have not had the experience of dealing with a dome, yurt or other atypical design and thus won't accept anything other than ICBO-approved plans. But you must check with your local department so see what their attitude is. If you can convince an inspector you know what you are doing, you may be able to get approval for an unconventional design.

## Temporary Dwellings

If you want to buy land but don't have the money to put up a house right away, most counties will allow you to live in a temporary dwelling while building a permanent dwelling. In some areas the building inspector does not have jurisdiction to regulate any temporary dwellings or canvas structures, such as tents or teepees. A tent usually means that 25 percent or more of the walls and roof are covered by canvas or other fabric.

If you have a bus, van, camper or trailer, you can usually live in it on isolated land indefinitely, except where zoning and building restrictions are strictly enforced. A fee is charged for a temporary dwelling permit, and a time limit is placed on the length of time you can house yourself temporarily. Many subdivisions have restrictions against living in any temporary facility, even while constructing a permanent dwelling. Read the subdivision covenants, conditions and restrictions to see if this is the case in your area.

## Land That Has Structures on It

If you want to purchase land with a structure already on it, be sure that it has been approved and that it meets current building and health code standards.

Two problems arise when you buy an older

house. The first occurs if the structure was built to code but is now substandard because the code has since been revised. Fortunately, new codes do not apply retroactively to buildings already approved in previous years. However, if the structure is determined to be a fire or health hazard or substandard because of revised code requirements after it was built, no permits will be issued for repairs, enlargements or modernization of the building. The theory is that if you are unable to touch the house as it is, you will tear it down and rebuild according to contemporary standards. This situation is usually encountered in areas close to urban centers.

A more frequent problem in rural areas occurs if a house was built prior to the institution of building codes in that locality and thus was never built to any set of standards. Whether you can live in it as it is or must first have it brought up to code will depend on your local building inspector. I have encountered inspectors who would take no pity in such a situation.

## How To Find Out If a Building Is Up to Code Standards

To discover whether a building meets the current standards, visit the county building inspector and see what he or she has on file with regard to the structure. You will have to give the inspector the name of the current owner and the location of the land. Do not say what you think is wrong with the place until you see what is in the file. The inspector should have a paid permit with all approvals having been granted. If you are talking to the official who inspected the house, ask what his or her opinion of the structure is. Then tell what you are going to pay for it and see what the reaction is. The official might reinforce your opinion or open your eyes to some defects in the property you had not considered.

## Appealing a Denial of a Building Permit

Every county that has building codes will have an established process for appealing decisions of building inspectors. The first level of appeal is often within the building codes department itself, where a board of appeals will hear your request for a modification of a specific ordinance. You must present your situation and explain why it is impractical for you to comply with the code. For example, you might have to completely rebuild an older house to meet the codes, or you might be located far from any other buildings so your structure will not decrease the value of surrounding buildings. In most cases it will be difficult to convince the board that it is not practical for you to comply with the ordinance, but it is always worth a try if you feel you are being harassed. Use the same method for preparing your case as you would use for a tax appeal. (See Chapter 17, "Property Taxes and Assessments.") If the appeal fails, you will probably have to go to court, which involves the expenditure of time and money.

Some people choose to ignore the codes and permit requirements altogether. I have been in many places where enforcement is insignificant. However, every area of the country is gradually becoming more efficiently regulated on all levels. Even if you manage to avoid the building inspector now, when you decide to sell your property in five or ten years, your buyers might not be willing to pay a good price for a structure that was not approved. Meeting code requirements in rural areas is often so easy that it is really only a matter of paying the fees.

## Enforcement

Most local laws permit inspectors to enter property at any reasonable hour to enforce the provisions of the local ordinances. If they are refused permission to enter, as some are, they may leave and return later with search warrants and an entire squadron of enforcers, including policemen, police dogs, sheriffs and deputies. Sometimes county agencies use small aircraft and helicopters that scan the countryside in search of new, illegal constructions. By checking the records they know if permits have been taken out on any new construction they spot from the air. If none have, they will pay the builders a visit.

Sometimes the building inspector will go to great lengths to enforce the regulations. In one place I visited, the building inspector used a helicopter to fly low over an area where many young people had recently immigrated and drop smoke bombs over the sites of illegal structures. A crew on the ground then followed the smoke to the buildings and issued citations. Obviously every county is not this efficient. But when large numbers of new residents move in, the authorities usually keep an eye on their activities.

Salaries of building inspectors depend on how much money they take in for permits. If they manage to increase local revenues, they will not only have a better chance of keeping their jobs, but also a good argument for salary increases. Much of the activity of building inspectors and other bureaucrats with a smattering of power is dependent on local politics.

There can be extreme monetary penalties for building illegally without a permit. You will not be able to get electric utilities to hook up to your building without a valid permit. Make sure you are ready to accept the penalties if you build without a permit.

## Health Codes and Permits

Regardless of where you buy land, you will have to deal with local health authorities. They are empowered to make sure that you have proper water and sewerage facilities and to issue permits and collect fees. A small fee buys a permit for the construction of an outhouse and later installation of a septic tank. Contrary to popular belief, outhouses are not outlawed by many health departments. In many areas if you do not have adequate running water under pressure to your house and the outhouse is not located within 200 feet of an adjacent residence, you are permitted to use an outhouse (privy). The following are standard health requirements for outhouses:

1.  It shall be unlawful to erect or maintain a privy or outhouse unless a suitable shelter be provided to afford privacy and protection from the elements. The door thereof shall be so constructed as to close automatically by means of a spring or other device.
2.  The vault shall not be permitted to become filled with excreta nearer than two feet from the surface of the ground and such excreta shall be regularly and thoroughly disinfected.
3.  The privy building shall be made flyproof.
4.  The pit privy shall be at least 4 feet deep.
5.  The pit privy shall be at least 75 feet from well or stream.
6.  All privy buildings shall be kept in a clean and sanitary condition at all times.

Most areas today require that permanent septic tanks and leach lines be installed when a residence is constructed. This is often a costly venture that requires a machine operator to come in with a backhoe to dig your septic tank hole. The required minimum capacity of a septic tank is usually 750 gallons for a two-bedroom house. If you purchase land with a house already on it, be sure that the waste disposal system has been approved by the county and is functioning properly. You will save yourself a lot of trouble and expense if you discover inadequacies at an early stage in the proceedings. In most counties, cesspools and sewer wells are strictly prohibited; and even where they are allowed, they are an inferior method of waste disposal. These facilities are very common in many parts of the country, so be sure that the local regulations have not rendered such systems obsolete if they are in use on the land you are buying.

If no septic tank exists on the property and you want to construct a home, never buy the property without first completing a percolation test and having the local health department approve the property for sewage disposal. If you buy the property without approval, you might not be able to obtain a permit later, and you will not be able to build on the land, making it worthless. I have seen this occur dozens of times over the past 15 years in my law practice. (See Chapter 5, "The Earth—Soil, Vegetation, Topography," for information on percolation tests).

Health codes also regulate the construction of water facilities, particularly wells. Sanitary seals of concrete are required around the tops of wells to prevent seepage, and a coliform potability test is taken of all running water before it receives health department approval.

## Road Encroachment Permits

Some counties are touchy about how private roads encroach on, or lead onto, a county road because such adjoining roads, if not constructed and maintained properly, can cause damage to public roads. Problems include automobiles tracking mud from a dirt road onto a paved county road, washouts of dirt roads and dirt washing down onto paved roads.

Some counties regulate the construction of private roads and require permits and fees before construction of a dirt road that will encroach onto a public road is begun. The private owner is required to bring his or her road up to the standards of the public road at the point where the two roads meet. To do this, the costs vary, but they often run from $300 to $500, which includes grading materials, culvert pipe, paving and labor. If you have to construct a road to get onto your land, figure this cost into the purchase price and adjust the figures accordingly. If there is a good road into the property you will pay for this "extra."

Check on all road and encroachment requirements by contacting the local department of public works. Often it has a special office for roads called the "Road Division." Find out if the seller has obtained the proper permits for his or her road and if it meets current county standards.

Many counties also have minimum requirements for unimproved roads that must be met before a building permit will be issued. For instance, there must be a minimum road width of 20 feet so emergency vehicles can pass each other on the road, a certain number of turnouts must be available and a minimum layer of gravel and rock must be in place.

## Warranty That No Code Violations Exist

Clause 16(f) of the Model Contract of Sale in Chapter 27 is a warranty by the seller that no codes are being violated by his or her use of the property or by the construction of any improvement on it. This warranty means that no building, health, road encroachment, zoning or other codes are being violated and that all permits have been issued and fully paid for. The fact that the seller signs this warranty as part of the contract should not relieve you of going to the relevant local departments to determine if the seller has met the required status and codes.

## Condition the Purchase on Your Ability To Obtain Necessary Permits

If you intend to build a house on the land you are buying, speak to all the various inspectors about the local codes and have them look at the land to determine if there will be any problems with the building site that could prevent the issuance of the necessary permits. Find out before you buy whether

you can put a road in, build a house and have adequate site conditions for sewage disposal. If there is any doubt about your ability to obtain a permit, insert the type of permit being sought in clause 17(c) of the Model Contract of Sale. If you cannot get approval by the close of escrow, you can terminate the purchase and have your money returned or postpone the close of escrow. You must make a reasonable attempt to obtain the permit by submitting appropriate forms.

## How One Homeowner Got Rid of the Building Inspector

Many people in the country deal with the myriad bureaucratic hassles, permits and fees by ignoring them and hoping they do not get caught. Paul, a good friend of mine, chose the exact opposite tactic in dealing with his local building inspector, who was one of the toughest I have met. When Paul bought his place, the largest structure on the land was a big, beautiful red barn that he wanted to convert into his family dwelling. Because in the eyes of the law a barn is not meant to be a house, many problems were involved in meeting the requirements of the building codes.

Knowing in advance that he would meet the building inspector sooner or later, Paul went to his office and told him what he was going to do. He drew up some fairly sketchy but basic plans, submitted them for approval and paid the first part of his fees. Then he began to modify the barn to make it his home. The inspector came to make an inspection and then began appearing on a regular basis. Each time, he hassled Paul about some aspect of the remodeling job until he really got on Paul's nerves. So Paul decided to give him some of his own medicine.

Any time Paul began a new part of his remodeling—a new wall, floor, beam, ceiling or fireplace—he called up the building inspector and asked what kind of materials he should use, how much he should buy, what kind of nails or cement he should get and how he should do the job. After several weeks of constant phone calls, the inspector had had enough. In complete exasperation he told Paul, "Dammit, I'm not your architect or contractor. Stop calling and bothering me." Paul then sent in the rest of his fees and never saw the building inspector again.

As long as you know that your house is going to have to be built to code and be inspected by someone who is being paid with your fees, you might as well get your money's worth. Bug the inspector. Maybe he will leave you alone. If you are way off in the hills, all the inspector probably cares about is getting those fees. As long as nobody is going to see your house and complain about it and his job will not be jeopardized, he will probably leave you alone. On the other hand, the building inspector can be very helpful in answering questions you might have. Inspectors have different philosophies and outlooks on their job, and many of them can be useful advisers. I hope you find an enlightened building official in your area.

## Useful Resources

All local codes and sample plans can be obtained at your local inspector's office. Check with the building inspector, department of roads and health inspector. The three national organizations that make up the various codes will send you information on any aspect of the requirements for house construction. Write to the following:

(Uniform Building Code)
International Conference of Building
   Officials (ICBO)
5360 S. Workman Mill Rd.
Whittier, CA 91061
Voice: (310) 692- 4226
Fax: (310) 692-3853

(Uniform Plumbing Code)
International Association of Plumbing
   and Mechanical Officials
20001 Walnut Dr., South
Walnut, CA 91789-2825
Voice: (800) 85-IAPMO
Fax: (909) 594-3690

(The Electric Code)
The National Fire Protection Association
1 Batterymarch Park
Quincy, MA 02269
Voice: (617) 770-3000  or  (800) 344-3555
Fax: (617) 984-7057

Although local building inspectors usually distribute the required building regulations and sample construction plans, you can obtain a complete set of the Uniform Building Code in an abridged version by sending $16.30 to the ICBO for the latest edition of *The Uniform Building Code*. They also have a catalog titled "Publications, Products and Services," which includes building, plumbing, electrical, zoning, manufactured home installation, fire and any other codes you might need to know. These products are available on CD-Rom.

Agencies have been established to enforce standards of construction, materials and occupancy for all buildings in every state. Check your telephone directory under one of these headings: "Building Commission," "Division of Codes and Standards," "Building Codes Administration" and so forth.

# CHAPTER

# 14 Subdivisions and Condominiums

*Friends, you are now in Coconut Manor, one of the finest cities in Florida. Of course, we still need a few finishing touches. But who doesn't? This is the heart of the residential district. Every lot is a stone's throw away from the station. As soon as they throw enough stones we're going to build a station. Eight hundred beautiful residences will be built right here. . . . You can have any kind of home you want to. You can even get stucco—Oh how you can get stucco. . . . And don't forget the guarantee—my personal guarantee. If these lots don't double in value in a year, I don't know what you can do about it.*

— Groucho Marx, portraying a land hustler in the movie *Coconuts*

## Beware of Vacation and Recreational Land Developments

You have seen ads in periodicals and heard commercials on the radio and television about "planned recreational subdivisions." You are enticed with talk and photos of golf courses, swimming pools, recreational activities of various types and "modern" homes in a country setting. Finally you are told that if you buy early, you will make a small fortune when you sell in a few years. Do not fall for the Madison Avenue come-ons that offer you free vacations, traveling expenses, drinks and other assorted sucker baits. Avoid these offerings, for they are Trojan horses.

Here's how the developers make a fortune off you. A group of wealthy businessmen combine finances and organize themselves into a partnership or syndicate for the purpose of buying and subdividing land for profit. They scout the country to locate a rural area they think is ripe for development. When they find a large piece of undeveloped land, their eyes begin to see houses, streets, sold signs and dollar signs. They purchase the land for a pittance compared with what they will sell it for.

For example, in New Mexico a land corporation bought 86,200 acres for $3 million and subdivided it into 86,176 lots. Without building any homes, they began reselling the land for ten times what they had paid for it. Profits from land sales and interest, by the time the last lot is sold, will be $112 million. Their expenses for advertising and meeting federal requirements were relatively minimal.

## Common Land Frauds

I have nothing against somebody making a profit, but not when it is done through fraudulent means, particularly when the people who are defrauded are those who can least afford it. Buyers of lots in these subdivisions rely largely on what they are told through the media and by real estate salespersons. They exercise little caution because they are not required to part with a large sum of money at once; rather, they pay in low monthly installments. In most cases, the information is misleading because of what is left unsaid or because what is stated is a half-truth. Because this type of misrepresentation does not meet the legal requirements for fraud, it is often difficult to bring a developer to court.

The most common fraud is the failure of developers to construct promised amenities, such as lakes, recreation centers, swimming pools, golf courses, stables, and the like. In small print, the contract states that the developers do not have to construct these things until 90 percent of the lots have been sold. After the developers sell 80 percent of the lots, more than enough to give them a healthy profit, they simply stop advertising and move their operation to a new development. Thus they have not violated the terms of the contract, and you are stuck with a lot in the middle of a thousand other lots with nothing to show for your investment of thousands of dollars.

Another scheme is the promise, never made in writing, that streets and other facilities will be installed by the county or municipality once the development gets built up. Most of these developments, however, are built in unincorporated areas outside town boundaries. The lots are sold, but the streets, sidewalks, utility lines and other expected facilities are never constructed. The average rural county cannot afford to build facilities for 3,000 new homeowners, even with the initial tax gain from property taxes. In addition, many rural areas do not welcome large subdivisions that intrude on their quiet communities, destroying the ecology and small-town mood of the area.

In a variation of this scheme, developers truthfully told buyers that the water table under the development was enough to supply one million people for 500 years. They forgot to mention that the utility company that was the only water supplier in the area had facilities for only 8,000 homes, whereas there were more than 60,000 lots for sale in the development.

Subdivision lots often are put up for sale before they have actually been surveyed into parcels and staked out on the ground; or if they have been surveyed, no roads have been put in. Salespeople will take prospective buyers to a hill overlooking the development and point out the distant lots that are for sale. The buyer never sets foot on the parcel he or she buys. When the time comes to put in a driveway and a house, the buyer discovers that his lot is steep, inaccessible and without a decent building site. Never forget that the developers' idea of a "building site" might be a mountain goat's idea of heaven. A lot advertised as "readily accessible" might be reachable only by foot or a four-wheel-drive vehicle.

Often salespeople fail to mention that maps of a development are available. They try to get people to buy lots already earmarked for a future public road. This information is part of the public records, so the buyer's ignorance is no defense. Anything that can be discovered from the records is held to be "constructive notice" to a land buyer.

Sometimes developers try to create a sense of urgency in prospective buyers by using two-way radio systems to give the impression that huge volumes of property are being sold, when actually this is not the case. Although these radios are also used for legitimate purposes of communication, be wary if you feel pressured.

Misleading advertising is rampant. A development might be advertised as "10 miles from town," which is true—if you are a crow. For people, it is 40 miles by car. Phony photographs and artists' conceptions of what a development will eventually look like are frequently used in ads. Small-print in advertising is another common technique that, though legal, should be carefully scrutinized. One of my favorite examples of this technique is a recent brochure distributed by Lakeworld Corporation for its new "environmental project" called "Tahoe Donner" at Lake Tahoe, California. In large print, the colorful pamphlet states that

> when the first snowfall comes, you'll head for Tahoe Donner's own private* ski resort, planned for family skiing. . . . Because Tahoe Donner is a private* ski resort, it's one of the few uncrowded places in the area.

If you look for the asterisk, you will find it at the end of the brochure, where the following statement is printed in the smallest type used in the advertisement:

Lakeworld reserves the right to open the Tahoe Donner Ski Bowl to the public at any time.

Several years ago the California attorney general brought suits against 80 individuals and firms for a scheme involving vacation certificates given by companies in league with land promoters. California firms sell inexpensive tickets to Las Vegas, and while the vacationers are in Nevada, they are confronted by hard-sell land sellers peddling desert and swampland, worth a dollar or less an acre, for $1,000 or more an acre. More than two million vacation certificates were sold for the undisclosed purpose of selling subdivisions in Nevada in an operation that would be illegal under California law.

The Federal Trade Commission clamped down on seven land sales companies because they were telling customers that their company's main interest was to provide real estate training, when they were actually trying to sell land. These companies were also saying that adverse economic conditions do not affect land values.

Many subdivisions are sold that include a "Lot Owners Association," which is supposed to maintain roads and other facilities in the development. These associations often sound better on paper than they work in actual practice. The administrator for HUD's Interstate Land Sales Full Disclosure Act (discussed later in this chapter) has stated, "Too often, the Lot Owners Association is a smoke screen established and controlled by the developer." You must read the conditions and agreements of any association before buying in a subdivision.

Many land promoters make a huge amount of money by selling land to which they do not have clear title. Promoters get together enough cash to make down payments on large pieces of land and give sellers a mortgage for the rest. Then they subdivide the land and sell the parcels under *land contracts*, whereby they do not have to deliver title for many years. They use the payments from their buyers to make their own mortgage payments. This is a dangerous situation for buyers, because if for any reason a promoter's loan gets foreclosed on, the buyers will never get title to the land. Other reasons why you should never buy land under a land con-

tract are discussed in Chapter 21, "Types of Financing: Land Contract, Mortgage, Deed of Trust."

A point continually stressed by subdivision salespeople is the profit a buyer can anticipate when the parcel is resold. Buyers will be told that the developer will buy back the lots if they do not make a profit as an investment. Of course, this promise is never put in writing. It doesn't occur to buyers that they cannot resell at a profit until the developer has sold every single lot; otherwise they will be competing with the developer's own salespersons and prices. Even when the developer is out of the picture, the buyers are in competition with thousands of other lot owners, all selling basically the same product. Look in the want ads of your local paper if you want an idea of how many people are trying to sell their lots. It is ridiculous. According to one estimate the average minimum amount of time a lot owner must wait before he or she can make any profit on a resale is ten years.

Every lot buyer figures that all the other buyers will build houses on their lots and that this will increase the value of his or her lot, which can be left undeveloped and sold at a profit when the surrounding land is built up. The trouble is, every other buyer is thinking the same thing. For example, in California the *build-out rate*, the percentage of lots in recreational land developments on which homes are actually erected is only 1 percent. For these reasons and because land in a development is often so overpriced, you may find out too late that your investment has turned into a financial liability.

If you are interested in making a good land investment, you would be much better off buying a nice-sized piece of undeveloped land for the same price you would have paid for that tiny lot in a development. You can hold onto it for a few years and then sell it as a whole piece or subdivide it up yourself to make a larger profit.

To buy land strictly as an investment and actually make any money, you will have to spend a little more time planning your purchase than you would if you simply send a check to a large developer for one of his lots. It is not that easy to make money. You will have to research the local subdivision laws in your area to see if your scheme is possible and profitable. If you are interested in making an investment, you should be willing to spend some time and energy to make it a good one. You will always be better off buying a parcel of land in an area near the recreational facilities you want, rather than in a planned recreational community. Most areas in the country now have golf courses, swimming pools, riding stables, bowling alleys, ski slopes and the other amenities most people desire. In the country, ten acres for $20,000 is almost always going to be a better investment than a one-acre lot for $20,000 in a recreational subdivision.

## Types of Frauds Prosecuted by the Federal Government

In the past ten years the federal government's Office of Interstate Land Sales Registration has taken action against land developers in hundreds of cases. The following ploys are some of the more interesting and flagrant examples of land fraud the government has pursued. Various developers have been caught

- painting grass to look greener and tying pine cones on trees to make the land more desirable for promotional movies.
- not revealing that raw sewage had been dumped into a pit in the development and that a building that was advertised as the golf and pro shop contained no golf equipment and had no golf pro.
- failing to disclose that it could cost owners up to $12,000 to have electricity extended to their lots.
- giving a figure for installing wells and septic tanks that was one-third of actual cost.
- misrepresenting to buyers that the Army Corps of Engineers was building a canal connecting the subdivision property in Florida with the Gulf of Mexico.
- harassing property owners who complained to the federal agency about land fraud.
- handing out brochures stating that two Florida subdivisions were conveniently located near shopping centers, hospitals and beaches, when in fact the facilities were 40 miles away.
- failing to state that lots were not accessible by ordinary automobile.
- showing roads on maps that were in fact unmarked open fields.
- failing to disclose that the developer was in foreclosure at the time parcels were being sold.
- failing to reveal that lots would need fill before structures could be built on them.
- failing to reveal that the state department of health had closed the subdivision swimming pool.
- failing to reveal that many of the lots in a Florida subdivision are covered with tidal waters.
- failing to reveal that the water in the subdivision was not potable.
- falsely representing that purchase of a lot was a way to achieve financial security and representing that prices were increasing without disclosing that the increase may be the result of the developers' pricing, unrelated to actual changes in the value of the land.
- telling buyers that a swimming pool was built for use by all property owners without revealing that the pool was a small backyard type that was soon closed.
- failing to reveal that the lake for boating and swimming was too shallow for either activity.
- presenting maps to customers showing many recreational amenities that did not exist.
- failing to reveal that lots in a Nevada subdivision were not accessible by any vehicle because of deep arroyos and fences, and that some lots were located in a floodplain.
- failing to inform purchasers of homesites that local laws prohibited the construction of homes on individual lots of the size they bought.
- telling purchasers that the property in the subdivision would remain in a natural wooded state for use as a recreation and retirement community, when in fact they had leased coal rights to an oil company that would permit the company to surface-mine coal in the subdivision.
- routinely giving buyers a "fast shuffle" closing, after which they left the sales office without copies of contracts, notes, property reports or any other important documents.
- falsely promising purchasers that a 20-acre lake would be built when, in fact, the developer had no plans for a lake and had never applied for a state permit to build one.

The above examples of fraudulent land sales techniques are only a few of the many that have been used by land promoters. You might think that a defrauded buyer always has the remedy available of suing the developer or salesperson. Unfortunately, this is often impossible because the corporation or syndicate that sold the land has since disbanded or has gone bankrupt by means of slick legal maneuvering. Even if the developer is available to be sued, a lot of money is needed to hire a lawyer and proceed with a civil suit in court. Most lawyers require fairly large retainers, which the average land buyer cannot afford because he or she has already dropped a bundle on the land. Of course, developers usually have several experienced and slick lawyers ready for their defense. Because recourse in the courts is expensive and there is certainly no guarantee of success, your best insurance, if you insist on buying land in a promotional subdivision, is to use every method of investigating subdivisions at your disposal. Many are discussed below.

## Laws Regulating Subdivisions

The first law regulating land subdivisions was passed in the late 1800s and required uniform land surveys. Then, in the 1920s, tremendous land swindles swept the country and more control was assumed by local governments. Many of the laws passed since then were full of loopholes, but the federal, state and local governments are closing the loopholes and the laws are getting tougher as time goes on.

Generally the purpose of subdivision laws is to prevent the creation of lots of inadequate size and poor design; to prevent the creation of building sites in areas where the topography, floods or other factors make safe and beneficial land use impossible; to prevent the creation of badly built roads; to prevent hazards from sewage effluent and inadequate drainage; to prevent the lowering of property values and loss of opportunity for good overall development of neighborhoods caused by successive, uncontrolled and haphazard land divisions; to prevent excessive cost to taxpayers of the county for providing services within the subdivision; and to prevent fraudulent land sales practices.

Not all subdivisions are large planned developments. Any land that is broken up into two or more parcels of any size is "subdivided." Many state and local laws apply to all types of subdivision—a 200-acre parcel being split into four pieces as well as a 2,000-acre parcel being split into 400 lots. If you are planning to buy any land that has been subdivided for the purpose of resale, read this chapter carefully and check into all the laws that apply in your state and county.

## The Federal Interstate Land Sales Full Disclosure Act

This act, passed by Congress in 1968, now regulates all land promoters who offer 25 or more undeveloped lots for sale through the mail or by advertising in any kind of interstate commerce. The seller must first submit a statement of record to the Office of Interstate Land Sales Registration, an agency within the United States Department of Housing and Urban Development (HUD). The statement must include information about the ownership of the land, the state of its title, its physical nature, the availability of roads and utilities, and other matters. All prospective buyers must receive a printed property report that contains extracts from the statement of record at least 48 hours before they sign a contract of sale. The sample Final Subdivision Public Report later in this chapter is an example of information that must be included in the property report. (See Figure 14–3.)

Every buyer shown a property report has a "cooling off" period of seven days after signing in which to cancel the agreement, get out of the deal and get a full refund. If the property report was not given to the buyer before signing the contract, the buyer may revoke the agreement at any time within two years of the date of signing.

If you want to receive a public report or any other information on an interstate land promotion, write to the Office of Interstate Land Sales Registration at the address given in "Useful Resources" at the end of this chapter.

### The Big Bust of 1972

In 1972, HUD came down on 450 land developers nationwide for alleged violations of the Interstate Land Sales Full Disclosure Act. One of the biggest subdivision frauds attacked involved Lake Havasu Estates in Arizona. It all began in 1964, when the McCulloch Corporation developed Lake Havasu City in the Arizona desert on the edge of Lake Havasu, one of the rare lakes in the arid Southwest. Since that time, the subdivision has become a self-contained city of more than 15,000 people, famed for its purchase and reconstruction of London Bridge.

This boom of Lake Havasu City prompted a group of unscrupulous investors to purchase 10,000 acres of desert 40 miles to the north, subdivide it, name it Lake Havasu Estates, and promote it in a national sales campaign. The sales brochures contained pictures of lake recreation and implied the land was near water and would soon have all types of facilities, just like Lake Havasu City. Potential buyers were shown a copy of the magazine *Arizona Highways,* which contained an article about the fine accomplishments at Lake Havasu City. Salesmen described Lake Havasu Estates as a great city of the future, although it had no known water supply, no electricity or telephone lines or paved streets, no sewage disposal system, no garbage collection, no hospital, and no shopping areas or schools. The only buildings it had were a large geodesic "dinesphere" that never opened for dining and a portable sales office.

The developers of Lake Havasu Estates easily sold the plots sight unseen to buyers in other states by setting the price of each lot at $3,000 to $5,000, with a down payment of $165 and monthly payments of $57.29. Buyers were given a year to get a refund if desired. Although many buyers did request refunds, none were given.

In response to complaints by the victims of this white-collar crime, a federal grand jury indicted nine of Lake Havasu Estate's officers and salespersons on charges of mail fraud, misrepresentation in selling and advertising, and failure to register lots and provide property records to purchasers, as required by the Interstate Land Sales Full Disclosure Act.

**The Feds Catch a Former U.S. Attorney**
One of the major convictions by the federal prosecutors was of one of their own people. A former Pennsylvania assistant U.S. attorney was convicted of 33 counts of violating federal law in connection with a land development in the Pocono Mountains in Pennsylvania. A federal jury found the defendant guilty of 21 counts of violating the Interstate Land Sales Full Disclosure Act and 12 counts of mail fraud.

Among many false representations made by the defendant, the following were the most flagrant:

• He gave completion dates for installing sewage disposal systems and paving roads, knowing the facilities could not be finished on schedule.
• He promised to put funds from the sale of each lot into an escrow account to cover the installation costs of roads and water and sewer lines with full knowledge the funds were insufficient.
• He asserted the subdivision had been surveyed and the lots were staked so they could easily be

identified. Actually, most of the lots were unmarked.
• He promised to build a heated swimming pool and tennis courts. The promises were not kept, despite the developer's claims in his reports. He said it was unnecessary to drain surface water or use fill to build on the lots. In fact, some of the lots were subject to flooding and needed drainage or fill to make them fit for construction.
• He withdrew more than $15,000 from an escrow account set up to build a bathhouse. The facility was not built. Similarly, money was taken from an escrow account for swimming-pool work not performed.

After conviction, the former U.S. attorney was sentenced to four years in prison and fined $11,550. The following statement was issued by the prosecutor's office after the conviction:

> The conviction is part of the federal government's program to protect consumers from dishonest land developers. In far too many instances, people invest their life savings in land for retirement or other purposes, only to see their dreams go down the drain. We urge the public to look at the land firsthand before buying it. Buyers should ignore gaudy pamphlets describing fancy facilities that may never be built. Would-be purchasers of unimproved land cannot be too careful in checking the credibility and business methods of some developers who offer land for sale. Although it is the duty of the developer to provide the buyer with a copy of the required report, this action is meaningless unless the consumer reads the report and fully understands its contents before signing the contract.

## State and Local Subdivision Laws

*State and local governments have authority founded in the Constitution to regulate and direct the future growth patterns of their communities. Therefore, they should shoulder their share of the responsibility to protect their land resources from profit-minded developers who not only bilk the buying public but devastate the land in the process.*

—George K. Bernstein, former head of the
Office of Interstate Land Sales Registration

Besides the federal government, most state and local governments also are concerned with the regulation of land splits or subdivisions and have enacted their own laws, usually referred to as *subdivision laws*. Different laws are required for various types of subdivisions, which are distinguished on the basis of the size and the number of parcels created. Legal requirements for land divisions vary both among the states and among areas within each state. However, these laws are becoming standardized, based on the federal laws. Check with your local planning commission, board of supervisors and building inspector to find out the laws that control your area. (See "Useful Resources" at the end of this chapter.)

Local governments usually control subdivisions in all stages of their development. Before a development can begin, its promoters must file a preliminary map or *plat* for approval by the public authorities. After the land is subdivided, they must get approval from the building inspector, health department, department of public works and other agencies before construction can begin on dwellings, if any are to be built, or land improvements. Before the selling of land and homes can begin, a sales permit must be issued. Finally, before anyone can live in any houses on the land, a certificate of occupancy must be issued for each dwelling by the local authorities. (See Chapter 13, "Building and Health Codes.") Some states also require that a bond be furnished, as a guarantee that the developers will complete all improvements promised to buyers. The problem is that only the county can sue on the bond if developers don't follow through on their promises. In general, the more parcels there are, the more regulations apply to the development.

### The Local Planning Commission
The city and county planning (or zoning) commissions throughout the country play a major role in what happens to real estate in their areas. The planning commission prepares a comprehensive long-term general plan for the development of land in the area of its jurisdiction. Once its conception of the area has been composed on paper, the group must approve all proposed land developments, using the plan as its guide.

The planning commission controls such matters as the location and intent of land use; the placement of roads, streets and utilities and the density of the population and intensity of building construction; and zoning variances and use permits. When a plan

for a subdivision is submitted to the planning commission for approval, it is supposed to conform to the master plan to be approved. Projected plans are never permanent, so rezoning, waivers or variances are often permitted for the purpose of allowing the proposed subdivision to go ahead with its plan.

You may become involved with the planning commission if you seek a variance of the zoning or a use permit to conduct certain activities on your land. If the commission's meetings are open in your area, you will learn much about the future plans and present attitudes of the local government by attending a commission hearing. More information on the planning commission is contained in Chapter 12, "Zoning Laws."

### Platting the Subdivision
*Platting* is the term used for the process of mapping out the planned development and plotting on paper the manner in which the land is to be divided. The plat must show the surveyor's layout of the parcels in relation to survey marks actually in the ground. Each lot must be numbered and its size indicated, and the length of all boundary lines and location of all streets, easements, open areas and facilities designated. Any aspect of the surrounding area affecting the subdivision must be shown.

Many states now require that a preliminary plat of a proposed subdivision be submitted and tentatively approved by the planning commission. Figure 14–1 is an example of a preliminary, or tentative, plat submitted for approval of a four-parcel land split, called a *minor division*. Once the plat is approved, the subdivision will almost certainly progress to completion. The plat will include a separate document containing any protective restrictions and covenants that are part of the development, including the types of dwellings permitted, in terms of style and quality and restrictions, if any, on businesses, fences and maintenance of open space. The plat and any accompanying reports must indicate the extent of utilities, streets, curbs, gutters, sidewalks, storm and sanitary sewers, fire hydrants, street lighting and other facilities to be provided.

If the parcels are several acres or more in size, the developer often is required to indicate only a few things on his plat. It must show that each parcel has been surveyed and laid out on the ground. Easements from each parcel to the public road must be shown; a soil report indicating the adaptability of the area to proper installation of sewerage facili-

**Figure 14–1. Example of a Minor Division Tentative Map**

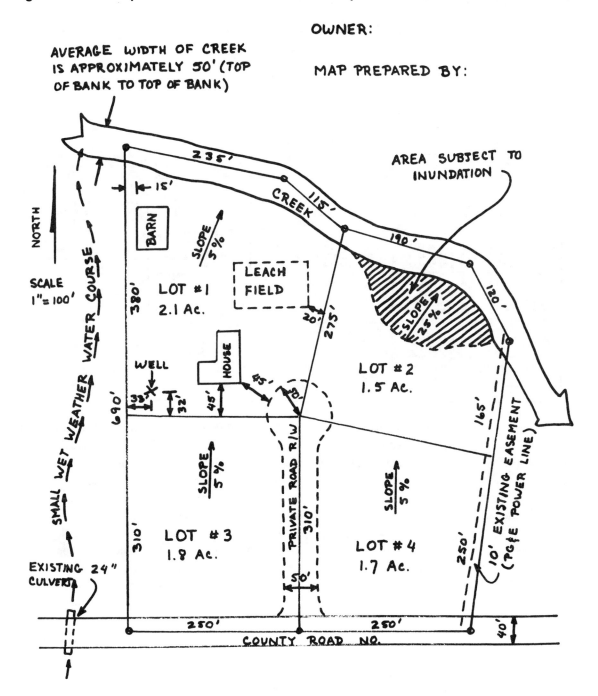

ties, usually septic tanks, must be included; and the available water supply must be located on the plat.

Those states that require the filing of a preliminary plat also require a final plat to be submitted after approval of the preliminary plat. This second filing is really just a formality. After it is approved and recorded, the building inspector must give his approval of any proposed buildings. He investigates whether the proposed plans meet the present zoning regulations with regard to the size of the parcels

and houses. If the plans do not meet these requirements, the planning commission will consider a request for rezoning or for a variance for the development. Assuming the okay is given, the building inspector must then approve the buildings.

All required plats must be placed on file with the local planning commission and recorded with the local government's recorder. There you can examine the submitted plans, if there are any, for the land you are interested in. You should be absolutely

**Figure 14–2. Example of a Parcel Map**

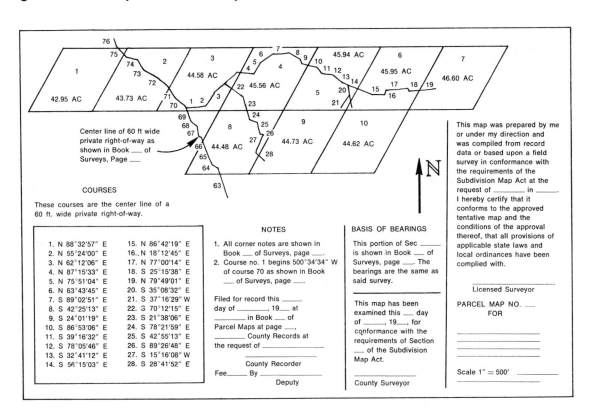

certain these plats have been approved and recorded because you can be refused building and health permits if your land is part of an unapproved subdivision. Always examine where your parcel will be in relation to the rest of the subdivision as indicated on the plat.

**Parcel Maps**

In some states, land splits containing fairly large parcels, usually 40 acres or more, require only parcel maps, which are much less detailed than full-scale plats or subdivision maps.

The parcel map must be drawn up by a licensed surveyor or registered civil engineer and submitted to the county surveyor or engineer for approval before filing. Usually, the map need indicate only the location of boundary lines for each parcel and easements from each parcel to the public road. Figure 14–2 is an example of a parcel map submitted for a subdivision of ten parcels of approximately 44 acres each.

**The Final Subdivision Public Report**

Because of increasing fraudulent activities of large-scale land developers, several states now require promoters to submit a public report covering all aspects of the planned subdivision. This is similar to

the Federal Property Report required under the Federal Interstate Land Sales Full Disclosure Act.

I have included the entire contents of a final subdivision public report here. (See Figure 14–3.) It indicates what a public report of this type must cover to meet the legal requirements of providing buyers with essential information concerning their proposed purchases, although some of the specific information in this report may not apply to your report. For instance, in this report the mineral rights have been reserved, whereas in yours they may not be. If you are buying in a state that does not require such a report, it will be up to you to make your own report to satisfy yourself that your purchase is a wise one. You will see after examining this final subdivision public report that it covers exactly those questions about land that I am detailing throughout this book. Of course, you should double-check the contents of any report, but if you can get a public report, much of your work will already be done for you. All you will have to do is read and analyze the report to understand what is involved in your purchase.

Unfortunately, many land developers don't file these reports even when they are required. State real estate enforcement agencies are usually understaffed and underfinanced and are unable to force the submission of such reports far many years, when much damage has already been done.

Always demand public reports from sellers or real estate agents who are handling the sale of subdivided land. If they say there are none, then go to the county planning commission and find out if such reports are required. You might uncover an illegal subdivision in the process.

Any legitimate land developer's advertising brochure will contain the following language: "Obtain the property report required by federal law and read it before signing anything. No federal or state agency has judged the merits or value, if any, of this property." The ad should also tell you how to obtain a public offering statement in those states where one is required. I cannot overemphasize the need to read these public reports and offering statements. They are required by the federal and state government for your protection.

## FHA and VA Approval

If subdividers want FHA and VA approval so that their markets will be increased by prospective buyers who need FHA-insured and VA-guaranteed home loans, their subdivisions must meet certain government standards. There are requirements on such things as housing design, taxes and assess-ments, restrictive covenants, physical plans for the area, housing needs, accessibility to public facilities and other essentials of a good loan risk.

## Property Owner's Associations and Covenants, Conditions and Restrictions

One of the major problems in subdivision and condominium development is that these operations are supposed to be run by all property owners banded together in an owners' association. This association is initially formed by the developer, who usually drafts articles of incorporation, bylaws and general rules.

Each property owner automatically becomes a member of the association, and the owner or owners of each parcel are entitled to one vote per parcel in the decision making. The association normally performs such tasks as maintaining the private roads in the subdivision, maintaining shared facilities—the swimming pool, tennis courts, golf course, boat ramp facilities and clubhouse—and hiring and firing employees of the association.

The association is run by a board of directors and a president, vice-president, secretary and treasurer. It is a small government, set up to manage the owners' affairs. It often suffers the same prob-

**Figure 14–3. Example of a Final Subdivision Public Report**

DEPARTMENT OF REAL ESTATE

OF THE

STATE OF _____

_____, Real Estate Commissioner

In the matter of the application

(SELLER'S NAME)

for a final subdivision public report on
(NAME OF THE SUBDIVISION)
COUNTY,

FINAL SUBDIVISION
PUBLIC REPORT

FILE NO. _____

ISSUED: _____(DATE)_____
EXPIRES: _____(DATE)_____

THIS REPORT IS NOT A RECOMMENDATION OR ENDORSEMENT OF THE SUBDIVISION BUT IS INFORMATIVE ONLY.

BUYER OR LESSEE MUST SIGN THAT HE HAS RECEIVED AND READ THIS REPORT. THIS REPORT EXPIRES ON DATE SHOWN ABOVE OR UPON A MATERIAL CHANGE.

**Figure 14–3. Example of a Final Subdivision Public Report** *continued*

SPECIAL NOTES

PROSPECTIVE PURCHASERS ARE URGED TO VISIT AND INSPECT THIS PROPERTY BE-FORE ENTERING INTO AN AGREEMENT TO PURCHASE.

THIS TRACT IS BEING OFFERED FOR SPECULATION ONLY.

THIS MEANS THE SUBDIVIDER HAS NOT BEEN REQUIRED TO MAKE ANY SHOWING THAT THE LOTS MAY BE USED FOR ANY OTHER USE, SUCH AS RESIDENTIAL.

SINCE NO PROVISIONS HAVE BEEN MADE FOR ANY OTHER USE THAN SPECULATION OF RAW LAND, THE SUBDIVIDER HAS NOT MET REQUIREMENTS FOR WATER, ROADS, UTILITIES, SEWAGE DISPOSAL, OR OTHER USUAL REQUIREMENTS FOR A RESIDENTIAL SUBDIVISION.

PURCHASERS WHO MIGHT CONTEMPLATE THE EVENTUAL DEVELOPMENT OF THEIR LOTS SHOULD CONSIDER THAT SUBSTANTIAL COSTS COULD BE INCURRED TO MAKE THE PROPERTY SUITABLE FOR ANY PROPOSED USE.

PURCHASERS SHOULD ALSO UNDERSTAND THAT WITHOUT THE COOPERATION OF OTHER PROPERTY OWNERS, INDIVIDUAL LOT OWNERS MIGHT FIND IT DIFFICULT AND EXPEN-SIVE TO DEVELOP THE PROPERTY.

ANY PERSON WHO PURCHASES FIVE OR MORE LOTS IN A SUBDIVISION WITH THE IN-TENT OF OFFERING THE LOTS FOR RE-SALE MUST OBTAIN A SUBDIVISION FINAL PUB-LIC REPORT FROM THE REAL ESTATE COMMISSIONER. IF THE LOTS ARE TO BE OF-FERED FOR SALE FOR RESIDENTIAL OR OTHER USAGE, IT WILL BE NECESSARY THAT THEY BE SUITABLE FOR SUCH USE BEFORE THE COMMISSIONER CAN ISSUE SUCH A PUBLIC REPORT.

IN A SUBDIVISION SUCH AS THIS, THE SUBDIVIDER'S PROMOTIONAL AND SALES COSTS ARE GENERALLY GREATER THAN IN OTHER TYPES OF DEVELOPMENT. A PERSON CON-TEMPLATING PURCHASE OF A PARCEL IN THIS SUBDIVISION WITH THE IDEA OF RESALE SHOULD CAREFULLY CONSIDER THE DIFFICULTIES OF RESELLING AT A PROFIT WITH-OUT A PROMOTIONAL CAMPAIGN OR A SALES ORGANIZATION. HE SHOULD ALSO REAL-IZE THAT IN ATTEMPTING TO RESELL, HE MAY BE IN AN UNFAVORABLE COMPETITIVE POSITION WITH THE SUBDIVIDER AND OTHER PROSPECTIVE SELLERS OF PARCELS IN THE SUBDIVISION AND IN THE VICINITY.

PURCHASERS WHO WISH TO RE-SUBDIVIDE THEIR LAND INTO FOUR PARCELS FOR SALE OR LEASE, MAY BE REQUIRED TO COMPLY WITH THE SUBDIVISION MAP ACT PROVI-SIONS REGARDING ROADS AND SHOULD CONTACT THE COUNTY DEPARTMENT OF PUB-LIC WORKS FOR THEIR REQUIREMENTS AND ESTIMATED COSTS OF FILING A PARCEL MAP.

THE ASSESSED VALUATION OF THIS LAND PRIOR TO SUBDIVIDING AND IMPROVING OF THE LAND IN CONNECTION WITH SUBDIVIDING IS $5.00 PER ACRE. ASSESSED VALUA-TION OF REAL PROPERTY IS 25% OF FULL CASH VALUE AS DETERMINED BY THE COUN-TY ASSESSOR. THIS MEANS THAT THE FULL CASH VALUE OF A 20-ACRE PARCEL OF THE LAND BEFORE IMPROVEMENTS ACCORDING TO THE ASSESSOR IS $400. THE ONLY IMPROVEMENTS OF THE LAND TO BE MADE IN CONNECTION WITH THE SUBDIVIDING ARE DIRT-GRADED ROADS. THE SUBDIVIDER IS OFFERING 20-ACRE PARCELS OF THE LAND AT PRICES RANGING FROM $9,500 TO $17,500.

THERE IS LITTLE OR NO DEVELOPMENT IN THE SUBDIVISION TO DATE. THERE IS NO ASSURANCE OF SUBSTANTIAL DEVELOPMENT IN THE NEAR FUTURE.

THE SUBDIVIDER HAS NOT DEMONSTRATED TO THE DEPARTMENT OF REAL ESTATE THAT HIS PROPERTY AS SUBDIVIDED HAS INVESTMENT MERIT OR PROFIT POTENTIAL TO OWNERS OF PARCELS THEREOF.

**LOCATION AND SIZE:** In _____ County. Twelve (12) miles southwest of _____(TOWN)_____, on County Road.

Approximately 400 acres divided into 20 lots or parcels.

**Figure 14–3. Example of a Final Subdivision Public Report** *continued*

**TITLE:** A title report shows title, among other things, to be subject to: A non-exclusive right of way for ingress and egress over the existing road lying within the North Half of the North Half of Section 24, and within the South Half of the Northeast Quarter and the Southeast Quarter of the Northwest Quarter of Section 13, Township 3 South, Range 2 East, _____ Meridian, as granted in the Deed dated January 4, 1971, executed by __(GRANTOR'S NAME)__ to _____(GRANTEE'S NAME)_____, and recorded March 17, 1971, in Book 895, Page 60, Official Records, under Recorder's Serial No. 12663, in the Office of the County Recorder of said County.

The above referred to Deed also contains the following: "The above right of way is conveyed on the condition that it shall be used only for normal ranch use, and there shall be no commercial hauling over said right of way."

**EASEMENTS:** Easements for utilities, drainage, ingress and egress, roads, rights of way, pipelines, transmission lines and other purposes are shown on the title report and parcel map recorded in the Office of the _____ County Recorder, Case 5, Drawer 12, Page 68.

**USES AND ZONING:** Zoned for 20 acre minimum (Upland-Recreation).

**RESTRICTIONS** There are no recorded restrictions, however, this subdivision is subject to the provisions of all applicable county ordinances.

**TAX ESTIMATES:** If the subdivider is unable to give you the current tax information for your lot, you may approximate your taxes as follows:

Take 25% of the sales price, divide by 100, and then multiply by the total tax rate. The tax rate for the 19___-19___ fiscal year is $9.046. The tax rate and assessed valuation may change in subsequent years. For example, any bonded debt or special district assessment approved after the above tax rate had been set could increase the future rate.

**MINERAL RIGHTS:** You will not own the mineral, oil and gas rights of every nature and kind under your land. These have been reserved to previous owners in a deed recorded in Book 3 of Official Records, Page 104, and by Correction Deed under Recorder's File No. 3124, _____ County Records.

The right to surface entry has not been waived, and the owners of the mineral rights may enter upon the land at some future date to extract minerals, etc. This right could affect your ability to obtain financing for building on your property.

**INTERESTS TO BE CONVEYED—CONDITIONS OF SALE:** Grant deed will include non-exclusive right of way for ingress and egress, water pipe lines and public utilities.

**PURCHASE MONEY HANDLING:** The subdivider must impound all funds received from you in an escrow depository until legal title is delivered to you. (Refer Section 11013.2(a), Business and Professions Code.)

**GEOLOGIC CONDITIONS:** The State Division of Mines and Geology reports: "Some parts of this area are underlain by relatively soft rock formations. In this rural area we assume that development will be concentrated on the more favorable sites avoiding the steeper slopes. However, if construction is planned on steep terrain in the area, precautions should be taken during site development to minimize slope-stability problems."

**WATER:** The subdivider does not intend to install any water system or wells in this subdivision.

Existing springs and private water wells are the only source of water in this tract and you will be required to pay all costs to have a well installed.

The subdivider's well driller has submitted the following information:

"Ample water for domestic use should be obtained in this area by drilling small diameter deep wells or, in some cases, through the development of existing springs.

"The small diameter deep wells, in which rock will have to be penetrated, could cost between $3,000 and $5,000, with the pressure system costing between $1,000 and $1,500.

"Some existing springs could be developed with a cost of from $300 to $500. In most cases, a pressure system for this type of well would cost less than $500.

"Well depths will vary from area to area with the deep wells averaging from 150 to 300 feet. The springs should be able to be developed within 8 to 20 feet."

**Figure 14–3. Example of a Final Subdivision Public Report** *continued*

However, there is no guarantee of the quality or quantity or availability of water on each lot or parcel.

The State Water Code requires every person who digs, bores, or drills a water well to file a notice of intent prior to commencement of work and a report of completion within thirty days after the work has been completed. Said notice and report are to be filed with the district office of the Department of Water Resources administering the area in which the well is located. Forms will be furnished upon request by any district office of the Department of Water Resources.

**FIRE PROTECTION:** Furnished by Forestry Service if equipment is available, from May 15 to November 1. No fire protection is available from approximately November 1 to May 15 of each year.

**ELECTRICITY:** There are no electric facilities within the subdivision. The nearest Pacific Gas and Electric Company electric facilities are approximately 15,300 feet to the farthest parcel in the tract and the cost to reach that parcel would be approximately $153,000.

**GAS:** Natural gas service is not available.

**TELEPHONE:** The local Telephone Company reports that the extension of existing phone service lines to the farthest parcel in this tract (about 37,000 lineal feet) would be approximately $3,750, based on a cost of $10 per each 100 lineal feet of line (with no charge for the first 300 feet). A decrease in these amounts would be made in the event additional orders for service were received along this distribution route.

**SEWAGE DISPOSAL:** Septic tanks will be used for sewage disposal. You must pay for your septic tank. Prior to commencing construction, you should contact the local health department for specifications, requirements and any local problems.

A General Contractor estimates that the cost of septic tank installation would be $500 for a 2-bedroom, 1-bath home and $600 for a 3-bedroom, 2-bath home.

**STREETS AND ROADS:** The roads within this subdivision are private. No provision for their repair and maintenance has been made by the developer, and it is not contemplated that he will do so. All repair and maintenance of these private roads will be your responsibility and expense individually and collectively proportionately to the use of the road easement by you.

If you and your neighbor cannot agree on pro rata shares or upon the need or extent of repair and maintenance, it will be necessary for you to appeal to the proper superior court for the appointment of an impartial arbitrator or for the determination of the court as to the pro rata shares.

An engineer estimates it will cost lot owners $40,000 per mile to bring roads to county standards and that the annual cost for maintaining roads as existing at time of sale will be $350 per lineal foot.

Purchasers should be aware and should fully investigate the possibility that the development of the ground and roads in this subdivision may alter the terrain so as to affect access to the building site and the views for particular lots in the subdivision.

**PUBLIC TRANSPORTATION:** Bus service is approximately 12 miles from the subdivision at the nearest town.

**SCHOOLS:** County Unified School District. You should contact the school district for information concerning schools, class schedules, and bus service.

**SHOPPING FACILITIES:** In Wilco, 12½ miles southeast of the subdivision with limited facilities.

lems as any government: lack of sufficient funds, good leadership, experienced personnel and longevity. It is initially formed by the developer, who owns all the properties and, therefore, runs the show. Once the developer is out of the picture, chaos often occurs. Because most of the owners are absentee, the few permanent residents tend to manage everything. They don't like to do anything that will "stir up the waters," because they have to live with each other. Generally, it is difficult to get anything done.

I prosecuted a lawsuit a few years ago against a property owner's association on behalf of an owner whose house was destroyed in a landslide caused by water running off a road above her house because of a lack of proper road maintenance, such as ditching and placement of rocks and culverts. For six months before her house was destroyed, she had written to her association and attended every meeting, demanding that they repair the road above her house. The directors declined to do anything because they said they lacked the funds to hire a road contractor. Fortunately for my client, every meeting was taped; the evidence was there loud and clear when her house was destroyed. We sued the association and the insurance company bought my client a new house. The association was lucky it had insurance, or it would have paid from its own account.

The association has the power to levy assessments against each property owner for funds to operate the subdivision. These assessments become liens against the property, like property taxes. The problem is that the directors hate to raise the assessment level to meet their needs because they take so much heat from their neighbors who don't want their "taxes" raised. As a result, most associations operate on a shoestring, and the turnover of officers and directors is very high, because nobody wants the responsibility of being in charge of such an operation.

One of the most difficult jobs for association leaders is to enforce the covenants, conditions and restrictions (CC&R's) that bind each property owner. Almost every subdivision and condominium has a set of regulations that are binding on each owner. Those rules can include the following:

- Prohibit commercial activities on the property.
- Require the prior approval of the house plans by the directors or by an architectural, design or environmental control committee.

- Prohibit occupancy of a trailer, mobile home or temporary structure.
- Prohibit keeping boats or cars parked in the street.
- Prohibit keeping of horses, dogs and other livestock.
- Prohibit shooting, hunting or cutting of trees.
- Prohibit the construction of outbuildings.
- Prohibit renting of the home or condominium unit.
- Require a certain level of maintenance of ground areas.

Generally, any individual property owner can bring a suit to enforce the CC&R's, but usually enforcement is left to the association. Often the rules look good on paper when you buy your parcel, but if they are not enforced, they are meaningless. Generally nobody likes to take on the job of enforcer, so the enforcement becomes very lax and the rules are often forgotten.

If you intend to purchase in a subdivision or condominium and you care about how things are run, then you had better be prepared to take an active role in the association and to spend a large part of your time in the country playing politics. If the thought of meetings and rules turns you off, then do not buy land in a subdivision or purchase a condominium.

While you are investigating the property, demand to see a copy of the articles of incorporation, the bylaws, the operating rules and the covenants, conditions and restrictions; read them thoroughly to see if you want to be part of such a project. A sample Declaration of Covenants, Conditions and Restrictions is shown in Figure 14–4.

## Getting Around Subdivision Laws

Of course, land developers have found ways of getting around existing subdivision laws. Some go ahead and subdivide without even attempting to comply with the laws, but there are quasilegal ways to avoid them as well, if the government is not watching.

Let's assume your state subdivision law applies only to land splits of more than four parcels. A seller wants to sell to eight separate buyers, but doesn't want to create eight parcels because he then would be obligated to meet the standards of the subdivision laws, which would mean added ex-

**Figure 14–4.   Sample Form: Declaration of Covenants, Conditions and Restrictions**

**Declaration of Covenants,
Conditions, and Restrictions**

CHUCK EDWARD and JERRY HERBERT, hereinafter called "Developers," are the owners of the following described real property, situated in the County of _____, State of _____:

Lots 1 through 90 of Tract No. 109, The
Pines, as per Map recorded in Book 116,
Pages 116 through 124, of Maps, in the
office of the County Recorder.

It is the desire and intention of Developers to sell the real property described above and to impose on it mutual, beneficial restrictions, covenants, and conditions, under a general plan or scheme of improvement for the benefit of all of the real property in the tract and the future owners thereof;

THEREFORE, Developers hereby declare that all of the property described above is held and shall be held, conveyed, hypothecated or encumbered, leased, rented, used, occupied, and improved, subject to the following restrictions, covenants, and conditions, all of which are declared and agreed to be in furtherance of a plan for the subdivision, improvement, and sale of the real property and are for the purpose of enhancing and protecting the value, desirability, and attractiveness of the real property and every part thereof.

All of the restrictions, covenants, and conditions shall run with the land and shall be binding upon all parties having or acquiring any right, title, or interest in the described real property, or any part thereof.

1.   Land Use and Building Type

No lot shall be used except for residential or church purposes. No building shall be erected, altered, placed, or permitted to remain on any lot other than one detached single family dwelling not to exceed two and one-half stories in height and a private garage for not more than three cars, with the exception that attached quarters may be used as a guest house, for the housing of hired help, or similar uses, but such quarters may not be rented or leased as separate units. Houses may be rented while waiting for a sale, but not to exceed 24 months. Lots 1 through 25, 34 through 36, 51 through 54, and 63 through 109 may have double wide mobile homes, provided a concrete foundation and a roof similar to a conventional home is provided. Garages and carports must be of wood construction with suitable roofing material to complement the proposed mobile home. The Developers' approval of all designs and location of improvements on a given lot must be obtained before obtaining a County permit. Permission to install a particular unit should be obtained before purchase, by submitting for Developers' approval the brochure of the manufacturer showing the unit that the applicant proposes to install.

2.   Architectural Control

No building or mobile home shall be erected, placed, or altered on any lot until the construction plans and specifications and a plan showing the location of the structure have been

**Figure 14–4.    Sample Form: Declaration of Covenants, Conditions and Restrictions** *continued*

approved by Developers, as to quality of workmanship and materials, harmony of external design with existing structures, and as to location with respect to topography and finish grade elevation. No fence or wall shall be erected, placed, or altered on any lot nearer to any street than the minimum building setback line unless similarly approved. Frontage fences shall be of a redwood product unless another design is specifically approved. Cyclone type fence, of a maximum height of 48 inches, with wood palings, will be considered equal to redwood.

Developers' approval or disapproval, as required herein, shall be in writing. If such written approval or disapproval is not accomplished within 30 days after submission of a plan and/or specification, then it shall be deemed approved and in compliance with this document.

3.    Dwelling Cost, Quality, and Size.

No dwelling shall be permitted on any lot at a cost of less than $45,000, based upon cost levels prevailing on the date these covenants are recorded. It is the intention and purpose of this covenant to assure that all dwellings shall be of a quality of workmanship and materials substantially the same or better than that which can be produced on the date these covenants are recorded at the minimum cost stated herein for the minimum permitted dwelling size. The ground floor area of the main structure, exclusive of one-story open porches and garages, shall be not less than 800 square feet for a one-story dwelling, nor less than 800 square feet for a dwelling of more than one story. All buildings and mobile homes will meet County Building Department Standards for High Density Subdivisions.

4.    Building Location

(a)    No building or mobile home shall be located on any lot nearer than 30 feet to the front lot line, nor nearer than 20 feet to any side street line. However, these front and side setbacks may be reduced to a minimum of 20 feet and 10 feet, respectively, by obtaining the prior written approval of Developers and a variance from the County Planning Commission.

(b)    No building shall be located nearer than 10 feet to any interior lot line. No dwelling or mobile home shall be located on any interior lot nearer than 10 feet to the rear lot line.

(c)    For the purpose of this covenant, eaves, steps, and open porches shall not be considered as a part of the building, provided, however, that such eaves, steps, and open porches shall not be located nearer than 5 feet to any lot line.

5.    Re-subdivision Prohibited

No lots shall be re-subdivided.

6.    Easements

Easements for installation and maintenance of utilities and drainage facilities are reserved as shown on the recorded plat. Within these easements, no structure, planting, or other material shall be placed or permitted to remain which may damage or interfere with the installation and maintenance of utilities, or which may change with the direction of flow of drainage channels in the easements, or which may obstruct or retard the flow of water through drainage channels in the easements. The easement area of each lot and all improvements on it shall be maintained continuously by the owner of the lot, except for those improvements for which a public authority or utility company is responsible. All natural drainages shall be kept free flowing.

**Figure 14–4.   Sample Form: Declaration of Covenants, Conditions and Restrictions** *continued*

7.   Nuisances

No noxious or offensive activity shall be carried on upon any lot, nor shall anything be done thereon which may be or may become an annoyance or nuisance to the neighborhood.

8.   Temporary Structures

No structure of a temporary character, trailer, basement, tent, shack, garage, barn, or other outbuilding shall be used on any lot at any time as a residence either temporarily or permanently, except that a travel trailer with proper sanitation facilities may be used as temporary housing during the construction of a home but not to exceed twelve months.

9.   Signs

No sign of any kind shall be displayed to the public view on any lot except one professional sign of not more than two square feet, one sign of not more than three square feet advertising the property for sale, or signs used by a builder to advertise the property during the construction and sales period. Professional people operating their businesses within their homes may use the above sign limitations.

10.   Livestock and Poultry

No animals, livestock, or poultry of any kind shall be raised, bred, or kept on any lot, except that dogs, cats, or other household pets, poultry not exceeding 10 in number, and sheep not exceeding 6 in number may be kept, provided that any such animals or poultry, other than household pets, must be contained not less than 50 feet from any frontage street. All dogs, animals, and poultry must be confined to their owner's lot at all times. Horses or cattle may be kept on parcels 1 through 11, 21, 22, 23, 68, and 69, provided adequate fencing is provided and conditions are provided for the animals to minimize flies and odors to neighbors. Additionally, this paragraph is subject to, and limited by, paragraph 7, above.

11.   Garbage and Refuse Disposal

No lot shall be used or maintained as a dumping ground for rubbish. Trash, garbage, or other waste shall not be kept except in sanitary containers. All incinerators or other equipment for the storage or disposal of such material shall be kept in a clean and sanitary condition.

12.   Water Supply

No individual water system shall be permitted on any lot unless such system is located, constructed, and equipped in accordance with the requirements, standards, and recommendations of the County Health Department. Approval of such system as installed shall be obtained from such authority.

13.   Sewage Disposal

No individual sewage disposal system shall be permitted on any lot unless such system is designed, located, and constructed in accordance with the requirements, standards, and recommendations of the Country Health Department. Approval of such system as installed shall be obtained from such authority.

**Figure 14–4.    Sample Form: Declaration of Covenants, Conditions and Restrictions** *continued*

14.    Term

These restrictions, covenants, and conditions are to have a term of thirty-five years from the date this document is recorded. After thirty-five years the term shall be automatically extended for successive periods of 10 years, unless an instrument signed by a majority of the then owners of the lots has been recorded, agreeing to change said term or otherwise modify the provisions of this document.

15.    Enforcement

Enforcement shall be by proceedings at law or in equity against any person or persons violating or attempting to violate any restriction, covenant, or condition. The remedy sought may be to restrain violation or to recover damages.

16.    Severability

Invalidation of any one of these restrictions, covenants, or conditions, by judgment, or otherwise, shall in no way affect any of the other provisions which shall remain in full force and effect.

17.    Mortgages and Deeds of Trust

Nothing herein contained shall defeat or impair the lien of any mortgage or deed of trust made in good faith and for value, but title to any property obtained through sale in satisfaction of any mortgage or deed of trust shall be held subject to all of the measures and provisions hereof.

18.    Enviromental

The beauty of this subdivision is in its mixture of trees and open space. Trees (defined as having a minimum trunk diameter of six inches, measured two feet above ground level) may only be cut if the following conditions are met: They must be dead or dying trees; or removal of the trees must be required to clear for building sites, access roads, or to enable installation of utilities. In any event, no trees may be cut without obtaining the prior approval of Developers.

DATED:


_____
CHUCK EDWARD


_____
JERRY HERBERT

pense and bother. So the developer makes four parcels and pairs the eight buyers. Each member of a pair of buyers will own half of a parcel, as specified in a contract between the two partners as drawn up by the seller. Because there are only four parcels, only four deeds will be issued, one for each pair of buyers. Thus, each buyer pays for his or her interest as if getting his or her own separate parcel; in fact, however, each person is a *tenant-in-common* in relation to the others and will suffer the problems of such a relationship. The developer sells the land for as much as if he had sold eight separate and independent parcels and has legally avoided legal responsibilities and legal safeguards for the buyer.

A variation on this scheme is the creation of a *campsite community*. A developer with a large piece of land advertises that all buyers will join with other buyers as tenants-in-common on a beautiful large piece of property and will have the right to have their own campsites on spots of their choice on a first-come, first-served basis. Often a certain amount of land is designated as open space. Thus, individual buyers share their land with many other people under the pretext that they are buying into a community, when in fact, the developer has bought a large parcel of land at a reasonable price and resold it to many buyers for a tremendous profit.

The above plan is often not considered a subdivision under the legal definitions of many states; therefore, there are no regulations that must be met. In a few areas of the country, state and local laws decree that where "five or more undivided interests" are sold, the development must comply with all normal subdivision requirements, such as plat approval and issuance of public reports.

## Condominium Developments

A condominium development is an apartment arrangement surrounded by open land and recreational areas owned in common by all persons who buy apartment units. The promotional literature emphasizes the ecological aspects of preserving open space. Aside from the fact that this "preserved" space includes golf courses, swimming pools and horse-riding trails and has hundreds of people tramping across it daily, the investment is often a poor one because the extremely high purchase price really buys only an apartment. The buyer could take his or her $50,000 to $250,000,

which is what one of these fancy apartments in the "country" costs, and get 50 or more beautiful acres of land near recreational facilities, and still have enough money left over to construct a comfortable house.

If you are nevertheless interested in a vacation or rural resort condominium, there are a few important things to know. Most people who buy into such projects use their condos for weekends and holidays. Therefore, you would not want to buy one for year-round occupancy, because your needs will likely be very different. You will not have full-time neighbors, and you may require a greater level of daily upkeep than the absentee owners.

The costs to you can become very high: First, you buy the condominium unit; then, you pay monthly assessments to maintain the common property as well as regular local property taxes. Always look at the operating budget of the development. It is available for public inspection. Study it to see if the developer retains ownership of the common area. For example, the developer will hang onto ownership of the recreational facilities and lease them back to the buyer. The sales pitch is that the lease arrangement means lower-priced condominiums. What often happens, though, is that owners get burdened with high rental charges that get higher every year. All of this information is available to you if you ask for it.

If you are buying into a new development, you will have to use your best estimate to project the future costs of ownership. If the condominium is several years old, look over past records, see the cost increases and project them into the future. Often the condominium is managed by a professional management firm, and that increases the costs. This is a necessity for vacation condos. The firm will also handle rental of your condo to third persons when you are not using it. This can help pay for the condo, but it also results in considerable wear and tear on the unit.

Because the development is managed by a board of directors, ask permission to sit in on a board meeting before you purchase, to judge for yourself how the project is run. These are your neighbors, and because you will all be living extremely close to each other, you should determine how compatible you are with other owners, not only in personality but in lifestyle and matters of taste.

The federal government recently completed an evaluation report called *Planned Unit Develop-*

*ments, Condominiums and Homeowner Associations,* which concluded:

> The most startling finding of this report is not how badly the Homeowners Associations are faring in the . . . condominium developments studied, but how they have even managed to survive, given the obstacles and barriers to their viability. It is indeed surprising to see haphazard groupings of . . . homeowners with little or no assistance from developers, HUD, mortgagees, local governments, or each other who have learned how to manage and care for what are in essence mini governmental jurisdictions.

## Some Final Advice

The Office of Interstate Land Sales has issued a list of warnings regarding the purchase of rural property, including the following:

- Don't buy land like you buy TV sets; buy it like the serious real estate purchase that it is.
- Don't buy land without first seeing it in person.
- Buy scared—don't buy on the spot on the first visit, or at a free dinner or when under pressure from a salesperson.
- Don't buy before asking for and reading the property report or, preferably, before showing it to an attorney or real estate authority.
- Know your rights in buying land.
- Look into the background of the developers what other projects have they done?
- Know the special risks involved, such as the chance that the land may not appreciate in value and the possibility that resale of the land may be subject to restrictions.
- Know how to deal with high-pressure sales tactics.
- Do your homework.

As a general rule, your money will be better spent purchasing your own piece of land outside a subdivision. You will not have to deal with petty internal politics, you will be in control of your environment and your property will appreciate in value faster. The more promises made to you in the slick brochures of the land and condominium developers, the more cautious you should be. If it sounds too good to be true, it is. Don't be swayed by low money-down deals. Money is money, and it should be spent as productively as possible, or not at all.

## Useful Resources

### The Office of Interstate Land Sales Registration

This office is under the U.S. Department of Housing and Urban Development (HUD). The addresses of the local HUD offices are given in "Useful Resources" at the end of Chapter 26. If you want information on a subdivision, also write to the main office:

> Land Sales Registration Division
> Assistant Secretary for Housing
> Federal Housing Commissioner
> Department of Housing and Urban
>  Development
> 451 7th St., S.W., Room 6278
> Washington, DC 20410
> Voice: (800) 569-4287
> URL: http://gopher.hud.gov

Send the name and location of the subdivision you are interested in and ask for any information the division has on the project. Write also for information on current federal laws. You should also write to the division if you feel you have been cheated in a deal. The division also has released a study entitled "Subdividing Rural America."

The following are available free from the above HUD office:

"Buying Lots from Developers," HUD-357-H(8)
 "Multi-Family Homesteading: A Guidebook
    for Local Government," ACCN-5286
"Before Buying Land . . . Get the Facts," HUD-
    183-H(10)

### Better Business Bureaus

The Better Business Bureau in the United States and Canada is a consumer protection and information resource. Check with the one nearest the subdivision or condominium you are interested in for information on real estate promotions and buying property.

You can find a local Better Business Bureau in most major cities. By writing to the national headquarters you can receive a list of addresses for all Better Business Bureaus.

National Headquarters
Council of Better Business Bureaus
4200 Wilson Boulevard, Suite 800
Arlington, VA 22203
(703) 276-0100

### FHA and VA

The FHA and VA have information on their own specifications for a proper subdivision. They also have separate reports on projects they have approved, and you can ask for these reports at any local office. Addresses for the regional offices of FHA and VA are given in "Useful Resources" at the end of Chapter 26, "HUD/FHA-Insured and VA-Insured Loans."

### State Real Estate Commissioner

Your state real estate commissioner's office has local offices throughout the state, and it can give you any information it has on a subdivision. Ask any real estate agent or planning commissioner for the address of the commissioner.

### County Agencies

The best place to start any investigation about land purchase, and particularly subdivision development, is at the county offices overseeing land use in the area.

The following officials or offices can give you the specified information:

- *Planning Commission (Director of Planing)*—the primary agency in charge of processing subdivision applications, plats and reports. It controls zoning and land use in general, and its information is available to the public.
- *Building Inspector*—information on the use of the land as a homesite, specifically grading, stability, erosion, drainage and building quality design for homes already constructed.
- *Health Officer or Department*—information on water supply, sewage disposal and health facilities.
- *Road Commissioner*—information on the quality of road construction in the subdivision, specifically surface materials, grading and easement provisions.
- *County Engineer*—must approve geological, drainage and flooding conditions of the subdivision.
- *County Surveyor*—processes all surveys, plats and maps submitted for a subdivision. You can copy any maps in the office.
- *Fire Officer*—can give you information on fire protection in the area.
- *County or District School Superintendent*—information on education facilities.
- *County Sheriff*—home protection and public safety information.

# CHAPTER
# 15 Eminent Domain and Condemnation

Federal, state, city and county governments; improvement districts; public utilities; and similar public and semipublic organizations have the power of *eminent domain*. This right permits them to take private property for a public benefit by condemning it. Private lands have been condemned for such things as public irrigation systems, railroads, electric power plants, parks, government buildings, airports, streets, highways, roads and sewage treatment plants.

## A True Condemnation Story

The following story is condensed from an article originally published in *Mother Earth News*.

A young married couple purchased 760 acres of fine farmland, bordered on two sides by federal land controlled by the Bureau of Land Management (BLM). The BLM is responsible for managing 400 million acres of government land. Like many land

buyers, this couple falsely assumed that it was an advantage to buy next to government land.

One month after they moved onto their farm, a neighbor told them that the BLM was preparing to construct two logging roads across their land to reach the timber on the federal land bordering their farm. Although the couple found this hard to believe, they checked with the local BLM office and, much to their astonishment, found out the sad truth. One road was to run behind their house and right through the source of their water supply. The other road was to start at their driveway, continue on a path between their barn and house, cross over their pasture and enter the BLM land. (See Figure 15–1.) Once constructed, these roads would be traveled by huge diesel trucks carrying cut logs from the BLM's "preserved" and "protected" woodlands.

The couple immediately registered a protest against the proposed plans and later prevented the entry of a government surveying team that wanted to survey the exact location for the roads. The government was forced to go to federal court to for-

**Figure 15–1. Example of a Condemnation**

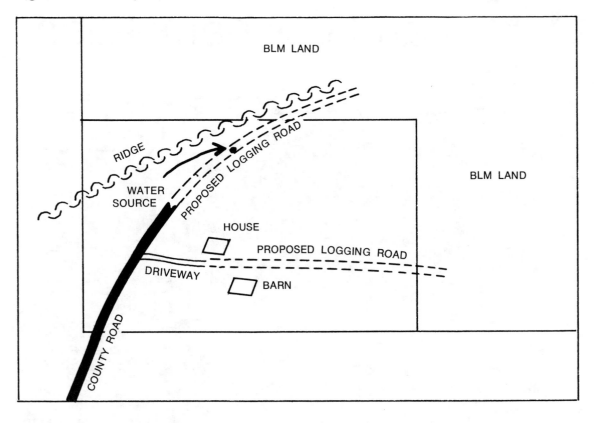

mally request condemnation actions against that part of the property needed for the road. They argued that they had to cross the farm rather than choose an alternative route because "the proposed roads are the easiest and cheapest routes for the logging companies." The court granted the BLM "the right to enter, survey and mark on-the-ground the location of an easement in relation to established property corners, and to appraise the market value of such an easement." In addition, "the United States of America, acting through the Bureau of Land Management of the Department of the Interior, its representatives, agents, or contractors [is allowed] to remove, sell, or otherwise dispose of any trees necessary to [do] such survey work."

The owners hired an attorney who forced the BLM to comply with some legal requirements they had ignored, and this postponed immediate action on the road. But after the government has complied with the regulations, the court will probably grant a permanent easement for the two logging roads. When this is done, the couple will be compensated an amount of money equal to the appraised value of the condemned land. But their

farm will no longer be the quiet, private place they had longed for.

The previous owner who sold this farm probably knew of the proposed plans for the logging roads and was aware of the diminished value the land would have after their construction. He was not legally required to inform the buyers of this fact, and they, unfortunately, did an inadequate job of researching the land before they purchased it. Had they spent only an hour at the nearest BLM office, they might have discovered what was in store for their land.

No private property is exempt from the government's power of eminent domain. However, the landowner can protest such action in court, in which case the government will have to bring a condemnation proceeding against the owner to prove that taking the land will benefit the general public and is required for public necessity. It is usually easy to prove to a court that the proposed action is for the "benefit of the public," so the primary dispute in almost all condemnation or eminent domain cases is over the amount of "just compensation" to be paid the property owner.

## "Just Compensation" on Condemnation

If the entire property is condemned, the owner will be paid its *fair market value*. (See Chapter 19, "Evaluating the Price of the Property.") This is called the owner's "just compensation" for the taking of his or her property. The amount of just compensation does not include expenses involved in moving and relocation, personal inconvenience, the necessity to buy more expensive land if nothing else is available in the area and loss of profits to any business conducted on the land. Generally the person whose property is condemned will not be happy about it, particularly when the entire parcel is not taken.

Most condemnations take only a part of a person's land. For example, in the condemnation story earlier, the government took only an easement for the logging roads across the couple's land. Therefore, the government has to pay them only the fair market value of the strips of land they condemn and an amount of money for *severance damages*. Severance damages are the loss in value of the land as a whole caused by the condemnation and taking of only a portion of it. The damages are usually figured as the difference between the original market value of the entire parcel and its reduced market value after the roads are put in. Although this might be a large sum of money, it will not be enough to allow the couple to buy a comparable piece of land, and no amount of money can make life satisfying in a home next to a logging road.

Even though none of your land is condemned, when property next to or near yours is condemned and you are injured in the process, you can be compensated for noise, smoke and loss of privacy. Because the value of such things is hard to determine, the affected person is rarely satisfied with his amount of "just compensation."

## My Favorite Eminent Domain War Story

I was able to help an elderly couple fight their local sewer district in Superior Court during a two-week jury trial. My clients, in their early seventies, had a beautiful, redwood-covered parcel of land with a small cabin and an orchard that had been in the wife's family for more than 50 years. They were good citizens and always believed that the things that happened to them could never happen in America, where property rights are sacred. That is, they believed it until they became the defendants in the case of *The Miranda Community Services District* vs. *Arnold and Helen Cooper*.

The service district, represented by its board of directors, was interested in putting in a sewerage system for the town, which had reached its limit for permissible septic tank installations. The town fathers decided that the sewerage plant would fit nicely right in the middle of the Coopers' family retreat.

But the Coopers liked their property just the way it was and were not interested in selling at any price.

The district hired a lawyer and filed a condemnation action to take the Coopers' property forcibly by eminent domain. The Coopers could not stop this action, so their option was to fight to get fair compensation for their land. In a condemnation case the trial becomes the battle of the appraisers, and this case was no exception. The government district had two appraisers who testified that the property was worth only $25,000. The Coopers had one appraisal of $58,000 and one of $52,000.

But what emerged during the preparation of the case was that one of the service district's appraisers had originally independently appraised the Cooper property at approximately $55,000. The district, not wanting to pay that price, agreed with the appraiser to destroy parts of that appraisal and to lower the value. Sections of the original appraisal were duly burned in the appraiser's fireplace, never to be seen again. The value was then reduced to $25,000.

Fortunately, a jury of 12 good citizens decided that the Coopers should receive $58,000 for their property, and rendered their verdict in less than two hours after a two-week jury trial. But the Coopers lost their property, for which no amount of money could truly compensate. Mrs. Cooper had been vacationing at her family hideaway since she was born and had a lifetime of fond memories.

The point of this story is not that the good guys won, but that the eminent government, successor to the Crown, has almost unlimited power to exercise its right to take back its "domain," if it is for the "general welfare" of its subjects. Never assume it can't happen to you. Be aware of any potential eminent domain possibilities in the area where you are looking at property. Going through a condemnation case in court takes thousands of dollars and years of aggravating time.

## Investigating the Possibility of Future Condemnation of Your Land

When you are ready to buy some land, search out every possible plan for future construction and development in your area. If the land is bordered by public lands of any kind, check with the agency controlling those lands. (The addresses of the BLM offices in charge of federal lands and the state agencies in charge of state lands are listed in Appendix B.) Look at its official maps, and see what is planned for the land adjoining your property. City and county land offices will be located in the city hall. The local planning commission and road department can give you much information and will show you the maps of proposed projects. The local and state water resources agencies and the local office of the Soil Conservation Service will have information on proposed water and irrigation projects. Read the local newspapers. Don't be afraid to ask a lot of questions.

Look for the most common causes of condemnation: roads, water and drainage canals, utilities and dams. By doing a little investigating, you can discover all the plans for the area that can affect your land. Look for proposals that have not yet been approved but that can cause problems if they are.

Of course, there is nothing you can do to prevent future actions by the government that have not yet been discussed. Regardless of your thorough investigation, your land might someday be threatened by eminent domain. If this happens, you may have to retain an attorney to fight against the condemnation or for just compensation.

## The Warranty for Condemnation and Eminent Domain

In many cases, longtime residents of rural areas have inside information on future condemnation actions to be levied against their properties, and they will sell out before this occurs. The unsuspecting buyer is left to suffer the consequences of eminent domain. The Model Contract of Sale in Chapter 27 has a warranty in clause 16(h) to protect you in such a case. After you take title, if the land is condemned, you can win a legal action against the seller if you can prove he or she had knowledge of the impending condemnation.

Clause 13 of the Model Contract of Sale deals with the possibility that the land may be taken by eminent domain after the signing of the contract and before the closing of escrow. If this occurs, the buyer may choose either to terminate the purchase or to get the purchase price reduced by the amount its value is reduced by the condemnation.

# CHAPTER 16
# Adverse Possession

## "Squatter's Rights"

Under certain circumstances you can lose title to part or all of your land by a legal device known as *adverse possession*. This has been referred to as "squatter's rights," and it is one of the legal traditions that gave rise to the expression, "Possession is nine-tenths of the law." Buyers who purchase land as investors and never use it often don't keep track of their properties and finally lose their titles by adverse possession. The law was established to encourage use of land and to clear up confusing title conflicts arising most often between owners of adjoining land.

For a person to take your title away from you, seven conditions must be fulfilled. That person's use of your land must be: (1) hostile, (2) actual, (3) open and notorious, (4) exclusive, (5) continuous and (6) under a claim of title; and (7) tax-paying.

Each of these elements must be satisfied by the person, or "squatter," in the following manners:

1. *Hostile.* The possessor must use your land without your permission and must deny the fact that you are the true owner. Thus, if you give persons permission to use or actually prevent the use of the land, they can never gain title by adverse possession. Their use must be hostile to you. Where there is no written proof of permission, it is difficult to defeat a claim of adverse possession.

2. *Actual.* The persons must be making actual use of your land. They must be living or working on the land in some fashion. Some activities that have led to adverse possession of portions of land in the past include clearing brush, cutting trees, planting crops, putting in ditches, erecting a building, fencing off a section of the land and living on the land.

3. *Open and notorious.* The user must be open and notorious in the manner in which they are on the land. They cannot sneak around your property in such a manner that they cannot he discovered, and their activities must be visible to you if you examine the land.

4. *Exclusive.* Exclusive possession means that users must be on the land alone. If they are there with you, they cannot get title to the land.

5. *Continuous.* Use of the land must be continuous from the beginning of the prescribed time period to the end, although seasonal use for the prescribed number of years is generally permissible.

6. *Under a claim of title.* Users must claim that they own the land, even if they are wrong. Their actions will speak for themselves in this

regard. If they are acting as if they believe they own the land, they are taking the property under a claim of title.

7. *Tax-paying.* The user must pay the property taxes on the land during the period of occupancy.

The time limit for acquiring adverse possession is called the *statute of limitations.* All of the above elements must occur for a minimum length of time before adverse possession "ripens" into title. The minimum period varies among the states; for example, in California the period is 5 years; in Louisiana, New York and Oregon, 10 years; in Minnesota, 15 years; in Colorado, 18 years; in Maine and Wisconsin, 20 years; and in Ohio and Pennsylvania, 21 years. It runs from the time the possessor begins to use the property and continues running even if the property is sold by the actual owner. Each person's use can "tack on" to the predecessor's use to make up the statutory time period.

## Acquiring the Land

The most common instance of acquiring land by adverse possession occurs when a neighbor unknowingly puts up a fence that encloses a portion of an adjoining landowner's property. If the neighbor meets all the above requirements and has the fence up for the prescribed period of time, when he or she discovers that the fence encloses part of the neighboring land, he or she can go to court and get a court order, or *declaratory judgment,* stating that he or she now owns the land so enclosed.

Another common situation that leads to adverse possession is when a part of a building, a section of an orchard or some other improvement encroaches on a neighbor's land, and this mistake is not discovered before the prescribed time period has elapsed. Usually the person whose fence, building, or other improvement is on a neighbor's property by mistake has been paying taxes on this property for years. This fact helps to prove his or her case in court.

The willingness of the courts to award title by adverse possession varies among the states. For example, some states require that the possessor have a document, such as a faulty deed, that appears to give good title but actually does not. This is referred to as possession under *color of title.* Other states simply require possession by the adverse user for any purpose.

## Precautions

A title report or abstract of title will not indicate that a person has met the requirements to adversely possess a piece of land, because the possessor's ownership will not be part of the public records until a claim is made. A standard owner's policy of title insurance will not ensure the buyer against adverse possession, because such activity can be discovered only by a correct legal survey and/or by inspection of the property. This shows the importance of having your land legally surveyed to discover where your boundaries are before you buy. (See Chapter 30, "The Title Search, Abstract of Title and Title Insurance Policy.")

If you look at land and discover that an adjoining landowner or anyone else is occupying the land, do not close the deal until you determine on what basis the user is occupying the land. Go talk to the user and ask. Tell the user you are buying the property and want to find out what his or her intentions are. You might find out you are walking into a potential lawsuit by purchasing the property. Tell the seller you want the trespassing squatter off the property prior to the close of escrow. Never decide to buy the property first and then to evict the squatter. You might end up in a very expensive battle that will ruin your dream of a peaceful life in the country.

If you encounter a situation like this before your purchase and are still interested in buying the property, seek out the advice of a good local real estate attorney, preferably one who has experience with adverse possession and prescriptive easement litigation.

Adverse possession involves taking title to a piece of land. There is a similar legal right that can be gained to allow a person to take substances such as water, minerals and timber from another person's land. This is called a *prescriptive profit* or *prescriptive right.* (See Chapter 10, "Water Rights," and Chapter 11, "Mineral, Oil, Gas, Timber, Soil and Other Rights.") An individual can also gain a legal right to cross over another person's land by a method called a *prescriptive easement* or *easement by prescription.* (See Chapter 9, "Easement Rights.")

## CHAPTER
# 17 Property Taxes and Assessments

## You Can't Live on the Land for Free, Even If It's Paid For

The tradition of taxing persons on the basis of the land they own began toward the end of the Middle Ages. The idea was that taxes should be paid by those who could afford them. Up until the last 100 years, most people earned the greatest part of their income from agriculture, and the amount and quality of land that a person owned was the most visible and reliable measurement of wealth. Land is difficult to hide, unlike stocks, bonds, money and other personal property, so it became an easy target for governments needing to raise money to run their operations.

## Real Estate Taxes on Land and Improvements

The purpose of taxes is to pay for services provided to people living within the taxed area. The police and fire departments, hospitals, schools, libraries, street and sidewalk maintenance, recreational facilities, local government and other public services are supported largely by property taxes. There is no doubt that these taxes will continue to increase in the future.

Fewer government services are provided the farther you are from large population centers, and the taxes drop accordingly. A recent study by the United States Department of Agriculture found that taxes on agricultural land in counties with a major city are three times higher than in the nearest neighboring counties and seven times higher than in the next group of counties.

Your local taxes may include a tax on real property (land and structures), a tax on personal property (appliances, machinery and so on), special assessment liens, special district taxes and possibly some others. There is no federal real property tax. The county tax assessor in each county maintains

189

all tax records and can give you information on all local taxes you will be responsible for. The assessor also determines the value of each parcel of property for purposes of levying taxes on it. The county tax collector, treasurer or other officer is responsible for collecting the tax. State laws specify when tax installments are due and what exemptions will be allowed.

## Appraised Value (Fair Market or Full Cash Value)

Tax appraisers must appraise the *fair market value* or *full cash value* of land in their counties each year for the purpose of levying taxes on it. This value is supposed to represent the amount of cash or its equivalent that the property would bring if it were put up for sale on the current market under conditions in which a willing buyer and seller knew all the facts of the situation. The assessor uses the same general standards for appraising property as I outline in Chapter 19, "Evaluating the Price of the Property." The basic method is the comparison analysis.

The assessor knows what property is sold each year by using the county recorder's deed index. He or she determines the sale price from tax stamps and the amount of transfer taxes paid, questionnaires filed when the deeds are recorded or sent to new buyers after the deed is recorded and personal interviews with real estate agents. If the assessor knows what a parcel sells for, he or she knows what its fair market value is. If surrounding property is similar, it will be assumed that the unsold land has the same value as the sold land.

For example, if a 20-acre parcel with an $80,000 house on it sells in 1996 for $120,000, a similar 20-acre parcel with a $80,000 house on it that is located a half-mile away and that has not changed hands in ten years will be appraised at, or near, $120,000 under the comparison test. Of course, this is a simple example, but it approximates the method used. Appraising property is not an exact science, but uniformity is supposed to he the goal of every appraiser.

In areas where most of the land is undeveloped, assessors look at current market conditions and establish a set market value for an acre of land. For instance, all land in a 100-square-mile area might be appraised at $500 per acre. Then the improvements on each parcel are examined and given separate appraisals. Conventional buildings are appraised higher than unusual structures, and older houses have a depreciated value placed on them. Because the assessor cannot look at all land each year, a parcel might have the same appraisal for several years, regardless of improvements. But in many areas, appraisers are notified every time a construction permit is issued and they make a point to visit the land and reassess its value based on the new improvements being constructed.

Alter a tax assessor appraises the property, your final tax is determined according to the property's assessed value and the current tax rate.

### Assessed Value

The assessed value is some percentage of the appraised value, usually 20 percent to 50 percent, although it can be 100 percent. The percentage is called the *assessment ratio*. For example, in a county that bases its property tax on an assessment value of 25 percent, if the tax assessor determines that a piece of land has a fair market value of $60,000, the tax levied on it will be based on 25 percent of that figure, or $15,000.

### The Tax Rate

The *tax rate*, or *mill rate,* is the percentage of assessed value that is levied in taxes. It is usually described as the tax rate per $100 of assessed valuation.

The county government determines the tax rate each year by first drawing up a budget of proposed expenses for the coming year. Let's assume your county budget requires $30 million. The treasurer then figures out how much money the county will receive from sources other than property taxes. Assume this income equals $6 million. This amount is subtracted from the total budget figure, and the remaining amount must be collected in the form of property taxes. This would be $24 million. The tax assessor adds up the appraised fair market value of all taxable land in the county and from this sum derives the total assessed value. Assume the fair market value of the land in your county is $2.4 billion. If the assessment ratio of assessed value to appraised value is 25 percent, the total assessed value of the land will be $600 million.

The $24 million needed by the county then is divided by the $600 million total assessed value. The result is the tax rate, which is 0.04, or 4 percent. Thus, your county will charge $4 on every $100 of assessed value. If your property is appraised at

$60,000 and then assessed at 25 percent of that, or $15,000, you will be charged $600 in taxes that year.

### A Decrease in the Tax Rate Does Not Always Mean Lower Taxes

When the county declares it is lowering the tax rate, this does not automatically mean your taxes will be lowered. If the percentage used to determine assessed value increases at the same time the tax rate decreases, your taxes may actually be greater. This is a common tax ploy. Compare these two examples:

1. Tax rate in 1993

   | | |
   |---|---|
   | | 12% ($12 per $100 of assessed value) |
   | Assessment ratio (assessed value to appraised value) | 20% |
   | True value of property | $80,000 |
   | Assessed value (20%) | $16,000 |
   | Tax rate times assessed value ($16,000 × 0.12) | $1,920 in taxes will be due |

2. Tax rate (lowered) in 1996

   | | |
   |---|---|
   | | 10% ($10 per $100 of assessed value) |
   | Assessment ratio (assessed value to appraised value) | 25% |
   | True value of property | $80,000 |
   | Assessed value (25%) | $20,000 |
   | Tax rate times assessed value ($20,000 x 0.10) | $2,000 in taxes will be due |

Even though the tax rate is lowered, taxes increase by $80 because the assessment ratio is increased.

## Property Taxes on Timber, Minerals and Water Rights

Your real property tax will be based on the value of the minerals, standing timber, water and other permanent fixtures on the land, as well as on the land itself. The value of each of these things is often determined separately and then added to the value of the bare land to find the overall worth of the property.

### Standing Timber

To determine the value of standing timber on land for tax purposes, a survey, often called a county cruise, is made of the trees on the property. Sometimes the survey will group several parcels together and evaluate the timber in a large geographic area. In that case, the timber tax assessment for each separate parcel is based on the value of the timber on the area as a whole, with no consideration given to the physical condition and accessibility of the timber. Usually, however, tax assessors rely on information supplied by the timber owners themselves, which is then corroborated by aerial photos and field sampling.

Only merchantable timber, mature trees capable of being cut and sold at the time of assessment, is considered. The definition of a mature tree varies, depending on state law. In California, a stand of trees can be declared mature 40 years after the time of planting or removal of the original timber growth, or when its average quality and volume per acre are at least equal to the quality and volume of timber stands in the area that are being converted into wood products. Values are usually determined by analyzing timber sales in the general area of the land.

Many landowners are forced to cut their trees to eliminate the excessive tax burden, which is the reason timber is taxed. If every rural landowner left his trees standing to provide beauty, preserve the soil and maintain the water table, the lumber industry would have a diminished source of timber. Although lumber companies own much of their own land, once it is logged it is worthless to them for many years until the second or third growth develops sufficiently to be logged again. Often after their land is logged, they subdivide and sell it. Forty years later, when the trees are ready to be cut again, the government begins taxing for marketable timber, regardless of whether the owner is cutting the trees. If the landowner cannot afford to pay the increased real property tax, the lumber companies are back in business with that same piece of land or the subdivision developers take it over. The factors of taxation in this situation are analogous to those that are causing vast farm acreage to be sold to developers by farmers who can no longer pay the exorbitant taxes. This is the main reason some states have enacted preferential assessment systems, which I discuss later in this chapter. As timber supplies diminish further in the future, the value of timber will increase, and many more property owners will be forced to log to be able to pay the increasing taxes on their land.

Ask the local tax assessor how timber is taxed in your county. He should show you a copy of the law regarding valuation of timber for tax purposes. Then find out if your state allows an *immature forest trees exemption,* which I discuss later in this chapter.

Fruit and nut trees are also assessed as part of the real property. If they are planted on a noncommercial basis, they increase the value of the property from the time they are planted. If they are part of a systematic planting in an orchard for commercial purposes, they may be exempt from taxation for a specified number of years. For example, in California fruit and nut trees that have been planted for less than four years are tax-exempt.

### Minerals

The value of minerals on your property will probably be slight and, therefore, have little effect on the real property tax. However, where the land has some proved mining value, the added tax assessment might be very high.

### Water Rights

In states that recognize riparian rights, the real property tax assessment will usually include the value of any riparian rights that go with the land. In appropriation states the value of the right to take water might be assessed differently. However it is done, the right of a landowner to take and use water on his or her land increases the value and, therefore, the property taxes. If water rights are shared with others, the value and taxes should be diminished somewhat. (See Chapter 10, "Water Rights.")

## Personal Property Taxes

More than half the states levy a tax on personal property. Although this tax affects mainly businesses, certain household items and farm animals may be taxed in you area. However, most household furnishings and personal effects are exempt from the tax, as are automobiles. Although many states exempt intangible property such as stocks, bonds and other paper assets, many areas do not exempt such intangibles as notes, deeds of trust and mortgages.

## School Taxes

School taxes, like general real property taxes, are levied according to the value of land. The tax rate may be different from the tax rate used for general real property taxes, however. Every school district has its own methods, but it is common to include school taxes within the general property tax bill. Check with the tax assessor's office for information on school taxes in your county.

These taxes support the schools in each district in the county and are levied regardless of whether the landowner has children in school. If the schools are old or inadequate for the growing rural population in your area, you can expect increased school taxes to finance new school construction.

## Special Tax Assessments

Property taxes pay the general expenses of running the local government and providing necessary services for the county's residents. Some services that are provided only to a particular group within the county are paid for by that group through another type of tax called a *special assessment.* These usually include water and irrigation systems, drainage and sewer systems, road construction, and sidewalk and curb improvement. These projects can be initiated either by the landowners who will benefit by the completion of such construction or by the city or county in which the area is located, which may have an election to set up a special improvement district. The cost of providing these services is usually split up among the landowners according to the amount of benefit each will receive. A separate tax bill may be issued by the special district, or the special assessment may be included as part of the county tax bill. If the tax is collected by the special district itself, you can go to the district office to determine the tax status of land you intend to buy.

Special assessments really hurt when your land is within a district that is providing sewers, water lines, new roads and other improvements for a new, or soon-to-be-built, housing development. Your land may be several miles away from the development, but if you are within the district, you must pay for the subdivision's improvements. Check with the tax assessor's office to find out what properties are included in your district and what the district's boundary lines are.

Assessments are usually levied over a period of several years. For example, if a sewerage district is installing sewer lines to replace septic tanks, each property owner's share in this improvement might be $300, payable over a period of three years at the rate of $100 annually.

Because special assessments support projects that increase the value of your land, you cannot deduct these taxes from your income tax, as you can general property taxes. If you are thinking about buying in an area that is developing rapidly, you should expect future special assessments, which will be an added burden on your funds.

### The Seller Should Pay the Entire Special Assessment Lien

A problem often arises when a seller has not completely paid off a special assessment tax, or lien, at the time he sells the property. For example, suppose the county has begun paving all the dirt roads in one section of the county. The value of this land increases immediately upon the announcement that the roads are to be paved, although the paving cannot be completed for three years. All affected property has a special assessment levied against it. You want to buy land in this area, and the seller is going to get a better price for the property than he or she could have gotten before the road paving began. Thus, when you buy the land, you are in effect paying the assessment by paying a higher price. If you also are to assume payment of the assessment on taking title to the land, you will pay twice for the improved roads. Therefore, a condition of the sale should be that the seller pay off all assessment liens before the closing of escrow.

The seller will probably resist this condition. A traditional solution of the conflict is for the seller to pay for special assessments levied on work started before the buyer made an offer to buy and the buyer to pay for assessments on work started after the offer was made. I do not like this remedy. Rather, I would insist that the seller pay the entire assessment before the close of escrow or subtract the amount due from the purchase price. Clause 10 of the Model Contract of Sale in Chapter 27 provides for this. But if the seller absolutely refuses to pay the entire assessment, of course you will have to pay it after you purchase the property.

## Tax Liens

When taxes are declared each year, the county has a lien, or claim, on the property until they are paid. Taxes are so important to the state and local governments, that laws have been passed giving tax liens precedence over all other claims by creditors of the property owner. When property is foreclosed, taxes are always the first debts paid.

Each county has its own remedy for collecting unpaid taxes. The most common method is by a tax sale. At the end of he year, if you have not paid your taxes, the county will sell your land at a tax sale to get its money. This is not usually as serious as it sounds. Often a municipality, anti sometimes a private party or commercial investor, purchases a certificate of tax sale that gives the buyer the right to take title and get a deed to your land if you do not pay the back taxes within a specified redemption period. The redemption period varies among the states, but is usually up to a year. Occasionally, no redemption period is allowed.

If you pay your taxes within this period, you will be charged penalty payments and interest on the unpaid taxes, and the county will cancel the lien on your land. You will be issued a redemption certificate showing that payment has been made and that title has been redeemed. The person who "bought" your land at the tax sale then gets his or her money back, plus interest, and the county gets its taxes plus a penalty charge. If you fail to pay the back taxes within the redemption period, the purchaser of the land at the tax sale receives title to the property. Always keep the redemption certificate, and when you buy land, get any that may be in the possession of the seller before escrow closes.

Before the close of escrow, examine the tax records book in the tax collector's office to see if any back taxes are due on the land. If so, find out if the seller can still redeem the property. If he or she can, then the taxes must be paid before the close of escrow, thus clearing the title to the land. This is stated in clauses 6 and 10 of the Model Contract of Sale in Chapter 27. Never buy land with any tax lien on it other than the current year's, which is a lien but not yet due and payable. A seller should always be able to clear the record before escrow closes, using your deposit if necessary. If the seller needs your deposit and part of the down payment to pay back taxes, the escrow holder will pay them and obtain a redemption certificate before giving the seller any money. (See Figure 29–1, Model Form for Buyer's Escrow Instructions, in Chapter 29, "Opening and Closing of Escrow and the Role of the Escrow Holder.")

In some states property taxes can be past due for a specified number of years before the property owner loses his land by a tax sale; for example, in California you will not lose your land for nonpayment of taxes until you are five years in arrears.

## Proration of Taxes

Prorating taxes divides the obligation to pay them between yourself and the seller, according to your respective periods of ownership during the tax year in which you buy the land. The proration date is usually the close of escrow. However, any date you and the seller agree on may be used. Because the owner of the property at the time the taxes became due will be responsible for paying the entire amount, provisions are made in the contract of sale to reimburse the party who pays the taxes for the period in which he or she does not own the property. (See clause 8 in the Model Contract of Sale, Chapter 27.) Tax periods usually extend from January 1 to December 31, or from July 1 to June 30. However, the term used varies from state to state; check with the local tax assessor for the dates used in your area.

Here's an example of how a proration is figured: Assume the taxable year is from July 1 to June 30 and escrow is to close on February 15. The seller will own the property from July 1 to February 15, or 7 months of the taxable year. If total taxes for the year are $750, taxes for each month would be $62.50. Figuring 30 days in a month, the taxes come to $2.08 per day. The seller will owe $437.50 for seven months and $31.20 for the 15 days of February, equaling $468.70 as his or her share of the proration. The buyer then owes $281.30 to make the total tax of $750. Thus, if the seller has already paid the taxes for the entire year, the buyer will be charged $281.30 at the close of escrow.

The escrow holder usually computes the proration, but you should always double-check the figures.

## Segregation of Taxes

When a landowner subdivides property for sale, the taxes for the year in which the land is sold will be based on the value of the original parcel. By filing for a *segregation of taxes,* the year's taxes will be apportioned among the new pieces of land according to their respective values. Do not confuse this with a proration of taxes, discussed above.

Here's an example of how a segregation is figured: Assume a seller subdivides 120 acres into three 40-acre parcels. The tax for the year of sale on 120 acres is $1,280. This amount must be divided among the three parcels. One of the "forties" has a house on it, and the other two are unimproved land. The tax assessor has appraised the fair market value of the land itself at $200 per acre and the value of the house at $40,000. Therefore, the appraised value of each of the two unimproved pieces of land is $8,000. The appraised value of the 40 acres with the house on it is $8,000 plus $40,000, or $48,000. In this particular county, the assessed value (assessment ratio) is 20 percent of the appraised value, and the tax rate is 10 percent. Thus, the assessed value of each of the two unimproved "forties" is $1,600, and the tax on each of them is $160. The assessed value of the remaining "forty" with the house is $9,600 and the tax on it is $960. Adding $960, $160 and $160 gives the total of $1,280 owed for the year.

Thus, when taxes become due on a parcel before segregation takes place, the buyer and seller will prorate on the basis of an agreed amount. Using the above example, if you buy the parcel with the house on it, you and the seller will prorate on the basis that your parcel represents 33 1/3 percent of the land tax and 100 percent of the tax on improvements, because your house is the only improvement on the 120 acres. When the taxes are finally assessed after escrow closes, if the proportions by which you agreed to segregate are different, then you and the seller must make reimbursements accordingly.

The best way to find out how the property taxes will be segregated is to talk to the tax assessor before the close of escrow and get an estimate of how the taxes probably will break down after segregation takes place. Let the assessor know exactly what you are buying so the values can be segregated correctly. Be absolutely certain the assessor understands where the boundary lines are for the new parcels and which parcels contain the improvements, or you could end up paying taxes on a house that is not on your land. The assessment will be based partly on what you are paying for the property, so the assessor will probably ask you for the figure. When you get your tax statement, check the assessments to see if they are in accordance with the agreement between you and the seller.

You and the seller must apply for segregation immediately on closing by filing all necessary forms with the tax assessor. The reason a segregation cannot be obtained before the close of escrow is because the title must be transferred to the buyer before a legal segregation can occur. The tax assessor always segregates parcels automatically when he or she gets a copy of a newly recorded deed; often, however, a deed may not be sent to the tax assessor by the county recorder for several months. To avoid this delay, file for segregation immediately on closing.

## Tax Impounds by Lenders

If you give a mortgage or deed of trust when purchasing land, the lender will take the responsibility for paying your property taxes on time each year until the loan is paid off. If the lender left the responsibility to you and you failed to pay your taxes, the land could be sold at a tax sale, and the only security for the loan would be lost. So that the lender can pay the taxes when they become due, the money must be collected from you in advance. This is done by having you pay impounds with your regular payments of principal and interest. Thus, you pay the taxes to the lender, pays them to the government.

Almost all commercial lenders collect impounds. However, if the seller finances the sale, the loan agreement usually provides that you are to pay the taxes yourself. Because the seller holds a mortgage or deed of trust, he or she might ask to be notified by the tax collector if you fail to pay the taxes. If that occurs, under the terms of most loan agreements the seller can foreclose.

## Estimating Your Future Taxes

Although taxes on the land you are buying may be low now, they will not necessarily stay that way. The more land being sold in the area, the faster the taxes will increase.

The best way to get an idea of what your future taxes might be is to determine how much taxes have been increasing in the past few years. Go to the tax assessor's office, find your land on the tax parcel map and get its parcel number. (Sometimes part of the land is in one tax district and the rest is in another. If so, the property will have two parcel numbers.) Look up the property's tax statements in the tax file or index. Check all parcel number records that cover the property. The tax records will indicate the amount of past property taxes (county, school, city, special districts and so on); when the property was last appraised; the breakdown of appraised value between improvements and the land itself; the ratio of assessed value to appraised value; the assessed value; the tax rate; and the existence of any tax liens, tax sales and other delinquencies. Figure 17–1 shows a typical tax statement with all the information you will find in the tax file or tax rolls.

Compare the current appraised value with the price you are planning to pay for the land. If the difference is great, you should expect an immediate substantial increase in the taxes. When you buy the land, one of the factors the tax assessor will use when reappraising the property is the price you paid for it. The tax assessor's office is informed when property is sold and often sends out a questionnaire to the new owner asking the price paid for the property. The next year, when the tax bills are sent out, the price you paid will be the value placed on the property. Trace the records back at least five years to see how much the taxes increased each year. Any changes in the appraisal of the property, in the ratio of assessed value to appraised value or in the tax rate will affect the amount of the tax. Note the assessments made on improvements. Are there any improvements that have not yet been assessed? If so, you can expect a tax increase the next time the property is reappraised.

Don't be afraid of the tax assessor or his or her office. All files are open to the public, and the chances are that the person who appraised your land will be in the office and available for discussion. Ask what factors the assessor considered in appraising the property, including improvements, recent sales in the area and the price being asked by the seller for the property. The assessor can give you a rough estimate of how much your taxes will probably increase, based on the amount you intend to pay for the land.

**Figure 17–1. Example of a Real Property Tax Statement**

| COUNTY TAX STATEMENT JULY 1 19 TO JUNE 30 19 | | | | | | PARCEL NO | TAX CODE AREA | ASSESSMENT NO |
|---|---|---|---|---|---|---|---|---|
| PROPERTY ASSESSED MARCH 1, 19 AT 25% OF FULL CASH VALUE | | | | | | 27-300-57 | 52-003 | 8366 |

| | LAND | IMPROVEMENTS | PERSONAL PROP | EXEMPTIONS | TOTAL | SPECIAL AND DIRECT ASSESSMENT | RATE | AMOUNT |
|---|---|---|---|---|---|---|---|---|
| FULL CASH VALUE → $ | 6000 | 2680 | | | 8680 | | | |
| ASSESSED VALUE → $ | 1500 | 670 | | | 2170 | | | |

PLEASE MAKE CHECKS PAYABLE TO TAX COLLECTOR

| | TAX RATE | COUNTY TAX | EDUCATION | CITY TAX | SPECIAL DISTRICTS | TOTAL GEN TAX |
|---|---|---|---|---|---|---|
| | 8.13 | 71.83 | 101.77 | .00 | 2.82 | 176.42 |

SOLD FOR TAXES 67 8272

| PAY THIS AMOUNT → | FIRST INSTALLMENT | SECOND INSTALLMENT | TOTAL TAX |
|---|---|---|---|
| | 88.21 | 88.21 | 176.42 |
| 6% PEN | | | |
| COST | | 3.00 | |
| TOTAL | | | |

ASSESSED TO →

YOUR CANCELLED CHECK IS YOUR BEST RECEIPT. IF YOU REQUIRE A RECEIPT IN ADDITION TO YOUR CANCELLED CHECK RETURN ENTIRE BILL WITH YOUR PAYMENT AND CHECK HERE — ☐

KEEP THIS UPPER PORTION OF BILL FOR YOUR RECORDS

SEE REVERSE SIDE FOR IMPORTANT INFORMATION

## IMPORTANT INFORMATION

1. Examine this bill carefully. The Tax Collector cannot be responsible for payments on wrong property.
2. ASSESSED VALUATIONS are established by the County Assessor at an announced ratio of 25% of full cash value. Questions regarding valuation should be addressed to the County Assessor, Courthouse,
3. PAYMENT OF TAXES should be made by mail by returning the appropriate stub or stubs with your payment in the return envelope.
   a. The Tax Collector acts only as the taxpayer's collecting agent and assumes no responsibility for the loss of any such items or the proceeds thereof in transit or for losses resulting from the failure of any bank used as a collection agency.
   b. IF A CHECK OR DRAFT WAS GIVEN IN PAYMENT OF A TAX BILL THE RECEIPT GIVEN SHALL BE VOID AND OF NO EFFECT SHOULD SAID CHECK OR DRAFT BE NOT PAID ON PRESENTATION. (Revenue and Taxation Code.)
4. THE FIRST INSTALLMENT IS DELINQUENT AFTER DECEMBER 10, 19 , 6% PENALTY ADDED THEREAFTER. THE SECOND INSTALLMENT IS DELINQUENT AFTER APRIL 10, 19 , 6% PENALTY PLUS $3.00 COSTS ADDED THEREAFTER.
5. If you find "SOLD FOR TAXES" on your tax bill, it is an indication of delinquent taxes for a previous year and thereafter, as provided by law, additional penalties will be charged. To ascertain the amount necessary to redeem, write directly to Treasurer-Tax Collector, Courthouse,
6. TAXES ARE LEVIED ON BOTH REAL AND PERSONAL PROPERTY as it exists the first day of March. Subsequent removal or change of ownership does not relieve the real estate of the personal property lien, and the tax collector cannot credit payments for real property taxes unless the personal property tax has been paid or is tendered.
7. Tax Statements are mailed only to addresses appearing on the Assessment Rolls of the County Assessor as of the First of March.
8. If you no longer own this property, please return this tax bill, giving the name and address of new owner, if known.

YOUR CANCELLED CHECK IS YOUR BEST RECEIPT     Complete the following information for your records:

1st Inst. Paid By Check No._____ Date_____ 2nd Inst. Paid By Check No._____ Date_____ or Total Tax Paid Check No._____ Date_____

In a subtle way, ask if the assessor thinks the seller's asking price is reasonable. His or her answer and analysis of the property might give you some valuable information to use when negotiating the purchase price. (See Chapter 19, "Evaluating the Price of the Property," and Chapter 20, "Bargaining To Get the Seller's Asking Price Down.") Do not rely completely on the tax assessor's opinion, however, because these officials are often behind on current market values.

## Keep Thorough Tax Records

Generally taxes are collected in installments during the year to ease the burden on the landowner. Different taxes may be due at different times of the year. Get a list of due dates for all taxes from the local tax collector. There is a penalty for late payment, and some taxing bodies reduce your tax as a reward for early payment.

The majority of tax delinquencies occur during

the first year of property ownership, usually because the new owner

- does not read or understand the title report or escrow papers as they pertain to taxes paid and taxes "subject to," meaning that the taxes are due but have not been paid before or at the close of escrow.
- does not know tax due dates and delinquent dates on real property taxes.
- misunderstands who is to pay the taxes—the property owner or the lending agency.

- erroneously believes the property is not subject to taxes or penalties unless a tax bill is rendered.
- does not inquire about taxes until billed.
- does not receive a tax bill because it is sent to the previous owner. Nonreceipt of a tax bill does not prevent the imposition of penalties after the delinquent date. It is the new owner's responsibility to see that the tax assessor has the current address to which future tax bills should be mailed.

# CHAPTER

# 18 Insuring Your Property for Yourself and Your Creditors

Even if you don't want to pay to have your property insured, you may not have a choice. Institutional lenders always require that insurance against loss by fire be taken out by the borrower to protect a mortgaged home. Most sellers who take back a mortgage or deed of trust will also want the house insured during the payment period. These creditors feel that if they do not require that you insure your house, if it were to burn down and you defaulted on your payments, it would be difficult to collect the money you owed them. Even if they were to foreclose, the value of the property would have greatly decreased.

If your property is not being held as security, your decision on whether to get insurance will depend mainly on your philosophy and your pocket book. Throughout this book I have strongly advised that you do many things to protect yourself when you buy land. I also recommend that you be properly insured.

Shop around to find the kind of coverage you want at the lowest price. Insurance premiums for the same amount of coverage differ among companies by as much as 20 percent. Never buy insurance from a mail-order company or from someone who sells insurance as a sideline. Avoid taking out a policy through the real estate agent who handles your deal until you have compared the cost of the agent's coverage with similar coverage available through other companies. Go to reputable insurance companies and individual insurance brokers, preferably in the area of your rural home. Ask around for recommendations. Compare types of coverage being offered and the cost of premiums being charged.

## Fire Insurance and the Lender's Insurance Requirements

If your lender requires that you get insurance, the amount and type of coverage will be dictated by its demands. The standard condition in a loan agreement states that

The Buyer agrees to keep all buildings now on, or that may hereafter be placed on, said property, insured in the name of the Lender (or Seller) against loss by fire in an amount not less than the fair replacement value thereof, and in no event for less than _____ Dollars ($_____), the policies to be in a form and in a company or companies satisfactory to the Lender (or Seller). The Lender (or Seller) may require that the Buyer deposit said policies with him.

If you fail to get insurance that fulfills the lender's conditions or to maintain premium payments, most loan documents allow the lender to make the payments and then add the amount to the total debt owed, making it subject to interest. Normally, however, the lender will start foreclosure proceedings if you fail to abide by the mortgage conditions. Most creditors require that the property be insured only against loss by fire, although some might require extended coverage. A single policy covering both yourself and your creditor can often be obtained at no greater cost than if just one of you were named as the beneficiary. Both you and your creditor will keep copies of the policy.

If you are in a rural area where water is scarce and fire protection is not readily available, you should assume that in case of fire your house will suffer a total loss. Therefore, you would probably want, and may be required, to insure it to its maximum value. When figuring its value, for instance, rather than using the price you paid for the house, you must determine the replacement value, that is, the amount that would be necessary to rebuild the house. When calculating the replacement value, do not figure in the value of the land, because most policies will not cover land. You would normally increase the coverage over the years to keep up with inflation.

Insurance companies usually require that you get minimum coverage of 80 percent of the replacement value of the house. Coverage can be extended upward for relatively little money above the minimum premium amount. Therefore, you should probably get the maximum coverage that you can afford, up to 100 percent coverage for fire.

Coverage cost is usually based on a certain dollar-per-square-foot value, based on local costs of construction. For example, if the size of your house is 1,500 square feet and building costs in your area are $50 per square foot, it would cost $75,000 to re-

build your house. Therefore, that would be the amount of coverage you would buy. Local insurance brokers know the current values for your area.

Insurance policies generally run for one year and then are renewed annually. The premium payment schedule can be arranged with the insurance agent, but the most common schedule is three annual payments. If the seller is financing your purchase, you will probably be responsible for paying the insurance premiums yourself, rather than paying through an impound fund. Your seller will order the insurance company to inform him or her if you do not make the required payments. If your loan is from a commercial lender, you will usually pay monthly *impounds* with your regular loan payments. These impounds cover the cost of the insurance premiums. The lender will make the premium payments when they become due from the money you have prepaid. (See Chapter 23, "Buying Property That Is Encumbered by a Loan Agreement.")

Most policies include a *deductible* clause, which requires that in case of loss you must pay the deductible amount and the insurance company will pay the rest, up to the total amount of coverage. The deductible amount is usually a few hundred dollars. For example, suppose you have a $500-deductible clause. If your house sustains $800 worth of damages from a fire, you pay $500 and the insurer pays $300. Most policies reduce the deductible amount as the total coverage increases. Before taking out a policy, be sure you understand all the terms regarding deductible items. Have the insurance agent explain anything you don't understand until it is completely clear. If the policy does not seem worth the price, go somewhere else.

If you suffer a partial loss of your home through a fire, the check issued for the loss is written in the names of both you and your lender. Normally the lender will endorse the check over to the appropriate party to pay for the repairs to the home. If the house is totally destroyed by fire, the lender can keep the entire loan proceeds up to the amount remaining due under your note or can allow you to use the funds to rebuild your home and continue to use it as security for the mortgage or deed of trust.

## Extended Coverage

For a small additional cost you can get extended coverage, which protects you against losses caused by hailstorms, tornadoes, wind, erosion, riots, aircraft damage, vehicle damage and smoke damage from cooking or heating units. Read the policy, because smoke damage from fireplaces may not be covered. A maximum amount to be paid for broken windows, such as $50, may be specified. If you want coverage for vandalism and malicious mischief or for earthquake damage, specify that it be included in your policy. An extended policy never covers loss or damage to personal property, only to the structures. Theft must be covered by a separate policy, which I discuss later.

## The "Risk of Loss" Rule and Property Insurance

If you take possession of your future home after the contract of sale is signed but before escrow closes, your insurance should cover you from the time you take possession rather than the time title is transferred to you. Consider the following possibility:

A family is buying a house in the country and is eager to move in. The contract of sale is signed, and the deal looks as if it is going to go through to everybody's satisfaction. Two weeks before closing of escrow, the seller allows the buyers to move into the house. A week before escrow closes, the house burns down in a fire of unknown origin while the family is away for the weekend. Do the buyers still have to complete the purchase? The seller does not want the property now that it is destroyed, and the buyers do not want to make payments for ten years on a pile of ashes. Most states have now adopted the standard Vendor and Purchaser Act, or Risk of Loss Rule, which places the loss on the party in possession before title is transferred. Thus, in this example, the buyers will be legally required to proceed with the deal. They did not get insurance coverage from the time they took possession, and the seller's insurance company is going to deny liability because its insured party, the seller, was not in possession of the property at the time the loss occurred.

If you are going to take over the seller's insurance policy, get the seller to place your name with the company as an insured beneficiary as of the date you are to take possession. Then get a certificate from the company stating that you are insured, as well as a copy of the policy with your name as a coinsured. If the seller cannot put you on his or her policy, you must get your own.

If you are not going to take possession early,

your policy should insure you as of the date of the closing of escrow, whether you move onto the property at that time or later. Once you receive title to the land, the responsibility for any loss will fall on you because you are then the owner, unless the destruction is caused by the seller's actions after you take title. Prior to the close of escrow, you should have a binder in your hands guaranteeing that you will be insured the moment escrow closes. Get this from the insurance agent who is selling you your insurance.

## Personal Liability Insurance

Insurance covering injuries to other people while they are on your property is the most important type of coverage to have in the country, whether or not you have a house on the land. The possibilities for accidents are numerous. Someone's child could fall out of a tree, someone could slip in your creek or fall into your well, get bitten by your dog or kicked by your horse. When you invite someone onto your land, you are under a legal duty to exercise care to prevent injury to that person. You could suffer great losses if a person were to sue you because of an injury suffered on your property.

Liability, or indemnity, insurance protects you up to the amount of coverage if legal action is taken against you for personal injury. The usual policy, costing several hundred dollars a year, can cover you for up to $300,000 for injuries to each person or $300,000 damages per incident or any other amount you purchase coverage for. If you intend to invite many people to your land, you might want greater coverage, because $300,000 is not much when you see the kinds of awards juries are giving to injured plaintiffs these days.

This type of policy does not cover injuries to yourself or your family. Those injuries are covered under your own medical insurance plan.

## Theft Insurance

If you are buying a country home you intend to occupy only part of the year, you might want theft insurance. The country, too, has burglaries, although they are not as prevalent as in the city. The type of coverage varies widely, as does the maximum amount of coverage available.

A program has been started by the federal government called the Federal Crime Insurance Program. The government provides crime insurance at a low rate in any state that does not have crime insurance available for homeowners. The insurance is sold through licensed insurance agents and brokers and through private insurance companies that act as servicing companies for the Federal Insurance Administration. Coverage includes loss from burglary, larceny and robbery. A licensed insurance broker should be able to provide you with the current information on this program and the appropriate application forms. Your local office of The Department of Housing and Urban Development (HUD) also has this information, or write to the Federal Insurance Administration, United States Department of Housing and Urban Development, Washington, DC 20410.

## The Homeowner's Insurance Policy

The most common type of policy today is the *Standard* or *Homeowner's policy,* which combines the features of fire, personal liability and theft insurance at a cheaper rate than such policies would cost if purchased individually. The policy covers the home, garage and other structures on the land as well as personal property. The policy should state the type and the value of the property covered, the maximum amount that will be paid in case of loss and the kinds of losses covered. Generally, damage to buildings other than the house and personal property outside the home will not be covered to their full replacement value. Find out what kind of proof you will have to provide as evidence of your loss. You should keep a list of all your personal property and its value in case of loss. I also advise having the inside and outside of your house videotaped in detail with the videotape stored off your property so you will have a visual record of your home and its contents in the event of a fire or theft loss.

The types of coverage and costs vary greatly throughout the insurance industry, so you will have to shop around for the best deal.

Most states now have workers' compensation laws that require you to provide insurance coverage for persons working on your property for you, for example, carpenters, gardeners, painters and housesitters. If they are injured while engaged in employment for you, they are entitled to have their medical bills paid, to receive disability payments and to receive a sum of money for any permanent disability.

If you are not insured, you can be sued and your insurance may not cover you, unless you specifically have workers' compensation coverage. This is normally added to your standard homeowner's policy for an additional premium. I advise getting this additional coverage if you intend to employ any persons on your property.

## The National Flood Insurance Program

Standard insurance policies never cover structural damage due to floods or mudslides. Because of the great losses that occur annually, the federal government decided to offer federally subsidized flood insurance, through the private insurance industry, to homeowners in areas that have met land use and flood control requirements and have been approved for this type of subsidy by HUD.

Any local property and casualty insurance agent or broker should have information regarding the availability of flood insurance in your area, or write to the Federal Emergency Management Agency (FEMA), United States Department of Housing and Urban Development, Washington, DC 20410, or to the National Flood Insurance Program, Box 450, Lanham, MD 20706. Ask if your state is in the subsidy program and if so, where the nearest office is that offers such coverage.

## Mortgage Life Insurance

This is a unique form of life insurance that provides that in the event of the death or disability of the head of a family, the insurance company will continue to make mortgage payments until the amount due is completely paid. The cost of the premium will depend on the age of the insured and the amount of the mortgage. Some lenders and sellers might require that you carry this type of insurance. Any reputable insurance broker can give you complete information.

## Assuming the Sellers' Insurance Policy

The sellers may already have the property insured, and you might find it to your advantage simply to take over their policy. Ask them to show you a copy of their policy with the schedule of premium payments. Sometimes an insurance company will want to increase the premium rates for the person assuming an existing policy. Find out if it intends to do so in your case. Then investigate to see if you can get a better deal elsewhere.

If you decide to assume the sellers' insurance, you must agree to do so in writing. This is specified in clause 8(b) of the Model Contract of Sale. (See Chapter 27.) The policy does not transfer automatically with the property; the insurance company must consent in writing to your assuming it. The local insurance broker or escrow holder can handle the problems involved in transferring the policy to you.

## Prorating the Prepaid Insurance Premium When You Assume a Policy

If you assume the sellers' insurance policy, the premium will have to be prorated according to the time you are to take possession of or title to the property. The sellers will probably have paid the premium in advance, so you will have to reimburse them for the amount of the premium that will cover your ownership of the property. Sometimes the insurance company will reimburse the sellers for the amount,

write a new policy for you, and have you pay them immediately.

The following example illustrates how such a proration is done. Assume that the sellers have a one-year extended coverage fire insurance policy and that they paid a premium of $600 on July 1, 1996, covering the next year from July 1, 1996 to June 30, 1997.

The policy will expire on June 30, 1997, but you are to take title on May 1, 1997. We want to figure out how many days the seller will have used the insurance, and how many days the buyer will benefit from it. Dividing the premium of $600 by 12, you get the monthly rate of $50.

The sellers were covered from July 1, 1996 to May 1,1997, a period of ten months. The premium is $50 per month, so they used $500 worth of insurance for the ten months. Thus, $500 of the $600 premium will have covered the sellers. Because you will be covered for the rest of the insuring period, you must reimburse the sellers for the remaining amount of the premium covering the two months of May and June, 1997. Subtracting $500 from $600 leaves $100, which you are to pay to the sellers at the closing of escrow. (See Chapter 29, "Opening and Closing of Escrow and the Role of the Escrow Holder.") This is the method of proration specified in clause 8(b) of the Model Contract of Sale. (See Chapter 27.)

# Deciding on a Fair Price

# Evaluating the Price of the Property

*The purpose of an appraisal is to estimate a defined value of any real property interest, or to conduct an evaluation study pertaining to real property decisions.*

—Dictionary of Real Estate Appraisal, 2nd ed.

When you find land that is right for you, that meets all your requirements and feels like home, you will want to evaluate what that land is worth and compare your results with the seller's asking price. Then you can begin the bargaining game described in the next chapter.

To evaluate the price of the land you want to buy, regardless of where it is located, you can do a number of things without employing a professional appraiser. This chapter tells you how to make your own appraisal of the property and how to hire a professional if you decide you need one.

Finally, I explain how the seller establishes his asking price.

## What Determines the Value of a Piece of Property?

Determining the value of a piece of land is a complex and ambiguous process. If there is any such thing as a formula for finding land value, it would have to be *Value is determined by the law of supply and demand*. Although the supply of land is ultimately finite, its availability is constantly fluctuating as large ranches, farms and other land parcels are split up for sale to the public. The desire for rural property has not diminished in the last 20 years.

The Bureau of the Census took a special survey

to determine where the average person prefers to have his or her primary residence. The results are shown below.

## Residential Location and Preferences

| | Where Do You Live Now? (%) | Where Would You Prefer To Live (%) |
|---|---|---|
| Open Country | 12 | 34 |
| Small Town or City | 33 | 30 |
| Medium-sized City or Suburb | 28 | 22 |
| Larger City or Suburb | 27 | 14 |
| Total | 100 | 100 |

Of the people questioned, 64 percent expressed a desire to live in a nonurban setting. Only 45 percent of the interviewees now live in this type of area. If you combine the 19 percent who wish to make a permanent move away from the cities and suburbs with the increasing number of second-home land buyers, it is clear that there is a tremendous demand for rural and semirural property.

All indications are that the rate of interested land buyers will continue to increase at a faster rate than land will become available, and prices will continue to rise at varying rates in all parts of the country.

### A List of Value Factors

Many elements must be considered in deciding whether the price of a piece of property is "worth it." A general list of the basic factors includes the following:

- Supply
- Demand
- Usability—for example, level land is more valuable
- State of the title—for example, what clouds, or defects, exist?
- Location—for example, neighbors, schools, shopping, public transportation, church, recreational facilities
- Directional growth of the area: industrial, commercial, recreational or residential
- Population and economic growth in the area
- Aesthetics: nice view, landscaping, beautiful house
- Road frontage
- Accessibility to the property, condition of the roads
- Water: quality and quantity
- Soil and drainage, for agricultural and/or building purposes
- Orchards and gardens: Have they been well cared for?
- Amount of timber and type of vegetation
- Availability of utilities
- Zoning and building codes
- Public health measures and regulations
- Condition and age of the house and other structures
- Size of the parcel—the larger the parcel, the smaller the price per acre
- Any stigma attached to the property
- Personal property included in the sale
- Climate
- Exposure to the sun—for example, north slope versus south slope
- Timing of the sale—for example, the owner must sell quickly because he is being transferred to a different location in his job.

Each of these elements has its own effect on the value of a parcel of land. For example, the closer property is to a populated area, the more desirable and expensive it will be. If it is close to employment, if it is accessible by a paved road, if utilities are supplied, if a house and other improvements are on the land, it will be more expensive than land without these features.

### Potential Use

One of the main determinants of value is the land's potential for development, meaning that it is valuable not for its own qualities but as a possible site for future activities of a profitable nature. Thus, if large numbers of people are moving into the area and the land is level or nearly so, more intensive use of the land may be expected. This potential increases the value of the land considerably, because level land can be subdivided into more usable parcels than steep land. The real estate agent may play up the land's suitability for subdivision to lure you with the thought of future profits, and thus make the present asking price seem more reasonable. If large timber is standing on the land, the price will be higher because you can cut and sell the trees. It is irrelevant whether you actually want to do so. The fact is that the potential is there.

When you evaluate the land, look at the potential uses for it and how soon the property will be in demand for such uses. How close is the nearest subdivision, and how well is it selling? Are any large industries planned nearby that might foretell a growing population? These things indicate the extent of the land's potential in determining the price.

### How the Tax Assessor Evaluates the Land and Its Improvements

A good place to start when determining the value of the land and its improvements is by checking the county tax assessor's records for the appraised market value. (The appraisal of land for tax purposes is discussed in Chapter 17, "Property Taxes and Assessments.") First, you must know how current the appraisal is. Talk to a tax assessor to see how recently he has been to your area. Several assessors usually work in the office, and you can ask to talk to the one who appraised the seller's land. The assessor will tell you what he or she thinks it is worth, which is usually somewhat more than its appraisal for taxes. You can tell the assessor what the seller's asking price is and get his or her opinion of it.

You can also ask for an opinion of any improvements on the land, their condition and value, independent of the land itself. The assessor will take into consideration factors of depreciation and appreciation.

Assessors are familiar with prices of land surrounding particular parcels, and can tell what kind of prices land has been going for in an area. They also know about developments being planned in an area and their possible effect on land values. This information is used in the most important and common of all appraisal techniques used by tax assessors and land appraisers, the comparison test.

### The Comparison Test

A parcel of land is compared with other parcels in the area that have been sold recently to determine its current value on the market, often called the *fair market value*. Find out the purchase prices of two or three separate pieces of land nearby that have been sold recently and that are similar in size and major features to the land you are interested in. For instance, if you are looking at land along a creek,

try to find out the price of the creek land above and below your prospective purchase.

Each parcel of land is unique, so you must be careful when comparing prices. Any improvements and other features, such as buildings, orchards, ponds and equipment, will raise the value of the property, so take these things into consideration. Two pieces of land that are basically similar, except that one has a house on it and the other does not, may be difficult to compare because of the added value of the house.

Where tax stamps are required on deeds, they can be used to find the purchase price of a piece of land. Prior to January 1, 1968, federal law required the placing of Internal Revenue Documentary Tax Stamps on every deed used to transfer property. Although there is no longer a federal land sales tax, many states have enforced their own tax stamp, or real property transfer tax, laws. If your state imposes a transfer tax, you can find out how the tax is computed from the county recorder and look up the deed of any land parcel to find out the purchase price either from the stamps affixed to it or from the stated amount of taxes that were paid. (See Chapter 32, "Deeds and Recording.") For example, under the old federal law, $0.55 worth of tax stamps was required for every $500 or fraction thereof of the purchase price. Thus, property that sold for $49,850 would have had $53.90 worth of documentary stamps affixed to the deed. To figure out the sale price from the stamps, divide the amount of the stamps by $0.55, then multiply that quotient by $500. This basic procedure can be used to determine the selling price wherever transfer taxes are required.

After looking at recent selling prices of comparable land, you will be able to price the land currently for sale. The more land you look at, the better idea you will have as to whether the land you like is priced high or low for the area. Ask other real estate agents who show you land if they are familiar with the land you are interested in. Tell them what the asking price is to see their reaction. Of course, you should not rely on their appraisal, but it will be interesting to hear what they say about it. When you compare the asking, price of other land for sale, remember that asking prices are almost always inflated.

As you compare the price of parcels similar to the land you are interested in, try to determine if there is justification for any difference in price. If a large discrepancy exists with no justification that you can see, keep it in mind to bring up during the bargaining and negotiations with the seller when you are pointing out why the price is too high.

If the seller bought the land within the past few years, try to find out the price he or she paid for it. You can simply ask, although he or she may be reluctant to tell you, especially if a large profit is possible. You can look up the deed and determine the purchase price by the amount of transfer taxes paid or the number of tax stamps, if they were required. Also compare the tax assessor's appraised value of the land the year before the seller bought the property with its appraised value after he or she took title. The increased amount reflects the amount paid for it.

Ask everyone familiar with the property his or her opinion of the reasonableness of the asking price. This includes the building inspector, tax assessor, other real estate agents, people living in the area and the farm adviser.

## Hiring a Professional Appraiser

A professional appraiser does not have access to any information you cannot get, but experience is on his or her side. The appraiser who works in one section of the country for many years should be thoroughly familiar with property values in the area and how they are set. But if you do a thorough job of comparing land prices and getting the opinions of people who have been in the area a long time, I believe you can efficiently appraise the value of the land yourself. Even professional appraisals vary.

Until recently real estate appraisers were not usually regulated by any state laws, so you had to be careful whom you selected. Congress has enacted regulations requiring all appraisers to be certified in the states where they practice. Appraisers may also belong to one or several national organizations and are supposed to abide by a code of ethics and pass some accreditation standards established by the group. If you look in the local telephone book under "Appraisers," those with memberships in a professional organization will be so designated. The group that seems to be preferred by professional lenders is the Appraisal Institute. The Appraisal Institute was formed with the unification of two industry groups, the American Institute of Real Estate Appraisers and the Society of Real Estate Appraisers. Its members may have such designations as RM, SREA, MAI, SRPA or SRA, de-

pending on their specialty or length of time with the organization. The American Association of Certified Appraisers, Inc. (AACA), and the American Society of Appraisers (ASA) are two other appraiser organizations. In "Useful Resources" at the end of this chapter you will find the addresses of these organizations. if you write them, they will send you lists of where their appraisers are located.

Appraisal fees are usually based on the amount of time needed to complete the job, and that depends on how thorough a job must be done. Undeveloped land will not take as long to evaluate as land that has a house on it. Costs vary throughout the country, but the minimum is usually around $300. A good report includes an evaluation of the house and other structures, the availability of utilities and other services, the value of the location, the potential for resale at a profit, present zoning and possible future rezoning, recorded restrictions, the expected economic and population growth in the community and comparison figures on other similar sales in the area. The result of this research will be a figure that is the appraised fair market value of the property in question.

Many real estate agents also work as appraisers. Thus, they sell property and make commissions, and also work for private parties and lending institutions as property appraisers on a fee basis. Most states now have a certification program where broker–appraisers and appraisers can be licensed. This requires the completion of educational classes and the passing of a test. You should try to use a certified real estate appraiser, whether it is a broker–appraiser or a full-time appriaser. However, never use the real estate broker who is selling the land as your appraiser because his or her commission depends on how much money the property sells for. You must also be careful that the appraiser you hire does not have a personal friendship with the broker handling the deal, which might sway the evaluation.

If you are a veteran, you can apply for a loan, and the Department of Veterans Affairs (VA) will appraise the property for a small fee as part of the loan. You must fill out a form called a "Request for Determination of Reasonable Value." You do not have to go through with the loan, but you will know, if it is approved, that the asking price is reasonable. The VA should also tell you what its appraisal is. (See Chapter 26.)

You can also apply for a regular commercial or FHA loan to get an inexpensive appraisal, but these organizations generally do not tell you the results of the appraisal. They will tell you only whether they accept or reject the application for the loan.

The seller might have had a professional appraisal done. If the seller presents you with an appraisal that equals the asking price, go to the appraiser yourself, talk to him and try to get a sense of how honest he or she is.

## How the Seller Sets His or Her Asking Price

The seller usually arrives at his or her asking price by combining four factors:

1.  the value of the property and the improvements;
2.  the costs of selling the land;
3.  the bargaining margin and the profit; and
4.  the psychology of numbers.

### The Value of the Property and the Improvements

Sellers may determine the value of the property and improvements by using the same methods as those explained above. However, sellers naturally will tend to estimate the value higher than you do, because of their sentimental attachment to the property. They will tend to emphasize appreciation caused by a greater demand to live in the area or to improvements made on the land and overlook depreciation caused by physical deterioration of the land and improvements, the obsolescence of structures because of stylistic trends and technological advances or the decline in the demand to live in the area. Sellers usually consider the price they paid for the land and add on whatever they spent on it to get its actual value. But it is possible they paid too much, especially if they bought in the early 1980s; so don't assume you automatically have to pay sellers at least whatever they paid. As land values decrease after the inflationary period of the late 1970s and early 1980s, people often are selling at a loss in various parts of the country.

### The Costs of Selling the land

Once sellers determine what they believe the actual value of the property to be, they will add on the costs involved in selling the land. These could include the real estate agent's commission; attorney's fees; escrow charges; taxes; and survey, appraisal and title insurance costs. By figuring them into the asking price, sellers pass these costs on to buyers. This is standard procedure, and brokers generally advise sellers to set their prices in this manner.

### The Bargaining Margin and the Profit

Sellers then add on a bargaining and profit margin figure, usually anywhere from 10 to 50 percent of the property's value as they see it. Part of the purpose of this additional figure is to give sellers room to negotiate with buyers. When buyers offer a low figure, sellers can compromise by coming down in the asking price and still realize a profit. They might allow buyers to talk them down in price several times, giving buyers the illusion that they are getting a steal. If sellers finance the purchase themselves, they will realize an additional profit in interest over the years, so they might reduce their initial profit margins by quite a bit. (See Chapter 22, "Terms of the Loan Agreement and Their Effect on the Total Price.") You will see how this works in negotiations in Chapter 20, "Bargaining To Get the Seller's Asking Price Down."

Real estate agents often play an important role in setting prices because sellers rely on their appraisals and judgment. One common practice is for agents to set prices high to convince sellers to give them exclusive listings. They make a few attempts to sell the property, then tell sellers the market is bad and they should lower their price. Sellers almost invariably follow the agents' advice. Then agents try to get quick sales and commissions. They will lower prices according to how desperately they need sales. Competition is so cutthroat in the rural real estate business that many agents would rather sell the property and take a small commission than risk losing the seller to another agent when the contract expires. You might come along at just the right time.

However, usually agents estimate high, hoping that buyers will pay the inflated price, which will increase their commissions, because they are based on a percentage of the sale price. Especially if agents know that sellers are not in a hurry to sell, they may let properties sit on the market until the right buyers come along to take them at high prices. In general, all the agents in an area try to keep prices inflated because that helps them all.

**The Psychology of Numbers**

Often a seller or an agent will use a figure that seems much lower than it actually is. For example, instead of setting the price at $47,000, the seller asks for $46,950. This is an old device that was first used by J. C. Penney and is now widely employed as a sales technique. The psychology of the odd price gives buyers the feeling that they are getting bargains and that prices have been cut as far as possible.

## The Appraisal as a Safety Valve in the Contract of Sale

A common safety valve put in buyers' contracts by attorneys is the condition that the purchase may be terminated if the buyer has the property appraised and is dissatisfied with the results. Clause 17(b) in the Model Contract of Sale in Chapter 27 allows this type of condition to be inserted. Always write in the parenthetical part that you are having an appraisal conducted on the property. You can use anyone you want as an appraiser. If you obtain an appraisal and you decide at some time after the seller has signed the contract and made it binding that you want out of the deal, all you have to do is write the seller a letter saying you do not approve the results of the appraisal that you had done—if it is lower than the price you agreed on.

## Useful Resources

You can get appraisal information and a directory of appraisers throughout the United States from each of the following professional appraiser organizations:

> Appraisal Institute
> 875 N. Michigan Avenue, Suite 2400
> Chicago, IL 60611-1980
> (312) 335-4100

American Society of Appraisers (ASA)
P.O. Box 17265
Washington, DC 20041
Voice: (703) 478-2228 or (800) ASA-VALU
Fax: (703) 742-8471
BBS: (703) 478-5502

American Association of Certified
Appraisers, Inc. (AACA)
800 Compton Rd., Suite 10
Cincinnati, OH 45231
(513) 729-1400

In addition to the pamphlets you will receive when requesting appraisal information, the following brochures are available free from the Appraisal Institute, listed above, with a stamped, self addressed business envelope:

"Estimating Home Value"
"Planning Home Improvements"
"Analyzing Rehab Potential"
"Statement of Purpose"
"Understanding the Appraisal"
"The Appraisal Institute—Organization and
 Services"
"Directory of Members"

The following are available with a stamped, self-addressed business envelope from the ASA, listed above:

| | |
|---|---|
| "Appraisal Publications" | free |
| "Information on the Appraisal Profession" | free |
| "The American Society of Appraisers" | free |
| "Directory of Accredited Professional Real Property Appraisers" | free |
| "Directory of Accredited Business Appraisers" | free |
| "Principles of Appraisal Practice and Code of Ethics" | free |
| "Information on the Appraisal Profession" | $.10 |

# CHAPTER

# 20 Bargaining To Get the Seller's Asking Price Down

## The Rules of the Game and Order of the Moves

The game of bargaining is an ancient one, and the rules and moves are well established. Because each piece of land is unique, uniform prices cannot be set, and bargaining has survived as the most common means of buying and selling land. Sellers usually set their prices higher than they hope to receive because they expect to bargain. Naturally, buyers and sellers will each be acting in their individual self-interests. The buyers' job is to lower prices so that they favor the buyer, which means keeping

sellers' profits as low as possible. Don't worry about a seller losing money on the deal. It rarely happens.

In the previous chapter, "Evaluating the Price of the Property," I outlined how sellers determine their asking prices and how buyers can appraise land to see if those prices are fair. Usually an *asking price* will be higher than the buyer wants to pay, and he or she will want to negotiate the price down. Bargaining is a game of endurance and coolness. I have isolated seven factors that influence all negotiations and affect the nature of your bargaining and the final purchase price. They are

1.  the willingness of both parties to play the game;
2.  the seller's eagerness to sell the property and the buyer's eagerness to find a home;
3.  the length of time a property has been up for sale;
4.  the current market for a property;
5.  the buyer's ability to point out deficiencies of a property versus the seller's ability to point out its desirable features;
6.  the buyer's ability to come up with more cash and the seller's desire to take more than he or she originally asked for; and
7.  the buyer's ability to know when he or she is getting a fair deal.

## The Willingness of Both Parties To Play the Game

The game is bargaining. If you and the seller are going to play, you both must be willing to make compromises. Unless you and the seller are willing to change your positions, the game cannot be played.

The seller always sets the asking price higher than he or she expects to get, for the specific purpose of establishing a position from which to bargain. The expectation of bargaining is implicit in the words *asking price*. In other words, the seller intends to play the game and will be very surprised if you don't play along by making a low offer in return. You will then bargain back and forth until either a stalemate or a common agreement is reached.

Unfortunately, every seller is not a game player. There are occasions when a seller sets a price with no intention of bringing it down, regardless of the circumstances. He or she intends to sit and wait until obtaining a buyer at the asking price, even if it takes four or five years. I have known such people, but there are not many. You should assume, until you find out otherwise, that the seller will come down in his or her price and that you will have to come up from your original offer. In other words, be prepared to play the game.

Needless to say, the real estate agents will play a part in this game. The agent has a vested interest in the results: His or her commission is based on the final selling price, but the commission will not be forthcoming until the property is sold. This places the agent in a curious position. Although the agent

will favor the seller as the principal, he or she will attempt to get the seller and you to compromise your positions so that the property gets sold and the commission gets paid. The average rural town agent dislikes a stubborn seller as much as an unwilling buyer. The longer the agent has to spend showing the property and dealing with buyers, the less monetary return he or she will get for the time spent. So the agent will be right there in the middle, pushing you and the seller, trying to get you to sign a contract. This is the essence of the bargaining game.

### The Seller's Eagerness To Sell the Property and Your Eagerness To Find a Home

This factor is closely related to the previous one. The less eager a seller is to get rid of the property, the less bargaining and compromising will be done. The seller may be holding the land as an investment and can afford to wait until he or she can make a killing. All the seller has to do is make the payments, pay the annual taxes and wait as long as necessary to get a buyer at the nonnegotiable price. You cannot negotiate with this type of landowner, and the real estate agent will not try very hard to sell his or her property.

However, even if the owner does not live on the land and is obviously an investor, this does not necessarily mean that it will be impossible to negotiate a price reduction. You do not know what the situation is. Perhaps the owner needs fast money for an emergency or a new investment, or land values in the area might not be increasing at the expected rate.

An owner presently living on the land or who recently moved from it will usually want to sell as soon as possible. A job may be waiting in another area, perhaps the family has outgrown the house, he or she may not be able to make payments or keep up with the taxes, or a bankruptcy or divorce may be involved. Sometimes land is sold at very reasonable prices when an owner dies and the beneficiaries want to sell as fast as possible to settle the estate. The greater the pressures on the seller to sell, the better the chances are of getting the price down.

It may be difficult for you to determine the seller's anxiety. One of the first things to do is ask the owner or the real estate agent why the land is for sale. Of course, you may not get an honest answer if the truth might dissuade you from buying the land or encourage you to drive a hard bargain. Verify what you are told by speaking to surrounding landowners and other real estate agents in the area. Local agents often know the facts about a piece of property even if it is not listed with them. If you can discover the seller's situation, you may feel more confident when bargaining with him or her.

Be conscious, too, of the fact that your own urgency can work to the seller's advantage. "Buyer's fever" has caused many to buy land at inflated prices simply because they were tired of looking for a place. Real estate agents often can scare people into believing that a land boom is on, that property is going fast, and that prices are soaring. This is their job. If an agent can convince you that the land won't be there tomorrow and therby increase your eagerness to buy, you will not be hard-nosed when it comes to bargaining. Notice as you look at land how many times you hear a phrase like "Someone else might beat you to the bargain if you delay." The real estate agent attempts to play on your insecurity to soften you up.

If you are unusually itchy to buy land because you have been looking for a long time or need to get settled quickly, do not fail to exercise your full bargaining power anyway. Be cool. Do not let on how long you have been looking and how tired and eager you are to find a home. The seller may be willing to go much lower than you realize. You will always be in the more secure position, because you can usually look at a lot of land for as long as you want until you find what you like. The seller has to patiently wait and hope to get a purchaser at the desired price.

If the agent and seller know that you hope to move out of the city or get a second home as soon as possible, they will plan their sales pitch with that in mind. For the sake of bettering your bargaining position, therefore, assume that any landowner who puts property up for sale is eager to sell, and never reveal your own desperation to buy.

### The Length of Time the Property Has Been Up for Sale

The longer a parcel of land has been on the market, the more realistic the demands of the seller tend to become. Sellers are at a disadvantage when their property does not sell for a long time because they know that prospective buyers will wonder if something is wrong with it. It is natural to assume that if property is worth the price, it will sell reasonably quickly. If it stays on the market for an excessive amount of time, the assumption is that it is overpriced or seriously deficient.

Ask the real estate agent how long the property has been for sale, not just how long he or she personally has listed it. Ask if the price has been reduced since it was first put on the market, and if so, how many times and by what amounts. This is another time when you should verify the answers you get with other agents and neighboring landowners.

If the property has just been placed on the market, you will not have the bargaining advantage of time on your side. However, if it has been listed for a long time, try to find out why it has not sold. It is possible that the market for such land, especially if it is rugged, is small. Point out the fact that something must be wrong if the land has not brought any acceptable offers in such a long time. Tell the seller or agent that you are willing to pay a fair price; then make your offer. If the agent is eager to get the owner to sell, your arguments and persistence might get him or her to increase pressure on the seller to lower the demands.

I have watched the attitudes of property owners who have been trying to sell their property over a long period of time. They always start out with tremendous demands and a great amount of optimism that they will get a buyer at their price. The longer their property stays on the market, the more nervous and malleable they become. For example, I know of 40 acres that were put up for sale at $80,000. In the first year, six offers were made in a range from $35,000 to $40,000. Then six months went by with no offers. The seller and agent began to get pessimistic and decided they would take the next reasonable offer. They did, and the land sold for $45,000. The owner and agent were glad to get rid of it after two years of trying, even at that price.

### The Current Market for the Property

Since the beginning of the 1900s, the demographic trend has been for more people to move from country farms to the city, although there have been a few back-to-the-land movements during this time. The last one was in the late 1940s. The present land rush started in the late 1960s and is still going on. Conditions in the cities and suburbs are getting worse, and emigration to more rural areas increases annually. In addition, the idea of a second home is increasingly more inviting to urban residents who finds themselves with more leisure time.

When looking at different areas you would like to live in, remember that the more people there are moving into an area, the higher the prices will be due to the old rule of supply and demand. You may feel more comfortable in an area where there are other people like yourself who are moving away from the city to begin a new life in the country or are discovering the pleasures of owning a vacation home. In those places your bargaining powers will be diminished because buyer competition will be high. However, if you venture into those parts of the country that have not yet become popular (and there are many), the market will be small, and prices will be lower and negotiable.

As land buying spreads to new areas, the buyers in the first rush always get the best deals. They buy when competition is low, before the demand for land increases. We bought our land just before our area started to attract a steady stream of homesteaders. Land selling for $200 an acre when we bought is now going for five to ten times that much, and will be even more expensive by the time you read this book.

Regardless of the area, if you are looking for extremely isolated and undeveloped land, the demand will always remain small. There are still very few people willing to build their own houses, live without electricity, develop their own water systems, haul their own garbage and live many miles from the nearest towns. Such areas will have the cheapest land and a relatively small market of purchasers. Undeveloped backwoods land for sale is usually a buyers' market.

However, if you avoid obviously popular and publicized areas, you can find land with more conveniences that is not yet affected by the inflated prices of a large market. Some of the nicest areas of the country have not yet been touched by the second-home boom. If you shop wisely you may find an undiscovered area that suits you.

### Your Ability To Point Out Deficiencies of the Property vs. the Seller's Ability To Point Out Its Desirable Features

As a prospective purchaser, you are on the offensive in the bargaining game. This is a strong tactical advantage when you begin to point out the deficiencies of the property. If you have read the first part of this book, you should be an expert at this. Every piece of property has some deficiencies—your job is to find and use them to get the price down when you bargain with the seller. Certain defects will be much costlier than others; these major items are the ones you should emphasize.

For instance, when downgrading a house, your first comments should be directed at structural weaknesses such as a cracked foundation, dry rot, termites, a leaky roof or basement, poor plumbing and old wiring. Emphasize the serious and expensive items first. Then bring in the smaller items broken windows, cracked tile, peeling paint and torn screens.

While you point out the bad points, the seller will counter with such desirable features as a beautiful fireplace, the isolation of the house, the gardens, the redwood shake exterior and other things that are plus factors to most people. If any of these factors is not a positive feature to you, let the seller know it. The real estate agent represents the seller, so you can be sure he will raise a vigorous defense to your criticisms.

Your complaints do not have to deal solely with the structures or land features. You can point out that the land is in a poor location or that there are no utilities available or anything else you can think of. If you can afford to get a complete house inspection and land appraisal, you can use these professional analyses in your bargaining; however, you have enough information from reading this book to do these things yourself. Take notes on what you learn, and get estimates of what it will cost you to correct existing defects in the property. At least try to decrease the asking price by the estimated amount needed to repair the major defects in the property. In the seller's defense, the real estate agent will tell you that all the deficiencies were taken into account when the asking price was set. You should then ask for the asking price to be broken down, to indicate just how these deficiencies were figured into it. How do the agent's figures compare with yours? What are the agent's estimates to correct the existing structures and other defects of the property? The agent might have an appraisal and inspection for the property. This appraisal will probably be different from yours. Read it carefully to find out when it was conducted and what items are covered. Was the appraiser a member of a professional organization? Even if the seller's appraisal concludes the property is worth more than your own appraisal does, yours is just as valid, and you should continue to press its results, assuming they are in your favor. If the seller's inspection report has underestimated the defects, say so. Use your evidence for all its worth when bargaining. Don't worry about being repetitive. Let the seller know you are a careful buyer.

There might also be clouds, or defects, on the title, such as a reservation of an easement across the property or a reservation of a right to take minerals or water. The structure might not have been properly approved by the building inspector or there might be a restrictive covenant in the deed that diminishes the future uses of the property.

If you can't find any deficiencies in the land, the improvements, the location or the title, you haven't looked hard enough.

**Your Ability To Come Up with More Cash and the Seller's Desire To Take More than He Originally Asks**

After you have made several offers and have brought the price down as far as possible, there is a final move left that you can make. You can offer a larger down payment or full cash in exchange for a lower price.

A seller who finances the sale generally asks for a cash down payment with monthly payments to continue until the principal and interest are paid. The requested down payment is usually 10 to 33 percent of the total asking price. However, sellers are often grateful to get more immediate cash than they ask for, even if it means they will get less money in the long run. If you think this seems unlikely, listen to our case.

When we were bargaining for our land, I got the seller down to what he claimed was his rock-bottom price. Then I asked him how large a discount he would give us if we paid the entire purchase price immediately in cash. He offered to reduce the price by an additional 30 percent. We got a loan at the same interest rate as our mortgage to the seller would have carried, and paid cash. Thus, not only did we reduce the price by 30 percent, but we reduced the total amount of interest we would have to pay because the amout of the principal was cut.

If you have to borrow the money at a higher interest rate, you will have to figure out if you actually will save by paying cash. Here are two simple illustrations of how this works:

Suppose the asking price of a parcel of land is $40,000 with a $10,000 down payment and monthly installments at the rate of 9 percent on the remaining $30,000. You. already have $10,000, and you can borrow another $20,000 at 12 percent interest from the bank. The seller offers to cut the price to $30,000 if you pay the entire amount in cash. If you accept this offer, you will pay 12 percent interest on the remaining $20,000 owed the

bank. The question is whether this is cheaper than paying 9 percent on $30,000. Figuring the interest for the first year you get:

9% interest $\times$ $30,000 = $2,700

whereas

12% interest $\times$ $20,000 = $2,400

The $2,400 interest is less at 12 percent than the $2,700 interest at 9 percent because the total price is less, so take the offer for $30,000 and finance it through the bank.

Now look at this example. The asking price for some land is, again, $40,000, with a down payment of $10,000 and monthly installments at the rate of 9 percent on the remaining $30,000. You offer to give the seller a total price of $30,000 cash because you can borrow $20,000 at 12 percent interest from the bank. The seller offers to cut the selling price by only $5,000, making it $35,000. You will have to give the seller a second mortgage for $5,000 at 9 percent in addition to the first mortgage to the bank at 12 percent. Figuring the first year's interest, you get

9% interest $\times$ $30,000 = $2,700

whereas

12% interest $\times$ $20,000 = $2,400
9% interest $\times$ $5,000 = $450

So

$2,400 + $450 = $2,850
$150 more than $2,700

Although this time the interest is higher by $150 the first year, there will be a smaller difference in succeeding years. In fact, if you pay off the loan over ten years, you will actually pay about $3,000 less by taking a loan from the bank, because your purchase price has been cut by $5,000. You can figure this out by using Figure 22-1 in Chapter 22 to figure the monthly payments, assuming a 10-year payoff period. Using the table to amortize a $1,000 loan, locate the factor in the column under 9 percent and in the row for 10 years. This factor is 12.6676. Multiply this number by 30 because the loan is for $30,000, not $1,000. Monthly payments for 9 percent on $30,000 are approximately $380.10. Do the same thing for 12 percent on $20,000 and 9 percent on $5,000. The monthly payments for 12 percent on $20,000 are $287; the monthly payments for 9 percent on $5,000 are

$63.35; the total is $350.35. Multiplying 12 payments per year times 10 years equals 120 payments.

$$\$380.10 \times 120 \text{ payments} = \$45,612$$

$$\$350.35 \times 120 \text{ payments} = \$42,042$$

Do this type of analysis on your own deal if you are in the position of being able to make a higher down payment than is asked for.

The seller will have a down payment established as part of the purchase price when he or she places the land on the market. Just tell the seller that you think you will be able to meet it if you decide to buy the land. Never reveal that you have a larger amount of cash available until the last minute, because you want to get the price as low as possible by the other methods before offering your final enticement.

Sometimes this strategy might not get you anywhere. There are landowners who don't want a larger down payment or full cash for their land because of their tax situation or because they prefer to make more money in the long run by the accrual of interest. But when the possibility of more cash is presented to the seller, he or she usually will make adjustments in the price to get it.

### Your Ability To Know When You Are Getting a Fair Deal

This is the most subtle part of effective bargaining. You must realize when you have pushed the price down as far as it is going to go. The buyer who continues haggling beyond the point where a fair deal has been reached often loses the property because another buyer comes along and makes a better offer that the seller accepts. Don't be greedy. The price is right when the seller stands to make a little money and you get a good piece of land at a reasonable sum. You will make your profit when you decide to sell. This is not to say that the seller always makes a profit, but he or she usually does; you should approach the negotiations with that in mind. Bargain strongly on your own behalf, but also be willing to compromise. Temper your self-interest when the price is just right and you can't go wrong. Don't hesitate to close the deal if you feel you have bargained wisely and you are getting a good deal.

Now that you understand the interacting elements, or "rules," that affect the bargaining process, you are ready to begin making the "moves," which consist of offers, rejections, counteroffers and, finally, acceptance.

## Your First Move— Your Offer

First, decide if you can afford to purchase the property you are looking at. A common formula states that a family should not buy a home that exceeds more than two times their annual family income. Another approach is that a homeowner usually should not pay more than 38 percent of income after federal tax for monthly housing expenses (payment on the mortgage loan plus the average cost of heat, utilities, repair and maintenance). You should also have the cash necessary to meet the down payment and closing costs such as title insurance, tax prorations and escrow fees. Once you have determined that the property you want is within your means, you are ready to start bargaining.

Your first move in the bargaining process is your offer to the seller to buy the property. Your offer should be made in a contract of sale that states all the terms you want and the price you are offering to pay. If you are dealing through a real estate agent, the agent must relay your offer to the owner. Just as the asking price is set high to give the seller room to bargain, your offer should be much lower than you expect to pay. You can always go up when the seller rejects your offer; but if you start high and your offer is accepted, it is too late then to bargain for a lower price. You never know how badly the seller wants to dispose of the property. Disregard any statements by the agent that the seller does not intend to reduce his price.

How low should your first offer be? In my experience the best way for you to begin bargaining is to offer somewhere between 50 percent and 80 percent of the asking price. Don't offer more than 80 percent initially, unless you know for sure that the asking price is fair already and that the property may be sold immediately. You might think this is ridiculous and will offend the seller. The agent may imply that you are crazy and attempt to dissuade you from "wasting everybody's time." But do not give in. Say that you have looked at a lot of land and feel your offer is a reasonable one.

The agent has a fiduciary duty to relay your offer to the seller. The worst thing that can happen is that the seller will reject your offer. Because you already expect that, you should not feel embarrassed. It is all part of the game. If you suspect that the agent hasn't relayed your offer, ask him for a written rejection from the seller.

Because you start low, you will have ample room to come up in later offers, giving the impression that the seller is forcing you higher. Being in this position gives you a psychological edge over the seller, particularly in the later stages of the negotiations.

Never tell a broker how high you will go. If you offer $50,000 against a $70,000 asking price, but tell the broker you will be willing to raise your offer to $60,000 if the seller doesn't accept the first offer, you can be sure the seller will find this out and know your $50,000 offer is meaningless. Always remember, the broker works for the seller because he or she is paid by the seller. The broker has a legal duty to disclose all information to the seller and cannot withhold information from the seller. It is hard to be discreet, because often you will develop a friendly relationship with the broker as he or she spends some time with you showing various properties.

But as hard as it is, never discuss your personal financial arrangements in front of the broker. Do not show any positive emotion when looking at properties. Try to remain passive, nonchalant and noncommittal. Never let on that underneath your cool exterior you are burning up with buyer's fever.

## The Seller's Rejection, Counteroffer or Final Acceptance

The response to your offer will come in one of three ways. First, the seller might accept it, and then you can move to close the deal. However, this is unlikely. Second, the seller might simply reject it and say it is not enough money and that he or she cannot afford to let the property go at your price. Third, the seller might start bargaining by rejecting your offer and making a counteroffer. That counteroffer will either be a new price lower than the original one or some added or deleted terms in the contract of sale. This is the usual response, and it means that he or she is willing to bargain with you. The seller might split the difference with you and go to the halfway point; usually, however, he or she will reduce the price by 5 percent or 10 percent. There is usually a 10 percent to 15 percent difference between the asking price and final selling price.

After the seller sends this new price to you through the agent, you can bring out the various de-

ficiencies in the property that you have been accumulating. Then make your second offer, which will be slightly higher than your first one. If the seller rejects it and makes a new counteroffer and you feel this is the lowest offer you will get, then you can offer a larger down payment or full cash (if you can get it) in return for a greater cut. Eventually you will force the seller to his or her lowest position, and you will be brought to your highest one. If your compromises are mutually satisfactory, then a deal has been made. If not, you had better start looking somewhere else.

Frequently during the bargaining process some thing occurs that can bring things to a head faster than anticipated.  For example, other interested buyers might enter the picture and force you to compete with them for the land. A well-known sales trick used by some real estate agents is to tell you that your offer has been surpassed by another prospective buyer, although this actually is not true. A variation on this trick is for the seller to arrange to have a friend or the broker telephone while you are inspecting the house. The call presumably is another interested buyer. Don't rush your decision unless you are certain you are getting what you want. Ask to meet the other buyer or see the other offer.

There are a few tricks you can use yourself. Pick out a piece of property that another agent in town is handling under a completely different deal, and announce to the original agent that you are preparing to buy the other property if the seller does not accept your present offer, which is your final one. This might scare the seller or make a compromise with you more like if the seller is anxious to sell and does not want to lose you as a prospective buyer.

## Your Deposit or Earnest Money Binder with the Contract of Sale

When you make your first and subsequent offers to the seller, you will do so using the Model Contract of Sale in Chapter 27, which you will adapt to your own situation, or you will use a form presented to you by the broker. When you present the broker with the contract, which is also an offer to purchase, you will include a small deposit to show your seriousness and whet the seller's appetite for more. This is usually called a deposit, or earnest money payment. (See Chapter 27, "The Model Contract of Sale.")

Usually the seller or real estate agent gives the buyer a *deposit receipt,* which contains no contingencies, to be signed before the final sales contract is drawn up. This is deceptive. The deposit receipt becomes a legally enforceable contract for the purchase of land as soon as both you and the seller sign it if it contains the date, names of the parties and description of the property. *Nothing you are told verbally is legally binding. Nothing that is not in writing is legally binding.* If you agree to some condition orally with the seller and if you then make a cash deposit and sign a binder or contract or deposit receipt without the condition written onto it, that condition is not binding on the seller. It does not have to be written into a more complete contract of sale later on. One of the most frequent complaints made to the local real estate departments comes from buyers who demand the return of their deposits. The buyer usually suffers because his or her terms or agreements with the real estate agent or seller were not in writing. Do not make the mistake of assuming, as many buyers do, that anything not called a contract will not be important. Contracts for the sale and purchase of land often are given such names as Conditional Sales Agreement, Offer to Purchase, Preliminary Sales Agreement, Deposit Receipt, Sales Deposit Receipt, Agreement for Sale of Real Estate, Binder, Installment Contract and Contract of Sale.

Instead of signing the usual deposit receipt, I recommend that you submit your deposit and your offer to purchase together with all the terms of the sale in a single document called the Contract of Sale, which is explained in detail in Chapter 27.

# Financing Your Purchase

# 21 Types of Financing: Land Contract, Mortgage, Deed of Trust

When you find land you want to buy, you must decide how you are going to pay for it. Unless you have enough money to pay cash, you will have to pay off your purchase gradually. Country land sales, particularly of undeveloped properties, are usually financed by the seller, because it is generally difficult to get a loan from a commercial lender. If the seller extends you credit, you will give a down payment and pay off the rest of the purchase price gradually under the terms of either a *land contract,* a *mortgage,* or a *deed of trust.* If you are able to borrow money from a third party to combine with your own money, you can pay the seller cash for the land and give the lender either a mortgage or a deed of trust.

Each type of financing is diagrammed in Figure

21–3 later in this chapter. As you read each of the following sections, refer to this illustration (pages 227–228).

## The Land Contract

Financing by land contract is the riskiest way to buy rural land. Do not confuse the land contract with the contract of sale. The contract of sale is the document that contains the terms and conditions of the sale. (See the Model Contract of Sale in Chapter 27.) The land contract details only the financial arrangements of the purchase and the rights and obligations of the seller and buyer during the payment period.

A land contract may also be called an *installment sale contract, second contract, land sale con-*

*tract, land contract of sale* or *conditional sales contract.* Regardless of the name used, the principle of *buying on contract* remains the same.

You give the seller a cash down payment and then make regular payments until the purchase price and interest are paid off. What makes buying on contract risky is that during the payment period, the seller gives you only possession of the land. You will not get a deed until after all payments have been made. (This is what differentiates this plan from a *mortgage* or *deed of trust,* as you will see below.)

The seller holds title to the land during this entire period. If you do not properly record the land contract, the seller can encumber the land with easements, mortgages and other liens that will seriously affect the title you are eventually to receive. Often a seller will convey land under a land contract while he or she is still paying for it. If the seller fails to make the payments, the loan may be foreclosed. If the seller loses the land, then you also will lose the land. If you go to court at that time, you may get your payments back, but it is very unlikely that you will get the land because the seller no longer has it. The situation is similar if the seller goes bankrupt while owing money on a prior mortgage on the property.

Sellers like land contracts because of the great advantages they offer if buyers are unable to make their payments. Under the *strict foreclosure action* generally used for land contracts, the seller simply asks you to leave the premises. The seller already has title to the land, so he or she does not have to go through a regular court foreclosure. At the end of the foreclosure, the seller has not only the land but also all the money you have already paid.

Although you can sue for the value of improvements you made on the land, such as buildings, septic tanks and water systems, you must hire a lawyer and initiate a costly court action. If you refuse to leave the property, the seller will be forced to go to court and obtain an *action for ejection* or *writ of possession* against you. He or she might be willing to make a settlement with you out of court to avoid this expense, in which case you can demand reimbursement for the improvements you have made on the land. Also ask for the money you have already paid under the land contract. You may get at least some of your money back in this manner. Never leave the land voluntarily unless the seller makes a deal.

Because of the nature of the land contract, sellers often require an extremely small down payment and low monthly terms. This might be the only way some of you can buy a piece of country land because of your poor financial condition. I recommend that you never buy on contract unless you have no alternative. If you have no other choice, at least be sure you have some essential protections written into the land contract.

- The land contract should state that the seller is to put the title to the land in trust with an escrow holder, or third-party trustee, until you either complete your payments or default on them.

- Have the seller write out a deed to you and place it with the trustee, with instructions to give it to you on the completion of your payments. This will ensure that a deed is ready to deliver to you as soon as you complete your payments.

- The land contract should state that your payments are to go to the trustee, who is to use the money to pay all taxes and other liens on the land, such as the seller's mortgage, before forwarding any money to the seller. This will prevent a foreclosure by the seller's creditor or a tax sale if your payments are sufficient to meet the sums due.

- Require that the land contract be recorded immediately with the county recorder so that the world is put on notice that you are buying that parcel, and the seller will not be able to encumber or sell the property.

- The land contract must specifically forbid the seller from encumbering the title in any way, so no loans can be made against the property.

- Get the seller to include a clause that promises to convey all or part of the title to you after you have completed a certain amount of the total payments. For example, after you have made half the payments, you will get full title to the land from the seller, who, and in turn, will get back a mortgage or trust deed for the remaining amount due. The earlier you get title to the land, the better.

- Never allow the seller to put a *prepayment penalty clause* into the land contract that penalizes you for paying off the balance at an earlier date than scheduled. For example, if your payments are to be $750 a month, you should be permitted to pay "$750 or more per month." (See Chapter 22 for more on this.)

- You will be required to keep the property in good repair and to pay for fire and hazard insurance on the property under terms to be approved by the seller. Be sure you, as well as the seller, are a named insured or beneficiary under the policy.

- Have the seller state, in detail, the conditions under which you can be forced off the land. Make sure you understand them.
- Use the information in Chapter 22 on the terms and elements of amortization to get the best financing arrangement possible.

## The Mortgage (Purchase Money Mortgage) and Deed of Trust

Unlike the land contract, when you give a *mortgage* or *deed of trust* in exchange for a cash down payment and credit, you receive title to the land immediately. The property is always held as security, or collateral, for the loan so that the lender has sufficient protection if you default on your payments.

A mortgage is technically called a *purchase money mortgage* when it is used for the specific purpose of buying land. (The term *mortgage*, as used throughout this book, refers to a purchase money mortgage.) The seller, who finances the deal herself or himself, does not actually give you money to buy the land. Instead, he or she allows you to pay off the purchase price over a period of time. The seller is giving you credit, which is like lending you the money.

When you borrow money from a third party, for example, a bank, in return for a mortgage or deed of trust, you actually receive cash to give to the seller for the land. You then pay back the lender over a period of time. (Throughout this and subsequent chapters, when I refer to the *lender,* I am talking about either the seller who finances the sale himself or a third party lender, unless I specify otherwise. It is assumed that the *borrower* is the buyer. A *creditor* is a person to whom money is owed. A *debtor* is the person who owes the money.)

### The Title Theory of Mortgages

Seventeen states use the title theory of mortgages. Under this financial arrangement you do not keep the title to the land during your payment period. For example, if the seller finances the sale, he or she delivers title to you at the close of escrow. Because you receive title at that time you can get the standard title protections, such as a title search and title insurance. You receive a deed specifying ownership in your name. Then, when you give the mortgage to the seller, it is as if you are giving the seller back your title to the land. The seller then holds title as security only, until you complete your payments. During that time, you have the right to the posses-

sion of the land. When you complete the required payments of principal and interest, the seller makes a new deed and redelivers the title to you. If you default on your payments, the seller merely keeps the title to the land. VA loans operate this way.

If you give a mortgage under this system to a third-party lender, the seller delivers title to you and you then deliver the title to the lender with a mortgage in exchange for cash, which you give to the seller. The terms of a title theory mortgage must specify that the creditor not alter the title in any way from the time you give it to the lender as security with the mortgage until it is redelivered to you at the time of your last required payment by recording a *satisfaction of mortgage.*

The difference between this system and a land contract is that in the latter form of financing you never receive title until you have completely paid for the property. With a title mortgage you receive title immediately, then give it back to the seller in the form of a mortgage. You have much greater protection under a title theory mortgage than with a land contract.

The states that use this title theory of mortgages are Alabama, Arkansas, Connecticut, Illinois, Maine, Maryland, Massachusetts, Mississippi, New Hampshire, New Jersey, North Carolina, Ohio, Pennsylvania, Rhode Island, Tennessee, Vermont and West Virginia. If your land is in any of these states you should determine whether the title theory is still observed at the time of your purchase.

### The Lien Theory of Mortgages

All other states, except trust deed states mentioned below, follow the lien theory of mortgaging property. When you give a mortgage, you do not give up title to the land but simply promise, in writing, that you will repay the lender or complete payments to the seller. The mortgage becomes a lien on the property, which means that a foreclosure action can be taken if payments are not made. Title and possession rights remain with you, the buyer, during the entire period. The seller's, or lender's, lien on the land will be removed on completion of all payments. Because you always keep the title in your possession, it is much harder for the lender to take your land from you if you default on your payments than it is under the title theory of mortgages, under which the lender already has title to the land if you default.

Under both mortgage theories, the buyer who gives the mortgage is called the *mortgagor.* The lender or seller who receives the mortgage is called the *mortgagee.*

### The Deed of Trust (Trust Deed)

Thirteen states and the District of Columbia prefer a system under which the borrower, or *trustor*, delivers a deed of trust to the seller rather than giving a mortgage to the lender or seller. Under this system, the lender is the beneficiary under the deed of trust. The third-party trustee is usually a commercial institution, such as a bank, title company or escrow company. The trustee, in essence, holds title to the property in trust, with the power to foreclose on the buyer if there is a default in payments. The buyer still owns the property and has full rights of ownership, subject to the conditions of the deed of trust. For example, the property cannot be logged or the improvements removed until the note and deed of trust are paid off. (See Chapter 29, "Opening and Closing of Escrow and the Role of the Escrow Holder.")

The trust is established in the following manner: The seller delivers title to you, the buyer, by giving you a deed to the land. If the seller is your creditor, you give him or her a down payment on the land and sign a note and deed of trust. If you borrow the money from a third party, you pay the seller the entire purchase price and sign a note and deed of trust to the lender. You then make your payments, pay the taxes and other liens on the land and keep the improvements insured, with the lender as coinsured. When the loan has been completely paid off, the trustee delivers clear title to you by recording a Deed of Reconveyance.

If you fail to make payments, the trustee has the right to sell the land at a foreclosure sale and deliver the title to the new purchaser or back to the seller if nobody bids at the foreclosure sale. Any money owed to the seller or lender, including interest and other expenses the seller has incurred as a result of the foreclosure action, is paid from the money received from this sale. The balance goes to you. This method of disposing of the title to the land on default makes the deed of trust the preferred security instrument from the point of view of the seller, who does not have to hire a lawyer or go to court for a judicial foreclosure.

Do not confuse a *deed* with a *deed of trust*. A deed is evidence of ownership of the property. The deed of trust, sometimes called the trust deed, is a method of financing and securing a sale of land. It is slowly being accepted throughout the country, although the mortgage remains the primary means of securing property for a loan. Either method is fine. The one you use will depend on which method is customary in your state.

The District of Columbia, California, Colorado, Idaho, Illinois, Mississippi, Missouri, Nevada, New Mexico, Tennessee, Texas, Virginia, West Virginia and Utah use deeds of trust. (Figure 21–1 is a sample deed of trust form.)

### The Promissory Note or Bond

The mortgage or deed of trust is always accompanied by a promissory note or bond, the document that actually specifies the debt and how it is to be paid. A mortgage and deed of trust only specify the security for the debt. In the note the borrower makes an unconditional promise in writing to the lender that the buyer will pay the loan according to a specified plan. The note or bond is signed and sometimes recorded with the county recorder at the same time as the mortgage or trust deed, which are always recorded.

Most notes are negotiable, which means they are as good as money and the holder of the note can sell or transfer it to another person and order the debtor to make all future payments to the new holder of the note.

A few states use a bond rather than a note as evidence of the debt. A bond generally contains the same information as a note and has the additional protection of a formal seal by a notary public. You might also encounter a document that incorporates both the security and the evidence of the debt. That is, the elements of a mortgage or trust deed and those of a note or bond are combined in the same form. Read every word and thoroughly understand the provisions of any document you sign. Always keep a copy.

## A Second, or "Junior," Mortgage and Deed of Trust

If you have more than one mortgage on your land, one is always junior to the other, which means that under a foreclosure action, the senior lender collects first and any surplus goes to the junior lender.

For example, say you want to buy some property for $60,000, but the seller wants 75 percent cash down payment and you have only $15,000. You find you can get a loan from a bank for $30,000 to make the $45,000 down payment, but you must then give the seller a *second mortgage* on the remaining $15,000 owed for the land. The seller will have to agree to *subordinate* the second mortgage to the bank's mortgage for the bank to make the loan. Commercial lenders always insist on having a lien on the property that is superior to all other credit liens. If you fail to make your payments, ei-

**Figure 21–1. Sample Deed of Trust**

## DEED OF TRUST

**This Deed of Trust,** made this _____(Date)_____ day of _____, 19___,
**Between** _____(Name of Borrower)_____
Whose address is _____(Address of Borrower)_____
_____(Number and Street)_____ _____(City)_____ _____(State)_____
herein called Trustor, _____(Name of Trustee)_____, a ___(State)___ corporation, herein called Trustee,
and _____(Name of Seller or Lender)_____
_____ herein called Beneficiary,
**Witnesseth:** That Trustor irrevocably GRANTS, TRANSFERS AND ASSIGNS to TRUSTEE IN
TRUST, WITH POWER OF SALE, that property in _____(City where land is located)_____
County of _____(County where located)_____, ____(State)____, described as

(Legal Description of the Property)

TOGETHER WITH the rents, issues and profits thereof, SUBJECT, HOWEVER, to the right, power
and authority given to and conferred upon Beneficiary by Paragraph 5 of Part B of the provisions
incorporated herein by reference to collect and apply such rents, issues and profits, For the Purpose
of Securing payment of the indebtedness evidenced by a promissory note, of even date herewith,
executed by Trustor in the sum of _____(Amount of Loan)_____
_____ Dollars, ($_____).
any additional sums and interest thereon which may hereafter be loaned to the Trustor or his successors or assigns by the Beneficiary, and the performance of each agreement herein contained. Additional loans hereafter made and interest thereon shall be secured by this Deed of Trust only if made
to the Trustor while he is the owner of record of his present interest in said property, or to his successors or assigns while they are the owners of record thereof, and shall be evidenced by a promissory
note reciting that it is secured by this Deed of Trust.

**By the execution and delivery of this Deed of Trust** and the note secured hereby the parties hereto
agree that there are adopted and included herein for any and all purposes by reference as though the
same were written in full herein the provisions of Section A, including paragraphs 1 through 6 thereof,
and of Section B, including paragraphs 1 through 10 thereof, of that certain fictitious Deed of Trust
recorded in the official records in the offices of the County Recorders of the following counties ___
(List of counties in state) _____

A copy of said provisions so adopted and included herein by reference is set forth on the reverse
hereof.

The undersigned Trustor requests that a copy of any notice of default and of any notice of sale
hereunder be mailed to him at his address given above.

(Name of Borrower) _____     _____
(Signature of Borrower)

State of
County of _____ } ss.

On this _____ day of _____(Date this agreement is signed)_____, 19___,
before me, the undersigned, a Notary Public in and for said _____(Name of County)_____
County, personally appeared _____(Name of Borrower)_____
_____

known to me to be the person(s) whose name(s) _____ subscribed to the within instrument, and
acknowledged that _____ executed the same.
WITNESS my hand and official seal.
(SEAL)

_____
(Signature of Notary)

Notary Public in and for said County & State

My Commission Expires: _____(Date of Expiration)_____   (Name of Notary)
_____
Type or Print Name of Notary

ther to the bank or to the seller, the loan will be foreclosed, and the bank will get to collect its money first. Any money left over goes next to the seller holding the second mortgage, up to the amount of his or her lien. If any money is left, it goes to you. If the seller takes a second mortgage, he or she runs a greater risk of not being able to collect the debt if a foreclosure becomes necessary. Therefore, you might be charged a higher rate of interest on the seller's mortgage. You usually will have to repay both mortgages simultaneously.

You might want a mortgage or trust deed to obtain money to construct a house or other improvements on the land after you take title. If you give the seller a mortgage on the land, you might convince him or her to subordinate it to enable you to obtain a bank loan to build a house. If you plan to do this, you must have a subordination clause in the note and mortgage you give the seller so you can get a construction loan at a later date. A house increases the value of the property and, therefore, the potential selling price of the land, so the risk of losing money in the event that a foreclosure becomes necessary diminishes for both the commercial lender and the seller. However, the seller might not want to run the risk of having to take back the property and pay off the construction lender, and might refuse to subordinate. In that case, you will have to do a total refinancing of the property.

When you have satisfied the loan by completing all your payments, you must request that your creditor issue a *certificate of satisfaction* or, if you have a title theory mortgage or deed of trust, a *deed of reconveyance*. This document must be recorded immediately with the county recorder. Once it is recorded, your title becomes clear of the lien against it. The original mortgage or deed of trust and the note or bond must be returned to the trustee by the beneficiary to have the property title cleared. That is why the original note should never be destroyed.

## Release Clauses

Release clauses in mortgages or deeds of trust come into play in two special circumstances.

Often a subdivider will purchase a large parcel of land and then subdivide it, selling off several parcels. The subdivider who purchases his large piece gives the seller a note and mortgage on the entire parcel. This is a much larger sum than the price for which each subdivided parcel will sell. If the subdivider has financed the purchased property, as each parcel is sold, the subdivider's seller will release that parcel from the overlying mortgage, and either be paid off with a set sum of money or take back a separate smaller note on the piece you are buying.

Some developers do not have a proper release clause and will attempt to sell you the parcel subject to a substantially larger mortgage that affects both your parcel and the other parcels in the subdivision. It is extremely risky to buy land in that manner. If the payments are not made by your seller to his or her mortgage holder, you and the other parcel owners could be foreclosed on, even though you have made all your payments to your seller.

Thus, you should never buy property subject to a mortgage that is a lien on other property besides your own. If you are tempted to do so, see an attorney for advice on how best to protect yourself.

The second circumstance in which release clauses are important is if you purchase land with the intention of subdividing. You want to have a clause in your note and deed of trust to your seller that allows you to release each parcel from your note as it is sold for payment of some cash; or you can have the seller, in essence, split your note among all of the parcels you sell, so that each buyer will make payments directly to the seller.

This is a complex matter; and if it is your intention to do this, you must consult an attorney to draft the appropriate release clause.

## Illustrations Comparing Types of Financing and Where They Are Used

Figure 21-2 shows which forms of financing are most common in each state. Figure 21-3 shows the different operations of the four types of financing: land contract, title theory of mortgage, lien theory of mortgage and deed of trust. By following this diagram as you read the text you will readily understand the different methods used.

## Checklist for Evaluating a Loan

___ How much will the lender give you? (What is the loan-to-value ratio?)
___ How soon can you get the loan?
___ Do you need a cosigner or any security other than the land you intend to buy?

**Interest Rate**
___ What is the annual interest rate?

**Figure 21–2. Common Financing Arrangements by States**

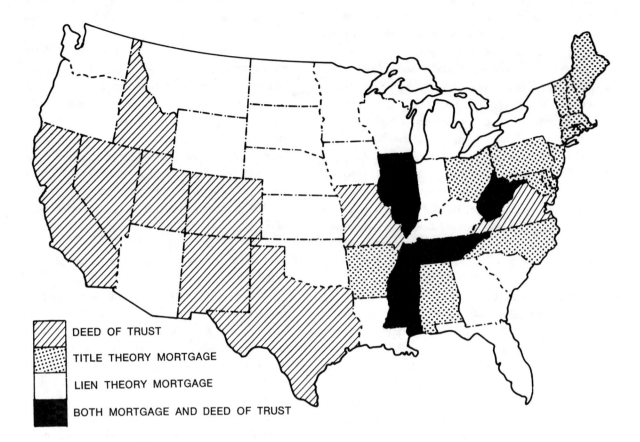

DEED OF TRUST

TITLE THEORY MORTGAGE

LIEN THEORY MORTGAGE

BOTH MORTGAGE AND DEED OF TRUST

___ Is the interest rate under a variable interest plan? (See the comparison factors under "Adjustable Rate Mortgages" in Chapter 22).

___ What will be the total amount of interest on the loan?

___ Is there an escalation clause that permits the lender to increase the interest rate in the future?

**Payment Plan**

___ How long is the amortization period (maturity date)?

___ When are the installments to be paid: monthly, quarterly, annually, and so on?

___ How much is each installment to be?

___ Is there a prepayment clause that allows you to make payments in advance and have them credited in the future if you cannot make a payment?

___ Are there any other prepayment privileges?

___ Is there a prepayment penalty? If so, what does it specify? Is prepayment prohibited altogether?

___ Is there a provision for a balloon payment? If so, how much is it?

___ Does the loan include an acceleration clause that permits the lender to force you to pay the entire amount due if you miss a payment, fail to pay taxes or assessments, attempt to sell the land or let the property fall into disrepair? Is there a due-on-sale clause?

___ Are you supposed to make impound payments for taxes and assessments along with your loan payments?

**Foreclosure**

___ What rights does the lender have if you get behind in your payments?

___ What procedure does the lender have to follow to foreclose your loan? Does the lender have to go to court first to foreclose?

___ Do you have a period of redemption? If so, how long is it and what period does it cover?

___ Does the loan specify that you are to be reimbursed for all money you have put into the land for improvements if there is a foreclosure?

___ Is it stated that you are to receive any surplus money from a foreclosure sale?

**Figure 21–3.  A Comparison of the Types of Financing**

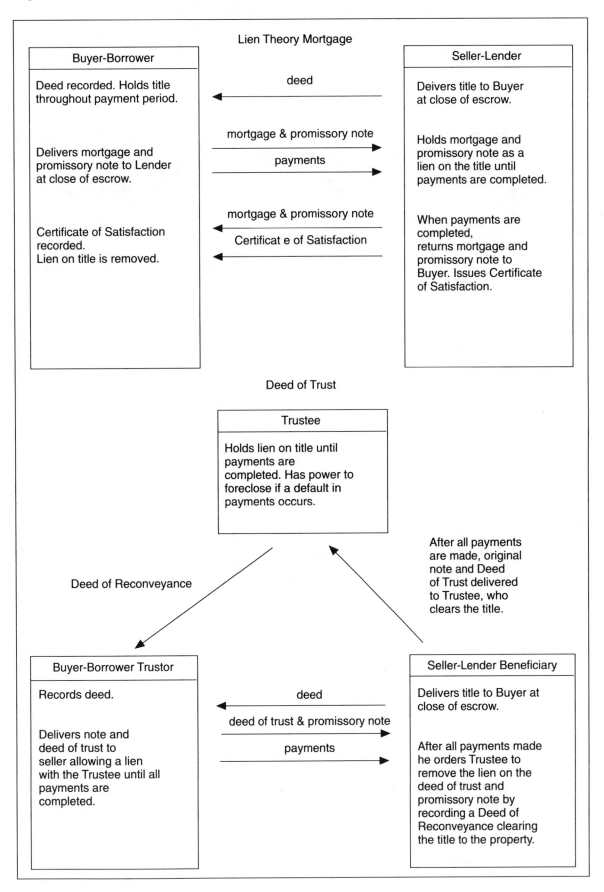

**Figure 21–3. A Comparison of the Types of Financing** *continued*

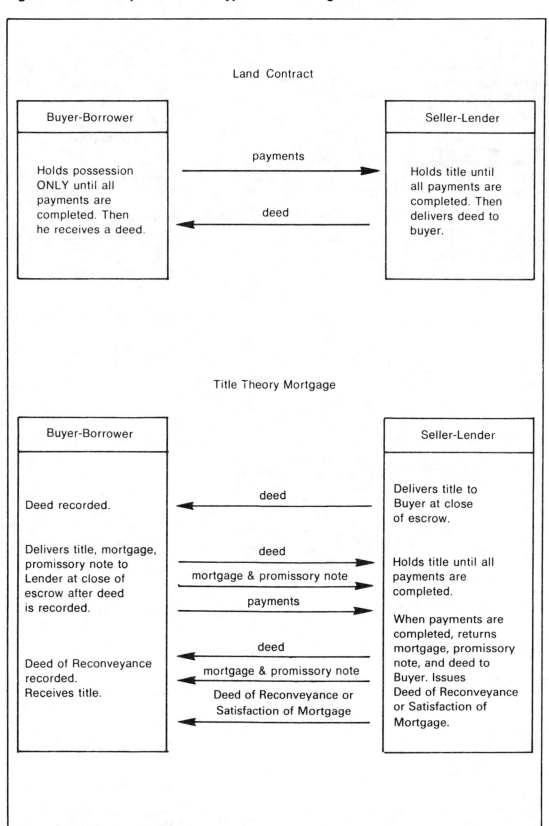

— If money received from a foreclosure is insufficient to meet the debt, can the lender get a deficiency judgment against you?

### Assignment Rights

— Is the note negotiable or nonnegotiable?

— Is the lender permitted to assign its interest under the loan?

— Can you sell or assign your interest in the property and have the buyer assume your debt? If so, are there any conditions, such as lender approval?

— Can you place a second mortgage or deed of trust on the property?

— Can you put other liens on the property during the loan period?

— Will you be allowed to borrow on your property and give a second mortgage to the same or another lender?

### Extra Fees

— Will you be charged for preliminary costs other than interest, for example, points, extras, origination fees? If so, how much will the charge be for each one?

— When do these fees have to be paid? Can they be included in the loan installments over a period of time?

— How much will you have to pay for having the loan documents drawn up?

— What type of insurance and how much coverage are you bound to carry on the property?

— How do you pay for the insurance?

— How much do you have to pay for a credit and employment report?

— How much do you have to pay for a property appraisal?

— Taking everything into account, how much will it cost you to borrow the money?

## Useful Resources

### Federal Land-Bank Loans

The following is a list of federal land banks, sometimes also called farm credit banks, and the states served by each. (See Figure 21–4.) You can contact your state office to obtain the bank nearest to your property.

Farm Credit Banks of Springfield
P.O. Box 141
Springfield, MA 01102
  (Connecticut, Maine, Massachusetts, New Hampshire, New Jersey, New York, Rhode Island, Vermont)

Farm Credit Banks of Baltimore
P.O. Box 1555
Baltimore, MD 21203
  (Delaware, District of Columbia, Maryland, Pennsylvania, Virginia, West Virginia)

Federal Credit Banks of Columbia
P.O. Box 1499
Columbia, SC 29202
  (Florida, Georgia, North Carolina, South Carolina)

Federal Credit Banks of Louisville
P.O. Box 32660
Louisville, KY 40232
  (Indiana, Kentucky, Ohio, Tennessee)

Federal Credit Banks of Jackson
P.O. Box 12468
Jackson, MS 39236-2408
  (Alabama, Louisiana, Mississippi)

Farm Credit Banks of St. Louis
Box 504
St. Louis, MO 63166
  (Arkansas, Illinois, Missouri)

**Figure 21–4. The Twelve Farm Credit Districts Containing the Federal Reserve Land Banks, and the States Served by Each**

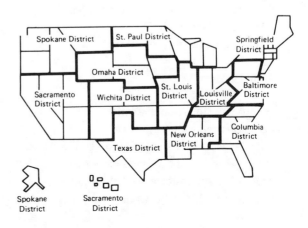

Federal Credit Services of St. Paul
Box 64949
St. Paul, MN 55101
　　(Michigan, Minnesota, North Dakota,
　　Wisconsin)

Farm Credit Banks of Omaha
206 S. 19th St.
Omaha, NE 68102
　　(Iowa, Nebraska, South Dakota,
　　Wyoming)

Farm Credit Banks of Wichita
Box 2940
Wichita, KS 67201-2940
　　(Colorado, Kansas, New Mexico,
　　Oklahoma)

Farm Credit Banks of Texas
P.O. Box 15919
Houston, TX 78723
　　(Texas)

Farm Credit Banks of Sacramento
P.O. Box 13106-C
Sacramento, CA 95813-4106
　　(Arizona, California, Hawaii, Nevada,
　　Utah)

Farm Credit Banks of Spokane
P.O. Box TAF-C5
Spokane, WA 99220-4005
　　(Alaska, Idaho, Montana, Oregon,
　　Washington)

For free information on obtaining a Federal Land Bank Loan and other loans through the Farm Credit Association, write to any of the above addresses.

　　The following are available from any of the above offices. Also ask for their current loan pamphlets.

"Country Home Loan—The Right Loan for a
　　Home in the Country"
"Production Credit Associations"
"The Farm Credit System"
"Farm Credit—All the Credit you Need"

## Federal Housing Administration (FHA) Insured Loans

Following is a list of area offices of the U.S. Department of Housing and Urban Development (HUD) and insuring offices of the Federal Housing Administration (FHA). These offices can supply you with in-

formation on lending policies in your area. The other source of FHA information is any FHA-approved financial institution. A list of these approved lenders is available from any HUD/FHA office.

### HUD Regional Offices

Contact the main Regional Offices for your region to obtain the address of your local HUD office.

*Region I*
　　Boston Regional Office
　　Boston Federal Office Building
　　10 Causeway St.
　　Boston, MA 02203-0801

　　Bulfinch Building
　　15 New Chardon St.
　　Boston, MA 02114-2598
　　　　(Connecticut, Maine, Massachusetts, New
　　　　Hampshire, Rhode Island, Vermont)

*Region II*
　　New York Regional Office
　　26 Federal Plaza
　　New York, NY 10278-0068
　　　　(New Jersey, New York)

*Region III*
　　Philadelphia Regional Office
　　Liberty Square Building
　　105 S. 7th St.
　　Philadelphia, PA 19106-3392
　　　　(Delaware, District of Columbia,
　　　　Maryland, Pennsylvania, Virginia, West
　　　　Virginia)

*Region IV*
　　Atlanta Office
　　Richard B. Russell Federal Building
　　75 Spring St., SW
　　Atlanta, GA 30303-3388
　　　　(Alabama, Florida, Georgia, Kentucky,
　　　　Mississippi, North Carolina, South
　　　　Carolina, Tennessee)

*Region V*
　　Chicago Regional Office
　　300 S. Wacker Dr.
　　Chicago, IL 60606-6765

　　547 West Jackson Blvd.
　　Chicago, IL 60606-5760
　　　　(Illinois, Indiana, Michigan, Minnesota,
　　　　Ohio, Wisconsin)

*Region VI*
Fort Worth Regional Office
1600 Throckmorton
P.O. Box 2905
Fort Worth, TX 76113-2905
(Arkansas, Louisiana, New Mexico, Oklahoma, Texas)

*Region VII*
Kansas City Regional Office
Professional Building
1103 Grand Ave.
Kansas City, MO 64106-2496
(Iowa, Kansas, Missouri, Nebraska)

*Region VIII*
Denver Regional Office
Executive Tower Building
1405 Curtis St.
Denver, CO 80202-2349
(Colorado, Montana, North Dakota, South Dakota, Utah, Wyoming)

*Region IX*
San Francisco Regional Office
Phillip Burton Federal Building and U.S. Courthouse
450 Golden Gate Ave.
P.O. Box 36003
San Francisco, CA 94102-3448

Indian Programs Office
Arizona Bank Building
101 N. First Ave., Suite 400
P.O. Box 13468
Phoenix, AZ 85004-2360
(Arizona, California, Hawaii, Nevada)

*Region X*
Seattle Regional Office
Arcade Plaza Building
1321 Second Ave.
Seattle, WA 98101-2054
(Alaska, Idaho, Oregon, Washington)

The following pamphlets are available free from any HUD or FHA office listed above or from the following address:

U.S. Department of Housing and Urban Development
451 Seventh St., SW, Room B-258
Washington, DC 20410
(800) 795-7915

"A Home of Your Own—Choosing, Buying, and Enjoying a Home"
"The HUD Home Buying Guide"
"How to Buy a Home with a Low Down Payment"

**Department of Veterans Affairs (VA) Federal Government Guaranteed Loans (GI Loans)**
The following is a list of Veterans Affairs (VA) Loan Guaranty Service Regional Offices. You can obtain information and necessary loan forms by sending a note to the director of any of these offices. These are also the offices that issue the Certificates of Eligibility.

For more information, contact the Department of Veterans Affairs at (800) 827-1000 or visit the VA Website at htpp://www.va.gov/vahowget/html.

Alabama
VA Regional Office
474 S. Count St.
Montgomery, AL 36104

Alaska
VAOC/Regional Office
2925 Dabarr Road
Anchorage, AK 99508

Arizona
VA Regional Office
3225 N. Central Ave.
Phoenix, AZ 85012

Arkansas
VA Regional Office
P.O. Box 1280
Building 65, Fort Roots
N. Little Rock, AR 72115

California (Northern)
Oakland Federal Building
1301 Clay Street
Oakland, CA 94612-5209

California (Southern)
VA Regional Office
Federal Building
11000 Wilshire Blvd.
Los Angeles, CA 90024

Colorado
VA Regional Office
Box 25126
44 Union Blvd.
Denver, CO 80225

Connecticut
Consolidated with Manchester, NH

Delaware
Consolidated with Philadelphia, PA

District of Columbia
VA Regional OFfice
941 N. Capitol St., NE
Washington, DC 20421

Florida
VA Regional Office
P.O. Box 1437
St. Petersburg, FL 33731

Georgia
VA Regional Office
730 Peachtree St., NE
Atlanta, GA 30365

Hawaii
VA Regional Office
P.O. Box 50188
Honolulu, HI 96850

Idaho
VA Regional Office
805 Franklin Street
Boise, ID 83702-5560

Illinois
VA Regional Office
P.O. Box 8136
536 S. Clark St.
Chicago, IL 60680

Indiana
VA Regional Office
575 N. Pennsylvania St.
Indianapolis, IN 46204

Iowa
VA Regional Office
5500 E. Kellogg
Wichita, KS 67218

Kentucky
VA Regional Office
545 South 3rd Street
Louisville, KY 40202

Louisiana
VA Regional Office
701 Loyola Ave.
New Orleans, LA 70113

Maine
Consolidated with Manchester, NH

Maryland
VA Regional Office
Federal Building
31 Hopkins Plaza
Baltimore, MD 21201

Massachusetts
Consolidated with Manchester, NH

Michigan
VA Regional Office
Federal Building
477 Michigan Ave.
Detroit, MI 48226

Minnesota
VA Regional Office
Federal Building
Fort Snelling
St. Paul, MN 55111

Mississippi
VA Regional Office
100 W. Capital St.
Jackson, MS 39269

Missouri
VA Regional Office
Federal Building
1520 Market St.
St. Louis, MO 63103

Montana
VA Regional Office
Fort Harrison, MT 59636

Nebraska
VA Regional Office
5631 S. 48th Street
Lincoln, NE 68516

Nevada
Consolidated with Oakland, CA

New Hampshire
VA Regional Office
Norris Cotton Federal Building
275 Chestnut St.
Manchester, NH 03101

New Jersey
VA Regional Office
20 Washington Pl.
Newark, NJ 07102

New Mexico
VA Regional Office
Dennis Chavez Federal Building
U.S. Courthouse
500 Gold Ave., SW
Albuquerque, NM 87102

New York (East)
VA Regional Office
252 Seventh Ave. at 24th St.
New York, NY 10001

NNew York (West)
VA Regional Office
Federal Building
111 West Huron St.
Buffalo, NY 14202

North Carolina
VA Regional Office
Federal Building
251 N. Main St.
Winston-Salem, NC 27155

North Dakota
Consolidated with Fort Snelling, MN

Ohio
VA Regional Office
Anthony J. Celebreze Federal Building
1240 E. Ninth St.
Cleveland, OH 44199

Oklahoma
VA Regional Office
1255 S. Main St.
Muskogee, OK 74401

Oregon
VA Regional Office
Federal Building
1220 S.W. Third Ave.
Portland, OR 97204

Pennsylvania (East)
VA Regional Office
P.O. Box 8079
5000 Wissahickon Ave.
Philadelphia, PA 19101

Pennsylvania (West)
VA Regional Office
1000 Liberty Ave.
Pittsburgh, PA 15222

Rhode Island
Consolidated with Manchester, NH

South Carolina
VA Regional Office
1801 Assembly St.
Columbia, SC 29201

South Dakota
Consolidated with Fort Snelling, MN

Tennessee
VA Regional Office
110 Ninth Ave., S.
Nashville, TN 37203

Texas (Northern)
VA Regional Office
1400 N. Valley Mills Dr.
Waco, TX 76799

Texas (Southern)
VA Regional Office
8900 Lakes at 610 Drive
Houston, TX 77054

Utah
VA Regional Office
P.O. Box 11500
1255 State St.
Salt Lake City, UT 84147

Vermont
Consolidated with Manchester, NH

Virginia
VA Regional Office
210 Franklin Rd., SW
Roanoke, VA 24011

Washington
VA Regional Office
Federal Building
915 Second Ave.
Seattle, WA 98174

West Virginia
VA Regional Office
640 Fourth Ave.
Huntington, WV 25701

Wisconsin
VA Regional Office
Building 6
5000 West Nation al Avenue
Milwaukee, WI 53295

Wyoming
> Consolidated with Denver, CO

The following pamphlets on VA loans are available free from any VA regional office listed above:

"How to get a VA loan"
"VA-Guaranteed Home Loans for Veterans"
"Manufactured (Mobile) Home Loans"
"Help in Planning the Purchase of a Home"
"Pointers for the Veteran Homeowner"

### Rural Housing Service and Farm Service Agency (both formerly part of Farmers Home Administration—FmHA)

For information on Rural Housing Service programs or Farm Service Agency programs available in your area, call or write to your local Rural Housing Service office or Farm Service Agency office (either of which may still be listed under Farmers Home Administration). To get the phone numbers, look under "Agriculture, Dept. of" under the U.S. Government Offices in the local phone book. To get the address of local offices write to:

> The Rural Housing Service
> U.S. Department of Agriculture
> Washington, DC 20250

and

> Farm Service Agency
> U.S. Department of Agriculture
> Washington, DC 20250

The following pamphlets are available free from any local Rural Housing Service office or the main office listed above:

"Technical Assistance for Self-Help Housing"
"Guaranteed Housing"
"Home Improvement Loans and Repair Loans and
   Grants"
"Home Ownership Loans"
"Rental Assistance Program"
"Rural Rental Housing"

They also have information fact sheets on Participation Loans, loans available partly from conventional lenders and party from the Rural Housing Service.

The following pamphlets are available free from

any local Farm Service Agency office or the main office listed above:

"Loans to Limited Resource Farmers"
"Farm Ownership Loans"
"Farm Operating Loans"
"Farm Loan Guarantees"
"Soil and Water Loans"

### Other Organizations

Following is a list of organizations, both private and governmental, and their publications to help you learn about financing your purchase. Publications are free unless otherwise noted.

From:   Building Research Council
        One E. Saint Mary's Rd.
        Champaign, IL 61820

"Financing the Home," A 1.3,                  $0.50

From:   R. Woods
        Consumer Information Center
        P.O. Box 100
        Pueblo, CO 810012
        URL: http://www.gsa.gov/staff/pa/cic/
            cic.htm

"The Mortgage Money Guide," 128B              $1.00
"Guide to Federal Government Sales,"
   143B                                        $1.75
"Are There Any Public Lands for Sale?,"
   109B                                        $1.00
"Consumer Handbook on Adjustable
   Rate Mortgages," 334B                       $.50
"Guide to Single Family Mortgage
   Insurance," 126B                            $.50

From:   Federal Trade Commission
        Washington, DC 20580
        URL: gopher//consumer.ftc.gov:2416

"Getting a Loan: Your Home as Security"
"Home Equity Credit Lines"
"Home Financing Primer"
"Mortgage Discrimination"
"Mortgage Money Guide"
"Mortgage Servicing"
"Real Estate Brokers"
"Reverse Mortgages"

The following is available from any savings and loan association office:

"Your Guide to a Savings and Loan Mortgage"

From:   Board of Governors of the Federal
        Reserve
        System Publications Services
        MS-138
        Washington, DC 20551
        Voice: (202) 452-3244
        URL: gopher://netec.mcc.ac.uk:70/
        11/netec/bibec/fedu

"Home Mortgages: Understanding the Process and
    Your Right to Fair Lending"
"Consumer Handbook on Adjustable Rate
    Mortgages"
"When Your Home Is on the Line: Home Equity
    Credit Lines"
"A Consumer's Guide to Mortgage Settlement
    Costs"
"A Consumer's Guide to Mortgage Lock-Ins"
"The Arithmetic of Interest Rates"
"A Consumers Guide to Mortgage Refinancing"

Your Real Estate Broker or local title company
in California has available from:

        California Land Title Association
        Box 13968
        Sacramento, CA 95853

"Understanding Foreclosure"
"Understanding Title Insurance:"
"Understanding the Language of Real Estate"
"Understanding Subdivision Public Report"
"Understanding Common Ways of Holding Title"

For information on the Fair Credit Reporting Act
or to register complaints regarding your credit application rights contact any of the offices of the
Federal Trade Commission listed below.

FTC Headquarters
6th & Pennsylvania Ave., NW
Washington, DC 20580
(202) 326-2275

FTC Regional Offices

1718 Peachtree St., NW
Atlanta, A 30367

101 Merrima St., Suite 810
Boston, MA 02114-4719

55 E. Monroe St.
Chicago, IL 60603

668 Euclid Suite 520A
Cleveland, OH 44114

100 N. Central Expressway, Suite 500
Dallas, TX 75201

1405 Curtis St.
Denver, CO 80202

11000 Wilshire Blvd.
Los Angeles, CA 90024

150 William St., Suite 1300
New York, NY 10038

901 Market Street
San Francisco, CA 94103

915 Second Ave.
Seattle, WA 98174

**General Information**

In addition to the lenders and financial agencies
listed above, you can get financial advice from your
local farm adviser and from your local agricultural
experiment station. (See addresses in "Useful Resources" at the end of Chapter 5, "The Earth—Soil,
Vegetation, and Topography.")

# CHAPTER
# 22 Terms of the Loan Agreement and Their Effect on the Total Price

The terms of a loan include the amount of the loan, the interest rate being charged, the length of time in which the loan is to be paid off, the amount of each payment and the payment plan (when each payment is to be made).

## Three Different Types of Amortization

Regardless of the type of financing you arrange, you will be making payments at regular intervals for a set length of time. This method of paying off a debt is called *amortization*. Each installment you make usually will consist of principal and interest.

The *principal* is the amount of money you borrow or owe. The *interest* is the price you are charged for the privilege of being allowed to pay

the principal over a period of time. Interest is charged as a percentage of the unpaid principal and should always be quoted to you on a *per annum,* or yearly, rather than a monthly or quarterly basis.

The three types of loan are the *unamortized*, the *partially amortized* and the *fully amortized* loan. Each type results in differing costs to the borrower. To illustrate how to figure out the different financial aspects of each kind of loan, I will use one simple example. Say you are buying 40 acres of undeveloped land for $40,000. You are to give the seller a down payment of 25 percent of the purchase price, or $10,000, and the seller will take back a note and mortgage for the remaining $30,000. The $30,000 is to be paid off in ten years, with 10 percent interest due per year on the outstanding principal. Here are the figures for easy reference:

| Total price | $40,000 |
|---|---|
| Cash down payment | $10,000 |
| Principal (to he paid off in ten years) | $30,000 |
| Interest rate | 10 percent |

### Figuring Interest Due

It is useful to know how to calculate interest on an annual, monthly and daily basis, and it's not hard to do. A calculator will be helpful.

Interest rates are usually quoted on a per annum basis. To calculate the annual interest due on a principal amount, multiply the principal amount, $P$, by the annual interest rate, $R$. $P \times R$ = Annual Interest. Using our example, $P = \$30,000$; $R = 10\%$ or $0.10$, so $\$30,000 \times 0.10 = \$3,000$ interest per annum.

If you want to know how much interest is due monthly, calculate the annual amount and divide it by 12 (months). So $(P \times R) \div 12$ = the monthly amount of interest. Using our example again ($\$30,000 \times 0.10$) $\div 12 = \$3,000 \div 12 = \$250$ interest per month.

If you want to know how much interest is due daily, calculate the monthly amount and divide it by 30 days (the commonly accepted number of days in a month for calculation purposes).

### Unamortized Loan

Because *amortize* means to pay off a loan in installments, under an unamortized loan the entire principal is paid in a lump sum at the end of a specified period of time. Interest on the principal is paid at regular intervals. The total amount of interest you will pay using this type of payment plan is large because the principal does not decrease as the interest is paid. Using our previous example, suppose the principal of $30,000 is to be paid in one sum at the end of ten years. During those ten years, interest may be paid once a year. Ten percent of $30,000 is $3,000 interest due each year. Interest of $3,000 per year for ten years will total $30,000 interest for the entire period of the loan. At the end of ten years, the principal amount of $30,000 is due. Because this is an interest-payment-only loan it is rarely used, but it is still possible to obtain such a loan under certain circumstances.

### Partially Amortized Loan

The partially amortized method of paying off a loan is rarely used, but it is much cheaper than the unamortized method. By this method you pay a fixed amount of the principal plus interest in regular installments. The amount of principal paid each time is always the same, but the amount of interest due gets progressively smaller as the debt is paid.

Say the $30,000 principal is to be paid in equal annual installments of $3,000 for ten years. At the end of the first year the amount of interest is 10 percent of the full $30,000, because none of the loan has been paid yet. Ten percent of $30,000 is $3,000. Thus, the first payment will consist of $3,000 principal and $3,000 interest, a total of $6,000. Subtracting the $3,000 payment of principal from the total borrowed leaves $27,000 of the loan left unpaid. The interest due at the end of the next year will be 10 percent of $27,000, or $2,700, and that year's payment will be $3,000 principal plus $2,700 interest, or $5,700. This leaves $24,000 of the principal unpaid. The interest the next year will be 10 percent of $24,000, or $2,400, so the payment will be $3,000 principal plus $2,400 interest, or $5,400.

As the amount of interest due gets smaller, each payment gets smaller. The last year's payment will consist of only $300 interest plus $3,000 principal, or $3,300. By adding up the interest paid each time, the total amount of interest for ten years is $16,500, considerably less than the $30,000 interest paid on the unamortized loan.

### Fully Amortized Loan

A fully amortized loan is the most common payment method used today. This loan plan, like the partially amortized method, combines the payments of principal and interest in each installment, but the amount of each payment is always the same. Because interest is charged as a percentage of the unpaid principal, the portion going to pay the interest is quite large in the first payments. As you pay off the loan, the portion of each payment allotted to the principal gradually increases, while the portion allotted to the interest gradually decreases. You will see how this works below.

Because payments are almost always made in monthly, rather than annual, installments, I will do the following example using a monthly payment plan. *An amortization table* (see Figure 22–1) is helpful in figuring out various aspects of the payment schedule.

For those of you interested in mathematics, the formula for getting those numbers is

$$mp(\$) = 1(\$) \times mir \times \left[ \frac{(1+mir)^n}{(1+mir)^n - 1} \right]$$

where $mp(\$)$ is monthly payment in dollars, $1(\$)$ is loan value in dollars, $mir$ is monthly interest rate (that is, annual interest rate divided by 12) and $n$ is the number of months over which the payments are to be made. For example, 9 percent means $9/100 = 0.09$; if the annual interest rate is 13 percent, say, then $mir = 13/100 \div 12 = 13/1200 = 0.0108333$. If you have a calculator that has an $x^y$ key, this formula is easy to calculate. However, without such a function it would be difficult to compute $(1+mir)^n$ if $n$ is a large number like 120, the number of monthly payments in a 10-year loan term.

*Figuring the amount of each payment.* To figure the amount of each monthly payment using our example, first look at Figure 22–1 under years for 10 years. Then move to the right to the 10 percent column, which is the interest rate. This amount, $13.2151, is the amount you must pay per month for each $1,000 due on the mortgage. You owe $30,000, so multiply this figure by 30. The result, $396.453, should be rounded up to the nearest penny, or $396.46. This is the amount of each monthly payment to pay off a loan of $30,000 at 10 percent interest over a period of ten years. When the seller or lender tells you what the terms are, you can plug in the figures to determine what each monthly payment will be.

*Figuring the length of the amortization period.* If the seller or lender tells you what your monthly payments will be but not how long you will be paying, you can determine this by working backward in Figure 22–1. Using the same example, if you are told that each payment is to be $396.46 per month, divide that figure by 30, because your principal is $30,000 ($396.46 $\div$ 30 = 13.2153). Look down the 10 percent column until you find the figure closest to the result; $13.2151 is closest to $13.2153. The chart shows that for this monthly payment you will be paying ten years.

*Figuring the total amount of interest on the loan.* Once you know what your monthly payments will be and how long you have to pay off the loan, you can easily determine how much the total interest will be. Using the same example, the payments will extend for ten years. Twelve monthly payments per year for ten years makes a total of 120 monthly payments. By multiplying $396.46 (each monthly payment) by 120 payments, you get the total amount of principal and interest you will pay on

your loan over ten years, which is $47,575.20. The principal amount of the loan is $30,000, so subtract that amount to see how much the total interest will be.

$$\$47,575.20 - \$30,000 = \$17,575.20$$

This is the amount of interest on the loan, and represents the true cost of your loan. This is the number that usually shocks the first-time property purchaser. It is expensive to pay interest on a loan. However, loan interest on a primary or secondary residence is deductible on your federal income tax.

*Figuring how much of each payment is allocated for principal and interest.* You will want to know how much of each monthly payment goes toward paying off the principal and how much goes toward paying the interest. Using our example, at the time of the first payment, the unpaid balance is the total loan amount of $30,000. (See Figure 22–2.) The interest rate is 10 percent per year on the unpaid principal, and 10 percent of $30,000 is $3,000. The interest for the entire year is $3,000, so divide this figure by 12 to get the amount due the first month.

$$\$3,000 \div 12 = \$250$$

Thus, out of a $396.46 payment, $250 will go to pay interest and $396.46 minus $250, or $146.46, will go to pay off the principal.

To figure the next month's ratio of interest to principal, subtract $146.46 (the principal already paid) from $30,000, which leaves $29,853.54. Multiply that figure by 10 percent, getting $2,985.35 interest for the next year.

$$0.10 \times \$29,853.54 = \$2,985.35$$

Divide that figure by 12 (months) to find the amount of interest in the second installment, which is $248.779, or $248.78 rounded off.

$$\$2,985.35 \div 12 = \$248.779 = \$248.78$$

The amount going to pay the principal is $396.46 (the monthly payment) minus $248.78 (the amount allocated to interest), which results in a payment toward principal of $147.68.

$$\$396.46 - \$248.78 = \$147.68$$

Each succeeding monthly payment can be computed in this same way.

You see from this example (see Figure 22–2) that the amount of interest paid when you first start

**Figure 22–1. Table of Monthly Payments Required To Amortize $1,000 Loan**

| Year | 6¾% | 7% | 7¼% | 7½% | 7¾% | 8% | 8¼% | 8½% | 8¾% | 9% | 9¼% | 9½% | 9¾% | 10% | 10¼% | 10½% | 10¾% | 11% |
|---|---|---|---|---|---|---|---|---|---|---|---|---|---|---|---|---|---|---|
| 1 | 86.4116 | 86.5268 | 86.6421 | 86.7575 | 86.8729 | 86.9885 | 87.1041 | 87.2198 | 87.3356 | 87.4515 | 87.5675 | 87.6836 | 87.7997 | 87.9159 | 88.0323 | 88.1487 | 88.2651 | 88.3817 |
| 1½ | 58.5715 | 58.6850 | 58.7987 | 58.9124 | 59.0263 | 59.1403 | 59.2545 | 59.3688 | 59.4832 | 59.5977 | 59.7124 | 59.8272 | 59.9421 | 60.0571 | 60.1723 | 60.2876 | 60.4030 | 60.5186 |
| 2 | 44.6594 | 44.7726 | 44.8861 | 44.9996 | 45.1134 | 45.2273 | 45.3414 | 45.4557 | 45.5702 | 45.6848 | 45.7996 | 45.9145 | 46.0297 | 46.1450 | 46.2604 | 46.3761 | 46.4919 | 46.6079 |
| 2½ | 36.3184 | 36.4320 | 36.5457 | 36.6597 | 36.7739 | 36.8884 | 37.0030 | 37.1179 | 37.2329 | 37.3482 | 37.4637 | 37.5794 | 37.6953 | 37.8115 | 37.9278 | 38.0444 | 38.1611 | 38.2781 |
| 3 | 30.7630 | 30.8771 | 30.9916 | 31.1063 | 31.2212 | 31.3364 | 31.4519 | 31.5676 | 31.6836 | 31.7998 | 31.9163 | 32.0330 | 32.1500 | 32.2672 | 32.3847 | 32.5025 | 32.6205 | 32.7388 |
| 3½ | 26.7993 | 26.9143 | 27.0295 | 27.1450 | 27.2609 | 27.3770 | 27.4935 | 27.6102 | 27.7272 | 27.8446 | 27.9622 | 28.0801 | 28.1983 | 28.3169 | 28.4357 | 28.5548 | 28.6742 | 28.7939 |
| 4 | 23.8305 | 23.9463 | 24.0625 | 24.1790 | 24.2958 | 24.4130 | 24.5305 | 24.6484 | 24.7666 | 24.8851 | 25.0040 | 25.1232 | 25.2427 | 25.3626 | 25.4829 | 25.6034 | 25.7243 | 25.8456 |
| 4½ | 21.5249 | 21.6416 | 21.7588 | 21.8763 | 21.9942 | 22.1125 | 22.2311 | 22.3502 | 22.4696 | 22.5894 | 22.7096 | 22.8302 | 22.9511 | 23.0725 | 23.1942 | 23.3162 | 23.4387 | 23.5615 |
| 5 | 19.6835 | 19.8012 | 19.9194 | 20.0380 | 20.1570 | 20.2764 | 20.3963 | 20.5166 | 20.6373 | 20.7584 | 20.8799 | 21.0019 | 21.1243 | 21.2471 | 21.3703 | 21.4940 | 21.6180 | 21.7425 |
| 5½ | 18.1798 | 18.2985 | 18.4178 | 18.5374 | 18.6576 | 18.7782 | 18.8993 | 19.0208 | 19.1428 | 19.2653 | 19.3882 | 19.5116 | 19.6354 | 19.7597 | 19.8845 | 20.0097 | 20.1354 | 20.2615 |
| 6 | 16.9293 | 17.0491 | 17.1694 | 17.2902 | 17.4115 | 17.5333 | 17.6556 | 17.7784 | 17.9018 | 18.0256 | 18.1499 | 18.2747 | 18.4001 | 18.5259 | 18.6522 | 18.7790 | 18.9063 | 19.0341 |
| 6½ | 15.8735 | 15.9944 | 16.1158 | 16.2377 | 16.3602 | 16.4832 | 16.6068 | 16.7309 | 16.8556 | 16.9808 | 17.1065 | 17.2328 | 17.3596 | 17.4870 | 17.6149 | 17.7433 | 17.8722 | 18.0017 |
| 7 | 14.9708 | 15.0927 | 15.2152 | 15.3383 | 15.4620 | 15.5863 | 15.7111 | 15.8365 | 15.9625 | 16.0891 | 16.2163 | 16.3440 | 16.4723 | 16.6012 | 16.7307 | 16.8607 | 16.9913 | 17.1225 |
| 8 | 13.5097 | 13.6338 | 13.7585 | 13.8839 | 14.0100 | 14.1367 | 14.2641 | 14.3922 | 14.5209 | 14.6503 | 14.7803 | 14.9109 | 15.0423 | 15.1742 | 15.3068 | 15.4401 | 15.5740 | 15.7085 |
| 9 | 12.3801 | 12.5063 | 12.6333 | 12.7611 | 12.8895 | 13.0188 | 13.1487 | 13.2794 | 13.4108 | 13.5430 | 13.6758 | 13.8094 | 13.9437 | 14.0787 | 14.2145 | 14.3509 | 14.4881 | 14.6259 |
| 10 | 11.4825 | 11.6109 | 11.7402 | 11.8702 | 12.0011 | 12.1328 | 12.2653 | 12.3986 | 12.5327 | 12.6676 | 12.8033 | 12.9398 | 13.0771 | 13.2151 | 13.3540 | 13.4935 | 13.6339 | 13.7751 |
| 12 | 10.1511 | 10.2839 | 10.4176 | 10.5523 | 10.6880 | 10.8246 | 10.9621 | 11.1006 | 11.2400 | 11.3804 | 11.5216 | 11.6638 | 11.8069 | 11.9508 | 12.0957 | 12.2415 | 12.3881 | 12.5356 |
| 15 | 08.8491 | 08.9883 | 09.1287 | 09.2702 | 09.4128 | 09.5566 | 09.7015 | 09.8747 | 09.9945 | 10.1427 | 10.2920 | 10.4423 | 10.5937 | 10.7461 | 10.8996 | 11.0540 | 11.2095 | 11.3660 |
| 20 | 07.6037 | 07.7530 | 07.9038 | 08.0560 | 08.2095 | 08.3645 | 08.5207 | 08.6783 | 08.8372 | 08.9973 | 09.1587 | 09.3214 | 09.4852 | 09.6503 | 09.8165 | 09.9838 | 10.1523 | 10.3219 |
| 21 | 07.4335 | 07.5848 | 07.7375 | 07.8917 | 08.0473 | 08.2043 | 08.3627 | 08.5224 | 08.6835 | 08.8459 | 09.0095 | 09.1744 | 09.3405 | 09.5079 | 09.6764 | 09.8460 | 10.0168 | 10.1888 |
| 22 | 07.2811 | 07.4343 | 07.5890 | 07.7452 | 07.9028 | 08.0618 | 08.2223 | 08.3841 | 08.5473 | 08.7118 | 08.8776 | 09.0447 | 09.2130 | 09.3825 | 09.5532 | 09.7251 | 09.8981 | 10.0723 |
| 23 | 07.1442 | 07.2992 | 07.4558 | 07.6139 | 07.7735 | 07.9346 | 08.0970 | 08.2609 | 08.4262 | 08.5927 | 08.7606 | 08.9298 | 09.1002 | 09.2719 | 09.4447 | 09.6187 | 09.7939 | 09.9701 |
| 24 | 07.0208 | 07.1776 | 07.3361 | 07.4961 | 07.6576 | 07.8206 | 07.9850 | 08.1509 | 08.3181 | 08.4867 | 08.6566 | 08.8278 | 09.0003 | 09.1739 | 09.3488 | 09.5249 | 09.7020 | 09.8803 |
| 25 | 06.9092 | 07.0678 | 07.2281 | 07.3900 | 07.5533 | 07.7182 | 07.8846 | 08.0523 | 08.2215 | 08.3920 | 08.5639 | 08.7370 | 08.9114 | 09.0871 | 09.2639 | 09.4419 | 09.6210 | 09.8012 |
| 26 | 06.8080 | 06.9684 | 07.1305 | 07.2941 | 07.4593 | 07.6260 | 07.7942 | 07.9638 | 08.1349 | 08.3073 | 08.4810 | 08.6560 | 08.8323 | 09.0098 | 09.1885 | 09.3683 | 09.5493 | 09.7313 |
| 27 | 06.7161 | 06.8782 | 07.0420 | 07.2074 | 07.3744 | 07.5428 | 07.7128 | 07.8843 | 08.0571 | 08.2313 | 08.4068 | 08.5837 | 08.7617 | 08.9410 | 09.1215 | 09.3031 | 09.4858 | 09.6696 |
| 28 | 06.6323 | 06.7961 | 06.9616 | 07.1287 | 07.2974 | 07.4676 | 07.6394 | 07.8125 | 07.9871 | 08.1630 | 08.3403 | 08.5189 | 08.6987 | 08.8797 | 09.0618 | 09.2451 | 09.4294 | 09.6148 |
| 29 | 06.5559 | 06.7214 | 06.8885 | 07.0573 | 07.2276 | 07.3995 | 07.5729 | 07.7478 | 07.9240 | 08.1016 | 08.2806 | 08.4608 | 08.6422 | 08.8248 | 09.0086 | 09.1935 | 09.3794 | 09.5663 |
| 29½ | 06.5202 | 06.6864 | 06.8544 | 07.0240 | 07.1951 | 07.3679 | 07.5421 | 07.7177 | 07.8948 | 08.0732 | 08.2530 | 08.4340 | 08.6162 | 08.7996 | 08.9842 | 09.1698 | 09.3565 | 09.5442 |
| 30 | 06.4860 | 06.6531 | 06.8218 | 06.9922 | 07.1642 | 07.3377 | 07.5127 | 07.6892 | 07.8671 | 08.0463 | 08.2268 | 08.4086 | 08.5916 | 08.7758 | 08.9611 | 09.1474 | 09.3349 | 09.5233 |

**Figure 22–1. Table of Monthly Payments Required To Amortize $1,000 Loan** *continued*

| Years | 11¼% | 11½% | 11¾% | 12% | 12¼% | 12½% | 12¾% | 13% | 13¼% | 13½% | 13¾% | 14% | 14¼% | 14½% | 14¾% | 15% | 15¼% | 15½% |
|---|---|---|---|---|---|---|---|---|---|---|---|---|---|---|---|---|---|---|
| 1 | 88.4984 | 88.6151 | 88.7319 | 88.8488 | 88.9658 | 89.0829 | 89.2001 | 89.3173 | 89.4347 | 89.5521 | 89.6696 | 89.7872 | 89.9048 | 90.0226 | 90.1404 | 90.2584 | 90.3764 | 90.4945 |
| 1½ | 60.6343 | 60.7501 | 60.8660 | 60.9821 | 61.0983 | 61.2146 | 61.3311 | 61.4476 | 61.5643 | 61.6812 | 61.7981 | 61.9152 | 62.0324 | 62.1498 | 62.2672 | 62.3848 | 62.5026 | 62.6204 |
| 2 | 46.7240 | 46.8404 | 46.9569 | 47.0735 | 47.1904 | 47.3074 | 47.4245 | 47.5419 | 47.6594 | 47.7771 | 47.8949 | 48.0129 | 48.1311 | 48.2495 | 48.3680 | 48.4867 | 48.6056 | 48.7246 |
| 2½ | 38.3953 | 38.5127 | 38.6303 | 38.7482 | 38.8662 | 38.9845 | 39.1029 | 39.2216 | 39.3405 | 39.4596 | 39.5789 | 39.6984 | 39.8181 | 39.9381 | 40.0582 | 40.1786 | 40.2992 | 40.4199 |
| 3 | 32.8573 | 32.9761 | 33.0951 | 33.2144 | 33.3339 | 33.4537 | 33.5737 | 33.6940 | 33.8145 | 33.9353 | 34.0564 | 34.1777 | 34.2992 | 34.4210 | 34.5431 | 34.6654 | 34.7879 | 34.9107 |
| 3½ | 28.9139 | 29.0342 | 29.1548 | 29.2757 | 29.3969 | 29.5183 | 29.6401 | 29.7621 | 29.8845 | 30.0071 | 30.1301 | 30.2533 | 30.3768 | 30.5006 | 30.6247 | 30.7491 | 30.8738 | 30.9988 |
| 4 | 25.9671 | 26.0891 | 26.2113 | 26.3339 | 26.4568 | 26.5800 | 26.7036 | 26.8275 | 26.9518 | 27.0764 | 27.2013 | 27.3265 | 27.4521 | 27.5780 | 27.7042 | 27.8308 | 27.9577 | 28.0849 |
| 4½ | 23.6847 | 23.8083 | 23.9323 | 24.0566 | 24.1813 | 24.3064 | 24.4319 | 24.5577 | 24.6839 | 24.8105 | 24.9374 | 25.0647 | 25.1924 | 25.3205 | 25.4489 | 25.5777 | 25.7068 | 25.8363 |
| 5 | 21.8674 | 21.9927 | 22.1184 | 22.2445 | 22.3710 | 22.4980 | 22.6254 | 22.7531 | 22.8813 | 23.0099 | 23.1389 | 23.2683 | 23.3981 | 23.5283 | 23.6590 | 23.7900 | 23.9214 | 24.0532 |
| 5½ | 20.3881 | 20.5151 | 20.6426 | 20.7706 | 20.8990 | 21.0278 | 21.1571 | 21.2868 | 21.4170 | 21.5476 | 21.6787 | 21.8102 | 21.9422 | 22.0746 | 22.2074 | 22.3407 | 22.4744 | 22.6086 |
| 6 | 19.1624 | 19.2912 | 19.4205 | 19.5502 | 19.6805 | 19.8112 | 19.9425 | 20.0742 | 20.2063 | 20.3390 | 20.4722 | 20.6058 | 20.7399 | 20.8745 | 21.0095 | 21.1451 | 21.2811 | 21.4175 |
| 6½ | 18.1317 | 18.2623 | 18.3933 | 18.5249 | 18.6570 | 18.7897 | 18.9228 | 19.0565 | 19.1907 | 19.3254 | 19.4606 | 19.5964 | 19.7326 | 19.8694 | 20.0066 | 20.1444 | 20.2827 | 20.4215 |
| 7 | 17.2542 | 17.3865 | 17.5194 | 17.6528 | 17.7868 | 17.9213 | 18.0564 | 18.1920 | 18.3282 | 18.4649 | 18.6022 | 18.7401 | 18.8784 | 19.0174 | 19.1568 | 19.2968 | 19.4373 | 19.5784 |
| 8 | 15.8436 | 15.9794 | 16.1158 | 16.2529 | 16.3906 | 16.5289 | 16.6678 | 16.8073 | 16.9475 | 17.0882 | 17.2296 | 17.3716 | 17.5141 | 17.6573 | 17.8011 | 17.9455 | 18.0904 | 18.2360 |
| 9 | 14.7645 | 14.9037 | 15.0437 | 15.1843 | 15.3256 | 15.4676 | 15.6103 | 15.7536 | 15.8977 | 16.0424 | 16.1877 | 16.3338 | 16.4804 | 16.6278 | 16.7758 | 16.9244 | 17.0737 | 17.2236 |
| 10 | 13.9169 | 14.0596 | 14.2030 | 14.3471 | 14.4920 | 14.6377 | 14.7840 | 14.9311 | 15.0789 | 15.2275 | 15.3767 | 15.5267 | 15.6774 | 15.8287 | 15.9808 | 16.1335 | 16.2870 | 16.4411 |
| 12 | 12.6840 | 12.8332 | 12.9833 | 13.1342 | 13.2860 | 13.4386 | 13.5921 | 13.7463 | 13.9014 | 14.0572 | 14.2139 | 14.3713 | 14.5295 | 14.6885 | 14.8483 | 15.0088 | 15.1701 | 15.3321 |
| 15 | 11.5235 | 11.6819 | 11.8414 | 12.0017 | 12.1630 | 12.3253 | 12.4884 | 12.6525 | 12.8174 | 12.9832 | 13.1499 | 13.3175 | 13.4858 | 13.6551 | 13.8251 | 13.9959 | 14.1675 | 14.3400 |
| 20 | 10.4926 | 10.6643 | 10.8371 | 11.0109 | 11.1857 | 11.3615 | 11.5382 | 11.7158 | 11.8944 | 12.0738 | 12.2541 | 12.4353 | 12.6172 | 12.8000 | 12.9836 | 13.1679 | 13.3530 | 13.5389 |
| 21 | 10.3618 | 10.5358 | 10.7109 | 10.8870 | 11.0642 | 11.2422 | 11.4213 | 11.6012 | 11.7820 | 11.9637 | 12.1463 | 12.3297 | 12.5139 | 12.6989 | 12.8847 | 13.0712 | 13.2585 | 13.4464 |
| 22 | 10.2475 | 10.4238 | 10.6011 | 10.7794 | 10.9587 | 11.1390 | 11.3202 | 11.5023 | 11.6853 | 11.8692 | 12.0538 | 12.2393 | 12.4256 | 12.6127 | 12.8005 | 12.9890 | 13.1783 | 13.3682 |
| 23 | 10.1475 | 10.3259 | 10.5053 | 10.6857 | 10.8671 | 11.0494 | 11.2327 | 11.4168 | 11.6018 | 11.7877 | 11.9743 | 12.1618 | 12.3500 | 12.5390 | 12.7287 | 12.9190 | 13.1101 | 13.3018 |
| 24 | 10.0597 | 10.2401 | 10.4215 | 10.6039 | 10.7872 | 10.9715 | 11.1567 | 11.3427 | 11.5296 | 11.7173 | 11.9058 | 12.0951 | 12.2851 | 12.4758 | 12.6673 | 12.8593 | 13.0521 | 13.2454 |
| 25 | 09.9824 | 10.1647 | 10.3480 | 10.5323 | 10.7175 | 10.9036 | 11.0906 | 11.2784 | 11.4671 | 11.6565 | 11.8467 | 12.0377 | 12.2293 | 12.4217 | 12.6147 | 12.8084 | 13.0026 | 13.1975 |
| 26 | 09.9144 | 10.0985 | 10.2836 | 10.4696 | 10.6565 | 10.8443 | 11.0330 | 11.2225 | 11.4128 | 11.6038 | 11.7956 | 11.9881 | 12.1813 | 12.3752 | 12.5697 | 12.7648 | 12.9604 | 13.1567 |
| 27 | 09.8543 | 10.0401 | 10.2269 | 10.4145 | 10.6031 | 10.7925 | 10.9828 | 11.1738 | 11.3656 | 11.5582 | 11.7514 | 11.9454 | 12.1400 | 12.3352 | 12.5310 | 12.7274 | 12.9244 | 13.1219 |
| 28 | 09.8013 | 09.9886 | 10.1770 | 10.3662 | 10.5563 | 10.7472 | 10.9389 | 11.1314 | 11.3246 | 11.5185 | 11.7132 | 11.9084 | 12.1043 | 12.3008 | 12.4978 | 12.6954 | 12.8936 | 13.0922 |
| 29 | 09.7543 | 09.9432 | 10.1330 | 10.3236 | 10.5151 | 10.7075 | 10.9005 | 11.0944 | 11.2889 | 11.4841 | 11.6800 | 11.8764 | 12.0735 | 12.2712 | 12.4693 | 12.6680 | 12.8672 | 13.0669 |
| 29½ | 09.7328 | 09.9225 | 10.1130 | 10.3043 | 10.4965 | 10.6895 | 10.8832 | 11.0777 | 11.2728 | 11.4686 | 11.6651 | 11.8621 | 12.0597 | 12.2579 | 12.4566 | 12.6558 | 12.8555 | 13.0556 |
| 30 | 09.7127 | 09.9030 | 10.0941 | 10.2862 | 10.4790 | 10.6726 | 10.8670 | 11.0620 | 11.2578 | 11.4542 | 11.6512 | 11.8488 | 12.0469 | 12.2456 | 12.4448 | 12.6445 | 12.8446 | 13.0452 |

**Figure 22–1.  Table of Monthly Payments Required To Amortize $1,000 Loan** *continued*

| Years | 15¾% | 16% | 16¼% | 16½% | 16¾% | 17% | 17¼% | 17½% | 17¾% | 18% | 18¼% | 18½% | 18¾% | 19% | 19½% | 20% | 20½% | 21% |
|---|---|---|---|---|---|---|---|---|---|---|---|---|---|---|---|---|---|---|
| 1 | 90.6126 | 90.7309 | 90.8493 | 90.9677 | 91.0862 | 91.2048 | 91.3235 | 91.4423 | 91.5611 | 91.6800 | 91.7991 | 91.9182 | 92.0374 | 92.1556 | 92.3954 | 92.6346 | 92.8740 | 93.1138 |
| 1½ | 62.7384 | 62.8565 | 62.9747 | 63.0931 | 63.2115 | 63.3301 | 63.4489 | 63.5677 | 63.6867 | 63.8058 | 63.9251 | 64.0444 | 64.1639 | 64.2835 | 64.5231 | 64.7633 | 65.0039 | 65.2450 |
| 2 | 48.8438 | 48.9632 | 49.0827 | 49.2024 | 49.3223 | 49.4423 | 49.5625 | 49.6829 | 49.8034 | 49.9242 | 50.0450 | 50.1661 | 50.2873 | 50.4087 | 50.6519 | 50.8959 | 51.1404 | 51.3857 |
| 2½ | 40.5409 | 40.6621 | 40.7835 | 40.9052 | 41.0270 | 41.1490 | 41.2713 | 41.3937 | 41.5164 | 41.6392 | 41.7623 | 41.8856 | 42.0091 | 42.1328 | 42.3808 | 42.6296 | 42.8793 | 43.1298 |
| 3 | 35.0338 | 35.1571 | 35.2806 | 35.4044 | 35.5285 | 35.6528 | 35.7773 | 35.9021 | 36.0272 | 36.1524 | 36.2780 | 36.4038 | 36.5298 | 36.6561 | 36.9094 | 37.1636 | 37.4189 | 37.6751 |
| 3½ | 31.1240 | 31.2496 | 31.3754 | 31.5015 | 31.6279 | 31.7546 | 31.8816 | 32.0089 | 32.1365 | 32.2643 | 32.3924 | 32.5209 | 32.6496 | 32.7785 | 33.0374 | 33.2973 | 33.5584 | 33.8206 |
| 4 | 28.2125 | 28.3403 | 28.4685 | 28.5971 | 28.7259 | 28.8551 | 28.9846 | 29.1144 | 29.2446 | 29.3750 | 29.5058 | 29.6370 | 29.7684 | 29.9002 | 30.1647 | 30.4304 | 30.6974 | 30.9657 |
| 4½ | 25.9662 | 26.0964 | 26.2270 | 26.3580 | 26.4894 | 26.6210 | 26.7531 | 26.8855 | 27.0183 | 27.1514 | 27.2849 | 27.4188 | 27.5530 | 27.6875 | 27.9577 | 28.2293 | 28.5024 | 28.7768 |
| 5 | 24.1855 | 24.3181 | 24.4511 | 24.5846 | 24.7184 | 24.8526 | 24.9872 | 25.1223 | 25.2577 | 25.3935 | 25.5297 | 25.6663 | 25.8032 | 25.9406 | 26.2165 | 26.4939 | 26.7729 | 27.0534 |
| 5½ | 22.7432 | 22.8782 | 23.0136 | 23.1495 | 23.2859 | 23.4226 | 23.5598 | 23.6974 | 23.8354 | 23.9739 | 24.1128 | 24.2521 | 24.3918 | 24.5320 | 24.8135 | 25.0968 | 25.3817 | 25.6682 |
| 6 | 21.5545 | 21.6919 | 21.8298 | 21.9681 | 22.1069 | 22.2462 | 22.3859 | 22.5261 | 22.6667 | 22.8078 | 22.9494 | 23.0914 | 23.2339 | 23.3768 | 23.6639 | 23.9529 | 24.2436 | 24.5360 |
| 6½ | 20.5607 | 20.7005 | 20.8408 | 20.9816 | 21.1228 | 21.2646 | 21.4068 | 21.5496 | 21.6928 | 21.8365 | 21.9807 | 22.1254 | 22.2705 | 22.4161 | 22.7088 | 23.0034 | 23.2998 | 23.5981 |
| 7 | 19.7200 | 19.8621 | 20.0048 | 20.1479 | 20.2916 | 20.4359 | 20.5806 | 20.7258 | 20.8716 | 21.0179 | 21.1647 | 21.3120 | 21.4598 | 21.6081 | 21.9062 | 22.2062 | 22.5083 | 22.8123 |
| 8 | 18.3821 | 18.5288 | 18.6761 | 18.8240 | 18.9725 | 19.1215 | 19.2711 | 19.4213 | 19.5720 | 19.7233 | 19.8751 | 20.0275 | 20.1804 | 20.3339 | 20.6425 | 20.9533 | 21.2661 | 21.5811 |
| 9 | 17.3741 | 17.5253 | 17.6771 | 17.8295 | 17.9826 | 18.1362 | 18.2905 | 18.4454 | 18.6009 | 18.7569 | 18.9136 | 19.0709 | 19.2287 | 19.3871 | 19.7057 | 20.0266 | 20.3496 | 20.6749 |
| 10 | 16.5959 | 16.7514 | 16.9075 | 17.0643 | 17.2217 | 17.3798 | 17.5386 | 17.6979 | 17.8579 | 18.0186 | 18.1798 | 18.3417 | 18.5042 | 18.6673 | 18.9953 | 19.3256 | 19.6583 | 19.9932 |
| 12 | 15.4948 | 15.6583 | 15.8225 | 15.9874 | 16.1530 | 16.3193 | 16.4863 | 16.6539 | 16.8223 | 16.9912 | 17.1609 | 17.3312 | 17.5021 | 17.6737 | 18.0187 | 18.3661 | 18.7159 | 19.0681 |
| 15 | 14.5131 | 14.6871 | 14.8617 | 15.0371 | 15.2133 | 15.3901 | 15.5676 | 15.7458 | 15.9247 | 16.1043 | 16.2845 | 16.4653 | 16.6467 | 16.8288 | 17.1948 | 17.5630 | 17.9335 | 18.3062 |
| 20 | 13.7254 | 13.9126 | 14.1005 | 14.2891 | 14.4782 | 14.6681 | 14.8585 | 15.0495 | 15.2410 | 15.4332 | 15.6258 | 15.8190 | 16.0127 | 16.2069 | 16.5967 | 16.9883 | 17.3816 | 17.7765 |
| 21 | 13.6351 | 13.8244 | 14.0143 | 14.2049 | 14.3961 | 14.5879 | 14.7802 | 14.9732 | 15.1666 | 15.3606 | 15.5551 | 15.7501 | 15.9455 | 16.1415 | 16.5347 | 16.9295 | 17.3260 | 17.7239 |
| 22 | 13.5587 | 13.7500 | 13.9418 | 14.1342 | 14.3272 | 14.5208 | 14.7149 | 14.9096 | 15.1048 | 15.3004 | 15.4966 | 15.6932 | 15.8902 | 16.0877 | 16.4839 | 16.8816 | 17.2808 | 17.6814 |
| 23 | 13.4942 | 13.6871 | 13.8807 | 14.0748 | 14.2695 | 14.4647 | 14.6604 | 14.8566 | 15.0533 | 15.2505 | 15.4481 | 15.6461 | 15.8446 | 16.0434 | 16.4423 | 16.8426 | 17.2442 | 17.6470 |
| 24 | 13.4394 | 13.6340 | 13.8291 | 14.0247 | 14.2209 | 14.4176 | 14.6147 | 14.8123 | 15.0104 | 15.2089 | 15.4078 | 15.6072 | 15.8069 | 16.0069 | 16.4081 | 16.8106 | 17.2144 | 17.6192 |
| 25 | 13.3929 | 13.5889 | 13.7855 | 13.9825 | 14.1800 | 14.3780 | 14.5765 | 14.7753 | 14.9746 | 15.1743 | 15.3744 | 15.5749 | 15.7757 | 15.9769 | 16.3801 | 16.7846 | 17.1901 | 17.5967 |
| 26 | 13.3535 | 13.5508 | 13.7486 | 13.9469 | 14.1456 | 14.3448 | 14.5444 | 14.7444 | 14.9448 | 15.1456 | 15.3467 | 15.5481 | 15.7499 | 15.9520 | 16.3571 | 16.7632 | 17.1704 | 17.5784 |
| 27 | 13.3199 | 13.5184 | 13.7173 | 13.9167 | 14.1166 | 14.3168 | 14.5175 | 14.7185 | 14.9198 | 15.1216 | 15.3236 | 15.5259 | 15.7286 | 15.9315 | 16.3382 | 16.7458 | 17.1543 | 17.5637 |
| 28 | 13.2913 | 13.4909 | 13.6909 | 13.8913 | 14.0921 | 14.2933 | 14.4949 | 14.6968 | 14.8990 | 15.1015 | 15.3044 | 15.5075 | 15.7109 | 15.9146 | 16.3226 | 16.7315 | 17.1412 | 17.5517 |
| 29 | 13.2670 | 13.4675 | 13.6684 | 13.8698 | 14.0715 | 14.2735 | 14.4759 | 14.6786 | 14.8816 | 15.0848 | 15.2884 | 15.4922 | 15.6963 | 15.9006 | 16.3098 | 16.7198 | 17.1306 | 17.5419 |
| 29½ | 13.2562 | 13.4572 | 13.6585 | 13.8603 | 14.0624 | 14.2648 | 14.4675 | 14.6706 | 14.8739 | 15.0776 | 15.2814 | 15.4856 | 15.6899 | 15.8945 | 16.3043 | 16.7148 | 17.1260 | 17.5378 |
| 30 | 13.2462 | 13.4476 | 13.6494 | 13.8515 | 14.0540 | 14.2568 | 14.4599 | 14.6633 | 14.8670 | 15.0709 | 15.2751 | 15.4795 | 15.6841 | 15.8890 | 16.2993 | 16.7102 | 17.1219 | 17.5341 |

**Figure 22–1.  Table of Monthly Payments Required To Amortize $1,000 Loan** *continued*

| Years | 21½% | 22% | 22½% | 23% | 23½% | 24% |
|---|---|---|---|---|---|---|
| 1 | 93.3540 | 93.5944 | 93.8352 | 94.0764 | 94.3178 | 94.5596 |
| 1½ | 65.4866 | 65.7287 | 65.9713 | 66.2144 | 66.4580 | 66.7022 |
| 2 | 51.6316 | 51.8782 | 52.1254 | 52.3734 | 52.6219 | 52.8711 |
| 2½ | 43.3811 | 43.6333 | 43.8862 | 44.1400 | 44.3946 | 44.6500 |
| 3 | 37.9323 | 38.1905 | 38.4497 | 38.7098 | 38.9709 | 39.2329 |
| 3½ | 34.0840 | 34.3484 | 34.6140 | 34.8807 | 35.1485 | 35.4173 |
| 4 | 31.2353 | 31.5061 | 31.7782 | 32.0515 | 32.3261 | 32.6019 |
| 4½ | 29.0526 | 29.3298 | 29.6084 | 29.8883 | 30.1696 | 30.4523 |
| 5 | 27.3354 | 27.6190 | 27.9040 | 28.1905 | 28.4785 | 28.7680 |
| 5½ | 25.9563 | 26.2461 | 26.5375 | 26.8305 | 27.1251 | 27.4213 |
| 6 | 24.8302 | 25.1262 | 25.4238 | 25.7232 | 26.0242 | 26.3269 |
| 6½ | 23.8982 | 24.2002 | 24.5039 | 24.8095 | 25.1168 | 25.4258 |
| 7 | 23.1182 | 23.4260 | 23.7357 | 24.0472 | 24.3606 | 24.6759 |
| 8 | 21.8981 | 22.2171 | 22.5382 | 22.8612 | 23.1862 | 23.5132 |
| 9 | 21.0024 | 21.3320 | 21.6636 | 21.9974 | 22.3331 | 22.6709 |
| 10 | 20.3304 | 20.6697 | 21.0112 | 21.3548 | 21.7005 | 22.0481 |
| 12 | 19.4224 | 19.7790 | 20.1377 | 20.4984 | 20.8612 | 21.2259 |
| 15 | 18.6809 | 19.0576 | 19.4362 | 19.8167 | 20.1989 | 20.5828 |
| 20 | 18.1729 | 18.5706 | 18.9698 | 19.3701 | 19.7716 | 20.1741 |
| 21 | 18.1231 | 18.5237 | 18.9254 | 19.3283 | 19.7322 | 20.1371 |
| 22 | 18.0832 | 18.4861 | 18.8901 | 19.2952 | 19.7011 | 20.1079 |
| 23 | 18.0510 | 18.4560 | 18.8620 | 19.2689 | 19.6766 | 20.0850 |
| 24 | 18.0250 | 18.4318 | 18.8395 | 19.2480 | 19.6571 | 20.0670 |
| 25 | 18.0042 | 18.4125 | 18.8216 | 19.2313 | 19.6418 | 20.0528 |
| 26 | 17.9873 | 18.3969 | 18.8072 | 19.2181 | 19.6296 | 20.0416 |
| 27 | 17.9737 | 18.3844 | 18.7958 | 19.2076 | 19.6200 | 20.0328 |
| 28 | 17.9627 | 18.3744 | 18.7866 | 19.1993 | 19.6124 | 20.0259 |
| 29 | 17.9539 | 18.3664 | 18.7793 | 19.1926 | 19.6064 | 20.0204 |
| 29½ | 17.9501 | 18.3630 | 18.7762 | 19.1899 | 19.6038 | 20.0181 |
| 30 | 17.9467 | 18.3599 | 18.7734 | 19.1874 | 19.6016 | 20.0161 |

1. Locate the monthly payment factor for the desired interest rate and term of years.

2. Multiply this number by the loan amount divided by $1,000 to obtain the MONTHLY PAYMENT. For instance, for a $75,000 Loan amount, multiply the factor by $75 ($75,000 ÷ $1,000 = $75).

3. Round up to the nearest penny.

The monthly payment of principal and interest for a $75,000 loan at 12% for 30 years is 10.2862 x $75 = $771.465 or $771.47.

to make payments is greater than the amount of principal being paid. However, as the principal is paid off, the portion of the payment going to pay interest drops steadily. By the time you have paid off half the principal, the amount of interest in each payment will be much lower than the amount going to the principal. Ten percent of $15,000, which is half of the principal, is $1,500 interest for a year. When you divide this figure by 12, you get $125 interest due for one month. Of the $396.46 payment now, only $125 goes to the interest and $396.46 minus $125, or $271.46, goes to pay the principal, a considerable increase in the ratio of principal to interest. By the time three-fourths of the loan is paid off, the interest portion will be quite low, only $62.50 out of the $396.46 payment.

## The Balloon Payment

Sometimes a balloon payment will be due during the period of a loan, usually at the end. It is called a *balloon* payment because it is much larger than the regular installment. For example, you may have amortized your loan over a 15-year or 20-year period to keep the monthly payments lower, but the loan is due and payable in 10 years. After 10 years the remaining principal due at that time must be paid in a lump sum, along with any interest due, usually only that due for that month.

Occasionally a loan has one or more balloon payments periodically during the loan period. For instance, your seller may allow you to amortize your loan over a 20 year period to keep your monthly payments down, but then may want you to pay, in addition to your regular monthly payments, a balloon payment at the end of, say, 5 years and another final balloon payment at the end of 10 years, so that the loan is paid in full in 10 years. These balloon payments will be credited almost entirely toward the principal.

For instance, if you were paying off a loan with an interest rate of 12 percent and monthly installments of $300, if the principal balance were

**Figure 22–2. Relationship Between Principal and Interest During Payment Period**

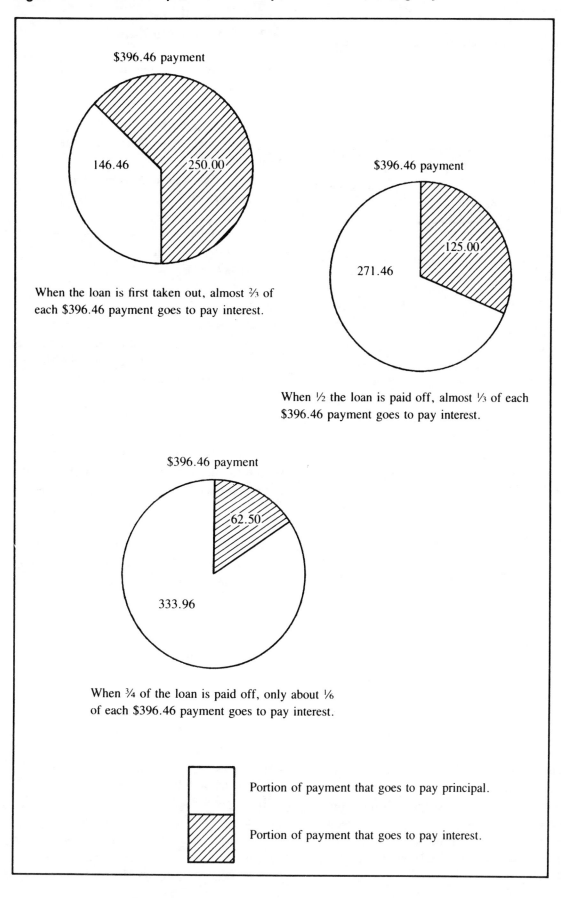

$396.46 payment

146.46    250.00

When the loan is first taken out, almost ⅔ of each $396.46 payment goes to pay interest.

$396.46 payment

271.46    125.00

When ½ the loan is paid off, almost ⅓ of each $396.46 payment goes to pay interest.

$396.46 payment

62.50

333.96

When ¾ of the loan is paid off, only about ⅙ of each $396.46 payment goes to pay interest.

Portion of payment that goes to pay principal.

Portion of payment that goes to pay interest.

**Figure 22–3. Effect of Interest Rate on Loan Cost**

| Interest Rate (%), Years | Monthly Payment of Principal and Interest | Total Interest for 10 Years |
|---|---|---|
| 9 | $506.71 | $20,805.20 |
| 10 | 528.61 | 23,433.20 |
| 11 | 551.01 | 26,121.20 |
| 12 | 573.09 | 28,770.80 |
| 13 | 597.25 | 31,670.00 |
| 14 | 621.07 | 34,528.40 |
| 15 | 645.34 | 37,440.80 |

$20,000, the usual monthly payment would consist of $200 interest

$$(\$20,000 \times 12\%) \div 12 \text{ months} = \$200$$

leaving $100 to go toward principal. If you paid a $5,000 balloon payment at this time, however, the same $200 would be credited against interest, and $4,800 would be credited against principal, leaving a principal balance on the loan of $15,200. Your next monthly installment of $300 would then break down as $152 toward interest

$$(15,200 \times 12\%) \div 12 \text{ months} = \$152$$

and $148 toward principal.

## The Loan Fees

Generally if the seller is financing your loan, no loan fees will be charged other than the interest rate. If you are financing your purchase through a commercial financial institution, however, there will be various charges, including an application fee, charges for credit checks, property appraisal, points that are generally calculated as a percentage of the total loan and charges for drawing up and recording the loan documents. loan fees may be called *debt service fees, loan brokerage fees, new loan fees, placement fees, origination fees* or *loan installment fees*. They are not standard from lender to lender, so it is possible to save hundreds, even thousands, of dollars by shopping around for a lender and comparing interest rates, loan fees and points charged. This will be discussed further in Chapter 25, "Borrowing from Third-Party Lenders."

## How To Get a Computerized Loan Amortization Schedule

Although knowing how to compute all the aspects of your loan yourself is essential, for a slight fee a computer company in Santa Monica, California (see below), will compute everything for you and send you a complete printout of your entire payment schedule.

Send your name and address and the information required with a check to

Delphi Information Sciences Corporation
2800 28th St., Suite 205
Santa Monica, CA 90405
(310) 425-7575

You must send the following information: the amount of the loan, the interest rate, the term of the loan in years and months, the amount of each payment and the payment schedule (monthly, quarterly, annually, and so on). You can omit either the term of the loan or the amount of each payment, and Delphi can still compute your loan. Indicate if the interest is to be paid as part of each installment. If you are to make monthly payments and escrow closes in the middle of the month, the first payment will not be for a full 30 days. Give the number of days accounted for in that first month.

A loan amortization schedule costs $20 for a straight loan schedule with a term of 19 years or less. If the term is more than 19 years or if there are any changes, such as a change in interest rate or balloon payments, the charge is $30. The printout the company sends you gives the terms of the loan and includes the number of payments, the amount of each payment, the breakdown of how much of each payment goes toward interest, the amount of the principal still unpaid at the end of each payment and the sum of the entire loan. If you are financing your purchase through the seller a loan amortization schedule might be very informative. The company responds to requests immediately.

Try to get the seller or real estate agent to furnish this essential information to you. Many brokers now have computer software that can give you a partial printout with the essential loan information you will need, as described above.

## Figure 22–4. Amount of Down Payment and Loan Cost

| % of $60,000 | Down Payment | Principal Amount To Be Amortized | Monthly Payments of Principal and Interest for 10 Years | Interest for 10 Years |
|---|---|---|---|---|
| | 0 | $60,000 | $830.83 | $43,299.12 |
| 10 = | $6,000 | 54,000 | 774.74 | 38,968.80 |
| 15 = | 9,000 | 51,000 | 731.70 | 36,804.25 |
| 20 = | 12,000 | 48,000 | 688.66 | 34,639.29 |
| 25 = | 15,000 | 45,000 | 645.62 | 32,474.34 |
| 30 = | 18,000 | 42,000 | 602.58 | 30,309.38 |
| 40 = | 24,000 | 36,000 | 516.50 | 25,979.47 |

## Factors That Affect the Cost of a Loan

### Effect of Interest Rate on Cost of Loan

When a loan is being paid off over a long period of time, a variation in the interest rate of even 1 percent can make quite a difference in the total amount you pay. Figure 22–3 shows the effect of 1 percent increases in the interest rate on a $40,000 loan over a period of ten years.

### Effect of Amount of Down Payment on Cost of Loan

The more cash you can afford for a down payment, the cheaper your loan will be in the long run. Figure 22–4 shows the amount of interest paid in relation to various down payments made on a $60,000 purchase at 12 percent interest paid off in monthly installments for ten years.

### Effect of Payment Period on Cost of Loan

Although the total amount of interest will be lower if you pay off your loan fast, most buyers like to spread their payments over a long period of time in order to keep the monthly payments at an easy-to-meet level. However, to give you an example of the effect of the payment period on the cost of a loan, Figure 22–5 shows the size of each payment and the total amount of interest on a $40,000 loan at 10 percent interest for four different payment periods.

## Advantages of Prepayment Without Penalty or Prohibition

You can cut down on the total amount of interest you will ultimately pay by making larger payments early in the payment schedule, because interest is figured as a percentage of the unpaid principal. You can do this only if your loan agreement includes a statement that "the principal and interest are payable in installments of _____ dollars *or more*." I have always been able to add this clause to a loan agreement if it was not already included. Often it is.

Your creditor may not want you to pay off your loan early because that would deprive him or her of interest. Another reason for prohibition of early payment may be that the creditor does not want to take in more money than expected because it would push him into a higher income tax bracket. A creditor might put a *prepayment penalty clause* in the note, which specifies that you are to be penalized if you pay off any part of the loan in advance. This penalty makes up for the interest lost by the early payment. Or the lender might insert a clause totally prohibiting prepayment, or early payoff, of the loan. Always fight to have such a penalty clause removed from the loan agreement and note. It is harder to have this clause removed from a commercial loan than from one financed by the seller. Also, the longer the term of the loan, the harder it is to get the penalty clause removed. Some states have laws that allow prepayment after the first year of sale for residential property. Check with the bank or mortgage company, title or escrow company, or lawyer to find out the laws in your state.

If you decide to sell your land before it is fully paid for, you will be in a better position if you can offer the buyer title free of encumbrances. If you are allowed to prepay your debt, when your buyer

## Figure 22–5. Effect Of Payment Period on Loan Cost

| Payment Period, Years | Monthly Payment of Principal and Interest | Total Interest Paid |
|---|---|---|
| 5 | $849.89 | $10,993.40 |
| 10 | 528.61 | 23,433.20 |
| 15 | 429.85 | 37,373.00 |
| 20 | 386.01 | 52,642.40 |

pays you for the land, you can pay off your creditor to get clear title. If you are not permitted to prepay your debt, you will be unable to clear the title for your buyer, and you might have trouble selling the land.

Sometimes a lender would be very happy to receive a large amount of cash early. If you come into some money, you can offer to prepay the total remaining due if your creditor gives you a discount on the remaining unpaid balance. If the lender could really use the extra cash and is anxious to have the mortgage paid off early, he or she should be willing to give you a discount. Such a situation frequently occurs when the seller self-finances the sale. Professional mortgage companies that purchase notes generally discount them for cash by as much as 40 percent. For example, if your seller holds a note with a balance of $40,000, a mortgage company might pay him or her $30,000 cash for the note. Certainly, your seller should give the same discount to you if he or she is interested in getting paid off early. Never offer to pay off a loan early without asking your lender to discount the note. You might easily save a few thousand dollars.

## Adjustable Rate Mortgages with Variable Interest Rates

*Adjustable rate mortgages (ARM)* are sometimes also called *variable rate loans* or *floating loans.* Shopping for a mortgage used to be a relatively simple process. Most home mortgage loans had interest rates that did not change over the life of the loan. Choosing among these *fixed rate* mortgage loans meant comparing interest rates, monthly payments, fees, prepayment penalties and due-on-sale clauses.

Today, many loans have interest rates (and monthly payments) that can change from time to time. To compare one ARM with another or with a fixed rate mortgage, you need to know about indexes, margins, discounts, caps, negative amortization and convertibility. You need to consider the maximum amount your monthly payment could increase. Most important, you need to balance costs against your future ability to pay.

With a fixed rate mortgage, the interest rate stays the same during the life of the loan. But with an ARM, the interest rate changes periodically, usually in relation to an index, and payments may go up or down accordingly.

Lenders generally charge lower initial interest rates for ARMs than for fixed rate mortgages. At first this makes the ARM easier on your pocketbook than a fixed rate mortgage for the same amount. It also means that you might qualify for a larger loan, because lenders sometimes make this decision on the basis of your current income and the first year's payments. Moreover, your ARM could be less expensive over a long period of time than a fixed rate mortgage—for example, if interest rates remain steady or move lower.

Against these advantages, you have to weigh the risk than an increase in interest rates would lead to higher monthly payments in the future. It is a trade-off—you get a lower initial rate with an ARM in exchange for assuming more risk. Be aware that if interest rates skyrocket as they did in the late 1970s, the mortgage payments could increase beyond your capacity to make them. Over the course of a variable rate loan, the payments could increase $500 per month or more. This is why you always want an interest rate cap on your loan.

An *interest rate cap* places a limit on the amount your interest rate can increase. ARMs with caps may cost more than ARMs without them. Caps are of two types: *periodic caps*, which limit the interest rate increases from one adjustment period to the next; and *overall caps*, which limit the interest rate increase over the life of the loan.

Some ARMs include *payment caps*, which limit the monthly payment increase at the time of each adjustment. For example, a 5 percent cap would mean that a mortgage payment of $400 could increase to no more than $420 during the first adjustment period and $441 in the second.

With most ARMs, the interest rate and monthly payment change every six months, every year, every three years, or every five years. However, some ARMs have more frequent interest and payment changes. The period between one rate change and the next is called the *adjustment period.* A loan with an adjustment period of one year is called a *one-year ARM,* and the interest rate can change once every year.

Most lenders tie ARM interest rate changes to changes in an *index rate.* These indexes usually go up and down with the general movement of interest rates. If the index rate goes up, so does your mortgage rate, in most circumstances, and you probably will have to make higher monthly payments. On the other hand, if the index rate goes down, your monthly payment may go down.

Sometimes the initial interest rate offered for ARMs is several points below the current market rate. In this case, you can be sure that unless market rates drop substantially, your interest rate and your monthly payment will rise the maximum amount allowed in the next few adjustment periods, until your interest rate reaches current market rates.

Lenders base ARM rates on a variety of indexes. Among the most common are the rates on one-year, three-year, or five-year Treasury securities, or the national or regional average cost of funds to savings and loan associations. A few lenders use their own cost of funds, over which—unlike other indexes—they have some control. You should ask what index will be used and how often it changes. Also ask how it has behaved in the past and where it is published.

An ARM loan may be valuable if interest rates are exceedingly high at the time you take out a loan. Usually, only institutional lenders offer ARMs, because calculating a varying interest rate is somewhat complicated.

In recent years, whenever interest rates have been very high, many commercial lenders have offered only variable rate loans and have deleted their fixed rate loans on real property.

You will see mortgages advertised that look extremely attractive. Ads will feature low initial interest rates without disclosing that substantial increases could occur over the course of the loan. (See information about truth in lending in Chapter 25.) Every lender should give you in writing the factors that will cause your rate to increase; what the effects of the increase will be; and limitations, if any, on the increases.

When comparing adjustable rate mortgages, obtain the following information:

> ARM annual percentage rate
> Adjustment period
> Index used and current rate
> Margin
> Initial payment without discount
> Initial payment with discount (if any)
> How long will discount last?
> Interest rate caps: periodic or overall
> Payment caps
> Negative amortization
> Convertibility or prepayment privilege
> Initial fees and charges

*Monthly Payment Amounts*
1. What will my monthly payments be after twelve months if the index rate
   a. stays the same?
   b. goes up 2 percent?
   c. goes down 2 percent?
2. What will my monthly payment be after three years if the index rate
   a. stays the same?
   b. goes up 2 percent per year?
   c. goes down 2 percent per year?

Take into account any caps on your mortgage and remember it may run as long as 30 years.

## Negative Amortization

Many commercial lenders are now offering a feature called *negative amortization,* usually in conjunction with variable interest rate loans. Negative amortization means that your monthly payment is not sufficient to pay the total amount of monthly interest due; therefore, your loan balance will actually increase. For instance, say you have a loan balance of $65,000 and your interest rate is 14 percent.

$$(\$65,000 \times 14\%) \div 12 \text{ months} = \$758.33$$
(interest due per month)

If, however, your monthly payment is $700, it wouldn't even pay the interest due, and the $58.33 left owing would be added to the principal. The next month's interest would be calculated

$$(\$65,058.33 \times 14\%) \div 12 \text{ months} = \$759.01$$

Notice that the amount of interest due is increasing, too. If your payments stay the same, you keep adding the extra interest to the principal each month, and you are then charged interest on the interest.

If interest rates are high, commercial lenders sometimes offer negative amortization on some variable rate loans for the first six months or one year to keep the payments lower and therefore more attractive to prospective borrowers. However, after the time period of negative amortization is up, you may find that your monthly payments are much higher than you can afford.

On the other hand, a lender might offer a fixed interest rate for the first six months; then, beginning with the seventh month, the interest rate begins to vary, while the payments stay the same for the rest

**Figure 22–6. Sample Payment Schedule**

Amount of Principal Indebtedness _____

Interest Rate of _____ % Payable _____ (e.g., monthly, quarterly) _____

Payments Made _____ (e.g., the first day of each month) _____ Beginning _____

| Date | Amount of Full Payment | | Amount of Interest Paid | | Amount Going Towards Principal | | Principal Balance Still Owed | |
|------|------|------|------|------|------|------|------|------|
|      |      |      |      |      |      |      |      |      |
|      |      |      |      |      |      |      |      |      |
|      |      |      |      |      |      |      |      |      |
|      |      |      |      |      |      |      |      |      |
|      |      |      |      |      |      |      |      |      |
|      |      |      |      |      |      |      |      |      |
|      |      |      |      |      |      |      |      |      |
|      |      |      |      |      |      |      |      |      |
|      |      |      |      |      |      |      |      |      |

of the year. If the interest rates go up, your payments may not cover the interest due. Then, every 12 months thereafter, the payments are adjusted to an amount sufficient to pay the unpaid balance in full by the maturity date. Again, you may find that your payments have increased so much that you cannot afford them.

If you cannot afford payments that at least pay the interest due, you cannot afford the loan. Always check to be sure there isn't a negative amortization clause buried in the text of your loan. And always check your monthly loan statement if you have a variable rate loan, to be sure that the payment has covered both the interest and some portion of the principal, even though very small at first.

## Loan Interest Is Tax Deductible

You are permitted to deduct any interest you pay on a loan from your state and federal income tax oblig-

ation. This, along with the right to deduct property taxes and to depreciate any improvements, makes land and home ownership easier for the average-income family. If you are planning to rent out a vacation home or second home, there are special rules that apply based on the number of days you rent out the dwelling and other factors. These are currently contained in Internal Revenue Code Section 280A, and you should consult an accountant if you plan to derive rental income from your country property.

## Maintaining a Payment Schedule

It is important to maintain an accurate schedule of your loan payments and the terms of your loan. Figure 22-6 can be used as a model when you set up your payment schedule. You can figure out what portion of each payment goes to principal and what portion goes to interest by using the methods explained at the beginning of this chapter.

# CHAPTER

# 23 Buying Property That Is Encumbered by a Loan Agreement

## Taking Subject to or Assuming a Loan

When you buy land, if the seller still owes money under a loan agreement that he or she cannot pay off before conveying title to you, you will either take the land subject to the loan or you will assume the loan.

If you buy *subject to* a loan, the seller continues to be personally responsible for making the payments until that loan is fully paid. You make a separate loan agreement with the seller. You then pay the seller, who pays his or her creditor and gets clear title to the land. When you finish paying your seller, you will get clear title. During this time, if

the seller fails to make the required payments, his or her creditor can foreclose on the loan. You will lose the land unless you jump in and take over the payments yourself. If you have to do this, you will stop making payments to your seller. The problem is that you might have to make larger payments than you expected. Here is an example of a case I was hired to deal with:

*A* bought a 120-acre piece of property for $120,000, paid $30,000 down, and gave back to the seller a note and mortgage for $90,000, payable $1,000 per month. *A* then divided the property into three 10-acre parcels and sold two of them for $80,000 each to *B* and *C*. *B* and *C* paid cash for their property, so *A* received $160,000 and paid the lender $310,000 cash for each of the two parcels that were sold to B and C. The lender then released those parcels from the $90,000 mortgage. Thus, the mortgage was reduced to $30,000, but the payments were still $1,000 a month.

A then sold D the third parcel for $60,000, because it was worth less than the other two. A took $15,000 down and a mortgage for $45,000, payable $500 per month, from D. Therefore, D was committed to paying A $500 a month, and A had to add another $500 to it to make the $1,000-a-month mortgage payments.

By this time A had received $175,000 from B, C and D, and had paid the lender only $90,000. So A was $85,000 ahead. A then either got in financial trouble and could not make the $1,000-per-month payments or simply walked away, leaving D holding the bag for the $1,000-per-month payments. D was greatly distressed when foreclosure was started on her land because she then had to come up with $1,000 per month to save the land.

How could this unfortunate situation have been avoided. When D bought her parcel for $60,000, giving back A a mortgage for $45,000, D should have found out that A still had a mortgage against the property for $30,000. D would have known this from a title report or abstract. D then should have demanded a full disclosure from A as to the existing mortgage. After discovering that the existing mortgage had payments of $1,000, D either should not have gone ahead with the deal or should have had A renegotiate the terms of the loan so that D's payments covered it.

Another way D could have dealt with this: D could have made A open a special collection account in the local bank and put in enough money to cover the extra $500-per-month loan payments for the balance of A's loan. The money would be placed in an account where A could not withdraw it. Thus, as long as D made the $500-per-month payments on time, D would be sure the other $500 was available to make the seller's $1,000-per-month mortgage payments. The bank with this type of account makes the payments directly to the mortgage holder, so no money goes through the hands of A.

On the other hand, if you *assume* a loan, you replace the seller and become personally liable to the seller's creditor for the remaining debt. You pay your seller a sum of money in cash and get the property, with the remaining obligation on the loan. You are then primarily responsible for paying the loan. If you fail to make your payments, the creditor can foreclose on your loan. If the creditor seeks a deficiency judgment, he or she can also sue *your seller*, unless the creditor signs a document relieving your seller of liability under the loan, once you assume it.

Most commercial loan agreements have a clause that prohibits transferring the debt without the written approval of the lender. If you are to assume a loan, be certain that the seller has his or her creditor's approval to transfer the property to you. Often a creditor will only allow the debtor to transfer the obligation if you qualify as a borrower and if the interest rate can be raised. If it will be raised before you are to assume the loan, shop around to see if you can get a new loan on better terms from someone else. If you can, borrow the money and pay for the land in cash, then give a mortgage to your lender under the terms you have received. If you cannot get a better deal than the loan you are to assume and you still want to purchase the land, try to get the seller to reduce the asking price by the amount of the increased interest you will be bound to pay.

## The Wraparound or All-Inclusive Mortgage

It is always better to *assume* a loan than to take *subject to* it. Sellers who will allow buyers to take title to land only if they take subject to the sellers loans rather than by assuming them may be planning to charge buyers a higher interest rate in their loan agreements than they are paying their lenders, so they can make a profit on the extra interest. This type of *secondary loan agreement* is taken subject to a seller's loan and is called a *wraparound* or *all-inclusive* loan agreement because the buyers mortgages with their sellers "wrap around," or include, the loan agreements sellers have with their lenders. In such a situation find out what the seller's interest rate is and whether she or he intends to overcharge you if you buy subject to her or his loan. Do not let the seller get away with this. Even if the seller's increased interest rate is no larger than you would get under a new loan agreement, you are always better off assuming a loan than taking subject to it, because you can deal directly with the creditor.

Wraparound mortgages are becoming more frequent so you should be sure you understand how they work. The illustration that follows shows how the mechanics operate.

Seller takes back a $40,000 mortgage from buyer, at 12 percent interest, payable $450/month, which wraps around the seller's existing mortgage.

Owes $20,000 to first mortgage holder *A* at 9 percent interest, payable $200/month.

Seller

Owes $10,000 to second mortgage holder *B* at 10 percent interest, payable $180/month.

Therefore, the buyer pays the seller 12 percent on a $40,000 mortgage, which wraps around the seller's preexisting mortgages at 9 percent and 10 percent. The seller thus makes extra money by charging the buyer 12 percent to pay the seller's loans at 9 percent and 10 percent. The buyer would be better off to simply assume the existing loans of $20,000 at 9 percent and $10,000 at 10 percent and give the seller back a third mortgage for $10,000 at 12 percent. Then the buyer is paying 12 percent on only a $10,000 mortgage, rather than on a $40,000 mortgage.

If the seller insists on a wraparound or all-inclusive mortgage, then be sure that you and the seller open a special collection account at the local bank, whereby the bank takes your payment of $450 every month and pays the $200 first mortgage and $180 second mortgage automatically before any money goes to the seller. It then pays the $70 due the seller under his third mortgage.

This way, you know that as long as you make your monthly payment, the mortgage holders will be paid. Never rely on the seller to make these payments. If the seller is lax in making them and foreclosure starts, you will have problems. Always open a special collection account in the local bank or savings and loan. The charge for this is minimal, usually a few dollars per month. The extra protection and security are well worth it.

If you do take title subject to a loan agreement, be sure the seller has permission from his or her lender to sell the property. Many loan agreements contain an *acceleration*, or *due-on-sale, clause,* which is activated if the borrower sells or encumbers the land without permission. If the land is sold to you without the lender's permission, the lender can demand immediate payment of the entire remaining principal and interest. If your seller cannot pay this amount, the loan can be foreclosed on, and you could lose the land. Under these provisions, the only way a seller can convey land is by paying the remaining money due before the sale. The due-on-sale provision is always contained in the note and deed of trust or mortgage.

The contract of sale should specify if you are to take title subject to or by assuming an existing loan. Either way, you should receive an offset statement or beneficiary statement from the creditor specifying the amount of interest and principal remaining on the loan, the amount of each payment and how much longer payments must be made. This is important. Never assume a loan without getting written confirmation from the lender as to the balance due on the loan. If you are assuming a loan held by a commercial lender, a fee will be charged for the necessary paperwork to transfer the documents.

## Prorating the Loan Agreement If You Assume the Obligation

If you assume the responsibility of paying off the seller's loan on the property, you will have to prorate the seller's payment during the month that escrow closes. For instance, say escrow is to close on the thirteenth day of the month, and payments are made on the first. If the monthly payments you are to assume are $450, including principal and interest, divide this figure by 30, the commonly accepted number of days in a month, to get the amount of the payment due per day, in this case $15. Multiply the $15 owed per day by the 17 days that you will own the land that month. You will credit the seller with this amount, in this case $255, because he paid the entire month's payment on the first of the month. To see how this fits into the pattern of closing of escrow, see Chapter 29, "Opening and Closing of Escrow and the Role of the Escrow Holder."

## Getting the Seller To Remove the Lien at the Time of Purchase

If you want title to the property free of an existing loan agreement, clause 6 of the Model Contract of Sale (Chapter 27) takes care of this. When you place your money in escrow, instruct the escrow holder to pay the lender the money due and request that a certificate of satisfaction or deed of reconveyance be recorded, clearing the mortgage lien from the title to the property.

## Assignment of the Loan Agreement

During the time you are making payments, your creditor might *assign* his or her rights to receive your payments to a third party in exchange for cash. Some commercial businesses buy loan agreement notes for an amount of cash that is less than the amount due on the loan. A person who needs money might be willing to sell his or her note at a loss for immediate cash. This frequently occurs with sellers who finance their own sales.

When an assignment occurs, a document is executed between your creditor and the person who has bought your note, which is recorded with the county recorder. When the recording takes place, you will be notified and bound to make all further payments to the new holder of the note. You might be required to sign a document, called an *owner's estoppel certificate* or *debtor's statement*, that certifies the amount of money you still owe on the loan and states that you are personally bound to pay the remaining amount. This document is executed to protect the person who is buying the right to receive your payments.

If you want to be able to sell your land before paying off your loan, you will also want the right to assign your obligation to your buyer. Your mortgage or trust deed and note will usually automatically be assignable, unless stated otherwise. Be sure to ask about this when you are in escrow.

## Paying the Insurance, Taxes and Assessments on the Land— Impounds

The basic security for a loan is the property, so your creditor wants to be certain that nothing happens to endanger his or her security. Therefore, your lender may require that you pay the money for insurance, taxes and assessments in advance, and he or she can then pay them as they become due. These additions to your normal payments are called *impounds*. Generally, in each payment you will be charged a portion of the annual insurance premiums and taxes for that year. The insurance premium and taxes are divided into 12 equal monthly installments, if that is how you pay your mortgage or deed of trust. Commercial lenders always require advance impound payments for the property taxes and insurance.

If the seller, rather than a financial institution, is your creditor, you may be responsible for paying these expenses yourself. But the tax collector will be instructed to notify the seller of any lapses in tax payments so that he or she can have a chance to pay them before the land is subjected to a tax sale. If you fail to pay the taxes or premiums, the creditor can legally foreclose on you.

If there is a house on the land, your creditor will probably require you to carry a basic policy of property insurance protecting the property against fire and other hazards. You will have to name the lender as a beneficiary in the policy and deliver a copy of the insurance coverage to him or her. If the house burns, you will negotiate with the lender as to whether the insurance will be used to rebuild the house or cover your debt to the lender. The loan agreement will specify the amount of insurance coverage you must buy. These impounds may increase your monthly payments by $100 or more per month over the principal and interest due.

## Recording a Request for Notice of Default

When a seller sells a parcel to you and you assume an existing mortgage and give a new mortgage to the seller, the seller wants to be sure of receiving notice if you fail to make your payments to the first mortgage holder. If the first mortgage holder starts to foreclose on you and the seller doesn't know it and if the foreclosure goes through and you lose the land, your mortgage to the seller is wiped out. Therefore, the seller will always want to record a request for notice of default. This ensures that if you start to get foreclosed, the seller will know about it. The seller will then make the payments to the first mortgage holder and start to foreclose on you. To stop the foreclosure, you will have to reimburse the seller for any payments he or she made to the first mortgage holder. The next chapter tells you more about the process of foreclosure.

# CHAPTER
# 24 Default, Foreclosure and Redemption

## Default

When you purchase your property and give a mortgage or deed of trust back to the seller or lender, you have certain obligations to meet during the term of the loan. You must keep the payments current on all your mortgages; you must keep the property taxes and fire insurance current; and you must not "commit waste," that is, damage the property or cause it to deteriorate, causing a lessening of the value of the property as security. For example, you will not be permitted to carry out a large-scale logging operation on forest land before the loan is substantially or totally paid off.

If you fail to meet any of your obligations outlined above, then you are in *default* on your loan, and the lender or seller can immediately start to foreclose on you. This is usually started by the lender's (or seller's) recording a *notice of default* and sending it to you and all other persons who

have an interest in the property, such as other mortgage holders, at the address specified in your security agreement. Be sure the lender or seller always has your current address. If you are not the current mortgage holder but you want to know if foreclosure proceedings start, you will want to record a *request for notice of default* with the county recorder. You can find out about this document through an attorney or a title or escrow company.

## Foreclosure

Once the default has occurred and foreclosure has begun, you will lose your land if you don't redeem your loan or cure the default.

Most states require a court or judicial foreclosure, which means that a notice of default must first be filed with the county recorder and a copy mailed to those interested in the property, stating that the buyer has not made the required payments or paid the taxes or is otherwise in default. The buyer is then given from one to three months to make up the missed payments or otherwise cure the default. If the payments are not made, the creditor can file a petition to foreclose in the county court. The court evaluates the creditor's claim, determines its validity, declares the amount of money due, and orders a foreclosure.

Then the creditor usually publishes a notice in a local newspaper that the property is to be sold to the highest bidder at a public auction. The sale is supervised by the court and often handled by a court-appointed commissioner. The proceeds from the sale are used to pay the creditor any money due on the land sale. If any surplus money remains, it goes to the defaulting buyer. This may not be a bad deal for the buyer if the land sells for a good price, but usually the lender bids in his or her note and simply takes the property back. It is rare that any money is left over for the defaulting owner.

Under other policies, such as *foreclosure without sale, strict foreclosure* or *foreclosure by entry and possession,* the creditor takes the entire property and can do with it as he or she wishes.

When executing a loan agreement, you should understand the type of foreclosure the creditor can use if you default. These vary, depending on the type of transaction involved. For example, if you are buying under a land contract, the seller can't simply come onto the property and retake it without any court proceedings. If you are buying with a mortgage, it might take as long as four or five months for the seller to foreclose. Ask your title company or attorney about the proceedings in your case.

## The Dangerous Acceleration Clause

A clause that creditors usually put into the loan agreement states that the creditor can immediately demand, or accelerate, the entire amount of the remaining principal and interest if you miss a payment. You cannot prevent foreclosure simply by making up back payments. The entire amount due must be paid. Although this is a standard clause in most loan agreements, you should try to have a grace period put in a loan with a late-payment penalty, just in case you get behind in payment. Even though the note has an acceleration clause, foreclosures are subject to state law. State laws often require a redemption period. Ask your title

company, escrow company, bank or lawyer if laws in your state allow for a redemption period.

## Curing the Default and the Right of Redemption

Most states have laws that allow a debtor a certain period of time after foreclosure proceedings have begun to make up payments, cure the default and keep the land. This grace period is referred to as the *right of redemption* or *equity of redemption.* To redeem after a foreclosure is begun, the owner must make up all back payments due plus penalties plus interest; pay all property taxes to bring them current; pay all insurance premiums; pay the costs of foreclosure, which are often between $500 and $1,500; and pay all legal fees incurred by the lender. There is a period of time after foreclosure commences when the payment of all of the above can stop a foreclosure. But after a certain time, according to state law, the foreclosure can be stopped only by the owner paying off the entire amount due on the loan, not just the back payments.

In some states the redemption period extends until the time of the sale by foreclosure, which might be anywhere from two months to a year after the buyer defaults. If you make up defaults and pay the penalties, no further action can be taken against you by the creditor, and the foreclosure is stopped. If you do not make up your payments by the time the foreclosure sale is initiated, you have little chance of keeping the land.

Some states allow a right of redemption even after sale or repossession of the land by foreclosure. When the land is sold at a foreclosure sale, the new buyer does not take full title to it but gets an *equitable right to the title* during the period of redemption. The new buyer will get full legal title only if the debtor does not make up the payments by the end of the redemption period. During this time, the debtor still retains the right of possession of the land.

## The Deficiency Judgment

Sometimes the lender has a right to sue the borrower to get a deficiency judgment if an insufficient amount of money is obtained from a foreclosure sale to make up the amount of money due. However, most states and courts will not permit a deficiency judgment when the loan was made for the purchase of a home or land. Such a loan is called a *purchase money mortgage*. Because the loan was made on the basis of the value of the security, the creditor cannot complain if it later turns out that the property is worth less than the loan. If enough money is not obtained at a resale of the land, the court assumes that the buyer probably paid too much for it in the first place and should not have to suffer further because of that circumstance.

For instance, the seller sells you land for $60,000, you pay off $10,000 worth of principal and then default. You still owe $50,000. The seller forecloses the loan and resells the land for only $40,000. In most states, the seller cannot obtain a deficiency judgment against you for the remaining $10,000.

## Advantages of a Partial Reconveyance or Partial Release Clause

If you purchase a large parcel of property or two or more adjacent parcels, you can have a clause in-serted that calls for a partial release of land with clear title after you make a specified number of payments. You can use the released portion of land as security for a new loan to finance construction of a house or meet other financial needs. You will have clear title to part of the land, so if you find it necessary, you may be able to sell the portion not encumbered by liens to finance the remaining portion.

For example, if you purchase two 20-acre parcels and give the seller one mortgage secured by both parcels, and if you make a down payment of 30 percent of the purchase price at the close of escrow, you can have a release clause in the note stating that after you have paid off 35 percent of the remaining principal you can have one of the parcels released from the mortgage lien, that is, reconveyed to you. That way you will have one of the 20-acre parcels free and clear of any liens so you can sell it or borrow against it.

# CHAPTER
# 25 Borrowing from Third-Party Lenders

Most commercial lenders will not loan money on remote improved or unimproved rural land because they consider remote country property to be a speculative security. Values on such land are not easily determinable since fluctuations in the supply and demand are great. Whereas a lot in a town or city with an $80,000 house on it is apt to sell quickly at a predictable price if a foreclosure becomes necessary, it is much harder to sell 20 acres of land 100 miles from the nearest big city, especially if the land has no structures, commercial electricity, running water or paved access.

If you are interested in rural land that has a house and basic amenities and is located in a developed rural area, your chances of getting a loan are improved because the lender's risk is reduced. If your country property is to be a second home and you have a mortgage on your first home, a commercial lender assumes that if you ever get into financial difficulty, you will default on your country property before you default on your regular home. When second-home loans are made, the lender often prefers to insure his loan by taking a first or

second mortgage on the borrower's city house. These mortgages are called *homeowner's loans* or *home equity loans*, and many lending agencies, particularly mortgage specialists, offer them. Nearly 65 percent of the householders in the United States own the houses they occupy, so homeowner loans are becoming a major method of financing. The loan is based on the amount of equity the owner has in the house. Equity is calculated as the difference between the current fair market value of the house and the remaining balance owed on the mortgage, if there is one. For example, if your house and lot is appraised by the lender at $180,000 and you still owe $60,000 on the existing mortgage, you have an equity of $120,000, and the amount of money you can borrow for a second home is based on this amount. Interest rates are usually higher on homeowner loans than on conventional first mortgages. The interest, however, is deductible on your taxes.

If you are buying a working farm, the commercial lender wants assurance that the income to be derived from it is enough to pay your family and business expenses, as well as your loan. As with most country land, productive farm property is usually financed by the seller.

When a commercial lender does give a loan for purchase of country property, the terms are stricter than usual. The standard loan rule is the greater the risk to the lender, the higher will be the interest rate, the shorter the maturity date and the lower the ratio of loan to value. The ratio of loan to value is the percentage of the appraised value of the property that will be given as a loan. For instance, if the appraised value of a parcel is $80,000 and the loan-to-value ratio is 75 percent, you can get a maximum loan of $60,000. You generally get a lower loan-to-value ratio for rural property than for urban property, because if the lender has to foreclose on you and sell the property to recoup the loan, it is generally more difficult to do this in rural areas than in urban areas. In urban areas, loan-to-value ratios may be as high as 90 percent.

When seeking a loan, go to as many different sources as possible and try to get the best terms you can. Because lending agencies located near the land you intend to buy will probably be familiar with the land and the local conditions, go to them first, unless you have established credit with, and are trusted by, an institution in your city.

Speak to the real estate agent handling the sale to see if she or he can offer some leads. Agents often have close ties with local banks and other lenders and can help you get a loan. But be cautious. Lenders often offer kickbacks or commissions to agents who bring them business, and these are ultimately and indirectly charged to the borrower through the loan fees. This problem is so rampant in the lending industry that the federal government submitted a proposal to Congress several years ago to deny FHA approval to any lender engaged in such practices. See what the agent can do for you, then try to find a loan on better terms. You always have the absolute discretion to choose your own lender, so never give in to pressure from the agent. Go through only the lender who gives you the best deal, but get an accounting of the loan fees first. (See "The Discount rate or Points Charge," later in this chapter.)

Your chances of obtaining a loan depend to a great extent on whether money is "tight" or "easy" at the time you are making your purchase. Lending agencies constantly change their loan policies, depending on the national and local economic situation and on the changes in the real estate market. Every lending agency has its own policies. For ex-

ample, many lenders prefer loans underwritten by the government and prefer to loan money for home purchases. It is never easy to get financing on rural property, except from the seller, but a commercial lender who thinks your credit is very good might place more emphasis on this aspect than on the property value, and lend you some money. This chapter tells you what is available on the loan market. Never assume you cannot get a loan before you try, particularly if the property has a house on it and your credit is good.

Each year the number of second-home buyers continues to increase. With this increasing demand for country property, there is every reason to believe that lending policies will continue to become more liberal with regard to the purchase of rural land.

## Your Financial History and Credit Rating

When you apply for a loan, you will be asked to fill out an application in which you are to give complete details of your financial condition and credit history, and you will be requested to produce documents relating to this information. Although the maximum amount of your loan will never be as much as the appraised value of the property, the lender is always concerned about your ability to repay the loan. Foreclosures are an expensive and time-consuming procedure. It is much easier for a creditor to work out feasible monthly payments than to go through an expensive foreclosure and the process of advertising and selling the property to have the loan repaid. Commercial lenders do not want to foreclose on a borrower. They want the borrower to make the mortgage payments because they make their profits on the interest they collect.

When answering questions, be as truthful as possible. The computerization of bank and credit accounts is becoming so thorough that any dishonest answers are likely to be uncovered when the lending institution does its independent investigation. If you have had some problems in the past repaying debts, you should explain this to the loan officer handling your case, rather than misstate the facts and have the lender discover the truth in some other manner.

Answers to eight major questions are required by all major lending institutions:

1. *How much cash and how many liquid assets do you own?* Liquid assets are things that can easily be converted to a known amount of cash, such as bonds and stocks, as opposed to real estate, which is a nonliquid asset. The lender will combine separate bank accounts of a married couple. He or she will request a copy of your bank balance, savings account balance, and an accounting of your stocks and bonds. You will also have to produce current and past state and federal income tax returns.

2. *What type of employment do you and your spouse have and what is your current income?*

3. *How many current debts do you have?* All current debts in your family will be considered, as well as possible future debts, such as schooling and common necessities. The lender will determine whether you have too many debts for the size of your income, which would prevent you from paying further debts. A common formula is used to determine the borrower's ability to repay a loan for the purpose of buying land: The borrower's combined total monthly income minus the payments due on other loans must be at least 4 to 4½ times greater than the amount of the monthly payments that will be required on principal, interest, taxes, assessments and insurance premiums.

4. *What type of credit history do you have?* This involves an investigation of your entire past with regard to loans and buying on credit. The lender will be looking to see whether you have always paid your bills on time, whether you borrow constantly for everything you buy, how many different persons you owe money to, whether you have ever declared bankruptcy, how often you move, whether you change jobs often and how long you have had your present job.

5. *What is your past banking experience?* Here you will be asked to list your bank(s). They will be contacted for information regarding the size of your accounts, the length of time you have been banking with them, the average amount of money you have on hand and any other information they can supply.

6. *Do you have adequate personal and credit references?* You will be required to bring in letters from creditors and acquaintances regarding your reliability and integrity. The amount of stress placed on these letters varies from lender to lender.

7. *How old are you and your spouse?* Age is often a relevant factor, because your earning potential usually declines as you get older. A common formula used in lending institutions is the *rule of seventy*, which states that the length of time you will be given to pay back the loan must not extend beyond the date when you will reach the age of 70. Thus, if you are 45 years old at the time you apply for a loan, the maximum time you will be permitted to repay the money is 25 years.

8. *How much do you want to borrow?* You will be asked to state the amount of money you wish to borrow and the repayment schedule you desire.

## The Fair Credit Reporting Act

In investigating your credit history, prospective lenders often use the services of a consumer reporting agency. This agency will issue a consumer report or investigative consumer report showing how you pay your bills; if you have ever been sued, arrested or declared bankrupt; what your neighbors' and employers' opinions are of your character, general reputation and manner of living; and any other information relating to your reliability as a borrower.

Sometimes an agency will give obsolete or inaccurate information that prevents you from obtaining a loan. Under the Federal Fair Credit Reporting Act of 1971, you can discover the type of information being distributed about you and your activities.

You have the right to be told the name and address of the agency that prepared the report that led to the denial of credit. Within 30 days of the denial of credit, you can approach the agency and discover the nature and sources of its information without paying a fee. You can request a reinvestigation of incomplete or incorrect information and have the revised information sent to your prospective lender. If you desire, you may include in your file your own version of any dispute with the agency and have it included in any future consumer reports. An agency is not permitted to report adverse information more than seven years after the occurrence unless it is a bankruptcy, which may be reported up to ten years later.

If you want more information about your rights under the Fair Credit Reporting Act, contact the

Federal Trade Commission, which oversees enforcement of the Fair Credit Reporting Act.

## Appraisal of the Property

Lending institutions often employ their own property appraisers to evaluate the fair price of houses and land to be used as security for a loan. These appraisers use the same criteria as other property appraisers (see Chapters 19 and 20): the location of the neighborhood, the size of the property, the physical soundness of the structures, the desirability of the architectural design, the sale prices of similar property in the area. However, they base their evaluation on the probable market value of the property during the entire life of the loan rather than on its value at the time you buy it because a foreclosure may have to be made at any time during the loan repayment schedule. Inflation and depreciation in the value of the structures during this period are also taken into consideration.

Usually within 60 days of filing a loan application, the lending agency will appraise the property, review your financial and credit history, and notify you as to whether it will grant your loan. Although you rarely will be able to see the results of the appraisal, if your application is rejected, the company probably feels the asking price is too high.

## The Letter of Commitment

If your application is accepted, the lender will issue you a letter of commitment detailing the terms of the loan and stating that the money will be delivered at a specific lime based on certain conditions that you must meet, such as getting title cleared and having a survey completed and approved. Be sure to get this commitment in writing because lenders sometimes refuse to grant the loan at the last minute, making it impossible for the prospective borrower to go ahead with the purchase.

Sometimes a commitment fee of 0.5 to 2 percent of the amount to be borrowed is required, which is usually refunded when you get the loan. Be sure to have a refund clause included in your letter of commitment that provides that your money will be returned in case you do not purchase the land or close the loan.

## The Finance Condition in the Contract of Sale

The Model Contract of Sale (Chapter 27) conditions the closing of escrow on your ability to obtain a loan under the terms you desire. (See clause 17[e].) This is an essential contingency when your ability to make the purchase is dependent on your obtaining a loan. Without this condition, if you sign the contract and then are unable to get a loan, you will lose your deposit or earnest money. Read the accompanying explanation of clause 17(e) in the Model Contract of Sale and use the information in Part V, "Financing Your Purchase," to fill in the blanks in the financing clause.

## Disclosure Statement under the Truth in Lending Law

The Truth in Lending Law requires that the lender supply you with a disclosure statement specifying the total amount of interest you will pay on the loan, the annual percentage rate (APR), the percentages of each payment going to interest and to principal, the amount of each payment, when payments are to be made, the number of payments to be made, the date of the last payment, the amount of any balloon payment and all loan fees and other extra costs. You will sign this disclosure statement as proof that you saw it and approved of its contents. The signed document is the lending agency's proof that it did not violate the law should a problem arise at a later date. Study the statement carefully before signing to be sure it contains all the terms you have agreed to.

## Private Mortgage Insurance

Most lending institutions today will lend the buyer only between 65 percent and 80 percent of the appraised value of the property. Because you must come up with the rest of the purchase price as well as all of the closing costs, on a land purchase of $80,000 you might have to supply from $16,000 to $52,000 in cash.

An innovation in the lending business allows lenders to obtain private mortgage insurance, which enables them to lend the borrower up to 95 percent of the purchase price. The mortgage insurance policy insures the lender for a certain portion of the mortgage loan, usually that amount above the normal loan amount. This is called "assuming the top of the risk."

The oldest and largest company offering this insurance is the Mortgage Guarantee Insurance Corporation, referred to as MGIC, or "Magic." Its insured funds are mostly available through savings and loan associations, savings banks and mortgage companies. Under the MGIC plan, you can borrow 90 percent of the purchase price, up to a maximum of $54,000.

Before MGIC insures the lender, it evaluates your credit and appraises the property, based on the documents you and the lender supply. You must pay the insurance company a fee of $50 to $100 for processing the application.

You must also pay a premium for the insurance policy, part of which is due at the closing of the loan (when you receive the money), with the rest to be paid in installments during the payment period of the loan. If you borrow 90 percent of the purchase price of the property, your annual MGIC premium will probably be 0.5 to 1 percent of the unpaid balance of the loan during the first year, and 0.25 percent of the balance remaining each year thereafter. You can also pay the entire premium at the closing of the loan, in which case it is usually 3 percent of the amount borrowed.

Although the interest rates are slightly higher than on uninsured loans, a MGIC loan might be the only way you can get enough money to make your purchase. Discuss the possibilities of obtaining mortgage insurance with the prospective lender if you need more money than it is willing to lend.

## Various Lenders

The "primary loan market" includes institutional and noninstitutional lenders. The four primary institutional lenders of residential loans for privately owned one-family to four-family homes are savings and loan associations, commercial banks, mutual savings banks and life insurance companies.

The noninstitutional lenders include mortgage companies, private individuals, and nonfinancial organizations. These lenders offer *conventional financing* by lending money directly to the borrower on a long-term basis and holding the land for security until the debt is discharged.

If you qualify, you can turn a conventional loan into a Department of Veterans Affairs (VA) Guaranteed Loan or a Federal Housing Administration (FHA) Insured Loan. (See Chapter 26.)

The Federal Land Bank System and the Farmers Home Administration (FmHA) are unique loan sources for rural property owners. (See Chapter 26.)

### Savings and Loan Associations

The largest home lenders in the United States are the federal and state savings and loan associations, which were established to promote the investing of money and the sound, economical financing of homes. The federally chartered associations are governed by the Federal Home Loan Bank Board, and the state-licensed associations are regulated by the savings and loan commissioner of the state.

Like most economical lenders, savings and loan associations believe that unimproved land is not a good form of security. Loans are not usually given on active farms and are only occasionally given on unimproved land. Unless a house already exists on the land you are planning to buy, it is not likely that a savings and loan association will lend more than 10 percent of the appraised value, if that much.

However, savings and loan associations are generally more amenable than other institutional lenders to financing second homes within 100 miles of a lending office, particularly with a VA or FHA loan. Because of the growing demand for second homes, this requirement is likely to be liberalized in the near future.

Loans for owner-occupied single-family dwellings average 70 percent of the appraised value of the house. The maximum loan permitted depends on the amount borrowed, with a maximum amortization period of 30 years. The opinions of two appraisers are required. Much importance is placed on the geographic location and age of the home.

Although the interest rate varies in different areas and at different times, it is generally higher than the interest rate on loans given by insurance companies and banks. However, savings and loan associations are generally more liberal in their lending policies. They will usually lend a higher percentage of the appraised value of the property than these other institutions will, and they will lend to persons having fairly small incomes. In recent years, interest rates have risen from 6.5 percent to 18 percent, and then dropped back to 8 percent.

Where they will be in the next ten years is pure speculation.

Loan fees of savings and loan associations are higher than those normally charged by other lenders, ranging from 1 percent to 10 percent or more of the full amount of the loan. In addition, a prepayment penalty of three to six months' interest is usually charged if more than 20 percent of the loan is repaid before maturity.

### Commercial Banks

Banks are general-purpose lenders, regulated by federal law and organized under federal and state charters. Loans by both federal and state banks are fairly similar. During the Great Depression of the 1930s, commercial banks were hit hardest because they had invested heavily in real estate, a nonliquid asset that cannot be quickly turned into cash to meet withdrawal demands. This experience left a bad taste in the mouths of bank presidents; therefore, home loans are low on their priority list of investments.

The most common type of bank loan is for the purpose of building a home. Loans for the purpose of buying land are given only for improved land or for unimproved land that is to be improved after the loan is granted. State banks are more amenable to lending for unimproved property than federal banks. Most banks will lend approximately 50 percent of the appraised value of a second home amortized for 10 to 20 years. Commercial banks are the most common financial institution outside urban areas, so they are the major source of loan funds in rural areas.

Although some banks will not make FHA and VA loans, most will do so at higher ratio of loan to appraised value for a longer maturity period than is given on a conventional loan.

### Mutual Savings Banks

Mutual savings banks are located predominantly in the Atlantic and New England states, where they replace the savings and loan associations. Their policies are similar to those of the latter, and they invest most of their assets in mortgages, with a heavy preference for government-underwritten loans.

### Life Insurance Companies

Approximately 30 percent of the assets of life insurance companies are invested in home mortgages. Many insurance companies will make only loans that are insured by the FHA or guaranteed by the VA.

The amount and terms of life insurance company loans are regulated by each state. Loans are usually restricted to an amount not more than two-and-a-half times the borrower's annual income with monthly payments lower than 20 percent to 25 percent of the borrower's monthly take-home pay. The normal loan has a maximum maturity of 25 years and a maximum of 75 percent of the appraised value of the house and land. Although financing is fairly liberal on farm property, insurance companies' appraisal policies tend to be conservative. Getting a loan on an old house is difficult, unless it is in exceptionally good condition. Life insurance companies' interest rates tend to be lower than those of other financial institutions, but this is highly variable.

Most life insurance companies require the borrower to purchase a life insurance policy insuring full payment of the loan if the borrower dies during the amortization period.

Life insurance companies lend money at lower interest rates if the borrower has a life insurance policy with the company. As you pay insurance premiums you build up cash value in the policy, which can be borrowed in the form of cash from the company. You will still need to be covered by your policy during the period of the loan if you do this. Find out the specifics from your insurance company on how you can use your life insurance policy to borrow money for the purchase of property.

### Mortgage Companies, Mortgage Banks and Mortgage Brokers

Mortgage companies and mortgage banks are considered to be noninstitutional sources of mortgage funds, and together with other noninstitutional lenders, they supply 25 percent of the loans for all property in the United States. Mortgage companies are regulated by each state and are generally much more liberal than other lending institutions.

In reality, mortgage companies are temporary lenders, in that they give loans and then sell the notes to insurance companies, commercial banks, savings and loan associations, other institutions and private individuals. After selling the notes, they continue to serve the note buyer by collecting the payments, paying the taxes, watching over the property, keeping it insured, and foreclosing when necessary. They charge the buyer of the note a fee of 0.5 percent of the outstanding loan balance for their services.

The mortgage companies prefer government-underwritten loans and generally restrict their loans to low-risk single-family dwellings in the low price range.

Mortgage brokers find investment for potential lenders and are paid a finder's fee, or brokerage fee, for this service. Often real estate agents are also involved in the loan brokerage business. Loan brokers can often obtain loans on types of rural land that nobody else will loan on and they always charge higher interest rates than commercial lenders charge. You can expect to pay interest rates of 12 percent to 20 percent on private loans. They usually find private lenders to make these loans, promising them fantastic returns on their investment. In fact, these loans are usually highly speculative and risky for the lenders. I have had cases where borrowers refinanced their rural property at high interest rates, borrowed on the basis of overinflated appraisals, took the loan funds and walked, abandoning the property to the poor lender-investor who had never even seen the property he or she loaned on through the mortgage broker. In general, this is an expensive way to borrow money.

### Borrowing from Individuals

The most common source of private loans is relatives and close friends. If they trust you to repay the loan, taking a mortgage is one of the best investments they can make, because the interest rate is higher than they can get by placing their money in a bank or savings and loan association. In fact, they can charge up to the maximum allowed by the state's usury laws, commonly 10 percent per year. (Banks, savings and loans and credit card companies are exempt from state usury laws.) Obtaining a high-interest loan from a relative might be the only way you can purchase a country home. Many states exempt loans for property purchase from the usury laws, so there is no limit on the amount of interest that can be charged.

Your relative-lender can take back a mortgage or deed of trust. If you make this type of arrangement, be certain that all the terms of the agreement are written in a legally binding contract between yourselves. Never agree to anything by a friendly handshake alone. If you deal with your relatives or friends, you should have an attorney do all the paperwork in a proper legal manner so that everyone has the usual protections. The best way to keep relatives and friends happy is to conduct your affairs in a businesslike manner.

### Credit Unions

Credit unions have recently begun to take a greater role in lending for housing purposes. Approximately 10 percent of the country's 18,000 credit unions now offer mortgages. You have to become a member of a credit union to borrow money from it, but because the credit union is a nonprofit organization, it can loan at lower rates, including lower down payments and fewer loan fees. If you have a credit union available through your place of employment, check out the possibilities of refinancing or borrowing.

### Other Nonfinancial Institutional Lenders

Title companies, REALTORS® and brokers lend money under certain circumstances. These institutional lenders are not regulated and can establish any terms they desire, unless they take an FHA or VA loan. Usually they do not have as rigid credit investigations as do institutional lenders, and often they conduct their own appraisals of property. They are often a good source for second mortgage loans.

### Loans from the Federal Land Bank System (Farm Credit System)

Although the federal land banks were originally funded for farmers, as of 1981 nonfarmers may borrow from the land bank for the purpose of buying, building, remodeling or refinancing a year-round, single-family, moderately priced home in the countryside. A rural resident can have only one loan outstanding, and the loan cannot be made if the owner intends to resell or rent the home.

Farmers, ranchers, nursery owners, timbermen and commercial fishermen, defined as persons engaged in the production of agricultural products on a full- or part-time basis, can borrow funds for the purchase of farms, farmland, and farm improvements.

In 1916, Congress passed the Federal Farm Credit Act, establishing the federal land banks and the National Farm Loan Association to provide long-term credit for farmers. In 1933 the Farm Credit Administration was created as an independent agency of the executive branch of the federal government to supervise the farm credit system, charged with making loans to farmers and prospective farmers through 12 federal land banks within the 12 farm credit districts set up around the country. These federal land banks have nearly 500 local federal land-bank association offices scattered throughout the United States, and these offices supply 23.5 percent of the loans on farm property.

Each land-bank association is owned cooperatively by the borrowers, who must be members to obtain a loan. When you become a land-bank borrower, 5 percent to 10 percent of the amount you borrow must be used to purchase shares in the association; the amount depends on the size of your loan. Stock purchase requirements are necessary to capitalize the associations and ensure investor confidence in the securities issued to raise loan funds. Sales of this stock and of federal land loan bonds are the source of the money for land-bank loans. Bonds are sold to private and commercial investors just like other securities. Like other banks, income from interest is exempt from state taxes, although subject to federal income taxes. As of 1983, the sales of all securities have been handled by one office, the Farm Credit Corporation of America. Like other investors, you will get dividends on the shares you purchased when you obtained your loan.

You can borrow money to purchase land or to make improvements on land you already own. Loans are made for up to 85 percent of the appraised value of the real estate security. But 97 percent financing is available if guaranteed by a state or federal agency. (See Chapter 26, "HUD/FHA-Insured and VA-Insured Loans.")

The loan must be secured by a first lien on the property. The amortization period can extend from 5 to 40 years, and payments can be made annually, semiannually, quarterly or monthly. There is no prepayment penalty. In fact, the land bank pays interest on money it receives in advance, and early payments can be put into a future payment fund to meet later installments if you run into trouble making payments later.

Interest rates on most federal land-bank loans are variable, being adjusted regularly to reflect the cost of funds. In certain regions of the country, fixed rates are available on certain types of loans.

If you are purchasing forest land rather than farmland, you can obtain a federal land-bail forest-land loan, which is based on the value of the marketable timber on the land. Check into the requirements for *marketable timber* in your area. Usually a tree must be 12 inches or more in diameter. Although you must be engaged in timber growing, you do not have to cut the timber to get the loan. The land bank simply wants to be sure that it can cut the timber to get their money back, should it have to foreclose. Forest-land loans are usually not made on

raw timberland, so some building, such as a house, must be on the property. This is an excellent way to finance a vacation home in the woods. You can borrow up to 65 percent of the appraised normal value of the timber and land, and the repayment schedules are the same as those on form loans.

To apply for a loan, go to the local federal land-bank association serving the area in which the property is located. Fill out all applications regarding your financial status and the purposes of the loan. The property is then appraised for its security value, and your credit worthiness is checked. When the loan is approved, a title search is done on the property, and if it is acceptable, the loan is closed.

Don't assume you will not qualify. Currently, 90 percent of all land-bank loans are made to individuals, and of that group, 98 percent have a net worth of less than $100,000.

To determine if there is a federal land-bank association in the area where you want to buy land, look in the phone book under "Federal Land-Bank Association."

## The Discount Rate or Points Charge

Commercial lenders, which includes everyone except private lenders, have developed a tricky thing called a *discount rate*, or *points charge*, to confuse the borrower, beat the legal interest rate ceilings and make more on their money.

Every state sets a maximum permissible interest rate, or ceiling, which financial institutions must adhere to. When the prevailing mortgage rates in the business world begin to rise and go higher than the state-controlled ceiling rate, loans may be "discounted" to permit the lender to make up the difference between the ceiling rate and the prevailing rate. Although the word *discount* usually connotes a savings, here the term means that the amount to be loaned will be decreased by an amount of discount or points, and the borrower must pay back on a larger principal than he actually receives in his pocket at the completion of the loan closing.

Each point is generally $1 for every $100, or 1 percent of the principal amount of your mortgage. For example, if you borrow $90,000 and are being charged four points at this rate, that is, 4 percent times $90,000, or $3,600, you will receive only $86,400 in cash from the lender, but you will have to repay on the basis of a $90,000 principal. If you need to receive a certain amount, like $90,000, to pay your seller, you may want to add the value of the points onto your loan rather than receiving less than you need. Often a higher interest rate is preferable to paying points. You will also pay interest on the points if you do not pay them at the time you take out the loan.

You must be aware of the amount of costs you will have to pay to obtain your commercial loan. On many loans, the fees—loan origination and application fees, title insurance, lawyer's and appraiser's fees, and points—could easily cost you as much as 6 percent of the sales price. So on a loan of $100,000, you pay $6,000 just to get the loan.

Of course, you can avoid most of these costs if the seller finances the sale himself, which is usually the case in the sale of rural property.

# CHAPTER
# 26

# HUD/FHA-Insured and VA-Insured Loans

## Department of Housing and Urban Development/Federal Housing Administration-Insured Loans

To enable people to purchase their own homes, the Federal Housing Administration, commonly referred to as the FHA, a subsidiary of the Department of Housing and Urban Development (HUD), has organized a program of mortgage insurance that protects the lender, enabling more liberal financing terms. The HUD/FHA insures the commercial lender against possible loss due to a defaulting borrower by allowing the lender to foreclose and give the property to HUD/FHA in exchange for cash or to assign the defaulted mortgage to HUD/FHA, which proceeds with the foreclosure and reimburses the lender after the foreclosure. Although

most of these loans are for urban housing and land, the HUD/FHA programs are available for use in all areas, both rural and urban, as long as a market exists for the property and it meets the objectives of HUD minimum standards. There are also special FHA loans for purchasing property in outlying areas, which I will describe later in this chapter.

To obtain a HUD/FHA loan, you first follow the same procedure used in obtaining a commercial loan. When you apply for a loan from a lending institution, it will order an appraisal of the property and check your credit history, employment and current bank account, and send this information, along with its lending terms, to the local FHA office. If you write or call your local HUD office, it will send you a list of approved lending institutions and additional information on its programs.

Using this information, HUD examines the applicant's credit history, motivation for wanting to buy the property, adequacy of income to meet future payments, adequacy of current assets to meet the down payment and closing costs, and integrity and motivation to carry through on the repayment of the loan. The incomes of both spouses are considered when it is certain that their employment will continue.

The property, too, must meet certain conditions. General requirements are that the house be soundly built and suitably located. Any defects in the property must be repaired before HUD/FHA will insure a mortgage on it. HUD/FHA makes its own appraisal of the value of the property, to determine the amount it is willing to insure the loan for. However, it does not warrant or guarantee the condition of the property, and HUD recommends that you have the property inspected for hidden defects. If the HUD office finds that the property is acceptable, it issues a *conditional commitment* to the lender.

The office then determines if the loan is reasonable for you. If both you and the property are acceptable, HUD issues a *firm commitment* to the lender, which states the estimate of the value of the property and the maximum loan it will insure. The lender then arranges with you to close the loan. The entire process generally takes two months.

HUD/FHA has approved certain housing counseling agencies in various locations around the country that offer free advice to people regarding the costs and steps involved in buying homes. Check with your local HUD office to get the address of any counseling agency near you.

The maximum interest rate permitted under HUD/FHA-insured loans is usually lower than the current interest rate on conventional loans. Also down payments are usually smaller. Because lenders do not like to accept the lower rates, they are allowed to *discount* the loan or charge *points* (discussed in Chapter 25, "Borrowing from Third-Party Lenders") to make up the difference between the HUD/FHA interest rate and the current interest rate on the mortgage money market. HUD/FHA prohibits the lender from collecting this discount from the buyer, because to do so would defeat the purpose of the HUD/FHA loan. Therefore, the seller is supposed to pay the points. (Often, however, sellers simply raise the purchase price to cover the amount they will have to pay, so buyers end up paying anyway.)

The borrower must pay a small HUD/FHA application fee; a lender's service charge of one percent or less of the loan; the charge for a title search and title insurance policy premium; a small fee for an appraisal; a small fee for a credit report; the fees charged to prepare, record and notarize the deed, mortgage and other documents; and other standard closing costs. The Model Contract of Sale specifies that the seller is to share the cost of many of these charges with you. (See Chapter 27, "The Model Contract of Sale.")

Under a HUD/FHA-insured loan, a special charge, called the *mortgage insurance premium*, which goes into the HUD/FHA fund to pay its expenses and insurance losses on defaults, is made on the outstanding balance of the mortgage. This premium is paid to the HUD/FHA at the time the loan closes. The amount of the premium at the time of this writing is 3.8 percent.

The borrower is to pay the taxes and special assessments on the property and will be charged for the premiums on fire and hazard insurance, taken out to protect the lender's security.

There is no prepayment penalty on an FHA loan, but the buyer who intends to make more than one month's payment at one time must give the lender 30 days' notice.

You can purchase a home that is already under an FHA-insured mortgage. If you buy *subject* to the mortgage, no FHA approval is needed because the seller's name remains on the mortgage and he or she bears the responsibility for the mortgage payments if you fail to make them. If you are approved by the FHA, the lender can release the seller from his or her obligation on the mortgage and substitute you, whereby you *assume* the mortgage.

The FHA has several different insurance programs that you might use. They are described below.

**One-to-Four Family Home Mortgage Insurance (Section 203, National Housing Act)**

The most commonly used program, Mutual Mortgage Insurance, Section 203(b) of the National Housing Act, provides for the purchase and construction of family homes. Up to four units are eligible under this program. The maximum amount you call borrow varies, depending on the area of the country the property is located. HUD will insure loans made by private financial institutions for up to 97 percent of the property value and for a term of up to 30 years. The loan-to-value ratio varies, depending on the age of the house and whether it was built under HUD/FHA approval. The loan may finance homes in both urban and rural areas—except farms. Less rigid construction standards are permitted in rural areas.

The HUD/FHA plan that probably is applicable to most people is the Outlying Area Properties Loan, Section 203(i) of the National Housing Act. Under this plan, HUD/FHA approval is given for mortgages on nonfarm housing on five or more acres adjacent to a highway in small communities. Many of the requirements regarding standards of construction and the condition of houses are much less rigid than those for mortgage insurance on housing in built-up urban areas. The maximum loan permitted is 97 percent of the appraised value of the property, up to a maximum loan amount permitted by HUD/FHA. If the purchase price is higher than the HUD/FHA estimate of the value of the property plus closing costs, the buyer must pay the difference in cash. You can choose among 10-year, 15-year, 20-year, 25-year or 30-year maturity periods.

**FHA Cooperative Housing Loan Insurance, Sections 213 and 221 (d) (3) and (4), National Housing Act**

Two unusual loan insurance plans that can be utilized by a group of people purchasing land together are the HUD/FHA Cooperative Housing Loan Insurance, Section 213, and the Multifamily Rental Housing for Low- and Moderate-Income Families, Sections 221 (d) (3) and (4). Under these plans HUD/FHA will insure financing for cooperative housing projects that will belong to, and provide housing for members of a nonprofit cooperative ownership housing corporation. These loans may finance new construction, rehabilitation, acquisition, or improvement or repair of homes already owned. Five or more dwellings must be purchased or constructed by the cooperative. Each purchaser may obtain HUD/FHA insurance. Although the most common users of this program are by large developers building low-cost cooperative housing, there is no reason why a group of people could not get together, form their own nonprofit cooperative and apply for loan insurance to finance construction of their homes. This program does not insure loans for the purchase of land, only for the construction of dwellings. Thus, if your group has only enough cash to purchase some inexpensive rural land, it might be able to borrow the money under one of these HUD/FHA plans to build your houses. The first thing to do if you are considering such a project is to discuss your plan with the local HUD/FHA insuring office. (For more information on cooperatives, see Chapter 31, "Types of Co-Ownership.")

**Graduated Payment Mortgage (GPM), Section 245, National Housing Act**

A fairly new HUD program can allow you to purchase a house with a reasonable down-payment and lower initial monthly payments in the early years of your loan. Your mortgage payments rise gradually for a set period of years, then level off and remain steady for the balance of the mortgage. There are five different GPM plans that vary the rate of monthly payment increases and the number of years over which the payments increase. The greater the rate or the larger the period of increase, the lower the mortgage payments are in early years. For example, your mortgage payments can start at $350 per month, slowly increase annually until the seventh year (when you might be paying $550 per month), then stay at that payment level for the duration of the loan.

**Adjustable Rate Mortgages (ARM), Section 251, National Housing Act**

This HUD-insured mortgage plan allows lenders to vary the interest rate and monthly payments during the life of the loan. The index used for determining the interest rate is the one-year Treasury Constant Maturities. Over the life of the loan, the maximum interest rate change allowed is five percentage points higher and lower than the initial rate of the mortgage, and the interest can change a maximum of one percentage point in any one year. The initial interest rate, the discount points charged and the margin vary from lender to lender.

**Insured Title 1 Manufactured (Mobile) Home Loan Program**

If you want to buy a manufactured (mobile) home after purchasing your land, or if you want to buy the home and lot together, you can get a HUD/FHA-insured loan from a private lending institution through the Insured Title 1 Manufactured Home Loans Program. You can borrow up to $40,500 for a single or multisection manufactured home and $54,000 for a developed lot and manufactured home. The interest rate varies, as does the down payment you must make, and the home must meet HUD standards of construction for a single- or multiple-unit home.

### Home Improvement Loan Insurance, Title 1

Once you own your land, you can get HUD/FHA insured loans under Title 1 Property Improvement Loan Insurance to finance major and minor repairs and improvements of existing homes and nonresidential structures and to build new, small nonresidential structures, such as agricultural buildings. Improvements can be do-it-yourself or through a contractor.

## Department of Veterans Affairs (VA)-Guaranteed Loans (GI Loans)

Since World War II, the Federal government, through the Veterans Administration (now the Department of Veterans Affairs) has been guaranteeing loans made by commercial lenders to honorably discharged veterans. Loans may be obtained for purchasing homes and farms; purchasing manufactured homes, certain condominiums and/or lots; constructing homes; and improving existing dwellings. These loans are called VA (or GI)-guaranteed loans.

The VA guarantees part of a loan that helps a home-buying veteran obtain a mortgage featuring

- an interest rate that is usually lower than conventional rates and
- no down payment, except for manufactured homes or if (1) required by the lender, (2) the purchase price exceeds the VA-determined reasonable value of the property or (3) the loan has a graduated payment feature.

There are various eligibility requirements depending on when the military service was performed. If you are a veteran, check with the VA regional office to determine if you are eligible for VA benefits.

A loan guarantee from the VA means that if you default on the loan, the VA will repay the lender for you. You then become liable for payment to the VA.

Your entitlement to loan guaranty benefits is available until used. Two or more veterans can put their entitlement together and purchase property as a group if both reside on the property as their permanent residence. Vacation homes do not qualify. A veteran may also use this entitlement with a nonveteran to purchase a home, but the VA will only guarantee the veteran's half of the loan. Under certain circumstances, you may be eligible to use the benefit more than once. Check with your local VA office.

The first thing a veteran must do is obtain a certificate of eligibility by filling out VA Form 26-1880, "Request for Determination of Eligibility and Available Loan Guaranty Entitlement," and submitting it with separation papers (DD214) to the local VA office or financial institution. Usually the VA automatically issues a certificate of eligibility to most newly discharged eligible veterans.

Eligible veterans must make their own arrangements for loans through the usual channels, such as banks, savings and loan associations, building and loan associations, mortgage loan companies, and the like. Real estate brokers will ordinarily assist veterans in finding lenders.

Before the VA will guarantee a loan, it appraises the property in the same way that HUD/FHA does. The appraisal report indicates the current fair market value by VA standards at the time the appraisal is made. It does not indicate the physical condition of the residence or whether the purchase is a good one or what the resale value will be at a future date. After completion of the appraisal, the VA sends a "Certificate of Reasonable Value" to the prospective lender. The maximum maturity allowed is 30 years for a house. The maximum interest allowed under a VA loan varies with market conditions.

First you must find the property you want to buy. Then make a deposit and sign a contract of sale that conditions the sale on your ability to obtain a GI loan. (See clause 17(e) in the Model Contract of Sale, Chapter 27.) A legal description of the property and a survey or sketch of its boundaries must be presented with your certificate of eligibility to the lending institution to which you apply for a loan. The lender will run a credit history check and employment report on you, and the VA will conduct its appraisal of the property and run a VA indebtedness check to see if you owe the VA for any other loans. The VA then sends the "Certificate of Reasonable Value" to the lender. If a lender decides to lend you the money, it gets a guarantee from the regional VA office, then gives you the money.

You will have to pay certain fees on a VA-guaranteed loan. The application fee includes a charge for the appraisal and for the credit report. You must also pay a VA funding fee, which could be as much as 1.875 percent of the loan amount, depending on your down payment. If the lender charges more points than allowed under the VA loan guarantee, the seller is supposed to pay them rather than the buyer. All other standard closing costs to be paid by the buyer and the seller are negotiable between the two of you.

In addition to VA loans, which are federally funded, many states have their own programs that make funds available to veterans through state bond issues. These state programs feature direct loans to veterans, who repay them at a low interest rate.

## Loans from the Farmers Home Administration (FmHA)

Leave it to the Federal government to create two separate financial agencies with the initials *FHA*. The Farmers Home Administration, referred to as the *FmHA* to distinguish it from FHA, makes housing loans available to low-income farm families and other people in rural areas of 10,000 people or less and in small communities with populations between 10,000 and 20,000. Its intent is to develop the resources of rural areas and upgrade the standard of living of people wishing to live in these places. The FmHA offers both direct loans and grants to very-low-income people as well as insured loans for up to $200,000 and guaranteed loans for up to $300,000 through private financial institutions. You can use money obtained from an FmHA loan to buy, improve or repair farm homes and farm service buildings, to drill wells, to develop energy conservation measures and to refinance debts. Purchasing forest land is permitted if you can show that it will produce income as a commercial or recreational enterprise. After the loan is made, the FmHA will give you technical advice for making profitable use of the land and its resources and help you manage your finances in general.

Insured funds are made directly from an FmHA revolving fund to the borrower. Guaranteed loans are made and serviced by usual commercial sources, such as federal land banks, local banks, insurance companies and savings and loan associations. FmHA provides lenders with guarantees against losses on loans.

FmHA also makes farm ownership loans in participation with other lenders and sellers of farms who supply a part of the needed loan funds. In these cases, FmHA loans may be secured by junior liens on properties.

Another purpose of the FmHA loan is to assist people who are unable to get reasonable credit elsewhere. Although special provisions are made for low-income families, usually the borrower is expected to have sufficient income to pay the installments, insurance premiums, taxes and other debts, as well as operating and living expenses. Borrowers also must have both a satisfactory history of meeting credit obligations and farm experience or training; in addition, they must possess the industry and ability needed to succeed in farming.

Eligibility for a loan is determined by a local committee of the FmHA, consisting of three persons who know local farming and credit conditions and what it takes to succeed. A standard credit and employment check is conducted, and veterans get preferential treatment for any FmHA loan. If your income is not sufficient, a cosigner might be necessary.

Repayment terms and interest rates vary, according to the type of loan made. Repayment is scheduled according to the borrower's ability to repay. The interest rate is set periodically, based on the cost to the government of borrowing.

A lower interest rate is available for borrowers with limited resources. Loans to limited-resource borrowers are reviewed after three years, and the interest rate will be increased if the borrower has sufficient repayment ability. Thereafter, these loans will be reviewed at least every two years. However, if at any time the borrower has sufficient income and repayment ability to pay the then-current rate being charged, the borrower's interest rate will be increased to the current rate.

For loans made by other lenders and guaranteed by FmHA, the interest rate and repayment terms will be agreed on by the borrower and the lender. Interest rates on these loans may not exceed a maximum set by the secretary of agriculture.

Each borrower who receives an insured loan is expected to refinance the unpaid balance of the loan when it is financially feasible to rely on commercial credit sources. Farm ownership borrowers are required to maintain their property and pay taxes and property insurance premiums when due.

A separate program that might be useful for a group of people buying land is the FmHA Self-Help Housing Loan, whereby funds are loaned to a group of people to buy building sites and materials. The majority of the construction is then done by the families themselves under an FmHA construction expert. The houses are expected to be modest in size and cost. You are encouraged to submit your own building plans but are advised to keep the house size around 1,100 square feet.

The best way to find out about the FmHA programs available in your area is to write to your local office.

## Changes Planned for FHA and VA Loans

There are some threats to government loan programs. The most serious proposals are to assess user fees on borrowers who participate in FHA and VA programs, and to require higher down payments and place limits on income eligibility. There also are plans to increase insurance premiums on loans guaranteed by the FHA and to increase the origination fee for VA mortgages. So get the latest information by contacting your local FHA and VA offices for current loan information.

You can also look in your phone book under "United States Government, Department of Veterans Affairs," for local toll-free numbers to obtain information on veterans' loans.

# The Contract of Sale

# 27 The Model Contract of Sale

This chapter is the heart of the book. It contains a Model Contract of Sale (Figure 27–1) that I present as a means of evaluating other contracts and that can be used in your land purchase. Some states, such as California, have standard form contracts formulated by reputable organizations that are extremely well done. In my own law practice, I regularly use the form called Real Estate Purchase Contract and Receipt for Deposit, originally drafted by the State Bar of California in conjunction with the California Association of REALTORS®, that includes every form of protection within it that I include in my Model Contract of Sale in this chapter.

However, most states do not have such standard form contracts available; even in California it is not mandatory to use the REALTORS® form. Many brokers in California and throughout the country use forms, purchased in stationery stores, that are usually inadequate.

Because my book is for use in all parts of the United States and Canada, my Model Contract is rather complex. It attempts to deal with as many conceivable situations as possible. If you use a contract submitted to you by your broker, be sure you

read and understand it. Compare its terms to the ones that I tell you are necessary to have in your contract. If you have any questions, I recommend that you consult an attorney who specializes in real property law. Its a lot cheaper to uncover problems before your purchase rather than afterward.

As stated previously, many times real estate agents will give documents to buyers to sign without making it clear that they are binding contracts. The *deposit receipt* is the most infamous example of this practice throughout the United States. *Any document that is dated, contains the name of the parties, states what is being sold and for how much, and is signed by the parties is a **legally binding contract**, regardless of what it is called.*

Each section of the Model Contract is accompanied by an explanation of what the terms mean, why they are included, and how you should fill in the blank spaces. When it is applicable, you are referred to the other parts of the book that have more information on that section of the Model Contract. First read the entire contract, then go back over each section while reading the explanation that goes with it. If you have read the rest of this book, you will then have an understanding of how to use this Model Contract in your purchase to protect yourself.

You will not use every clause in this contract. Many sections will be deleted for your purposes, as explained in the discussion of each section. For example, if there is no house on the land, delete each section of the contract that relates to the purchase of a house.

This contract serves three purposes. First, it is a receipt for your deposit money, which you and the broker sign as evidence you have paid it. There is no reason why you should give the real estate agent any money unless you are ready to make an offer to buy the land according to your terms. Second, the contract serves as an offer to purchase the land. Third, the contract becomes the final agreement between the parties if the seller accepts your offer. When you fill in the amount of money to be paid for the property, this is really the amount you are offering to pay. The seller who rejects your offer will return the contract unsigned. It will not be surprising if this contract passes back and forth between the two of you several times before a final agreement is reached. The seller can cross out or change anything in your offer and sign and return the contract to you. All changes, additions and deletions in the document must be initialed or signed by both parties. (See Chapter 20, "Bargaining To Get the Seller's Asking Price Down.")

When a buyer makes an offer and puts a deposit on a piece of property, the real estate agent normally offers a deposit receipt or contract of sale for the buyer to fill out and sign. You can tell the agent that you wish to use your own form or you can write the contingencies you want included on the agent's form. If you have time, get all the information from the agent that you need to complete your own contract. Then, go through the contract; delete and add whatever is necessary. Type the resulting contract on regular typing paper, fill in the blanks and sign it, and give it to the agent or seller, whichever party you are dealing with. He or she will probably be shocked. Compared to the simple form that the agent usually gives a buyer, your contract of sale will look like a manifesto. Don't worry about a thing. The purpose of all this is to protect your investment. Should anything go wrong during or after your purchase, forcing you to proceed with legal action against the seller, you will be glad you used this contract. If you decide to include your contingencies on the agent's form, be sure to check

through the Model Contract of Sale for those contingencies that are important to you. They can be written out on a separate sheet or sheets of paper labeled "Conditions of Purchase," attached to the form, and referred to in the form with words such as "close of escrow is contingent on Buyer's approval prior to the close of escrow of the conditions specified in 'Conditions of Purchase,' attached hereto and made a part hereof."

If you submit your own contract to the agent, he or she is bound by law to deliver it to the seller. You may get resistance from the seller about accepting it. However, I mention areas where you can make compromises with the seller without jeopardizing your basic protections. If the seller absolutely refuses to deal with this contract, ask him or her to give you a contract form that is acceptable. Take that contract and compare it with the Model Contract. Where the seller's contract has omitted protections you must have, write in the clauses directly from the Model Contract. If the seller's contract has clauses you do not like, cross them out and initial the change. Then you can return the contract to the seller. Never allow yourself to be buffaloed by the seller or agent. A fair and honest seller will allow you the basic and adequate protections provided for in this Model Contract of Sale. If the agent or seller balks at all the conditions, simply use the one condition that the purchase is subject to the approval of your attorney, who can then tell you what you should have in the deal before it closes.

Do not be surprised if the form is a little difficult to understand the first time through. By the time you have finished reading the book, looked at some land and talked to some real estate agents and public officials, everything will fit into place. Even if you decide to retain the services of an attorney, this chapter will give you a good understanding of what the attorney should be doing for you. It provides you with the information you need to ask intelligent questions about the transaction. Compare this Model Contract with the contract your lawyer prepares for you. If you find anything omitted from your lawyer's contract, or if any clauses are in conflict, point this out. Lawyers are not infallible.

It is always risky to purchase real estate without consulting an attorney because of the complexity of the laws regarding rural property. If you feel unsure at any point, go to an attorney for a consultation to have it checked over. The minimal expense of

**Figure 27–1. Model Contract of Sale**

(d) Installments of principal and interest on the following personal property: _____ which are to be included with this transaction.

9. If impounded funds are held by the lender in connection with a mortgage, deed of trust or other encumbrance remaining of record at close of escrow, Buyer shall be charged and Seller credited with the full amount.

10. If at the close of escrow, all or any part of the property is affected by any assessment liens, or bonds, all or part of which are or may become payable, all the unpaid installments of these, including those that are to become due after close of escrow shall, for purposes of this agreement, be considered due and liens on the property, and except for _____ , Seller shall pay and discharge them before close of escrow or, at Buyer's election, allow them as a credit against the _____(cash or note)_____ due Seller at close of escrow.

11. Buyer shall pay____% and Seller shall pay ____% of each of the following: the escrow fee; the escrow holder's and customary charges for document-drafting, recording, and miscellaneous charges; the title insurance premium or charge for the Abstract of Title and Certificate of Title; and local transfer taxes.

   In addition, each party will pay reasonable compensation to the escrow holder for extraordinary or unusual services rendered to or for that party, if any, plus costs and expenses incurred in connection with those services.

12. Seller shall deliver possession of the property, all improvements thereon and all personal property, if any, to Buyer in substantially the same condition, reasonable wear and tear excepted, as on the date of this agreement:
   (strike out inapplicable alternatives below)
   (a) on close of escrow; or

   (b) not later than _____ days after close of escrow; or

   (c) _____ ; or

   (d) If the Seller has not vacated the property by the date Buyer is to take possession, the Seller shall be liable to the Buyer for a daily rental equal tot he sum of_____ Dollars ($ _____) per day for each and every day the Seller remains on the property as a holdover Seller in possession; or the Buyer, at his option, may terminate this agreement and any deposit and other money deposited in escrow shall thereupon be returned to him.

13. If, when neither legal title nor possession of the property has been transferred to the Buyer, any part of the property is destroyed, materially damaged or taken by eminent domain, the Buyer, at his option, may be relieved of his obligation to complete the purchase, or he may obtain a reduction to the purchase price to the extent of the cost of repairing or replacing the damage from destruction or the diminution in value resulting from eminent domain.

14. Seller recognizes the Buyer will spend time and effort preparing for the acquisition of this property, and Buyer recognizes that Seller's property will be removed from the market during the existence of this agreement. Both parties agree that if either fails to perform under this contract, the other should be entitled to compensation for the detriment described above, and the parties agree to liquidate damages as follows:

   If Seller fails to perform for any reason, Buyer shall be entitled to recover his deposit and any other money he has deposited into escrow or paid to or for Seller's account and shall also recover from Seller the sum of _____ Dollars ($ _____) as liquidated damages. If Buyer fails to perform for any reason, Seller shall be entitled to recover the sum of___(amount of deposit or less)___ ($_____) as liquidated damages and shall be entitled to obtain the sum out of any deposit made by Buyer to Seller or his agent or into escrow and out of any other money Buyer has deposited into escrow or paid to or for Seller's account.

   Both parties agree that these sums stated as liquidated damages shall be in lieu of any other monetary relief to which the parties might otherwise be entitled by virtue of this contract or by operation of law.

15. The Seller, for himself, and his heirs, representatives, and assignees, covenants with the Buyer and his heirs, representatives, and assignees as follows:

   (a) That the Seller is lawfully seised of the described property in fee simple, and has the right to convey the same;

**Figure 27–1. Model Contract of Sale** *continued*

(b) That the property is free from all liens and encumbrances, except as aforesaid;

(c) That the Buyer shall quietly enjoy the property;

(d) That the Seller will do any further acts or procure any further necessary assurance of the title for the purpose of perfecting the title to the property;

(e) That the Seller forever warrants and will defend the title of the property against the lawful claims and demands of all persons.

(f) All of the above covenants shall survive delivery of the deed.

16. The Seller warrants and represents the following:

(a) That the land title conveyed to the Buyer contains legal access rights from the most accessible public road to the building sites on the conveyed land which is the subject of this agreement. These access roads shall include, but not be limited to, the existing access roads to the building sites on the conveyed land if any are in existence at the time of this conveyance.

(b) That as of the closing of escrow the property will have a legal survey completed by a licensed surveyor or registered civil engineer with all corners staked on the ground and all boundaries marked and visible on the ground; and will include within its boundaries the following structures and land features: _____ _____.

(c) That as of the closing of escrow the property will include a spring, well, creek or other water supply with a year-round output of at least _____ gallons per_____ .

(d) That at this time and as of the close of escrow the property is and will be zoned _____ , under the laws of the City of _____ , the County of _____ , and the State of_____.

(e) That as of the closing of escrow the structures will be free of any damage from infestation by wood-destroying pests and organisms, including but not limited to termites, dry rot and fungi.

(f) That at present and as of close of escrow no violation exists or will exist with respect to the property or any improvements, of any statute, ordinance, regulation or administrative or judicial order or holding, whether or not appearing in public records.

(g) That the property is not, and at the close of escrow shall not, be the subject of any proposed liens, assessment liens, or bonds other that those expected in Clause 10 above, by reason of any work or improvement completed or installed at or before the close of escrow, or to be completed after the close of escrow.

(h) That at present and as of close of escrow the Seller has no knowledge of any intent to take any part of the property by condemnation or eminent domain.

(i) That at present and as of close of escrow the Seller owns, in full, those items listed as personal property to be conveyed to the Buyer according to this agreement. The following such items are not owned in full by the Seller: _____ .

(j) That no poisonous sprays, insecticides, pesticides or herbicides have been used in any way on said property or applied to any vegetation growing on said property.

(k) All of the above warranties and representations shall survive delivery of the deed.

17. Buyer's obligation to perform this agreement is subject to the following terms and conditions:

(a) If Buyer notifies Seller that Buyer disapproves any matter set out in this Clause, or that the condition has not been satisfied, Buyer, at his election, can terminate the agreement without liability on his part, and his deposit shall be immediately returned to him. Buyer shall notify Seller of his disapproval of a condition herein within _____ days of the signing of the agreement. The close of escrow is contingent upon the Buyer approving of all the conditions herein or meeting those conditions prior to the close of escrow.

**Figure 27–1. Model Contract of Sale** *continued*

(b) Buyer's approval, within _____ days after the date of this agreement, of _____ (survey, soil test, termite and house inspection, appraisal of land and improvements, etc.) . The cost of this is to be paid _____ (equally, by Buyer and Seller, by Seller, by Buyer) . Buyer and his representatives shall have the right from this date to enter on the property to obtain the pertinent information and for any other purposes reasonably related to carrying out the provisions of this agreement.

(c) Buyer's ability to secure the right, under applicable zoning and land use laws, regulations and ordinances, to (zoning, or use designation being sought, building permits, etc.) . Buyer shall file the documents and pay the fees necessary to obtain the change. If Buyer has proceeded with reasonable diligence but has not obtained a final determination by the time scheduled for closing, on Buyer's written election the closing shall be extended until final determination, provided Buyer is diligently pursuing a determination. Seller may terminate this agreement on _____ days notice if Buyer is not diligent in pursuing a determination. If the final determination is adverse, Buyer alone shall have the election either to terminate this agreement or to waive this condition. Buyer shall make his election within _____ days after final determination.

(d) Buyer's approval within _____ days after execution of this agreement, of a structural pest control inspection from _____ (name of company) , a licensed structural pest control operator, selected by the Buyer, certifying that normally accessible areas of the property are free from infestation by wood-destroying pests and organisms, including but not limited to termites, dry rot and fungi, and that no corrective work is required, the cost of the report to be borne _____ (equally, by Buyer and Seller, by Seller, by Buyer) .

Buyer shall notify Seller by _____, 19 ___, if the condition is not satisfied, and Buyer may, at his election, terminate the agreement, unless Seller agrees to pay the cost of completing all recommendations made in said report.

(e) Buyer's obtaining from a lender of his choice within _____ days of execution of this agreement a loan of not less than _____ Dollars ($ _____) secured by _____ (first deed of trust mortgage) on the property on terms no less favorable to the Buyer than the following: Interest at _____ % per year, principal and interest payable in equal monthly installments of _____ Dollars ($ _____) for a term of _____ years, privilege of prepayment at any time without penalty, loan fees and costs of not more than _____ %, acceleration provisions to be approved by Buyer and _____ (guaranteed by VA or insured by FHA) .

Buyer shall make diligent application to at least two lending institutions and execute and furnish documents and supply all information reasonably requested by the lending institutions in connection with his applications.

(f) The Seller shall make a diligent effort to locate and develop a year-round adequate water supply for the Buyer's needs on the property. If necessary, the Seller shall drill a well to a maximum depth of _____. The water supply must have a year-round output of at least _____ gallons per minute. If the Seller cannot locate and develop an adequate water supply, then this agreement shall be terminated immediately and all funds deposited and paid by the Buyer shall be returned immediately and the Buyer shall suffer no further liability under this agreement.

18. The prevailing party in any action or proceeding between the parties shall be entitled to reasonable attorney's fees in addition to all other relief to which he may be entitled

19. As used in this agreement, the masculine, feminine, or neuter gender, and the singular or plural number shall each be deemed to include the others whenever the context so indicates, and the words Buyer and Seller shall include the respective successors in interest of each, whenever the context so requires.

20. All Exhibits to which reference is made are deemed incorporated in the agreement, whether or not actually attached.

21. The waiver by either or both parties of the performance of any covenant, condition or promise shall not be considered a waiver of any other covenant, condition or promise. The waiver by either or both parties of the time for performing any act shall not constitute a waiver of the time for performing any other act required to be performed under the agreement.

22. All notices and demands shall be given in writing by registered or certified mail, postage prepaid and return receipt requested. Notices shall be addressed as appears below for the respective person unless one party notifies the other of a change of address. Notices to any party of any transaction, sent after escrow is opened, shall also be sent to the escrow holder.

**Figure 27–1. Model Contract of Sale** *continued*

23. This agreement shall apply to and bind the heirs, executors, administrators, successors and assignees of the respective parties.

24. Any change in or modification of this agreement must be in writing and signed by the parties thereto.

25. Time is of the essence in this agreement.

_____
Name of Seller's Agent

_____
Address

_____
Telephone

The undersigned Buyer offers and agrees to buy the above described property on the terms and conditions above stated and acknowledges receipt of a copy hereof. Upon acceptance by the Seller and delivery to the Buyer of the copy signed by both Buyer and Seller, this instrument becomes a binding contract between Buyer and Seller.

| | |
|---|---|
| Dated | Address |
| Telephone | |
| Buyer's signature | Signature of Buyer's partner |
| Name of Buyer | Buyer's spouse/partner |

Acceptance

The undersigned Seller accepts the foregoing offer and agrees to sell the property described therein on the terms and conditions therein set forth.

The undersigned Seller has employed the Agent above named and for the Agent's services agrees to pay the Agent as a commission the sum of_____ Dollars ($_____) payable as follows:

(a) On recordation of the deed or other evidence of title,

(b) If completion of sale is prevented by default of Seller, upon Seller's default, or

(c) If completion of sale is prevented by default of Buyer, only if and when Seller collects the damages from Buyer, by suit or otherwise, and then in an amount not to exceed one half that portion of the damages collected after first deducting title and escrow expenses and the expenses of collection, if any. The undersigned acknowledges receipt of a copy hereof and authorizes the Agent to deliver a signed copy of it to Buyer.

| | |
|---|---|
| Dated | Address |
| Telephone | Name of Seller |
| | Seller's signature |

Agent consents to the foregoing.

| | |
|---|---|
| Dated | Agent's signature |
| | Name of Agent |

**Figure 27–1. Model Contract of Sale** *continued*

City of _____     County of _____
State of _____     Date _____, 19 __
Received from _____ (herein called Buyer), the sum of _____ Dollars ($ _____ ) evidenced
by _____(personal check or cashier's check)_____ as deposit on account of purchase price of _____ Dollars
($ _____ ) for the purchase of property, situated in City of _____,County of _____,
State of _____ , described as follows _____(Describe real property and personal property, if any)_____
_____
_____

Said deposit will be held uncashed until acceptance of this offer. Buyer will deposit in escrow with _____
the balance of purchase price as follows:

The sum of _____Dollars ($ _____ ), to be deposited prior to close of escrow, as a down payment,
which shall include the above deposit;

The sum of _____ Dollars ($ _____ ), to be represented by a __(note and mortgage or deed of trust)__ , to be
payable_____ Dollars ($_____ ) or more per month with interest on all unpaid principal of
_____% per annum, from close of escrow, payable with each monthly payment as part of the same. First payment is due
30 days after close of escrow.

1. Buyer's signature hereon constitutes an offer to Seller to purchase the real estate and personal property described
   above. Unless acceptance hereof is signed by Seller and the signed copy delivered to Buyer, either in person or by
   mail to the address shown below within _____ days hereof, this offer shall be deemed revoked and the deposit shall
   be returned to Buyer within 48 hours.

2. The price of said property is _____ Dollars ($ _____ ) per acre. The total number of acres is _____.

3. The total acreage on which the purchase price is computed shall be based on a legal survey completed by a licensed
   surveyor. The results of the survey are to be approved by Buyer before the close of escrow. The expense of the survey
   is to be paid by the Seller.

4. Within _____ days of the Seller's acceptance hereof, escrow instructions signed by Buyer and Seller shall be delivered
   to _____(name and address of escrow holder)_____ .

   Escrow instructions signed by both parties shall provide for closing within _____ days from the opening of escrow,
   subject to written extensions signed by Buyer and Seller.

   Close of escrow means the time when the documents transferring title are recorded.

5. Unless otherwise designated in the escrow instructions of Buyer, title shall vest as follows: _____ .
   _____ .

6. Seller shall by Warranty Deed or a Grant Deed convey to Buyer a marketable fee simple title as approved by Buyer in
   the following manner: Title is to be free of liens, encumbrances, easements, covenants, reservations, restrictions,rights
   and conditions other than current property taxes and those items approved of by Buyer after inspection of a current
   preliminary title report or abstract of title. Within_____ days of the Seller's acceptance hereof, Seller shall cause to
   be delivered to Buyer a Preliminary Title Report issued by _____(title company)_____ describing the property, and
   copies of all documents referred to in it. Within _____ days after Buyer's receipt of the Preliminary Title Report
   and all documents referred to in it, Buyer shall give Seller notice specifying the matters disapproved by Buyer. If these
   matters are not corrected by the Seller to the satisfaction and approval of the Buyer before the close of escrow, the
   Buyer may, at his election, terminate this agreement and any deposit shall immediately be returned to him.

7. Seller shall furnish to Buyer a marketable fee simple title as evidenced by a _____(standard or extended)_____ Owner's Title
   Insurance Policy insuring title in Buyer for the amount of the purchase price of said property and issued by
   _____(title company)_____ .

8. The following prorations shall be made in escrow on the basis of a 30-day month and shall be prorated as of the date of
   recordation of the deed:

   (a) Real property taxes;
   (b) Premiums on insurance policies approved by Buyer and to be assumed by Buyer;
   (c) Interest on obligations secured by encumbrances to which the property will remain subject after close of escrow;

doing this is well worth it, considering the amount of money you are about to invest.

## Explanation of Clauses in Model Contract of Sale

Where appropriate, an explanation will be followed by an example showing you how the blanks on the contract can be filled in. Reference will be made to other chapters that include more details and information on the subject of each clause.

### Place and Date of Signing

Write in the city, county and state in which this transaction occurs and the date you sign this contract. This date is important because it starts the time period in which the seller must accept your offer, according to clause 3.

### Buyer's Name

Insert your name here.

### Amount and Form of Deposit (Earnest Money)

Next, specify the amount of your deposit. Any time money amounts are given in the contract, they should first be written out, then given numerically, for example., "Two Hundred Dollars ($200.00)." This avoids any possibility of confusion due to a typographical error, because the amount written out always takes priority over the numerical figure.

Although the deposit can be for any amount, it is generally between $200 and $1,000. The seller will want the amount to be as large as possible, because the seller gets to keep it as a penalty if you break the contract and back out of the deal later. Naturally, you, as the buyer, will want to make it a small amount in case of such eventuality. Never deposit more than 1 percent. Generally, on an offer of less than $100,000 I would never deposit more than $1,000. There is a common conception that a contract is not legally binding without a deposit. This is not true. I have handled transactions in excess of $500,000 in which no deposit was ever made before the close of escrow. The deposit is basically a means of "hooking" a buyer into a deal. It is standard throughout the country to request a deposit nowadays, but keep it reasonable.

Pay the deposit in the form of a personal check rather than cash. If the seller won't accept a personal check, use a cashier's check. Make the check payable to the intended escrow holder. Give it to the real estate agent to hold until the seller accepts your offer and escrow is opened. Because the check is made out to the escrow holder, neither the agent nor the seller can cash and misuse it before the agreement becomes final. When escrow opens, the deposit will go in as part of the purchase price.

If the seller rejects your offer or at any time breaches the contract, the deposit will be returned to you, as indicated in clauses 1 and 14. If the seller accepts your offer but the deal does not close because some condition is not met, you will get the deposit back. You did not submit cash or endorse the check to the seller or agent, so you should have no problem getting your deposit back. You can instruct your bank at any time to stop payment on the check. If you default on the agreement, the deposit will go to the seller, as indicated in clause 14. (See Chapter 20, "Bargaining To Get the Seller's Asking Price Down.")

### Amount of Full Purchase Price (Your Offer to the Seller)

You must also fill in the purchase price here, which is really only an offer until the seller accepts and signs this contract without changing any of its terms. Once the seller accepts the contract, this figure becomes the final purchase price. (See Chapter 20, "Bargaining To Get the Seller's Asking Price Down.")

### Location and Description of the Property

Write in the name of the city, county and state in which the land is located. After "described as follows," you must give the description of the property as it is to appear on the deed. The real estate agent will give you a copy of this description, which you can copy into the contract. The description must identify the land so that it cannot be confused with any other piece of land. If the property has not yet been surveyed, this can be done after you sign the contract and before the close of escrow, as a condition of the contract. This is provided for in clauses 3, 16(b) and 17(b). (See Chapter 8, "Land Descriptions and Surveys.") If the description is long, it can be attached to the contract as Exhibit A. If that is the case, write in here, "See Exhibit A attached hereto."

This description will sometimes include what will be excluded from the title to the property, such as mineral and timber rights. (See Chapter 11, "Mineral, Oil, Gas, Timber, Soil and Other

Rights.") Usually, the description is copied from the seller's deed and includes easements and reservations. It does not matter if it is incomplete, because your purchase is subject to approval of a title report or abstract, and that is where you will get all the details on the title.

Sometimes, the broker has only the tax assessor's number for the property and uses that as the legal description. It is preferable, but not mandatory, to attach the entire legal description.

List all personal property to be included in the deal. This is everything except the *real property*, that is, the land and the things permanently attached to the land, such as structures and vegetation. *Personal property* can include such things as machinery, tools, furniture, rugs, appliances and animals. Make this list complete, because if you omit any item that you expect to receive, this could be construed to mean that it is not included in the sale. This list should he an inventory of everything you are buying that could he removed and taken by the seller. If you wish, you can list the property on a separate piece of paper and attach it to the contract as an Exhibit. You would refer to it here. See clause 20.

For example, the following is a property description by reference to the United States Rectangular Survey. Mineral rights are excluded from the title to the land. An easement across the neighbor's land is included, as are several items of personal property.

> PARCEL ONE: The South Half of the Northwest Quarter of Section 21, Township 4 South, Range 2 East, New Mexico Meridian.

> EXCEPTING therefrom all coal and other mineral rights in said land together with the right to prospect for, mine, and remove the same as reserved by the United States of America in Patent recorded June 8, 1928, in Book 24, Page 214, of Patents in the office of the County Recorder of said County.

> PARCEL TWO: A nonexclusive easement in the Southerly portion of the Northeast Quarter of the Northeast Quarter of Section 21, in Township 4 South, Range 2 East, New Mexico Meridian, and extending Easterly to the West line of the County Road, together with the right to convey said easement to others.

> PERSONAL PROPERTY included in this purchase shall include:

> One (1) Homelite Chain Saw, Model 14, Serial Number A246415.
> One (1) Servel Propane Refrigerator.
> Fifteen (15) Rhode Island Red Chickens: four (4) roosters, eleven (11) hens.

### Deposit Held Uncashed

The deposit check should not he cashed until there is a contract between the parties. As soon as there is a signed contract, the deposit will be placed with the escrow holder.

### Name and Location of Escrow Holder

Locate a reputable escrow company to manage the escrow proceedings. Every real estate agent has one or two companies that handle his or her deals, but you do not have to use that company. Often a particular title company regularly acts as the escrow holder for the agent. If the agent is a good friend of the title officer, you might not get as much help from that title company as you would from another. Title companies rely on escrows to make their money, and they cater to brokers for their business. Although escrow companies are supposed to be neutral, there is no question that some will give you more information and advice than others. In addition, escrow fees vary, and you might be able to find a better deal than the agent's company can offer. It is best for the buyer to pick out the escrow holder. If you are familiar with the local ones, find a properly licensed and reputable escrow or title company or bank and insert its name and location here. (See Chapter 29, "Opening and Closing of Escrow and the Role of the Escrow Holder.") Example: Home Land Title Company of Bronwood, Georgia.

### Details of the Purchase Price and Financing

Detail here how you will pay the purchase price. This is actually the amount of your offer and the terms you are offering to pay. State the down payment you are offering to pay the seller, usually 10 percent to 30 percent of the total price. (For example, it could be $25,000 down on a total of $80,000.)It is paid at the closing of escrow. The down payment will include the deposit money you are making with this offer. If you are paying all cash, there will be no down payment; if that is the case, omit the down payment and write in the full amount of cash.

If a down payment is made, the rest of the purchase price will be paid under some kind of financing arrangement. A buyer usually pays the seller for the land over a period of time. After you fill in the amount of the down payment, state the remaining amount of the mortgage sum and how you will pay it.

For example, "The sum of Fifty-Five Thousand and 00/100 Dollars ($55,000.00)," to be represented by "a Note and Purchase Money Mortgage" or "a Note and Deed of Trust."

Then specify the amount of money you want to make with each payment, and when each payment is to be made (usually monthly). If you want to pay quarterly, semiannually or annually, then write it in that way.

If you are assuming an existing mortgage, then you will have to write in the approximate balance of the mortgage or mortgages you are assuming and the approximate amount of the mortgage you will he giving back to the seller, if any.

Then give the rate of interest paid on the principal on a yearly, that is, per annum, basis. Interest starts accruing on the unpaid principal on the date escrow closes.

This section gives you the right to prepayment without penalty. It also specifies that each payment will include both principal and interest. The essential words *or more* allow you to prepay any amount you desire and should *always* be included in your contract.

Example:

The balance of purchase price as follows:
The sum of Twenty-Five Thousand and 00/100 Dollars ($25,000.00), to be deposited prior to the close of escrow as a down payment, which shall include the above deposit;

The sum of Fifty Thousand and 00/100 Dollars ($50,000.00), to be represented by a Note and Mortgage to be payable Five Hundred Thirty-Seven and 31/100 Dollars ($537.31) or more per month, with interest on all unpaid principal of 10% per annum, from close of escrow, payable with each monthly payment as part of the same. First payment is due 30 days after the close of escrow.

## Clause 1—Buyer's Offer and Seller's Procedure for Accepting

This contract is not binding on either party unless the seller signs it without making any changes and returns it within the specified time limit. If you decide to withdraw your offer, you can do so without penalty until you receive the signed contract from the seller. If you want to revoke your offer after you submit it, you must notify the seller in writing that your offer is no longer open and that your deposit should be returned to you.

You will write your address at the end of the contract. You must state the amount of time the seller has to accept or reject your offer. You do not want to give him too much time, because he may stall around waiting for other buyers. Five to ten days is a standard time limit for a response. If you are really anxious to know where you stand, you can make the time limit shorter.

## Clause 2—Price per Acre and Number of Acres

Sometimes land is advertised and sold on the basis of a specified amount of money per acre, rather than a price for the total piece of land. If this is true of your deal, leave this clause in the contract. Otherwise, omit it. Most sellers are reluctant to state an exact acreage figure because they often don't know how much it is themselves. This is why you will sometimes see a figure like "40 + acres." The advantage of the clause is that if you have the land surveyed during escrow and find that the number of acres actually included in the parcel is less than the amount advertised, you can terminate the deal or get the price reduced accordingly. This relates to clause 16(b). (See Chapter 8, "Land Descriptions and Surveys.")

## Clause 3—Requirement of a Survey To Be Approved by the Buyer

This protective clause should not be removed from the contract. It provides that a legal survey must be furnished with the land and that the purchase is contingent on your approval of it. If the survey shows that the land does not include what you thought it did, you will notify the seller in writing that you disapprove of the results, and you can terminate the deal.

This clause states that the seller is to pay for the cost of a survey. In some cases, a survey will already have been done and there will be no problem. But if the land has not been surveyed, this can be a point of conflict between you and the seller, who will not want to pay the added expense of a survey. This is a point where you can compromise, if you wish, by offering to pay half the cost. In some cases, the real estate agent will pay for it to make the sale. If you cannot afford to pay for a survey and the seller refuses to supply one, you can tell the seller to increase the purchase price by the cost of a survey and you will pay for it over a period of time, should the deal be finalized. However you work it out, get the land surveyed before you buy. If you buy unsurveyed land, you have no precise idea of what you are buying. (See Chapter 8, "Land Descriptions and Surveys.")

### Clause 4—Escrow Instructions and Opening and Closing of Escrow

*First Paragraph:* This provides for delivery of escrow instructions. After the seller accepts your offer to purchase and signs the contract, both of you will submit written escrow instructions to the escrow holder on how to go about closing the deal. A 20-day time limit for submission of instructions is reasonable. Fill in the name and address of the escrow holder, as given in the beginning of this contract. Normally, a copy of the contract is delivered to the escrow holder, who prepares escrow instructions for the buyer and seller based on the terms of the contract.

*Second Paragraph:* You can set any closing date you desire. Provide enough time for any condition that must be completed, such as a loan arrangement, pest report and survey. Usually 30 to 60 days is sufficient time to complete necessary arrangements for the closing of escrow. If you need more time, both parties can mutually agree to a extension.

*Third Paragraph:* The purchase is final when the deed is recorded and escrow closes. (See Chapter 29, "Opening and Closing of Escrow and the Role of the Escrow Holder.")

### Clause 5—How Title Shall Vest

Vesting title refers to the form of ownership by which the buyers will take the property; for example, as husband and wife, as community property or joint tenants, tenants-in-common, or a corporation. The method used is important for legal reasons. Give the buyers' names and the way they will own the property here. If you do not have this information yet, fill in "to be designated prior to close of escrow." (See Chapter 31, "Types of Co-Ownership.") If you are buying with partners, you should have your co-owner's agreement drafted and signed during the purchase process.

Example:

> Gerald Herbert, a single man, an undivided one-half interest; and Daniel and Louise Varre, husband and wife, as community property, an undivided one-half interest.

### Clause 6—Condition of Title, Type of Deed, Preliminary Title Report and Buyer Approval

*Title* indicates legal ownership. Many things can interfere with your absolute ownership of a piece of property. There may be liens or encumbrances on the title.

*Liens* include any taxes, bonds, assessments, mortgages and judgments that have not yet been paid and that could lead to a forced sale of the land in order to obtain money for their payment. (See Chapter 17, "Property Taxes and Assessments"; Chapter 18, "Insuring Your Property for Yourself and Your Creditors"; and Chapter 23, "Buying Property That Is Encumbered by a Loan Agreement.")

*Encumbrances* can include many of the same things as liens but are more general. An encumbrance can be anything that affects or limits your title to the property.

An *easement* is a legal right-of-way belonging to other persons over your land. (See Chapter 9, "Easement Rights.")

*Covenants* are usually included in the deed as *restrictive covenants* that specify what uses will he permitted or prohibited on the land. (See Chapter 32, "Deeds and Recording.")

*Reservations* are rights held by the seller or other persons to do certain things on your land, such as remove minerals or trees from the property. (See Chapter 11, "Mineral, Oil, Gas, Timber, Soil and Other Rights.")

*Restrictions*, like covenants, include anything that limits what you can do with or on your land.

*Rights and conditions* is a catchall for anything that can't be included under the other terms.

All of these items, if they are recorded, will be uncovered and indicated by a title search or abstract of title. However, certain possible encumbrances such as *prescriptive easements*, are not recorded but may still be legally binding against the property owner if proved in court. (See Chapter 30, "The Title Search, Abstract of Title and Title Insurance Policy.")

This clause is drafted so that you must approve of any items that affect the title to the property. You will do this after you receive a title report or abstract. Always ask the title company or abstractor to give you complete copies of every document referred to in the report so that you can review them for yourself. After reviewing them, you can tell the seller if you disapprove of anything. For example, if the title company indicates that there is a cloud on the title from a prior lawsuit, tell the seller or broker you disapprove of that and you want it cleared up before the close of escrow.

Example: An easement over the property held by someone else would state that the title is subject to

> a nonexclusive easement 60 feet in width for ingress and egress and public utilities over the existing road located in the Northeast Quarter of the Southeast Quarter of said Section 21 as granted to John Doe by deed recorded June 19, 1970, in Book 4710 of Official Records, page 122, Elk County Official Records.

The warranty deed gives the buyer good protection. (See Chapter 32, "Deeds and Recording.") You must know what your deed will convey before escrow closes. The best way to get this information is by a preliminary title report, which is usually included free as part of the policy of title insurance and is given to you during the escrow. The report will indicate all recorded items that affect the title to the property. If you want an item removed, ask the seller to clear it up before the purchase is finalized and escrow closes. A seller can remove defects, or *clouds*, on the title more easily than the buyer, because the seller knows the parties involved. You should be able to get a preliminary title report within a couple of weeks of the opening of escrow, but you can fill in the blank with any time period. Give yourself a week or two to notify the seller of those things you want cleared, and state that time limit in the third blank space. The report will also state those items that the title company will not insure. Find out why they are not being insured. There might be a serious problem that you should know about.

You must state the name of the title company that is to conduct the title search and issue the report and policy. You can choose any title company you desire.

An important part of this clause is the requirement that the seller must provide you with copies of each document referred to in the preliminary title

report. For example, if the land is subject to an existing mortgage, you must receive a copy of the mortgage so that you can see what its terms are, how much is left to be paid and who holds the note.

In some areas of the country, title reports are replaced by abstracts of title. In that case, substitute "Abstract of Title" for "Preliminary Title Report" and fill in the name of the abstract company or lawyer who is to prepare the abstract. (See Chapter 30, "The Title Search, Abstract of Title and Title Insurance Policy.")

No matter what contract you use, the following contingency is essential:

> The close of escrow is contingent upon buyer's approval of (1) a preliminary title report or (2) an abstract of title issued in the name of buyer prior to the close of escrow.

### Clause 7—The Title Insurance Policy

Marketable *fee simple* title means that the seller owns the property, and there is no question about his or her rights of ownership. A policy of title insurance is to be delivered to you by the seller, guaranteeing marketable fee simple title. Although a standard policy has limited coverage, it is the most common buyer's policy. For more money you can get extended coverage offering greater protection, as is sometimes required by lending institutions. (See clause 11.)

The usual amount of coverage of the standard policy is equal to the purchase price of the property. Thus, if you build a house after escrow closes and a title problem later develops, the title company is liable to reimburse you only for the price of the land. The value of the house is not included. If you want greater coverage, you will usually have to pay for it later. (See clause 11.)

State the company that is to issue the title insurance policy. It should be the same company named in clause 6. If you are dealing with an abstract of title and opinions of an attorney, instead of a title search and title policies, amend this paragraph accordingly. (See Chapter 30, "The Title Search, Abstract of Title and Title Insurance Policy.")

### Clause 8—Prorations

This clause specifies the proportional breakdown between the seller and yourself of taxes, insurance premiums, interest on existing loans and installment payments on personal property. The amount each party pays depends on that party's respective periods of ownership possession. Proration occurs at the closing of escrow, because that is the date on which the property is transferred to the buyer. In cases where the buyer moves onto the property before escrow closes, the date the buyer takes possession might be used as the proration date. In that case cross out "the date of recordation of the deed" and write in "the date Buyer takes possession."

a. Because property taxes are calculated on an annual basis, under the proration you should pay taxes for only that part of the year you own the land. (See Chapter 17, "Property Taxes and Assessments.")

b. The proration of insurance premiums occurs only when you take over insurance held by the seller. If the seller is not transferring his or her policy to you, omit this section.

If you decide to take over the seller's insurance policy, your name must be placed on it as the insured. If the seller or a third-party lender is taking a mortgage or trust deed, the creditor usually must be named as a coinsured of the policy. Because the property is the creditor's only form of security for the loan, as a beneficiary under the policy it will be protected should the property be destroyed. (See Chapter 18, "Insuring Your Property for Yourself and Your Creditors.") During the escrow period, speak to the insurance agent and get a binder guaranteeing that you will be insured the moment you take title to, or possession of, the property, whichever occurs first.

c. If you are taking title subject to a preexisting encumbrance, such as a mortgage or deed of trust, prorate the interest to be paid by you and the seller. You do not want to pay interest on the loan for the period before you take title to the land. If you are taking title to the land free of any existing encumbrance, omit this section. (See Chapter 23, "Buying Property That Is Encumbered by a Loan Agreement.")

d. If the sale includes personal property, such as appliances and machinery, that is not fully paid for, prorate the installment payments so that you will begin to take over payments as of the close of escrow. If you are not taking over payments on any personal property as part of the purchase, omit this section.

Any other item that you want to prorate with the seller can be included in clause 8 by adding a statement identifying what is to be prorated. (See Chapter 29, "Opening and Closing of Escrow and the Role of the Escrow Holder.")

**Clause 9 —Credit for Impounded Funds**

When land is bought under a mortgage or deed of trust, the party who holds the land as security, if it is a commercial lender, usually continues to pay the taxes, assessments and insurance premiums so that it can be certain these obligations get paid. To pay these expenses, the institutional lender takes payments from the buyer, called *impounds*. These impounds are prepaid by the borrower so money will be available for upcoming payments. For instance, the buyer might pay the lender for taxes a year in advance.

When escrow closes, some funds that the seller has already paid will be in this account. The seller will be credited with this amount, and the prorations listed in clause 8 will determine the breakdown of payments between buyer and seller. When you see a copy of the existing mortgage or deed of trust and discuss assuming the loan, you will be given a list of impounded funds.

If you are not assuming or taking title subject to an existing loan, this clause should be deleted from the contract. (See Chapter 23, "Buying Property That Is Encumbered by a Loan Agreement.")

**Clause 10—Payment of Liens, Assessments and Bonds**

Clause 10 indicates that the seller is to pay all money due on liens, assessments and bonds before the close of escrow. This clause is used when the county has enacted a special assessment against the property. This is commonly done by local governments to pay for roads, sewage treatment facilities and other major improvements.

It is always best to get the seller to (1) pay these assessments before you take title to the land, or (2) allow you to subtract the amount due from the purchase price. These assessments and liens often are prorated as part of clause 8, because they are almost always included as part of the normal real property tax bill.

**Clause 11—Apportionment of Escrow Charges and Title Insurance Premium**

Usually, the buyer and seller each pay half of the escrow charges, in which case "50" would be inserted in both spaces here. When you first submit this contract to the seller, you can stipulate that he or she pay 100 percent of the fee. Later, you can "compromise" and offer to pay half.

The real estate agent may tell you that these charges are apportioned according to local custom, but you can come to any agreement with the seller that you want. For example, you and the seller can split the escrow fees and the title insurance premium equally, or you can pay the recording and drafting fees and the seller can pay the insurance premium. If you use an abstract of title, omit the reference to title insurance, and vice-versa. (See Chapter 29, "Opening and Closing of Escrow and the Role of the Escrow Holder," and Chapter 30, "The Title Search, Abstract of Title and Title Insurance Policy.")

### Clause 12—Delivering Possession of Property and Penalty for Holdover

Possession is "delivered" when the buyer moves onto the property or when he or she has the right to do so. The seller call give the buyer the right to possession at any time, even before the buyer takes title to the land. Parts (a), (b) and (c) of clause 12 fix the date when possession will be delivered. Fixing a date for possession is important because liability for property damage and personal liability usually follows possession.

The person in possession bears the risk of property destruction, being the only person in a position to protect the property. Many states have laws called *Risk of Loss Acts*, which expressly state this rule. Once title has passed, the buyer will always be the one to bear the loss, regardless of who is in possession, unless specified otherwise in the contract.

If you move into a house before title is transferred to you and the house burns down, you are still legally required to go ahead with the purchase. I don't think it is wise to take possession before the close of escrow, but sometimes this can't be avoided when the buyer is desperate for a place to live. Specify here when you are to take possession.

If you are going to take over the seller's property insurance, have your name added to the policy as an insured person as of the date you take possession, and adjust the proration of the premium accordingly it, clause 8. Never permit the seller to insert a clause that states that you are to assume the burden of insuring the land before you take possession of the property. (See Chapter 18, "Insuring Your Property for Yourself and Your Creditors.")

Part (d) of this clause provides for a penalty to be levied on the seller if possession of the property is not delivered on the specified date. A fee of $50 per day is usually considered a reasonable amount to be paid by a *holdover seller*. If you choose, you can terminate the entire deal and have your money

returned. To ensure that money will be available for the fine or refund, instruct the escrow holder to keep all money paid into escrow until notified that the seller has vacated. If you are buying land that is already vacant, you can delete this part of this clause.

To avoid a problem, never allow a seller or a seller's tenant to remain in possession after the escrow closes. I have had to legally evict a seller who refused to vacate after he got his money. Although I do have provisions for penalties here, the best policy is always to refuse to close escrow until the seller vacates the property. Of course, the seller will want all of your money in escrow before vacating the property, and that is perfectly acceptable. (See Chapter 29, "Opening and Closing of Escrow and The Role of the Escrow Holder.")

### Clause 13—Buyer's Option If Property Is Destroyed or Taken by Eminent Domain

This section permits you to terminate the deal or have the purchase price reduced if anything happens to the property before you receive possession or title. It is important that you have both of these choices. (See clause 14; Chapter 15, "Eminent Domain and Condemnation"; and Chapter 29, "Opening and Closing of Escrow and the Role of the Escrow Holder.")

### Clause 14—Default and Liquidated Damages

When the seller accepts the terms of your offer by signing this contract, each of you has specified obligations to perform as stated in the contract. This clause states the damages that will be levied if one of the parties breaks the agreement. Because the amount of damages is specified before any damages actually occur, this is referred to as a *liquidated damages* clause.

If the seller fails to carry through on the contract, you get the deposit and any other money returned, in addition to a penalty amount that is to be inserted here. You call make this any figure you wish, but it should approximate what your actual damages will probably be. For example, if you are paying for an appraisal of the property, you would insert the amount you pay here so that you can get your money back if the seller later backs out. If you have no expenses and the return of your deposit is sufficient, you can leave this space blank. But it is preferable to penalize the seller the same amount of money you will be penalized if you back out.

If you wish to reserve your right to sue the seller if he or she breaches the contract, then, to get a court order compelling the seller to specifically perform the sale to you, you should delete the portion of the liquidated damages clause that deals with the buyer's rights upon the breach of the seller to perform.

If you default, the seller can keep the amount specified in the blank. Fill in the amount of your deposit (or, perhaps, less if you put down a large amount). It is standard procedure that a buyer who defaults loses the entire deposit, but you should not permit the seller to take any more than that.

Most courts will overlook this clause if the stated amounts do not represent the actual damages that occur later. The courts can always adjust the amount up or down if a party protests that an inequity exists. Because court costs are so high, however, it is unlikely that either you or the seller will want to go to court, and that is the purpose of this clause. Try to keep the figure as reasonable as possible.

This clause offers only monetary damages for breach of contract. In another type of remedy, called *specific performance*, the court can force a party to go through with the deal, that is, to perform the contract. Thus, if the seller refuses to sell you the land after this agreement has been signed and you have met all the conditions, you do not have to accept money if it is really the land you want. But you will have to get a court order to force the seller to give you the land. In like manner the seller who feels monetary damages are not sufficient can force you to complete the purchase. These legal options are available even though they are not specifically mentioned in the contract.

### Clause 15—Comprehensive Title Covenant and Warranty

Paragraphs (a) through (e) state that (a) the seller owns the land he or she is selling and has the right to sell it, (b) no liens or encumbrances exist other than those stated in the contract, (c) your ownership will not be disturbed by any other person with a valid title to the land, (d) the seller will fulfill any other condition you require to clear the title to the land, and (e) the seller will pay for costs involved if you have to defend your right to the land.

If you get title insurance, the same warranties will be covered and insured by the title company. The title company will defend you if your title is challenged. In states where title insurance is available, this type of clause is often excluded from the

contract. But I see no reason why the seller should not warrant these things, regardless of whether you are insured. Thus, I have included them.

When the seller is vehemently opposed to including this clause, if he or she intends to give you warranty deed or grant deed and if you can obtain title insurance, or certificate of title, you can remove this clause from the contract and still be adequately protected. The reason for the seller's opposition is that he or she will be liable to pay for your defense if anybody challenges your ownership.

Paragraph (f), that these covenants will survive delivery of the deed, means that they will still be binding on the seller after you accept the deed for the property. Once the deed is accepted, the terms of the contract of sale usually are superseded by the terms of the deed and are no longer binding. The court assumes that if you accept the deed, you cannot complain later that the terms of the contract have been violated. But the warranty negates the assumption that you intend to let the seller "off the hook" by accepting his or her deed. (See Chapter 32, "Deeds and Recording.")

### Clause 16—Warranties and Representations by the Seller

Insert in this clause any elements of the sale for which you want the seller to give a warranty. If you insert a provision the seller refuses to warrant, find out why. You might discover something that should discourage you from making the purchase. I have included here a list of the most common warranties used in sales agreements. If the seller accepts the contract and an item that is included as a warranty is later discovered to be untrue, this clause will be extremely useful to you in a court action. If you want the seller to warrant something that is not included here, write out the details of your warranty, using this as a model, and insert it into your contract. If any of the warranties are irrelevant in your case, simply omit them from your contract.

a. Clause 16(a) is a warranty that you have a legal right-of-way to your building site from the public road. You may very likely have trouble getting a seller to agree to this, because many pieces of land are sold with inadequate access. Do not purchase such a parcel. If you don't have good access, you cannot use the land. Make sure this warranty stays in the contract. (See Chapter 9, "Easement Rights.")

b. The only part of this warranty you might allow the seller to modify is that specifying surveyed boundaries. On a small parcel or a flat piece of land, you will be fairly safe if only the corners of the property are marked by a licensed surveyor, because you can often estimate from them where the boundary lines run. However, if you have any doubt about whether an item such as a spring, a house or a creek is on the property, you definitely want the entire boundary marked by a licensed surveyor. You gain additional protection by listing those things that are essential to your purchase—structures, waterfalls, springs, creeks, and so on. (See Chapter 8, "Land Descriptions and Surveys.")

c. This is your guarantee that there is a year-round water supply on the land. Estimate the amount of water you will need for anything you plan to do on the land, or use the figures the seller gives you. The seller who says a well produces two gallons a minute every day of the year must be willing to allow this warranty in the contract. This is a warranty that will be difficult and probably impossible to get the seller to make. But the discussion it generates will give you some idea of the seller's feelings about the water situation. (See Chapter 4, "Is There Enough Water on the Land?")

d. If the zoning of the area is changed before the close of escrow, this warranty makes the seller, rather than you, bear the risk that the change might prohibit your intended use of the land. (See Chapter 12, "Zoning Laws.")

e. If there is a house or other structure on the land, this warranty should be inserted for your protection, especially if the structure represents a large portion of the purchase price. Because it does not require freedom from pest infestation until the closing of escrow, the seller has time to get the house sprayed or fumigated before you buy in (See Chapter 6, "Evaluating Houses, Manufactured Homes and Other Structures.")

f. This warranty is important if there are structures or sewerage facilities on the land, because it ensures that these conform to the local building and health codes and zoning ordinances. Violations that have not yet been cited by the local authorities also are covered. (See Chapter 13, "Building and Health Codes.")

g. This warranty ensures that there are no liens on the property, including assessments and bonds levied for past and future improvements or mechanics' liens for work completed and not paid for. A title search or abstract will not cover unrecorded items, but the seller might know of liens, assessments or bonds that will be levied against the land and are not yet part of the public records. These should be inserted here. For example, if the seller had construction work done and owes a materials supplier money, does not pay the bill, then sells you the land, the supplier could place a mechanic's lien against the property, even though you did not own it at the time the bill was incurred. This should be needed only if recent construction has been done on the property. (See Chapter 17, "Property Taxes and Assessments," and Chapter 30, "The Title Search, Abstract of Title and Title Insurance Policy.")

h. Often, a seller who discovers that the government has plans to take all or part of a property by eminent domain will try to sell that property quickly at a higher price than is expected from the government. The ignorant buyer then suffers the consequences of the condemnation. This warranty is excellent protection should such circumstances arise after you take title. If you had to go to court, however, you would have the burden of proving the seller knew that condemnation was imminent. But at least with this warranty in the contract, you would be able to *get* to court. (See Chapter 15, Eminent Domain and Condemnation.")

i. This warranty refers to the complete list of personal property included in clause 8(d) with the description of the property to be conveyed. The seller is to list those items that will not be fully paid for by the time escrow closes. If personal property is not included in the sale, omit this warranty.

j. For those interested in back-to-nature or organic living, this warranty will be very important. It is self-explanatory. (See Chapter 5, "The Earth—Soil, Vegetation, Topography.")

k. See clause 15(f).

**Clause 17—Conditions to the Agreement**
This clause, in which you list all conditions or contingencies that you want met before the close of escrow, is one of the most important in the contract. You can specify essential elements for your protection, as well as any aspect of the deal you are unsure of and want to approve before escrow closes.

Some lawyers prefer to list these conditions in a separate document called a *contingency contract*; however, I list these items right in the contract of sale. When the seller signs the contract of sale, he or she agrees to those conditions. The seller who crosses out anything before signing the contract, according to the law of contracts, rejects the entire offer and makes you a counteroffer.

In this clause of the Model Contract I include

the most common conditions used for the protection of the buyer. You can insert any conditions you like in your contract and hope the seller accepts them. If he or she will not, you will have to decide whether these conditions are absolutely essential for your protection or whether you should compromise on them. If the conditions the seller will not accept are necessary for your protection, you had best not buy the land. Irrelevant conditions listed here should be omitted from your contract. If you want a condition that is not here, write it up in the same manner as those that are here and insert it into your contract.

a. If you do not approve of any matters specified in the following conditions or if the conditions are not satisfied, clause 17(a) states that you are to tell the seller of your objections and can then terminate the deal and get your money back. Sometimes, when a condition is not satisfied, you and the seller can renegotiate the deal rather than terminate it. For example, if a pest report says that $2,000 worth of work is needed and you refuse to buy the property, the seller and you might agree to split the cost or to reduce the purchase price of the property by $2,000 to make the deal go. Perhaps the broker might agree to pay for the work out of his or her commission to make the sale.

b. State any report you want made on the property, such as a survey, soil test, pest report, termite and structural inspection, potability test or property appraisal. You can choose who will do these reports and set your own standards for approval. The only rule generally followed in the law is that you cannot disapprove a survey, test or report *unreasonably*. If the seller is to have a survey run before closing and it does not include something you want on the property, you can send your disapproval to the seller in writing and terminate the deal. You can also insert a condition here that the close of escrow is subject to your attorney's approval.

The time limit you allow should be inserted in the blank in clause 17(b). The time allowed will depend on what is to be done, for example, a survey usually takes longer than a termite inspection. Give yourself at least 30 days to be on the safe side, and 60 days is more reasonable. (Things in the country tend to move at a slower pace.) Also insert here how the survey, tests or reports will be paid for. If you disapprove of the results of any of these reports, you can legally terminate the deal within the terms of the contract and get your deposit back. (See Chapter 6, "Evaluating Houses, Manufactured

Homes and Other Structures"; Chapter 8, "Land Descriptions and Surveys"; and Chapter 19, "Evaluating the Price of the Property.")

c. This condition protects you if you need to get the land rezoned or if you need a permit for something you intend to do or build on the property. For example, some areas permit only one dwelling for each 20 acres of land. If you know that you want to build two houses on your 20-acre parcel, you may extend the close of escrow to give you time to seek a variance. If you cannot get the variance and permit you seek, you have the option to terminate the deal or waive the condition. If you need a permit to run a commercial venture on the property, *before the deal closes* you want to be sure you can get the permit. The contract states that you are to pay the costs of getting a permit or whatever you are after. Of course, you should try to get the seller to help with the fees. You must proceed with haste and diligence, or the seller can terminate this contract. Usually, the seller will not agree to allow this process to proceed for very long, because it could take months to get a variance from the local government. (See Chapter 12, "Zoning Laws," and Chapter 13, "Building and Health Codes.")

d. You need this condition if there are buildings on the land. The pest inspection must take place after the date the contract is signed, so that the seller won't attempt to show you an old report. You can write in the name of the company you want to do the inspection if you have selected one by the time you sign the contract. Otherwise, put in the words: "a company of Buyer's choice." You should try to get the seller to pay for it. You also may offer to share the cost with him or pay the entire cost yourself. I have written in all three options, and you call choose whichever you want. But first submit a contract that specifies that the seller has to pay for the test. If the seller objects, you can offer to pay half or you can try to get the real estate agent to pay for it. (See Chapter 6, "Evaluating Houses, Manufactured Homes and Other Structures.")

e. If your purchase depends on getting a loan from a party other than the seller, that is, a commercial lender, have this condition in the contract. If the seller is taking back a mortgage or deed of trust, the payment provision at the beginning of the contract will be sufficient, and you will not need this lending clause. The condition states that you must obtain *the loan*, rather than just a commitment for one, because the lender could change its mind before the papers are signed. The date inserted as a time limit for obtaining the loan should allow you enough time to get all the paperwork done. It can easily take 60 days for a loan to he approved.

Specify the terms under which you are willing to take a loan. Keep them low for your initial attempt to obtain financing. You can always raise them later. If you are seeking an FHA-insured or a VA-guaranteed loan, you should insert this as part of the condition.

After attempting to get a loan, if it is obvious you cannot get the financing, inform the seller of that fact; do not delay his or her sale of the property unnecessarily.

If you cannot get a loan, you will get your deposit back. *Never* let the seller omit this clause from the contract if your purchase is dependent on obtaining a loan. Investigate your loan possibilities before signing the contract so you do not waste your time. For example, it is almost impossible to get a loan on undeveloped, raw land. If your purchase is contingent on your first selling your present home, then you will want to write that in as a condition. (See Part V, "Financing Your Purchase.")

f. If the seller does not want to give the warranty specified in clause 16(c), clause 17(f) must be included in the agreement. One or the other is absolutely essential. Under this clause, the seller must make a "diligent effort" to search for water, meaning that he or she must dig a well, if necessary, to a depth not greater than that which you insert here. If you don't obtain the minimum rate of flow you specify, the agreement will be terminated and any money you have paid the seller should be repaid. This condition must be met before escrow closes. The problem is that you will not know whether the flow of water will be adequate in the driest time of year until that time. You have to decide whether you want to go ahead and risk the chance that it will be sufficient. (The well-driller might have a well log that indicates the flow during the dry season.) The condition and warranty specify year-round supply; if the supply proves to be insufficient, you can always attempt to rescind the contract and get your money back. Of course, the seller will put up a fight. The figures you use here for maximum depth should be at least the average depth for your area, and the output should be the amount you will need.

Sellers often are reluctant to allow this condition in a contract for obvious reasons. Regardless of how beautiful the land is and how good the price is, if no visible means of water supply exists, do not sign a contract without a condition of this type. Even if 90 percent of the landowners in the area located adequate water by drilling a well, you could be in the unlucky 10 percent, in which case the land will be worthless to you. A seller who will not allow this condition in the contract is out to cheat you. Your only compromise should be that you will pay either half or all of the costs of water development. I don't think you should pay more than half, but if you are hooked on the land, go ahead and get a well drilled. If no water is found, you can still get out of the contract, and you will lose only the cost of drilling, which is better than buying a dry, worthless piece of land. (See Chapter 4, "Is There Enough Water on the Land?")

**Clause 18—Liability for Attorney's Fees in Case of Lawsuit**

If you ever have to sue the seller because of breach of this agreement, you will get your attorney's fees paid as part of the damages. Of course, the same thing applies if the seller sues you and wins. This is a standard clause in a contract of sale.

**Clause 19—Explanation of Terms in this Agreement**

This is a standard clause in any contract of sale.

**Clause 20—Incorporation of Exhibits**

Insurance policies, copies of a mortgage or deed of trust, surveys, lists of personal property and anything else specified in the agreement and included on separate sheets of paper or in other documents are called *exhibits*; according to this clause, such items are part of the contract, whether or not they are directly attached. Label attached forms Exhibit A, B, C, and so on. This is a standard clause in any contract of sale.

**Clause 21—Waiver of Performance, Time for Performance and Remedies**

This is a standard clause in any Contract of Sale.

**Clause 22—Requirements of Valid Notice**

You must give notice by the means specified here if you want such notice to be valid. This is a standard clause in any contract of sale.

**Clause 23—Other Persons Bound by This Agreement**

This is a standard clause in any contract of sale. It protects both you and the seller in the event either of you dies or assigns your rights under the contract after it becomes binding. At that time your successors or assigns also will he bound by the contract.

### Clause 24—Requirements for Change or Modification of This Contract

This is a standard clause in any contract of sale. If you submit this contract to the seller and he or she deletes or adds anything, you must sign your initials or your name next to the change, signifying you agree to the change, before it will become binding.

### Clause 25—Time Is of the Essence

Each time limit specified in this agreement is to be strictly enforced. Any extensions must be agreed to by all parties in writing. If a provision has no time limit indicated, the period allowed is to be a "reasonable" amount of time. It is always preferable to specify exact time limits whenever possible. This is a standard clause in any contract of sale.

## Identification of Escrow Holder and Real Estate Agent

Insert the names, addresses and phone numbers of the escrow holder and the agent. These are needed in case any of the parties must contact them regarding an element of the transaction. If there is no agent, this is unnecessary.

## Buyer Signs the Contract of Sale and States Form of Acceptance by Seller

You, the buyer, sign here. If you are married, both you and your spouse should sign the contract. Be sure to keep a copy of this agreement for yourself and give a signed copy to the seller. The seller's acceptance is not valid until you receive the returned contract signed by him or her.

Before you sign this contract or any other document, be absolutely certain that everything you want has been expressed in writing, including all conditions of purchase and warranties by the seller. No oral statements made to or by the real estate agent or seller are binding in any way, unless they can be proved, and that is difficult. That is why you want everything in writing.

## Acceptance—Details of Real Estate Agent's Commission

Here the seller fills in the commission he has agreed to pay the real estate agent, if any. The commission will be paid only if the deal closes, if the seller breaks the contract or if the seller recovers money from you because you default. Sometimes the broker does not include the details of the commission because it is part of a separate listing agreement between seller and broker.

## Seller Signs the Contract and Accepts Your Offer

Finally, the seller signs his name in acceptance of your offer and of the contract of sale. If the seller is married, both husband and wife must sign. Once the seller signs and delivers a signed copy to you, the contract becomes legally enforceable; both you and the seller are bound by its terms. If all conditions and terms of the agreement are met by both parties, the transaction will close as scheduled on the day escrow closes.

If the seller alters the document in any material way, it is invalid until the changes have been approved and initialed by you. If the seller makes changes and sends the altered contract back to you, he or she is making a counteroffer for you to purchase the land on the basis of the contract as changed. Or the seller might return your offer unsigned and submit his or her own contract to you for acceptance. You will have to decide whether the new terms are acceptable. The contract of sale may be sent back and forth several times before a final agreement is reached, if one is reached. So many alterations may be made during the course of your bargaining that you might have to type up a new contract three or four times. Usually, though, you will have negotiated enough verbally with the seller before you submit your contract that it will merely put in writing what you have already agreed to verbally. (See Chapter 20, "Bargaining To Get the Seller's Asking Price Down.")

If the seller signs the contract, the real estate agent signs below the seller's name as evidence that he or she consents to the amount of commission stated and then returns the contract to you as a representative of the seller. If you are buying directly from the seller, omit all reference in this section to a real estate agent and a sales commission.

# 28 Option Agreements

## Option To Purchase

The purpose of an option to purchase is to get the land off the market while you decide if you want to buy it. This option is created when the buyer gives an amount of money, called the *option money* or *consideration*, to the seller, who promises, in return, not to sell the property until the end of the specified option period. The amount of consideration can be any amount of money. For instance, suppose you are interested in buying a certain piece of land but cannot decide if you really want it, and you don't want to commit yourself to the extent of offering the seller a contract of sale. You know that several other prospective buyers are also interested in the land, so you want the seller to take the land off the market for awhile. You offer to pay the seller $500 if he or she does not sell the land for three months, and the seller gives you an option to

purchase the land. The seller (or *optionor*), gives the option to you, the possible buyer (or *optionee*), and you sign an option-to-purchase contract. In the option the entire purchase agreement is detailed, including price, terms, conditions, cost-sharing arrangements and warranties.

During the next 90 days, you can exercise that option by offering to buy the land at any time. The seller must not sell the property during that time to anyone but you. If the seller breaches the option, you can successfully sue for damages. If you do exercise the option and buy the land within the time period, the contract of sale becomes binding as of the date the option agreement is exercised; generally, the option payment of $500 is credited toward the purchase price. If you do not exercise the option by the time 90 days pass, the seller keeps your consideration of $500 and puts the property back on the market.

Because the option to purchase is a contract, it

should contain all essential elements in writing: the names and addresses of the seller and potential buyer; the date the option goes into effect (usually on signing); the amount of payment, or consideration, given by the potential buyer to the seller for the option; the express statement that an option has been created; the period the option is for and the date of expiration; how the option is to be exercised (usually by written notice to the seller); the full purchase price and terms of the sale; a statement that the option money is lost if the option is not exercised; the right for you to give, or sell, your rights under the option to someone else during the option period; and the signatures of parties.

The option should be stated in a short contract with all the required details attached to it in the unsigned contract of sale, which is signed if and when the option is exercised. Personally, I do not recommend the use of an option to purchase in the standard land purchase because it is often a waste of money and destroys much of the flexibility needed for negotiation. An option is almost always taken on the basis of the seller's asking price.

However, if you would like complete freedom to back out of the purchase and are willing to pay the option price, an option to purchase might give you the flexibility you need.

It is important to get notice of the option, if you use one, into the public records. If during your option period the seller sells the property, the buyer will have the greater right to the land, unless you have recorded the option-to-purchase document or a memorandum that an option has been granted with the county recorder's office. (See Chapter 32, "Deeds and Recording.") An option to purchase is a separate transaction from the signing of a contract of sale. Be sure you are not signing a contract of sale under a different name or some other type of sales contract under the impression that what you are signing is an option. Because of the unique legal aspects of an option to purchase, check the whole deal out with your lawyer before signing or promising anything. For this reason I am not including a Model Option-To-Purchase agreement in this book.

## The Lease with an Option To Purchase

The *lease with an option to purchase*, or *lease option*, is an excellent way for a person who is un-

sure whether he or she really wants to live in the country, to buy land. This option allows you to move onto the property, live in the dwelling and pay rent for an agreed-on time, the lease period. You also have to pay an additional sum of money for the option itself. If you decide to buy the property during that time, you can exercise an option to purchase the property, and all or part of the rent money and/or option money you have paid should be credited toward payment of the total purchase price. Be sure the lease option has that written into it as part of the deal. If you do not exercise the option during the period of your lease, you lose nothing except the option money. You have had the privilege of living on the property during the lease period.

The purchase price is determined as of the date the lease option is entered into.

A binding contract occurs when the option is exercised, so the original lease option agreement must contain all the essential items of a contract of sale. A contract of sale should be used with the lease agreement. Most options that are handled on standard preprinted forms by agents are not sufficient. You would be wise to obtain legal advice if you have any questions about the validity of your agreement or if you intend to draft your own lease option agreement. All terms of the lease option must be in writing and a memorandum of the agreement must be recorded with the county recorder in order to give the public notice of your rights and to protect you should the seller make a deal with anybody else after signing a lease option with you.

A lease option occasionally gives the tenant only the *first right of refusal*. A first right of refusal means that if the landlord-owner decides to sell his property during the terms of your lease, you, as holder of the option, will have the first chance to purchase it at the same price and terms that the third party has offered. This is probably not worth paying extra money for. In the normal lease option, the landlord-owner agrees to sell the tenant the land when the lease option is signed. The final sale depends solely on whether the tenant exercises the option, not on whether the seller offers to sell the property to the tenant during the lease period. If you want a regular lease option, be sure you don't get a first right of refusal instead. Read the agreement carefully, and seek the advice of a competent real estate attorney.

# Going Through Escrow

# 29 Opening and Closing of Escrow and the Role of the Escrow Holder

One of the most important aspects of your land purchase is the function of *escrow*. the finalization of a real estate transaction is characterized by different terminology around the country. In the west, where buyer and seller may never meet, the paperwork is handled by an *escrow agent* or *officer* and the process is known as *closing escrow*. Other parts of the country may refer to this critical moment in the transaction as *closing, settlement, transfer (of title)* or, as in the Northeast, the descriptive term *passing papers*. Whether the closing occurs face-to-face or through escrow, the main concerns are that the buyer receive the marketable title, that the seller receive the purchase price, and that certain other items be adjusted properly between the two. I describe the escrow process used by title companies or escrow companies. Your state may have variations of this process that can be explained to you by your real estate agent or attorney.

Although an escrow may be used for many kinds of business transactions, it is primarily used in the sale of real estate. Through escrow, title to land is transferred from the seller to the buyer according to the written escrow instructions of each party. These escrow instructions constitute the escrow agreement and are submitted to the *escrow holder*, also called the *escrow agent, escrow officer* or *escrowee*, who is bound to carry them our before the deed can be transferred to the buyer, the purchase price conveyed to the seller and the sale consummated. Escrow is *opened* when a file escrow number is given to the parties and the instructions are given to the escrow holder; escrow is *closed* when the deed is transferred to the buyer.

The most commonly used escrow agents are title insurance and abstract companies, trust companies, banks, savings and loan associations, escrow companies and attorneys. The functions of all escrow agents are the same, although specific procedures may differ. Lawyers are sometimes used as escrow holders, but institutional agents usually can perform the necessary escrow services at a lower fee than an attorney can, because they have escrow departments that specialize in these services.

It is best to use a different escrow agent from the one normally used by the real estate agent handling the sale, because the agent and the escrow holder have probably become close friends after working together over a long period of time; the necessary element of "disinterest" on the part of the escrow holder might be lacking. Fees charged by escrow agents vary considerably. Look for the most reputable and professional escrow holder you can find who charges a reasonable fee.

## There Must Be a Valid Contract of Sale Before Escrow Can Open

You and the seller must complete your negotiations and sign a valid contract of sale before going into escrow. The contract will state when escrow is to open and the parties are to submit escrow instructions; when escrow is to close; and who the escrow holder shall be, giving the name and address of the individual or institution involved. These items would be included in clause 4 of the Model Contract of Sale in Chapter 27.

## Parties Submit Escrow Instructions, and Buyer Includes a Deposit

Separate instructions to the escrow holder are submitted by both buyer and seller, as well as by the lender if a third-party loan is involved. Each set of instructions must be in writing and signed by the party who submits it. They are legally binding on the parties as soon as the buyer and seller have signed identical forms of instructions. Escrow opens and remains open until the transaction is terminated according to the terms of the contract of sale and the instructions. Therefore, be certain that the instructions contain everything you expect to

receive in the purchase. In some areas, both the buyer's and the seller's instructions are included on a single form, but usually both parties submit separate documents.

Escrow holders generally have standard preprinted forms of escrow instructions that the parties are supposed to fill in with the necessary information or that come to the parties already completed, based on the contract of sale. However, the best way to protect your interest is to read carefully any escrow instructions submitted to you for signing. Chapter 27 included a Model Contract of Sale that you could use in your transaction by inserting appropriate information or could compare to a contract used by the broker. This chapter includes a Model Form for Buyer's Escrow Instructions (Figure 29–1), which is meant to be used in conjunction with the Model Contract of Sale for you to either fill in and submit or use as a sample for comparison with instructions submitted to you. The information you give in these two forms should never be contradictory. As a safety measure, the escrow instructions should specify that any inconsistency is to be interpreted in favor of the contract of sale. (See clause 9 of the Model Escrow Instructions.) Although it is not required, I think you should submit a copy of the contract of sale with your escrow instructions as Exhibit B (see Model Form for

### Figure 29–1. Model Form for Buyer's Escrow Instructions

To_____ (name of escrow holder) _____          Escrow No. _____

_____ (address of escrow holder) _____          Escrow Officer _____

Date: _____, 19____

These Escrow Instructions constitute part of an agreement by which _____, called Buyer, agrees to buy, and _____ , called Seller, agrees to sell the real property described in Exhibit A, attached hereto and made a part hereof.
Buyer delivers to you with these instructions ___(amount of deposit)___ Dollars, ($ _____._) by___(cashier's or personal check)___ to your order as part of the total purchase price of_____ Dollars, ($ _____._).

Buyer will also hand to you or cause to be handed to you, on or before ___(date escrow closes)___ :

   (Describe how the remaining purchase money is to be paid. For example, "Balance of the purchase price in Buyer's promissory note and mortgage in the form attached, or placed in your hands before the close of escrow, bearing interest at____% per year, principal in ___(number of payments)___ equal ___(monthly, etc.)___ installments including interest on the unpaid balance, beginning on or before _____ , 19____."
   At the end of these instructions you should attach a copy of the mortgage or deed of trust and promissory note. If you don't have these at this time, give them to the escrow holder as soon as you have them. For samples of these documents, see Chapter 21: *Types of Financing: Land Contract, Mortgage, Deed of Trust.*)

**Figure 29–1. Model Form for Buyer's Escrow Instructions *continued***

Buyer will also hand to you or cause to be handed to you, on or before _____ (date escrow closes) _____ all additional funds and documents necessary on the part of Buyer to enable you to comply with these instructions.

1. You are authorized to use the foregoing money and documents when each of the following conditions have been fulfilled:
   (a) You have received notice of approval of all conditions in this transaction, as called for in Exhibit B, attached hereto and made a part hereof, or the time for notice of approval has expired without notice of disapproval of the conditions. Each requirement of notice to a party in Exhibit B and the Contract of Sale shall be construed also as a requirement of notice to the escrow holder.
   (b) You can issue or obtain at _____ (Buyer's or Seller's) _____ expense a _____ (standard or extended coverage) _____ Policy of Title Insurance with liability equal to_____ Dollars, ($_____ . ___ ) showing title to the described property vested in _____ (Buyer's name and marital status, and manner by which title is taken, e.g., joint tenancy, husband and wife, tenants-in-common, etc.)
   _____
   _____
   _____

   subject only to exceptions approved by Buyer in writing. You are authorized to record any instruments delivered through this escrow if necessary or proper for issuance of the Policy of Title Insurance called for above.

2. Prorate as of_____ (date escrow closes or date of possession) _____ on the basis of a 30-day month:
   (a) Real property taxes based on the most recent official information applicable to the fiscal year in which the proration date occurs, and obtainable in the office of the particular taxing authority.
   (b) Premiums on existing transferable insurance policies approved by Buyer by notice delivered to escrow covering damage to or destruction of the property transferred to Buyer through escrow.
   (c) Interest on obligations secured by encumbrances to which the property will remain subject after close of escrow. All new notes shall be dated as of close of escrow. If any new notes are dated before closing, they shall be "Interest to run only from _____ , 19 ___ ."
   (d) Installments of principal and interest on the following personal property:_____ (List any personal property that will be transferred to you with the sale that you will continue to make payments on.)
   _____

3. If impounded funds are held by the lender in connection with a mortgage, deed or trust, or other encumbrance remaining of record at close of escrow, Buyer shall be charged and Seller credited with the full amount.

4. Buyer shall pay_____% of the escrow fee; the escrow holder's customary charges to Buyer for document-drafting, recording, and miscellaneous charges; and the title insurance premium to the extent that it exceeds the premium for standard coverage with a liability equal to the purchase price.

5. Seller shall pay_____% of the escrow fee; and the escrow holder's customary charges to Seller for document-drafting, recording, and miscellaneous charges, including local real property transfer taxes; and the title insurance premium to the extent that it does not exceed the premium for standard coverage with a liability equal to the purchase price.

   (In the above two clauses, it is assumed that the Seller will pay for the Policy of Title Insurance. If this is not the case you can change the statement to apply to your situation.)

6. In addition each party shall pay reasonable compensation to the escrow holder for extraordinary or unusual services rendered to or for that party, if any, plus costs and expenses incurred in connection with these services.

7. These Escrow Instructions are to be construed with the instructions of Seller placed in this escrow with you.

8. If conflicting demands are made or notices served on you, you may, at your election, withhold and stop all further proceedings in this escrow without liability and without determining the merits of the demands, notices, or litigation.

9. As a matter of agreement between the parties, with which you are not to be concerned, any inconsistency between these Escrow Instructions and the Contract of Sale is to be resolved in a manner consistent with the Contract of Sale unless the inconsistent provision of the agreement is expressly waived by a writing specifically referring to the inconsistent provision in the Contract of Sale.

10. Time is of the essence for these instructions. If for any reason other than my failure to comply with the foregoing instructions this escrow cannot be closed by_____ , 19_____ , I may, by written notice to you, demand the return of all money and/or documents that I have placed herein. If both parties fail to comply within the said time limit, then neither party shall be entitled to the return of money and/or documents until, after demand, a five-day notice shall have been given to the other party by ordinary mail at address given you. If no demand for the return of money and/or documents is given, close this escrow as soon as possible.

**Figure 29–1. Model Form for Buyer's Escrow Instructions** *continued*

11. Any provision requiring an act to be performed or a condition to be satisfied at or before close of escrow refers to the date above; provided that the time for closing shall be extended if and to the extent that any time limit expressly given in the Escrow Instructions or the Contract of Sale between the parties has not expired on the above date.

12. Close of escrow means the time when the documents transferring title are recorded.

13. As soon after close of escrow as possible, deliver funds and documents to the parties respectively entitled to receive them. Make delivery to the address given below.

    (Here list what money and documents are to be given to each party. For example: "Seller gets purchase money or down payment, mortgage, promissory note. Buyer gets deed, Title Insurance Policy, Fire Insurance Policy.")

    _____

    _____

    _____

    _____

14. Buyer is to pay the following charges: ____(For example: "drawing up and recording the deed.")_____

    _____


I acknowledge receipt of a copy of these instructions.

Buyer, as referred to in these instructions, consists of the undersigned:

_____

(signature of Buyer)

_____

(typed name of Buyer)


_____

(signature of Buyer)

_____

(typed name of Buyer)


Buyer's address for notice is the following:

_____

(City and State)

_____

(Zip Code)

_____

(Telephone Number)

**Figure 29–1. Model Form for Buyer's Escrow Instructions** *continued*

---

**EXHIBIT A**

**(DESCRIPTION OF REAL PROPERTY AND PERSONAL PROPERTY THAT IS THE SUBJECT OF THE CONTRACT OF SALE)**

**EXHIBIT B**

**TERMS AND CONDITIONS OF THE PURCHASE BY BUYER:**

1. The total acreage on which the purchase price is computed shall be based on a legal survey completed by a licensed surveyor or registered civil engineer. The results of the survey are to be approved by Buyer before the close of escrow. The expense of the survey is to be paid by the Seller. (May be Buyer and Seller equally.)

2. Seller shall by grant or full covenant and warranty deed convey to Buyer a marketable fee simple title as approved by Buyer in the following manner: Within_____days of the Seller's acceptance of the Contract of Sale, Seller shall cause to be delivered to Buyer a Preliminary Title Report issued by____(name of the title company)____of ___(city and state)___ describing the property. Within _____ days after Buyer's receipt of the Preliminary Title Report and all documents referred to in it, Buyer shall give Seller notice specifying the matters disapproved by Buyer. If Buyer fails to give notice of approval or disapproval, his silence shall terminate the agreement.

3. (List further conditions which the sale is subject to. See Clauses 19(a) through (f) of the Model Contract of Sale in Chapter 28.)

---

Buyer's Escrow Instructions, clause 1 [a]), so that the escrow holder will have both documents at its disposal for clarification of the terms of the transaction. Again, if you have any questions, always consult a real estate attorney.

## Closing of Escrow

The Model Escrow Instructions are meant to be a guide to protect you. You may use a preprinted form given to you by the escrow holder if you make changes and additions to it that specify all of the necessary information included in the Model Escrow Instructions. The most important fact to remember about the instructions to the escrow holder is that all the facts of the purchase must be made known to the agent so that the expectations of both parties can be carried out to their satisfaction.

If you decide to use the escrow holder's preprinted form, beware of clauses that relieve the escrow holder of liability, such as a clause specifying that the escrow holder is not bound to inform the parties regarding facts within its knowledge. Also beware of any clauses that might be against your interests, such as a clause specifying that the buyer is to "take title subject to all easements, reservations, liens, encumbrances, covenants, conditions and restrictions of record" without giving you either a detailed list of what these are or copies of the recorded documents themselves.

The seller's instructions basically will require that before the close of escrow you must deposit the amount of money you and he or she have agreed on, either the full purchase price or a down payment and mortgage or deed of trust. The contract of sale specifies that if you give the real estate agent any earnest money as a deposit on the land when you sign the contract of sale, he or she must submit that money into escrow when escrow is opened or instructions are submitted. This money is to be held until the terms of the contract of sale are met and escrow closes. The seller's instructions should not be in conflict with your instructions or the terms of the contract of sale. Any conflict must be resolved before escrow can close.

If you are borrowing money from a third party such as a commercial bank, the lender will submit separate lender's instructions to the escrow holder explaining its role in the transaction and what the escrow holder is to do for the lender.

When you submit your instructions, an escrow number will be issued that will be written at the top of the instructions. If an institution is to be the escrow holder, it will assign an escrow officer, who will personally handle your transaction. Ask for this escrow officer and use your escrow number whenever you need to discuss your transaction with the escrow holder.

In some states, the parties submit their instructions in person and meet with the escrow holder to discuss what is to be done before the closing of escrow. It is becoming common, however, for parties to give their instructions to the real estate agent, who delivers them to the escrow holder. The buyer and seller may never meet the escrow holder. To protect your interests to the fullest extent, I think you should maintain personal contact with your escrow holder throughout the entire escrow process. Figure 29–2 is a simple diagram of how escrow works and what the duties of each party are.

## Summary of Things You Must Check Before Closing of Escrow

Before escrow closes, be certain that you have examined every aspect of the purchase and that everything meets your approval. Once you accept the deed, it will be difficult to complain later about anything that has not been performed according to the contract of sale, because closing the transaction and accepting the document implies that you approve of the transaction. Therefore, be sure you check each of the following points before the day escrow is to close.

- *Make a complete inspection of the land and structures and give your approval or disapproval to the seller.* If someone is living on the land, determine his or her status and have the seller ask the person(s) to leave before escrow closes. Look for and investigate any roads or paths across the land that could be unrecorded easements. Find out if the sale of the land creates an implied easement for the seller or anyone else. Match the description of any easement in your deed with its physical location on the ground to be sure you have access to your building site. If you notice recent repairs or construction when you examine the structures, be sure all costs of the work have been paid by the seller so that future liens cannot be brought against the title. If the closing is contingent on your approval of an appraisal or report of any kind, be sure the report covers the subject to your satisfaction. Check the water source to determine if it supplies the quantity and quality of water warranted by the seller.
- *Check any surveys of record to be sure that your land has been surveyed or check with the local surveyor.* Use a legal survey to locate the land's boundaries on the ground, and be sure that all the structures and physical features you expect to get are within those boundaries. Also use the survey to check the location of easements.

**Figure 29–2. Diagram of How Escrow Works**

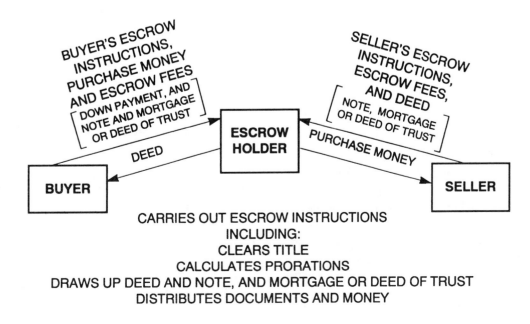

CARRIES OUT ESCROW INSTRUCTIONS
INCLUDING:
CLEARS TITLE
CALCULATES PRORATIONS
DRAWS UP DEED AND NOTE, AND MORTGAGE OR DEED OF TRUST
DISTRIBUTES DOCUMENTS AND MONEY

- *Examine any personal property that goes with the real estate.* If you are buying machinery or tools, operate them to see if they are in working condition. Ask the seller to show you records that all personal property is paid for. If any payments are still due, find out how much is owed and whether you are to assume them.
- *Check building, health and zoning codes to be sure no violations of ordinances or regulations exist regarding the land.* Find out whether permits have all been paid for.
- *Examine the title and order the seller to clear any defects you object to.* The escrow instructions state that the title must be searched, cleared and insured before the close of escrow. The seller must furnish you a preliminary title report, abstract of title or similar document showing the results of a title search, along with all documents representing encumbrances on the title, that is, easements, reservations, mortgages or other liens. When escrow opens, the first thing the escrow holder will do is order a title search and preliminary title report. It will charge this search to the seller, according to your instructions. The title search will be done by the escrow holder itself if the escrow holder is a title company.

If you have any objection to the state of the title as shown by the preliminary title report or abstract, inform the escrow holder that the seller is to have the encumbrances removed before escrow closes. For example, if back taxes are due on the land, you want them paid; if money is still owed on a mortgage, you want it satisfied; if a judgment exists against the seller's land, it should be paid off; or if someone has timber rights, you want the reservation removed. The escrow holder usually will obtain the money from the seller to pay and clear these liens. If the seller does not have sufficient funds to remove existing encumbrances but is willing to do so as soon as he or she obtains the purchase money from you, the escrow holder can take your purchase money on closing day and pay off the liens before closing escrow and delivering the purchase money to the seller. The escrow holder will then be able to convey a satisfactory, insurable title to you along with documents that show the encumbrances have been removed. These documents might include, for example, a receipt for taxes paid to the tax collector or a satisfaction of mortgage from the seller's creditor.

Regardless of what encumbrances exist, escrow should never be closed as long as you have objections to the title you are to receive. Provisions for making objections to the title are contained in clause 6 of the Model Contract of Sale and in exhibit B, clause 2, of the Model Escrow Instructions. If all defects in the title to which you object are not cleared within a specified time, you are entitled to have your money returned and the transaction terminated.

When all terms and conditions of escrow have been performed and the title is ready to be transferred, the escrow holder will order the title insurance company to issue a policy of title insurance that insures your title up to the exact minute that the deed is recorded. The policy must show that your title is free of any defects you previously disapproved of. If you cannot get title insurance in your state, you will have to determine from the abstract and certificate of title or similar document that the title is satisfactory. (See Chapter 30, "The Title Search, Abstract of Title and Title Insurance Policy.")

## Escrow Holder Transfers the Insurance Policy to Buyer

If the seller has the property insured and you agree to assume the insurance policy, the seller will give a copy of the policy to the escrow holder. If the escrow holder obtains permission from the insurance company to assign it to you, the holder draws up the document of assignment and gets the insurance policy and assignment form ready to deliver to you at the close of escrow. Sometimes the insurance company draws up a new policy in your name and delivers it to the escrow holder. (See Chapter 18, "Insuring Your Property for Yourself and Your Creditors.")

## Escrow Holder Makes Prorations and Adjustments

Prorations between you and the seller of property taxes and assessments, insurance premiums and interest on an existing mortgage are usually made by the escrow holder according to the date escrow closes. The method used in prorating each obligation is explained in Chapter 17, "Property Taxes and Assessments"; Chapter 18, "Insuring Your

Property for Yourself and Your Creditors"; and Chapter 23, "Buying Property That Is Encumbered by a Loan Agreement."

## Buyer Pays Purchase Price or Down Payment and Submits Loan Agreement and Note

The escrow holder will receive your deposit when escrow opens. You can submit into escrow any other cash you are to pay the seller at any time after escrow opens. However, wait until after you receive a preliminary title report or abstract of title and after all other conditions of the contract of sale and the escrow instructions have been met. It is best to submit purchase money on the day escrow is to close.

When the escrow holder receives your funds for the purchase, it will use them to clear up any encumbrances on the title as specified in the escrow instructions, pay the charges owed by the seller and deliver the rest to the seller after closing.

I caution you against giving the seller any money outside escrow. The purpose of escrow is to protect you in your dealings with the seller. The seller should not receive your money until you receive what you are paying for. The escrow holder can see that both sides meet their obligations before the money, deed and other documents are disbursed.

If you have arranged a loan from a commercial lender, it will not want to pay you until you have received clear title, because the lender wants to be sure to receive good security for the loan. The seller, on the other hand, does not want to give up title to the land until, and unless, he or she is certain of receiving the full purchase price. An escrow holder handles this situation to everybody's satisfaction in the following manner:

Before closing, the escrow holder receives the deed from the seller, a signed mortgage or deed of trust and note from you and the money from the lender. If all terms and conditions of the sale have been satisfied, the escrow holder records the deed and delivers it to you. It then delivers the purchase money to the seller. Thus, all parties are protected during the period of escrow, and everything is managed by the disinterested escrow holder without the possibility of fraud or violation of any terms of the agreement.

Be sure all financial documents are prepared and ready to be signed before escrow closes. If you are getting an FHA or VA loan, finalize all arrangements with the appropriate agency. If the seller is financing the sale, be sure the mortgage or deed of trust and the note or bond are prepared and approved by you before you sign them.

## Closing Costs

The closing costs are expenses in addition to the purchase price that must be paid before you take title. Before escrow closes be certain of how much you will be expected to pay and be sure you will actually receive what you are paying for. Believe it or not, I have met buyers who paid for title insurance and never received a copy of the policy. This should never be allowed to happen.

Your closing costs can be anywhere from $50 to over $1,000. Figure 29–3 lists all the items that can be included in closing costs. (Your transaction probably will not include all of them.) With each item, the figure states which party most often pays the charges involved. In many instances, this will be a matter of negotiation between you and the seller, and it is your goal to keep your costs as low as possible. I have not indicated the amount each will cost because prices are not standard.

In rural areas, closing costs are usually pretty standard within each community. As you get closer to major metropolitan areas, however, closing costs can vary widely from company to company.

Before engaging an escrow holder, shop around and ask what charges will be levied and particularly how escrow fees are determined. Even after you have an escrow holder, before escrow closes ask for an itemized accounting of every single charge that is to be levied against you, and make sure you receive a complete preliminary closing statement prior to the close of escrow.

Congress passed the Real Estate Settlement Procedures Act (RESPA) to protect home buyers from unnecessarily high settlement costs. RESPA requires advance estimates of settlement costs, limits the size of escrow accounts and prohibits referral fees and kickbacks. The act requires that all applicants for federally related mortgage loans receive from the lender a HUD-prepared booklet containing information about real estate transactions, settlement services, cost comparisons and relevant consumer protection laws when applying for a loan.

One day before the settlement, or closing, the

**Figure 29–3. Possible Closing Cost**

PAID BY (B=Buyer) (S=Seller)

| | |
|---|---|
| 1. Fees for a title search, title examination, or abstract of title (seller pays to clear existing liens on demand of buyer) | B or S or shared |
| 2. Premium for the policy of title insurance | B or S or shared |
| 3. Escrow fee | Usually shared |
| 4. Fee to draw up and notarize the deed | S |
| 5. Fee to record the deed | B |
| 6. Real property transfer tax | S or shared |
| 7. Termite and structural inspection fee | S or shared |
| 8. Cost of survey | B or S or shared |
| 9. Cost for water drilling and water quality test | B or S or shared |
| 10. Buyer's attorney's fees | B |
| 11. Seller's attorney's fees | S |
| 12. Real estate agent's commission | S |
| 13. Prorations (see 14(h) below) | |
| 14. Possible loan costs | |
|    (a) Fees charged by the escrow holder or the lawyer representing the seller or lending institution to draw up, notarize, and record the mortgage or deed of trust and note or bond | B |
|    (b) Amount of an existing loan to be paid off before closing with possible prepayment penalty fee | S |
|    (c) Credit report fee | B |
|    (d) Appraisal fee | B |
|    (e) "Point" charge | S |
|    (f) Assumption fee charged by the lender, if you are assuming a loan | B |
|    (g) State mortgage tax, in some states, based on the amount of the mortgage (usually 0.5–1 percent of the mortgage amount) | B |
|    (h) Prorations to seller for prepaid taxes, assessments, insurance, and loan impounds | B |
|    (i) First impound installment for taxes, assessments, and insurance to a third party lender | B |
|    (j) FHA insurance premium | B |

borrower may request information on the settlement costs; and both buyer add seller are entitled to a statement itemizing the costs they paid in the transaction. To find out mere about the Real Estate Settlement Procedures Act you may write to

> Assistant Secretary for Consumer Affairs and Regulatory Functions
> Office of Finance and Regulatory Enforcement
> Attention: RESPA Office, US/HUD
> 451 7th St., SW, Room 9262
> Washington, DC 20410
> (202) 708-9983

## The Closing Statement

The closing statement shows the facts and figures of the closing of escrow for both buyer and seller. This document is usually prepared by the escrow holder, although the real estate agent or the seller's attorney might do it in some areas.

A separate closing statement may be used for each party or both parties may be included on one statement. I recommend using a single closing statement that enumerates the charges for each party on one sheet of paper, with the buyer and seller each receiving a duplicate copy. All parties should have a complete knowledge of the costs in-

**Figure 29–4. Sample Closing Statement**

Statement of Escrow No. _____    Office _____

To _____    Date _____

| Seller | | Item | Buyer | |
|---|---|---|---|---|
| Charge | Credit | | Charge | Credit |
| | $60,000.00 | Purchase Price | $60,000.00 | |
| | | Deposit (3/5/97) | | $    500.00 |
| | | Deposit (5/1/97) | | $14,500.00 |
| $45,000.00 | | By First Mortgage | | $45,000.00 |
| | | | | |
| | | Prorations as of 5/1/97 | | |
| | 100.00 | Taxes for One-half Year | 100.00 | |
| | 78.00 | Insurance (Premium $468.00) | 78.00 | |
| | | | | |
| 365.00 | | Policy of Title Insurance | | |
| 10.00 | | Deed | | |
| 66.00 | | Real Property Transfer Tax | | |
| | | Recording Deed | 7.00 | |
| | | Drawing Mortgage | 10.00 | |
| | | Recording Mortgage | 7.00 | |
| | | Notary | 5.00 | |
| 150.00 | | Escrow Fee ( Each) | 150.00 | |
| 4,800.00 | | Realtor's Commission (8%) | | |
| | | Buyer Owes at Closing | | 357.00 |
| 9,787.00 | | Due Seller at Closing | | |
| | | | | |
| $60,178.00 | $60,178.00 | | $60,357.00 | $60,357.00 |

volved, what services are provided and who is expected to pay for each service.

Figure 29–4 is a sample closing statement that includes many of the typical charges and credits for a buyer and seller. Study the sample and read the accompanying explanation so you will be fully prepared to examine your own closing statement for accuracy and understand how the itemization system of *charges* and *credits* functions.

## Explanation of Closing Statement

Figure 29–4 is an example of a closing statement. The buyer and seller each have a column of charges and credits. Amounts that must be paid into escrow by each party are charged against that party. Amounts that have already been paid into, or that are to be paid out of, escrow are credited to each party. The amount charged to each party must equal the amount credited to that party. This accounting method is the one most commonly used. It may not make complete sense to a nonaccountant, but it works.

### Purchase Price

In our example, the buyer is paying $60,000 for the property. This amount is charged to the buyer and credited to the seller. The buyer made an initial earnest money deposit of $500, which was submitted into escrow when escrow opened, and has since submitted into escrow a down payment of $14,500. The buyer has arranged to pay the remainder of the purchase price by giving the seller a mortgage and note for $45,000. Although no cash actually changes hands, the seller is "charged" for "lending" the $45,000 to the buyer. In return, the buyer signs the mortgage and note and is credited with having agreed to "pay back" this amount to the seller.

### Prorations

Prorations are to be made as of the date of closing, which is May 1, 1997. The property taxes for the year of sale, from July 1, 1996, to June 30, 1997 are $600, to be paid in two equal installments of $300 each. The seller has already paid the first installment, covering the time from July 1, 1996 to December 30, 1997. The second installment was due and paid by the seller before March 10, 1997, so the seller should get credit for the taxes for two months from May 1, 1997 to June 30, 1997 since the closing date is May 1, 1997. Thus, the taxes must be prorated. Since the second tax installment is $300, by dividing this amount by 6 (months), we find that the taxes are $50 per month. Thus, on the closing statement the seller is credited the $100 worth of taxes he has paid for the two months during which he will not own the land. The buyer is charged this $100.

A similar proration is performed for a fire insurance policy that the buyer is assuming. The policy extends for a one-year period dating from July 1, 1996 to June 30, 1997. The seller has already paid the premium of $468. At the closing date, he will have been covered under the policy for ten months, from July 1, 1996 to May 1, 1997. Since the policy extends for a total of 12 months, the buyer will be covered for two months. The entire premium must be divided into monthly amounts to prorate it: $468 divided by 12 equals $39. The buyer owes $39 times 2 (months), or $78, for the period he will own the land under the policy. He is charged this amount

on the closing statement, and the seller is credited this amount.

### Remaining Fees

The remaining fees are divided between the seller and buyer according to the terms agreed to in the contract of sale and specified in the escrow instructions. The charges shown here are the average fees charged for these services. Separate fees are usually charged for drawing up, notarizing and recording documents, as done in this statement. The *escrow fee* is usually based on either the amount of money passing through escrow or the total price of the transaction. In this example, the escrow fee is 0.5 percent of the purchase price and is shared by the buyer and the seller. The state in which this sale occurs has a *real property transfer tax*. This tax requires that for each $500 of the purchase price, $0.55 in taxes must be paid to the state. This item will be written on the deed or evidenced by tax stamps on the deed. The $66 transfer tax required in this purchase is charged to the seller. These taxes vary among the states. Of course, the seller is charged for the real estate agent's commission, given here as 8 percent of the purchase price. The commission usually varies between 6 percent to 10 percent of the purchase price.

Because the buyer must pay his or her charges into escrow at closing, all the items from the prorations down to and including the escrow fee are added to get $357, which the buyer is credited with paying at the close of escrow. The seller must pay all of his or her charges out of money *due him or her* that the buyer pays into escrow, in this case the $15,000 down payment plus $78 and $100 from the two prorations. Because the seller's charges equal $5,391, the escrow holder deducts this amount from the money paid in by the buyer ($15,178), leaving $9,787 to be distributed to the seller by the escrow holder after closing.

### Checking the Statement

You can personally check the mathematics of the closing statement by using the same system that the escrow holder uses. This check is done by balancing the money the escrow holder takes in against the money it will pay out. Using our Sample Closing Statement, you see that the escrow holder will receive $15,000 in cash from the buyer as part of the purchase price and $357 for the various fees charged to the buyer. Thus, the escrow holder's total receipts from the buyer on closing day equal $15,357.

Now the escrow holder adds up the total amount of disbursements that it will have to make according to the closing statement. These are listed in Figure 29–5. The escrow holder takes in $15,357 and pays out $15,357, and the figures balance as they should. Never leave the job of calculating your costs and totaling your money to the escrow holder or anyone else without double-checking all the figures yourself.

## Preparation of Documents for Closing

When the title has been cleared to your satisfaction and all other conditions of the sale have been met, the escrow holder will prepare forms necessary to complete your purchase. The escrow holder, or possibly the seller's attorney or title company, will prepare a new deed in your name. If the contract of sale calls for a warranty deed, that type of deed must be prepared. If the title cannot be cleared as specified in the contract, thus preventing the delivery of a proper deed, escrow cannot close. The deed should be signed by the seller and be ready to be recorded before the day of closing arrives. Many states impose a tax on the transfer of all real estate. Evidence of the payment of this tax is tax stamps affixed to the deed or the amount paid written somewhere on the deed. The escrow holder pays the tax and affixes the stamps, if required. (See Chapter 32, "Deeds and Recording.") If the seller finances your loan, the escrow holder or the seller's attorney prepares the mortgage or deed of trust and note. All forms are sent to the parties for proper signatures and acknowledgments before escrow closes, unless the parties all meet together on closing day.

## Closing (Settlement) Day

The *close of escrow* is the last of the "closings" during your land purchase. The first, the *closing of the sale*, occurs when you and the seller sign a legally binding contract of sale. The *financial closing* occurs when you have negotiated a loan and signed all the necessary documents. The close of escrow or *legal closing*, occurs when all terms and

**Figure 29–5. Escrow Holder's Balance Sheet**

| | |
|---|---|
| Policy of Title Insurance | $365 |
| Drawing up deed | 10 |
| Real Property Transfer Tax | 66 |
| Recording deed | 7 |
| Drawing up mortgage | 10 |
| Recording the mortgage | 7 |
| Notary | 5 |
| Escrow Fee | 290 |
| Realtor's commission | 4,800 |
| Seller to receive | 9,787 |
| | $15,357 |

conditions of the sale have been met by both parties and the title to the land is officially transferred to you by recording the deed with the county recorder. You then own the land, although you may still be obligated to pay off a mortgage or deed of trust for many years to come.

The day of legal closing, also called settlement day or paper signing day, is the day on which the deed and other documents are recorded. This will happen anytime from a few weeks to a few months after both parties sign the contract of sale. Although the contract will specify a closing date, this date can be, and often is, postponed or extended, if both parties agree to an extension. (See clause 4 of the Model Contract of Sale in Chapter 27.) Occasionally the party granting a requested extension might penalize the other. If the seller has not met all your conditions specified in the contract of sale by the closing date, you have several options. You can grant him an extension or you can terminate the deal if you desire, because the contract of sale specifies that "time is of the essence." Any expenses you incur by the seller's delay in closing and transferring possession to you should be charged to the seller.

The closing is generally handled either by mail or in person. If it is to be done by mail, the escrow holder draws up and sends each party the documents to be signed and completes its other duties according to the escrow instructions, such as clearing the title and making the various prorations. Before closing day, each party returns the documents and pays the money charged against her or him. On closing day, the escrow holder records the documents with the county recorder and mails copies to each of the parties, together with any money due.

If the closing is to be done in person, all parties, including the buyer, the seller, the real estate agent, the escrow holder, any attorneys and, if a loan is involved, the lender's representative, meet to sign the documents. This meeting usually occurs at the escrow holder's office. However, the office of the real estate agent, the buyer's or the seller's attorney or the lender, if the buyer is borrowing the money from a financial institution, may be used.

The person handling the closing presents a closing statement to each person. The buyer submits the money he or she is obligated to give the seller at closing for the purchase price and other expenses. These payments are usually made by cashier's check or money order, with each check marked as to what it covers. If you plan to pay by personal check, send it to the escrow company at least 11 days before closing so that the check will have 10 days to clear. The escrow holder will not close escrow until all checks clear. It can then disburse the money as stipulated on the closing statement.

If the seller is financing the purchase, the buyer will sign and give the seller a mortgage or deed of trust and a promissory note. If a third-party lender is involved, its representative will deliver the loan money at closing and take back a mortgage or deed of trust and promissory note from the buyer. The lender will want to see the policy of title insurance and get copies of the binders on the fire and other insurance before handing over the money. The buyer will pay any money due the lender at this time, such as loan fees and impounds. When all documents have been signed and all money has been submitted into escrow, the documents will be brought to the county recorder to be recorded, after which time all parties will be paid and will receive their documents according to the escrow instructions.

## Review Documents for the Close of Escrow

At the closing you must be certain that everything is done exactly right and that the terms are as you have negotiated them. Before closing day, you should receive copies of all documents involved in the purchase. *Read every word* of these documents.

Look for clerical errors, and double-check all mathematical figuring. Never let yourself be rushed through these procedures. There is a great temptation to just sign the papers, pay your money and "get the thing over with." Never become casual about any part of your purchase, particularly these final and extremely important details. You should receive 13 items and assure yourself that they are in order. (All 13 may not be applicable in every case.)

1. *A deed to the property from the seller that should be signed by her or him and notarized.* The description of the property and encumbrances in the deed must conform to the contract of sale. Check every word in the deed to see that it is exactly as it should be. A mistake in the property description or a misspelling of any name can cause complications in the future. At closing, the deed is recorded with the county recorder, who will make a copy of it and return the original to you, usually by mail.

2. *A copy of the final title report or abstract of title and the policy of title insurance.* Check the date and time on which the policy is to take effect to be sure the title insurance covers you from the exact moment that the deed is recorded. If you are to receive other evidence of title, such as a certificate of title, you will get it at the closing. Your lender also will want a copy of the policy, and he will be named as a cobeneficiary in the policy. You should postpone closing until all actual or potential liens on the title have been cleared, as specified in the contract of sale.

3. *A bill of sale signed by the seller listing all personal property* (if any) included in the sale. Generally, personal property is not included in the deed, so it must be provided for separately. Get all available instructions and warranties for appliances, machinery and equipment, and get a list of the people who have been servicing them. You should get all keys for all locks on the property.

4. *A copy of the survey of the property and copies of any blueprints of the buildings.*

5. *A check for the loan amount.* If you are borrowing money from a third-party lender, you will sign a mortgage or deed of trust and a promissory note to the lender, who will give you a check for the loan amount. You will en-

dorse it and deliver it to the seller with your own cash contribution to the purchase price. If the seller is financing the purchase, you will give the escrow holder the down payment, less the amount of earnest money already paid. The escrow holder should give you a receipt for this payment. You will then sign the mortgage or deed of trust and promissory note to the escrow holder. These documents will be recorded with the county recorder and remain as lien against your title until all payments have been completed.

6. *All documents pertinent to assuming an existing mortgage or deed of trust.* These documents must include the seller's receipts for payments already made, because you will need these to receive a release deed or reconveyance of title after all payments have been completed. You also want a statement, called a *beneficiary's statement, certificate of reduction of mortgage,* or *estoppel certificate,* signed and notarized by the seller's lender, specifying the amount still due on the existing mortgage or deed of trust, so the lender cannot later claim that more is due than you expected. This statement should contain all the terms of the loan that you are to accept and the nature of the lien on the property, such as a first mortgage. Examine the document carefully. Check all the figures to see that they are correct, according to your contract of sale. If there is a due-on-sale clause in the note and mortgage or deed of trust, it is advisable to ask the lender for a written statement stating that it is aware that you are to take over payment on the loan and that this arrangement is satisfactory.

7. *Any necessary government forms.* If you are borrowing under an FHA or VA plan, you will have to fill out government forms on or just before closing day as part of the loan.

8. *Receipts showing the disposition of all liens that you have asked the seller to remove before you take title.* For example, you might want the current receipts as evidence that taxes, special assessments, utilities, and propane have been paid for. If you are to pay any bills, you should get a copy of the bill that indicates what is due and the final date payment can be made. The bills should be computed to the date of closing in line with the prorations that are to be made by the es-

crow holder, according to the contract of sale and escrow instructions.

9. *A list of prorations.* Double-check the prorations made on the taxes, insurance premiums, interest on assumed mortgages, utilities and other items to see that the escrow holder has figured them properly.

10. *An authorization to the tax collector.* If you are borrowing money from a commercial lender who is going to take impounds, you will have to sign an authorization that instructs the tax collector to have all tax bills on your property sent to the lender for payment. Your lender may have you sign a similar document covering premium payments on insurance policies.

11. *A legal copy of the insurance policy and a binder on closing day.* If you are taking over the seller's insurance policy, the seller should assign this policy to you in writing, and the insurer should give written recognition that it is aware of this transfer and approves of it. A cover note from the insurance company should state that your property will be protected by the insurance policy from the time of closing until your new policy is prepared and delivered to you. The seller or your lender will be named as a cobeneficiary. Your lender, if you have one, will also want a copy of this document.

12. *Copies of any permits or certificates, such as building and sanitation permits, road encroachment permits or certificates of occupancy.* If the seller has paid for and received any such documents, have him or her give you copies of them. If the seller does not have copies in his or her possession, it is the seller's responsibility to go to the appropriate agencies and have copies made.

13. *Tax segregation form(s).* If you are purchasing a subdivided parcel, you and the seller may have to complete tax segregation forms at the closing so that you can proceed as quickly as possible with the segregation of your land for purposes of proper taxation of the individual subdivided parcels. If it is possible, the seller should have the segregation completed before the closing and should give you a statement from the tax collector that the segregation has been completed, with a breakdown of how it was computed.

## Role of the Lender's Escrow Department When Money Is Borrowed—Loan Payments and Impounds

If the seller is financing your purchase, a third-party escrow holder will generally not be used for collecting impounds and land payments. You will make your payments to a bank or the seller, and you or the seller will take care of paying taxes and insurance premiums.

If you borrow from a commercial lender, however, you will make your payments to the lender's special escrow department. These payments will not only include principal and interest on the loan but will also include the property taxes, assessments and insurance premiums that will become due during the year. These impounds are usually divided up equally among the number of payments you will make each year and will be added to those payments. The lender's escrow officer pays the taxes, assessments and insurance bills, thus insuring the protection of the lender's security. The lending institution often acts as the escrow holder throughout the entire purchase and is responsible for preparing all closing documents. (On impounds, see Chapter 23, "Buying Property That Is Encumbered by a Loan Agreement.")

### Long Term Escrows and Land Contracts

As explained in the section on land contracts (Chapter 21, "Types of Financing: Land Contract, Mortgage, Deed of Trust"), you must be certain to have title held in escrow during the entire payment period if you are buying land under a land contract. Because the seller keeps the title to the land until you complete all of your payments, you must protect yourself against the seller's transferring title to someone else or otherwise encumbering the title before your payments are completed. Require that the seller make out a deed in your name and give it to the escrow holder, with instructions to deliver it to you when you make your final payment. If you are to have part of the title conveyed to you after a specified number of payments have been made, this should be noted in the escrow instructions. Also instruct the escrow holder to record the land contract in the county records, so that public notice is given that the seller is not free to encumber the title. In spite of these precautions, because title to the land does remain with the seller during the payment period, he or she could have a judgment rendered against the title in a lawsuit, a federal income-tax lien could be placed against the title or the seller could go bankrupt, in which case his or her creditors would be able to attach the title or, at least, create some legal problems for you. For these reasons, among others, it is risky and foolish to buy property under a land contract. Always demand a mortgage or deed of trust.

## Escrow Is Necessary

It is absolutely essential that you use an escrow holder in your purchase. Never avoid using an escrow holder to save a little money on escrow fees. A reputable and intelligent escrow holder can be of tremendous assistance to you through all stages of your purchase, and you should maintain close personal contact with your escrow holder at all times.

## Useful Resources

Several sources offer publications that will be helpful in dealing with questions of escrow. These publications are free, except as noted.

From:    American Land Title Association (ALTA)
           1828 L St. NW
           Washington, DC 20036

"Closing Costs and Your Purchase of a Home"

From:    California Land Title Association
           P.O. Box 13968
           Sacramento, CA 95853

"Closing Costs-A Primer"
"Escrow"

From:    The Superintendent of Documents
           Government Printing Office
           Washington, DC 20402

"Settlement Costs" (A HUD Guide)
    S/N 023-000-00699-5           $3.50

# 30 The Title Search, Abstract of Title and Title Insurance Policy

When you buy a parcel of land, you are purchasing *title*, or legal ownership, to the land. The deed is the instrument by which title is passed from one person to another.

An owner of land might not have clear title, even though he or she has a deed and a right to legally possess the land. A *defect*, or *cloud*, on the title might exist because someone has a legal right to claim all or part of the property or to make demands on the owner. For example, the owner who has mortgaged property still owns it, but the mortgagee has a lien against the title and can foreclose

and take the property to a foreclosure sale if the owner defaults on the mortgage payments; or if a landowner does not pay property taxes, the county will bring a lien against the land for the collection of back taxes.

The terms *marketable* or *merchantable title* mean that the seller has the legal right to sell the land. Any defect that makes the title unmarketable must be removed before you buy the land. To find defects that may exist against a seller's title and to determine the title's marketability, you must look at its history by researching the public records.

This chapter tells you how to do this to protect yourself as much as possible when buying title to a piece of land. First, there is a list of the types of defects that can cloud a title. Second, there is a description of how a title is searched, going back through the chain of title. Third, the types of documents that you need to determine the state of the title—the abstract of title or title report—are described. Finally, the importance of obtaining a title insurance policy or other title coverage is discussed.

## Liens and Encumbrances

Liens and encumbrances are the two most common defects on a land title. They do not make the title unmarketable, because the seller has the legal right to sell the land subject to the liens and encumbrances. Encumbrances include anything that limits or affects the title, for example:

- *Mineral, timber* or *water rights held*, or *reserved*, by the seller or a third party. These can be in writing or by prescription. (See Chapter 11, "Mineral, Oil, Gas, Timber, Soil and Other Rights," and Chapter 10, "Water Rights.") prescriptive rights will not show up on the public records and are never insured against.
- *Easement rights* that permit others to cross your property. These can be in writing, by implication and necessity or by prescription. (See Chapter 9, "Easement Rights.")
- *Restrictive covenants* in the deed that limit what the property can be used for. (See Chapter 32, "Deeds and Recording.")
- *Liens* are also encumbrances, but a lien arises only when the property becomes security for the payment of a debt or obligation, for example:
- When the owner gives a *mortgage* or *deed of trust*, using the land as security. The title will have a lien on it until the debt is paid. If the debt is not paid in the prescribed manner, the creditor can foreclose on the loan. (See Chapter 21, "Types of Financing: Land Contract, Mortgage, Deed of Trust.")
- *Federal, state* and *local taxes* can become liens against the property when they have not been paid. *Real property taxes* are automatically liens against the property at all times. *Special assessments* remain liens against the land until they are paid. The property can be sold for nonpayment of taxes and assessments. (See Chapter 17, "Property Taxes and Assessments.")

- A *mechanic's lien* can be held against the property by anybody who furnished labor or material for improvements to the property and was not paid by the owner. This lien could force the sale of the land to satisfy the debts if they remain unpaid.
- A plaintiff who initiates a lawsuit against the owner can attach the property, by an *attachment*, to prevent the owner from disposing of the property for the duration of the lawsuit. The plaintiff who wins a *judgment* against the owner can force the owner to sell the property to satisfy the judgment.
- A *lis Pendens* puts the buyer on notice that there is litigation in progress concerning one aspect of the title to the property. Anybody who brings a lawsuit claiming an interest in the property, such as a suit to establish prescriptive rights or to establish a boundary line or right to water, will file and record a lis pendens, which becomes a lien on the property.
- *Liens for debts of the decedent* can exist against his or her property if they remain unpaid. If the creditors cannot get their money from personal property, then the real estate can be sold to satisfy their liens.
- *Federal and state inheritance tax liens* can exist against the property of deceased persons. The property can be sold by court order to meet these taxes.

Clause 6 of the Model Contract of Sale (see Chapter 27) states that the title conveyed to the buyer is to be free of any defects, including liens, encumbrances, easements, covenants, reservations, restrictions, and rights and conditions of the title, except those approved by the buyer prior to the close of escrow. In addition to this protection, you must always search the title and receive an abstract of title or policy of title insurance.

## Searching Back Through the Chain of Title

All land in this country was originally in the possession of the Native Americans. Their various conquerors took their land from them, divided it up, and kept records of who took ownership of each parcel. The transfer of title from owner to owner established a *chain of title* from the present back to the first recorded document of ownership.

The history of New Mexico is a good example of how far back records were kept in this country and how a chain of title develops. In 1539 the area around the present city of Gallup, New Mexico, was claimed by a Franciscan friar from Spain. The fact that American Indians already lived on this land did not deter the missionaries from taking it and extending the boundaries of the huge Spanish colony of Mexico. The king of Spain offered large parcels of property to those who would colonize the new land. These gifts were recorded in documents called the Crown Land Grant Records. Spanish immigrants began to move into the area, and the province of New Mexico was established.

Mexico gained its independence from Spain in 1830, and in 1846 the Mexican War began between the United States and Mexico. That war ended in 1848 with the Treaty of Guadalupe Hidalgo, which passed sovereign control of the northern part of Mexico, including the province of New Mexico, to the United States. Spanish and Mexican land records were transferred with the land.

In 1912 the territory of New Mexico became a state. At that time, the federal and state governments traced land ownership back as far as they were recorded to settle all existing claims to title and took control of the rest of the public lands, which were eventually sold to private owners or retained as government lands. Accurate records of all land transfers have been kept since that time, and make up the chain of title.

After you sign the contract of sale, you will hire an abstract of title company, a title insurance company or a lawyer to search, or trace back, the land through the chain of title, to determine whether the current owner has legal ownership with the right to sell the land and to discover what, if any, defects exist on the title.

The title does not have to be searched back to the first colonizers. Each state has its own laws (*statutes of limitations*) that specify how far back a title search must extend to be legally *sound*. This period ranges from 22 years in Nebraska to 50 years in Minnesota, to the federal land patents in California.

The primary sources of information that form the links in the chain are the documents recorded with the county recorder or clerk, the tax collector, the various courts and other government agencies. The person doing the search will trace all of these documents back for the specified number of years to locate anything that affects the title to the land.

Because all these records are public, you can do your own title search. However, because of its importance, I don't recommend that you rely solely on your own examination. You must obtain a professional title search before the close of escrow, which I discussed in the previous chapter. Nevertheless, I will tell you how a title search is performed so that you will understand this vital aspect of your purchase, and I hope you will do your own search, even though you have a professional examination to confirm it. This is one of the most interesting aspects of your investigation, because you will learn the history of the land you are preparing to buy.

The deed is the basic instrument for transferring ownership of land, and it includes a description of the title being conveyed. Every state has recording statutes that require that valid deeds be publicly recorded with the county recorder or similar official. When escrow closes on a property transaction, the deed is photocopied by the county recorder, who places it in the deed index, which is arranged chronologically. (See Chapter 32, "Deeds and Recording.") Other documents affecting the land are similarly recorded in separate indexes. Each index consists of a set of books or microfilms that together form the official record.

There are two systems of recording and indexing documents affecting real estate. These are the *Grantor-Grantee Index* and the *Tract Index*.

## Grantor-Grantee Index

The most common system used to index recorded documents is the *grantor-grantee index*. The grantor index alphabetically lists the name of every seller, or *grantor*, according to the year of the land sale; the grantee index lists every buyer, or *grantee*, in a similar manner. Leases, mortgages, trust deeds, assignments, wills, liens, lis pendens (that is, pending legal actions involving the property) and judgments may also be indexed in this general grantor-grantee index. Never hesitate to ask the county recorder to describe the indexing system used in the office.

As an example of how to do a title search using the grantor-grantee index, assume that you are buying a parcel of land from a seller by the name of Daniel Lawrence.

Names are listed in the indexes alphabetically for the year the document was recorded. Before you can look up Lawrence's name in the grantee index, you must know the year in which he bought the land. Ask the real estate agent or Lawrence for the date. The tax assessor also has this information in the tax rolls.

In the county recorder's office, locate the grantee index for the year in which your seller bought the land, and look under the section containing last names beginning with *L*. Entries within this section are made according to the date the documents are received for recording during the year. Thus, they are not alphabetical. The first thing you want to locate is the seller's deed. If Lawrence took title on May 9, 1970, the page on which you will find Daniel Lawrence's name as it was recorded when he received his deed might look like the list in Figure 30–1. The book and page number refer you to the location of Lawrence's deed.

This index also refers you to the location of other documents in Lawrence's name that have been recorded, such as mortgages. The county recorder can show you where to find the book referred to in the index and how to use it. The book might be a general index of all the county records, or it might contain only copies of deeds.

Look up Lawrence's deed in Book 310 on page 3. Read the deed in its entirety. Does it include a description of the land you are planning to buy from Lawrence? The description might be of a larger parcel that has been subdivided, but it should definitely include the entire parcel you are buying. (If it does not, then Lawrence is not the owner of the land.) Note what kind of deed was given, whether it was a quitclaim deed, a warranty deed or some other kind. (See Chapter 32, "Deeds and Recording.") Are there any easements; reservations of mineral, timber, water or other rights; restrictive covenants; or other encumbrances written into the deed? Write down the names of the sellers who signed the deed to Lawrence.

If there is any indication that the property was conveyed by an administrator or executor after the death of the owner, you must examine the probate court records (ask the county recorder to tell you where they are located) to determine whether the property was properly distributed to the heirs. Keep notes on everything in the deed, including notations that refer to the location of other documents.

Next, look up all these other documents and copy their contents. For example, there might be a copy of a mortgage Lawrence gave a lender. If so, you want to see a copy of a satisfaction of mort-

### Figure 30–1. Sample List in a Grantee Index

| Grantee | Grantor | Date | Book (Liber) | Page |
|---|---|---|---|---|
| Leifer, William | Fresauet, Victoria | May 2 | 308 | 89 |
| Leland, Kathy | Inkeles, Gordon | May 4 | 309 | 95 |
| Lutz, Grace | Martin, Arnold | May 4 | 309 | 120 |
| Ladrini, Duncan | Herbert, Geraldine | May 8 | 309 | 142 |
| Lawrence, Daniel | Charles, Edward | May 9 | 310 | 3 |
| Lambert, Vivian | Howard, Robert | May 12 | 311 | 54 |
| Lynn, Mary | Glickman, Raymond | May 20 | 312 | 122 |
| Lund, David | Akselsen, Susan | May 20 | 312 | 132 |

gage or deed of reconveyance to determine if the loan was paid off.

After you have examined the deed and all other documents referred to in it, search the records to be sure Lawrence hasn't already sold the land to some other party. This part of the title search is tedious. It involves looking in the grantor index to see if Lawrence has ever sold the land he is selling you. Go to the grantor index for the current year and look for Daniel Lawrence's name as a grantor. This index is arranged in the same manner as the grantee index, except that the grantor and grantee columns will be reversed. If you find Lawrence's name listed in the grantor column, look up the document referred to and see whether it is a deed selling the same parcel you intend to buy. If it is, you cannot get title because he no longer has title to pass to you. If this is the case, you are being defrauded. However, he may have owned and sold a different parcel of land. Read the description to see if the deed is for another piece of property. If it is, go back to the grantor index and continue looking for Lawrence's name by going backward until you reach the date he received title, May 9, 1970.

If you determine that Lawrence has not sold the land to anyone else and that he still owns it, you must then carry your search back another link in the chain of title by repeating the entire process for Lawrence's seller, Edward Charles. If you are lucky, Lawrence's deed in some way referred you to the location of Charles's deed. If not, you must either go through the grantee index starting with the year in which Charles sold the land to Lawrence and search backward through each year's list looking for reference to his deed or get the date from the tax assessor. When you find Edward Charles's name in the grantee index, his seller's name will be given, with the date the deed was recorded and the book and page number of its location in the index. Look up Charles's deed and check all those things that you checked in Lawrence's deed. Remember to take notes and to examine all other documents referred to in the deed. Then go backward through the grantor index, from the time Charles sold the land to Lawrence to the time Charles bought the land, and look for Charles name, to be sure he did not sell the land to anyone other than Lawrence. Repeat this procedure for each owner of the land as far back as is required by the law of your state.

The grantor-grantee index usually includes indexing of recorded leases, assignments, mortgages, deeds of trust, attachments and judgments. The grantor index might include the names of defendants in legal actions involving real property, of assignors of loans, of mortgagors and of trustors. The grantee index would include plaintiffs, assignees, mortgagees and beneficiaries of deeds of trust.

Instead of a general, all-inclusive grantor-grantee index that refers to the location of all documents, the county recorder might use a *multiple index system.* In this case you must cheek through each type of index to uncover relevant documents. This makes the general title search much more difficult. For example, there will be a *mortgagor-mortgagee index,* which you must examine to determine whether anyone who ever owned the land gave a mortgage on the property and, if so, whether any mortgage still exists as a lien against the title.

Let's assume that Edward Charles gave a mortgage on the property during the period of his ownership. By checking through the mortgagor index, you find that he gave a mortgage to a savings and loan company on July 2, 1984. Note the book and page numbers where a copy of the mortgage can be found, and look it up. If it has been paid off, you will be referred to a book and page number where you will find a copy of the satisfaction of mortgage. Sometimes the satisfaction will be attached to the copy of the mortgage. If you can't find any evidence that the mortgage has been paid off, then it may be a lien on the title.

Often these counties have a separate *lis pendens index* that lists all pending legal actions initiated in the county according to plaintiffs and defendants and refers you to the location of the documents filed in those actions. If such an index exists, cheek to see whether any previous owner of the land had an action such as a foreclosure, mechanic's lien or civil suit pending against him or her. If a name

shows up, check the files to be sure that the property has been cleared of any connection with the legal action. Do not buy land with a lis pendens filed against it because you must take the property subject to that pending action. If an action has been resolved, sometimes the parties forget to withdraw a lis pendens. An attorney can draft the papers to clear the title if that is the case.

There also may be a separate *judgment roll* or *judgment index* that lists creditors and debtors named in judgments resulting from lawsuits. This index usually names the attorney of the creditor and indicates whether the debt has been paid. Look for the name of any previous owner of the property in the column of debtors for the years he or she owned the property. If a former owner is listed, examine the recorded document to determine the status of the debt. Never purchase land subject to a judgment lien. In some areas, you might have to ask the clerk of the local courts to check for proceedings affecting the property if court records aren't kept in the county recorder's office.

There will also be separate indexes for *federal tax liens, lessors-lessees, assignors-assignees, wills* and *deeds.*

Finally, you must examine the *county tax rolls* located in the tax collector's office to see if any back taxes are due on the land. These lax liens are indexed according to the parcel number, which can be found in the tax books. Ask the tax assessor to show you how to use the books.

The above description of how a title search is conducted probably has you rather confused. Don't worry about it. You will have it done by a professional anyway. But if you go to the county records and start looking through them, you will become familiar with the system of indexing for your area, and everything in this chapter will begin to make sense. The records are always open to the public, and there is no substitute for actually going and investigating on your own. If you are confused, the clerks are there to assist you.

## Tract Index

A much simpler system used to index recorded documents affecting a piece of land is the tract index. Unfortunately it is found in only a few states: Iowa, Louisiana, Nebraska, North Dakota, Oklahoma, South Dakota, Utah, Wisconsin and Wyoming. This system has a page for every single parcel or tract of land in the county. Every transaction affecting each particular parcel is indexed on that parcel's page with the locations of the recorded documents referred to. For example, if you look up the parcel you are buying, the index page states the location of every deed used to convey the land since it was first sold by the government. Every mortgage and other recorded instrument affecting the title also is referred to.

Thus, the papers for the entire chain of title are in one spot, unlike the grantor-grantee index system, in which you must trace every transaction yourself. As land is subdivided, the new parcels are added to the tract index.

### The Title Company or Abstractor's Plants

A title company maintains its own records at its title office. Today, this is usually done by a computerized system. Every day the title company orders copies of every document recorded at the recorder's office. Then it sees what property is affected by each document. In its private *title plants* it has a file page for each separate parcel of property in the

county or parish. Each recorded document is noted on the file page for the parcel it affects with a note of the type of document and the book and page where it is recorded.

When you order a search for a particular parcel, the title or abstract company simply looks up the parcel in its private files at its plant. It can turn to the file page and see notes on every recorded document that affects the property. All these are on one page. Thus the job of the title company is relatively easy. The escrow fees you pay go for paying the overhead or maintaining this system.

### Unrecorded Items That Affect the Title

Some things that affect land title will not be found in the indexes: building and health code regulations, zoning restrictions, renters leasing the land without a recorded lease, persons with a legal right to title by adverse possession, prescriptive easements or prescriptive profits, changes in the boundaries due to erosion or accretion, water rights laws and work that has been done on the land that could

**Figure 30–2. Type of Title Proof Used by Each State**

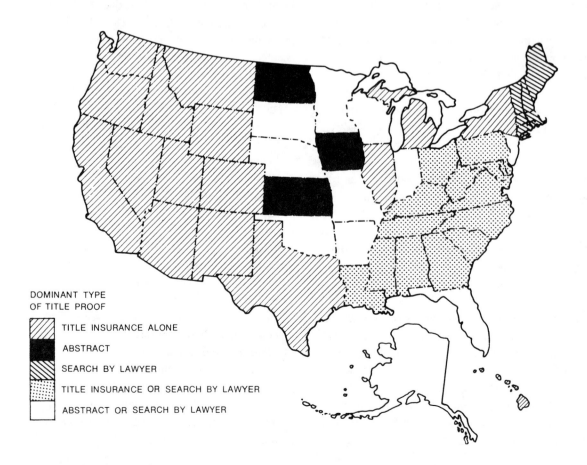

DOMINANT TYPE
OF TITLE PROOF

- TITLE INSURANCE ALONE
- ABSTRACT
- SEARCH BY LAWYER
- TITLE INSURANCE OR SEARCH BY LAWYER
- ABSTRACT OR SEARCH BY LAWYER

lead to a mechanic's lien being filed after you buy the land.

Therefore, an important aspect of your investigation will be to determine the laws that apply to your land and to inspect the property personally to see what is happening to it. How to do these things was explained in previous chapters.

## Types of Title Proof

A professional title search must be conducted before you can receive proof of good title by an abstract of title, a title insurance policy or a title certificate by an attorney. Figure 30–2 shows which forms of title proof are mainly used in the various states.

## The Abstract of Title

In many parts of the United States, particularly in rural parts of the Midwest, land buyers commonly get an abstract of title after signing a contract of sale. An abstract is a summary of the title history of a parcel of land, based on recorded documents for as far back as is required by the state or the buyer. It is prepared by an abstract company that uses its own records of all transactions in that area. These private files, called *title plants*, are often better organized and more up-to-date than the public records in the county recorder's office. An abstract of title tells the effect of all deeds, mortgages, trust deeds, release deeds, satisfactions, recorded leases, mechanic's liens, foreclosure actions, special assessments, wills, attachments and judgments, tax sales, encumbrances and other items of record on the title. The contents of each document affecting title are summarized in chronological order in the abstract, and any irregularities in them will be pointed out by the abstractor.

An entry in the abstract will look like the example in Figure 30–3.

When the abstract company delivers the complete abstract, it issues a *certificate of title*, which states that the property title is held by the seller, subject to the encumbrances of record shown in the abstract. This certificate is the guarantee that the abstractor's research and examination of the public records are correct. However, the abstract company is liable for a mistake only to the person who contracts for the abstract. Therefore, if the seller has

**Figure 30–3. Sample Abstract Entry**

| Martin Berman and Deborah R. Berman, husband and wife to Arnold Berschler | Warranty Deed dated July 23,1970 ack. July 23,1970 rec. July 26,1970 Liber 43, p.92 |

Conveys lot #43 of the Map of Happy Acres Development Company.

the abstract done and shows it to you as evidence of his or her title, you have no claim against the abstract company if you later discover that an error was made in it. If you must use an abstract of title, have it performed in your own name, even if the seller pays for it, so that the company is liable to you.

Unless you are buying a newly subdivided parcel, an abstract of title probably already exists for the property, completed when an earlier buyer purchased the land. If this is the case, you do not have to have a complete abstract done. Simply have the abstract company bring the existing one up to date. It will examine the title from the time the last abstract was completed and show any new encumbrances. The company will then give you a certificate called a *reissue* or *recertification*, which guarantees that the entire abstract, including the former one and the newly completed section, is correct. This is much cheaper than getting an entire abstract done, and the recertification makes the company liable to you if it is done in your name.

Never accept an old abstract as proof of good title from the seller unless it has been brought up-to-date and recertified with your name as the insured. Be sure the abstract company is bonded with the state or federal government and is licensed and reputable. Although abstract companies are usually regulated by state agencies, if you must use one, exercise care in choosing.

### Preliminary Title Report and the Policy of Title Insurance

An abstract of title informs you only about the contents of documents in public records exactly as they appear there and guarantees you that the search is complete. The title to the land you are buying is neither guaranteed nor insured. You are not protected against title defects not shown by the records or documents that are part of the records but improperly executed. Only the owner's policy of title insurance insures the title you are being sold and protects you against defects not shown in the records or forged documents. I strongly recommend that you get title insurance if it is available, rather than an abstract of title. Ever since the first title company was founded in Philadelphia on March 28, 1876, real estate purchasers and lenders have been able to obtain protection against land title problems.

Many kinds of defects are so serious that they can render your title unmarketable. Title insurance protects you if any such defects exist. Some defects not shown by examining the public record are

- *Clerical errors*—A clerk in any of the public offices responsible for recording the documents in the chain of title could have made an error in transcription or filing, or a document could be misstated, incomplete or misplaced. For example, after you take title, if a lien appears that was misfiled by the recorder, the title insurance company will pay your losses up to its coverage if the lien results in your losing title to the land.
- *Forgery*—The deed or any other document might be a forged instrument or fraudulent in some other way.
- *Incorrectly given marital status*—A former owner may have been a married person whose spouse was not named in a transaction that conveyed title to the property during the marriage. The unnamed spouse might later claim an interest in the property under a state law regarding marital rights of spouses to joint property. (See Chapter 31, "Types of Co-Ownership.")
- *Undisclosed heirs*—If a former owner died while he or she owned the property and the estate was improperly distributed, the title could be disturbed later by a legal action brought by an undisclosed heir.
- *Postdeath deed delivery*—A deed might have been signed by the seller but not legally delivered to the buyer before death. The date of delivery on the deed in the records would not indicate a prior death of the seller, and a suit could be brought at a later time by an heir claiming title or by the government claiming estate taxes.
- *Lack of capacity of a party to a transaction*—If a deed or other document affecting title was executed by a person who was a minor, insane, in-

toxicated or drugged, or acting without the authority of the owner although otherwise a proper agent-employee of the owner, the deed does not properly convey a valid title to the property.
- *Improper interpretation of wills*—Most lands have been conveyed at least once in their history by a will, which may have been improperly interpreted so that title was not conveyed correctly, leaving open the possibility that someone might contest the transaction after you take title to the land.

The possibility of any of the above events occurring may not be great, but anyone can bring a court action against your title, causing you much grief and expense, even if the plaintiff does not have a valid and proper claim. Title insurance will pay for court costs and legal fees in the event this happens. Besides insuring you against any possible claim that might arise hostile to your claim of title, the title company insures you against errors made in its title search.

Before issuing insurance, the title company conducts a title search to determine the soundness of the title it will be insuring and the existence of liens and encumbrances. Just as a life insurance company will not insure a person without a thorough physical examination, a title insurance company will not issue a policy without doing a thorough search. Thus, if the title company issues you an insurance policy, you know that it is convinced that the seller has valid marketable title to give to you, subject to any liens or encumbrances on the title that it lists in the policy.

## What Do Title Companies Pay under the Policy?

The usual situation in which a title company will pay money to the insured is one in which it fails to disclose a recorded lien in its title policy. Although this is a mistake rarely made, it does occur. I have collected thousands of dollars for my clients over the years by filing claims under their policies. For example, one title company failed to disclose a water rights reservation in the policy through negligence of a title searcher, who forgot to note it on the policy. I have also seen policies that failed to show restrictions on cutting timber, easements through property, reservations of mineral rights and judgments on record affecting the title.

I have also had title companies pay my attorney fees when my clients have sued over a title matter. Sometimes the title companies use their own attorneys to defend legal actions or to get the title problems cleared up, but it never costs the policyholder any money. That is why you buy title insurance.

Other recent cases of how purchasers have been protected by title insurance policies are quite interesting.

In the East, a buyer purchased real estate from heirs named in the will of its deceased owner. Years later, another will by the same owner was discovered that named different heirs. The second will was probated and found to be valid, leaving the buyers under the first will with no title to the real estate. The title insurance company protected its insured by paying the full amount of the purchase price, as provided in its policy of title insurance.

In the Southwest, an affidavit obtained in a title search showed that the owner of an undivided one-sixth interest in real estate was deceased with no heirs. Some time after the transaction was completed, this supposedly deceased person appeared and filed a claim against the buyer for one-sixth of the purchase price. The claim proved to be valid, and the title company insuring the buyer paid the claimant for his interest under its policy of owner's title insurance, to settle the matter and avoid loss for the insured.

In the Midwest, a home buyer encountered trouble when the seller paid for two years of taxes on his house with a personal check that later was rejected because of insufficient funds. Because the buyer had obtained owner's title insurance before completing the real estate purchase, the title insurer contacted the seller—who had moved to another state—and collected the full amount of the bad check. When an attempt was made to pay the taxes on the home, it was learned that the amount had been miscalculated in the county office, and as a result, additional taxes were owed on the property. The insuring title company paid the initial amount collected from the seller and the additional amount due, thus sparing the buyer a financial setback.

## Preliminary Title Report

Before issuing the insurance policy, the title company will give you, at your request, a preliminary title report showing the status of the seller's title to the land. Often this report is included as part of the final title insurance policy, and both are covered by a single fee or premium. All encumbrances and liens on the land will be indicated, and the title company will inform you of the basis on which it is willing to issue you a final policy. It will indicate which encumbrances are of record and shown as exceptions to the policy of title insurance. The preliminary title report does not insure the title. It simply describes the condition of the title as of the date the report is issued. Never rely solely on this report as a reason for not getting an insurance policy.

Clause 6 in the Model Contract of Sale specifies that the seller is to have a preliminary title report made and delivered to you. (See Chapter 27.) If a defect such as a lien or encumbrance is shown by the report and you want it removed before the close of escrow, you must notify the seller of your disapproval. If the seller has not removed the defect by the closing date, you can terminate your purchase and have any money you have paid returned to you.

In areas where an abstract of title is used, rather than a title report and title insurance policy, clause 7 of the contract of sale should be changed to state when you are to get the abstract for inspection. The abstract of title, as well as the preliminary title report, should cover the title up to the date you receive it. After examining the abstract, notify the seller of any objections you have; the seller should clear the defects before closing. Clause 6 states that at the time you get the abstract or preliminary title report, the seller must include copies of all documents listed as encumbrances on the title so you can examine them in their entirety before the close of escrow. You can often obtain copies of all documents listed in the preliminary title report from the title company that prepared the report.

## The Policy of Title Insurance

Unlike other insurance policies, a policy of title insurance is paid for at one time only and continues as long as you and your legal successors hold title to the property. The premium for a policy is based on the amount of coverage, which is usually the amount paid for the property. Each title company has its own fee schedule. Generally, a $50,000 policy will cost about $400.00.

Clause 7 of the Model Contract of Sale in Chapter 27 states that the seller is to furnish and pay for the insurance policy, which is to be issued in your name with you as beneficiary. Sometimes the seller objects to paying the entire premium. If you choose, you can compromise and split the cost. I do not think you should pay the entire amount, because the seller has a duty to provide you with a valid and insured title.

A title insurance policy issued in your name is never assignable or transferable to subsequent purchasers of the property. For instance, the seller cannot transfer his or her policy to you. Each new buyer of a piece of land must purchase a completely new policy, regardless of how recently the seller had a title search conducted. A title company needs to search back only to the date that the seller's policy was issued to bring the title up-to-date for the buyer. Whether the amount of work involved in the search is great or small, the premiums always remain the same.

A standard coverage title insurance policy usually insures the buyer for the price paid for the land. Therefore, if the title company has to defend you in a court action, it will be responsible for bearing costs only up to the amount paid for the property. After you have owned the land for a period of time and have made improvements on it, its value will increase. You can then pay the title company to increase its liability to you based on the increased market value, or you can obtain an inflation endorsement to the policy when you initially purchase it at the close of escrow.

## Example of a Title Insurance Policy and an Explanation of Its Contents

The type of title insurance usually taken by a buyer is the standard coverage policy of title insurance. (I discuss extended coverage later in the chapter.) Although each state has its own policy form, the type of coverage granted is basically the same. Figure 30–4 is a copy of a standard coverage policy. The policy you receive will be similar to this one. The following is an explanation of the terms of the policy.

### Liability

The policy lists four instances in which the company will be liable for loss or damage to the insured owner plus three instances in which it will be liable to a lender insured under the policy.

1. Guarantees that title is actually in the person being insured.
2. Protects the insured if the title company makes any mistakes in searching the title. If defects not specified in the policy are later found to exist, the damages caused by them are covered. Defects that have been found and are thus excluded from coverage are listed in Schedule B, Part II. Other items not covered are listed in the Conditions and Stipulations.
3. Protects you against the existence of a defect that would make the title unmarketable, which means the seller did not have a right to sell the land. These are such things as forgeries, undisclosed heirs and the other defects listed earlier in this chapter. Never accept any policy that does not ensure that the title is marketable.
4. Guarantees legal access and right-of-way to the property.
5. Protects the lender, named as an insured, that has a lien on the buyer's title as security for the loan. This could be a seller who has taken back a mortgage from the buyer; both seller and buyer are insured under this policy. The company is liable for a defect in the execution of a mortgage or deed of trust that adversely affects the resulting lien on the property. Before insuring the lender, the company examines the executed mortgage or deed of trust for completeness. If you borrow from a bank or other lending institution, a different type of policy, called a mortgage or lender's or ALTA (American Land Title Association) policy, is often used. (See "The Lender's Policy of Title Insurance," later in this Chapter.)
6. Insures against the existence of any prior lien or encumbrance, such as a mortgage, not excepted in Schedule B, that would adversely affect the mortgage held by the lender or seller insured by the policy. For example, under this policy, if a lender makes a loan to the buyer and thinks it is the only mortgage on the property, if another mortgage exists that is superior and not excepted by this policy, any losses suffered by the insured lender will be paid.
7. Insures a person who has received an assignment of a mortgage from another person.

### Schedule A

First, the policy number, date of issuance (the day escrow closes), amount of coverage and cost of the policy are inserted.

**Figure 30–4. Example of Policy of Title Insurance**

*CALIFORNIA LAND TITLE ASSOCIATION*
*STANDARD COVERAGE POLICY 1990*

SUBJECT TO THE EXCLUSIONS FROM COVERAGE, THE EXCEPTIONS FROM COVERAGE CONTAINED IN SCHEDULE B AND THE CONDITIONS AND STIPULATIONS, CHICAGO TITLE INSURANCE COMPANY, a Missouri corporation, herein called the Company, insures, as of Date of Policy shown in Schedule A, against loss or damage, not exceeding the Amount of Insurance stated in Schedule A, sustained or incurred by the insured by reason of:

1. Title to the estate or interest described in Schedule A being vested other than as stated therein;
2. Any defect in or lien or encumbrance on the title;
3. Unmarketability of the title;
4. Lack of a right of access to and from the land;

and in addition, as to an insured lender only:

5. The invalidity or unenforceability of the lien of the insured mortgage upon the title;
6. The priority of any lien or encumbrance over the lien of the insured mortgage, said mortgage being shown in Schedule B in the order of its priority;
7. The invalidity or unenforceability of any assignment of the insured mortgage, provided the assignment is shown in Schedule B, or the failure of the assignment shown in Schedule B to vest title to the insured mortgage in the named insured assignee free and clear of all liens.

The Company will also pay the costs, attorneys' fees and expenses incurred in defense of the title or the lien of the insured mortgage, as insured, but only to the extent provided in the Conditions and Stipulations.

*In Witness Whereof*, CHICAGO TITLE INSURANCE COMPANY has caused this policy to be signed and sealed as of Date of Policy shown in Schedule A, the policy to become valid when countersigned by an authorized signatory.

CHICAGO TITLE INSURANCE COMPANY
By:

*President*

By:

*Secretary*

Issued by:
**HUMBOLDT LAND**
**TITLE COMPANY**
Eureka, CA 95501

**Figure 30–4. Example of Policy of Title Insurance** *continued*

## CLTA STANDARD COVERAGE

### SCHEDULE A

| OFFICE FILE NUMBER | POLICY NUMBER | DATE OF POLICY | AMOUNT OF INSURANCE | PREMIUM AMOUNT |
|---|---|---|---|---|
| 1 | 2 | 3 | 4 $ | 5 $ |

1.  Name of Insured:

2.  The estate or interest in the land which is covered by this Policy is:

3.  Title to the estate or interest in the land is vested in:

4.  The land referred to in this Policy is described as follows:

SCHEDULE A
CLTA Standard Coverage
Reorder Form No. **3243** (Rev. 2/91)

**This Policy valid only if Schedule B is attached.**

**Figure 30–4.  Example of Policy of Title Insurance** *continued*

## SCHEDULE  B

File Number _____

### EXCEPTIONS  FROM  COVERAGE

This policy does not insure against loss or damage (and the Company will not pay costs, attorneys' fees or expenses) which arise by reason of:

### PART I

1.  Taxes or assessments which are not shown as existing liens by the records of any taxing authority that levies taxes or assessments on real property or by the public records.
    Proceedings by a public agency which may result in taxes or assessments, or notices of such proceedings, whether or not shown by the records of such agency or by the public records.

2.  Any facts, rights, interests or claims which are not shown by the public records but which could be ascertained by an inspection of the land or which may be asserted by persons in possession thereof.

3.  Easements, liens or encumbrances, or claims thereof, which are not shown by the public records.

4.  Discrepancies, conflicts in boundary lines, shortage in area, encroachments, or any other facts which a correct survey would disclose, and which are not shown by the public records.

5.  (a) Unpatented mining claims; (b) reservations or exceptions in patents or in Acts authorizing the issuance thereof; (c) water rights, claims or title to water, whether or not the matters excepted under (a), (b), or (c) are shown by the public records.

### PART II

SCHEDULE B
CLTA Standard Coverage
Reorder Form No. 12201

**Figure 30–4. Example of Policy of Title Insurance** *continued*

## EXCLUSIONS FROM COVERAGE

The following matters are expressly excluded from the coverage of this policy and the Company will not pay loss or damage, costs, attorneys' fees or expenses which arise by reason of:

1. (a) Any law, ordinance or governmental regulation (including but not limited to building and zoning laws, ordinances, or regulations) restricting, regulating, prohibiting or relating to (i) the occupancy, use, or enjoyment of the land; (ii) the character, dimensions or location of any improvement now or hereafter erected on the land; (iii) a separation in ownership or a change in the dimensions or area of the land or any parcel of which the land is or was a part; or (iv) environmental protection, or the effect of any violation of these laws, ordinances or governmental regulations, except to the extent that a notice of the enforcement thereof or a notice of a defect, lien or encumbrance resulting from a violation or alleged violation affecting the land has been recorded in the public records at Date of Policy.

   (b) Any governmental police power not excluded by (a) above, except to the extent that a notice of the exercise thereof or a notice of a defect, lien or encumbrance resulting from a violation or alleged violation affecting the land has been recorded in the public records at Date of Policy.

2. Rights of eminent domain unless notice of the exercise thereof has been recorded in the public records at Date of Policy, but not excluding from coverage any taking which has occurred prior to Date of Policy which would be binding on the rights of a purchaser for value without knowledge.

3. Defects, liens, encumbrances, adverse claims or other matters:

   (a) whether or not recorded in the public records at Date of Policy, but created, suffered, assumed or agreed to by the insured claimant;

   (b) not known to the Company, not recorded in the public records at Date of Policy, but known to the insured claimant and not disclosed in writing to the Company by the insured claimant prior to the date the insured claimant became an insured under this policy;

   (c) resulting in no loss or damage to the insured claimant;

   (d) attaching or created subsequent to Date of Policy; or

   (e) resulting in loss or damage which would not have been sustained if the insured claimant had paid value for the insured mortgage or the estate or interest insured by this policy.

4. Unenforceability of the lien of the insured mortgage because of the inability or failure of the insured at Date of Policy, or the inability or failure of any subsequent owner of the indebtedness, to comply with applicable doing business laws of the state in which the land is situated.

5. Invalidity or unenforceability of the lien of the insured mortgage, or claim thereof, which arises out of the transaction evidenced by the insured mortgage and is based upon usury or any consumer credit protection or truth in lending law.

6. Any claim, which arises out of the transaction vesting in the insured the estate or interest insured by this policy or the transaction creating the interest of the insured lender, by reason of the operation of federal bankruptcy, state insolvency, or similar creditors' rights laws.

## CONDITIONS AND STIPULATIONS

**1. DEFINITION OF TERMS**

The following terms when used in this policy mean:

(a) "insured": the insured named in Schedule A, and, subject to any rights or defenses the Company would have had against the named insured, those who succeed to the interest of the named insured by operation of law as distinguished from purchase including, but not limited to, heirs, distributees, devisees, survivors, personal representatives, next of kin, or corporate or fiduciary successors. The term "insured" also includes

(i) the owner of the indebtedness secured by the insured mortgage and each successor in ownership of the indebtedness except a successor who is an obligor under the provisions of Section 12(c) of these Conditions and Stipulations (reserving, however, all rights and defenses as to any successor that the Company would have had against any predecessor insured, unless the successor acquired the indebtedness as a purchaser for value without knowledge of the asserted defect, lien, encumbrance, adverse claim or other matter insured against by this policy as affecting title to the estate or interest in the land);

(ii) any governmental agency or governmental instrumentality which is an insurer or guarantor under an insurance contract or guaranty insuring or guaranteeing the indebtedness secured by the insured mortgage, or any part thereof, whether named as an insured herein or not;

(iii) the parties designated in Section 2(a) of these Conditions and Stipulations.

(b) "insured claimant": an insured claiming loss or damage.

(c) "insured lender": the owner of an insured mortgage.

(d) "insured mortgage": a mortgage shown in Schedule B, the owner of which is named as an insured in Schedule A.

(e) "knowledge" or "known": actual knowledge, not constructive knowledge or notice which may be imputed to an insured by reason of the public records as defined in this policy or any other records which impart constructive notice of matters affecting the land.

(f) "land": the land described or referred to in Schedule A, and improvements affixed thereto which by law constitute real property. The term "land" does not include any property beyond the lines of the area described or referred to in Schedule A, nor any right, title, interest, estate or easement in abutting streets, roads, avenues, alleys, lanes, ways or waterways, but nothing herein shall modify or limit the extent to which a right of access to and from the land is insured by this policy.

(g) "mortgage": mortgage, deed of trust, trust deed, or other security instrument.

(h) "public records": records established under state statutes at Date of Policy for the purpose of imparting constructive notice of matters relating to real property to purchasers for value and without knowledge.

(i) "unmarketability of the title": an alleged or apparent matter affecting the title to the land, not excluded or excepted from coverage, which would entitle a purchaser of the estate or interest described in Schedule A or the insured mortgage to be released from the obligation to purchase by virtue of a contractual condition requiring the delivery of marketable title.

**2. CONTINUATION OF INSURANCE**

(a) **After Acquisition of Title by Insured Lender.** If this policy insures the owner of the indebtedness secured by the insured mortgage, the coverage of this policy shall continue in force as of Date of Policy in favor of (i) such insured who acquires all or any part of the estate or interest in the land by foreclosure, trustee's sale, conveyance in lieu of foreclosure, or other legal manner which discharges the lien of the insured mortgage; (ii) a transferee of the estate or interest so acquired from an insured corporation, provided the transferee is the parent or wholly-owned subsidiary of the insured corporation, and their corporate successors by operation of law and not by purchase, subject to any rights or defenses the Company may have against any predecessor insureds; and (iii) any governmental agency or governmental instrumentality which acquires all or any part of the estate or interest pursuant to a contract of insurance or guaranty insuring or guaranteeing the indebtedness secured by the insured mortgage.

(b) **After Conveyance of Title by an Insured.** The coverage of this policy shall continue in force as of Date of Policy in favor of an insured only so long as the insured retains an estate or interest in the land, or holds an indebtedness secured by a purchase money mortgage given by a purchaser from the insured, or only so long as the insured shall have liability by reason of covenants of warranty made by the insured in any transfer or conveyance of the estate or interest. This policy shall not continue in force in favor of any purchaser from an insured of either (i) an estate or interest in the land, or (ii) an indebtedness secured by a purchase money mortgage given to an insured.

(c) **Amount of Insurance.** The amount of insurance after the acquisition or after the conveyance by an insured lender shall in neither event exceed the least of:

(i) the amount of insurance stated in Schedule A;

(ii) the amount of the principal of the indebtedness secured by the insured mortgage as of Date of Policy, interest thereon, expenses of foreclosure, amounts advanced pursuant to the insured mortgage to assure compliance with laws or to protect the lien of the insured mortgage prior to the time of acquisition of the estate or interest in the land and secured thereby and reasonable amounts expended to prevent deterioration of improvements, but reduced by the amount of all payments made; or

(iii) the amount paid by any governmental agency or governmental instrumentality, if the agency or instrumentality is the insured claimant, in the acquisition of the estate or interest in satisfaction of its insurance contract or guaranty.

**3. NOTICE OF CLAIM TO BE GIVEN BY INSURED CLAIMANT**

An insured shall notify the Company promptly in writing (i) in case of any litigation as set forth in Section 4(a) below, (ii) in case knowledge shall come to an insured hereunder of any claim of title or interest which is adverse to the title to the estate or interest or the lien of the insured mortgage, as insured, and

## Figure 30–4.  Example of Policy of Title Insurance *continued*

which might cause loss or damage for which the Company may be liable by virtue of this policy, or (iii) if title to the estate or interest or the lien of the insured mortgage, as insured, is rejected as unmarketable. If prompt notice shall not be given to the Company, then as to that insured all liability of the Company shall terminate with regard to the matter or matters for which prompt notice is required; provided, however, that failure to notify the Company shall in no case prejudice the rights of any insured under this policy unless the Company shall be prejudiced by the failure and then only to the extent of the prejudice.

#### 4.  DEFENSE AND PROSECUTION OF ACTIONS; DUTY OF INSURED CLAIMANT TO COOPERATE

(a) Upon written request by an insured and subject to the options contained in Section 6 of these Conditions and Stipulations, the Company, at its own cost and without unreasonable delay, shall provide for the defense of such insured in litigation in which any third party asserts a claim adverse to the title or interest as insured, but only as to those stated causes of action alleging a defect, lien or encumbrance or other matter insured against by this policy. The Company shall have the right to select counsel of its choice (subject to the right of such insured to object for reasonable cause) to represent the insured as to those stated causes of action and shall not be liable for and will not pay the fees of any other counsel. The Company will not pay any fees, costs or expenses incurred by the insured in the defense of those causes of action which allege matters not insured against by this policy.

(b) The Company shall have the right, at its own cost, to institute and prosecute any action or proceeding or to do any other act which in its opinion may be necessary or desirable to establish the title to the estate or interest or the lien of the insured mortgage, as insured, or to prevent or reduce loss or damage to the insured. The Company may take any appropriate action under the terms of this policy, whether or not it shall be liable hereunder, and shall not thereby concede liability or waive any provision of this policy. If the Company shall exercise its rights under this paragraph, it shall do so diligently.

(c) Whenever the Company shall have brought an action or interposed a defense as required or permitted by the provisions of this policy, the Company may pursue any litigation to final determination by a court of competent jurisdiction and expressly reserves the right, in its sole discretion, to appeal from any adverse judgment or order.

(d) In all cases where this policy permits or requires the Company to prosecute or provide for the defense of any action or proceeding, an insured shall secure to the Company the right to so prosecute or provide defense in the action or proceeding, and all appeals therein, and permit the Company to use, at its option, the name of such insured for this purpose. Whenever requested by the Company, an insured, at the Company's expense, shall give the Company all reasonable aid (i) in any action or proceeding, securing evidence, obtaining witnesses, prosecuting or defending the action or proceeding, or effecting settlement, and (ii) in any other lawful act which in the opinion of the Company may be necessary or desirable to establish the title to the estate or interest or the lien of the insured mortgage, as insured. If the Company is prejudiced by the failure of an insured to furnish the required cooperation, the Company's obligations to the insured under the policy shall terminate, including any liability or obligation to defend, prosecute, or continue any litigation, with regard to the matter or matters requiring such cooperation.

#### 5.  PROOF OF LOSS OR DAMAGE

In addition to and after the notices required under Section 3 of these Conditions and Stipulations have been provided the Company, a proof of loss or damage signed and sworn to by the insured claimant shall be furnished to the Company within 90 days after the insured claimant shall ascertain the facts giving rise to the loss or damage. The proof of loss or damage shall describe the defect in, or lien or encumbrance on the title, or other matter insured against by this policy which constitutes the basis of loss or damage and shall state, to the extent possible, the basis of calculating the amount of the loss or damage. If the Company is prejudiced by the failure of an insured claimant to provide the required proof of loss or damage, the Company's obligations to such insured under the policy shall terminate, including any liability or obligation to defend, prosecute, or continue any litigation, with regard to the matter or matters requiring such proof of loss or damage.

In addition, an insured claimant may reasonably be required to submit to examination under oath by any authorized representative of the Company and shall produce for examination, inspection and copying, at such reasonable times and places as may be designated by any authorized representative of the Company, all records, books, ledgers, checks, correspondence and memoranda, whether bearing a date before or after Date of Policy, which reasonably pertain to the loss or damage. Further, if requested by any authorized representative of the Company, the insured claimant shall grant its permission, in writing, for any authorized representative of the Company to examine, inspect and copy all records, books, ledgers, checks, correspondence and memoranda in the custody or control of a third party, which reasonably pertain to the loss or damage. All information designated as confidential by an insured claimant provided to the Company pursuant to this Section shall not be disclosed to others unless, in the reasonable judgment of the Company, it is necessary in the administration of the claim. Failure of an insured claimant to submit for examination under oath, produce other reasonably requested information or grant permission to secure reasonably necessary information

from third parties as required in this paragraph, unless prohibited by law or governmental regulation, shall terminate any liability of the Company under this policy as to that insured for that claim.

#### 6.  OPTIONS TO PAY OR OTHERWISE SETTLE CLAIMS; TERMINATION OF LIABILITY

In case of a claim under this policy, the Company shall have the following additional options:

(a) **To Pay or Tender Payment of the Amount of Insurance or to Purchase the Indebtedness.**

(i) to pay or tender payment of the amount of insurance under this policy together with any costs, attorneys' fees and expenses incurred by the insured claimant, which were authorized by the Company, up to the time of payment or tender of payment and which the Company is obligated to pay; or

(ii) in case loss or damage is claimed under this policy by the owner of the indebtedness secured by the insured mortgage, to purchase the indebtedness secured by the insured mortgage for the amount owing thereon together with any costs, attorneys' fees and expenses incurred by the insured claimant which were authorized by the Company up to the time of purchase and which the Company is obligated to pay.

If the Company offers to purchase the indebtedness as herein provided, the owner of the indebtedness shall transfer, assign, and convey the indebtedness and the insured mortgage, together with any collateral security, to the Company upon payment therefor.

Upon the exercise by the Company of the option provided for in paragraph a(i), all liability and obligations to the insured under this policy, other than to make the payment required in that paragraph, shall terminate, including any liability or obligation to defend, prosecute, or continue any litigation, and the policy shall be surrendered to the Company for cancellation.

Upon the exercise by the Company of the option provided for in paragraph a(ii) the Company's obligation to an insured lender under this policy for the claimed loss or damage, other than the payment required to be made, shall terminate, including any liability or obligation to defend, prosecute or continue any litigation.

(b) **To Pay or Otherwise Settle With Parties Other than the Insured or With the Insured Claimant.**

(i) to pay or otherwise settle with other parties for or in the name of an insured claimant any claim insured against under this policy, together with any costs, attorneys' fees and expenses incurred by the insured claimant which were authorized by the Company up to the time of payment and which the Company is obligated to pay; or

(ii) to pay or otherwise settle with the insured claimant the loss or damage provided for under this policy, together with any costs, attorneys' fees and expenses incurred by the insured claimant which were authorized by the Company up to the time of payment and which the Company is obligated to pay.

Upon the exercise by the Company of either of the options provided for in paragraphs (b)(i) or b(ii), the Company's obligations to the insured under this policy for the claimed loss or damage, other than the payments required to be made, shall terminate, including any liability or obligation to defend, prosecute or continue any litigation.

#### 7.  DETERMINATION AND EXTENT OF LIABILITY

This policy is a contract of indemnity against actual monetary loss or damage sustained or incurred by the insured claimant who has suffered loss or damage by reason of matters insured against by this policy and only to the extent herein described.

(a) The liability of the Company under this policy to an insured lender shall not exceed the least of:

(i) the Amount of Insurance stated in Schedule A, or, if applicable, the amount of insurance as defined in Section 2 (c) of these Conditions and Stipulations;

(ii) the amount of the unpaid principal indebtedness secured by the insured mortgage as limited or provided under Section 8 of these Conditions and Stipulations or as reduced under Section 9 of these Conditions and Stipulations, at the time the loss or damage insured against by this policy occurs, together with interest thereon; or

(iii) the difference between the value of the insured estate or interest as insured and the value of the insured estate or interest subject to the defect, lien or encumbrance insured against by this policy.

(b) In the event the insured lender has acquired the estate or interest in the manner described in Section 2(a) of these Conditions and Stipulations or has conveyed the title, then the liability of the Company shall continue as set forth in Section 7(a) of these Conditions and Stipulations.

(c) The liability of the Company under this policy to an insured owner of the estate or interest in the land described in Schedule A shall not exceed the least of:

(i) the Amount of Insurance stated in Schedule A; or,

(ii) the difference between the value of the insured estate or interest as insured and the value of the insured estate or interest subject to the defect, lien or encumbrance insured against by this policy.

(d) The Company will pay only those costs, attorneys' fees and expenses incurred in accordance with Section 4 of these Conditions and Stipulations.

**Figure 30–4. Example of Policy of Title Insurance *continued***

**8. LIMITATION OF LIABILITY**

(a) If the Company establishes the title, or removes the alleged defect, lien or encumbrance, or cures the lack of a right of access to or from the land, or cures the claim of unmarketability of title, or otherwise establishes the lien of the insured mortgage, all as insured, in a reasonably diligent manner by any method, including litigation and the completion of any appeals therefrom, it shall have fully performed its obligations with respect to that matter and shall not be liable for any loss or damage caused thereby.

(b) In the event of any litigation, including litigation by the Company or with the Company's consent, the Company shall have no liability for loss or damage until there has been a final determination by a court of competent jurisdiction, and disposition of all appeals therefrom, adverse to the title or, if applicable, to the lien of the insured mortgage, as insured.

(c) The Company shall not be liable for loss or damage to any insured for liability voluntarily assumed by the insured in settling any claim or suit without the prior written consent of the Company.

(d) The Company shall not be liable to an insured lender for: (i) any indebtedness created subsequent to Date of Policy except for advances made to protect the lien of the insured mortgage and secured thereby and reasonable amounts expended to prevent deterioration of improvements; or (ii) construction loan advances made subsequent to Date of Policy, except construction loan advances made subsequent to Date of Policy for the purpose of financing in whole or in part the construction of an improvement to the land which at Date of Policy were secured by the insured mortgage and which the insured was and continued to be obligated to advance at and after Date of Policy.

**9. REDUCTION OF INSURANCE; REDUCTION OR TERMINATION OF LIABILITY**

(a) All payments under this policy, except payments made for costs, attorneys' fees and expenses, shall reduce the amount of the insurance pro tanto. However, as to an insured lender, any payments made prior to the acquisition of title to the estate or interest as provided in Section 2(a) of these Conditions and Stipulations shall not reduce pro tanto the amount of the insurance afforded under this policy as to any such insured except to the extent that the payments reduce the amount of the indebtedness secured by the insured mortgage.

(b) Payment in part by any person of the principal of the indebtedness, or any other obligation secured by the insured mortgage, or any voluntary partial satisfaction or release of the insured mortgage, to the extent of the payment, satisfaction or release, shall reduce the amount of insurance pro tanto. The amount of insurance may thereafter be increased by accruing interest and advances made to protect the lien of the insured mortgage and secured thereby, with interest thereon, provided in no event shall the amount of insurance be greater than the Amount of Insurance stated in Schedule A.

(c) Payment in full by any person or the voluntary satisfaction or release of the insured mortgage shall terminate all liability of the Company to an insured lender except as provided in Section 2(a) of these Conditions and Stipulations.

**10. LIABILITY NONCUMULATIVE**

It is expressly understood that the amount of insurance under this policy shall be reduced by any amount the Company may pay under any policy insuring a mortgage to which exception is taken in Schedule B or to which the insured has agreed, assumed, or taken subject, or which is hereafter executed by an insured and which is a charge or lien on the estate or interest described or referred to in Schedule A, and the amount so paid shall be deemed a payment under this policy to the insured owner.

The provisions of this Section shall not apply to an insured lender, unless such insured acquires title to said estate or interest in satisfaction of the indebtedness secured by an insured mortgage.

**11. PAYMENT OF LOSS**

(a) No payment shall be made without producing this policy for endorsement of the payment unless the policy has been lost or destroyed, in which case proof of loss or destruction shall be furnished to the satisfaction of the Company.

(b) When liability and the extent of loss or damage has been definitely fixed in accordance with these Conditions and Stipulations, the loss or damage shall be payable within 30 days thereafter.

**12. SUBROGATION UPON PAYMENT OR SETTLEMENT**
**(a) The Company's Right of Subrogation.**

Whenever the Company shall have settled and paid a claim under this policy, all right of subrogation shall vest in the Company unaffected by any act of the insured claimant.

The Company shall be subrogated to and be entitled to all rights and remedies which the insured claimant would have had against any person or property in respect to the claim had this policy not been issued. If requested by the Company, the insured claimant shall transfer to the Company all rights and remedies against any person or property necessary in order to perfect this right of subrogation. The insured claimant shall permit the Company to sue, compromise or settle in the name of the insured claimant and to use the name of the insured claimant in any transaction or litigation involving these rights or remedies.

If a payment on account of a claim does not fully cover the loss of the insured claimant, the Company shall be subrogated (i) as to an insured owner, to all rights and remedies in the proportion which the Company's payment bears to the whole amount of loss; and (ii) as to an insured lender, to all rights and remedies of the insured claimant after the insured claimant shall have recovered its principal, interest, and costs of collection.

If loss should result from any act of the insured claimant, as stated above, that act shall not void this policy, but the Company, in that event, shall be required to pay only that part of any losses insured against by this policy which shall exceed the amount, if any, lost to the Company by reason of the impairment by the insured claimant of the Company's right of subrogation.

**(b) The Insured's Rights and Limitations.**

Notwithstanding the foregoing, the owner of the indebtedness secured by an insured mortgage, provided the priority of the lien of the insured mortgage or its enforceability is not affected, may release or substitute the personal liability of any debtor or guarantor, or extend or otherwise modify the terms of payment, or release a portion of the estate or interest from the lien of the insured mortgage, or release any collateral security for the indebtedness.

When the permitted acts of the insured claimant occur and the insured has knowledge of any claim of title or interest adverse to the title to the estate or interest or the priority or enforceability of the lien of the insured mortgage, as insured, the Company shall be required to pay only that part of any losses insured against by this policy which shall exceed the amount, if any, lost to the Company by reason of the impairment by the insured claimant of the Company's right of subrogation.

**(c) The Company's Rights Against Non-insured Obligors.**

The Company's right of subrogation against non-insured obligors shall exist and shall include, without limitation, the rights of the insured to indemnities, guaranties, other policies of insurance or bonds, notwithstanding any terms or conditions contained in those instruments which provide for subrogation rights by reason of this policy.

The Company's right of subrogation shall not be avoided by acquisition of an insured mortgage by an obligor (except an obligor described in Section 1(a)(ii) of these Conditions and Stipulations) who acquires the insured mortgage as a result of an indemnity, guarantee, other policy of insurance, or bond and the obligor will not be an insured under this policy, notwithstanding Section 1(a)(i) of these Conditions and Stipulations.

**13. ARBITRATION**

Unless prohibited by applicable law, either the Company or the insured may demand arbitration pursuant to the Title Insurance Arbitration Rules of the American Arbitration Association. Arbitrable matters may include, but are not limited to, any controversy or claim between the Company and the insured arising out of or relating to this policy, any service of the Company in connection with its issuance or the breach of a policy provision or other obligation. All arbitrable matters when the Amount of Insurance is $1,000,000 or less shall be arbitrated at the option of either the Company or the insured. All arbitrable matters when the Amount of Insurance is in excess of $1,000,000 shall be arbitrated only when agreed to by both the Company and the insured. Arbitration pursuant to this policy and under the Rules in effect on the date the demand for arbitration is made or, at the option of the insured, the Rules in effect at Date of Policy shall be binding upon the parties. The award may include attorneys' fees only if the laws of the state in which the land is located permit a court to award attorneys' fees to a prevailing party. Judgment upon the award rendered by the Arbitrator(s) may be entered in any court having jurisdiction thereof.

The law of the situs of the land shall apply to an arbitration under the Title Insurance Arbitration Rules.

A copy of the Rules may be obtained from the Company upon request.

**14. LIABILITY LIMITED TO THIS POLICY; POLICY ENTIRE CONTRACT**

(a) This policy together with all endorsements, if any, attached hereto by the Company is the entire policy and contract between the insured and the Company. In interpreting any provision of this policy, this policy shall be construed as a whole.

(b) Any claim of loss or damage, whether or not based on negligence, and which arises out of the status of the lien of the insured mortgage, or of the title to the estate or interest covered hereby, or by any action asserting such claim shall be restricted to this policy.

(c) No amendment of or endorsement to this policy can be made except by a writing endorsed hereon or attached hereto signed by either the President, a Vice President, the Secretary, an Assistant Secretary, or validating officer or authorized signatory of the Company.

**15. SEVERABILITY**

In the event any provision of this policy is held invalid or unenforceable under applicable law, the policy shall be deemed not to include that provision and all other provisions shall remain in full force and effect.

**16. NOTICES, WHERE SENT**

All notices required to be given the Company and any statement in writing required to be furnished the Company shall include the number of this policy and shall be addressed to the Company at the issuing office or to:

**Chicago Title Insurance Company**
**Claims Department**
**111 West Washington Street**
**Chicago, Illinois 60602**

The names of the parties being covered by the policy, the *Insured*, are inserted next.

1. Each buyer's name must be inserted.
2. Indicates the form of title to be given to the buyers. The type of *estate* or *interest* you should get is called a *fee simple* title, which means you will have complete ownership of the land to sell, give away or encumber as you wish, subject to the terms of your mortgage or deed of trust.
3. The type of ownership by which the buyers are taking title is then given, for example, tenants-in-common, joint tenants, husband and wife as community property.
4. This is the complete legal description of the land you have purchased. A complete description of the property is given and should specify any easements, water rights or other property rights to be included in your purchase so that they will be insured by the policy. If any parts of the property are to be excluded from the conveyance, such as mineral or timber rights, they also should be specified here. Often water rights will be included as part of the description but will not be insured by the title company.

**Schedule B**

*Part I*

Lists the five common exceptions from coverage in standard coverage policies. That is, the policy does not insure against the following:

1. Any taxes or assessments levied against the property before the close of escrow but not indicated on the public, or tax authority, records are not insured against by this policy.
2. Encumbrances that can be discovered only by physically inspecting the property and by asking questions of people living on it are not covered by the policy. For example, because you could discover an adverse possessor or prescriptive user only by inspecting the land, you will not be insured against a claim for adverse possession or prescriptive use after you purchase the property. (See Chapter 16, "Adverse Possession.") Another common unrecorded instrument is a lease held by a renter that is not recorded but that would be binding on the purchaser of the land. Thus, you must talk to any

people living on the land to ascertain if they have a lease. The policy will not defend you against any legal claims made by such persons in possession after you take title because you had notice they were there by your own inspection of the property.

3. The seller of the property may have granted easement rights to an adjoining landowner or other person without recording this grant in the public records, or a person might have gained a prescriptive easement by meeting the requirements for obtaining this right. (See Chapter 9, "Easement Rights.") This policy does not insure against easements that can not be discovered by searching the public records. It is your responsibility to determine the status of any right-of-way roads crossing the property or pipelines taking water from the property that are not recorded easements to insure yourself against future claims against the land. The seller is supposed to list all existing easements in clause 6 of the Model Contract of Sale. (See Chapter 27.)

4. This policy does not require a legal survey and thus ensures only that you will receive the seller's title to the property described in this policy and the deed. It does not insure the exact location of that property on the ground. Thus, if you buy land without a survey and later discover that the boundary lines are not where you thought they were, the policy does not protect you. The amount of acreage you will receive is not insured, nor are unrecorded "boundary line agreements" made between an owner and an adjoining landowner. Thus, you should get a survey, as provided in clauses 16(b) and 17(b) of the Model Contract of Sale.

5. Here the policy excludes from coverage one of the most complicated areas of land ownership, water rights (among others). Many rights to take water are based on the riparian nature of the property rather than on the recording of any documents, so the policy does not take any liability for future water disputes. (See Chapter 10, "Water Rights.") Title companies never insure your right to take water. You must do your own investigation to satisfy your ownership of water rights. Mining claims and mineral rights that exist against the property are also excluded from coverage. (See Chapter 11, "Mineral, Oil, Gas, Timber, Soil and Other Rights.")

*Part II*

Any liens and encumbrances against the title that the title company found during its title search are listed here, including tax, assessment and mechanics' liens; mortgages or deeds of trust on the property; easements on the land; covenants, conditions and restrictions of ownership binding on the owner; and attachments and judgments. These are defects in the title, but they do not make the title unmarketable. If an encumbrance did make the title unmarketable, the title company would not issue a policy of title insurance, because it insures the marketability of the title.

### Exclusions from Coverage

Further exclusions from the coverage of this policy are listed here. The policy does not insure the buyer against any losses he or she might suffer because of:

1. (a) Governmental regulations and laws, such as building codes and zoning regulations, that restrict the use of the property. If the property has been illegally subdivided or the house does not have a legal building permit, any losses you suffer are not covered by this policy. (See Chapter 12, "Zoning Laws," and Chapter 13, "Building and Health Codes.")

    (b) Unrecorded police power right, such as a forfeiture action against the property for illegal activities by a prior owner.

2. Acts of eminent domain condemnation, unless this action has been recorded prior to issuance of the policy. (See Chapter 15, "Eminent Domain and Condemnation.")

3. (a) Any matters that the buyer agrees to accept with the purchase as part of the purchase agreement.

    (b) Unrecorded defects known about or agreed to by the buyer but not reported to the title company, or defects that do not result in loss to the insured or that were created after the date the policy was issued. For example, suppose the seller sells the land to someone else before selling it to you, and the first buyer does not record the deed. If you record your deed before the first buyer does and you do not know that the land is already sold, you are the only person with a legal right to the land because you are a *purchaser without knowledge*. If the first buyer sues you, the policy pays for your defense. But if you buy the land knowing it has already been sold, you do not have a legal right

to the property because you are a *purchaser with knowledge*. If you are sued, this policy does not cover you, because you knew and assumed the risks when you bought the property.

    (c) If there is an error made in the title policy but you suffer no loss, no liability accrues to the title company.

    (d) Obviously, there is no coverage for any lien placed on the property after the policy is issued.

    (e) The buyer who is a bona fide purchaser (pays the actual worth of the property) would be covered if he or she did not know about a prior lien. The policy does not insure you if you don't pay fair value for the property, and you thereby suffer a loss that you would not otherwise have suffered.

4. If a lender is not properly licensed in the state in which the loan is made, it is not covered under this policy.

5. A lender that suffers losses because it violates consumer protection laws, such as the truth in lending law, is not covered under this policy.

6. Title companies do not insure title against any claim made in a bankruptcy proceeding, for example, that the property was sold to avoid the rights of creditors.

### Conditions and Stipulations

These conditions are common to most standard coverage title insurance policies.

1. (a) through (i) The terms used in the policy are defined.

2. (a) The insurance policy will continue to cover *assignees of the lender* under certain circumstances.

    (b) The insurance coverage ends when the purchaser of the property sells or transfers his interest in the property.

    (c) Limits the coverage of a lender to the amount of the policy, even if the amount of money owed, including interest, exceeds the amount of the policy.

3. The insured person must notify the title insurance company as soon as he discovers any problem with the title.

4. (a) through (d) This clause establishes the obligation of the title insurance company to protect your title by bringing and defending actions. An interesting part of the defense obligation stipulates that if you make a contract to sell the property and your prospective

buyer terminates the purchase because he or she discovers a defect in your title not excluded from coverage in this policy, the company will cover your damages from the loss of the sale up to the amount of the policy coverage. The company also has the right to commence an action to clear the title on its own initiative. Finally, the policy states that the company shall be allowed to use the insured's name in the prosecution or defense of a case and that the insured shall give the company full cooperation, should it have to meet a challenge to the title it is insuring.

5. Additional requirements of notice to the company of its liability are given here. The insured has 90 days after discovery of any loss or damage to notify the company in writing of a claim under the policy. The insured also must submit to any request for his or her business records or other documents.

6. The company has the obligation to meet its obligations to the insured by either paying the insured's loss up to the amount of coverage or securing the title so that the insured does not suffer a loss.

7. (a) through (d) This section specifies the elements involved in determining and paying for any losses covered by the policy: (a) and (b) deal with the liability owed to an insured lender and the amount of money that must be paid for any loss; (c) deals with the liability owed to an insured owner. This would be either the entire amount of the insurance policy or the difference in value between the land with the lien or title defect and what the land would be worth without the defect or title problem. (d) specifies that the title insurance company is liable to pay only the costs and attorney's fees incurred in defending or prosecuting the title. It does not have to pay the insured's personal attorney fees.

8. The company has no liability to pay damages until after a final determination of any lawsuit, including appeals. Only if the problem remains unsolved after all of the company's efforts have failed, does it have to pay money to the insured.

9. If the company pays a claim, the amount of insurance available is decreased by the amount of the payment, should another claim be made. If the company pays out the entire policy amount, then it is released from any further liability under the policy.

10. If you have given a mortgage on the land and a judgment later renders your title unmarketable, or if it is discovered that a lien or encumbrance exists that is covered by the policy, the company must first pay any money to the lender-mortgagee before it can pay you, the insured. If the defect results in a partial loss only, the amount paid, whether to the lender or to you, will reduce the future liability of the company by that amount to prevent the accumulation of liabilities beyond the amount of the policy.

11. The insured should turn in the original title insurance policy to be paid for a loss. Once the insured's loss is determined, payment must be made within 30 days.

12. To *subrogate* means to substitute. For example, assume that the seller did not reveal an unrecorded defect in the title in the contract of sale when he or she sold the land to the insured buyer, and the insured buyer suffers a loss because of the defect. After the title company pays the insured for his or her loss, if it is covered by the policy, the company then has the right to subrogate, or substitute, itself in the place of the insured and sue the seller for breach of contract of sale and fraudulent activity. The company can sue in its own make and in the name of the insured. If any damages are awarded, the title company keeps the money

13. If there is a dispute between the insured and the company, it may go to arbitration rather than to a judge in a court if both parties agree to arbitration. If the amount being asked for by the insured is less than $1,000,000, it must go to arbitration.

14. All liability that the insurance company has to the insured is contained in this policy. No oral statements made to the insured by a title company are binding, unless they are backed up by the policy.

15. If, for any reason, a legal challenge is raised regarding some aspect of the policy and a provision is determined to be nonbinding on the insured, that court ruling will not invalidate the rest of the policy.

16. The address given here should be used if you have to make a claim or notify the company for any reason.

## Why You Need Title Insurance in Addition to the Contract of Sale

The Model Contract of Sale includes every protection that you receive in the policy of title insurance. Under the contract the seller is liable to you for your damages, whereas under the policy of title insurance, the title company assumes liability. Therefore, it might appear that getting a policy of title insurance is an unnecessary expense. However, if you are not insured and you have to proceed against the seller for any defect in title and breach of the contract of sale, you will have to pay the legal expenses prior to a judgment, you might not be able to locate the seller to collect a judgment, and the seller might not have any money to pay a judgment. A title insurance policy pays your legal costs, ensures coverage for any losses included in the policy, and pays for your defense if you are sued over any title problems after your purchase. At this time, it is the best insurance you can have when buying land. It should be an essential part of your purchase, and must always include a preliminary title report issued to you during escrow, so that you will know what liens exist on the title to the land, well before you pay your money and take title. Then you will be able to demand the removal of those liens that you do not accept; if they cannot be removed, you can cancel the transaction and get your deposit returned to you.

## The Lender's Policy of Title Insurance

If the seller takes back a purchase money mortgage or deed of trust and note when he or she sells you the land, usually the seller is included as an insured party in your standard coverage owner's policy of title insurance. But if a commercial lender extends a loan to you for the purchase and takes back a mortgage or deed of trust with the land as security, you will be charged for obtaining a more inclusive form of title insurance, called a *loan policy* or *lender's policy*, which was established by the American Land Title Association (ALTA) for the protection of lenders.

All items excluded from coverage in the owner's policy are included in the loan policy, which includes a legal survey and physical inspection by the insurer before a policy will be issued. The cost of this type of coverage is much greater than that of a standard coverage policy, but a lender usually wants as much protection for its security as possible, so it will demand an ALTA Policy.

The buyer usually pays for the lender's policy as part of the loan. This policy insures only the lender-mortgagee; it does not protect the buyer. Thus, you also must get your own policy of title insurance. The amount of coverage is for the amount of the debt owed to the lender, because that would be the extent of its loss, should there be a defect in the title to the land. As the amount of the debt is paid off by the buyer, the amount of coverage decreases by an equal amount. When the debt is totally paid, the lender's policy terminates, because there is no longer anything to insure the lender against.

If you order a lender's policy at the same time you order an owner's policy, a discount is usually given by the title company. A few states combine the owner's policy and the lender's policy in a joint protection policy, issued in the amount of the purchase price. As the buyer pays off his loan, the company's liability to the lender decreases, and its liability to the buyer increases. When the loan is completely paid, the buyer remains as the only party insured by the policy.

## Extended Coverage Owner's Policy of Title Insurance

The greater protection given to a lender by the loan policy can be obtained by a buyer who extends the standard owner's policy to cover these possible defects. The extended coverage owner's policy generally gives buyers what the ALTA Policy gives lenders, except that insured access rights are usually not included. The main advantage of extended coverage is that it insures a survey and everything that can be found by a physical inspection of the property. But the survey taken by the title company is usually more expensive than any survey you can have done elsewhere. Therefore, because it is easy to inspect the property for unrecorded easements and to determine the state of persons in possession of the land, if you get your own legal survey done, you will get adequate coverage with a standard owner's policy of title insurance. Of course, if the seller is willing to pay for it, get the extended coverage policy.

If you desire, you can specify that the seller is to

pay the entire amount of an extended policy. It is very easy to change the clause in the contract of sale, if you want to provide for this. (See Chapter 27, "The Model Contract of Sale.")

If you want any information about title insurance in your state, write to your state insurance commissioner or the land title association listed in the "Useful Resources" at the end of this chapter.

## Attorney's Certificate of Title

In a few states in the East (see Figure 30–2), abstracts of title by abstract companies and title insurance policies are not commonly used. Instead, an attorney, hired to examine all of the recorded documents relating to the title, makes up the abstract of title. The attorney issues the results of the title search in a certificate of title that details what records were examined and what encumbrances exist against the title, if any. This certificate is basically the same as an abstract of title certificate. It is not insurance of marketable title, and it does not insure against undisclosed defects, such as forgery and the others listed earlier. Thus, like an abstract of title, it is not an adequate form of protection for the buyer.

If the attorney makes a negligent mistake in the title search, you will have to sue him or her for any losses you suffer due to that negligence. In contrast, under a title insurance policy, you will be compensated if the company is negligent and for unknown defects in the title, subject to any exception in the policy.

Always insist on a policy of title insurance if it is available in your area. If the real estate agent or seller tells you that such policies are not issued in your area, do some investigating on your own to determine the location of the nearest title company. Title insurance is becoming more widespread every year. Look in the yellow pages under "Title Companies." If you can't locate a title company, send an inquiry to

The American Land Title Association
  (ALTA)
1828 L St., NW
Washington, DC 20036

## The Torrens Title System and Torrens Certificate

Less than 1 percent of the country uses a completely different method of guaranteeing title to land, called the *Torrens Title System*. In this system, the county recorder maintains a record of all encumbrances that exist on the title to each piece of property in the county. Before a parcel of land can be sold or mortgaged, the buyer and seller must go to court for a hearing. The county recorder sends a notice of the hearing to anybody whom the recorder determines could have a claim against the title, according to the county records. Anybody with a claim must sue to have that claim settled before title is passed to the buyer. The court dismisses or settles all the claims, orders the title to be registered in the buyer's name and issues the new owner a Torrens Certificate, which lists any liens and encumbrances against the title. If a Torrens Certificate is issued, the title is declared marketable, and no undisclosed defects can be used later to cause a loss of title.

## Useful Resources

The listed titles are available from

American Land Title Association (ALTA)
1828 L St., NW
Washington, DC 20036

"The Importance of the Abstract in Your Community"
"Buying a House of Cards?"
"Protecting Your Interest in Real Estate"
"Land Title Insurance—Consumer Protection Since 1876"
"Blueprint for Home Buying"

There is no charge for any of the above.

The titles that follow are available free from

California land Title Association
P.O. Box 13968
Sacramento, CA 95853

"Why Do You Need Title Insurance?"

"Solar Access: A Potential Title Problem"

"Closing Costs: A Primer"

'Title Insurance: Where Does Your Dollar Go?"

"Understanding Foreclosure"

"The Function of an Escrow"

"Mechanics' Liens"

"Forgery: A Cause for Alarm"

"Creative Financing: Carrying Back a Second? You Need a Lender's Title Policy"

"The Title Consumer—Understanding Supplemental Property Taxes"

"Understanding Closing and Title Costs"

# CHAPTER
# 31 Types of Co-Ownership

In this chapter, I describe the advantages and disadvantages of the various types of co-ownership by which a married or unmarried couple or a group can take title to a parcel of land. Today more and more people are joining together with others willing and able to share the costs of owning country land and are buying as a group. Generally, the larger the parcel of land, the cheaper it is per acre. As a group, individuals can pool their funds to buy a larger parcel. Even if you do not want to share ownership of your land with anyone else, you might agree to buy a large parcel of land with some other people and then subdivide the property among yourselves, with each of you taking separate title to your individual parcel. However, you must check the local zoning regulations first to be sure that you will be allowed to subdivide, or partition, your land after purchasing it. Some areas have minimum acreage laws for parcel splits and limits on the number of residences per parcel. (See Chapter 12, "Zoning Laws.")

Whenever two or more people plan to buy land together, before signing the contract of sale all buyers should understand what each person's goals and desires are regarding the land. It is often useful to draw up an owner's agreement that specifies the group's goals and desires in writing. I have included a Model Owner's Agreement at the end of this chapter that your group can use as a basis for drawing up your own contract. Then the group should decide on the form of co-ownership best suited to it.

The two most common forms of land co-ownership are tenancy in common and joint tenancy. People can also join together in a corporation, nonprofit association or cooperative. All the legal aspects of these legal entities could fill another book of this size, so I will merely summarize their advantages and disadvantages to give you a basic idea of the possibilities available to your group.

I also include some information pertaining to property ownership by a husband and wife, specifically tenancy by the entireties, dower and curtesy, and community property rights.

## Owning Land as Tenants in Common

When buying land as tenants in common, each purchaser shares an undivided interest in the total parcel of land. This means that one party cannot claim any specific portion of the land as his or hers alone unless it is specified in a contract among all the owners. Each cotenant does not necessarily have to own an equal share. For instance, one person might have a quarter interest, another a half interest and two others might each have a one-eighth interest in the land. Usually, each person is financially responsible only to the extent of his ownership.

A cotenancy in a deed might read as follows: "Gordon Iris, a single man, an undivided 1/3 interest, and Wendi Campbell, a single woman, an undivided interest, as tenants in common."

The only way one tenant can destroy the tenancy in common, or cotenancy, without the other owners' approval is by going to court and filing an action to *partition* the land among the owners. There is no way to stop such an action unless all parties have waived these rights by a legal agreement among themselves. The judge will appoint a commissioner, or referee, who will equitably divide the land into separate parcels, according to the amount of interest held by each tenant. Each person then becomes the sole owner of his respective portion. If, for geographic or legal reasons, the land cannot be split up in this manner, the court will order that the entire piece of land be sold and the proceeds split up among the owners, according to their respective interests. If all the owners are willing, of course, they can partition the land themselves as local law permits or sell it and divide the proceeds without initiating a court action, although getting everyone to agree on a fair division of the land is usually difficult. The owners can also mutually agree in writing to replace the cotenancy with another form of co-ownership.

Each individual cotenant can sell or mortgage his or her interest in the land but acts only for his or her own share and cannot bind anyone else's interest. Thus, if a person's mortgage on her share were to be foreclosed, her lender would take its share as a tenant in common with the other owners. Because the lender would then have to either sell its interest in the land or file for a partition to sell the land and get the money owed, a commercial lender will not likely grant a loan to just one cotenant in a tenancy in common.

To avoid possible problems with lenders or a purchaser of a cotenant's interest, the owners can specify in a contract among themselves that no tenant may sell or mortgage his or her share or that the remaining owners have the *right of first refusal* if one tenant wants to sell. The right of first refusal means that the cotenant who wants to sell an interest must first offer to sell it to the other owners before it can be offered to anyone else. The Model Owner's Agreement at the conclusion of this chapter illustrates how such an agreement can be written.

If a cotenant fails to make payments on the land and other expenses, the other co-owners can sue, get a judgment and foreclose on that owner's interest in the property. If a cotenant dies, his or her interest in the property goes to the heirs, who take that cotenant's place as a tenant in common with the other owners. This inheritance rule is the most important legal aspect of a tenancy in common and differentiates it from other forms of co-ownership. Under a joint tenancy (see next section), if one owner dies, his or her interest in the property goes to the surviving owners. Because most people want their property to go to their heirs, unrelated land buyers usually buy as tenants in common rather than joint tenants. Most states assume that unless stated otherwise, title to property will be under a tenancy in common. Nevertheless, you should specify in your contract of sale, in your escrow instructions and in your deed that you are to take the property as tenants in common if that is your choice.

## Owning Land as Joint Tenants

Whereas tenants in common may hold undivided unequal interest in the land, joint tenants always share an undivided equal interest in the land. The major legal difference between these two types of co-ownership is that under a joint tenancy the coowners have the *right of survivorship* which means that if one of the parties dies, that party's interest automatically passes to the surviving owners. Joint tenants cannot will their interests to their heirs or anyone else, and their interests do not become part of their estates at death. The surviving joint tenants inherit the deceased's interest free from personal debts and liens. No will is involved, so an expensive and lengthy probate proceeding is unnecessary. Depending on the state, an inheritance tax may be levied, based on the value of the deceased person's interest in the land.

Because each person owns an equal interest in the land, all expenses, including land payments, taxes, repairs, insurance and other items, must be shared equally. If one party fails to contribute his or her share, the other joint tenants can sue for contribution or breach of contract, obtain a judgment against the defaulting tenant, place a lien against his or her interest in the property and eventually obtain a writ of possession against that share of the property.

Once a joint tenancy has been created, no joint tenant can get out of it without destroying that form of ownership. If a party sells his or her interest, the buyer comes in as a tenant in common, rather than a joint tenant with the others. For example, if X, Y and Z hold a piece of land as joint tenants and Z sells his interest to A, A buys in as a tenant in common. If A dies, her share goes to her heirs, rather than to X and Y. X and Y remain joint tenants, and each has a right of survivorship to the other's interest. On death, their interests never go to A. If X and Y choose, they can change their arrangement to become tenants in common with A. If only two people are joint tenants and one sells his or her interest, the joint tenancy is automatically terminated and transformed into a tenancy in common when the new owner takes title. (See Figure 31–1.) A joint tenant who chooses to sell his or her interest can do so without the consent of the other owners, unless the owners specify otherwise in a contract among themselves.

Like a tenant in common, a joint tenant who wants to borrow money for a private loan can mortgage his or her interest in the property. However, if the loan is foreclosed the lender will take his or her interest as a tenant in common, and the remaining tenants then automatically become tenants in common. A joint tenant, like a tenant in common, would probably have a hard time finding a lender willing to lend money solely on the security of a joint tenancy interest.

If a money judgment is rendered against one tenant for personal debts, that tenant's interest can be split off from the others and used to pay the obligation.

Any owner or creditor can go to court to file an action for partition of the individual interests, just as in a tenancy in common, or the owners can mutually agree in writing to change the arrangement.

If you choose to take ownership under a joint tenancy, you must specify in your contract of sale, escrow instructions and deed that you are to take title as *joint tenants* or as *joint tenants with the right of survivorship.* A few states, Florida, Georgia, Kentucky, North Carolina, Ohio, Oregon, Pennsylvania, South Carolina, Tennessee, Texas, Virginia, Washington and West Virginia, have abolished the right of survivorship in joint tenancy. Title passes to the heirs on the death of joint tenants as if they were tenants in common.

A typical joint tenancy would read as follows: "John Rael, a single man, an undivided 1/2 interest, and Mary Smith, a single woman, an undivided 1/2 interest, as joint tenants."

## Owning Land as Tenants by the Entireties

This type of ownership applies only to a husband and wife. In some states—Arkansas, Delaware, Florida, Indiana, Kentucky, Maryland, Massachusetts, Michigan, Missouri, New Jersey, New York, North Carolina, Oklahoma, Oregon, Pennsylvania, Rhode Island, Tennessee, Vermont, Virginia, West Virginia, Wisconsin and Wyoming—a sale to a married couple can create a tenancy by the entireties between the spouses. In some states it is automatic, unless specified otherwise; in other states it must be specifically stated in the deed. Under a tenancy by the entireties, title is held by both persons as if they were one owner. Each has complete ownership of the property, and when one dies the other keeps full ownership rights. Thus, like joint tenants, they have the right of survivorship. If the deceased spouse had individual debts, creditors cannot get a lien against the property. However, if the debtor spouse is the one who survives or if the husband and wife had common debts, the creditors can attach the property.

If a married couple buys land with a single person, another couple or a group of people, each mar-

**Figure 31–1. How a Joint Tenancy Operates**

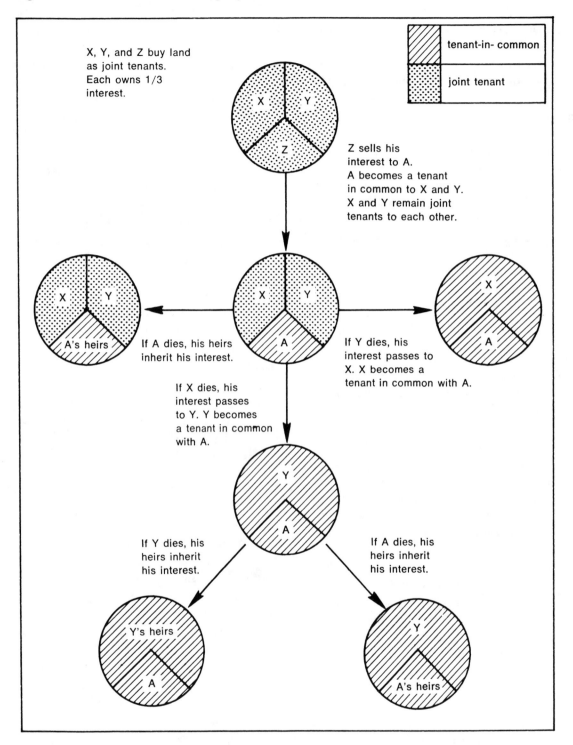

ried couple may be considered as tenants by the entireties within a group of joint tenants. For instance, if *X* and *Y*, a husband and wife, buy land with *Z*, a single person, *X* and *Y* can be considered one person under the law of tenancy by the entireties and own an undivided half interest in the property as a joint tenant with *Z*, who also owns an undivided half interest in the land. Compare this with a strict joint tenancy, under which *X*, *Y* and *Z* would each own an undivided one-third interest in the land. If a divorce occured, *X* and *Y* would split their half interest and become tenants in common with *Z*, and the right of survivorship would terminate.

No action for partition can be forced by only one

of the spouses in a tenancy by the entireties, and no sale of the property can be made by one spouse without the written consent of the other.

## Dower and Curtesy Rights and Community Property

Several states recognize either dower and curtesy rights or community property rights of a husband and wife, which, like a tenancy by the entireties, require both spouses' consent to a sale of their mutual property. Although these rights are not a type of ownership, strictly speaking, they will affect your title if you are a married couple, and they could affect the title of the land you are buying if the sellers include a married couple.

### Dower and Curtesy Rights

Where recognized, dower rights give a widow one-third of her husband's real estate on his death. (Some states have increased this to a half interest.) On the other hand, curtesy is the husband's right to one-third of his wife's real estate on her death, but he only obtains this right if a child was born during the marriage.

Dower and curtesy rights cannot be cut off by one spouse's selling the land without the permission of the other. Both parties must consent to the sale in writing and must sign the deed. For instance, in a dower and curtesy state, if you buy land from a husband and the wife does not sign the deed, you run the risk that if her husband dies before she does, she can collect her share of her husband's estate from you, because she never signed away her dower interest in the land. To be sure both parties will agree to sign the deed, get both the husband and the wife to sign the contract of sale. If both parties do not sign the contract of sale, either party can refuse to sign the deed without legal liability.

The states that still recognize dower and curtesy rights are Alaska, Arkansas, Delaware, Georgia, Hawaii, Kentucky, Maryland, Massachusetts, Ohio, Oregon, Rhode Island, Tennessee, Virginia, West Virginia and Wisconsin. New Jersey abolished dower and curtesy rights as of May 28, 1980.

### Community Property

Eight states—Arizona, California, Idaho, Louisiana, Nevada, New Mexico, Texas and Washington—regard any property purchased during a marriage as community property. Both husband and wife have an equal right to own and possess the property purchased during marriage. On the death of either spouse the survivor automatically receives half of the community property and the other half passes to the lawful heirs. In some states the surviving spouse automatically receives the entire amount of community property. Check with a lawyer to determine what the law is in your state if you are in a community property state. Of course, the deceased spouse may will the other half to the surviving spouse, regardless of the state law. In a divorce the community property is always split in half between the spouses. Community property laws, like dower and curtesy laws and tenancy by the entireties, were enacted to prevent a surviving spouse from being totally deprived of property under the will of the deceased.

It is now common for a married couple to take title as follows: "Victor Marci, husband, and Mary Marci, wife, as community property."

Be sure that both the husband and the wife sign the contract of sale and the deed when conveying any community property to you. Regardless of the state law, you must always have both spouses sign a contract of sale and deed if you are purchasing land from a married couple.

## Forming a Corporation To Buy Land

If you have a fairly large group that wants to purchase land together, you might consider corporate ownership. Its unique feature is that a corporation has all legal aspects of a single person. When a corporation is formed, each person puts in a sum of money in return for shares of stock and becomes a shareholder in the corporation. This money goes to make the down payment for the land. The shares are issued as in any other type of corporation, and the shareholders' agreement can entitle the shareholder to live on the land and obligate him or her to pay assessments to the corporation to cover its cost of owning the property.

The shareholders must draw up articles of incorporation, bylaws and a shareholders' agreement. Each state has its own requirements regarding the proper legal form of these documents, but every state requires, at least, the filing of the articles of incorporation with the secretary of state (of the state) for approval. A filing fee is required, and in most states an annual corporation tax, or franchise tax, is due.

The corporation is managed according to the by-laws and by a board of directors. Each shareholder can be a member of the board and thus take part in all the decision making. The voting power of each member will depend on the number of shares of stock he or she owns. For simplicity, it is preferable in a large group to keep things equal. The group will specify in the bylaws the number of votes required to approve an action taken by the board. For instance, the group might decide that 75 percent of the shareholders must agree on any decision. The shareholders pass resolutions authorizing the corporation's officers, including a president, vice-president, secretary and treasurer, to handle particular problems involving the land, such as paying taxes and insurance premiums, hiring someone to do roadwork, and paying off the mortgage. Each board member can take turns being an officer.

The shareholders' agreement specifies any terms the group wants binding on the shareholders. It must be in writing, but it does not have to be filed with the secretary of state. The agreement is a contract signed by all shareholders and states their rights and obligations. For example, the agreement can specify that no share can be sold or transferred by a shareholder without the approval of the board or that the use or occupancy of the land by any person other than, a shareholder is prohibited unless approval is granted.

To form a corporation, it is not necessary to have an income-producing business. I have had articles of incorporation approved that state that "the specific business in which the corporation is primarily to engage is to own and occupy certain real property." This type of corporation will have no income and, therefore, will be charged no federal income tax. Of course, a profit will be made when the land is sold, and a tax will be levied at that time. Although the corporation has no regular income, it will have regular expenses such as mortgage payments, property taxes and maintenance costs, which the individual shareholders must pay according to the terms in the shareholders' agreement. Thus, the corporation operates at a loss each year.

Some states permit shareholders to deduct from their annual personal income tax returns the amount of the corporation's net loss in proportion to the number of shares of stock owned; for example, a subchapter S corporation in California allows this.

Thus, the shareholder receives all annual tax benefit because the corporation "loses" money. If the shareholder lives on the land, an amount equal to the appraised rental value of the land must be subtracted from the above allowed deduction unless the shareholder can show that he or she is living on the land to perform duties for the corporation, such as maintenance and care of the property.

The board of directors can vote to sell the shares of any shareholder who fails to pay any obligations, as specified in the shareholders' agreement, to recoup the money owed to the corporation. When a buyer is found and approved, the transfer of ownership merely necessitates changing the name of the shareholder in the corporate books instead of the usual foreclosure procedure. A reserve "slush" fund is always maintained by the corporation for use if any shareholders fall behind in their payments to prevent a default on the mortgage payments.

If the shareholders vote to sell the entire corporate land, the profits will be divided according to the amount of stock each shareholder owns.

An advantage of a corporation is that the shareholders do not have personal liability for the acts of the corporation; conversely, the corporation does not have liability for the acts of individual shareholders. Thus, land owned by a corporation cannot be attached for personal debts or judgments rendered against any of its shareholders. A creditor can only attach the debtor's shares in the corporation. The creditor then becomes a shareholder and must abide by the rules of the corporation. In this way, the landowners are protected against having their ownership disrupted by an unwelcome stranger. If the board of directors must approve the sale of any stock, the creditor might find it difficult to collect on the debt.

On the other hand, if the corporation cannot pay its debts, none of the shareholders can individually be forced to pay a creditor, although the corporation's assets, such as its land, can be reached and sold to make up a debt. If the land is worth less than the amount of debts, the creditor cannot get a deficiency judgment against the shareholders.

The major disadvantage of a corporation is the cost involved in incorporating. You will probably need an attorney to draw up the documents and you will have to pay state filing fees and state corporation taxes. But the corporate form of ownership has many advantages for a group that wants to own a large, undivided parcel of land.

### Cooperative Corporation

If your group plans to buy land primarily for the purpose of living on it rather than for the purpose of investment, you might see whether your state recognizes a specific corporation called a cooperative corporation. Under a cooperative corporation the corporate organization is seen as a landlord and the individual shareholding members are viewed as tenants. Because this arrangement is more a type of property ownership than a true corporation, some states have placed the cooperative corporation under the supervision of the real estate commissioner, rather than the secretary of state, who normally oversees corporations. Instead of issuing shares of stock, the cooperative corporation issues a certificate entitling the holder to a vote in the corporation's management and the right to live on the land. Everything else in this type of corporation is arranged in basically the same way as the profit-type corporation. Each state has its own laws regarding cooperatives, particularly with regard to their tax status.

### The Nonprofit Corporation

Another type of corporation you might investigate if you are not planning to make money on the land is the *nonprofit corporation.* Your group must fit into one of the special nonprofit and nonpolitical categories, such as religious, educational, scientific or charitable. If you qualify, the nonprofit corporation may not have to pay income taxes, and in many states, will also be exempt from paying property taxes. However, you will have to maintain thorough financial records and file detailed tax returns covering the nature of your nonprofit operation.

Instead of issuing stock, the nonprofit corporation may sell or give "memberships" to individuals, who elect a board of directors and vote on the operation of the corporation. Like a profit-oriented corporation, articles of incorporation and bylaws are required, and an additional application for nonprofit status must be made to the Internal Revenue Service and to the appropriate state agency, which determine whether the corporation is truly nonprofit and, therefore, eligible for tax exemptions.

Once formed, the nonprofit corporation remains in existence until it is dissolved. This dissolution process could present problems to the individual owners of the corporation, because the secretary of state or state corporation official will likely determine that the corporation's assets were held in trust for the nonprofit purpose the corporation claims to represent. This causes delays and legal problems when you try to sell the property and divide the profits among yourselves, because the secretary will attempt to prevent the profits from going to private individuals. If your group is, or wants to become, a church or other nonprofit organization and buy land, you will need a lawyer to get you through the legal paperwork involved in setting up the corporation in the best manner possible to meet your needs.

## Forming an Unincorporated Nonprofit Association

A religious, social, educational or other nonprofit group also can form an *unincorporated nonprofit association* to buy land. Although the group must appoint one of its members as a trustee who takes the title to the land in his or her name, the organization, rather than the trustee or other members of the group, retains liability for its own debts. The trustee only acts according to the charter and bylaws of the organization.

In a nonprofit association, no single person owns any part of the land. The members of the group usually agree to pay rent to the association for living on the land. This rent can be used by the association to pay its mortgage and other expenses without making a profit. This type of purchase appeals primarily to communes, ecological groups interested in preserving open space, and people interested in forming some type of community in the country without actually being personal landowners.

Arrangements must be made in writing at the time the association is formed as to how the funds from a future sale of the property will be disbursed. Each state has its own rules regarding the formation of an unincorporated nonprofit association, and you can get all the necessary information from your secretary of state or commissioner of corporations. Forming such an association is usually easy, but you will require the services of an attorney. Associations are easier to form because the regulations for corporations are avoided. You must be sure the zoning will allow the construction of multiple dwellings on a single parcel of property.

## A Model Owner's Agreement

If you are going to buy land with other people, get together to discuss and write out in detail the terms of the co-ownership before you make the purchase. The entire group should understand as completely as possible the intentions and desires of each person. The best of friends one year can become bitter enemies the following year over conflicts involving such things as mate switching, being a vegetarian versus being a meat eater, whether to hunt or not, nudity versus modesty, religious fervor versus atheism, or other basic personality clashes. Or the issues. could be more ordinary—failure or inability to pay the mortgage, tax or insurance payments or disagreement over where the houses are to be built. The best-intentioned people cannot possibly predict what will happen to them when they become co-owners of land, with all the responsibilities that entails, particularly if they are living in the country for the first time.

Often people who have never lived together in the city think they will automatically be able to commune together in the country. Actually, life in the country is more difficult, because you must rely to a much greater extent on yourselves, not only for the basic necessities of survival, such as providing water, heat and shelter, but also for more subtle psychological reinforcements. The distractions of the city, which help relieve the pressures of living and working together with the same people day after day, are gone; individual levels of awareness and personal conflicts are, therefore, emphasized. Although you cannot prevent problems from arising, you can eliminate basic misunderstandings and decide how to deal with potential future problems in an owners' agreement. If you are a married couple and you want to define your respective interests in your property differently from the way they are specified by the laws governing marital property rights, you will need to make a postnuptial agreement.

Each buyer signs the agreement, which should state in writing all the details of the purchase, including such items as each person's rights and obligations regarding the property and its use; the construction of improvements; future resale of the property; financing; decision making; the sale of one person's interest; individual personal liability; and what happens in the event of a death, divorce, separation or insolvency.

All financial aspects of the purchase should be specified. Some people might want to live on the land year-round, whereas others might want to use the property only as a vacation home. Are you all going to want to pay an equal share? Each person should understand the financial obligations, including mortgage payments and maintenance costs, and must be willing and able to meet them.

The group must decide how the members want to live on the land. For instance, is the group going to build one communal house and share a portion of the land without dividing it up? Are the members of the group going to build houses on separate building sites and share a portion of the land communally? Or is the group going to divide up the entire land into proportionate sections for each person with none of the land shared by the group? Regardless of how it is done, be sure that adequate building sites exist for everyone who wants to construct his own house. Every site is not equally inviting so decide who gets what before you take title to the property.

The Model Owners' Agreement (Figure 31–2) included at the end of this chapter covers the two basic areas of any co-owner's agreement. First, it details each buyer's ownership rights and obligations; second, it states the rules to be observed relating to the land. This model agreement assumes there are three partners, each having an equal third interest in the land, and that agreements will be made on the basis of a simple majority. You can use any figure you want for approval of co-owner decisions. If there are married couples or partners sharing an interest, you may want to give the couple only a single vote between them.

You should have no problem understanding the agreement. Each owner is responsible for building his or her own house, and the respective values of each house will be paid to its owners on the sale of the total property. It provides for the possibility that one owner might want to sell his or her interest and get out of the agreement, in which case the remaining owners have the "right of first refusal."

I include three alternative methods of setting up the first right of refusal. Select the one you and your partners wish to use, and remove the other two from the agreement. You can also change the interest rate of 8 percent to any figure you desire. The contract specifies the terms under which the remaining owners can buy the seller's interest and also that if they decide not to buy it, they have the right to approve a new buyer.

To preserve the natural environment as much as possible, it specifies in great detail what can and cannot be done on the land.

You can use this agreement as a guide to your

specific group needs, whether there are 2 or 20 of you. You can insert and omit specific clauses depending on your situation. Whatever agreement you make, it must be in writing, dated and signed by all owners. It is always advisable to notarize all the signatures. This is a simple, inexpensive process.

You should also prepare a *memorandum of agreement* for recording, so it will be of record that there is an agreement affecting the rights of the owners of the property. I also include here a Model Memorandum of agreement (Figure 31–3). The agreement should be drawn up and signed before you buy the

### Figure 31–2. Model Owner's Agreement

This Owners' Agreement is made this _____ day of _____ , 19 ___, by and between _____, _____ , _____ , whereby it is agreed as follows:

1. The purpose of this Owners' Agreement is to specify the rights and obligations of the undersigned Owners with regard to that certain real property situated in the County of _____ , State of _____ , described as _____ .

2. The purpose of this Owner's Agreement is also to specify the rules and regulations regarding the use and enjoyment of said property.

3. Each Owner shall have one vote in any decision regarding said property or any condition specified in this Agreement.

4. Each Owner shall pay an equal amount of the principal and interest on the existing mortgage; and each Owner shall pay an equal amount of the property taxes, assessments, insurance and maintenance costs, including road repair.

5. If any owner is in default in any obligation under the terms of this Agreement, any Owner may bring an action in court for breach of contract or other appropriate causes of action. If a judgment is obtained against a defaulting owner, it shall be recorded as a lien against his or her interest in the property, and legal recourse may be had to seek to execute against the interest of the defaulting owner, and cause his or her interest to be sold in order to satisfy the judgment for the breach.

*Right of First Refusal–Alternative 1*

6. In the event any Owner should desire to sell his or her interest in said property, the first right of refusal shall be accorded to the remaining Owners. The option vested in the remaining Owners shall entitle them, individually or as a group, to purchase all rights and liabilities of the selling Owner at a price equivalent to the total investment to date made by the selling Owner in said property, plus interest on that investment. The interest shall be computed at a rate of eight percent (8%) per annum from the date of investment. The term "investment" shall include all money paid in the form of mortgage payments, including that portion of the payment which is accorded to principal and that portion of the payment which is accorded to interest.

The selling Owner shall also be entitled to reimbursement for his or her portion of the investment in any improvements made on said property. The term "improvement" shall include structures, orchards, gardens, development of water systems, sewerage systems and drainage systems, and any other construction or development on said property which increases its value for sale. For this Agreement, the term "improvements" shall also include any items which will remain on said property, such as machinery, tools and animals. The term "investment," with regard to improvements, shall include all money paid for the improvement. The value of an Owner's labor shall not be included in the computation of said Owner's investment.

The selling Owner shall be entitled to have all monies due him or her to be paid in a period not to exceed four (4) years at a rate of one-fifth (1/5) of the principal amount due, or more, per year, plus eight percent (8%) interest per annum on the unpaid principal, with a cash down payment of one-fifth (1/5) of the selling price.

*Right of First Refusal–Alternative 2*

6. In the event any Owner should decide to sell his or her interest in said property, the first right of refusal shall be accorded to the remaining owners. The option vested in the remaining Owners shall entitle them, individually or as a

**Figure 31–2. Model Owner's Agreement** *continued*

group, to purchase all rights and liabilities of the selling Owner at the same price and the same terms as those offered to the selling Owner by any third person.

Should the selling Owner receive an offer to purchase his or her interest, the Owner must immediately notify the remaining Owners as to the terms of the offer, and allow the Owners fifteen (15) days to exercise their first right of refusal to purchase the interest of the selling Owner. If the Owners elect not to purchase the interest, then the selling Owner must sell to the third party on the same terms previously offered, subject to paragraph 7 below. If the terms are changed, then the selling Owner must again offer his or her interest to the remaining Owners, who have fifteen (15) days to exercise their first right of refusal.

If one or more Owners elect to purchase the selling Owner's interest, they shall have thirty (30) days to close escrow on the sale. If they fail to close escrow in a timely manner they shall be held to be in breach, and the selling Owner shall be free to sell his or her interest to any third party on any terms the selling Owner desires, subject to paragraph 7 below.

*Right of First Refusal–Alternative 3*

6. In the event any Owner should desire to sell his or her interest in said property, the first right of refusal shall be accorded to the remaining Owners. The option vested in the remaining Owners shall entitle them, individually or as a group, to purchase all rights and liabilities of the selling Owner on the following terms:
   a. The selling Owner and the Owner or Owners who desire to purchase the seller's interest shall mutually agree on a real estate appraiser to appraise the selling Owner's interest in the said property, including his or her share of the value of the land and the value of his or her improvements on the land, such as a house. Once the written appraisal has been submitted by the appraiser, the purchasing Owner has fifteen (15) days to exercise his or her first right of refusal to purchase the seller's interest.
   b. If an Owner elects to purchase the seller's interest, the Owner shall close escrow in thirty (30) days and shall pay the Seller's price over a period not to exceed four (4) years at a rate of one-fifth (1/5) of the principal amount due, or more, per year, plus eight percent (8%) interest remaining on the unpaid principal, with a cash down payment of one-fifth (1/5) of the selling price.
   c. If no Owner elects to exercise his or her right of first refusal the selling Owner is free to sell his or her interest on any terms he or she desires to any third person, subject to paragraph 7 below.

7. Any Owner desiring to sell his or her interest in said property shall so advise the other Owners in writing, and subject to the rights granted in paragraph 6 above, all Owners shall use their best efforts to locate a buyer for the interest. No interest shall be sold to any person without the written consent and approval of the majority of all the Owners.

8. No Owner shall encumber or permit the encumbrance of his or her interest in said property by any person or legal entity without the written consent of a majority of Owners, which consent shall not be unreasonably withheld.

9. No Owner may make a gift or donation of his or her interest in said property without the written approval and consent of a majority of all the Owners.

10. No Owner shall split or divide his or her interest in said property with any other persons for any reason. Should an Owner attempt to do so, such action will be interpreted as a desire to sell his or her interest in said property, and the rules of this Agreement regarding the sale of an interest shall apply.

11. In the Event of the death of an Owner, the heir or devisee to his or her interest shall be bound by the terms of this Agreement.

12. This Agreement secures for each Owner the right, should he or she choose, to construct a habitation on said property. A majority approval is required with regard to the exercise of said right to the extent that the Owners may consider aesthetic, environmental and other considerations relevant to the location and construction of said habitation.

13. Any physical alteration of said property must be approved by a majority of the Owners. "Physical alterations" shall include, among other things, the construction of any structures, such as houses, barns, garages, greenhouses, roads, dams, wells, water tanks and other forms of land development. The term "physical alteration" shall also include the cutting of any trees and vegetation and the clearing of any part of said property.

14. There must be approval by a majority of the Owners before any gas, water or sewer pipes, or electric lines can be installed on said property from outside sources.

15. There shall be no use of pesticides, herbicides or other poisons at any time or any place on said property without the approval of all the Owners.

**Figure 31–2. Model Owner's Agreement** *continued*

16. The hunting and killing of wildlife shall be absolutely and strictly prohibited on said property at all times and during all seasons, except that killing of wildlife will be permitted for the protection of dwellings. The wildlife in the category of animals that threaten dwellings shall include mice, rats and skunks. Under no circumstances shall bears, wildcats, deer or birds be killed. The taking of any fish from the creeks on said property shall be in accordance with state and local regulations.

17. The keeping of all domestic and farm animals shall be subject to approval by a majority of the Owners.

18. There shall be no unnecessary discharge of firearms at any time or place on said property. The term "unnecessary discharge" shall include the use of firearms for target or practice shooting.

19. If, at any time, none of the Owners is willing or able to live on said property, then the Owners will allow one or more persons to act as caretakers of said property. The caretakers must be approved by a majority of said Owners. If any caretakers operate to the dissatisfaction of the majority of Owners they shall be asked to leave. Under no circumstances may an Owner permit a nonowner to live on said property without the prior approval of all Owners living on said property.

20. The entire property may be sold if approval for such sale is given by a majority of the Owners in writing. In the event the entire parcel of said property is sold, a majority of the Owners shall agree on a selling price. The Owners may hire a licensed appraiser to determine the fair market value of said property and improvements. The fees and cost of said appraisal, and the fees and cost of any other expenses involved in the selling of said property, shall be borne by each Owner in proportion to his or her ownership interest in the property.

21. In the event the entire parcel of said property is sold, the proceeds shall be divided equally among the Owners, with regard to the portion of the selling price attributed to the value placed on the real estate. Each Owner shall be entitled to receive a separate share of the proceeds based on the value of each Owner's respective improvements, as determined by agreement between the Owners or by an appraisal of the respective improvements.

22. In exercising the majority approval and vote rule of this Agreement, the Owners shall make all reasonable efforts to contact and consult with an absentee Owner and accord to him or her the right to exercise a vote whenever any matter subject to approval should arise. "Reasonable efforts" shall include express mail and telegrams, if necessary. Should the absentee Owner be unavailable after the expenditure of a reasonable amount of time and effort to locate him or her, then the remaining Owners shall proceed with the granting or denying of approval.

23. Any Owner shall have the right to initiate legal action against any Owner who violates the terms of this Agreement.

24. If any legal action arises due to a violation of the terms of this Agreement, the prevailing party shall be entitled to reasonable court costs and attorney fees.

25. Any amendments or additions to this Agreement must be approved in writing by a majority of the Owners of said property.

26. This Agreement is written and approved in the spirit of fairness to all the Owners in the hope that no Owner shall derive any benefit at the unfair expense of any other Owner.

27. This Agreement is binding on the heirs and successors-in-interest of the parties hereto.

28. A memorandum of this Agreement shall be recorded in the county records which shall state that there is an agreement between the Owners relating to their rights to sell or encumber their interest in the property.

(Owner's Signature)

_____

(Owner's Signature)

_____

(Owner's Signature)

_____

land, so that you can iron out basic problems in advance. Some group members may come to realize that they do not see eye to eye with the other members on major issues and will decide to drop out of the deal before it is too late. I have seen this happen many times. My agreement is very formal and legal sounding, but yours can be expressed in any manner you choose. Informality or choice of language is irrelevant, as long as you express clearly and thoroughly what each individual's rights, obligations and expectations will be after the group takes title to the property.

If necessary, consult an attorney as a group to work out your own specific agreement.

**Figure 31–3. Sample Model Memorandum of Agreement**

## MODEL MEMORANDUM OF AGREEMENT

When Recorded, Return To:

> [name]
> [street]
> [city & state]

### Memorandum of Agreement

_____ and _____

and _____, Owners of that real property, in the County of _____, State of _____, described in Exhibit A, (legal description of the property) attached hereto and made a part hereof, have executed an agreement among themselves which gives certain rights of first refusal and which contains other terms and conditions regarding the subject real property. A copy of the Owners' Agreement, dated _____ should be inspected to determine all the matters regarding the subject real property.

Dated:

_____
(signature)                    Owner

_____                    (NOTARY SEAL)
(signature)                    Owner

_____
(signature)                    Owner

# CHAPTER
# 32 Deeds and Recording

The development of the deed as a method of transferring title is perhaps the most important element to evolve during the history of private land ownership. Not until 1676, when the Statute of Frauds was enacted in England, were written documents required and widely used as evidence of land ownership. Prior to that time, the transfer of land titles was mainly done orally and symbolically. A seller simply handed the buyer a stick, an acorn, a rock or a handful of dirt from his land and pronounced that he was passing title to the land.

Many problems arose under this system, the most common of which was the lack of evidence of the conveyance. Nothing prevented the seller from returning to his land and claiming he never sold it. Buyers, demanding greater protection, began to call on neighbors to witness land transac-

tions. The seller, standing on his land, made a public statement to the buyer and the witnesses, who stood a short distance off the land. After stating that he was selling his land to the buyer, the seller walked off the land and the buyer walked onto it. Thus, many witnesses heard and saw the seller convey his land to the buyer. But witnesses eventually died and moved away, and a better system had to be found.

The first written documents showing land transfers eventually evolved into what we now call deeds. A deed is not the title to the land being conveyed. *Title* represents ownership. A *deed* is the instrument used to transfer the title to or ownership of property from one person to another. A person holding the deed to a parcel of land holds the title as represented by the writing in the deed, which states that title was transferred by the former owner to the party now holding the deed.

A deed is not a contract between the buyer and seller and should never be used as one. The terms and conditions of the sale are stated in the formal contract of sale. (See Chapter 27, "The Model Contract of Sale.") Do not confuse a deed, which transfers title, with a *deed of trust*, which is a means of financing a land purchase in some states. (See Chapter 21, "Types of Financing: Land Contract, Mortgage, Deed of Trust.")

## Basic Provisions of Any Legal Deed

Although various types of deeds are used to convey property, any deed must contain 14 basic elements to be legally valid.

1.  A deed must be in writing, and all of its terms must be contained within it. The seller, who must be legally and mentally competent, is responsible for having the deed drawn up and delivered to the buyer.
2.  The date of the conveyance must be stated.
3.  The name of each person who shares ownership of the land, including both spouses, must be given in full.
4.  The names of all buyers must be given in full and their marital status specified. The deed also must state how title is to be taken, for example, joint tenants, tenants in common or husband and wife as community property. (See Chapter 31, "Types of Co-Ownership.") If there are several buyers, their interests in the property should be specified; for example, "to *A*, a single man, an undivided one-half (½) interest, to *B*, a single man, an undivided two-sixths (⅔) interest; and to *C*, a single woman, an undivided one-sixth (⅙) interest."
5.  All owners, including both spouses, must sign the deed as sellers, using the same names by which they took title to the property. If a buyer was single at the time he bought the property but is now married, both spouses must sign the deed, unless one spouse has previously deeded his or her interest in the property to the other spouse. Some states require witnesses to sign the deed also. The buyer does not usually sign the deed.

6.  Words of conveyance must be used in a *granting clause* that states that the seller is conveying, or transferring, title to the buyer. For example, the seller does hereby "bargain and sell," "grant and convey," or "quitclaim and release" his or her title.
7.  Although most states do not require that the purchase price be given, the deed must state that something of value was given. The phrase "good and valuable consideration" or "for value received" is often used in place of an actual monetary figure.
8.  The property being conveyed must be described in full, preferably including easements, water rights and other property rights that the buyer is getting. The description should also include reservations, exceptions and restrictive covenants in the title. For example, if mineral rights will not be included in the conveyance, the deed might state that they are excepted from the title and identify the person in whose name the rights are reserved. Because these are not always mentioned in the deed, it is essential to get a title report or abstract of title to determine the nature of the grants and reservations.
9.  Depending on the type of deed, various warrants and covenants of title must be included, either specifically in the document or implied by law. These are described later in this chapter.
10.  If the title is being conveyed "subject to" an existing encumbrance, such as a mortgage, deed of trust, tax or other lien, the encumbrance might be stated and fully described in a "subject to" clause. This is not a legal requirement for a valid deed.
11.  The deed must be authenticated by an "acknowledgment," whereby the seller declares before a public official, usually a notary public, that he or she is in fact the person who signs the deed. This method helps prevent forgeries. The notary signs the deed and stamps it with his or her official notarization.
12.  Real property transfer tax stamps must be placed on the deed, or the amount of taxes must be written on the deed in states that levy such a tax. (See Chapter 19, "Evaluating the Price of the Property.")
13.  Before the transfer of title is valid, the deed must be delivered to the buyer. Acceptance of the delivery is considered complete when the

deed is recorded in the county records, whereby notice is given to the world that the seller has transferred title to the buyer.

14. Some states require buyers to state their addresses on deeds to facilitate communication with them for purposes of sending them property tax bills.

## Restrictive Covenants in a Deed

Restrictions, binding on anybody who purchases the land thereafter, are often placed in a deed to a piece of land. A restrictive covenant limits what you can do on the property. For example, a covenant might specify that the land can be used only for residential purposes, or only during certain times of the year. Only private dwellings or only one building per parcel might be permitted. A line might be established, called a building line restriction, beyond which no buildings can be constructed. These are not government restrictions, like zoning, building and health codes. Restrictive covenants are established and enforced by private parties to a transaction, usually a subdivider or seller.

If any restrictions exist, they should be listed in clause 4 of the Model Contract of Sale. (See Chapter 27.) The real estate agent should show you what restrictions exist, and you also can look them up in tie seller's deed in the county records. Chapter 30, "The Title Search, Abstract of Title and Title Insurance Policy," tells how to look up deeds.

Restrictive covenants might be written in a declaration of covenants, conditions and restrictions, a form used when land is being subdivided and all the parcels are to be bound by the same restrictions. The declaration of restriction is filed with the subdivision public report and plat and may not appear in your deed. (See Chapter 14, "Subdivisions and Condominiums.") Instead, the deed may refer to the location of the recorded restrictive covenants. For example, the deed might state "title is conveyed subject to the restrictions listed in the Declaration of Covenants, Conditions and Restrictions recorded in the Office of the County Recorder, Case 5, Drawer 12, Page 68." Locate and examine this document thoroughly, to see what restrictions exist. The document also is referred to in your title report or abstract of title.

How will existing restrictions affect your intended use of the land? If a subdivision is formed with the same restriction included in each buyer's deed, any landowner in the subdivision can bring a legal action against any other owner who violates the restrictions.

If the restriction will hinder your use, ask the seller to either release the restriction himself or get it released by whoever initially placed the restriction on the land before you agree to purchase. If that cannot be done and you will be prevented from using the land as you wish, you had better look elsewhere.

A restriction might not be to your disadvantage. Particularly in a subdivision, you may want restrictions prohibiting commercial development or placing a minimum size on subdivided parcels. If other landowners in the subdivision violate a restriction, you can take legal action against them if the restriction has been established for the entire subdivision as shown in the plat and report. If the restriction is made only in each individual purchaser's deed or contract of sale, the seller alone can take action for violations.

## Warranty Deed

In clause 6 of the Model Contract of Sale in Chapter 27, I specify that the seller shall convey title by a grant deed or warranty deed, because these deeds offer the best protection to the buyer in the states that use this kind of deed. A variety of deeds are used throughout the United States. You might be told by the real estate agent or title company that local custom or law favors the use of a different kind of deed. If you find out that a deed other than a warranty or grant deed is customarily used in your state, ask what protections are included in your deed, and fill out your contract of sale accordingly. For example, California uses a grant deed, Wisconsin uses a warranty deed and New Jersey uses a bargain and sale deed.

The advantage of the warranty deed (also called *full covenant* and *warranty deed* or *general warranty deed*) is that when the seller gives title to the land, five specific warranties, called *covenants of title*, must be included. These warranties must be written into the deed as covenant of seisin, covenant against encumbrances, covenant of further assurance, and covenant of warranty of title.

1. The *covenant of seisin* guarantees that the seller is *seised* of the full title to the land,

which means the seller has possession of a *fee simple estate*. In this covenant the seller also warrants that he or she has a legal right to sell the land and that it has not been previously sold to any other person.

2. The *covenant against encumbrances* assures the buyer that the only encumbrances existing against the title are listed in the deed. Encumbrances include mortgages, deeds of trust, tax and assessment liens, judgment liens, restrictions, easements, rights of spouses and all other liens. If you should find out later that a lien does exist against the property that is not included in the deed, the covenant is breached; you can take legal action against the seller.

3. The *covenant of quiet enjoyment* assures the buyer that neither the seller nor any other person will have a better title to the land than the buyer has and that the buyer's "quiet enjoyment" of the land will not be disturbed by the actions of anyone after he or she receives the deed to the property. A buyer who is forced to leave the property because of a court order can take legal action against the seller for breach of this covenant. Furthermore, if the buyer sells the property, his or her buyer will also be covered by this covenant.

4. The *covenant of further assurance* guarantees that the seller will do anything necessary to give the buyer the title promised in the deed. For example, if the seller is to pay off an existing mortgage before the deed is delivered and later it is discovered that a mistake was made and the mortgage was not legally paid, the seller must clear the defect on the title. If there is a mistake in the deed, the seller must rewrite the deed to correct the error. Regardless of when the mistake is discovered in the title, the seller must do whatever is necessary to put the title to the land in the condition in which he or she promised to deliver it to you.

5. The *covenant of warranty of title* guarantees the buyer good title and possession of the land forever. If a third party presents a rightful claim to the title of the land, the seller must defend the buyer's title. If the buyer loses title, the seller must pay the buyer damages for the loss.

These five warranties give basically the same protection as a standard owner's policy of title insurance. But title insurance places liability for a de-

fective title on the title company, whereas a warranty deed makes the seller responsible to you. Thus, you get double protection if you have both—and it is always desirable to get as much protection as possible. In an area where title insurance is not available, a warranty deed is essential.

You will notice that clause 15 in the Model Contract of Sale also includes the five covenants of title. A sixth provision states that the covenants survive delivery of the deed, thus protecting the buyer after receiving title to the land. (See Chapter 27.) A seller who wants to delete the warranties from the contract might have some reservations about the state of the title. If you detect this in the seller's actions, you must proceed with extreme caution to determine the cause of that reluctance.

## Grant Deed

A few state legislatures have established a special warranty deed called a *grant deed*. The law states that a grant deed automatically includes certain warranties that do not have to be written into the document. Find out from the title company or escrow holder what warranties are included in the deed by state law. A grant deed usually includes only some, not all, of the five warranties I have discussed above. For example, in California the grant deed signifies that the seller has not previously sold the property to anyone else and that a fee simple title is being conveyed, unless specified otherwise. Figure 32–1 shows a typical form of grant deed.

### Bargain and Sale Deed

Most bargain and sale deeds make two warranties. First, the seller warrants that he or she owns the land being conveyed. The second guarantee is "that the seller has not done or suffered anything whereby the said premises have been encumbered in any way." Under the warranty, called a *covenant against grantor's acts*, the seller is liable only if he or she has caused a defect to be placed on the title, whereas in a warranty deed the seller is also liable if any other person, including the seller's seller, has placed an encumbrance on the title to the land.

For example, if your seller intends to use a bargain and sale deed and has given a mortgage on the property, that mortgage must be paid off before title is conveyed to you. However, if your seller's seller mortgaged the property during his or her ownership, your seller would not be liable under a bar-

**Figure 32–1. Example of a Grant Deed**

RECORDING REQUESTED BY

LES SCHER, ESQ.

AND WHEN RECORDED MAIL TO

NAME

ADDRESS

CITY & STATE

Title Order No._____Escrow No._____

MAIL TAX STATEMENTS TO

NAME

ADDRESS    BUYER'S NAME & ADDRESS

CITY & STATE

——— SPACE ABOVE THIS LINE FOR RECORDER'S USE ———

Documentary transfer tax $.........................
☒ Computed on full value of property conveyed, or
☐ Computed on full value less liens and encumbrances remaining thereon at time of sale.

.........................................................
Signature of declarant or agent determining tax — firm name

## Individual Grant Deed

FOR VALUE RECEIVED,    [SELLERS]

GRANT__S__to   [BUYERS]

all that real property situate in the

County of                                State of California, described as follows:

[Legal description of property being sold.]

_____

_____      [SELLER'S SIGNATURE]

STATE OF CALIFORNIA

_____ County of _____ } ss.

On _____, 19___, before me, the undersigned, a Notary Public in and for said State, personally appeared _____
_____
_____, personally known to me or proved to me on the basis of satisfactory evidence to be the person_ whose name ____ _____ subscribed to the within instrument, and acknowledged to me that _ he _ executed it.

_____
NOTARY PUBLIC

FOR NOTARY SEAL OR STAMP

MAIL TAX STATEMENTS AS DIRECTED ABOVE

gain and sale deed for giving you the title subject to the mortgage, whereas under a warranty deed he or she would. This type of deed is also called a *bargain and sale deed with covenant against grantor's acts*; a *grant, bargain, and sale deed with covenant against grantor's acts*; or, because the protection is less than a warranty deed, a *special warranty deed* or *limited warranty deed*.

There can also be a bargain and sale deed without covenant against grantor's acts. The only warranty in this deed is that the seller owns the land being conveyed. No guarantees are made against liens and encumbrances on the title.

## The Quitclaim Deed

In the quitclaim deed, the seller makes no warranties or guarantees about anything. Whenever you see the word quitclaim in a deed, such as "the seller does hereby quitclaim and release" or "remise, release and forever quitclaim," that deed transfers to the buyer only whatever interest the seller has in the land. If the seller has full title, the buyer will get full title. If the seller has nothing, the buyer will get nothing. *When you are buying land never, under any circumstances, accept a quitclaim deed.* Somebody could legally sell you the Grand Canyon with such a deed. Regardless of what the title search shows and despite the fact that the seller is willing to give you a policy of title insurance, do not buy land under a quitclaim deed. Quitclaim deeds are usually used for transfers between spouses or partners.

## Patents

When the federal or a state government transfers or sells land it owns, a patent, rather than a deed, is used. A patent serves the same function as a deed and also gives notice that the land was formerly owned by the government. Almost every parcel of land in the United States has a patent in its chain of title because most land was originally owned by the government. If you buy land that has oil, mineral, timber or other rights reserved by the government, your deed will generally state that those rights are reserved in a patent recorded in the county recorder's office. Ask the county recorder how to look up this patent so you can read it.

## Recording Your Deed and Other Documents

The deed to your land must be recorded as soon as you receive title to the property. Only recording it protects you against the possibility that the seller will convey the title to another person after selling it to you.

For instance, suppose escrow closes and Buyer *A* receives a warranty deed to the land on May 1 and does not record it. On May 2 the seller sells the same land to another person, Buyer *B*, and gives *B* a warranty deed. *B* knows nothing about the sale to *A* the day before and because *A* is not living on the property, cannot tell by inspecting the land that it has already been sold to *A*. On the same day *B* receives the deed, May 2, *B* records the deed with the county recorder. On May 3, *A*'s deed is recorded. Under every law regarding title to land, *A* will not have legal title to the property because *A*'s deed was not recorded first. If *A* and *B* were to go to court, the judge would undoubtedly declare that *B* holds the only legal title to the land.

The first person to record a deed to a parcel of land is the owner. Once a deed is recorded, the law declares that everybody in the world has full knowledge, that is, *constructive knowledge*, of the deed. Thus, if *A* had recorded the deed first, *B* could not claim a lack of knowledge that the land had already been sold, because *A*'s deed would be part of the public record. The recording system was established to show the chronological sequence of the land transfers and other actions affecting title to the land.

If your name is not on a recorded deed and the seller died or is sued and has a judgment against her or him, this will impair your ability or get clear title to the property.

When you are receiving a deed to property, all owners must sign it, including both husband and wife.

A deed is recorded in the recorder's office of the county where the land is located. The county recorder will photograph, photocopy, microfilm or microfiche the deed, and the original will be returned to you. The copy is filed with the other documents and indexed in the grantor-grantee index or the tract index. (These indexes are discussed in detail in Chapter 30, "The Title Search, Abstract of Title and Title Insurance Policy.") A recording fee, usually $10 or less, will always be charged, usually to the buyer.

The escrow holder usually records the deed as a routine part of escrow. Be sure your escrow holder does this and that your policy of title insurance goes into effect at exactly the same time. The burden of making sure the deed is recorded is on the buyer. If, for any reason, the deed is returned to you before it is recorded, you must take it to the county recorder and have it recorded immediately. Generally, the title insurance company will also be watching to be sure the deed is recorded because the policy of title insurance insures the title up until the moment the deed is recorded. The insurer's representative usually walks the deed over to the recorder's office and personally records it.

Most deeds contain a space in which the buyer is to write an address where all tax statements and other official notices are to be sent. Be sure to give a current address, where you are certain to receive your mail, and keep the county informed of any changes. Nonreceipt of mail is not a good defense for failure to pay property taxes.

Any other document affecting title to land is also recorded and open to public inspection in the county recorder's office. Some of these documents include mortgages; deeds of trust; release deeds; satisfactions of mortgages or deeds of trust; deeds of reconveyance; assignments of mortgages or deeds of trust; easement grants; and covenants, conditions and restrictions.

## A Final Note and a Warning

I have included a copy of one type of deed in this chapter. You can see copies of the types of deeds used in your state by looking through any of the record books in your local county recorder's office. I cannot urge you strongly enough to become familiar with these records. Look up the seller's deed to the land you are planning to buy. (See Chapter 30, "The Title Search, Abstract of Title and Title Insurance Policy.") What kind of deed did the seller receive, and what is included in it?

You must specify in your contract of sale the type of deed you want the seller to give you. Your escrow instructions should specify the same type of deed. I recommend that you state you want a warranty deed, a grant deed or a bargain and sale deed, depending on the laws in your state. You can find out what is customary in your state from a real estate attorney, a title or escrow company, a bank or another financial institution. If the seller tells you he or she cannot give you such a deed, find out why. What is the seller afraid of? Does the seller doubt that he or she has full and clear title to the land or does he or she have good title but simply wants to avoid liability by giving you a policy of title insurance that places liability on the title company? If you do not specify what type of deed you are to receive, the seller might deliver you a quitclaim deed. Maybe you'll buy part of the Grand Canyon, too, while you're at it.

# VIII Canada

# 33 Canada

*There has often been, on the part of Canadians, a desire to own a piece of land. Land, air and space were perceived as free or public goods. Today, increased land costs are a major component of high house prices, but the desire for land and space, engendered generations ago, is still with Canadians.*
—Canada's Special Resource Lands

*In Canada all roads lead away from cities. We have an extraordinary urge to build in the bush, as witness the lemming rush to cottage country at the end of the school term, an urge to cleanse ourselves outside the city. . . . Seemingly revitalization comes from lakes and trees, bracken, brush and rock.*
—Harold Town, *Canada with Love*

Canada is the second largest country in the world with regard to land mass, with an area of more than 4 million square miles. The population is now more than 26 million, and more than 80 percent inhabit urban areas within 100 miles of its 3,000-mile border with the United States. Sixty-two percent of its population lives in two provinces—Ontario and Quebec. This concentration is mainly because of the Canadian climate but also because of trade and transportation access. Only about 10 percent of the land is viable farmland, with the balance being forest and tundra with rich mineral deposits. Canada is divided into ten provinces and two territories, each with its own legislative body that can enact laws on land ownership. Because of the complexities of land purchase, it is essential to retain an attorney to help you in any Canadian land purchase.

## General Information

Canada is commonly seen as being divided into six geographic regions, as shown in Figure 33–1.

**Figure 33–1. Geographical Region of Canada**

1. *The Atlantic Region*—The maritime provinces and the island of Newfoundland have lower income and less expanding economy. This is a rural area with few densely populated areas, characterized by low hills and mountains and a rugged, irregular coastline.
2. *The Great Lakes–St. Lawrence Lowlands*—A high-intensity agricultural and urban area, with the highest density of industry, commerce and population in Canada. This area holds more than half of Canada's population. This is the area of French-speaking Canadians, with a rural landscape of long, narrow farms and rural villages.
3. *The Canadian Shield*—Occupies half of the mainland of Canada and contains few people. It is a region of forests, lakes and rocks where people come mostly for recreation or holidays.
4. *The Interior Plains*—The largest area of nearly level land in Canada, consisting mostly of large grain farms. A main characteristic is the geometric spacing of its villages, towns and cities that provide the service needs of the surrounding farms.
5. *The Cordillera*—The mountainous region, with most of its population concentrated in the southwestern corner of British Columbia. Many variations exist in its mountainous terrain.
6. *The Northwest Territories*—Characterized by its diversity of natural environment, lack of developed resources, scanty population and different government. This is a wild, unspoiled area of Canada, where hunting and trapping are still practiced as a livelihood.

## Population and Immigration

For many years Canada's center of population has been moving slowly westward; central Canada, especially in Ontario, is growing faster than the eastern part of the country but less vigorously than the western region. In the 70s, British Columbia and Alberta, in particular, experienced rapid population growth. But this westward flow declined at the end of the oil boom in the early 1980s. Presently, British Columbia leads the provinces in net interprovincial migration, while Quebec loses in population exchanges.

The population of Canada has more than doubled since World War II. Its rate of growth has not been steady, however, gradually subsiding from the high levels of the late 1940s and the 1950s to a very low level in recent years.

Historically, immigration has been a key factor in the growth of Canada's population. As a result of the economic slump that recently affected the entire western world, the Canadian government cut immigration levels to less than 100,000 in 1983 and 1984. But, since 1984, the new policy direction has been one of continued increase in annual immigrant admissions. In 1986, Canada's immigrants represented 15.6 percent of the country's population. In 1989, approximately 190,000 immigrants were admitted, a significant increase over the previous decade.

Traditionally, the majority of immigrants came from Europe, especially England. In the past ten years, however, there has been much greater diversity in the countries of origin of those who come to settle in Canada. In particular, there has been a sharp increase in the number of Asian immigrants.

Of course, Canada continues to be a popular place for Americans to live, either permanently or seasonally. Many Americans maintain vacation homes in Canada, and that is becoming an increasingly popular idea, because land prices are so much lower in Canada than in the United States.

Canada is primarily an urban country, with more than 75 percent of the population in urban areas. The most urbanized provinces are Ontario, Quebec, British Columbia and Alberta. At the other end, Prince Edward Island has a majority of its population in rural areas.

According to Canadian real estate investors, the most popular areas for Americans buying Canadian rural property are in British Columbia, Ontario and the Maritime Provinces of Nova Scotia and New Brunswick.

## Tax Sales

There are some municipal tax sales being held in towns and cities across the country. In general, however, the famous rural tax sales have been discontinued because of a number of factors, mainly the realization of provincial governments that they have to acquire large tracts of land for their own use as provincial parks, game refuges and open space. Other reasons include the many legal challenges to tax sales because of incorrect data and im-

perfect titles. There were also cases of manipulation by local officials, as well as sales of properties that did not exist or, in some cases, that were under water!

One notable exception to the discontinuation of tax sales is the Province of Ontario. Under 1984 legislation, Ontario requires tax authorities to offer for sale by tender all properties taken for nonpayment of taxes that are not required for official use. These properties are listed throughout the year in the Ontario Government's *Gazette*, obtainable from

> The Queen's Printer
> Parliament Buildings
> Toronto, Ontario, Canada

The *Gazette* is published weekly, and listings are sporadic and located all over this large province. Therefore an annual subscription is really required if one is interested in a specific area.

## Canadian Property Tax Features

It is a common misconception in Canada that if people are paying taxes on properties, the land belongs to them. These people base their stand on the fact that they receive tax bills each year, with their names on them, from a local tax office.

What they do not understand is that the Registry of Deeds Office has nothing to do with the Tax Office—both are entirely separate and distinct from one another. A Tax Office will gladly deal with anyone who is willing to pay the taxes; after all, its main objective is to collect as much tax as it can for the municipality, and it does not concern itself with ownership. Many persons pay taxes on a parcel of land without going through the formalities of deed registration and never become the legal owners.

In most provinces, you will receive one tax bill a year covering all charges on the property, but there are exceptions. In some northern Ontario areas, there are three taxing authorities and, therefore, three bills each year. These are for land tax, which is collected by the Ontario Provincial Government; Statute Labor Tax, which is usually collected by the local Roads Board of the Township where the land is located (this is really a road maintenance tax); and school board tax, which is collected by the local district school board.

There may be other taxes imposed by these authorities, such as a wolf bounty tax (to keep the local wolf population under control, mainly for the sheep farmers) and a fence tax (to keep the neighboring farmer's cattle on his property). If title to the property includes mining rights as a separate parcel, there also will be a tax bill for these.

If any of these taxes are outstanding for the prescribed legal period, the taxing authority can take over the property and sell it to the highest bidder if it is not required for public use.

The Province of Nova Scotia recently enacted a change-of-use tax, based on the classification (forest, resources, farming, and so forth) into which the county assessors had categorized each and every property. When a property changes hands, they may deem a "change of use" has occurred and impose a one-time tax of 20 percent of the assessed value. Therefore, one has to find out what the category of the property is before buying, because the purchaser is responsible for the additional cost.

Canadian provinces also impose certain restrictions on land sales to non-Canadians. the main ones are show in Figure 33–2.

## Without Question Every Buyer of Canadian Land Must Use a Lawyer

Because of the complex manner in which Canada has developed, systems of real estate practice differ widely from province to province. In Quebec, local buyers don't use a lawyer, they use a notary. A notary is similar to a lawyer, but is used especially for real estate deals. It is not similar to what is known as a notary in the United States.

In Canada, the lawyers prepare the abstract of title or the lawyer's opinion regarding the condition of title to a piece of property. This is the equivalent of the American title search or abstract of title. Figure 33–3 is a sample portion of an Abstract of Title typical for lands in Nova Scotia and other provinces using abstracts. Figure 33–4 is a sample of a lawyer's opinion letter regarding the condition of title of an Ontario parcel of land.

Usually a deed is transferred from the seller to the buyer, and then a certificate of indefeasible title is issued by the land title office or land registry. Figure 33–5 is a sample of a certificate of indefeasible title and Figure 33–6 is a sample of a warranty deed.

Different recording systems are used in some

**Figure 33–2. Rules Regarding Land Purchased by Nonresidents**

| | |
|---|---|
| Alberta | Nonresidents cannot purchase more than ten acres of land without provincial approval. |
| British Columbia | None, but province records citizenship data. |
| Manitoba | Nonresidents cannot purchase more than ten acres of land without provincial approval. |
| New Brunswick | None at present, but ownership statistics are recorded. |
| Newfoundland | None at present. |
| Nova Scotia | None at present, but ownership statistics are recorded. |
| Ontario | Non-Canadians must pay a provincial one-time tax of 20 percent of the value of the property at the time of deed registration, which occurs after the property is fully paid for. |
| Prince Edward Island | Nonislanders cannot purchase more than 10 acres or 330 feet of water frontage without the approval of the Legislative Assembly of Prince Edward Island. |
| Quebec | Non-Canadians are subject to a provincial one-time tax of 33 percent of the value of the property at time of deed registration. |
| Saskatchewan | Nonresidents cannot purchase more than ten acres of land without provincial approval. |
| Yukon Territory | No restrictions on the sale of privately held lands to nonresidents. Government land sales are only made to Canadian citizens who have lived in the Yukon for one full year. |

provinces. For example, in Ontario the rural northern tracts are under the Land Titles Act, and the urban areas in the south are under the Registry System. The method of deed and document recording

**Figure 33–3. Sample Portion of an Abstract of Title (Canada)**

ABSTRACT OF TITLE TO LANDS OF EDWARD
BENOIT'S ISLAND, TRACADIE,
ANTIGONISH COUNTY, NOVA SCOTIA

Searched For:     Purchaser
Searched By:     Attorney

Searched:
File:

1. DEED                                  Francis L. Jones & wife,
    58/16                                    Jennifer
    June 2, 1900                          - to -
    July 4, 1900                         Sarah J. Landon
    $375.00

Conveys, inter alia, lands under search. Refers to Book 27, Page 192.

2. WILL                                    Will of Sarah Jean Wilcox
    81/728
    Sept. 2, 1929
    Jan. 7, 1930

Leaves everything to her husband, Samuel Wilcox.
NOTE: It would appear that Sarah J. Landon became Sarah J. Wilcox.

3. DEED                                    Samuel Wilcox & wife, Georgina
    91/25                                     - to -
    April 19, 1948                      Edward Johnson and Weldon Berman
    May 17, 1948
    $1.00

2nd lot describes lands under search. Refers to Book 58, Page 16 and Will in 81/728.

4. QUIT CLAIM DEED                   Weldon Berman & wife, Myrtle
    95/31                                     - to -
    July 8, 1953                          Edward Johnson
    July 22, 1953
    $1.00

Second lot appears to describe lands under search.

5. PETITION FOR ADMINISTRATION       Est. of Edward Johnson
    100/300                                     - to -
    July 12, 1962                     Mildred Johnson
    July 16, 1962

**Figure 33–3. Sample Portion of an Abstract of Title (Canada)** *continued*

Recites that Edward Johnson died intestate on June 26, 1962, leaving his widow, Mildred Johnson, and three children: William, Claire, and Richard, surviving.

6. DEED                          William Johnson, one of the heirs of Edward
   104/219                     Johnson
   May 16, 1968           - to -
   June 6, 1986           Mildred Johnson
   $1.00

Lot #2 describes lands under search.

7. ORDER OF SALE           In the matter of the interest of Claire Johnson
   104/220                     and Richard Johnson, infants
   June 5, 1968
   June 6, 1968

Authorizes the sale of the interests of Claire and Richard Johnson in lands, including lands under search to Mildred Johnson, for the sum of $8,371.50. Appoints Mildred Johnson as next friend of infants. Lot 2 describes lands under search.

**Figure 33–4. Sample of Lawyer's Opinion Letter (Canada)**

BARRISTER, SOLICITOR

Re: H. M. _____ purchase from
The Royal Bank of Canada - Lot 1,
Township of Harvey, County of Peterborough

I would advise that the above transaction was completed in accordance with the provisions of the Agreement of Purchase and Sale, the Statement of Adjustments, and your instructions on October 22, 1986, at which time a conveyance under Power of Sale by The Royal Bank of Canada pursuant to the provisions of its First Mortgage on the subject lands, as Transferor in favour of H. M. _____ as Transferee with respect to Lot 1, _____ for the Township of Harvey, was registered as Instrument Number _____ for the Registry Division of Peterborough on the 22nd day of October, 1986.

In my opinion, you have a good and marketable title in fee simple to the lands set out therein without encumbrance and without execution and subject only to the reservations as set out in the original conveyance from the Subdivider, Sumcot Development Corporation Limited, as contained in its conveyance being Instrument Number _____, a copy of which is enclosed herewith and which was discussed with you by telephone and in particular the reservation of mines and minerals as a Vendor's Lien for unpaid purchase money in favour of Sumcot Development Corporation Limited. This conveyance was in favour of _____ and _____ at which time a Mortgage back from Messrs. _____ and _____ was given in favour of Sumcot Development Corporation Limited as Instrument Number _____ and which was later Discharged by Instrument Number _____.

I am enclosing herewith a copy of that portion of the Plan pertaining to the subject lands together with the duplicate registered conveyance.

is very different from the system used in the United States.

The method of surveying in Canada is not based on the rectangular survey method, as it is in the United States. Instead, three-dimensional coordinates are used as property identifiers. Boundary lines are described in metes and bounds, bearings and distances. All land should be positively defined on the ground by a licensed surveyor before the purchase of any parcel of property.

In Canada, land size is offered measured in hectares, rather than acres. A hectare is a metric unit of area measure equal to 10,000 square meters. 1 hectare = 2.471 acres and 1 acre = 0.4047 hectares.

Figure 33–7 is a sample of a real estate purchase agreement as used in British Columbia. However, it is important to use an attorney in Canadian land purchases.

## Useful Resources

For general information regarding Canada, see the Canadian Government Web site at http://www.emr.ca/home/nrcanhpe.htm#canada. Government addresses can be found at http://www.lib.uwaterloo.ca/discipline/government/CanGuide/.

Most of the publications printed by the Canadian government are distributed in the United States by the International Specialized Book Services (ISBS) at the following address.

5804 NE Hassalo Street
Portland, OR 97213-3644
Voice: (800) 547-7734
Fax: (503) 280-8832
E-mail: orders@isbs.com

**Figure 33–4. Sample of Lawyer's Opinion Letter (Canada)** *continued*

The Power of Sale documents were deposited on title at the time of closing as Instrument Number _____, and I am enclosing the duplicate copy herewith, for your records.

A search of executions initially carried out at the time of the completion of the search of title on _____ indicated no executions outstanding against the previous owners as evidenced by the enclosed Certificate of the Sheriff of the County of _____ being Certificate Number _____ which was updated at the time of closing with a search of executions against the Transferor, _____, on the _____ day of _____ which indicated no executions outstanding as evidenced by the enclosed Certificate of the Sheriff of the County of _____ being Certificate Number _____.

I would advise that we carried out a search of work orders and zoning and find no outstanding work orders issued against the property and that the property is zoned Recreational Residential as evidenced by the enclosed Report of the Clerk of the Municipality dated _____.

Pursuant to the provisions of the Agreement of Purchase, we have determined the arrears of taxes for the years _____, _____, and _____ totalling _____ and have paid same from the proceeds received on closing and I am enclosing a copy of my letter to the Municipality paying the aforementioned tax arrears and further advising them of the change of ownership. I would advise that the final installment of _____ taxes is due _____ in the sum of _____, which said installment has been paid to the Municipality together with the arrears of taxes as reflected in my letter to the Municipality dated the _____ day of _____.

I would like to take this opportunity to thank you for permitting me to act on your behalf in this matter and I hope that everything has been handled to your satisfaction.

Yours very truly,

**Figure 33–5.  Sample Certificate of Indefeasible Title (Canada)**

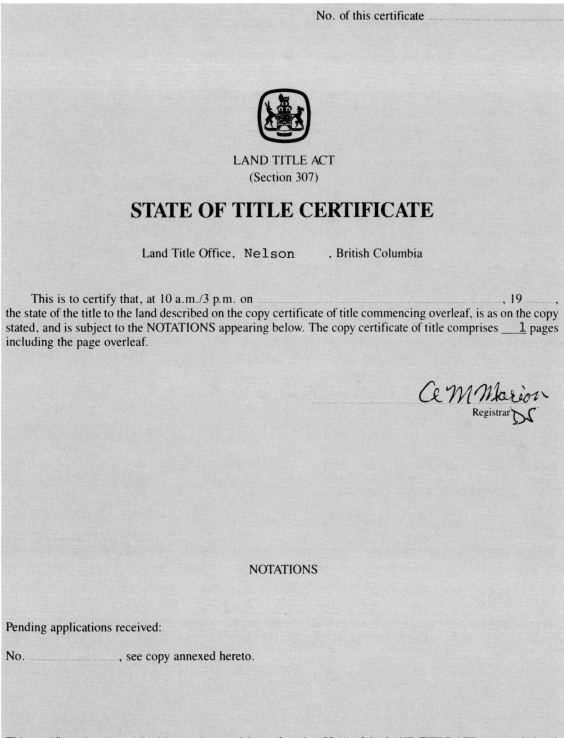

No. of this certificate .............................................................................

LAND TITLE ACT
(Section 307)

# STATE OF TITLE CERTIFICATE

Land Title Office, Nelson        , British Columbia

This is to certify that, at 10 a.m./3 p.m. on ...................................................................., 19........., the state of the title to the land described on the copy certificate of title commencing overleaf, is as on the copy stated, and is subject to the NOTATIONS appearing below. The copy certificate of title comprises ___1 pages including the page overleaf.

*C. M. Marion*
Registrar

NOTATIONS

Pending applications received:

No. ........................., see copy annexed hereto.

This certificate is to be read subject to the provisions of section 23 (1) of the *LAND TITLE ACT* as amended and may be affected by the *LAND ACT* sections 52–55 (*see* R.S.B.C. 1979, chapter 214).

**Figure 33–5. Sample Certificate of Indefeasible Title (Canada)** *continued*

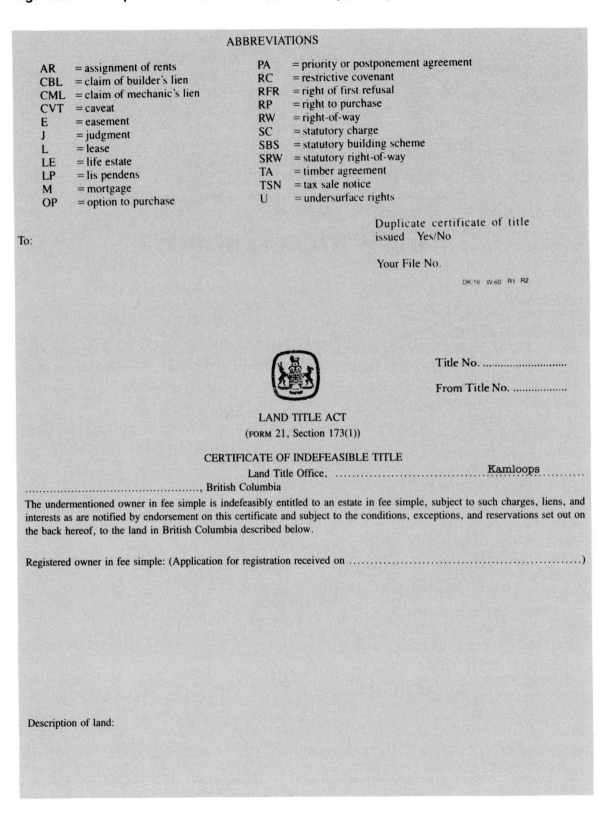

ABBREVIATIONS

AR = assignment of rents
CBL = claim of builder's lien
CML = claim of mechanic's lien
CVT = caveat
E = easement
J = judgment
L = lease
LE = life estate
LP = lis pendens
M = mortgage
OP = option to purchase

PA = priority or postponement agreement
RC = restrictive covenant
RFR = right of first refusal
RP = right to purchase
RW = right-of-way
SC = statutory charge
SBS = statutory building scheme
SRW = statutory right-of-way
TA = timber agreement
TSN = tax sale notice
U = undersurface rights

Duplicate certificate of title
issued    Yes/No

Your File No.

DK-16  W-60  R1  R2

To:

Title No. ............................

From Title No. .................

LAND TITLE ACT
(FORM 21, Section 173(1))

CERTIFICATE OF INDEFEASIBLE TITLE
Land Title Office, ..................................... Kamloops ...........
................................................., British Columbia

The undermentioned owner in fee simple is indefeasibly entitled to an estate in fee simple, subject to such charges, liens, and interests as are notified by endorsement on this certificate and subject to the conditions, exceptions, and reservations set out on the back hereof, to the land in British Columbia described below.

Registered owner in fee simple: (Application for registration received on ..................................................)

Description of land:

**Figure 33–5. Sample Certificate of Indefeasible Title (Canada)** *continued*

```
Minerals only F to C R5496 17.3.82
```

## CHARGES, LIENS, AND INTERESTS*

| Nature of Charge; Number; Date and Time of Application | Registered Owner of Charge | Remarks |
|---|---|---|
|  |  |  |

Signed and sealed by me, this ............ day of ................................................, 19 ................

## DUPLICATE CERTIFICATE OF TITLE

| Date Issued | Name and Address of Person to Whom Delivered | Filing Reference of Request for Duplicate Certificate of Title | Date of Cancellation of Duplicate Certificate of Title |
|---|---|---|---|
|  |  |  |  |
|  |  |  |  |
|  |  |  |  |

| Title Cancelled and Interests Disposed of as Follows | Date | Signature of Registrar |
|---|---|---|
|  |  |  |
|  |  |  |
|  |  |  |

450.161

*Each endorsement affects all the land described, unless otherwise indicated in "Remarks." See back hereof for abbreviations.

**Figure 33–6. Sample Warranty Deed (Canada)**

THIS WARRANTY DEED      made this          day of

BETWEEN:

being the Owner of the lands described in Schedule "A" herein
(hereinafter called the "GRANTOR")

- and -

(hereinafter called the "GRANTEE")

- and -

being the spouse (of the Grantor) who holds no title to the said lands
(hereinafter called the "RELEASOR")

WITNESSETH THAT in consideration of One Dollar and other good and valuable consideration;

THE GRANTOR hereby conveys to the GRANTEE the lands described in Schedule "A" to this Warranty Deed and hereby consents to this disposition, pursuant to the Matrimonial Property Act of Nova Scotia.

THE GRANTOR covenants with the GRANTEE that the GRANTEE shall have quiet enjoyment of the lands, that the GRANTOR has good title in fee simple to the lands and the right to convey them as hereby conveyed, that the lands are free from encumbrances, and that the GRANTOR will procure such further assurances as may be reasonably required.

THE RELEASOR hereby consents to the within conveyance and releases any claim that the RELEASOR had, has, or may have pursuant to the Matrimonial Property Act of Nova Scotia and hereby conveys any land and all right, title, and interest which the RELEASOR may have with respect to the lands described in Schedule "A."

IN THIS WARRANTY DEED the singular includes the plural and the masculine includes the feminine, with the intent that this WARRANTY DEED shall be read with all appropriate changes of number and gender.

IN WITNESS WHEREOF, the Grantor and Releasor have properly executed this deed on the date first shown above.

SIGNED, SEALED, AND DELIVERED   )
                                      )
    in the presence of         )
                                        )
                                        )
                                        )  _____

_____

A Notary Public in and for
the State of _____      _____

SAMPLE WARRANTY DEED

**Figure 33–7. Sample Real Estate Purchase Agreement (Canada)**

PLEASE PRESS HARD FOR COPIES

# MULTIPLE LISTING BUREAU
## INTERIM AGREEMENT

LIST No. ____________

Salesman ____________

OFFER TO PURCHASE

I (WE) the undersigned, ____________ Occupation ____________

____________ Occupation ____________

Address ____________ Phone No. ____________

(herein called "Purchaser(s)"), having inspected the real estate property listed by ____________ Agent for the Vendor,

and owned by ____________ Occupation ____________

____________ Phone No. ____________

(herein called "Vendor(s)"), hereby offer and agree to purchase the property at ____________ (Place)

and known as ____________
(Street Address)

and described as (Legal Description) ____________

____________

free and clear of other encumbrances except restrictive covenants, existing tenancies, reservations and exceptions in the original grant from crown, easements and/or rights of way in favour of utilities and public authorities and except as set above. ____________

and save existing tenancies at the price of ____________ $ ____________
payable as follows:
Cash Deposit paid herewith ____________ $ ____________

Balance of Cash Payment on or before ____________ $ ____________

All cash funds to be held in trust until completion of registration on ____________

of the necessary documents and the balance if any as follows

____________ $ ____________

____________ $ ____________

____________ $ ____________

____________ $ Total Purchase Price $ ____________

____________

AND adjustment of taxes, tolls, local improvement rates, irrigation taxes and tolls, insurance premiums and water rates, sewer and garbage rates as hereinafter provided, such price to include all existing blinds, awnings, screen doors and windows, fixed floor coverings, electric, plumbing and heating fixtures and attachments as owned by the vendor.

____________

____________

____________ as shown to me by your agent on or about ____________
(Date)

Possession (subject to existing tenancies) shall be given to me on, and taxes, local improvement rates, rentals, insurance premiums and water rates shall be adjusted as of ____________
(Date)

THE PROPERTY SHALL BE AT MY RISK FROM ____________ (Date) Registerable documents shall be prepared at my expense and shall contain the terms herein set out and shall contain, in addition thereto such covenants, terms and conditions not inconsistent therewith as may be agreed upon between us or, failing such agreement, as may be specfied by the solicitor for the time being of the Multiple Listing Bureau of the Kootenay Real Estate Board. Time shall be of the essence

I/WE HAVE READ AND CLEARLY UNDERSTAND THE ABOVE OFFER TO PURCHASE, ACKNOWLEDGE THAT IT ACCURATELY SETS OUT ALL THE TERMS OF MY/OUR OFFER, THAT I WAS/WE WERE NOT INDUCED TO MAKE IT BY ANY REPRESENTATIONS, WARRANTIES, GUARANTEES OR PROMISES NOT CONTAINED THEREIN, AND ACKNOWLEDGE HAVING RECEIVED A COPY OF THE SAID OFFER ON THIS DATE.

This offer shall be open for acceptance by you until 11:59 p.m. on ____________ 19____

DATED at ____________ on ____________, 19____
WITNESS:

____________ ____________
Purchaser

____________ ____________
Purchaser

RECEIPT FOR DEPOSIT

To(Purchaser) ____________

I/We (Agent) ____________
(Selling Broker)

acknowledge receipt of the sum of ____________ ($ )
being the deposit referred to in the above Offer to Purchase.

Dated at ____________ on ____________ ____________
(Selling Broker)

Per ____________

ACCEPTANCE

To (Purchaser) ____________

And to (Listing Broker) ____________

I/We Vendor ____________
hereby accept the above offer and its terms and covenants and agree to pay to my/our said agent a commission as heretofore agreed upon.

____________

Dated at ____________ on ____________, 19____
WITNESS:

____________ ____________
Owner

____________ ____________
Owner

1 White—Selling Broker 2 Green—Purchaser 3 Blue—Vendor 4 Red—Bureau 5 White—Purchaser

For information about publications, of national scope, contact

> Environment Canada
> Inquiry Centre
> Ottawa, Ontario
> K1A 0H3 Canada
> Voice: (819) 997-2800 or (800) 668-6767
> Fax: (819) 953-2225
> EnviroFax: (819) 953-0966
> E-mail: enviroinfo@cpgsv1.am.doe.ca

The following are some of the publications available free of charge from the Canada Communications Group. Send requests to:

> Canada Communication Group
> Publishing Canada
> Ottawa, Canada
> K1A 0S9
> Voice: (819) 956-4802
> Fax: (819) 994-1498
> URL: http://www.dow.on.doe.ca/
>     climate/climate.html

"Primer on Freshwater," IWDM-266
"Water—Here, There and Everywhere," WFS-2E
"Water—Groundwater Nature's Hidden Treasure," WFS-5E
"The Climate: What a Difference a Degree Makes!" AESM-9
"Surface Water and Acidification in Atlantic Canada," IWD-FS-91-1E
"Acid Rain: A National Sensitivity Assessment," IWD-M-272
"How Safe Is Our Water?" IWDM-245
"Water-Wise Tips for the Summer Season," IWD-WW-9
"Leaking Underground Storage Tanks," EPS-FS-18
"Fighting Mercury Pollution," EPS-FS-19
"Ground Level Ozone in Canada," SOE-FS-92-1E
"Smog in Canada," SMOG-FS-2E
"Health Effects of Smog," SMOG-FS-5E
"Climate and Canadians," AES-FS-9
"Probability and Precipitations," AES-FS-11
"Canada's Weather Service: Much, Much More Than Weather," AES-FS-18
"Climate Change and Variability," AES-FS-26
"Toxic Chemicals in the Arctic," AES-FS-30
"Tornados," AES-FS-38
"Drought," AES-FS-43

An index and list of all available maps and aerial photographs for every region in Canada is available from

> Canada Map Distribution Office
> Department of Energy, Mines, and Resources
> 130 Bentley Ave.
> Ottawa, Ont. K1A 0E9, Canada
> Fax: (800) 661-6277 or (613) 952-7000

**Soil Survey Information**

Soil Survey information is available for many areas throughout Canada. Write to the province you are interested in at the following addresses:

> Canada Soil Survey Research Branch
> Agriculture Canada
> P.O. Box 7098
> St. John's West, Newfoundland A1E 3Y3

> Canada Soil Survey Research Branch
> Agriculture Canada
> Nova Scotia Agricultural College
> Truro, Nova Scotia B2N 5E3

> Canada Soil Survey Research Branch
> Agriculture Canada
> P.O. Box 1210
> Charlottetown, Prince Edward Island C1A 7M8

> Canada Soil Survey Research Branch
> Agriculture Canada
> P.O. Box 280
> Fredericton, New Brunswick E3B 4Z7

> Equipe Pedologique Federale
> Complexe Scientifque C.1.208
> 2700, rue Einstein
> Ste-Foy, Quebec G1P 3W8

> Ontarion Institute of Pedology
> Guelph Agricultural Centre
> P.O. Box 1030
> Guelph, Ontario N1H 6N1

> Canada-Manitoba Soil Survey Research Branch
> Agriculture Canada
> University of Manitoba
> Winnipeg, Manitoba R3T 2N2

Saskatchewan Institute of Pedology
University of Saskatchewan
Saskatoon, Saskatchewan S7N 0W0

Canada Soil Survey Research Branch
Agriculture Canada
6660 N.W. Marine Drive
Vancouver, British Columbia V6T 1X2
Voice: (604) 224-4355
Fax: (604) 666-4994

Canada-Yukon Soil Survey, Research Branch
Agriculture Canada
c/o Yukon Department of Renewable
    Resources
Box 2703
Whitehorse, Yukon Y1A 2C6

Northwest Territories, Agriculture Canada
Land Resource Research Centre
Ottawa, Ontario K1A 0C6

The following pamphlets are available free from any of the above offices:

"Home buyers—Soil Surveys Can Help You"
"Septic Tank Filter Fields"
"Recreation Area Planner"

### Canadian Geological Survey Offices

The Canadian Geological Survey Offices can be found at the following addresses:

Geological Survey of Canada
Commission geologique du Canada
601 rue Booth St.
Ottawa, ON K1A 0E8
(613) 996-3919

GSC Atlantic / CGC Atlantique
P.O. Box / B.P. 1006
Dartmouth, NS / N-E B2Y 4A2
(902) 426-3225

GSC / CGC Quebec
2700 rue Einstein
Ste-Foy, Quebec G1V 4C7
(418) 654-2601

GSC / CGC Calgary
3303 rue 33 ST. N.W.
Calgary, Alta T2L 2A7
(403) 292-7000

GSC / CGC Vancouver
100 West Pender St.
Vancouver, B.C. / C-B V6B 1R 8
(604) 666-0529

GSC / CGC Victoria
9860 West Saanich
Sidney, B.C. / C-B V8L 4B2
(604) 363-6500

### Public Land

Some Provinces still have public land available for private use. You can find them listed in the phone book under "Crown Lands," or through the Department of Natural Resources or Lands Division, under the Ministry of Lands, Forests and Water Resources. Each province makes their own laws regarding requirements for ownership of this land. In Manitoba you must be a resident of Manitoba to own Crown Land, whereas in British Columbia that is not the case. Also, Crown Land in some regions is just leased and not purchased. So check the province you are interested in for their requirements and restrictions. Local REALTORS® may have information about Crown Lands.

### H.M. Dignam Corporation

This unique company is probably the premier national rural property seller in Canada. It has been offering Canadian Recreational properties since 1916, and from all accounts is a trustworthy outfit to deal with. It is not a broker. It owns and sells its own land. The average price is around $10,000. Dignam puts out a monthly catalog of its offerings, with complete details for each parcel. Dignam will also send you aerial photographs, road maps, and a sectional map for any parcel in the catalog in which you are interested.

Dignam specializes in buying land at tax sales to resell for profit. You can buy for all cash or on time, and a deed conveying clear title is guaranteed by the firm after you have made all your payments. Dignam has a unique exchange program under which you can exchange your parcel for another of equal or greater value within two years of purchase. Below is a sample ad from one of their recent land catalogs.

Atlantic Provinces
Property 320-PE
Stephen Lank Property, Parcel 784652, Glen Road, Part of Township 67, Glen Valley,

Queens County, Prince Edward Island, 21.50 acres or 8.7 hectares. With a panoramic view of Pleasant Valley to the north and Glen Valley to the South, this acreage is newly reforested with pine and spruce. It offers over 1,650 feet of frontage on the south side of graveled Glen Road, just east of Highway 227. On the eastern border is a five-foot stream, a branch of the Dunk River, and the parcel has a depth of about 530 feet. The area is characterized by prosperous farms and pride of ownership is very evident. However, more than half of the residents live on small holdings and work in the capital city of Charlottetown, just 20 minutes east via Route 2, the Trans Canada Highway. Topographically, this acreage slopes fairly rapidly from its western end to its eastern side, well over a quarter mile away. It exhibits good percolation and surface drainage. Electrical and telephone services are available just 120 feet east. General services may be obtained at Hunter River, five miles away, or Kensington, just ten minutes distant. World famous Cavendish Beach is ten miles north. Price $18,880.00 payable $1,880.00 cash with order and 50 monthly payments of $340.00 each, and interest; or $16,992.00 (being 10% off) if paid $1,995.00 cash with order and $14,997.00 within 30 days thereafter.

Remember, as much care should be used in purchasing land from Dignam as in any other purchase of real estate. The burden is always on you to check out your land purchases.

Properties for sale can be obtained from the address given below:

H.M. Dignam Corporation
65 Cedar Pointe, Unit 807
Barrie, ON L4N 5R7
Voice: (705) 721-1515
Fax: (705) 721-1519

The current prices of the H.M. Dignam sale lists are as follows: One year (twelve issues) by 1st Class Airmail, $18.00 Canadian. ($18.00 U.S. funds for United States addresses and $25.00 Canadian funds outside Canada and the U.S.A.) All prices include GST. (General Sales Tax).

The staff at Dignam is extremely helpful and will answer any questions you have about purchasing land in Canada.

**Real Estate Agents**
Information on buying land in Canada can be obtained from

The Canadian Real Estate Association
Education Department
Suite 2100, Place de Ville, Tower "A"
320 Queen Street
Ottawa, Ontario
K1R 5A3
(613) 234-3372

To get lists of real estate agents for each Province, write to the following offices:

The British Columbia Real Estate
   Association
309-1155 West Pender Street
Vancouver, B.C. V6E 2P4
Voice: (604) 683-7702
Fax: (604) 683-8601

The Alberta Real Estate Association
828 12th Avenue South West
Calgary, AB T2R 0J3
Voice: (403) 264-5581
Fax: (403) 266-1597

The Saskatchewan Real Estate Association
231 Robin Crescent
Saskatoon, SK S7L 6M8
Voice: (306) 373-3350
Fax: (306) 373-5377

The Manitoba Real Estate Association
1240 Portage Ave., 2nd Floor
Winnipeg, MB R3G 0T6
Voice: (204) 772-0405
Fax: (204) 775-3781

The Ontario Real Estate Association
99 Duncan Mill Road
Don Mills, ON M3B 1Z2
Voice: (416) 445-9910
Fax: 416) 445-2644

Federation des Chambres Immobilieres du
    Quebec
990, avenue Holland
Quebec, QC G1S 3T1
Voice: (418) 682-6102
Fax: (418) 682-8107

The New Brunswick Real Estate Association
P.O. Box 774 Station A
358 King Street, Room 204
Fredericton, NB E3B 5B4
Voice: (506) 459-8055
Fax: (506) 459-8057

The Nova Scotia Real Estate Association
7 Scarfe Court
Dartmouth, NS B3B 1W4
Voice: (902) 468-2515
Fax: (902) 468-2533

Prince Edward Island Real Estate Association
75 St. Peter's Road
Charlottetown, PE C1A 5N7
Voice: (902) 368-8451
Fax: (902) 894-9487

Newfoundland Real Estate Association
251 Empire Avenue
St. John's, NF A1C 3H9
Voice: (709) 739-8600
Fax: (709) 726-4221

Yukon Real Estate Association
P.O. Box 5292
Whitehorse, YK Y1A 4Z2
Voice: (403) 668-2070

# Using a
# Lawyer

# Do You Need a Lawyer?

*In a profession where unbounded trust is necessarily reposed, there is nothing surprising that fools should neglect it in their idleness, and tricksters abuse it in their knavery, but it is the more to the honor of those, and I will vouch for many, who unite integrity with skill and attention, and walk honorably upright where there are so many pitfalls and stumbling blocks for those of a different character.*
—Sir Walter Scott, *The Antiquity*

If you follow the course I outline in this book, you should have no problems handling your land deal with minimal assistance from an attorney. Every transaction is unique, however, and you might have an unusual problem involving complicated legal questions I do not cover. If there is any matter you do not fully understand, do not sign anything at any stage until you see a lawyer.

Because laws and practices vary throughout the country and are constantly being revised, you will have to investigate which laws apply to your area. Some of you will not have the time or the inclination to do a thorough job of investigation and negotiation yourselves, and you will want a lawyer to do some of this for you. Although a lawyer cannot tell you if the property is satisfactory with reference to location, water, soil, climate, amenities and condition of the structures or if the price is reasonable, he or she can help you write the contract of sale, negotiate

with the seller or decide whether you have the necessary easements, water rights and other legal rights.

It you retain a lawyer to handle your real estate deal, he or she will work exclusively on your behalf and do everything possible to see that you receive what you expect to get. All other parties—the title company, mortgagee, lending institution, local and state government officials, the seller, the real estate agent—will have interests contrary to your own. As explained in Chapter 2, "Real Estate Agents and Salespersons," real estate agents work for sellers. They cannot give you legal advice and may, in fact, give you false advice due to ignorance or intent. Beware of agents who discourage you from obtaining an attorney or who ask you to rely on their own advice. Some brokers are only interested in making a quick and easy sale so that they can collect a commission. A lawyer's interest is in protecting the client who employs him or her.

## What a Lawyer Can Do for You

You can retain a lawyer to do anything from drafting or double-checking your contract of sale to handling all the legal aspects of the purchase from start to finish.

By the time you start negotiating to get the price down, you might be too friendly with the agent to become a hard bargainer. Sometimes it is to your advantage to have an attorney negotiate on your behalf with the real estate agent and the seller. (When the agent tells you that your demands are unreasonable, you can blame your lawyer for insisting on them.) A lawyer also might have connections with a bank or finance company and be able to help you obtain a loan.

Drawing up contracts and examining forms you are asked to sign are important functions of a lawyer. In many states, real estate agents are permitted to write contracts, but these contracts will not give you sufficient protection. The Model Contract of Sale in Chapter 27 is drafted to protect the interests of the buyer, but its details must be carefully studied and adjusted to fit your situation. If you have doubts about any document involved in the transaction, a lawyer can determine its legality and explain its contents.

You can have an attorney investigate the zoning and other ordinances that affect your property and tell you whether your intended use is permissible. An attorney can do a title search or obtain one for you. Most important, the attorney can read all the legal documents pertaining to your property, such as easements, reservations and restrictions, and explain them to you. He or she can ensure that you have adequate water rights and easements and can personally examine the land for any constructive defects of title that would not be recorded in the county records, such as prescriptive easements or adverse possession claims. (See Chapter 9, "Easement Rights" and Chapter 16, "Adverse Possession.") Then, before you buy, an attorney can help you get the seller to clear any defects of title, such as an unwanted easement or tax lien.

The means by which you take title and the financial terms of the purchase have tax consequences that can be to either your benefit or your detriment, and you might want to ask an attorney's advice on these matters if you have an unusual situation. The retention of a lawyer is mandatory if you belong to a group that plans to incorporate or form a non-profit organization such as a church or foundation. Certain state regulations must be satisfied and the legal problems involved can be complex.

## Choosing Your Lawyer

You must decide whether to use a city or a country lawyer. Then you must choose between a general practitioner or a real estate specialist.

If you already have a lawyer in the city who has handled other matters for you, you may want him or her to handle your land deal. This usually is not advisable. Most attorneys are reluctant to oversee a real estate transaction more than 100 miles away, because it is difficult to inspect the land and speak with the parties involved. Your regular attorney will probably recommend that you retain local counsel, and that is my advice also. A local lawyer not only knows the land and can easily reach it, he knows everybody in town and has established a working relationship with surveyors, well-diggers, appraisers, inspectors, government officials, title company officials, bankers and other lending institution officials, escrow holders, sellers and real estate agents. Your city lawyer may be able to refer you to a local attorney whom he or she knows personally or by reputation. If you still want your regular attorney's aid, you can make an arrangement whereby he or she will double-check the local country lawyer's work and advice, but that really is not necessary if you find a competent attorney in the area where the land is located.

You must be careful that a lawyer's association with the local residents does not interfere with his or her work on your behalf. For example, some lawyers will try to work out a deal in the real estate agent's interest by recommending that you make the purchase without researching certain matters that could complicate the deal. Be careful to recognize when, and if, a lawyer is trying to talk you out of necessary protections such as surveys, appraisals and contingencies in the contract. If you read anything in this book that the lawyer does not mention to you, question him or her on the matter and try to determine if any ties with the real estate agent, seller or other party exist that might lead to a conflict of interest.

Many lawyers in the country specialize in real estate law, because the majority of their cases involve land problems. Often such specialists charge more than a general practitioner, but it is worth the extra expense because they are the most knowledgeable. They are more familiar with the problems and laws involved and will have to do less research and spend less time on a case than lawyers who handle such deals only occasionally. Compare the estimated fee of the local specialist with that of the local general practitioner. Beware of attorneys who tell you they have to research the law on some point that you feel they should know. These are not specialists, and they should be avoided.

In most rural areas, your choice of attorneys will be limited because of the scarcity of lawyers practicing in the country. Usually several lawyers practice in the county seat; the farther you go from that base, the fewer lawyers you will encounter. If a local, state or federal legal assistance office is located in the area, ask for recommendations and information on who are the most trustworthy and reasonable lawyers in the area. Call the county bar association and ask for a list of real estate specialists. If you know a lawyer in the city, ask if he or she can recommend a good lawyer in the area in which you intend to purchase land. Talk to local people and try to get an idea of the reputations of local attorneys. You may find that one lawyer will be consistently referred to as being the most honest and knowledgeable one in town.

Whatever you do, never pick a lawyer by his or her ad in the Yellow Pages of the telephone book. Any lawyer can take out an ad, but the best lawyers continue to operate on the basis of reputation.

Sometimes large real estate agencies have attorneys who work for them, drawing up papers and overseeing the legalities of sales. Do not rely on them to represent you. If they draw up any documents, examine them very carefully yourself, and if you hire an attorney, he or she also must inspect them.

## How To Relate to Your Lawyer

Good feelings between you and your lawyer are essential. If you do not feel comfortable with a lawyer after you retain one, fire him or her and go to someone else. Your lawyer needs to be able to contact you, so keep him or her notified of your whereabouts at all times. Keep your lawyer up-to-date regarding all conversations you have with the real estate agent and the seller; give your lawyer copies of every document you receive; and inform him or her of any other matters relating to your purchase. When giving information, do not reveal only what you think is relevant. Tell your lawyer everything. Conversely, he or she should also keep you informed about everything being done for you.

Sometimes a lawyer will put you off when you try to contact him, or her or will seem to be very slow in getting the job done for you, probably because he or she has many clients. If you do not think your lawyer is giving your case enough atten-

tion, do not hesitate to prod him or her along at a reasonable pace.

## How To Know Whether Your Lawyer Is Doing a Good Job

Check everything the lawyer does against the information contained in this book. If legal advice or information conflicts with what I say, bring it to your lawyer's attention and resolve the problem. No attorney necessarily has to agree with everything I say, but he or she should give you an adequate explanation for any disagreement. New laws may have been passed, or practices may be different in your area.

If your lawyer uses standard forms, which are preprinted forms containing blank spaces for inserting the necessary information, be certain that they protect you adequately. Forms drawn up specifically for your individual situation are much better because preprinted forms often do not satisfactorily deal with your individual circumstances. Nevertheless, most lawyers will use them to save time. In some states, the bar association and/or REALTORS® have established preprinted forms that are completely adequate. In California I use the printed contracts supplied by the California Association of REALTORS® daily, without hesitation. Check the forms used by your attorney against those in this book for completeness. After any forms are drawn up, carefully review them with your attorney to be sure they include everything you expect to get out of the deal, particularly regarding conditions of the sale and financing. Show my Model Contract of Sale to your attorney so he or she can use it, making the appropriate changes. (Of course, the purpose of including it is to enable you to draw up your own contract, but have it double-checked by an attorney if you are uncertain about something.)

## How Much Will a Lawyer Cost?

A lawyer's fee is based on several factors, including the time and labor that he or she estimates will be required, the difficulty of the problems involved, the amount of skill involved and the level of his or her expertise, the standard fees of lawyers in the community, the amount of money and benefits that you will receive from his or her services and whether you are an established or a new client.

When you see a lawyer, after explaining what you want done, ask what the fee is. Depending on the situation, the lawyer will either quote you a single fee as a package price or an hourly fee with an estimated time involved. The method he or she chooses will largely depend on what you want done. A lawyer who handles the whole purchase, including all negotiations, execution and examination of documents, will probably give you a package rate. If you simply want to consult him or her whenever a problem arises that you think you cannot deal with, the attorney will charge by the hour—and probably keep track of every letter, every phone call, and every minute spent talking to you, either in person or on the phone. If you run into any time-consuming problems in the middle of the transaction, the amount of the fee could easily be as much as, or more than, it would have been if the lawyer had handled the entire purchase for a package price. In a legally complicated land deal you might find that it is cheaper to pay a set fee and let the lawyer handle it entirely.

Lawyers are often retained to process the entire sale where the seller and buyer have negotiated between themselves without a real estate agent being involved. The lawyer usually charges a single fee that is often based on the purchase price of the property, with a set minimum. The common fee is 1 percent to 3 percent of the purchase price, with a minimum of $1,500.00. Thus, on an $80,000 purchase price, a lawyer's fee would be $1,500, and on a $200,000 purchase price, the fee would be $2,000 to $6,000. All fees are negotiable, but the seller usually comes out better than he or she would if he or she used a real estate agent, and the price should probably be lower to reflect the fact that no real estate commission will have to be paid. Hourly fees usually start at a minimum of $100 and can go as high as $200 per hour. Remember, you may also have fees and costs to pay to a title or escrow company, and for title insurance and recording costs.

If you simply want to consult an attorney to review the sales contract and to examine the legal documents that affect the title to the property, you will be charged an hourly rate. A competent real estate attorney will be able to review all the documents and render an opinion of the title in a few hours. A complete review of the contract and title documents should cost you between $500 to $1,000.

If you are buying as a group and want to form a corporation, nonprofit entity or partnership, you will have to retain an attorney to draw up and file the proper documents. This service could cost several hundred dollars, in the case of a simple partnership agreement or into the thousands of dollars for a simple corporation.

Whatever your decision is regarding the use of a lawyer, one thing is certain: It will cost you more time and money to go to court after the transaction is completed than to pay a lawyer to oversee your purchase from the beginning or to double-check your own legal work. Buying property is the largest investment you will make in your life; paying a few hundred dollars to ensure that you are proceeding properly is a small price to pay for security.

By considering your responses to the following questions you will be better able to determine whether or not you need to retain an attorney:

- What is your business experience in general and your prior experience in land and real estate transactions?
- How large is your purchase, and what could you lose if something were to go wrong?
- Is a good lawyer available?
- What are his or her fees?
- What do you want a lawyer to do for you?
- After reading this book, do you feel confident that you can handle the entire deal on your own?

If you do retain an attorney, this book can be used to help you understand what is involved in the purchase and to enable you to oversee your attorney's work.

# Property Evaluation Checklist

# 35 The Property Buyer's Complete Checklist

The following pages contain a complete summary of all essential points to consider when evaluating any piece of property, whether improved or unimproved.

Nothing should be overlooked. Room has been left for you to write in the necessary information. A blank line has been placed next to each number for you to check off the information as you proceed

with your research. If a particular point does not apply to your parcel, write in N/A ("Not Applicable").

Remove this list from the book so you can carry it with you on a clipboard. You might even show it to the real estate agent so he or she knows what information you will want to evaluate for your prospective purchase.

## General Information

—    I. Location:

—    II. Property owner, if being sold by seller:

—      A. Address:

—      B. Phone:

—    III. Acreage and/or size of property:

—    IV. Legal description:

—    V. Tax Assessor's Parcel Number:

—    VI. Improvements:

— VII. Special qualities:

—VIII. Income produced by land:

—    IX. Lay of land:

     Hilly ——————    Flat ——————————

     Open —————    Steep ————————

     Tillable ———    Forested ——————

—    X. Availability and cost of power, telephone, cable TV, sewer and water

## Real Estate Agent

—    I. Name of broker or salesperson and real estate agency:

—    II. Address of agency:

—    III. Phone:

—    IV. Type of listing, if known:

     Exclusive —————————————

     Open listing ————————————

     Multiple listing ———————————

## Facts for Price Negotiation and Financing

—    I. Asking price:

—      Total: ——— Per acre: ———————

—    II. Terms:

—      A. All cash or cash down payment plus mortgage or deed of trust?

—      B. How much money down?

—      C. Assume existing mortgage or deed of trust?

—      D. How much will note to seller be?

—    III. When did the seller buy the property, and how much did seller pay (if you can determine this)? See tax stamps on deed, and seller's existing mortgage on the property.

—      Why is seller selling the property?

—    IV. Does seller or broker have a written appraisal of the property? Get a copy. What does tax assessor have the land and buildings appraised at for tax purposes?

—    V. How firm is seller on price?

—    VI. Can you afford this property?

—    VII. Existing mortgage to be assumed by you:

—      A. *1st*

—        1. Amount to be assumed:

—        2. Interest rate:

—        3. When each payment is due and amount of payment:

—          a. Balloon payments?

—          b. Acceleration clause or prepayment penalty?

—          c. Who is trustee or title company?

—          d. Any other liens to be assumed?

—      B. *2nd*

—        1. Amount to be assumed:

—        2. Interest rate:

—        3. When each payment is due and amount of payment:

—          a. Balloon payments?

—          b. Acceleration clause or prepayment penalty?

—          c. Who is trustee or title company?

—          d. Any other liens to be assumed?

—VIII. New note and mortgage or deed of trust given back to seller:

—      A. Amount:

—      B. Interest rate:

___ C. When each payment is due and amount of payment.

___ D. Balloon payments?

___ E. Acceleration clause or prepayment penalty?

___ F. Can it be subordinated to construction loan?

___ G. FHA/VA

___ IX. Third-party lenders

___ A. Name

___ B. Branch

___ C. Address

___ D. Attention

___ E. Loan Number

___ F. Verbal commitment received

from _____

date _____

___ G. Written commitment date

___ H. Terms:

Amount _____

Points _____

Fees:

Points and fees paid by

Seller _____

Buyer _____

___ I. Interest Rate

___ J. Monthly payments

___ K. FHA/VA

## Water

___ I. Above-ground source:

___ Springs _____ Creek _____

___ Lake _____ Pond _____

___ River _____ Other _____

___ Year-round supply _____

___ Flood hazards?

___ Property in flood zone?

___ A. Amount (during dry season). Ask:

___ 1. Neighbors

___ 2. Farm adviser

___ 3. Well driller

___ B. Potability—Health Department

___ C. Location

___ 1. Within boundaries

___ 2. In relationship to sewage disposal system—Health Department

___ D. Others' rights to use water—see seller's deed, title report, abstract of title. Do you get water from someone else's land? Do others get water from your land? What are terms? Enough water for everyone at *all* times of the year? Do you really want to share water?

___ E. Prescriptive rights—water being taken by surrounding landowners?

___ F. Provided by irrigation district or water company?

___ Talk to supplier about costs and amounts available.

___ II. Underground source (existing well)

___ A. Observe system in use

___ B. Check well driller's log

___ C. Health department and building department—permits

___ D. Others' right to use water. See seller's deed, title report, abstract of title. Do you get water from someone else's land? Do others get water from your land? What are terms? Enough water for everyone at *all* times of the year? Do you really want to share water?

___ III. Underground source (no existing well)

___ A. Check with local well drillers—compare with other wells in the area

___ 1. Depth

___ 2. Estimated cost (drilling, casing, pump, holding tank and so on)

___     3. Probability of getting water

___     B. Health department and building department

___       1. What permits required

___       2. Percolation test

___       3. Potability

___     C. Condition in contract that water be obtained prior to close of escrow.

___     D. Others' right to use water. See seller's deed, title report, abstract of title. Do you get water from someone else's land? Do others get water from your land? What are terms? Enough water for everyone at *all* times of the year? Do you really want to share water?

___   IV. Contamination potential

___     A. Waste disposal sites in area

___     B. Pesticide, insecticide or chemical fertilizers used? What is upstream—livestock, homes, industry, farms? Test water before escrow closes. What is result?

## Soil

___   I. Type of soil:

Clay _____    Rocky _____

Acid _____    Hardpan _____

Sandy _____    Other _____

How much topsoil? _____

Tillable? _____

___   II. Soil test reports available?

___     A. By whom?

___     B. Summary of tests

___     C. Additional testing needed?

___     D. Any foreseeable problems caused by soil conditions: special site engineering creating extra building costs, drainage problems for septic systems and so on?

___   III. Vegetation growth:

moderate ____ heavy ____ light ____

What kind? _____

___   IV. Timber: Marketable? _____

___     Anyone else have timber rights?

___     Kind of trees _____

___     Firewood supply _____

___   V. Is USGS topo map available? _____

___     Aerial photos _____

___     Timber and soil maps _____

___   VI. Drainage, irrigation and agricultural potential. Talk to neighbors and surrounding farmers; see USGS data, farmer adviser and so on.

## Boundaries and Surveys

**(Not covered by title insurance—only by survey by licensed surveyor or registered civil engineer.)**

___   I. Existing survey

___     A. Copy of recorded survey—county recorder's office and/or local surveyor

___     B. Find markers on ground; use aerial photographs and topographical maps with survey

___     C. If doubt that something is within boundaries, put condition in contract

___       1. Line(s) to be surveyed—flagged and approved by buyer prior to close of escrow.

___       2. Specify that improvements, water supply, and so on, are within boundary lines of property

___   II. No existing survey

___     A. Estimated cost of survey from licensed surveyor

___     B. Condition in contract that survey be completed and approved—paid for by seller

___   III. Talk to neighbors to see if any boundary conflicts exist

## Mineral and Timber Rights

___ I. Check deeds, preliminary title report, abstract of title

___ II. Evaluate reserved/excluded rights carefully to determine if they are so undesirable you do not want the land

## Easements and Road Access

___ I. Your easement

___ A. Existing easement

___ 1. Check deed, preliminary title report or abstract of title

___ 2. Check deed description against available maps

___ 3. Maintenance

___ a. Check with neighbors

___ b. Examine road condition (culverts, gravel, ditching, and so on)

___ c. Accessible year-round?

___ B. Easement needed

___ 1. Condition in contract requiring recorded easement in deed. Never buy land without deeded access rights. If none, cancel purchase now.

___ 2. Road construction company

___ a. Possibility of construction

___ b. Estimated cost of construction and annual maintenance

___ c. Seller should pay for road construction as part of sale

___ II. Others' easements over the land

___ A. Check deeds, preliminary title report, or abstract of title

___ B. Decide whether they will interfere with your enjoyment of land

___ C. Prescriptive easements (not covered by title insurance)—examine land for evidence of access usage by adjoining owners. Talk to them regarding their rights and future intentions.

## Sewage Disposal System

___ I. Public or private? If public available: cost of running pipes, hook-up fees, monthly charges

___ II. Existing septic tank on property

___ A. Observe location of tank and leach field, open lids, concrete, wood or metal

___ B. Pumping information

___ 1. Who installed system?

___ 2. Who does pumping?

___ 3. How often is system pumped?

___ 4. When last pumped?

___ C. Health department and building department

___ 1. Permits and percolation test results

___ 2. Relationship to water source

___ 3. Size of tank for needs, size of lot, flush toilets, run shower and faucets

___ 4. Is system legal?

___ III. No existing septic tank

___ A. Health department and building department

___ 1. Percolation test rules

___ 2. Permits required

___ 3. Estimated cost

___ B. Condition in contract requiring approval of percolation test and permits before close of escrow. Never buy land without prior approval of percolation test—or might not be able to build

## House

___ I. Condition in contract

___ A. Pest and structural report

___ B. Appraisal

___ C. Cost to do improvements on house (if needed)

__ Subordination clause needed in mortgage?

__ D. Personal property included: Check conditions of equipment and appliances; list everything in contract

__ II. Bargaining over conditions of property. Get price lowered if repairs are needed; or get repairs done before deal closes

House Inspection Checklist: Number each blank 1–10: 1 = excellent condition—10 = rebuild

## I. Structural Integrity

Foundation:

| | |
|---|---|
| __ Concrete perimeter | __ Concrete slab |
| __ Pole frame | __ Chemically treated |
| __ Sinking | __ Floor joint sag |
| __ Cracked concrete | __ Irregularities |
| __ Termites | __ Wood rot |
| __ Is all wood in the house above level of soil? | __ Does crawl space have adequate ventilation? |
| __ Was soil under house treated with insecticide during construction? | __ Is soil covered with moisture barrier? |
| __ Afterward? | __ Soil under any addition covered with moisture barrier? |
| __ Any termite shelter tubes visible on foundation? | __ Does crawl space contain stumps or wood debris? |
| __ On pipes? | __ Any small holes in any unfinished wood with powder in them indicating infestation? |
| __ If house in zone of high termite hazard, is structural pest control contract on it? | |
| __ Include guarantee? | |

Comments _____

Basement:

| | |
|---|---|
| __ Cement | __ Dirt |
| __ Wood | __ Rock |

| | |
|---|---|
| __ Floor evidence | __ Mud |
| __ Sump pump | __ Water stains |
| __ Drains | |

Comments _____

Roof:

| | |
|---|---|
| __ Wood | __ Gutters and downspouts intact |
| __ Shingle | |
| __ Tarpaper | __ Gravel |
| __ Leader condition | __ Plywood |
| __ Leaks | __ Flashing |
| __ Fireproof | __ Is roof decking completely covered, especially at roof edge? |
| __ Roof extension over walls sufficient? | |

__ Roof sag (rafter decay)?

__ Water stains on ceilings under roof indicating leaks?

Comments _____

Exterior walls:

| | |
|---|---|
| __ Sagging? | __ Paint peeling or blistering due to condensation? |
| __ Square? | |
| __ Pest damage? | __ Wood rot? |
| __ Interior walls buckling | __ Caulking around windows, doors and joints? |
| __ Are decorative and other items attached to house likely to admit or trap moisture? | |

Comments _____

Drainage:

__ Grading slope away from house?

__ Leaders drain proper distance away?

__ Drainage ditches?

Comments _____

Attic:

___ Insulation under roof

___ Insulation on floor

___ Louver ventilation in attic

___ Leaks?

___ Water stains?

___ Beam ceiling: insulated?

Comments _____

Porches:

___ Earth-filled porches separated from house?

Comments _____

## II. Efficient Insulation
Insulating material:

| | |
|---|---|
| ___ Foil | ___ Condition |
| ___ Fill | ___ Thickness |
| ___ Slab | ___ Clammy? |
| ___ Board | ___ Mice damage? |
| ___ Other | ___ Drafts? |
| ___ Snow on roof? | ___ Under floors? |
| ___ In ceiling? | ___ In walls? |

Comments _____

## III. Interior
Doors, windows, floors:

| | |
|---|---|
| ___ Doors or windows sag or stick? | ___ Floors level? |
| ___ Frames decayed? | ___ Spongy spots in floor, particularly in bathroom or kitchen |

Comments _____

Electrical:

| | |
|---|---|
| ___ Fuse box | ___ Meets code standards? |
| ___ Circuit breaker | ___ Frayed or loose wires? |
| ___ Number of outlets in kitchen? | ___ Other rooms? |
| ___ Capacity (120, 240 volt) | ___ Rewiring necessary? |

Load system can carry:

| | |
|---|---|
| ___ Number of amps? | ___ Estimated costs? |

Comments _____

Plumbing:

___ Water pressure—turn several faucets on at once and flush toilet

| | |
|---|---|
| ___ Toilets flush well? | ___ Ask about all appliances—dishwasher, washing machine, and so on |
| ___ Floors feel spongy when walked on in bathroom or kitchen? | |
| ___ Faucets drip? | ___ Caulking around tubs, sinks, showers intact? |
| ___ Standing water indicating poor drainage? | ___ Leaks anywhere, including drains? |
| ___ Water stains on ceiling? | ___ Rusty water? |
| | ___ Rusty pipes? |
| ___ Separate shutoff? | ___ Main shutoff valves for individual rooms? |
| ___ Valves for individual rooms? | |
| ___ Frozen pipes or valves? | |

Comments _____

## IV. Chimney

| | |
|---|---|
| ___ Code freestanding wood stove? | ___ Smoke or burn marks? |
| ___ Code fireplace? | ___ Loose or missing bricks? |
| ___ Good draft? | |
| ___ Good location? | |

Comments _____

## Commercial Farming Capabilities

___    I. Kinds of crops/livestock or animals

___      A. Annual Income: (for last 5 years)

___        1. Net profit

___        2. Overhead breakdown

   B. Equipment for crops/livestock or animals

      1. List items and examine condition, age, repair history

   C. Who gets existing crops and animals?

   D. Who has been buying crops? Talk to them

  II. Get complete profit-and-loss statements and seller's tax returns for past five years, reflecting farming income and expenses.

  III. Talk to neighbors, farm and agriculture officials, and read as much as possible about the current economic situation in the area for your intended business.

## Contract, Title Examination, Restrictions on Development

  I. Current preliminary title report or abstract of title available?

   A. Get copy of title report

   B. Read entire report of abstract

  II. Put all conditions of sale in contract to purchase. Sale is subject to:

   A. Buyer's approval of preliminary title report or abstract of title

   B. Guarantee of water availability (reports by soil and water engineers, hydrologists, well-drillers)

   C. Guarantee property buildable (percolation and engineering study)

   D. Pest, termite, structural report and approval

   E. Review by buyer's attorney

   F. Buyer's approval of survey of property

   G. Buyer obtaining building permit for the property

   H. Buyer's obtaining financing or selling home in city to obtain purchase money

  III. If deal is made, order preliminary title report or abstract of title in your name.

  IV. Get copies from title company of all documents contained in preliminary title report or abstract of title necessary to evaluate condition of your title. Read every document. If you don't understand some thing, see an attorney.

  V. Anything detrimental in report which cannot be cleared before escrow closes, for example, property subject to easements, reservation of water rights, timber rights, mineral rights? If detrimental and can't be cleared, stop the deal and do not buy the property.

  VI. Anything detrimental that can be found only by physical inspection of property that cannot be cleared before escrow closes; for example, prescriptive water rights, boundary line in dispute, present or prospective dispute with a neighbor?

   A. Physically examine property carefully; talk to neighbors

   B. If problem cannot be taken care of by seller now, stop deal and don't buy property.

  VII. Any back taxes due? Judgment liens, mechanic's liens, other monetary liens on property paid by seller prior to close of escrow?

  VIII. Restrictions on development of property by property owners' association or government agency.

   A. Building or architectural and design restrictions

   B. Lot size restrictions

   C. Zoning (commercial or industrial) restrictions

   D. Have existing buildings been condemned for violation of health codes?

  IX. Taxes/Assessments

   A. Sewerage or water assessments?

   B. Property taxes?

   C. Proposed easements?

  X. Obtain and read public report if one has been issued.

  XI. If part of homeowners' association, obtain

and read all documents pertaining to the operation, rights and powers of association.

## Your Offer

\_\_\_ I. Date your made offer.

\_\_\_ II. How much offered.

\_\_\_ III. What terms offered.

\_\_\_ IV. Seller's response to offer.

\_\_\_ A. Silence

\_\_\_ B. Rejection

\_\_\_ C. Counteroffer

\_\_\_ Are you willing to respond to seller's counteroffer?

\_\_\_ 1. How much?

\_\_\_ 2. What terms?

\_\_\_ 3. Date you respond to counteroffer.

If no deal is made—don't worry. There is plenty of good land available. Keep looking. Don't get buyer's fever.

## Agencies with Information

1. County recorder's office:
   Deeds
   Surveys
   Liens
   Any other recorded documents
2. Tax assessor:
   Delinquent taxes
   Value of land and improvements by tax assessor
   Amount of yearly taxes
3. Planning department:
   Zoning
   Use permits
   Mobile homes
   Violations
4. Building department:
   Permits already granted
   a. Well
   b. Septic tank
   c. House
   d. Other buildings
      Permits needed
      Violations
5. Health department:
   Permits already granted
   a. Well
   b. Septic tank
   c. Percolation tests
   Permits needed
   Violations
6. BLM (Bureau of Land Management)
   If land is near federally owned lands, find out BLM's future plans for the area; have mineral information.
7. Farm adviser, soil conservation agent, Forest Service, U.S. Geological Service, Department of Water Resources.

# 36 Country Property Buyer's Top Ten List

I hope that the information in this book has not only made you more aware of the complexities involved in finding and buying your place in the country but also has given you the confidence to handle many aspects of your purchase yourself. By referring to this book, you should be able to find the answers to any questions and the solutions to any problems that might arise. If you encounter a unique problem or an example of a fraudulent real estate practice I have not discussed, I would be interested to learn of it. Your information might be

useful to include in future editions of this book. You can write or call me at my office.

Les Scher, Attorney at Law
293 Sprowel Creek Rd.
P.O. Box 780
Garberville, CA 95440
Voice: (707) 923-2128
Fax: (707) 923-2176

Even after you buy your land, you will find that

much of the information in this book will continue to be useful. When you decide to sell your property, for instance, you can take this book from the shelf and refresh your memory on many aspects of buying and selling real estate. You will find that by having been a wise land buyer, you will also be a successful land seller.

In closing, I give you:

## The Country Property Buyer's Top Ten List of Essential Things To Know Before Closing the Purchase

1. Remember, the seller's real estate agent works for the seller and does not get paid without making a sale.
2. The price and terms are always negotiable.
3. Never buy land without a proven source of adequate water, which includes recorded water rights if it is from somebody else's land. Test the water for potability.
4. Never buy land without first securing the necessary permits for installing your own sewage disposal system, or insuring that you can hook up to a public sewage system if one is available.
5. Be certain of where your boundary lines are located by conducting a survey of the property.
6. Don't buy land that does not have deeded easement rights from the public road to the property.
7. Be sure the zoning will permit you to use your property as you intended to use it.
8. Determine the legal status of any uses being made of the property by other persons. Investigate any sign of roads, grazing, or the taking of water.
9. Review all documents referred to in a preliminary title report or abstract of title. Hire a lawyer to review and interpret these documents if you are unable to do so yourself.
10. Avoid partnerships if at all possible.

# Appendixes

# Appendixes

## APPENDIX A

## Real Estate Catalogs and Useful Magazines for the Country Property Owner

Many real estate agencies put out catalogs and brochures of their properties for sale. Check through the classified ads in magazines specializing in country land, and you will see free and low price catalogs offered.

The definitive rural property real estate catalog for properties in the United States is United Country, America's Catalogue of Country Real Estate for Sale. You can order it by sending $4.95 to:

United National Real Estate
1600-MO N. Corrington Avenue
Kansas City, Missouri 64120
(800) 999-1020. Ext. 92

The definitive rural property real estate catalog and listings for properties in Canada can be ordered by sending $18.00 for twelve months of sales lists to:

H.M. Dignam Corporation Ltd.
370 Dunlop St. West, Unit 807
Barrie, Ont. L4N 5R7, Canada

A catalog of books about country living is:

*Storey's How-To Books for Country Living*
Schoolhouse Road
Pownal, Vermont 05261
(800) 441-5700

## Magazines of Special Interest for People in the Country:

*Back Home*
P.O. Box 70
Hendersonville, NC 28793
(800) 992-2546
4 issues/$16

*Caretaker Gazette*
2380 NE Ellis Way, Suite C16
Pullman, WA 99163-5303
Voice:(509) 332-0806
E-mail: garydunn@pullman.com
6 issues (bi-monthly)/$24

*Country*
5400 S. 60th St.
Greendale, WI 53129-1404
Fax: (414) 423-1143
6 issues/$17

*Country Accents*
GCR Publishing Group, Inc.
1700 Broadway
New York, NY 10019
6 issues/$13

*Country Almanac or Country Decorating Ideas*
1115 Broadway, 8th Floor
New York, NY 10010-2897
Quarterly/$10

*Country Home*
1716 Locust St.
Des Moines, IA 50309-3023
6 issues/$18

*Country Journal*
4 High Ridge Park
Stanford, CT 06905
(203) 358-9900
6 issues/$24.00

*Country Living*
224 W. 57th Street
New York, NY 10009-5905
Fax: (212) 581-7605
6 issues/$18

*Fine Homebuilding*
63 S. Main St.
Box 355
Newtown, CT 06470
7 issues/$26

*Harrowsmith Country Life*
Ferry Rd.
Charlotte, VT 05445
6 issues/$25

*Home*
1633 Broadway
New York, NY 10019-6741
Monthly/$15

*Home Buyers Monthly*
7080 Donton Way #108
Dublin, CA 94568
Monthly/$24

*Home Energy*
2124 Kittridge St., #95
Berkeley, CA 94704
(510) 524-5405
6 issues/$19

*Home Power Magazine*
Box 520
Ashland, OR 97520
Fax: (916) 475-0830
6 issues/$15

*Log Home Living*
4451 Brookfield Corporate Dr.
Chantilly, VA 22071
6 issues/$22.00

*Log Homes Design Ideas*
2900 N. Meade St., Suite #4
Appleton, WI 54911-9928
6 issues / $ 19.00

*Mother Earth News*
24 E. 23rd St.
New York, NY 10010
Voice: (212) 260-7210
Fax: (212) 727-2326
1 yr./$17.95

*Muir's Original Log Home Guide*
164 Middle Creek RI.
Cosby, TN 37722-3222
6 issues/$24

*New Farm*
222 Main St.
Emmuas, PA 18049-2749
Voice: (215) 967-8497
Fax: (215) 967-8959
7 issues/$15.00

*The New Settler Interview*
P.O. Box 730
Wilits, CA 95490
12 issues a year/$12

*Organic Gardening*
33 E. Minor St.
Emmaus, PA 18098
9 issues/$25

*Practical Homeowner*
656 Bair Island Road
Redwood City, CA 94062
Bi-monthly

*Small Farmers Journal*
P.O. Box 1627
Sisters, OR 97759-1627
Voice: (503) 549-2064
Fax: (503) 549-4403
Quarterly/$22.00

*The Whole Earth Review*
FULCO
30 Broad Street
Denville, NJ 07834
(800) 783-4903
Quarterly/$20

# APPENDIX B

# Bureau of Land Management (BLM) State and District Offices

The following offices are state and district branches of the BLM. They will have the information you need about present and future uses of federal land adjoining or near the land you wish to buy. Look at their maps and studies of projected multiple uses. They also have much useful information, which is referred to throughout this book.

Main Office
United States Department of the Interior
Bureau of Land Management
1849 C St., NW
Washington, DC 20240-0001
Voice: (202) 208-5717
Fax: (202) 208-4152

Alaska
Alaska State Office
222 W 7th Ave., # 13
Anchorage, AK 99513-7599
(907) 271-5076

*District Offices*
Anchorage, AK 99507
Fairbanks, AK 99707

Arizona
Arizona State Office
3707 N. 7th St.
P.O. Box 16563
Phoenix, AZ 85011
(602) 650-0206

*District Offices*
St. George, UT 84770
Phoenix, AZ 85017
Stafford, AZ 85546
Yuma, AZ 85364

California
  California State Office
  Federal Office Building, Room E-2841
  2800 Cottage Way
  Sacramento, CA 95825-1889
  (916) 979-2845

  *District Offices*
  Bakersfield, CA 93301
  Folsom, CA 95630
  Redding, CA 96001
  Riverside, CA 92507
  Susanville, CA 96130
  Ukiah, CA 95482

Colorado
  Colorado State Office
  2850 Youngfield St.
  Lakewood, CO 80215-7076
  (303) 239-3900

  *District Offices*
  Canon City, CO 81212
  Craig, CO 81625
  Grand Junction, CO 81502
  Montrose, CO 81401

Idaho
  Idaho State Office
  3380 Americana Terrace
  Boise, ID 83706-2500
  (208) 384-3001

  *District Offices*
  Boise, ID 83702
  Burley, ID 83318
  Coeur d'Alene, ID 83814
  Idaho Falls, ID 83401
  Salmon, ID 83467
  Shoshone, ID 83352

Montana, North Dakota, South Dakota
  Mountain States Office
  P.O. Box 36800
  222 N. 32nd St.
  Billings, MT 59107-6800
  (406) 255-2904

  *District Offices*
  Butte, MT 59701
  Dickinson, ND 58601
  Lewiston, MT 59457
  Miles City, MT 59301

Nevada
  Nevada State Office
  850 Harvard Way
  P.O. Box 12000
  Reno, NV 89520-0006
  (702) 785-6590

  *District Offices*
  Battle Mountain, NV 89820
  Carson City, NV 89701
  Elko, NV 89801
  EIy, NV 89301
  Las Vegas, NV 89102
  Winnamucca, NV 89445

New Mexico, Oklahoma, Kansas, Texas
  New Mexico State Office
  1474 Rodeo Drive
  P.O. Box 27115
  Santa Fe, NM 87502-0115
  (505) 438-7501

  *District Offices*
  Albuquerque, NM 87107
  Las Cruces, NM 88001
  Roswell, NM 88201
  Socorro, NM 87801

Oregon, Washington
  Oregon State Office
  1300 NE 44th Ave.
  P.O. Box 2965
  Portland, OR 97208-2965
  (503) 280-7024

  *District Offices*
  Baker, OR 97814
  Burns, OR 97720
  Coos Bay, OR 97420
  Eugene, OR 97440
  Lakeview, OR 97630
  Medford, OR 97501
  Prineville, OR 97754
  Roseburg, OR 97470
  Salem, OR 97302
  Spokane, WA 99201
  Vale, OR 97910

Utah

    Utah State Office
    324 S. State St.
    Salt Lake City, UT 84111-2303

    *District Offices*
    Cedar City, UT 84720
    Moab, UT 84532
    Richfield, UT 84701
    Salt Lake City, UT 84119
    Vernal, UT 84078

Wyoming, Nebraska

    Wyoming State Office
    2515 Warren Ave.
    P.O. Box 1828
    Cheyenne, WY 82003
    (307) 775-6001

    *District Offices*
    Casper, WY 82601
    Rawlins, WY 82301
    Rock Springs, WY 82901
    Worland, WY 82401

States East of the Mississippi River, Plus Iowa, Minnesota, Missouri, Arkansas, Louisiana

    Eastern States Office
    7450 Boston Blvd.
    Springfield, VA 22153
    (703) 440-1700

B.L.M. Service Center

    Denver Service Center
    Denver Federal Center, Bldg. 50
    P.O. Box 25047
    Denver, CO 80225-0047
    Voice: (303) 236-1975
    Fax: (303)236-0845

# APPENDIX C

## Federal Lands for Sale

*Businesses and householders do not retain items they do not need, neither should the Government.*

        —Official Federal Government
                Policy Statement

The federal government, through the Bureau of Land Management (BLM), regularly disposes of excess public lands. Almost all are in the western states of Alaska, Arizona, California, Colorado, Idaho, Montana, Nevada, New Mexico, Oregon, Utah and Wyoming.

There are also small amounts in Alabama, Arkansas, Florida, Illinois, Kansas, Louisiana, Michigan, Minnesota, Missouri, Mississippi, Nebraska, North Dakota, South Dakota, Oklahoma, Ohio, Washington and Wisconsin.

There are no public lands managed by BLM in Connecticut, Delaware, Georgia, Hawaii, Indiana, Iowa, Kentucky, Maine, Maryland, Massachusetts, New Hampshire, New Jersey, New York, North Carolina, Pennsylvania, Rhode Island, South Carolina, Tennessee, Texas, Vermont, Virginia and West Virginia.

The excess lands have been identified as unneeded by the federal government or as better utilized in private ownership. By law, these lands are made available for sale at no less than fair market value.

The law states that BLM can select lands for sale if, through land use planning, they are found to meet one of three criteria.

1. They are scattered, isolated tracts, difficult or uneconomic to manage.
2. They were acquired for a specific purpose and are no longer needed for that purpose.
3. Disposal of the land will serve important public objectives, such as community expansion and economic development.

Land types vary widely. Some may be desert; some higher elevations. Some are close to towns; some are rural. Some are small parcels of just a few acres; some are several hundred acres in size.

Any lands with agricultural potential will be clearly identified in the sale notice. However, most public lands have little or no agricultural potential.

The source of information for these sales is the local BLM office (see Appendix B, "Bureau of Land Management [BLM] State and District Offices") or the General Services Administration (addresses at the end of this appendix).

The sales are held near where the land is located. Details of any sale are specified in the sale notice available from BLM. By writing to any BLM office you can find out what sales are currently scheduled. It will send you a description of the property, method of sale, bidding procedure, a general map, special conditions of sale and other facts. More detailed information, such as land reports, and environmental assessments are available on request for a small copying fee.

In the late 1980s and the early 1990s, there was a major sale of public lands by the BLM. For example, in California, the federal government sold 2 percent of the public lands, or approximately 330,500 acres.

The following types of land were sold:

- Land in or near population centers that can be used for community expansion;
- Isolated or scattered land tracts that are expensive and difficult for BLM to manage;
- Land whose appropriate use is agricultural, commercial or industrial development by non-federal entities; and
- Other types of land identified for disposal in existing or future land use plans.

The fair market value of these lands was advertised in advance. They were then sold by sealed bids. You can obtain all information regarding those sales free from the BLM. You do not have to pay any commercial service to obtain this information.

*There is no free land.* Never believe any source that tells you otherwise. There has been no "free" land since the Homesteading Act was repealed in 1976 by the passage of the new Federal Land Policy and Management Act.

Just as much care should be used in buying these federal sale properties as in buying any land, including obtaining a title report, examination of easements and reservations (such as timber, water and minerals), and suitability for residential construction.

## National Forest Lands

The U.S. Forest Service has limited authority for the sale of National Forest System lands. New legislative authority will be necessary to allow the sale of National Forest System lands. In the unlikely event that any forest lands are offered for sale, you can find out about it through the local U.S. Forest Service Office or the National Forest Service, P.O. Box 2417, Washington, DC 20013 (see "Useful Resources" in Chapter 5 for addresses). There are

areas of private lands intermingled with National Forest Lands in most areas. Local real estate brokers are generally a good source of information regarding such land. Check with those brokers operating in the area nearest the forest lands you are interested in. If Congress authorizes the sale of forest system lands, details can be obtained from the Forest Service, P.O. Box 2417, Washington, DC 20013.

The publication below is available for the specified price from

> Superintendent of Documents
> U.S. Government Printing Office
> Washington, DC 20402

"Are There Any Public Lands for Sale,"
  S/N 024-011-00177-8               $1.00

Important information about the federal program to sell excess undeveloped public land. Explains why there are no more lands available for homesteading.

Two publications are available free from

> California State Office
> Bureau of Land Management
> 2800 Cottage Way, Room E-2841
> Sacramento, CA 95825

"Questions and Answers on the Public Land Sales
  Program in California"
"California Desert: Occupying Public Lands"

Inquiries regarding sale information about public lands managed by the BLM may be obtained by writing any of the BLM offices listed in Appendix B.

## The General Services Administration (GSA)

The GSA does not maintain a mailing list for each property sale. You must request a list each time, as indicated in its brochures. Each list tells you when, where and how surplus properties will be sold and where to go for more information on specific pieces of property. To get the latest free issue of *U.S. Real Property Sales* List write to

Properties
H, Consumer Information Center
Pueblo, CO 81009

For information on properties listed in "U.S. Real Property Sales List," GSA now has an electronic bulletin board. The phone number is (800) 776-7872; in Washington, DC, dial (202) 501-6510.

In addition to the sales listings in the above material, the GSA also provides information on specific upcoming sales through the "GSA Real Property Mailing List." This list affords prospective buyers the opportunity to receive notices of government sales of property in which they are interested. A copy of the Real Property Mailing List Application Card is free from

General Services Administration (7KYT-6)
1500 East Bannister Road
Kansas City, MO 64131

You can get notices of individual sales of federal real property by writing to one of the four regional real estate offices:

Office of Real Estate Sales (2PR-1)
U.S. General Service Administration
10 Causeway Street
Boston, MA 02222
(617) 565-5700

Office of Real Estate Sales (4PR)
U.S. General Service Administration
Peachtree Summit Building
Atlanta, GA 30365-2550
(404) 331-5133

Office of Real Estate Sales (7PR)
U.S. General Service Administration
819 Taylor Street
Ft. Worth, TX 76102
(817) 334-2331

Office of Real Estate Sales (9PR)
U.S. General Service Administration
525 Market St.
San Francisco, CA 94105
(415) 744-5952
(800) 421-7848

# APPENDIX D

## Special Uses of the National Forests, Including Habitation for Summer Homes and Sale to the Public

Long-term exclusive private use of National Forest System lands involving erection of a building for residential or second-home use is no longer authorized by the Forest Service. Some years ago, a limited number of summer home lots were made available in National Forests to persons interested in building a recreation residence for seasonal use. All of these lots have now been developed. While the special-use permits authorizing summer homes on those lots continue, no new lots are being established, and there are no plans to establish additional lots in the future. Annual rental fees for the existing lots are based on fair market value and range from a few hundred dollars to more than $2,000 a year. The improvements on these lots are frequently offered for sale by the owners. When this happens, a special-use permit may be reissued to the new owners.

At this time there are approximately 6,500 recreational residences (summer homes) in the National Forests in California alone. Most recreational residences are in tracts established long ago when public recreation in National Forests was just beginning. The current owners are using their property under a permit and own only their improvements on the land, not the land itself. The special-use permits for this use are issued for a maximum term of 20 years.

If you are interested in buying the improvements from a permittee, you should meet with the seller and a local Forest Service representative to discuss preparing new special-use permit conditions and requirements before completion of the sale.

Be very careful, because there is no guarantee that a new special-use permit will be issued or renewed at the end of the stated term. If it is not, you will be required to remove all improvements from the lot and restore it to the original condition at your sole expense. Remember, residences under these special-use-permits are for recreational use only. They may not be used for primary residences. A permittee must have a primary residence elsewhere.

For current information on these kinds of permits, the listed pamphlets are free from

Forest Service
U.S. Department of Agriculture
Washington, DC 20250

"Field Offices of the Forest Service," FS-1 3

The Forest Service does not handle the sale of recreation residences or keep track of them. This information can be obtained from a local real estate broker or from "For Sale" signs posted on recreation residence sites. There is a national organization of thousands of persons who own recreation resident permits on National Forest Service lands. They have banded together to protect their rights as permits. If you are interested in this program or want information on permits that might be for sale, contact the organization and ask for a copy of the N.F.R.A. Newsletter:

National Forest Recreation Association
P.O. Box 191455
Sacramento, CA 95819
(916) 344-5050

For information on leasing summer homes in National Forests in each state, write to the United States Forest Service Regional Field Office for your state. All addresses are given in the "Useful Resources" at the end of Chapter 5.

# APPENDIX E

# Federal Information Centers

If you have questions about any service or agency of the federal government, you may want to call the Federal Information Center (FIC) nearest you for a free call or minimum long-distance charge. FICs are prepared to help consumers find needed infor-

matin or locate the right agency for help with problems.

Alabama
Birmingham, Mobile
(800) 366-2998

Alaska
Anchorage
(800) 729-8003

Arizona
Phoenix
(800) 359-3997

Arkansas
Little Rock
(800) 366-2998

California
Los Angeles, San Diego, San Francisco, Santa Ana
(800) 726-4995

Sacramento
(916) 973-1695

Colorado
Colorado Springs, Denver, Pueblo
(800) 359-3997

Connecticut
Hartford, New Haven
(800) 347-1997

Florida
Fort Lauderdale, Jacksonville, Miami, Orlando, St. Petersburg, Tampa, West Palm Beach
(800) 347-1997

Georgia
Atlanta
(800) 347-1997

Hawaii
Honolulu
(800) 733-5996

Illinois
Chicago
(800) 366-2998

Indiana
Gary
(800) 366-2998

Indianapolis
(800) 347-1997

Iowa
All locations
(800) 735-8004

Kansas
All locations
(800) 735-8004

Kentucky
Louisville
(800) 347-1997

Louisiana
New Orleans
(800) 366-2998

Maryland
Baltimore
(800) 347-1997

Massachusetts
Boston
(800) 347-1997

Michigan
Detroit, Grand Rapids
(800) 347-1997

Minnesota
Minneapolis
(800) 366-2998

Missouri
St. Louis
(800) 366-2998

All other locations
(800) 735-8004

Nebraska
Omaha
(800) 366-2998

All other locations
(800) 735-8004

New Jersey
Newark, Trenton
(800) 347-1997

New Mexico
Albuquerque
(800) 359-3997

New York
Albany, Buffalo, New York, Rochester,
Syracuse
(800) 347-1997

North Carolina
Charlotte
(800) 347-1997

Ohio
Akron, Cincinnati, Cleveland, Columbus,
Dayton, Toledo
(800) 374-1997

Oklahoma
Oklahoma City, Tulsa
(800) 366-2998

Oregon
Portland
(800) 726-4995

Pennsylvania
Philadelphia, Pittsburgh
(800) 347-1997

Rhode Island
Providence
(800) 347-1997

Tennessee
Chatrtanooga
(800) 347-1997

Memphis, Nashville
(800) 366-2998

Texas
Austin, Dallas, Fort Worth, Houston,
San Antonio
(800) 366-2998

Utah
Salt Lake City
(800) 359-3997

Virginia
    Norfolk, Richmond, Roanoke
    (800) 347-1997

Washington
    Seattle, Tacoma
    (800) 726-4995

Wisconsin
    Milwaukee
    (800) 366-2998

# APPENDIX F

# Alternative Energy Resources

If you have any interest in developing alternative energy on your property, water, wind or solar, you must take this into account when evaluating a piece of property. To properly assess the layout of the land, some basic knowledge of energy systems is essential.

The resources in this Appendix provide a good source of basic information to help you gain the knowledge necessary to purchase a parcel appropriate for alternative energy production.

Start by checking with your local library because numerous books and periodicals have been written on this subject in the past ten years.

The best mail-order catalogs of alternative energy supplies are the following:

*Alternative Energy Engineering Catalog*
    *and Design Guide*            $3.00
P.O. Box 339
Redway, CA 95560
Voice: (800) 777-6609
URL:  http://www.nando.net/
    prof/eco/aee.html

*Alternative Energy Source Book*      $14.00
Real Goods Trading Corporation
966 Mazzoni St.
Ukiah, CA 95482
Voice: (800) 762-7325
URL: http://www.well.com/user/realgood/

*Solar Design Catalog*
2021 Zearing Ave., N.W.
Albuquerque, NM 87104
(800) 245-0311 or (505) 243-3212

Write to the following agency for a list of its publications, written for the lay person, on all areas of alternative energy, building construction ideas and energy saving in all aspects of your life:

National Center for Appropriate Technology
(NCAT)
Box 3838
Butte, MT 59702
(406) 494-4572

The Energy Efficient and Renewable Energy Clearinghouse (EREC) offers information and assistance to a broad audience (consumers, educators and students, builders, business, government agencies, entrepreneurs) on a wide range of topics by providing publications, customized responses and referrals to energy organizations.

Energy Efficient and Renewable Energy
    Clearinghouse (EREC)
U.S. Department of Energy
P.O. Box 3048
Merrifield, VA 22116
Voice: (800) DOE-EREC (363-3732)
TDD: (800) 273-2957
Fax: (703) 893-0400
BBS: (800) 273-2955
E-mail  energyinfo@delphi.com
URL: http://www.eren.doe.gov/

Cited below are EREC fact sheets that will introduce you to some of the many technology options that exist for saving energy and money and using renewable resources.

"Energy-Saving Tips for Small Businesses"
"Advances in Glazing Materials for Windows"
"Cooling Your Home Naturally"
"Energy Efficient Water Heating"
"Energy-Efficient Windows"
"A Guide to Making Energy—Smart Purchases"
"Heating Your Home With an Active Solar Energy
    System"
"Heat Pumps"
"Landscaping for Energy Efficiency"

"Learning About Saving Energy (for grade school students)"
"Passive Solar Heating"
"Selecting a New Water Heater"
"Solar Heat Storage"
"Sun Space Basics"
"Caulking and Weatherstripping"
"Efficient Air-Conditioning"
"Fans and Ventilation"
"Home Energy Audits"
"Insulation Materials and Strategies"
"Passive Solar Home Design"
"Small Renewable Energy Systems"
"Water Heating Systems"
"EREC Fact Sheets in Adobe PDF Format"

The following is available for the specified cost from

Primary Glass Manufacturers Council
3310 Harrison
White Lakes Professional Building
Topeka, KS 66611-2279
(913) 266-3666

*Builders Guide to Passive Solar Home Design and Land Development*          $12.00

The Government Printing Office (address can be found in Chapter 4) has available:

*Affordable Housing Through Energy Conservation*
S/N 061-000-00729-6          $26.00

The E.P.A.(address in Chapter 4) has available:

"Buying an EPA-Certified Woodstove"

The National Association of Home Builders puts out a catalog of books on various subjects. For a copy of their free catalog write to:

NAHB Bookstore
15th & M St., NW
Washington, DC 20005

## Magazines

*Custom Builder* (Formerly *Progressive Builder Magazine*)
Energy Efficiency and Quality Home Construction

Willows Publication Group
38 Lafayette St.
Yarmouth, ME 04096
Voice: (207) 846-0970
Fax: (207) 846-1561
12 issues/$38

*Architectural Design*
Davis Publications Inc.
380 Lexington Ave.
New York, NY 10168-0035
2 issues / year, no subscriptions

## Wireless Telephone System

Many places in the country, especially in more remote regions, do not have telephone service available, or the telephone company may not want a large line extension charge to provide service. Cellular telephone service is an option in some areas, but the per minute charges can make this very expensive if it is your only telephone. A company that makes high-quality remote telephone systems and may be able to offer an alternative is:

OptaPhone Systems (formerly Carlson Communications, Inc.)
P.O. Box 4000
Redway, CA 95560
Voice: (800) 283-6006
Fax: (707) 923-2655

## Wind-Driven Electrical Systems

A publication about a specialized use of wind energy is available from

National Technical Information Service
U.S. Department of Commerce
5285 Port Royal Rd.
Springfield, VA 22161

*Solar Wind-Powered Irrigation Systems*, 36pp.
PB 82-177486          $ 4.50

## Pumping and Raising Water and Hydro Power

Catalogs and information about pumping and raising water with various alternative energy sources, such as windmills and hydraulic rams, can be obtained from several sources.

Dempster Industries Inc.
Box 848
Beatrice, NE 68310
Voice: (800) 777-0212 or (402) 223-4026
Fax: (402) 228-4389
(free catalog)

Baker Manufacturing Company
133 Enterprise St.
Evansville, WI 53536-1497
Voice: (608) 882-5100
Fax: (608) 882-6776
(free catalog)

Heller-Aller Co.
Corner of Perry & Oakwood
 Napoleon, OH 43545
(information, $1.50)

The definitive resource catalog is still *The Whole Earth Catalogue*. The new edition, titled *The Millennium Whole Earth Catalogue* (1994) available in bookstores, or send $30.00 U.S. or $42.00 Canada for softcover or $50.00 for a hardcover edition (postpaid) to:

Whole Earth Access
Point Foundation
27 Gate 5 Road
Sausilito, CA 94965
Voice: (415) 332-1716
Fax: (415) 332-2416

# Index

# Start Enjoying Greater Financial Freedom
# Triple Your Investment Portfolio

# SAVE Thousands on Real Estate as a Buyer or Seller

# Successfully Start & Manage a <u>NEW</u> Business

### Small Business

## The Business Planning Guide
### *Plan for Success in Your New Venture*

**With this multimedia kit:**
- Just plug in your financials to plan your dream business
- Point and click to automate planning and financial forecasts
- Start, expand, or buy a business

**Order No. 1800-0101**
**$34.95**

**David H. Bangs, Jr.** is founder of Upstart Publishing Company, Inc.

## How To Form Your Own Corporation Without a Lawyer For Under $75

**With this multimedia kit:**
- Save thousands of dollars in legal fees
- Limit your personal liability and protect your assets
- Access the complete set of forms, certificate of incorporation, minutes, and more

**Order No. 1800-1601**
**$34.95**

**Ted Nicholas** owns and operates four corporations of his own and acts as a consultant to small businesses.

## Starting Your Home-Based Business
### *39 Million People Can't Be Wrong*

**With this multimedia kit:**
- Position your home-based business for long-term success
- Deal effectively with zoning, labor laws, and licenses
- Answers to the 20 most-asked questions

**Order No. 1800-2801**
**$34.95**

**Linda Pinson** and **Jerry Jinnett** are consultants and speakers as well as successful business owners and authors.

## The Start-Up Guide
### *Everything You Need to Create a Smart Start in Your New Business*

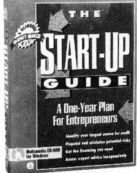

**With this multimedia kit:**
- Create your own 12-month interactive start-up plan
- Access interactive management, bookkeeping, and marketing forms
- Learn the best ways to deal with bankers, vendors, and investors
- Get the financing you need

**Order No. 1800-1001**
**$34.95**

**David H. Bangs, Jr.** is a frequent speaker and acknowledged expert on small business management topics.

---

## 3 Easy Ways to Order

**1. By Mail:**
Mail to:
Dearborn Multimedia
155 N. Wacker Drive
Chicago, IL 60606

**2. By FAX:**
FAX your order
(with credit card information)
to: 1-312-836-9958

**3. By Phone:**
Call Toll-Free
(credit card orders only)
1-800-638-0375
Have your Visa, MasterCard, or American Express handy.

Name_____

Address_____ City_____

State_____ Zip_____ Phone (      )_____

❑ Personal Check Enclosed (checks payable to: Dearborn Financial Publishing)

**Credit Card Information**   ❑ Visa   ❑ MasterCard   ❑ AMEX

Account #_____ Exp. Date_____

Signature_____

| Order No. | Title | Price | Qty. | Total |
|-----------|-------|-------|------|-------|
|           |       |       |      |       |
|           |       |       |      |       |
|           |       | Subtotal | | |
|           |       | Sales Tax (CA, FL, IL and NY only) | | |
|           |       | Shipping & Handling   $5.00 | | |
|           |       | Total | | |

**Dearborn Multimedia**
155 North Wacker Drive
Chicago, IL 60606
**1-800-638-0375**

Source Code 605107